Where to

Europe and Russia

THE *WHERE TO WATCH BIRDS* SERIES

Where to watch birds in Africa
Nigel Wheatley

Where to watch birds in Asia
Nigel Wheatley

Where to watch birds in Australasia and Oceania
Nigel Wheatley

Where to watch birds in Europe and Russia
Nigel Wheatley

Where to watch birds in South America
Nigel Wheatley

Where to watch birds in

Europe and Russia

Nigel Wheatley

Princeton University Press
Princeton, New Jersey

Published in the United States, Canada, and the Philippine Islands
by Princeton University Press, 41 William Street,
Princeton, New Jersey, 08540

In the United Kingdom and the European Union, published by
Christopher Helm (Publishers) Ltd, a subsidiary of
A & C Black (Publishers) Ltd, 35 Bedford Row, London WC1R 4JH

Library of Congress Catalog Card Number 00-100076

ISBN 0-691-05729-X

Printed in Italy

This book has been composed in Cheltenham

www.pup.princeton.edu

1 3 5 7 9 10 8 6 4 2

CONTENTS

Contents

Contents

Contents

Contents

Contents

ACKNOWLEDGEMENTS

It would have been impossible to produce this book without the help of the many birders who have not only travelled to Europe and Russia in search of birds, but who have also been unselfish enough to record their experiences for the benefit of others. Most of these people have made their information generally available, and, to me, are some of the pillars of the birding world.

I would like to express my heartfelt thanks to the following birders and organisations who have generously allowed me to use their information and/or covered some country accounts in honest red ink: Gordon Avery, Greg Baker, Phil Benstead, Marek Borkowski (Wildlife Poland), Chris Bradshaw, Dave Gosney (BirdGuides), BirdLife International, Birdquest, David Brewer, John Cantelo, Josef Chytil, Stephane Claerebout, Alan Clamp, Steve Fisher, Annika Forsten, Alberto Garcia, Sandra Gardeslen, Bob Gibbons, Rob Goldbach, Igor Gorban, Gerard Gorman, Ian Green (Greentours), John Hale, Mark Hardwick, Tim Herfurth, Jon Hornbuckle, Mike Inskip, Guy Kirwan, Frank Laessing, Aivar Leito, 'The Colonel' (Paul Macklam), Eileen Marsh, Karel Mauer, Anthony McGeehan, Dominic Mitchell (*Birdwatch* magazine), Dirk Moerbeck, William Oliver, Jean-Yves Paquet, Ian Phillips, Terry Pickford, Dirk Raes, David Rosair, Marco Sacchi, Stefan Schleuning, Martin Scott, Heikki Seppanen, Andrej Sovinc, Tadeusz Stawarczyk, Joe Sultana, Sunbird, Bryan Thomas, David Tomlinson, Arnoud van den Berg, Frank van Groen, Bernard Volet, Will Wagstaff, Duncan Walbridge, Peter Walding, Richard Webb, Steve Whitehouse (Foreign Birdwatching Reports and Information Service) and Paul Willoughby (Bird Holidays).

Naturally, many thanks also go to the many birders who accompanied these people in the field, helped to find the birds, and no doubt contributed their own information. I have spoken to numerous other people on the telephone, in the field and in the pub about minor, but important, matters, who I have unwittingly omitted from the above list. I sincerely hope these people will accept my profuse apologies if I have failed to acknowledge their help in this edition, and hope they will let me know before the next edition.

Unfortunately, it has to be said at this juncture that there are some birders, including a few with a wealth of experience in Europe and Russia, who have never written any trip reports. Or, if they have done so, they have not made their information generally available. Fortunately such people are few and far between, and sharing information comes naturally to the vast majority of birders. Writing a trip report can be a very enjoyable undertaking, because it enables the author to relive the experience, absorb as many birds as possible and cement the memories, hence I can only say to those who don't bother, have a go next time.

Once I had come up with the idea for the book I had to convince a publisher it would be popular. Fortunately Robert Kirk, the editor at Christopher Helm, saw the potential and deserves thanks for taking on the original idea and developing it. When I started compiling the basic information for the book it seemed as though every bird had at least three different names. This major headache was cured by James

Clements, to whom I am very grateful for giving me permission to use his *Check List* as the baseline for this book.

Finally, I thank my birding companions, past and present, many of whom have contributed to the book, but, more importantly, without whom I would never have been able to see so many great birds and the wild places they inhabit, and birding would not be anywhere near so enlightening, entertaining and entirely enjoyable. There are too many to list in full here, but foremost amongst them are, in alphabetical order, Ando (Paul Anderson), Carolyn Atkins, Chief (Nick Cobb), Nige Crook, Foggy (Simon Fogg), Chris Gibbins, Mark Golley, Martin Hallam, Alun Hatfield, Steve Howat, Roy Hunter, Nick Lever, Leigh Lock, Georgie Malpass, Rob Roberts, Spotter (John Mason), Barry Stidolph, Nick Wall, Trevor Williams and last, but certainly not least, my parents, Pam and Tony Wheatley.

INTRODUCTION

As my friend Ando and I entered the wood at dawn in late May 1980, it appeared to be lifeless apart from a few Garden Warblers which were singing their heads off. Further in however, we thought we could hear, drifting eerily through the trees, the mellow whistles of the birds we had travelled so far to see. We had never heard one before. We were very, very tired, having already spent a few days hitch-hiking and, mostly, walking, around the rest of East Anglia, England, pitching our tent wherever took our fancy. The calls seemed so far away and so like a Blackbird's that we remained unsure. We carried on, with the mysterious magical music drawing us deeper and deeper into the wood, listening intently to what we decided had to be the birds we were after. For a while we saw virtually nothing, but the wood was far from devoid of avian life—it was now a wonderfully spellbinding, exotic place which resounded with the yodelling 'Weelo-Wee Weeo's' of invisible orioles. We had been warned that seeing these birds would be very difficult, if not impossible, on a single visit, and sure enough hour after hour passed without so much as a glimpse of black or yellow. The birds were so perfectly camouflaged in the canopy of the pale-leaved poplars that we decided to settle in one particularly noisy place, looking into a glade. Suddenly, just as we discovered the field craft necessary to see Golden Orioles, we were treated to the unforgettable spectacle of four jet-black and deep yellow males chasing two apple-green females just a few paces in front of us, for the best part of half-an-hour. Nothing we had ever seen before, in books, in life, on television or in our imagination, was so fantastic.

Twenty years and as many countries later, there has been little to match that moment, which goes to show that Europe and Russia are just as capable of producing brilliant birding as anywhere else on earth. In fact, many European birders travel back and forth across the globe to enjoy such experiences without realising that such great birds grace some of the wildest places on the planet right on their doorstep.

Take Scotland for example, where in early June 1984 life seemed as though it could never be better: falling asleep in the soft machair of the Outer Hebrides to the sound of rippling Dunlins, after spending a long summer day watching a couple of Short-eared Owls, a stunning male Hen Harrier and a Golden Eagle together in a sunny sky, a delightfully dainty Red-necked Phalarope spinning on a loch, Corn Crakes, strolling for all the world to see between iris beds, and a drake Steller's Eider amongst a flock of equally gorgeous Common Eiders, to boot. And all in one of the most beautiful places on earth. A few days later my friend Chief and I danced down a Scottish mountain in delight, having just seen our first Eurasian Dotterels on the wild top of Cairngorm.

A year later we were lying on our stomachs amongst the tame Puffins at Bluescudda Kame, Herma Ness, in the Shetlands, looking down at the clouds of screaming auks, kittiwakes and gannets swirling over cliffs packed with just as many birds, and a grey sea, far, far below, which was covered with even more birds. It was our first experience of a seabird city and came complete with a bombardment from the Bonxies, nesting nearby, and a Black-browed Albatross. That night, having spent the afternoon in the close company of three wonderful Red-necked Phalaropes, we walked out to a headland on the island of Fetlar to watch European Storm-Petrels return to their burrows. It was well past midnight when we began the walk back to our caravan in the middle of the island but the Bonxies were still wide awake and their attacks were more terrifying now in the thin light. It soon got brighter though, for as we breached the brow of the Scord of Grunnigeo, a monstrous moon rose before us, a moon so massive we could see its craters with the naked eye. It was yet another reminder provided by a far-flung island that there was so much more to birding than the birds. However, our sojourn in the Shetlands would not have been complete without the main bird we had gone all that way to see. For three long, damp days every white, owl-sized rock on those rock-strewn islands did indeed turn out to be a rock, until, on what we decided would be our last lengthy scan, one of those million rocks moved a little, and what's more it had two big bright yellow eyes. It was our first Snowy Owl and, of course, the best bird we had ever seen.

Britain and Ireland have more than their fair share of the top birding spots in Europe and Russia, thanks mainly to their position at the north-western edge of the landmass next to the Atlantic. Their rugged head-lands and offshore islands are not only perfect for millions of breeding seabirds. they are also some of the best promontories in the region for observing wintering seabirds up from the south Atlantic and, to cap it all, some of the very best places to see great rarities, whether they originate 3000 miles to the west in North America or 3000 miles to the east in Siberia. I have been fortunate enough to witness all three phenomena, thanks to the aforementioned visits to Scotland and its offshore islands, thanks to choosing the right day to visit Porthgwarra in Corn-wall—13 August 1989, when the birds passing included a *Pterodroma* petrel now believed by many to be a Fea's Petrel, as well as Great, Cory's, Sooty, Manx and Mediterranean Shearwaters—and thanks to fre-quent visits to the Isles of Scilly, where on my first full day in that archi-pelago I saw, in order of appearance, Rough-legged Buzzard, Eurasian Dotterel, Blackpoll Warbler and Yellow-browed Warbler, a combina-tion of east and west which would be nigh on impossible to see any-where else in the world, let alone Europe and Russia, and another reminder of how exciting birding in this region can be.

Flicking through a European field guide in the mid-1980s I started to think, ten years down the birding line, that it was about time I ventured across the English Channel, for there were some amazing birds 'just across the water'. So, soon after I was standing overlooking the marsh-es in La Camargue, southern France. Rain was pouring out of a gloomy grey sky, pounding the poor flamingos, thunder had silenced the teem-ing masses of other birds, and lightning was hitting the ground in the distance. It was not how I had imagined the Mediterranean would be, or for that matter how I thought my first Bee-eater would look, but the bedraggled bird, with drops of water running down its skyward-pointing bill, perched on the telegraph wire next to the road, was still the most beautiful thing I had ever set eyes on. It was only when the storm passed though and I saw flocks of them, calling constantly as they caught drag-onflies in mid-air with such casual ease, that I was sure I had never seen anything so stunning. We are blessed in Europe with the best bird in the world: the brilliant bird the Russians used to call the Golden Bee-eater.

One of my most memorable birding experiences in Europe was a fine autumn day in the Pyrenées. When an Eleonora's Falcon dashed up the valley below us as we drove up to the car park at Port de Gavarnie, on the french side of the mountains, my friend Nick and I knew it was going to be a special day, and so it was. From the car park we ascended stark scree slopes, crossed cascades of melt-water and traversed a small glacier to reach Breche de Roland, a remarkable rectangular gap in the mountain wall high above Gavarnie. As we breached the breche, several Alpine Swifts zoomed past our heads so close we could hear the rush of air sweeping across their scythe-shaped wings. On the Spanish side of the bare jagged crest of the Pyrenées we turned right, on to a narrow dusty trail which ascended Le Doigt, a towering pinnacle of rock. To our left was a massive bare high valley with a steep scree slope sweeping down from our feet. To our right was a sheer rock wall which went straight up to the icy-blue sky. It was a magnificent setting for a very special bird, and shortly after leaving the breche behind we flushed, almost from our feet, what appeared at first to be a massive carmine-winged butterfly, but which I soon realised was my first Wallcreeper, for I had fallen asleep on many a night before then with the Hamlyn *Field Guide to the Birds of Europe* open at the Wallcreeper page. The bird flew up on to the rock wall and during the next hour it was joined by up to four more, all flitting around that stone canvas to paint one of nature's finest works of art with their carmine wing patches and white primary spots flashing away, just a few paces in front of me. I had to be dragged away, down the mountain, to also see, as it happened, a Lammergeier dropping a bone on to a slope where there were a few snowfinches and a couple of Alpine Accentors. At the end of that day, when the sun fell below the peaks of the Pyrenées and the sky turned pink as we pitched our tents on a high grassy whaleback, I had never felt so glad to be alive.

These personal memories and the hope of many more have inspired me to research and compile the information contained within this book, and in sharing this information I hope I might encourage fellow birders to travel to the region's wild places and help them in their search of the birds about which they dream. One reason why I personally wanted the information was to find out where I could see the highest percentage of the birds I have yet to see in Europe in one area, and now that my research is complete I have discovered that I should head for the Black Sea coastal plain of Bulgaria and/or Romania. Hopefully, the information contained in the following pages will help other birders to work out where they can look for the birds they most want to see. It is in fact fairly easy to see most of the region's birds, time and funds permitting, but to ensure success it is essential to prepare thoroughly, hence I have aimed to include all the information that will help birders to plan their own successful and enjoyable birding trips to Europe and Russia. Unlike another 'Where to watch' guide for which the author states, in his tour company's newsletter, 'some of our favourite niches are not included on the sensible grounds that we want to keep them to ourselves', this guide has no such policy and I have attempted to include every 'favourite niche' of every birder I know or have corresponded with in the course of compiling this book.

Birders who want to organise a trip to Europe and Russia will probably want to know, first and foremost, where to look for certain species, in which case, in Europe they may be thinking about such birds as divers, shearwaters, storm-petrels, pelicans, Greater Flamingo, Red-breasted Goose*, King and Steller's* Eiders, Smew, Lammergeier, Cinereous Vulture*, Spanish* and Imperial* Eagles, Eleonora's Falcon, Rock Partridge, Common Crane, Little* and Great* Bustards, Eurasian Dotterel, Audouin's* and Slender-billed Gulls, Atlantic Puffin, Pin-tailed and Black-bellied Sandgrouse, owls, European Bee-eater, European Roller, Azure-winged Magpie, Eurasian Nutcracker, choughs, Eurasian Golden-Oriole, shrikes, Collared Flycatcher, Bluethroat, wheatears, Corsican* and Rock Nuthatches, Wallcreeper, Firecrest, Olive-tree, Rüppell's and Marmora's Warblers, Eurasian Penduline-Tit, White-winged Snowfinch, Alpine Accentor, Citril Finch, Scottish Crossbill* and Cretzschmar's Bunting.

In Russia most of the species birders may wish to see are confined to the far east, with the exception of birds such as Caucasian Snowcock and Demoiselle Crane, and they include Spectacled Eider*, Scaly-sided Merganser*, Steller's Sea-Eagle*, Siberian Grouse*, Hooded* and Red-crowned* Cranes, Nordmann's Greenshank*, Great Knot, Spoonbill Sandpiper*, Aleutian Tern, auks, Blakiston's Fish-Owl*, White-throated Needletail, Japanese Waxwing*, thrushes, Yellow-rumped and Mugimaki Flycatchers, Siberian Rubythroat, Siberian Blue Robin, warblers, Reed Parrotbill*, Japanese Grosbeak and buntings.

Once birders have decided on what they would like to see, further questions spring to mind. Which country, island or region supports the best selection? Is it safe? When is the best time to visit? Where are the best sites? How easy is it to get from one to the other? How much time will be needed to bird each one thoroughly? What other species are there at these sites? Which birds should I concentrate on? The list goes on.

Such questions need careful consideration if the proposed birding trip is going to be an enjoyable success, and without months of pains-taking preparation a trip may not be anywhere near as exciting as it could be. Hence, this book's major aim is to answer those questions birders may ask themselves before venturing to Europe and Russia for the first or fortieth time. It is not meant to direct you to every bird in the minutest detail, but to be a first point of reference, an aid to your own research and planning, a guiding light. It is no substitute for up-to-date reports and I urge readers to seek these reports out (see Useful Addresses, p. 393) once they have decided on their destination, and to write their own reports on their return.

Birders are notoriously hard to please, so writing this book has been all consuming. I began by compiling a list of sites and the species recorded at them, from every imaginable source. Reports written by independent birders were the major goldmine and without the gener-ous permission of the writers the book you are now reading would not exist (see Acknowledgements, p. 11). Whilst compiling the site lists it became apparent that many species were known by more than one name, hence I needed a baseline list to cure what was fast becoming a bad headache. So I began looking for the world list of species which I thought was the most logical, easy to use and popular, in terms of indi-vidual species names and taxonomic order, and it did not take long to settle on *Birds of the World: A Check List* (Fourth Edition). Clements J, 1991, and its supplements, and I am most grateful to James Clements for being kind enough to allow me to use it. Some of the names James uses are different from those used in other books covering the region, and in some birders trip reports, hence I have compiled a table to compare these (see p. 401). In addition, where the names used by James are significantly different from those still in common use by European birders I have retained these popular names. They are as follows:

Name used in this book	Name used in 'Clements'
Slavonian Grebe	Horned Grebe
Fea's Petrel	Cape Verde Island Petrel
Mediterranean Shearwater	Yelkouan Shearwater
Bewick's Swan	Tundra Swan
Brent Goose	Brant
Ferruginous Duck	Ferruginous Pochard
Common Scoter	Black Scoter
Velvet Scoter	White-winged Scoter
Goosander	Common Merganser
Hen Harrier	Northern Harrier
Rough-legged Buzzard	Rough-legged Hawk
Red-knobbed Coot	Crested Coot
Grey Phalarope	Red Phalarope
Lesser Sandplover	Mongolian Plover
Common Gull	Mew Gull
Pomarine Skua	Pomarine Jaeger
Arctic Skua	Parasitic Jaeger
Long-tailed Skua	Long-tailed Jaeger
Little Auk	Dovekie
Common Guillemot	Common Murre
Brünnich's Guillemot	Thick-billed Murre
Red-throated Diver	Red-throated Loon
Black-throated Diver	Arctic Loon
Great Northern Diver	Common Loon
White-billed Diver	Yellow-billed Loon
Tengmalm's Owl	Boreal Owl
Grey-headed Woodpecker	Grey-faced Woodpecker
Isabelline Shrike	Rufous-tailed Shrike
White's Thrush	Scaly Thrush
Red-breasted Flycatcher	Red-throated Flycatcher
Red-flanked Bluetail	Orange-flanked Bush-Robin
Eversmann's Redstart	Rufous-backed Redstart
Guldenstadt's Redstart	White-winged Redstart
Pallas's Grasshopper Warbler	Pallas' Warbler
Pallas's Warbler	Lemon-rumped Warbler
Yellow-browed Warbler	Inornate Warbler
Reedling	Bearded Reedling
Citrine Wagtail	Yellow-hooded Wagtail
Radde's Accentor	Spot-throated Accentor
Arctic Redpoll	Hoary Redpoll
Two-barred Crossbill	White-winged Crossbill
Grey-necked Bunting	Grey-hooded Bunting
Lapland Bunting	Lapland Longspur

Although the 'English' names of New World birds should be spelt in the American way (eg. 'colored' should be used instead of 'coloured', and 'gray' instead of 'grey') I have written all bird names in English, simply because my busy fingers refused not to press the 'u' in 'coloured' or to press the 'a' in 'grey' instead of the 'e', whilst whizzing (no, stumbling) across the keyboard.

Using birders trip reports and a wide variety of other sources as my database, most, if not all, of the best birding sites, spectacular, endemic and near-endemic species, as well as those birds hard to see beyond the region's boundaries, have been included, albeit in varying amounts of detail. Absolute coverage and precision would have resulted in the staggered publication of several thick volumes. The major sites, of which there are over 250, are listed in the Site Index (p. 403) and all species mentioned in the text are listed in the Species Index (p. 000).

The Layout
After much consideration the book has taken the following shape. Countries have, on the whole, been split according to political boundaries, with the exception of Eire (southern Ireland) which has been included in Britain and Ireland, and the Balearic Islands (under Spanish administration), the Bay of Biscay, the Channel Islands (a British Crown Dependency), Corsica (under French administration), Crete (under Greek administration), the Faroes (a self-governing Island Region of Denmark), Sardinia (a Special Autonomous Region of Italy) and Svalbard (under Norwegian administration), which are all dealt with separately. The countries, islands and archipelagos are treated alphabetically and details for each are dealt with as follows.

The **Introduction** to each country, island or archipelago includes:
A brief **summary** of the features discussed below.
The **size** of the country, island or archipelago in relation to England and Texas.
The basics of **getting around**.
The range of **accommodation and food** available.
Details relating to **health and safety** where, although general advice is given, it is still important to find out the latest information on immunisation requirements and personal safety levels before travelling.
A section on **climate and timing**, where the best times to visit are given (these are summarised in the Calendar, p. 390).
An outline of the **habitats** present.
A brief outline of **conservation** issues.
The total number of **bird species** recorded (where known), followed by a short list of notable species which is intended to give a brief taste of what to expect (rarely seen species are not usually included in this brief list).
Expectations, where an idea of how many species to expect, usually on a short trip lasting one to three weeks, is given.

Some of these sections may be missing for the less well-known destinations, and the details given for all places on getting around, accommodation and food, and health and safety, are intended to be as brief as possible because there seems little point in repeating here the vast amount of information now available in the numerous travel guides. It makes much more sense to save room for more information on the birds and birding in this book.
At the beginning of each country, island or archipelago account there is a map showing the **Sites**, which are then discussed in detail, after the introduction: (i) along a more or less logical route through the country; or (ii) in 'bunches'. Naturally, different birders will prefer their own routes, but I felt that arranging the sites in these ways was more

practical than dealing with them alphabetically, mainly because those birders intending to: (i) follow the same route I have chosen or (ii) visit just one region, will find all the sites they intend to visit dealt with in the same section of the book.

The **Sites** accounts within each country, island or archipelago include:

(1) A **Site name**, which usually refers to the actual site, or, if it involves a number of birding spots which are in close proximity, the name used is that of the best city, town or village from which to explore all of these spots.

(2) A **Site introduction**, which includes a brief breakdown of the site's general location, size, main physical characteristics, habitats and most notable birds (that is those which are worth concentrating on the most at the given site).

(3) A **Species list**, which includes **Endemics** (species endemic to the country, island or archipelago, not the site), **Localised Specialities** (species which are not site specialities, but have: (i) restricted ranges which cross country boundaries; (ii) wider distributions throughout Europe and Russia, but are generally scarce, rare, or threatened; or (iii) rarely been mentioned in the literature consulted in preparing this book), **Other Localised Species** (species which almost meet the above criteria), **Others** (species that are widely distributed but uncommon, spectacular or especially sought after for a variety of reasons), and **Other Wildlife** (notable mammals, listed in alphabetical order, and, if appropriate, a reference to other flora and fauna).

The **Others** section is not comprehensive and many more species than those listed may have been recorded at a given site. Such species are relatively common or widespread in small numbers and therefore occur at many sites throughout the relevant country, island or archipelago, or indeed across much of Europe and/or Russia. By restricting the numbers of species listed under **Others** I have hoped to avoid repetition and saved a considerable amount of space, not least in the Species Index. Species not normally mentioned include the following:

The grebes, Mute Swan, Greylag Goose, Common Shelduck, most ducks, Little Egret, Grey and Purple Herons, Great Bittern*, Eurasian Spoonbill, several raptors, Grey Partridge, Common Quail, Common Pheasant, Water Rail, Common Moorhen, Eurasian Coot, most shorebirds, gulls, terns, pigeons and doves, Common Cuckoo, European Scops-Owl, Tawny, Little, Long-eared and Short-eared Owls, Eurasian Nightjar, Common Swift, Common Kingfisher, Eurasian Hoopoe, Eurasian Wryneck, Lesser Spotted, Middle Spotted, Great Spotted, Eurasian Green and Grey-headed Woodpeckers, most corvids, Eurasian Golden-Oriole, most shrikes, White-throated Dipper, Ring Ouzel, Eurasian Blackbird, Fieldfare, Redwing, Song and Mistle Thrushes, Common Starling, Spotted, European Pied and Red-breasted Flycatchers, European Robin, Common Nightingale, Black and Common Redstarts, Whinchat, Common Stonechat, Northern and Black-eared Wheatears, Eurasian Nuthatch, both treecreepers, Winter Wren, Sand Martin, Barn Swallow, House Martin, Goldcrest, Firecrest, most warblers, Reedling, most tits, Crested and Wood Larks, Sky Lark, House and Eurasian Tree Sparrows, most wagtails and pipits, Dunnock, most finches including Hawfinch, Yellowhammer, and Cirl, Corn, Ortolan and Reed Buntings.

No one, not even the most experienced observer, is likely to see all the species listed under each site in a single visit, or over a period of a few days, or in some cases, during a prolonged stay of weeks or more. This is because a number of species, even some which are relatively common and widespread, are very thin on the ground or highly elusive and thus difficult to find.

Although you may not wish to take this book into the field once you have decided on your destination and itinerary, it, or a photocopy of the relevant section, may prove useful if you are prepared to scrawl all over it. For, by crossing out those species you have seen on a previous trip, or at a previously visited site, or already at the site you are at, you will be able to see what species you still need to look for. It is all too easy, in the haze of excitement generated by birding in a new country or at a new site, to see a lot of good birds and be satisfied with your visit, only to discover later that you have missed a bird at that site which does not occur at any other, or that you have just left a site offering you the last chance to see a certain species (on your chosen route) and are unable to change your itinerary.

Within the lists of species those marked with an **asterisk (*)** have been listed as threatened, conservation dependent, data deficient, or near-threatened by BirdLife International/IUCN in *Birds to Watch 2: The World List of Threatened Birds*. Collar N *et al.*, 1994. BirdLife International's Threatened Birds Programme aims to gather the most up-to-date information on these species, raise awareness of their plights among governments, decision-makers and the public, and initiate action to protect them, hence it is important to report any records of these species, and those described as rare in the text, to **BirdLife International, Wellbrook Court, Girton Road, Cambridge, CB3 0NA, England, UK.** The excellent BirdLife book deals in detail with Europe and Russia's rarest and often most spectacular species, hence all birders planning a trip to the region should seriously consider using it for their pre-trip research.

The sites accounts also include:

(4) Details of **Access**, where directions to the site from the nearest large city, town, village or previous site, are given, followed by more detailed information on where to look for the birds, especially those which occur at few, if any, other sites. Distances are usually given to the nearest km or mile because speedometers and tyres vary so much, and directions are usually described as points of the compass rather than left or right so as not to cause confusion if travelling from a different direction from that dealt with.

If the access details seem scant this is usually because most birds are easily seen or one or more endangered species are present at the given site. The directions are aimed at birders with cars, since this is the most effective mode of transport in the majority of places. I have decided not to repeat the vast amount of information available about public transport, in order to allow more room in this book to talk birds.

(5) **Accommodation**—places recommended by birders for their safety, economy, comfort, position and, in some cases, opportunities for birding in their grounds. Once again, in order to save space and to avoid repeating the very detailed descriptions of accommodation which can be found in the various travel guides, I have not listed all types of accommodation available at every site. The prices of accommodation (per person per night) are marked as follows:

(A) = Over £10/US$15 (usually a long way over); (B) = £5 to £10/US$8 to 15; (C) = Under £5/US$8. In a few cases these price codes have been used to indicate other costs, such as boat hire and guide fees.

There are many good birding sites and numerous nooks and crannies where some scarce and difficult birds may be found, which have not been included in this book, due to the lack of space, so if you find it impossible to see certain species, even with the help of this book, it is time to put your exploring boots on and track them down. If successful please send the details to me for inclusion in the next edition (see Request, p. 389).

Where appropriate, at the end of each country, island or archipelago account there is a section called **Additional Information**, which includes: (i) a list of **Books and papers**, recommended for further reading, research and field use; and; (ii) a list of **Addresses**, to contact for more information, permits, booking accommodation in advance, and so on.

Finally, it is important to remember that this book is not an up-to-the-minute trip report. Some sites will have changed when you get there, some may not even be there, and some new ones will be discovered. Still, a little uncertainty is what makes birding so fascinating. It would be one hell of a poor pastime if every bird was lined up on an 'x' on the map, and whilst some birds are lined up like that in this book, I hope there are not too many. I have aimed to provide just the right amount of guidance to help you to plan a successful and enjoyable birding trip to Europe and Russia, and, hopefully, left enough leeway for you to 'find' your own birds.

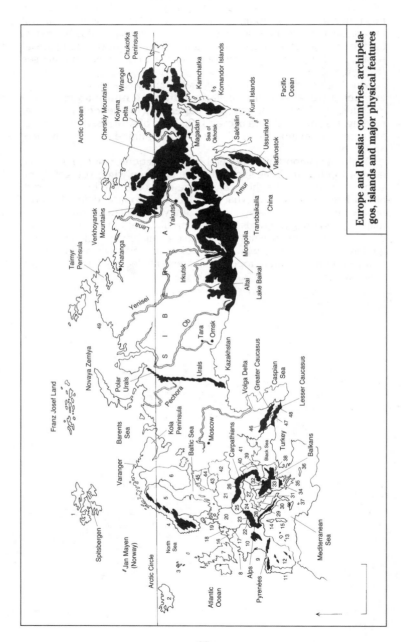

Europe and Russia: countries, archipelagos, islands and major physical features

Species Diversity

Less than 10% of the world's bird species occur on a regular basis in Europe and Russia, only 5% in the case of Europe, and 7% in Russia. A total of 688 species regularly occur in this region, 22 more than North America, but nearly 2,400 fewer than in South America, 2,000 fewer than in Asia and over 1,600 fewer than in Africa. The total number of species which occur regularly in North American minus the species with ranges which just reach into that region from Mexico to the southern states (66) and from the Caribbean to Florida (14), as well as those restricted to Alaska (35), is 551, a total of 84 more than the 467 species which occur on a regular basis in Europe. However, when including nearly 60 species which are regular vagrants from North America and Siberia, Europe's list is 525, just 26 fewer than the number of species which occur regularly in the main body of North America.

Within Europe and Russia 94 species occur east of the Urals only and a further 151 are confined to the Russian far east, including 75 which occur only in the Amur-Ussuriland area. The total for North America including the species restricted to Alaska but not those which are typically central American or Caribbean is 586, 74 fewer than the total of 660 species which occur in Russia on a regular basis. However, remove the 75 species which are restricted to the Amur-Ussuriland area (and essentially Asian) from the total of 660 for Russia and the total for that country becomes 585, just one less than the total of 586 for North America minus the essentially Caribbean and Central American species.

Leaving the Amur-Ussuriland area aside, birders hoping to see the widest possible diversity of species on a short trip to Europe and Russia should head for the northern shores of the Mediterranean, and the Black and Caspian Seas, at the southern edge of the region, where diversity peaks. The range of species then decreases to the north and east.

Europe and Russia: countries, archipelagos, islands and major physical features (key to map opposite)

1 Svalbard	17 Luxembourg	33 Macedonia
2 Iceland	18 Netherlands	34 Albania
3 Faroes	19 Denmark	35 Greece
4 Norway	20 Germany	36 Crete
5 Sweden	21 Poland	37 Malta
6 Finland	22 Switzerland	38 Bulgaria
7 Britain and	23 Liechtenstein	39 Romania
Ireland	24 Austria	40 Moldova
8 Channel Islands	25 Czech Republic	41 Ukraine
9 *Bay of Biscay*	26 Slovakia	42 Belarus
10 France	27 Hungary	43 Lithuania
11 Portugal	28 Italy	44 Latvia
12 Spain	29 Slovenia	45 Estonia
13 Balearic Islands	30 Croatia	46 Georgia
14 Corsica	31 Bosnia-	47 Armenia
15 Sardinia	Herzegovina	48 Azerbaijan
16 Belgium	32 Yugoslavia	49 Russia

FIGURE 1: SPECIES LISTS OF SIX OF THE WORLD'S MAJOR ZOO-GEOGRAPHICAL REGIONS

The figures below relate to regularly occuring species. They are approximate and based on *Birds of the World: A Check List* (Fourth Edition). Clements J, 1991, together with its supplements, which list some 9700 species.

Region	List	% of world total	% of Europe and Russia total
EUROPE and RUSSIA	688	7.1	–
NORTH AMERICA	666	6.9	97
AUSTRALASIA and OCEANIA	1,563	16	227
AFRICA	2,313	24	336
ASIA	2,689	28	391
SOUTH AMERICA	3,083	32	448

Family Diversity

Europe and Russia supports representatives of 71 regularly occurring different bird families, two of which are confined to Europe and five of which are represented only by one or two species in extreme southeast Russia (see Fig 2, below). The total minus the five restricted to the Amur-Ussuriland area is 66, three fewer than North America and at 34% the lowest portion of the world total (see Fig 3, p. 25). The revised total of 66 families is 50 fewer than Asia, the most diverse region on earth, 42 fewer than Africa, 34 fewer than Australasia and Oceania, and 26 fewer than South America.

There are no endemic or near-endemic families in Europe and Russia, as is the case with North America, whereas Asia supports six, Africa 15, Australasia and Oceania 20, and Central and South America 25, endemic families.

FIGURE 2: A LIST OF THE 71 BIRD FAMILIES REPRESENTED IN EUROPE and RUSSIA

The 64 families represented in Europe and Russia

Grebes	Kites, Hawks and Eagles
Petrels and Shearwaters	Falcons
Storm-Petrels	Pheasants and their allies
Cormorants	Buttonquails
Pelicans	Rails and Coots
Waterfowl	Cranes
Flamingos (Greater)	Bustards
Egrets, Herons and Bitterns	Sandpipers
Ibises and Spoonbills	Thick-knees (Eurasian)
Storks	Oystercatchers (Eurasian)
Osprey	Stilts and Avocets

Pratincoles	Waxwings
Plovers	Dippers
Gulls and Terns	Thrushes
Skuas	Starlings
Auks	Old World Flycatchers
Divers (Loons)	Nuthatches
Sandgrouse	Treecreepers
Pigeons	Wrens
Old World Cuckoos	Long-tailed Tit(s)
Barn Owls	Swallows
Owls	Crests (Kinglets)
Nightjars	Old World Warblers
Swifts	Parrotbills
Kingfishers	Tits
Bee-eaters	Penduline-Tits
Rollers	Larks
Hoopoes (Eurasian)	Old World Sparrows
Woodpeckers	Wagtails and Pipits
Crows	Accentors
Old World Orioles	Finches
Shrikes	Buntings

The two families represented in Europe only
Gannets (Northern), Cisticolas (Zitting).

The five families represented in Russia only
Painted-snipes (Greater), Monarch Flycatchers (Asian Paradise-Flycatcher), Cuckoo-Shrikes (Ashy Minivet), Bulbuls (Brown-eared), White-eyes (Chestnut-flanked and Japanese).

FIGURE 3: FAMILY LISTS OF THE WORLD'S MAJOR ZOOGEO-GRAPHICAL REGIONS

The figures below are based on *Birds of the World: A Check List* (Fourth Edition). Clements J, 1991, together with its supplements, which lists 195 families.

Region	List	% of world total	% of Europe and Russia total
EUROPE	66	34	93
RUSSIA	69	35	97
EUROPE and RUSSIA	71	36	–
NORTH AMERICA	69	35	97
CENTRAL AMERICA and the CARIBBEAN	90	46	127
SOUTH AMERICA	92	47	130
AUSTRALASIA and OCEANIA	100	51	141
AFRICA	108	55	152
ASIA	116	60	163

Habitat Diversity

For the purposes of this book the Europe and Russia region includes Iceland, Britain and Ireland, mainland Europe, from Portugal in the west to Romania in the east, the islands in the 3700-km-long Mediterranean Sea east to Lesbos off Turkey's west coast, the former Russian republics, including Armenia, Azerbaijan and Georgia, mainland Russia, and Russia's offshore islands east to the Kuril Islands which lie between Japan and the Kamchatka Peninsula. The total land area covered is 23,204,596 km^2, 52% of which is taken up by the vast expanse of Siberia.

Since the thawing of the ice sheet which covered much of northern Europe and Russia during the last ice age, about 10,000 years ago, the climax vegetation of the region, from north to south, became dominated by the Arctic **tundra**, the gloomy coniferous boreal forests of the **taiga**, which extends from the Baltic to the Pacific and is broken only, here and there, by large rivers, raised bogs and marshes, and forms the greatest belt of forest on earth, temperate **mixed forests** and **broad-leaved forests** (both mainly west of the Urals), **evergreen forest and scrub** in the Mediterranean, and **steppe and semi-desert**, mainly east of the Mediterranean in southern Russia. However, once these major habitats became established they were soon populated by human beings, especially in Europe, who then felled the forests to graze cattle, grow food and make shelter. In time, other habitats such as **grasslands** and **wetlands** were also destroyed or degraded and by the end of the 20th Century only a few remnant areas of pristine climax vegetation were left, hence many of the bird populations in the region, especially those west of the Urals, were severely depleted.

Aside from the main vegetation types, Europe and Russia's major habitats also include: coastal cliffs, stacks and offshore islands which still support huge numbers of seabirds; a multitude of estuaries alive with massive flocks of passage and wintering waterbirds; and some huge bird-rich deltas, including those at the mouths of the Río Guadalquivir in southern Spain (the Coto Doñana), the River Rhône in southern France (La Camargue), the 2850-km-long River Danube in eastern Romania and the 3688-km-long River Volga which forms a delta at the north end of the Caspian Sea.

Europe's main mountain ranges, which support foothill forests and grazed alpine grasslands, are the Pyrenées, which extend along the border between France and Spain for about 435 km and rise to 3404 m (11,168 ft) at Aneto; the Alps which extend from eastern France to eastern Austria and rise to 4809 m (15,778 ft) at Mont Blanc on the border between France and Italy, the highest peak in Europe; the Carpathians, which extend 1450 km from the Czech Republic southeast to Romania and rise to 2663 m (8737 ft) at Gerlachovka in the Tatry Mountains on the border between the Czech Republic and Poland; and the Balkans, which rise to 2925 m (9597 ft) at Musala in Bulgaria and lie between the Adriatic Sea and the Black Sea.

At the eastern end of the Black Sea the Lesser and Greater Caucasus rise to 5642 m (18,511 ft) at El'bruz on the border between Georgia and Russia. To the northeast of the Caspian Sea the 2000-km-long Urals, which rise to 1894 m (6214 ft), form a relatively low and narrow border between low-lying European Russia and low-lying Siberia. The next mountains to the east of the northern Urals, the Verkhoyansk, are thousands of kms away, but to the south the borders with Mongolia and northeast China are almost entirely mountainous, rising to 4506 m (14,784 ft) in the Altai. Amidst these rather barren border ranges lies Lake Baikal, the deepest lake on earth, which reaches a maximum depth of 1640 m (5381 ft).

The remote and rugged Chukotka and Kamchatka peninsulas, where many a mystical bird, not least Spoonbill Sandpiper*, breeds, are situated at the extreme eastern end of Russia, while in the far southeast of the region, in the Amur and Ussuriland area, the diverse broadleaved woodlands support an exceptionally rich avifauna which includes many Asian species at the northern limits of their breeding ranges.

Country Lists

With the exception of Britain and Ireland (c.535), the Netherlands (c.450) and Finland (c.430), where numerous rarities, many of which are now found on a regular basis by large numbers of highly skilled birders, bolster the country lists, and Russia (c.660), the top country lists for the region, most of which exceed 400, belong to the countries bordering the Mediterranean, and Black and Caspian Seas, notably Spain, France, Italy (480+), Greece (420+), Bulgaria (c.400) and the Ukraine (400+), although over 400 species have also been recorded in Poland. Hence, many European countries have richer avifaunas than places such as New Zealand (320+) and Madagascar (250+), and the total of 660 species which occur in Russia on a regular basis compares favourably with the total of 650 regularly occurring species in Australia. However, even the best European country totals fall a long way short of the best in the world. For example, Colombia's total of 1853+, which is the world's highest, is well over a thousand more than the total recorded in the whole Europe and Russia region. Furthermore, avian diversity decreases northwards from the Mediterranean and this is reflected in Iceland's total, which, despite being boosted by North American vagrants, barely exceeds 240.

Trip Lists

Birders in search of maximum variety on trips to Europe lasting around two weeks during the spring and early summer should head for Bulgaria, where 220–240 species may be seen; Spain, where 220+ is possible if the whole country is covered, in which case three weeks would be preferable; or Finland and Varangerfjord (in nearby northern Norway), where the 200-mark may also be broken. All of these destinations compare favourably with most of those slightly further afield, including Morocco (220), Israel (200), Turkey (200), and Churchill and Manitoba (200). Up to 200 is also possible in Armenia, Britain and Ireland, Estonia, Hungary and Slovakia, Poland, and northern Spain. In southern Spain birders in search of big lists could manage 170, and a similar total is also possible in Romania, La Camargue and Pyrenées, northern Greece, Hungary, and Portugal, all of which would be as productive as a winter trip to Florida. One hundred to one hundred and fifty is the going rate at most other destinations, although don't expect to see many more than 80 on Corsica and 70 on Iceland.

During the autumn the best two-week trips for diversity are La Camargue and Pyrenées, and Hungary, where it is possible to see up to 180 species, although Bulgaria is almost as good. During the winter the best places to be are Britain and the Netherlands where up to 140 species may be seen on trips lasting one to two weeks. At the other end of the scale those brave enough to have visited Varangerfjord during the winter have struggled to crack 40 in two weeks.

The record total for a three-week trip to Russia (and the whole region) is 316 species, which was recorded by Birdquest on their mammoth early summer excursion to Siberia and far east Russia in 1991. It included over 20 ducks, 40+ shorebirds, 30+ warblers and more than ten types of bunting. The 300-mark is very difficult to achieve, however, and in 1993 a similar trip could only muster a total of 289 species. On shorter two-week early summer trips to Ussuriland around 225 species are possible.

Most trip totals for Europe and Russia fall well short of those possible on excursions to the best countries in the world. Indeed, it is possible to see more birds during a few weeks in some countries than it is in a lifetime of birding in Europe and Russia, especially in South America and Africa. The world record total for a trip lasting up to a month is 1,040, set in Colombia in October 1997 by a team led by Paul Salaman, shattering the previous best, held by the Danish Ornithological Society which managed to record 844 during a 27-day trip to Ecuador in 1992. The African record belongs to the trip led by Brian Finch which notched up 797 on a 25-day tour to Kenya in 1991. Such numbers must be almost beyond belief to birders who have yet to breach the boundaries of Europe, and to them it must be hard to comprehend that the people on that month-long trip to Colombia saw or heard twice as many species than regularly occur in the whole of Europe.

Although such immense totals are usually possible only on organised tours led by leaders equipped with masses of experience of the sites, the birds and the best birding techniques, as well as the latest high-tech tape-recorders to lull out the many skulkers, the great advantage of birding in Europe, where so much more is known about the birds and the information on their whereabouts is relatively easier to get hold of, is that a thoroughly prepared team of independent birders can see just about every bird possible at their chosen destination.

Site Lists

There are plenty of sites in Europe with lists in excess of 250, including the Biebrza Marshes in Poland (260+), the Quinta da Rocha area of the Algarve in Portugal (c.275), Neusiedler See in Austria (nearly 300), the Ebro Delta in northeast Spain (300+), and Flevoland in the Netherlands (325+), while La Camargue in southern France and the Coto Doñana in southern Spain both have lists of 340 or so. There are a number of other sites west of Russia which may not have large overall totals, but whose richness is expressed in the number of breeding species they support. These include Pripyatsky National Park in Belarus (195 breeding species), Matsalu Bay in Estonia (170), the Danube Delta in Romania (160+), Puszcza Bialowieska, a forest on the border between Poland and Belarus (159), and the Black Sea Nature Reserve in the Ukraine (150+).

However, in Europe it is the sites which lie on the major migration routes and attract vagrants on a regular basis, and are thus birded intensively, which boast the longest lists; they include Fair Isle (350+), Cley (362), the Shetlands (363), Helgoland (400) and, best of all, the Isles of Scilly, where the list zoomed past the 400-mark in 1999. Only the comparatively underwatched Amur-Ussuriland area can compete with Europe's birding hotspots. Over 400 species have been recorded there, while the island of Sakhalin off the coast of far east Russia has a list of 355, and about 200 species have been recorded in the Kronotskiy Reserve on the Kamchatka Peninsula, to the north. Over 250 species have been recorded breeding in Ussuriland which, surprisingly, is about 35 fewer than the total for Spain.

While Europe and Russia's top site lists struggle to compete with the best in the world, including the highest total of 1,000 (at Manu Biosphere Reserve in Peru, and, probably, Madidi National Park in adjacent Bolivia), Africa's best, which is 535 (at Ruwenzori National Park in Uganda), and Asia's peak of 480 (at Chitwan National Park in Nepal), they are more than a match for several exotic locations, including Lake Nakuru in Kenya (400+), Bharatpur in India (400), Taman Negara in Malaysia (350+) and Kakadu National Park in Australia (275); and even the migration hot-spots of Beidaihe in China (400+) and Eilat in Israel (420+) are not far ahead.

Day Lists

During the spring and summer it is possible to see over 100 species on foot at sites across the whole of Europe, including the Coto Doñana in southern Spain, La Camargue in southern France, Minsmere in England, Flevoland in the Netherlands, Helgoland off the north coast of Germany, the Hortobâgy in Hungary and the Dobrudja in Romania. There are plenty more areas where it is easy to see over 100 species in a day, with the aid of a vehicle, even as far north as Kuusamo in Finland, but, apart from in Estonia where the European day-record of 190 was set on 25th May 1998, it will be necessary to attempt the land speed record to see many more than 150, even in the top areas such as East Anglia in England. Such totals are equally difficult to achieve in North America, although 150 shouldn't be too difficult in spring along the Texas coast, and during the annual New Jersey Bird Race some teams have managed to pass the 200 barrier, albeit while covering over 500 miles.

Elsewhere in the world it is possible to record over 180 species during a day's walk at Bharatpur in India or Lake Naivasha in Kenya. Impressive totals but still meagre when compared to the 331 species recorded during 24 hours at Manu Biosphere Reserve in Peru, in 1986—the world's top single-site day list. Even this incredible total is not the world day-list record, however. That belongs to Kenya in Africa, where with the aid of a small aircraft, a team recorded 342 species on a November day, also in 1986. Both of these amazing totals are on a par with the site lists for La Camargue and Coto Doñana, built up over many years.

Endemic Species

Regions of the world with concentrations of restricted-range birds have been identified as Endemic Bird Areas (EBAs) in BirdLife International's *Putting Biodiversity on the Map,* 1992. Out of the world total of 221 EBAs, Europe and Russia has just one (in the Caucasus), the same as North America, which shares its EBA with northwest Mexico, but far, far fewer than Asia (57), South America (55), Australasia and Oceania (46), Africa (37), and Central America and the Caribbean (25).

Just ten species are endemic to Europe and Russia, a tiny total when compared to those of other large landmasses such as North America (47) and Australia (313), and even large, nearby countries such as China (59). In order to see all ten endemics it will be necessary to visit

Corsica, Spain, Azerbaijan, Georgia or Russia, the Alps, Appenines or Balkans, Scandinavia or northwest Russia, and Scotland. During a single trip the highest number of the region's endemics (four out of ten) can be seen in Corsica, Spain and the Alps. By combining trips to Spain and Corsica it would be possible to see six of the ten endemics, leaving Caucasian Snowcock (endemic to the Caucasus), Rock Partridge (endemic to the Alps, Appenines and Balkans), Parrot Crossbill (endemic to Scandinavia and northwest Russia) and Scottish Crossbill* (endemic to Scotland).

FIGURE 4: THE 10 ENDEMIC BIRDS OF EUROPE and RUSSIA

Species	Range
Spanish Eagle*	Spain (occasionally Portugal and Morocco)
Caucasian Snowcock	Azerbaijan, Georgia and Russia
Rock Partridge	Alps, Appenines and Balkans
Red-legged Partridge	Western Europe
Corsican Nuthatch*	Corsica
Marmora's Warbler	Balearic Islands, Corsica and Sardinia (possibly local on east coast of Spain, and some winter in north Africa)
Crested Tit	Europe, east to the Ural Mountains in Russia
Citril Finch	Spain, France, Alps, Italy, Corsica and Sardinia
Parrot Crossbill	Scandinavia, east to the River Pechora in Russia
Scottish Crossbill*	Scotland

Five endemic forms, currently treated by most taxonomists as races, may be designated full species status in the future. They are:

Dark-bellied Brent Goose	*bernicla* breeds in west Siberia and winters in the southern North Sea area.
Red (Willow) Grouse	*scoticus* is resident in Britain and Ireland.
Mediterranean (Citril) Finch	*corsicana* is resident on Corsica and Sardinia.
Lesser Redpoll	*cabaret* breeds in northwest Europe south to the Alps and may disperse in winter as far south as the Mediterranean.
Icelandic Redpoll	*islandica* breeds in Iceland and may disperse to Scotland during the winter.

Near-endemic Species

Almost 60 species are nearly endemic to Europe and Russia. In order to see the 25 possible in Europe it will be necessary to travel to Spain, Scotland (during the winter), Finland and northern Norway, where at least 11 near-endemics are present in each area, although seven to nine near-endemics also occur in the Balearic Islands, Corsica, Sardinia and France.

The remaining 33 near-endemics occur in the Caucasus (four), south-central Russia (five) and far east Russia (24). In order to see these birds it will be necessary to visit Azerbaijan or Georgia, where the four Caucasian near-endemics, as well as the endemic Caucasian Snow-cock, occur; the steppes and nearby Altai Mountains, where the five species which are near-endemic to south-central Russia can be seen; the Amur-Ussuriland area, where it is possible to see 17 of the 24 near-endemic birds of the Russian far east; and the Kuril Islands (Red-faced Cormorant, Japanese Accentor and Grey Bunting), the Komandor Islands (Red-legged Kittiwake*) and the Chukotka Peninsula (Emperor Goose, Spectacled Eider* and Least Auklet) in order to clear-up the remaining seven.

FIGURE 5: THE 58 NEAR-ENDEMIC BIRDS OF EUROPE and RUSSIA

The 12 Near-endemic birds of western Europe and the Mediter-ranean

Mediterranean Shearwater	Black Wheatear
European Storm-Petrel	Firecrest
Pink-footed Goose	Dartford Warbler
Great Skua	Dupont's Lark
Audouin's Gull*	Thekla Lark
Spotless Starling	Rock Pipit

The 13 Near-endemic birds of Europe and Russia

European Shag	Slender-billed Curlew*
Barnacle Goose	Ural Owl
Steller's Eider*	Eurasian Pygmy-Owl
Red Kite	Siberian Jay
Black Grouse	Willow Tit
Eurasian Capercaillie	Siberian Tit
Hazel Grouse	

The Four Near-endemic birds of the Caucasus Region

Caspian Snowcock	Armenian Gull
Caucasian Grouse*	Radde's Accentor

The Five Near-endemic birds of the Russian South-Central Region

Altai Falcon	White-winged Lark
Altai Snowcock	Black Lark
Pallas's Sandgrouse	

The 24 Near-endemic birds of the Russian Far East

Japanese Cormorant	Siberian Grouse*
Red-faced Cormorant	Black-billed Capercaillie
Emperor Goose	Swinhoe's Rail*
Spectacled Eider*	Slaty-backed Gull
Scaly-sided Merganser*	Red-legged Kittiwake*
Steller's Sea-Eagle*	Spectacled Guillemot

Kittlitz's Murrelet	Horned Puffin
Ancient Murrelet	Blakiston's Fish-Owl*
Parakeet Auklet	Japanese Waxwing*
Crested Auklet	Reed Parrotbill*
Whiskered Auklet	Japanese Accentor
Least Auklet	Grey Bunting

Five near-endemic forms, currently treated as races by most taxonomists, may be designated full species status in the future. They are:

The 'Balearic' *mauretanicus* race of Mediterranean Shearwater
The 'Scopoli's' *diomedea* race of Cory's Shearwater
The 'Pale-bellied' *hrota* race of Brent Goose
The 'Common' *nigra* race of Common (Black) Scoter
The 'Velvet' *fusca* race of Velvet (White-winged) Scoter

Exploration

Those birders keen to add the little-known and rarely seen species to their burgeoning European and Russian lists, or those birders in search of something new and exciting, will be busy planning possible trips to the region's remote nooks and crannies, having carried out extensive and painstaking research into old records, habitat preferences and the present-day distribution of the relevant habitats. Surprisingly, for such a supposedly well-known region of the world, remote and rarely visited areas do still exist, especially in the potentially very exciting Caucasian countries of Armenia, Azerbaijan and Georgia, as well as in Moldova, the Ukraine and Russia, where it may even be possible to rediscover Crested Shelduck* (not reported in east Russia since 1985, and the last sighting before that was of at least three on islands in the Bay of Peter the Great in 1964), Crested Ibis* (not seen in southeast Siberia since 1983) and even the current breeding grounds of Slender-billed Curlew* (no nests have been found since 1924 despite extensive searching).

Alternative ways to contribute new information on the region's avifauna include going to sea in search of seabirds, the mysterious movements of which still need unravelling, and while working out what's what why not look out for potential new birds for the region? If southern hemisphere species such as Black-browed Albatross can make it, then so can many more. The first White-tailed Tropicbird may even be seen from some exposed headland, probably in southwest England or Ireland. Most of such headlands are also migrant hot-spots and these together with the islands of northwest Europe famous for great rarities, may also harbour a new landbird for the region, so, while enjoying the movements of common and scarce migrants, which is such a speciality of birding in Europe and Russia, remember that someone somewhere may just be fortunate enough to bump into the first Yellow-throated Warbler to successfully cross the Atlantic.

TAXONOMY

Taxonomy, or classification, is the arrangement of organisms into kingdoms, phyla, classes, orders, families, genuses, species and subspecies (or races), based on their anatomical, biochemical, morphological and physiological characters. There are several systematic classifications of birds, reflecting the various ways in which the evolutionary paths and relationships of their characters are interpreted by different taxonomists, but the two most popular arrangements are based on the Phylogenetic and Biological Species Concepts. Phylogeny is the historical sequence of changes that occur in a given species during the course of its evolution. The Phylogenetic Species Concept (PSC) is based on the idea that by tracking the evolution of a bird's adaptations or characters it is possible to ascertain how different birds are related historically, and that it is this history which distinguishes between different species. PSC thus regards a species as the smallest population of individuals within which there is a pattern of ancestry which is different from that of another population, and since many current subspecies exhibit different historical sequences of changes the application of PSC results in these subspecies becoming full species. For example, the PSC shows that the traditional arrangement of Yellow Wagtail, with its many subspecies, does not accurately reflect the evolutionary relationships between the subspecies, and that the different evolutionary histories of these subspecies means that they should in fact be treated as full species.

However, not all taxonomists believe PSC is the concept which should be applied when deciding what is a species and what is not. Some taxonomists believe the traditional Biological Species Concept (BSC) is better. Basically, the BSC regards a species as those populations of birds which can produce fertile offspring if they interbreed. So, in the case of allopatric populations, that is geographically separated and reproductively isolated populations of what are currently the same species, if it is believed that these populations could interbreed and produce fertile offspring if they came into contact, then the application of BSC results in those populations being regarded as the same species, even though an ocean may separate them and the likelihood of them meeting up, let alone interbreeding, is minimal. So, based on the BSC, Common Teal, which breeds on the east side of the Atlantic, is the same species as the allopatric Green-winged Teal, which breeds on the west side of the Atlantic, because if they ever came into contact there is a chance that they might breed and produce fertile offspring. Whereas, based on the PSC they are different species because they exhibit different patterns of ancestry.

If PSC is applied to all current bird species it has been estimated that the world list will double, since there is a current average of two subspecies per species, or, to put it another way, two phylogenetic species for every biological species. Hence PSC is likely to prove very popular with birders, since there will be more birds to look for (and list), and, much more importantly, with conservationists, since the case for saving what are currently regarded as subspecies by BSC becomes much stronger when these are made into full species.

Both concepts have their faults. The main problem with PSC is that it could result in species being split into so many new species that it will be impossible to identify them in the field. For example, research by Groth on Crossbills in North America suggested that Red Crossbill should be split into about eight different species, none of which could be reliably identified in the field. In fact the only way to tell them apart was by the subtle differences in their calls. If PSC did spiral out of control, future birders may only be able to identify individual species by taking a blood sample. Seriously though, the main problem lies with conservation, because the more species there are, the more there are to save, and with funding already stretched to the limit it may prove very difficult to conserve twice as many threatened species, let alone those which are of current concern. Furthermore, if PSC proves to be an ephemeral phenomenon, funds used to save PSC species will have been wasted. The main problem with BSC is that it relies on guesswork, in that it assumes allopatric species could breed and produce fertile offspring, and this means many allopatric populations and, crucially, island forms, are lumped together, thus resulting in less conservation concern for what would be full species if the PSC was applied. Taxonomists working in the fields of botany and entomology have found BSC, on the whole, to be unworkable. Hence some sort of compromise seems inevitable and, indeed, has already been suggested, by Charles Sibley, who calls it the Allopatric Species Concept (ASC).

PSC was ahead on points at the end of the 20th Century, and, so long as the taxonomists working with it continue to secure funding, the splits they have proposed so far may just represent the tip of a very large iceberg. However, since the PSC has yet to be universally accepted, the site bird lists in this book are based on *Birds of the World: A Check List*, Clements, 1991, with the proposed splits resulting from work on the PSC (up to the end of 1998) included in parentheses after the relevant 'super' species name, as shown below.

Cory's Shearwater—three species: Cory's Shearwater *Calonectris borealis*. Cape Verde Shearwater *Calonectris edwardsii*. Scopoli's Shearwater *Calonectris diomedea*.

Mediterranean (Yelkouan) Shearwater—two species: Yelkouan Shearwater *Puffinus yelkouan*. Balearic Shearwater *Puffinus mauretanicus*.

Bewick's (Tundra) Swan—two species: Bewick's Swan *Cygnus bewickii*. Tundra (Whistling) Swan *Cygnus columbianus*.

Bean Goose—(at least) two species: Taiga Bean Goose *Anser fabalis*. Tundra Bean Goose *Anser rossicus*.

Canada Goose—(at least) two species: Canada Goose *Branta canadensis*. Lesser Canada Goose *Branta hutchinsii*.

Brent Goose (Brant)—three species: Dark-bellied Brent Goose *Branta bernicla*. Pale-bellied Brent Goose *Branta hrota*. Black Brant *Branta nigricans*.

Common Teal—two species: Common Teal *Anas crecca*. Green-winged Teal *Anas carolinensis*.

Common (Black) Scoter—two species: Common Scoter *Melanitta nigra*. Black Scoter *Melanitta americana*.

Velvet (White-winged) Scoter—two species: Velvet Scoter *Melanitta fusca*. White-winged Scoter *Melanitta deglandi*.

Willow Ptarmigan (Grouse)—two species: Willow Grouse *Lagopus lagopus*. Red Grouse *Lagopus scoticus*.

Purple Swamphen—three species: Western Swamphen *Porphyrio porphyrio*. Grey-headed Swamphen *Porphyrio poliocephalus*. African Swamphen *Porphyrio madagascariensis*.

Common Snipe—two species: Common Snipe *Gallinago gallinago*. Wilson's Snipe *Gallinago delicata*.

Iceland Gull—two species: Iceland Gull *Larus glaucoides*. Kumlien's Gull *Larus kumlieni*.

Lesser Black-backed, Yellow-legged and Herring Gulls—eight species: Lesser Black-backed Gull *Larus graellsii*. Baltic (Black-backed) Gull *Larus fuscus*. Heuglin's (Siberian) Gull *Larus heuglini*. Yellow-legged Gull *Larus michahellis*. Caspian (Pontic) Gull *Larus cachinnans*. Herring Gull *Larus argentatus* (and *argenteus* (British Herring Gull)). Vega Gull *Larus vegae*. American Herring Gull *Larus smithsonianus*.

Isabelline (Rufous-tailed) Shrike—three species: Turkestan Shrike *Lanius phoenicuroides*. Daurian Shrike *Lanius speculigerus*. Chinese Shrike *Lanius isabellinus*.

Great Grey (Northern) Shrike—three species: Northern Grey Shrike *Lanius excubitor*. Southern Grey Shrike *Lanius meridionalis*. Steppe Grey Shrike *Lanius pallidirostris*.

Dark-throated Thrush—two species: Red-throated Thrush *Turdus ruficollis*. Black-throated Thrush *Turdus atrogularis*.

Dusky Thrush—two species: Naumann's Thrush *Turdus naumanni*. Dusky Thrush *Turdus eunomus*.

Common Stonechat—two species: European Stonechat *Saxicola rubicola*. Siberian Stonechat *Saxicola maura*.

Black-eared Wheatear—two species: Western Black-eared Wheatear *Oenanthe hispanica*. Eastern Black-eared Wheatear *Oenanthe melanoleuca*.

Eurasian Reed-Warbler—three species: European Reed-Warbler *Acrocephalus scirpaceus*. Caspian Reed-Warbler *Acrocephalus fuscus*. Mangrove (African) Reed-Warbler *Acrocephalus avicennia* (occurs around the Red Sea).

Booted Warbler—two species: Booted Warbler *Hippolais/Acrocephalus caligatus*. Sykes's Warbler *Hippolais/Acrocephalus rama*. These two species (as well as Olivaceous Warbler) are now believed by some taxonomists to belong to the *Acrocephalus* genus (not *Hippolais*) and to be most closely related to the large unstreaked members of that genus.

Chiffchaff—five species: Chiffchaff *Phylloscopus collybita*. Iberian Chiffchaff *Phylloscopus brehmii*. Mountain Chiffchaff *Phylloscopus sindianus*. Caucasian Chiffchaff *Phylloscopus lorenzii*. Canary Islands Chiffchaff *Phylloscopus canariensis*.

Bonelli's Warbler—two species: Western Bonelli's Warbler *Phylloscopus bonelli*. Eastern Bonelli's Warbler *Phylloscopus orientalis*.

Yellow-browed Warbler—two species: Yellow-browed Warbler *Phylloscopus inornatus*. Hume's (Leaf-) Warbler *Phylloscopus humei*.

Greenish Warbler—three species: Greenish Warbler *Phylloscopus trochiloides*. Two-barred Greenish Warbler *Phylloscopus plumbeitarsus*. Green Warbler *Phylloscopus nitidus*.

White Wagtail—four species: White Wagtail *Motacilla alba*. Pied Wagtail *Motacilla yarrellii*. Masked Wagtail *Motacilla personata*. Moroccan Wagtail *Motacilla subpersonata*.

Yellow Wagtail—ten species: Yellow Wagtail *Motacilla flavissima*. Blue-headed Wagtail *Motacilla flava* (and *beema* (Sykes' Wagtail)). Grey-headed Wagtail *Motacilla thunbergi*. Black-headed Wagtail *Motacilla feldegg*. Spanish Wagtail *Motacilla iberiae*. Ashy-headed Wagtail *Motacilla cinereocapilla*. Yellow-headed Wagtail *Motacilla lutea*. Green-headed Wagtail *Motacilla taivana*. Kamchatka Wagtail *Motacilla simillima*. White-headed Wagtail *Motacilla leucocephala*.

Citril Finch—two species: Citril Finch *Serinus citrinella*. Mediterranean Finch *Serinus corsicana*.

Arctic (Hoary) Redpoll—two species: Hornemann's Redpoll *Carduelis hornemanni*. Arctic Redpoll *Carduelis exilipes*.

Common Redpoll—four species: Mealy Redpoll *Carduelis flammea*. Lesser Redpoll *Carduelis cabaret*. Greenland Redpoll *Carduelis rostrata*. Icelandic Redpoll *Carduelis islandica*.

CONSERVATION

Most of the natural habitats of Europe and Russia have been destroyed or degraded. That is a wretched fact, but what is even more depressing is that this destruction and deterioration continues apace at the beginning of the 21st Century. One of the major reasons why about 40% of the birds which occur in Europe are declining is agricultural intensification, leading to the loss of grassland, forest, woods and wetland, and resulting in pollution, through the excessive use of fertilisers, herbicides and pesticides, and the creation of, what are in effect, vast areas of sterilised crops devoid of avian life. However, the long list of reasons why even supposedly common birds such as Eurasian Blackbird (down over a million between 1988 and 1997 in Britain) are decreasing in numbers also includes the spread of built development, poor forestry management, the number of domestic cats (over seven million in Britain alone), airborne pollution such as acid rain (which has damaged 30–50% of forests in central and eastern Europe), overfishing, overgrazing, trapping and, believe it or not, even in this day and age, hunting, which, especially in the Mediterranean, takes a terrible toll.

When birds such as the Sky Lark disappear from our lives, we know we are in trouble. The British population of this species fell by four million between the mid-1970s and mid-1990s, and, as is the case with many other species across Europe, its decline is primarily linked to the Common Agricultural Policy (CAP), which rewards European Economic Community (EEC) farmers according to how many crops they produce, not how they go about producing them. Just 3% of the CAP budgets are spent on conservation, a terrible reflection on where the policy's priorities lie, and the CAP reforms (Agenda 2000) which were finalised in early 1999 did little to encourage farmers to employ methods which are more environmentally sustainable. A great opportunity to address the problem, which will perhaps spiral out of control when a number of eastern European countries join the EEC in the early 21st Century, has therefore been missed.

However much we rant and rave about making sure large landowners farm food, and not money, it is still little more than whistling in the dark when one considers that the human population of Europe continues to rise (by 320,000 in 1998), making less and less land available for farming anyway. If we wish to live in a world where we can enjoy all the modern appliances while listening to the Sky Lark singing outside, we will have to live in harmony with the planet *and* make more room for wildlife, but if the human population continues to rise, the only way it may be possible to hear Sky Larks outside our windows will be if those windows lie between a wild world and a concrete box on the umpteenth floor of a tower block. Some people would be more than happy to live in a centrally-heated concrete box at the top, or bottom, of a skyscraper, whether it is encompassed by flower-filled fields and bird-rich woods or chemically sterilised, lifeless farmland and tarmac, but given the choice, surely most of us would rather live in a modern detached house surrounded by the former. However, most of us don't have a choice ...because there are so many of us crammed into Europe that there just isn't the room. So, unless the quality of our lives is to sink to even greater depths, with people living in smaller and smaller boxes, stacked higher and higher, we need to stabilise, or, better still, reduce human population growth.

Unfortunately, however, stemming population growth seems impossible, and indeed, undesirable to some governments. In the long term, if the population of Europe continues to grow, what is the point in trying to persuade the EEC to reform CAP and to convince governments to protect areas, when the same authorities advocate increasing human populations as a necessary prerequisite of economic growth and stability? The point is that one day they will come to realise that growth where the environmental costs outweigh the environmental benefits is uneconomic.

So, in the meantime, conservationists are trying to save what little remains of the region's wildlife with a variety of small-scale projects. One of these, ecotourism, especially in the form of birding where Europe is concerned, has the potential to protect many of the best habitats throughout the region. If local people can be shown that birds are just as valuable to their local economies as, say, hunting, poor forestry or overgrazing, via the injection of visiting birders' cash into their local economy, then they may be persuaded to manage their natural resources accordingly. An excellent model of the sustainable utilisation of natural resources for the benefit of wildlife, the local people and visiting birders is provided by the raptor feeding station at the Dadia-Soufli Forest Reserve in Greece, which has attracted hundreds of visitors since it was established, all of whom have contributed significantly to the local economy. Hopefully, many other places will follow suit and perhaps even convince their respective governments that the sustainable use of their country's dwindling natural resources is the only logical way ahead. A good example is the forest at Puszcza Bialowieska in Poland, already a popular birding destination, and yet the Polish government has so far failed to realise that maintaining and increasing the annual influx of birders, which contributes greatly to the local economy, is a far better way of exploiting the forest than logging it, as they are currently doing.

I hope this book, in its own small way, will help to encourage as many birders as possible to visit as many sites as possible in Europe and Russia, and, ultimately, help those birders not only to enjoy the region's birds but also to contribute to conserving them. So, when visiting any of the sites described in this book please make sure every local person, especially business people, knows why you are there and why more birders will follow.

GENERAL TIPS

The following words of advice are by no means comprehensive. They are little more than a mishmash of miscellaneous points resulting from personal experience and birding tales shared between friends. However, they may help to maximise the enjoyment of a birding trip to Europe and Russia.

The best birding trips usually result from extensive research and months of planning. Take the time necessary to find out where you are most likely to locate the species you wish to see before embarking on any trip and work out an itinerary very carefully—the best itineraries are normally the result of several drafts.

When in the field, walk quietly and slowly, especially in forest, and make use of vegetation for patient stalking. These basic field skills are well known to most birders, but they are all too easily forgotten in the frenzy of new and exciting birds. Early morning is usually the best time for birding anywhere in the world and Europe and Russia is no exception, especially in the hot Mediterranean, and Black and Caspian Sea lowlands where heat-haze can seriously hamper birding from mid-morning to late afternoon, but during the short Arctic summer, when it is possible to bird for 24 hours, the first few hours after midnight are usually the most productive. The middle of the day is a good time to move from one site to another, or, if this is not appropriate, to take a siesta before a late afternoon bash, the evening owl and nightjar search, and the appropriate celebration of another great day in the field. Some fanatical birders will argue that it is still possible to see plenty of birds around midday, especially where there is some shade or water, and the hours of darkness after the owls and nightjars have been seen are the best time to move from site to site. Travelling by road between sites at night could be dangerous in some countries, especially where the roads are bad, but overnight drives do help to keep accommodation costs down and they may produce a few otherwise unexpected birds and mammals. However, while a couple of night drives may save some money and be good fun, too many may result in overtiredness which could impair your enjoyment of the whole trip. It's not much fun returning home after a successful and enjoyable trip full of glorious moments only to discover that you can't remember much because you were too tired.

Forest birding in Europe and Russia, especially in central and eastern Europe, Scandinavia, and Russia, can be very frustrating, and several hours may pass without seeing a single bird, although many may be heard. The woods of western Europe can also appear to be devoid of avian life during the winter months, but when a wave (feeding flock) appears, or a skulker such as Hazel Grouse pops out on to the trail or track, all those hours of pre-trip planning and patient stalking will suddenly seem worthwhile. Bird waves are a feature of European and Russian woods and forest during the winter. Birds often seem to appear from nowhere and move all too quickly, but try sticking with the flock as long as possible, even after it seems like they have all moved on, because the stragglers sometimes turn out to be the more unusual species.

Tracking down every unknown call is essential, but more often than not requires the patience of a saint. It is easy to get the tape recorder out in such a situation, but this devious birding method which, lets face it, requires very little field skill, is *not* appropriate for use with threatened or near-threatened species (not knowing the call means it could be such a species), if any species at all. Tape-luring birds out interrupts behaviour, distracting them from defending their breeding and feeding territories, and this inevitably affects food intake, a potentially lethal outcome if the bird is busy feeding its young. Furthermore, birds which eventually stop responding to tapes may also stop responding to real intruders, in which case their food supply could be diminished, and this may ultimately lead to them leaving the area altogether. Trying to pin down a bird which you can hear but cannot see is extremely frustrating, but surely there is more joy and satisfaction to be gained from seeing the bird after a long and hard hunt than by standing next to a tape recorder waiting for the unfortunate creature to come and peck at it. Good birders don't need tapes; they use their own knowledge of birds' habitats and habits, and their field skills, to find birds.

Seawatching arguably requires more experience and skill than any other type of birding, so the more hours you spend getting to know the jizz and finer identification points of the commoner species, the more you are likely to get out of this extremely enjoyable branch of birding. Deciding on the time to seawatch is crucial and, unfortunately, even birders who double up as amateur meteorologists don't always get it right: seabird movements are still a mystery to most. Onshore winds, the stronger the better, are usually the best, but this is not always the case, and, once again, in order to find out the best conditions for seawatching at a particular site, it is best to spend as much time there as possible (in all conditions). Serious seawatchers know one thing is certain— exceptional seawatches are rare, and vagrant seabirds even harder to connect with, so the old maxim 'persistence pays', which applies to all birding, is probably most appropriate to seawatching.

Thrushes, warblers, tits, finches and buntings are good examples of birds which are attracted to flowering and fruiting trees, and areas of woodland and farmland where there is an abundance of seed. On first impressions such trees, woods and fields may seem to be lacking in avian life, as the birds feed quietly, but by waiting a while these areas can slowly come alive. In some cases, there may be so many birds in a particular tree, an area of trees or in a field, that watching these for a couple of hours or so will probably prove to be more productive than frantic wandering.

Most countries, islands and regions of Europe and Russia are some of the safest places in the world to go birding, but even at the end of the 20th Century there were still a few areas which were definitely best avoided, including Yugoslavia, especially the Kosovo region and its adjacent areas of Albania and Macedonia, and much of the Russian Caucasus, especially the breakaway republic of Chechnya. Before even considering a visit to these areas it is crucial to contact the relevant foreign office for details on the latest situation.

Apart from civil and ethnic wars, and crime in general, the most likely form of danger a birder will face in Europe and Russia may be presented by some of the birds themselves. Arctic Terns, Great Skuas and, especially owls, all defend their young very aggressively, and female Ural Owls have been known to rip shirts and draw blood, so protect your precious eyes and enjoy the many pleasures of birding in Europe and Russia.

GLOSSARY

2WD: Two-wheel-drive vehicle.

4WD: Four-wheel-drive vehicle.

Acid Rain: Rain containing sulphur dioxide, formed by the burning of fossil fuels such as coal, and nitrogen oxides, produced by various industries and motor vehicles.

Afforestation: The planting of trees in areas which have not previously been forested.

The Arctic Circle: Line which encircles the North Pole within which there is at least one day during the summer when the sun never sets and at least one day during the winter when the sun never rises. In Europe and Russia this line lies across northern Norway, Sweden, Finland and Russia

Bog: Acidic, waterlogged soil where the decomposition of dead matter proceeds at a slower than normal pace and accumulates as peat. The typical vegetation of bogland includes cotton grass, rushes and sphagnum mosses. A raised bog builds up above the surrounding peat where there is high rainfall but poor drainage.

Calcareous: Usually used to describe soil which is rich in calcium, usually in the form of chalk or lime.

Carr: A woodland which has grown on a bog or fen, typically containing Alder and willows.

Cirque: A mountainside hollow with steep walls, formed by glaciation, and also known as a corrie or a cwm.

The Common Agricultural Policy (CAP): The system used by the European Economic Community (EEC) to increase productivity, provide a fair standard of living and stabilise markets within the agricultural community, as well as to ensure reasonable consumer prices. In many cases the policy has resulted in environmental degradation and destruction, overproduction and high subsidies.

Eutrophication: The excessive enrichment of soils or waterbodies with nutrients and pollutants, often as a result of nitrate and phosphate fertilisers running off farmland, which encourages the growth of algae and bacteria which lower oxygen levels and thus cause a decrease in the diversity of flora and fauna.

Fen: Predominantly alkaline peatland which receives relatively high amounts of mineral salts and water from the ground.

Fjord (Fiord): A narrow sea inlet with high, steep walls, formed by rising seas filling over-deepened glacial valleys.

Garrigue: Low, often thorny, open scrub, which usually results from the overgrazing of maquis, and is typically found on Mediterranean slopes.

Heathland: Land with vegetation dominated by evergreen dwarf shrubs which usually grow on well-drained, acidic, gravelly or sandy soils in lowlands near the Atlantic. It is sometimes distinguished from moorland by having an average annual total precipitation of less than 1000 mm (3.3 ft).

Karst: Limestone country, which may be complete with caves and limestone pavements, and which takes its name from the Karst region on the Adriatic coast in Croatia and Slovenia.

Machair: Flower-rich dunes, grazed grassland and wet hollows formed where calcareous sand has been blown over soil, usually near the coast in northwest Europe.

Maquis (Macchia): Tall, mostly evergreen, dense scrub, up to 4 m (13 ft) high, usually including species such as gorse, heather, mastic, rosemary, sage and broom, and typically found on Mediterranean slopes where it supports birds such as Orphean, Rüppell's, Sardinian, Subalpine and Marmora's Warblers. Overgrazing of maquis leads to the formation of garrigue.

Marsh: Land which usually remains wet throughout the year and is seasonally flooded.

Meadow: Land which is composed of grassland and which is traditionally maintained by cutting (for hay) or grazing.

Mire: Plant and soil communities characterised by an accumulation of peat. Acidic mires are known as bogs and alkaline mires are known as fens.

Moorland: Acidic peatland in northern European uplands dominated by grasses, heath-like plants or sedges, and sometimes distinguished from heathland by having an average annual total precipitation of over 1000 mm (3.3 ft).

Peat: Partly decomposed plant matter which accumulates in waterlogged soil, mainly due to a lack of oxygen.

Polder: A low-lying area of farmland which has been reclaimed from the sea.

Re-afforestation: The planting of trees in areas which have been deforested.

Saltmarsh: A marsh which is periodically flooded by the sea or which contains water which is rich in salt for some other reason.

Steppe: Extensive, usually treeless plains where the vegetation is dominated by grasses or dwarf shrubs.

Taiga: Russian name for the boreal forest zone which lies south of the tundra and is composed, for the most part, of dense coniferous forests.

Tundra: Arctic land with a permanent layer of frozen subsoil (permafrost) which means the vegetation consists almost entirely of grasses, Heather, lichens, mosses and sedges.

MAPS

Before embarking on a birding trip, it is essential to obtain the best maps available of the intended destination. Many detailed maps of Europe can be found in good book shops throughout the region, but to avoid missing the best available and to track down those which cover the more remote regions of Russia contact the specialist map sellers listed under Useful Addresses on p. 395.

The maps in this book are simplified, since they are intended to give a quick impression of (i) how the major birding sites are distributed within in a country, archipelago or island; and (ii) where the best places for birds are at individual sites. Each country, archipelago or island account has a map at the beginning which shows the location of the major cities and towns, road routes and birding sites. In some accounts there are also maps of regions within countries, archipelagos and islands to show how 'bunches' of sites are distributed. Most accounts also contain individual site maps.

When in the field, birders are more interested in finding and watching birds than making detailed notes on distances and directions, so although every effort has been made to make the site maps in this book as precise as possible, most of them are not perfect. Since their main purpose is to help birders to orientate themselves and to get to the best spots for birds, more often than not 'direction-pointers' such as buildings, roads and rivers, and on-site detail such as trails, have been exaggerated, and are not usually drawn to scale.

It is also important to remember that site details change. Signposts may have fallen down or been taken away, new signposts may have been put up, trails may have become tracks, tracks may have become roads, buildings may have been knocked down or put up, marshes, lakes and rivers may have dried up or been drained, rivers may even have changed course, steppe grasslands may have been turned over to agriculture, woods and forest may have been felled, new woods and forest may have been planted etc. Furthermore, some sites may no longer exist by the time you come to use these maps, so if you arrive at a site which looks totally different from what you have perceived as a result of reading this book, or that site no longer exists, don't blame the birders who have been before you and don't blame me, blame the ever increasing human population of the planet.

The **map symbols** used are as follows:

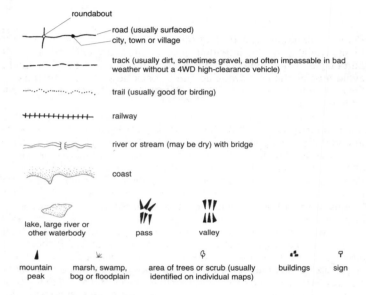

ALBANIA

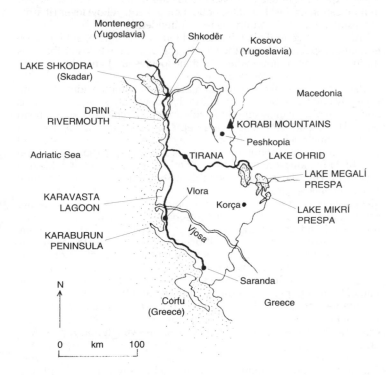

INTRODUCTION

This small country, which borders the eastern Adriatic, was virtually sealed off from the outside world until the fall of its own brand of communism in 1990, and it seems likely to remain one of the least visited countries in the world well into the 21st century, since outbreaks of violence were still occuring within the country and nearby in the late 1990s. Hence it would be wise to find out the latest details on whether or not it is safe to travel in Albania (with the relevant foreign office) before embarking on a trip. If and when it is safe to visit this country and the tourist infrastructure is developed, birders may wish to consider visiting Albania to look for elusive high-altitude specialities such as Rock Partridge and some species which, within Europe, breed only in the eastern Mediterranean, such as Olive-tree Warbler.

At 28,750 km2, Albania is one fifth the size of England and 4% the size of Texas. Even in the capital, Tirana, finding a vehicle for hire is likely to prove very difficult, and this, coupled with a skeletal public transport network, makes getting around Albania without the assistance of a local or international organisation almost impossible. Many Albanians speak

Italian, and being able to converse in this language would be a great help in getting to the best sites, sorting out accommodation and food once there, and, if necessary, arranging the services of guides. There are a few expensive hotels and basic foods are available in most places. Immunisation against hepatitis, polio, typhoid and yellow fever (if arriving from an infected country) is recommended.

The Adriatic coastal plain has a Mediterranean climate, but it is cooler inland, especially during the winter. The peak time to visit Albania is during the early summer when resident species are joined by summer visitors such as Olive-tree Warbler.

The narrow coastal plain, which reaches a maximum width of 60 km, is largely cultivated but there are also dunes, estuaries, lagoons, salinas and pine woods which support a wide variety of typical Mediterranean birds. The inland river valleys and depressions are also cultivated, but as the terrain rises, farmland gives way to beech and fir forests, and grasslands on the mountains which rise to 2753 m (9032 ft) in the Korabi Mountains on the border with Macedonia and the Kosovo region of Yugoslavia. In the southeast there are three large natural mountain lakes, the waters of which are shared with Greece and Macedonia, all of which are very important for waterbirds. There are some national parks and nature reserves in Albania but the seven threatened and near-threatened species as well as the relatively common and widespread birds which occur in the country almost all look likely to decline in the future, due to agricultural intensification (especially around the natural mountain lakes), hunting (Albania is a popular destination for Italian shooters), pollution and the highest annual rate of human population growth in Europe and Russia (1.7%).

Notable species include Pygmy Cormorant*, Great White and Dalmatian* Pelicans, Rock Partridge, Semicollared Flycatcher, Wallcreeper, Olive-tree Warbler, White-winged Snowfinch and Alpine Accentor.

The huge, mainly shallow, freshwater **Lake Shkodra** in northwest Albania, extends northwards into Montenegro, southwest Yugoslavia, where it is known as Lake Skadar (p. 388). The lake and its surroundings support a wide range of waterbirds, including what may still be the world's second most important colony of Pygmy Cormorants*, after the Danube Delta/Dobrudja area in Romania, a colony of Dalmatian Pelicans* and passerines such as Olive-tree Warbler. Other species recorded here include Ferruginous Duck*, Squacco Heron, Glossy Ibis, Collared Pratincole, Whiskered Tern, European Bee-eater, Lesser Grey Shrike, Rock Nuthatch, Moustached, Olivaceous and Orphean Warblers, Spanish Sparrow, Yellow Wagtail ('Black-headed' *feldegg*) and Black-headed Bunting. The lake is accessible via the town of Shkodër at the eastern end.

The coastal lagoons and marshes around the **Drini Rivermouth** in northwest Albania support a similar avifauna to that of Lake Shkodra and Rock Partridge occurs on the nearby mountain slopes. Rock Partridge also occurs in the **Korabi Mountains**, northeast of Tirana, along with Wallcreeper, Sombre Tit, White-winged Snowfinch and Alpine Accentor.

LAKES OHRID, MEGALÍ PRESPA AND MIKRÍ PRESPA

These three large, natural mountain lakes in southeast Albania, about 85 km southeast of Tirana, together with the scrub and forest on the slopes which surround them, support a wide range of waterbirds and some eastern Mediterranean passerine specialities such as Cretzschmar's Bunting.
The species listed below occur during the summer unless otherwise indicated.

Localised Specialities
Rock Partridge, Olive-tree Warbler, Cretzschmar's Bunting.

Other Localised Species
Pygmy Cormorant*, Dalmatian Pelican*.

Others
Great White Pelican, Ferruginous Duck*, Squacco Heron, Glossy Ibis, Egyptian Vulture, Lesser Kestrel*, Collared Pratincole, Alpine Swift, European Bee-eater, European Roller, Syrian Woodpecker, Lesser Grey Shrike, Rufous-tailed Rock-Thrush, Rock Nuthatch, Eurasian Crag-Martin, Moustached, Olivaceous and Orphean Warblers, Sombre Tit, Yellow Wagtail ('Black-headed' *feldegg*), Black-headed Bunting.

Rock Partridge, Olive-tree Warbler and Cretzschmar's Bunting occur around **Lake Ohrid** (Ohridsko Jezero), the northernmost water which extends into Macedonia (p. 253). To the southeast, **Lake Megalí Prespa**, which also extends into Macedonia, as well as Greece (p. 208), supports a pelican colony, although the birds are more likely to be seen south of here on **Lake Mikrí Prespa**, which also extends into Greece.

The breeding stronghold of Dalmatian Pelican* in Albania is at **Karavasta Lagoon**, about 100 km southwest of Tirana. Between 50 and 60 pairs were present here in the early 1990s, but only 25 birds were present in May 1996. About 200 species have been recorded on this reserve in total, including Pygmy Cormorant*, Great White Pelican, White-headed Duck*, Pallid Harrier* (passage), White-tailed* and Greater Spotted* (winter) Eagles, and Collared Pratincole (summer). To the south, a stretch of the Adriatic coastal plain known as Pishe Poro, the large coastal lagoon known as Gjol i Nartes, the **Karaburun Peninsula** a few km to the southwest, the small rocky island off this peninsula known as Sazan and the nearby salinas, are all worth birding as well. In extreme southwest Albania, Squacco Heron and Olive-tree Warbler have been recorded around the large, brackish, coastal **Butrintit Lagoon**.

ADDITIONAL INFORMATION

Books and papers
Ornithological research in Albania: an annotated bibliography. Bogliani G, Barbieri F and Prigioni C, 1987. *Avocetta* 11: 63–66.
Karavasta Lagoon: Ecoguide. Ecotourism Limited, 1996. Karavasta Lagoon Wetland Management Project.

ARMENIA

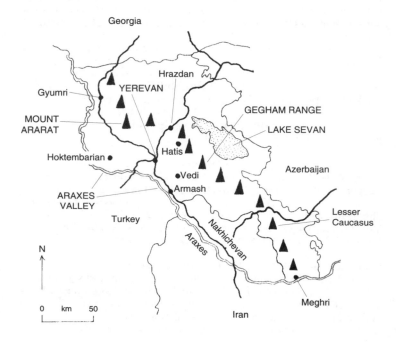

INTRODUCTION

This small former Soviet Republic to the east of Turkey supports such restricted-range species as Caspian Snowcock and Caucasian Grouse*, along with some mouthwatering 'Middle Eastern' breeding specialities such as White-throated Robin, all of which can be seen in eastern Turkey. However, since access to that part of Turkey is often restricted, if the compact country of Armenia, which has an excellent field guide, improves its tourist infrastructure early in the 21st century it may soon become a popular birding destination.

At 30,000 km², Armenia is roughly one quarter the size of England and about 5% the size of Texas. The region in which the country is situated experienced outbreaks of war in the early 1990s, and although Armenia has been largely free of such trouble since the mid-1990s, it would be wise to find out the latest details on whether or not it is safe to travel from the relevant foreign office before arranging a trip. Such offices should also be able to give information on the latest situation regarding the infrastructure, for Armenia also lies in an earthquake zone and in 1988 a serious shift in the earth's crust led to the loss of about 25,000 human lives and caused extensive damage. Most visitors arrive in the capital, Yerevan, by air, since the borders with Azerbaijan,

Georgia, Nakhichevan and Turkey are often closed. Vehicles, with driver/guide/interpreters, can be hired at the Hotel Armenia or the US-run Levon Travel in Yerevan. Most sites are also accessible by bus. There are few places to stay beyond the capital, although many sites are within a day's reach of there and although almost all of the land is privately owned the offer of a bottle of vodka usually results in permission to camp. Western food is available in Yerevan but elsewhere the major crops (bulgar wheat, chick peas and nuts) form the major ingredients of meals, although lamb (especially in the form of grilled kebabs) and soups are also usually on sale at roadside cafes. Grapes are grown on the plains, some of which are used to make Armenian wine, but the national drink is vodka. Immunisation against hepatitis, polio and typhoid is recommended. Although Armenia is reputed to be malaria-free it may be wise to take all the necessary precautions against this disease, since there are many mosquitoes around the fishponds in the subtropical south.

Armenia has a continental climate with wet springs, hot summers (the temperature in the southern lowlands may rise to almost 50°C (122°F)) and cold winters. The peak time to visit the country is during July and August, when summer visitors such as White-throated Robin are present, it is still relatively easy to see the high-altitude specialities such as Caucasian Grouse* and the autumn shorebird passage is in full swing.

Landlocked Armenia is dominated by the lofty Lesser Caucasus, a rugged mountain range with fragmented beech forest, rocky gorges and mountain steppe, which rises to 4090 m (13,419 ft) at Mount Ararat. Most of the country lies above 1000 m (3281 ft) and the lowest point is the Araxes Valley, which is situated at at 600 m (1969 ft) in the west. This rather arid valley supports usually dry canyons and semi-desert terrain, as well as fishponds and fig orchards. To the east lies a huge lake known as Lake Sevan, which at 1300 km² is the second largest alpine lake in Europe and Russia, after Lake Geneva (Lac Leman). The use of traditional agricultural methods is widespread, but problems such as massive irrigation projects, hunting, pollution and the equal second highest annual increase in human population in Europe and Russia, spell trouble for the nine threatened and near-threatened species, as well as the relatively common and widespread birds which occur in the country.

Over 346 species have been recorded in Armenia, including Pygmy Cormorant*, White-headed Duck*, Marbled Teal*, Lammergeier, Cinereous Vulture*, Levant Sparrowhawk, Imperial Eagle*, Caspian Snowcock, Caucasian Grouse*, Armenian and Great Black-headed Gulls, Blue-cheeked Bee-eater, White-throated Robin, Finsch's and Red-tailed Wheatears, Rock and Persian Nuthatches, Wallcreeper, Paddyfield and Upcher's Warblers, Chiffchaff ('Caucasian' *lorenzii*), Greenish ('Green Warbler' *nitidus*) and Ménétries's Warblers, Bimaculated Lark, White-winged Snowfinch, Alpine and Radde's Accentors, Fire-fronted Serin, Crimson-winged Finch and Grey-necked Bunting. During July and August it is possible to see up to 200 species during a trip lasting one to two weeks.

Few capitals of the world can boast the presence of such a wonderful bird as Wallcreeper within the city limits, but this is true of **Yerevan**, the capital of Armenia, where, during the winter, Wallcreepers occur in the

Hrazdan Gorge which splits the city in two. Cities across the world are inhabited by Peregrine Falcons, but here they are replaced by Saker Falcons which hunt feral pigeons from the tower blocks during the autumn. Furthermore, the city parks support Levant Sparrowhawk (summer) and, in spring, Rosy Starlings are regular visitors, while Eurasian Eagle-Owl and Rock Nuthatch also occur in Hrazdan Gorge.

GEGHAM RANGE

This section of the Lesser Caucasus, between the Araxes Valley, where Yerevan is situated, to the west and the Lake Sevan basin, to the east, supports such spectacular birds as Lammergeier and White-throated Robin, while in the autumn these mountains are a good place to look for southbound raptors. On one mid-September day in 1995 for example, 16 Pallid Harriers*, 18 Levant Sparrowhawks, 61 Lesser Spotted Eagles and 167 Steppe Eagles were seen passing over Gree Gorge.

The species listed below occur during the summer unless otherwise indicated.

Localised Specialities
Lammergeier, White-throated Robin, Radde's Accentor, Crimson-winged Finch.

Other Localised Species
Cinereous Vulture*, Lanner Falcon, Rosy Starling.

Regular Autumn Passage Migrants
Pallid Harrier*, Levant Sparrowhawk, Lesser Spotted (some also breed) and Steppe Eagles, Red-footed Falcon, Broad-billed Sandpiper, Greenish Warbler ('Green Warbler' *nitidus*, some also breed), White-winged Snowfinch.

Others
Egyptian Vulture, Eurasian Griffon, Rufous-tailed Rock-Thrush, Chiffchaff ('Caucasian' *lorenzii*), Barred Warbler, Black-headed Bunting.

The mountains are accessible by road east from the capital, Yerevan, but no roads traverse the range. The area around the village of **Hatis** on the west flank is a good place to look for White-throated Robin. The open scrubby woods on the cliffs in the 234 km² **Khosrov Reserve**, at the southern end of the range, are excellent for raptors. Radde's Accentor and Crimson-winged Finch (a flock of 330 were present here in December 1995) occur in **Gree Gorge**, 8 km west of Kamo on the east flank. This is also the best place to look for passage raptors and passerines during the autumn.

The huge **Lake Sevan**, which has a 200-km-long shoreline, about 70 km east of Yerevan, supports few breeding birds, apart from a large colony of Armenian Gulls, but during the autumn this localised larid is joined by impressive numbers of passage migrants, which have included Ruddy Shelduck and over 1,000 Demoiselle Cranes (numbers peak in early September), and during the winter, large numbers of Great Black-headed Gulls (over 600 in December 1995). Most of the Armenian Gulls breed along the northwestern shore. During the winter most Great Black-headed Gulls usually concentrate around Cape Noratoos on the western shore. The opposite side of the lake, at Gilli Marsh in the south-east corner, is the best place to look for Demoiselle Cranes. The south-ern shores are the best for passage shorebirds such as Broad-billed Sandpiper and the reedbeds here attract large numbers of 'Caucasian' Chiffchaffs during the autumn. The area around the village of Lichk at the southwest corner of the lake is another passage migrant hot-spot which is particularly favoured by Red-footed Falcons. This is one of the few sites with accommodation, in the form of Motel Sevan (B), which is on the northwest shore near the town of Sevan, and other lakeside lodgings.

Caucasian Grouse* occurs in northeast Armenia, although it was recorded at only two sites in 1995 despite extensive searching and both of these were near the city of **Hrazdan**. The best place to look is along-side the dangerous 4WD-only track which traverses the saddle of Mount Tezhler and passes through the favoured alpine grasslands above the tree-line on north-facing slopes.

MOUNT ARARAT

This extinct volcano, a couple of hours by road northwest of Yerevan, rises to 4090 m (13,419 ft), high enough to support such truly montane specialities as Caspian Snowcock, Wallcreeper and White-winged Snow-finch, as well as an impressive variety of raptors and White-throated Robin on the lower slopes.

The species listed below occur during the summer unless otherwise indicated.

Localised Specialities
Caspian Snowcock, White-throated Robin, Radde's Accentor, Crimson-winged Finch.

Other Localised Species
Wallcreeper, White-winged Snowfinch.

Others
Long-legged Buzzard, Lesser Spotted and Imperial* Eagles, Syrian Woodpecker, Lesser Grey Shrike, Rufous-tailed Rock-Thrush, Bluethroat (*magna*), Chiffchaff ('Caucasian' *lorenzii*), Horned Lark, Rock Petronia, Yellow Wagtail ('Black-headed' *feldegg*), Twite, Alpine Accentor, Rock Bunting.
(Other species recorded here during the autumn include Pallid Harrier* and Steppe Eagle.)

It is possible to reach most of the habitat zones via the road which reaches as far as **Lake Kari** and the adjacent weather station at 3200 m (10,499 ft). The roadside juniper scrub about 9 km below Lake Kari is the best place to look for White-throated Robin and Radde's Accentor.

Above the lake the boulder fields support Crimson-winged Finch, and, higher still, the precipitous heights surrounding the crater are the best place to look for Caspian Snowcock and Wallcreeper.

The Araxes Valley, which forms the border between Armenia and Turkey to the west, is, on average, about 20 km wide, and the largest valley in the country. Volcanic basalt dominates the **Northern Araxes Valley** where, during the summer, temperatures can reach 35°C (almost 100°F), making it an inhospitable place for humans. However, birds are much more adaptable and some species even manage to eke out an existence here, including, as one might expect, some larks, which in this part of the world include Bimaculated and Lesser Short-toed. Other species present during the summer include Black-bellied Sandgrouse, Finsch's Wheatear and Ménétries's Warbler, while rarities have included Caspian Plover. The areas around Hoktembarian and Vanand are arguably the best for birding.

THE CENTRAL ARAXES VALLEY

The low, sun-baked, rugged, rocky hills near Vedi, 40 minutes by road southeast of Yerevan, support a select band of birds, including Upcher's Warbler. Lower down the valley there are nearly 350 km² of fishponds and marshes which have attracted up to 2000 Pygmy Cormorants* and a fine selection of passage shorebirds, including Black-winged Pratincole* and Sociable Lapwing*. The tamarisks surrounding some of the ponds support Ménétries's Warbler and, to complete the valley's extraordinary avifauna as many as 145 Blue-cheeked Bee-eaters have been seen together in late summer around Armash.

The species listed below occur during the summer unless otherwise indicated.

Localised Specialities
White-headed Duck*, Marbled Teal*, Armenian Gull, White-throated Robin, Rufous-tailed Scrub-Robin, Persian Nuthatch, Paddyfield, Upcher's and Ménétries's Warblers, Pale Rockfinch, Trumpeter Finch, Grey-necked Bunting.

Other Localised Species
Pygmy Cormorant*, Slender-billed Gull, Blue-cheeked Bee-eater, Fire-fronted Serin (Nov).

Regular Passage Migrants
Lesser White-fronted Goose*, Pallid Harrier*, Levant Sparrowhawk, Steppe Eagle, Great Snipe*, Marsh, Terek and Broad-billed Sandpipers, Red-necked Phalarope, Collared Pratincole, Greater Sandplover, Sociable Lapwing*, White-winged Tern, Moustached Warbler, Chiffchaff ('Caucasian' *lorenzii*).

Others
Ferruginous Duck*, Squacco Heron, Rock Nuthatch, Olivaceous Warbler.

(Other species recorded here include Little and Baillon's Crakes, Black-winged Pratincole*, Spur-winged Plover and White-tailed Lapwing.)

There is a spring near the town of **Vedi** which may repay hours of observation since it is one of the few sources of water in this arid area of Armenia. The rugged hills around **Dashtakar**, a village 4 km south of Vedi, support Pale Rockfinch. Most of the fishponds and marshes are situated near the villages of **Armash**, **Masees** and **Yeghegnoot**, where many fishpond complexes are fenced off. 'Officially' they are only accessible with prior permission but a bottle of vodka may be as good as a permit if presented politely to the gatekeepers, and this tactic has proved to be much more successful in the 1980s and 1990s than any attempts to track down the fishpond owners. The best place to look for Pygmy Cormorant* is around Armash where there is a breeding colony. Late summer flocks of Blue-cheeked Bee-eaters occur around Armash and Masees. Take plenty of mosquito repellent.

In the **Southern Araxes Valley**, where summer temperatures have approached 50°C (122°F), the usually dry canyons and rocky gorges, together with the odd fig, peach and pomegranate orchard, support such hardy birds as Black Francolin, Finsch's and Red-tailed ('Eastern Red-tailed' *chrysopygia*) Wheatears, Rock and Persian Nuthatches, and Sombre Tit. Bird around the city of Meghri which is situated on the north bank of the River Araxes.

ADDITIONAL INFORMATION

Books and papers
A Field Guide to the Birds of Armenia. Adamian M S and Klem D, 1997. AUA, USA.
Handbook of the Birds of Armenia. Adamian M S and Klem D, due 1999. AUA, USA.

AUSTRIA

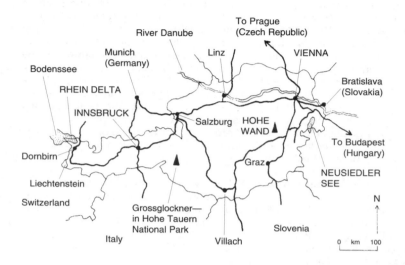

INTRODUCTION

Summary
Birders who like to look for a wide variety of birds from a single base may wish to consider visiting eastern Austria where the close combination of a huge shallow lake, known as Neusiedler See, steppe farmland and forests offers an opportunity to see anything from Little Crake to Great Bustard*, within an hour's drive of the lake. Slightly further afield it is possible to add most high-altitude alpine specialities.

Size
At 83,855 km², Austria is under half the size of England and one eighth the size of Texas.

Getting Around
The best birding areas around Neusiedler See are all within an hour's drive of the town of Neusiedl-am-See. Using a vehicle would save time but hire costs are amongst the most expensive in Europe and most of these areas are accessible on the modern public transport system. At all but the remotest railway stations it is possible to hire bicycles which do not have to be returned to the same station. Travelling across country on the motorways will add to expenses due to the tolls and heavy policing (speeding fines are common), so it is wise not to avoid paying the tolls since on-the-spot fines are substantial. Proof of payment comes in the form of stickers on sale at border posts, petrol stations and some shops.

Accommodation and Food

Hotels, guesthouses and pensions are expensive, especially in and around the major tourist centres such as Salzburg and Vienna, where they are also often full to overflowing during July and August. Cheaper alternatives throughout the country include many excellent campsites and about 100 youth hostels. Food is also rather expensive so eating out can work out cheaper than self-catering. Meat dishes, which include various sausages and veal (schnitzel), tend to dominate menus but it is also possible to find meat-free bean soups and sandwiches. Wine is usually cheaper than beer.

Health and Safety

The Danube Plain area of eastern Austria is full of mosquitoes during the height of summer so take plenty of repellent.

Climate and Timing

Austria has a continental climate with short warm summers and long cold winters. Late May to early June is the peak of the breeding season, an excellent time for passage migrants and a good time for alpine flowers, while late August to early October is a good time for passage shorebirds and raptors, although at this time Neusiedler See is often enveloped in mist.

Habitats

Austria is almost all alpine, especially in the west, and since the steep mountain slopes which rise to 3798 m (12,461 ft) at Grossglockner support extensive coniferous forest, this is the major habitat in the country, accounting for about 45% of the land surface, the highest country coverage outside Scandinavia. Most of these forests have been planted for commercial purposes, but they still support a typical alpine forest avifauna. Lowland areas are few and far between, but they include the small Rhein Delta at the southeast end of Bodenssee (Lake Constance) at the extreme west end of the country and the much more extensive Danube (Donau) Plain at the east end of the country near Vienna and Neusiedler See.

Conservation

Most of the lowland and submontane forests in Austria were replaced with arable farmland a long time ago, leaving the remaining five threatened and near-threatened species as well as the relatively common and widespread birds which occur in Austria to cope with further habitat loss and degradation, dams, eutrophication, hunting and pollution.

Bird Species

Notable species include Saker Falcon, Little Crake, Great Bustard*, Collared Flycatcher, Wallcreeper, Moustached Warbler, White-winged Snowfinch, Alpine Accentor and Citril Finch.

Expectations

During the spring it is possible to see 120–150 species on a trip lasting one or two weeks to eastern Austria, and during the autumn about 120 species could be expected on a similar trip.

The capital **Vienna** is situated on the banks of the River Danube in the northeast corner of the country and is a good gateway to the southern Czech Republic, western Slovakia and western Hungary. Further along the Danube, in the town of **Bad Deutsh Altenburg**, Collared Flycatcher occurs in the small riverside park and alongside the adjacent river.

NEUSIEDLER SEE, SEEWINKEL AND HANSAG

The 30-km-long and 8-km-wide lake known as Neusiedler See, an hour by road southeast of Vienna, rarely reaches depths greater than 2 m (6.6 ft) and it is surrounded by a sea of reeds, up to 6 km wide in places. Its well-vegetated waters support a wealth of waterbirds, including Great Egret (at least 737 pairs were present in 1997, the most ever) and Little Crake, while the nearby woods are inhabited by Collared Flycatcher and, perhaps best of all, the steppe farmland of Seewinkel and Hansag, which extend eastwards from the lake into Hungary, is graced by Saker Falcon and Great Bustard*. Numerous passage migrants also stop to rest and refuel here; nearly 300 species have been recorded in total.

The species listed below occur during the summer unless otherwise indicated.

NEUSIEDLER SEE, SEEWINKEL and HANSAG

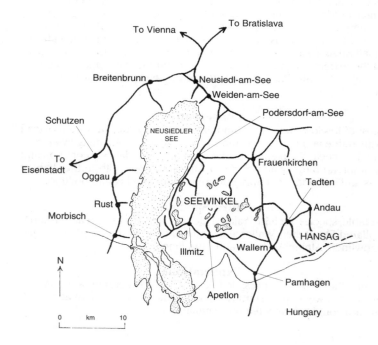

Localised Specialities
Saker Falcon, Great Bustard*.

Regular Passage Migrants
Temminck's Stint, Little Gull, Whiskered, White-winged and Black Terns.

Others
Ferruginous Duck*, Great Egret, Black-crowned Night-Heron, Black and White Storks, Red Kite, Little Crake, European Bee-eater, Syrian and Black Woodpeckers, Eurasian Nutcracker, Collared Flycatcher, Blue-throat ('White-spotted' *cyanecula*), Eurasian River, Moustached and Barred Warblers.

(Other species recorded here include Squacco Heron, Glossy Ibis, Lesser Spotted and Greater Spotted* Eagles, Red-footed Falcon (early May), Common Crane, Marsh and Broad-billed Sandpipers, Red-necked Phalarope, Caspian Tern and Lesser Grey Shrike (formerly more common, but only one breeding pair in 1997).)

The northern end of **Neusiedler See** is about 50 km southeast of Vienna. Due to the lake's virtually complete reedy shoreline there are only a few places where it is possible to view the shallows and open water. These include: (i) the north shore near Neusiedl-am-See; (ii) the west shore near Oggau; and (iii) the east shore between Podersdorf-am-See and Illmitz. To look for Black Woodpecker, bird alongside the road outside the zoo (tiergarten) near Schutzen. Syrian Woodpecker occurs in the grounds of Esterhazy Castle (best around Leopold Temple) in Eisenstadt and the best place for Collared Flycatcher is in the woods near Rust, a town where White Storks nest.

The vast reedbeds surrounding Neusiedler See support the delightful Reedling, the only representative of the parrotbill family in Europe

There are a number of small lakes in the western **Seewinkel** which is situated to the east of Neusiedler See, and many waterbirds are easier to see here than at the main lake. To the south, the Einser Canal near Pamhagen is worth walking along, in search of soaring storks and raptors, as well as Eurasian River and Barred Warblers. The plains east of Pamhagen and south of Tadten support a few Great Bustards*, some of which occur at the **Hansag Reserve** between Tadten and the border with Hungary. It is best to look for the bustards from the road south of Andau, early in the day before the heat-haze makes viewing difficult, and there are observation towers to enhance viewing distances. Look out for raptors here too, including Saker Falcon.

Accommodation: Neusiedl-am-See—Hotel Wende (within a short walk of good birding habitat).

The seasonally flooded meadows and damp deciduous woods alongside the River March in the 800-ha WWF **Marchauen-Marchegg Reserve**, 40 km northeast of Vienna, support breeding Black Stork, Collared Flycatcher and Eurasian River Warbler. At the north end of the village of Marchegg, which is on Route 49, take the track which leads east to the reserve car park, looking out for Collared Flycatcher alongside the entrance track, then walk north from the car park along the floodbank to look for Black Stork and Eurasian River Warbler.

The high **Eastern Austrian Alps** are within a couple of hours by road and rail southwest of Vienna and they support high-altitude specialities such as Rock Ptarmigan, White-winged Snowfinch and Citril Finch, as well as Golden Eagle, Black Woodpecker, Eurasian Nutcracker, Yellow-billed Chough, Eurasian Crag-Martin and Alpine Accentor. The 12-km-long and 3-km-wide forested limestone outcrop known as **Hohe Wand** (High Wall) is a popular tourist attraction and a fairly good birding area where many of the species listed above occur, but almost all of which can be very difficult to track down. To try, head out of Stolhof on the road which ascends the outcrop and once on top head for the western escarpment where there is a car park and walking tracks. Rock Ptarmigan, White-winged Snowfinch, Alpine Accentor and Citril Finch also occur in the **Schneeberg Mountains**, southwest of Hohe Wand, where they are arguably easier to find. To reach the high tops take the rack-and-pinion railway from Puchberg to the top station, which is situated at about 2000 m (6562 ft), 1.5 hours from Puchberg, and bird from there up to and around the summit which is 600 m (1969 ft) higher up.

In central Austria the **Niedere Tauern Mountains**, southeast of Salzburg, support Eurasian Nutcracker, a disjunct population of 'Redspotted' *svecica* Bluethroats, White-winged Snowfinch and Alpine Accentor, and **Hohe Tauern National Park**, southeast of Innsbruck, is the site of a Lammergeier reintroduction scheme. It is still difficult to see this bird here, however, and most visitors have to be happy with Eurasian Griffon (summer only) and Golden Eagle.

Few birders bother with the **Western Austrian Alps** and yet the beautiful mountains which surround towns such as Innsbruck are complemented by such great birds as Alpine Swift, White-winged Snowfinch, Alpine Accentor and Citril Finch. Those who have birded the area have tended to do best in the 720 km² Karwendel Reserve, which rises to 2700 m (8858 ft) at Birkkarspitze between the A12 and the border with Germany to the north, and is accessible via numerous minor roads. Other productive spots in the past have included the slopes above Achensee, the glacial lake to the east of Karwendel; the high tops (accessible via cable-car) at Penkenbahn, above the small resort of

Mayrhofen about 70 km southeast of Innsbruck; and around the ski-resort at Hintertux to the southwest.

The **Rhein Delta** at the southeast end of Bodenssee (Lake Constance) on the north flank of the Alps is an excellent place for passage migrants, especially during the autumn, when on wet and cloudy days birds on their way south prefer to wait in the delta before attempting to cross the high mountains before them. Hence, on a good day it is possible to see over 100 species, including Little Bittern, Whiskered and Caspian (up to seven in September 1997) Terns, and Red-throated Pipit. The delta has also provided refuge for several rare shorebirds, including Slender-billed Curlew*, Cream-coloured Courser, and Sociable* and White-tailed Lapwings, and during the winter Smew is a regular visitor. Some of the water in the River Rhein is redirected into a channel and it is the area between this channel, known as the New Rhein, and the original

RHEIN DELTA

river, known as the Old Rhein, which is the best for birds. The east end is accessible via the village of Fussach and the west end is accessible via Gaissau. This road leads to the Seerestaurant on the lakeshore; a good place to scan the lake from. East of the restaurant (northwest of Fussach) the dyke which separates Bodenssee from the delta runs alongside Fussacher Bucht, a large bay which is always worth grilling thoroughly. The long spits which penetrate the lake from the ends of the Old and New Rheins are also worth birding.

The cliffs behind **Dornbirn**, near the Rhein Delta, are worth checking for Eurasian Eagle-Owl and Wallcreeper, and the road up to **Ebnit** from here reaches the subalpine zone above 1000 m (3281 ft) where Three-toed Woodpecker occurs.

ADDITIONAL INFORMATION

Addresses

Please send records of rarities to the Avifaunistische Kommission, Bird-Life Osterreich, Museumsplatz 1/10/8, A-1070 Vienna, Austria. The rarities report is published in *Egretta*, in German with an English summary.

Books and papers

Finding Birds in Eastern Austria. Gosney D, 1994. Available from Bird-Guides (address, p. 395).

Atlas of Breeding Birds in Austria (English summary of *Atlas Der Brutvogel Osterreichs*). BirdLife Osterreich, 1994.

AZERBAIJAN

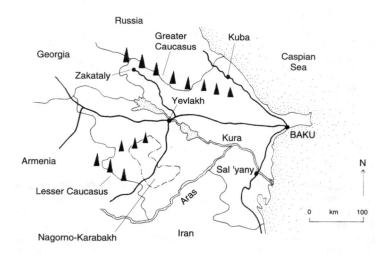

INTRODUCTION

This former Soviet Republic, independent since 1991, supports a very diverse avifauna thanks to the wide variety of habitats. Both the Lesser Caucasus and Greater Caucasus mountain ranges penetrate the country's boundaries, hence both Caucasian (in the Greater) and Caspian (in the Lesser) Snowcocks are present, along with Caucasian Grouse*, but seeing these restricted-range species could prove difficult to say the least, for, up until early 1997 at least armed conflicts were still taking place in some areas. Much of the east, including the capital Baku, was relatively safe by the end of the 1990s, but it would be wise to find out the latest details on whether or not it is safe to travel around Azerbaijan, from the relevant foreign office, before planning a trip here.

At 87,000 km², Azerbaijan is a relatively small country which is just under half the size of England and nearly one eighth the size of Texas. Getting around without a vehicle, preferably a 4WD, could be difficult, although there are some buses. Apart from the hotels in Baku it may also be hard to find accommodation elsewhere, although there is always the possibility of arranging to stay with local people. There are plenty of restaurants and teahouses, serving casseroles, caviar (ikra) and fish and lamb kebabs. Immunisation against hepatitis, polio and typhoid is recommended, as are precautions against malaria if visiting certain areas.

Azerbaijan has a continental climate with warm to very hot summers and cold winters. The best time to look for the snowcocks and Caucasian Grouse* is in late May and early June, when many summer visitors should also be present, but many waterbirds, as well as bustards, are usually only present during the winter.

The heavily cultivated, wide River Kura valley runs northwest to southeast through the middle of the country, between the Greater Caucasus to the northeast, which rise to 4480 m (14,698 ft) at Bazar Dyuzi, and the Lesser Caucasus to the west. South of Baku the valley becomes very broad and rather arid, especially next to the Caspian Sea. Azerbaijan is a sparsely populated country but habitat loss and degradation, hunting and pollution are still major problems facing the eleven threatened and near-threatened species, as well as the relatively common and widespread birds which occur in the country. Notable species, not mentioned before, include Pygmy Cormorant*, Dalmatian Pelican*, Lesser White-fronted* and Red-breasted* Geese, Marbled Teal*, Lammergeier, Cinereous Vulture*, Chukar, Purple Swamphen ('Grey-headed' *poliocephalus*), Great Bustard*, Caspian Tit (in the Talyshskiye Gory range) and Radde's Accentor (in the west).

Very little up-to-date information on the avifauna is available, especially passerines, although these are likely to be very similar to those present in adjacent Armenia (p. 48), hence one can only assume the sites outlined below are still present and continue to support the species for which they were once considered important.

Little* and Great* Bustards may still winter on the **Shirvanskaya Steppe**, south of the capital, Baku, and the well-vegetated irrigation dams here may still support an important breeding population of Purple Swamphen.

During the 1950s an incredible ten million ducks and coot wintered in and around **Kirov Bay** on the Caspian Sea, south of Baku, but numbers fell to three million by the 1960s and only up to about a million were present in the 1980s. The bay also used to be a very important wintering area for up to 25,000 Red-breasted Geese*, but their food supply was cut off when grain and rice crops were replaced with cotton, grapes and vegetables, and by the 1980s only 25–200 were present. Other species recorded here include Pygmy Cormorant*, Great White and Dalmatian* Pelicans, Lesser White-fronted Goose* (winter), Ruddy

Shelduck, Greater Flamingo, Squacco Heron, Glossy Ibis, Purple Swamphen and Little Bustard* (winter), while old records also exist for Siberian Crane*. The site includes Kyzyl-Agach Bay and Maly Kyzyl-Agach Bay, which is separated from the Caspian Sea by a dam.

Lake Akgyel, a saline lake inland from Kirov Bay, used to be the most important breeding site in Russia and its former Republics for Marbled Teal* (about 250 pairs), and used to support about 100,000 wintering waterfowl, as well as breeding Ruddy Shelduck and Purple Swamphen.

The foothills of the Greater Caucasus around Agdash, Evlakh and Turian-Chai in the **Bozdag Ridge Reserve** in northern Azerbaijan may still support Eurasian Griffon, Cinereous Vulture*, Chukar and European Roller. Northwest of here the southern Greater Caucasian slopes around **Belokany and Zakataly**, which rise to 3648 m (11,969 ft), may still support Caucasian Snowcock and Caucasian Grouse*, as well as Lammergeier and Cinereous Vulture*. Farmland and forests at **Karayazi** in northwest Azerbaijan, between the Tbilisi-Baku railway to the north and the Kura Waterway to the south, may still support Black Stork, and White-tailed*, Imperial* and Golden Eagles.

Species recorded in the forest and grassland around Geigelski, Kirovobad and Khanlar on the deeply incised slopes of **Mount Kyapaz** in the Lesser Caucasus of western Azerbaijan, include Caspian Snowcock, as well as Lammergeier, Egyptian Vulture, Eurasian Griffon, Cinereous Vulture* and Chukar.

BALEARIC ISLANDS

INTRODUCTION

Summary

Millions of tourists visit Mallorca, Menorca and Ibiza, the three main Balearic Islands, in the western Mediterranean, every year and yet it is possible to leave behind the crowded beaches and bars on these islands, and go birding amongst some splendid scenery in search of such localised and spectacular species as Cinereous Vulture*, Eleonora's Falcon, Audouin's Gull* and Marmora's Warbler. However, these birds and the prospect of a wide variety of passage migrants, especially during the spring, inevitably attract large numbers of birders too, in search of a cheap but exciting Mediterranean birding break.

Size

The largest island, Mallorca, is 80 km at its widest, Menorca reaches a maximum width of 40 km and the islands of Ibiza and Formentera are much smaller. Hence each one can be covered from a single base.

Getting Around

Most visitors arrive by air on very cheap package holidays. There are ferries from mainland Spain and Marseille in France, and between the islands, but they are very expensive. During the peak tourist season, mid-June to mid-September, it may be difficult to find a suitable vehicle for hire, so it is wise to book in advance from outside the archipelago, but this is not usually a problem during the best birding period. Hiring a vehicle or a taxi will save time because the bus network is more or less restricted to the main routes between the major towns on all four islands.

Accommodation and Food

Very cheap accommodation and food are available on the numerous package holidays. Otherwise both are rather expensive and independent travellers may struggle to find a room during the peak season, from mid-June to mid-September. There are a few campsites on Ibiza and Mallorca, one on Menorca and none on Formentera.

Health and Safety

During the summer it is wise to take sunglasses, a sunhat and sunscreen.

Climate and Timing

Fortunately the best time for birding the Balearics is during the spring, from mid-April to early May, between the horrendously busy easter and summer holiday periods, and during the autumn, at the end of the main tourist season, when passage peaks in late September and early October.

Habitats

The 3640 km^2 island of Mallorca is generally flat apart from in the northwest where there are 37 peaks over 1000 m (3281 ft), rising to 1445 m (4741 ft) at Puig Major in the Tramuntana Mountains. These mountains are primarily composed of limestone, hence there are some spectacular gorges with precipitous crags and rugged peaks. Below the garrigue and maquis-covered mountain slopes lie pine woods, almond orchards, fig fields and olive groves, while in the lowlands there are marshes and salinas, as well as a long coastline made up of cliffs, rocks and beaches. The other islands are basically small-scale versions of Mallorca without the high mountains.

Conservation

Habitat loss and degradation, mainly as a result of residential and tourist development projects, as well as hunting and pollution, are the main problems facing the four threatened and near-threatened species, as well as the relatively common and widespread birds which occur in the Balearic Islands. Red Kite has already suffered, having declined to 12 pairs on Menorca in 1995, compared to about 135 pairs which were present in the 1980s.

Bird Species

Over 309 species have been recorded in the Balearic Islands, including Cory's ('Scopoli's' *diomedea*) and Mediterranean (mainly the endemic breeding 'Balearic' *mauretanicus*—nearly 75% of the world population of about 3,300 pairs breeds on Ibiza) Shearwaters, Cinereous Vulture*, Eleonora's Falcon, Audouin's Gull* (1,650 pairs in 1997), Moustached and Marmora's Warblers, and Thekla Lark.

Expectations

It is possible to see 110–140 species on a trip to Mallorca which lasts a week or two during the spring or autumn, but not many more than 100 on the other islands.

MALLORCA

Make no mistake, Mallorca is a marvellous island. It would be better if approximately three million sex and sunseekers didn't descend on it every year, but nevertheless it is still a splendid place to go birding. Fortunately the vast majority of bar and beach lovers rarely escape from the 40-km-long stretch of coast around Palma in the southwest. Furthermore, the best time to visit the island for birds is during the spring, before the peak tourist season, so visitors such as birders who venture further afield may be forgiven for thinking that they are on a different island, or, on Mallorca not 'Majorca'. However, birders who like to have places more or less to themselves should be aware that they are almost certain to encounter crowds even outside the peak tourist season, and that these crowds may well be birders, for many tour companies run organised trips to Mallorca, especially during the spring.

The island's mountains rise to 1445 m (4741 ft) at Puig Major in the northwest and they provide a fine backdrop to the S'Albufera, one of the largest freshwater marshes in the western Mediterranean. This and other lowland wetlands on the island support what is reputed to be the greatest breeding concentration of Moustached Warblers in the world, with a resident population of up to 4,000 birds. On the mountain slopes, Marmora's Warblers occur in the garrigue and maquis, and high above Cinereous Vultures* soar over the crags. Further variety is provided by dashing Eleonora's Falcons which commute between the coastal cliffs and inland marshes, and seabirds such as shearwaters and Audouin's Gulls*, which grace the coastal waters.

The birds listed below occur during the spring unless otherwise indicated.

Localised Specialities

Audouin's Gull*, Marmora's Warbler.

Other Localised Species

Cinereous Vulture*, Eleonora's Falcon, Thekla Lark.

Regular Spring Passage Migrants

Temminck's Stint, Collared Pratincole, Whiskered and Gull-billed Terns,
European Bee-eater (also breeds), Ortolan Bunting.

Others

Cory's ('Scopoli's' *diomedea*) and Mediterranean Shearwaters, Euro-
pean Storm-Petrel, European Shag ('Mediterranean' *desmarestii*), Great
Egret, Black-crowned Night-Heron, Little Bittern (also known to winter),
Osprey, Red Kite, Booted Eagle, Red-legged Partridge, Black-winged
Stilt, Snowy Plover, Alpine and Pallid Swifts, Woodchat Shrike, Rufous-
tailed and Blue Rock-Thrushes, Eurasian Crag-Martin, Zitting Cisticola,
Moustached, Sardinian and Spectacled Warblers, Rock Petronia, Red
Crossbill ('Balearic' *balearica*).

(Other species recorded here include Marbled Teal* (bred at S'Albufera in 1997 (for the first time) and one pair was present during the summer of 1998), Greater Flamingo, Squacco Heron, Glossy Ibis, Egyptian
Vulture (a few birds), Eurasian Griffon (one bird), Common Crane,
Marsh Sandpiper, Slender-billed Gull, Caspian Tern, European Roller,
Rufous-tailed Scrub-Robin, Red-throated Pipit and Alpine Accentor
(wintering on top of Tomir in Tramuntana Mountains). Reintroduced
species include White-headed Duck*, Red-crested Pochard and Purple
Swamphen ('Western' *porphyrio*).)

Mallorca, with a maximum width of 80 km, can be covered from one
base, the best being **Puerto de Pollensa** at the north end of the island,
one hour by road from the airport near Palma and the main tourist areas.
From mid-April to the end of May and from mid-September to mid-
October the local ornithological society in conjunction with the RSPB
hold meetings with log calls every Monday and Friday at 2100 hours in
the Hotel Pollentia in Pollensa (tel: 971 862418). Audouin's Gull* occurs
along the seafront in Pollensa, which is a short walk from the **Vall de
Bocquer**, a 2.5-km-long rocky pass with fields, orchards, dry garrigue
and pine woods, which runs from the Pollensa–Cabo Formentor road
west through the mountains to the northwest coast. This valley is a good
place to look for passage migrants early in the morning, as well as Blue
Rock-Thrush. To reach it from the main road take the rough track which
leads between two rows of pine trees and follow this through a farm.
Birding can be good almost anywhere alongside the road from Pollensa
to the tip of **Cabo Formentor**, especially where it nears the western
cliffs (Marmora's Warbler) and just before the lighthouse (Eleonora's
Falcon). The path from the lighthouse (check the garden for passage
migrants) leads to a good seawatching spot, from where it is possible to
see the rafts of shearwaters which are usually present offshore, along
with a few Audouin's Gulls*. Tripper boats from Pollensa to Cala San
Vicente may produce better views of seabirds and Eleonora's Falcon.

There are about 60 Cinereous Vultures* (six breeding pairs in 1997) on Mallorca and the best place to look for them, as well as the island's other vultures, is in the **Tramuntana Mountains**, particularly at Gorg Blau, about 5 km northeast of Cuber Reservoir. View from the long lay-by south of the tunnel when coming from Pollensa. The north end of Cuber Reservoir is the best area on the island for Rufous-tailed Rock-Thrush and Spectacled Warbler.

The brilliant Firecrest occurs at only a few places outside Europe

The small freshwater marsh known as **Albufereta**, which lies on Pollensa Bay, supports Zitting Cisticola and attracts passage waterbirds, but it is nowhere near so good as **S'Albufera**, a large reserve complete with a visitor centre, an observation tower and hides, which is situated near the coast south of Puerto de Alcúdia and is signposted from the C712. Together with the adjacent sewage works and salinas, this reserve supports most of the wetland species which occur on the island including Moustached Warbler. S'Albufera is also a favoured foraging site of Eleonora's Falcons and at times it can seem as if the air above the marshes is full of these elegant raptors. A loose flock of 82 birds was seen hunting over the reserve in late May 1999 and the largest ever gathering was 102.

The sewage works (**Depuradora**) on the southern flank of S'Albufera is a good place for waterbirds, including Marbled Teal*. The best place on the island for Alpine Swift is the **Castell de Santueri** where there is a small colony (up to 15 birds in 1999).

At the south end of Mallorca the **Salinas de Levante** (Lagunas de Salobrar de Campos) area is a major resting and refuelling site for passage shorebirds, gulls and terns. It also regularly attracts passing passerines such as Red-throated Pipit and small numbers of Greater Flamingo and Common Crane have overwintered here. Access to many of the salinas is often restricted to working days or denied outright but birding is still good from the PM604 and other minor roads which traverse the area. Audouin's Gull*, Pallid Swift, Marmora's Warbler and Thekla Lark occur at and around **Porto Colom**, at the southeast end of the island, and this is another good place to look for passage migrants. On reaching the old harbour check it for Audouin's Gull* (which also occurs on Cala Marsal Beach) then head left along the rocky peninsula, good for Pallid Swift, to the lighthouse where the scrub supports Marmora's Warbler. The nearby fields are worth checking for Thekla Lark and the bay to the northeast of the peninsula is a good back-up site for Audouin's

Gull*. **Cabo de Salinas**, the island's southernmost tip, is a good place to look for shearwaters and Audouin's Gull*, while Thekla Lark occurs alongside the access road. The shearwaters and Audouin's Gull* breed on the **Cabrera Archipelago** to the south, along with European Storm-Petrel and Eleonora's Falcon, and in August 1997 a Swinhoe's Storm-Petrel was trapped here. One of the two main islands, Cabrera, is accessible by boat from Colonia Santa Jordi.

Accommodation: Puerto de Pollensa—Flora Apartments (five minutes walk from the Vall de Bocquer), Hotel Daina, Hotel Uyal. Cala San Vicente—Oriola Hotel. Porto Colom—Hotel Cala Marsal.

MENORCA

This small, rugged island, which is about 40 km long and 20 km wide, attracts fewer tourists than Mallorca but, unfortunately, it is not so good for birds as its larger neighbour. Nevertheless, most of the Balearic specialities are present, and in 1998 Spotless Starling bred here for the first time in the archipelago.

The species listed below occur during the spring unless otherwise indicated.

Localised Specialities
Audouin's Gull*.

Other Localised Species
Eleonora's Falcon, Spotless Starling, Thekla Lark.

Others
Cory's ('Scopoli's' *diomedea*) and Mediterranean Shearwaters, Black-crowned Night-Heron, Red Kite, Egyptian Vulture, Booted Eagle, Red-legged Partridge, Alpine and Pallid Swifts, European Bee-eater, Wood-chat Shrike, Blue Rock-Thrush, Zitting Cisticola, Moustached, Sardinian and Subalpine Warblers.

(Other species recorded here include Squacco Heron, Rufous-tailed Scrub-Robin and Marmora's Warbler.)

About 20 Spotless Starlings raised 18 young near **Ciudadela** at the western end of the island in 1998. The south coast resort of **Cala Santa Galdana** is situated by a small estuary and the gorge upriver is good for raptors, with Thekla Lark on the arid farmland above. To the west of the resort Blue Rock-Thrush occurs on the cliffs. One of the best places to look for Audouin's Gull* on Menorca is in the natural harbour at **Mahón** at the eastern end of the island. The large lake known as **Albufera**, just west of El Grao, 8 km north of Mahón, supports Black-crowned Night-Heron and attracts passage shorebirds. At the north end of the island the marshes, sewage works, tamarisk scrub and woodland at **Son Parc**, 6 km south of Fornells, attracts a wide variety of species including Eleonora's Falcon, and passage migrants have included Rufous-tailed Scrub-Robin. Flocks of Cory's Shearwaters gather off the north coast most evenings, preparing to visit their nests here on their

Balearic stronghold. Other sites worth visiting on the island include the wetlands at Es Grau, Son Bou and Tirant, the salinas at Addaya and Fornells, and Cala Blanca, Cala Morell, Cap d'Artrutux and Mercadal.

Accommodation: there is one campsite, at Cala Santa Galdana on the coast south of Ferrerias.

IBIZA

This small island is renowned for its thriving nightclub scene, which attracts streets full of young hedonists in search of the sensual, rather than the local avifauna, but there is much more to this well-vegetated island and birds such as Audouin's Gull* and Marmora's Warbler are capable of providing birders with plenty of pleasure.

The species listed below occur during the spring unless otherwise indicated.

Localised Specialities
Audouin's Gull*, Marmora's Warbler.

Other Localised Species
Thekla Lark.

Others
Cory's ('Scopoli's' *diomedea*) and Mediterranean Shearwaters, Blue Rock-Thrush, Eurasian Crag-Martin, Rock Petronia.

The best sites to visit are the harbour of Ibiza town (Audouin's Gull*), Ses Salinas near El Cuartel (Marmora's Warbler and passage shorebirds, gulls and terns), Cala Codolar (Thekla Lark and Rock Petronia) and Cala San Vicente (Blue Rock-Thrush). Naturally, any suitable looking areas are worth checking for migrants which could include any of those listed for Mallorca.

Accommodation: there are five campsites.

The island of **Formentera**, three nautical miles south of Ibiza, is rather barren apart from the large areas of wild rosemary. There are also some good cliffs, dunes near La Mola and salinas at the northern tip, all worthy of attention.

ADDITIONAL INFORMATION

Addresses
Please send records of rarities to the Comite de Rarezas de la SEO, Facultad de Biologia, Universidad Complutense, 28040 Madrid, Spain. The rarities report is published in *Ardeola*, in Spanish with an English summary, and can be obtained from SEO/BirdLife, Carretera de Humera, 63-1, 28224 Pozuelo, Madrid, Spain.

Books and papers

A Birdwatching Guide to Mallorca (second edition). Hearl G and King J, 1999. Arlequin Press.

A Birdwatching Guide to Menorca, Ibiza and Formentera. Hearl G, 1996. Arlequin Press.

Finding Birds in Mallorca (revised edition). Gosney D, 1991. Available from BirdGuides (address, p. 395).

Where to watch birds in Spain and Portugal. Rose L, 1995. Hamlyn.

The Mallorca Bird Report (annual since 1990), available from Mark Thompson, 29 Leith Road, Beare Green, Dorking, Surrey, RH5 4RG, UK.

The Birds of the Balearic Islands. King J and Hearl G, due late 1999. Poyser.

The Birds of Menorca. Ramos E, 1996. Spain.

Videos

Gosney in Mallorca. Gosney D. Available from BirdGuides (address, p. 395).

BAY OF BISCAY

The ferries which run between England and northern Spain cross the Bay of Biscay, presenting a great opportunity to look for some superb seabirds and cetaceans. Although many seabirds can be seen elsewhere in Europe, there is always the chance of a rarity, although while looking for the likes of Little Shearwater there are likely to be plenty of distractions, for nearly a quarter (20) of the planet's dolphins and whales have been recorded in the Bay of Biscay, including striped dolphin, and Cuvier's beaked and northern bottlenose whales, all three of which are difficult to see elsewhere in the world. Both seabirds and cetaceans are often recorded in large numbers, with return journey totals in the late 1990s having reached around 300 Cory's Shearwaters, over 2,000 Great Shearwaters, over 400 common dolphins and 20 fin whales.

The best time to cross the Bay of Biscay is from May to October, especially between mid-August and early September, and the species listed below occur during this period unless otherwise indicated. Passengers who take a vehicle, or hire one on arrival in Spain, need only drive a short distance to look for birds such as Wallcreeper in the Picos de Europa (p. 352).

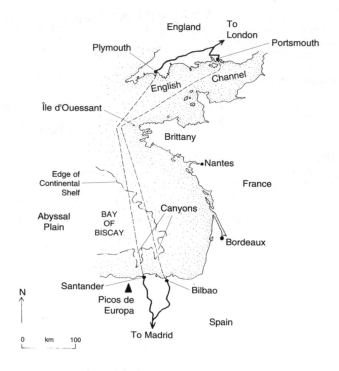

Regular Seabirds

Cory's (*borealis*), Great, Sooty, Manx and Mediterranean ('Balearic' *mauretanicus*) Shearwaters, European Storm-Petrel, Grey Phalarope, Sabine's Gull, Long-tailed Skua.

Other Wildlife

Bottlenose, common and striped dolphins, harbour porpoise, leathery sea-turtle, basking shark, sunfish, Cuvier's beaked, fin, minke, northern bottlenose and long-finned pilot whales.

(Other birds recorded include Wilson's and Band-rumped Storm-Petrels, and Little Shearwater. Other wildlife recorded includes white-beaked, white-sided and Risso's dolphins, and false killer, blue, humpback, killer, sei, Sowerby's beaked, sperm and True's beaked whales.)

There are two ferry routes; the Brittany Ferries trip between Plymouth and Santander (24 hours) and the P&O European Ferries trip between Portsmouth and Bilbao (36 hours). The water depth beyond the continental shelf in the northern Bay of Biscay reaches 3500 m (11,483 ft) within a few km, and the upwelling of nutrients at the narrow edge of this shelf produces the richest feeding grounds for cetaceans and seabirds in the whole bay. However, while most of the action takes place here, it is also worth seawatching during the rest of the trip, especially where the ferries travel through the two deep-water canyons at the shelf edge near the Spanish coast.

From Bilbao and Santander it is a short distance to the Picos de Europa (p. 352) where the possibilities include Eurasian Griffon, Black Woodpecker, Wallcreeper, White-winged Snowfinch, Alpine Accentor and Citril Finch.

ADDITIONAL INFORMATION

Addresses

For more information contact the Company of Whales, 17 Stanmore Road, Thorpe St Andrew, Norwich, NR7 OHB, UK (tel: 01603 294058). Please send records (preferably as timed counts) to The Editor, *Sea Swallow*, M. B. Casement, Dene Cottage, West Harting, Petersfield, Hampshire, GU31 5PA, UK. *Sea Swallow* is the journal of the Royal Naval Birdwatching Society.

Books and papers

The Bay of Biscay Cetacean Report, an annual publication available from Graeme Cresswell, 35 Melrose Road, Norwich, NR4 7PN, UK.
Whale-watching Begins at Home. Walker D, 1998. *British Wildlife* 9(5): 291-297 (June 1998).

BELARUS

INTRODUCTION

With its tourist infrastructure improving steadily at the end of the 1990s, Belarus, which still has vast forests and wetlands, looks set to become a popular alternative birding destination to its western neighbour, Poland, thanks to the presence of that country's two star attractions; Great Snipe* and Aquatic Warbler*, as well as additional goodies such as Pallid Harrier* and Azure Tit.

At 208,000 km², Belarus is 1.6 times larger than England and about one third the size of Texas. The capital, Minsk, is accessible by air from some European capitals. It is possible to hire vehicles here. Most roads are in good condition but most road signs are in cyrillic, so a basic understanding of this alphabet would help in getting around. There is also an extensive rail network and some bus services. Cheap accommodation is thin on the ground since most hotels cater mainly for business people and are therefore expensive, but there are some guesthouses. Major foods include dumplings, and pork and sour cream dishes, which are washed down with beer and vodka. Immunisation against hepatitis, polio and typhoid is recommended.

The climate is continental with warm summers and cold, snowy winters. The wettest time of year is late summer and autumn. The best time of year to be in Belarus is mid-May when Great Snipe* are lekking, Aquatic Warblers* are singing and most of the summer visitors have arrived. Any later and visitors run the risk of masses of midges and mosquitoes spoiling the birding.

Belarus is predominantly a low-lying, rolling, sparsely populated country with over 25% forest cover and extensive wetlands, the most impressive of which lies alongside the southern rivers which drain into the River Pripyat. The main types of tree cover are birch woods and coniferous forests, although some of the forest which straddles the border with Poland is part of the largest remaining area of virtually untouched lowland temperate mixed forest in Europe. Apart from the thousands of square km which were contaminated by a leak of radioactive isotopes from the nuclear power station at Chernobyl, just across the southern border in the Ukraine, in April 1986, habitat loss and degradation, as well as hunting, are the main problems facing the seven threatened and near-threatened species as well as the relatively common and widespread birds which occur in Belarus.

Notable species include Pallid Harrier*, Greater Spotted Eagle*, Great Snipe*, Terek Sandpiper, Ural Owl, Collared Flycatcher, Aquatic Warbler* (6,700–9,700 singing males were recorded at 12 sites in 1996) and Azure Tit. It is possible to see around 120 species during a trip last a week or so in mid-May.

Birders with time to spare while in the capital **Minsk** may wish to take a stroll around the Botanical Gardens (Black Woodpecker, Collared Flycatcher) and Comsomolsky Park (White-winged Tern, Eurasian River Warbler and Blyth's Reed-Warbler) or, better still perhaps, take a taxi to the **Priluksky Reserve**, 15 km southeast of the city, where European Bee-eater and European Roller occur, and where Greater Spotted Eagle* has been recorded. There is an Intourist Hotel known as Yubiliyana in Minsk. About 90 minutes by road from the capital, over 200 species have been recorded in the 1200 km² **Berezinsky Biosphere Reserve**, including resident breeding species such as White-tailed Eagle*, Ural Owl, Eurasian Pygmy-Owl, Tengmalm's Owl, White-backed and Three-toed Woodpeckers, and Eurasian Nutcracker, and winter visitors which often include Bohemian Waxwing and Pine Grosbeak. This reserve is also renowned for its wide range of mammals which includes grey wolf, as well as brown bear, Eurasian beaver (500), European bison, elk, lynx, European mink, pine marten, racoon-dog and wild boar. The Reserve Hotel is in Domzheritsy and it is also possible to stay at a hunting lodge within the reserve.

BELOVEZHSKAYA PUSHCHA

The only remaining substantial tract of virtually untouched lowland temperate mixed forest in Europe straddles the border between Belarus and Poland (where it is known as Puszcza Bialowieska, p. 277). That part which lies within Belarus is situated here, amidst a much larger expanse of less pristine forest and marshes which together support about 160 breeding bird species, an amazing total for somewhere so far north in the temperate zone, and which includes Great Snipe*, 15 raptors, eight owls, nine of the ten European woodpeckers (Syrian is the only one missing) and 18 warblers.

The species listed below occur during the summer unless otherwise indicated.

Localised Specialities
Great Snipe*.

Others
Black and White Storks, Lesser Spotted Eagle, Eurasian Capercaillie, Hazel Grouse, Corn Crake*, White-backed, Three-toed and Black Woodpeckers, Eurasian Nutcracker, Collared Flycatcher, Eurasian River and Barred Warblers.

Other Wildlife
Eurasian beaver, wild boar, elk, beech and pine martens.

(Other species recorded here include Greater Spotted* and Booted Eagles, Ural Owl, Eurasian Pygmy-Owl, Tengmalm's Owl and Bohemian Waxwing (winter). Other wildlife rarely seen include lynx, Eurasian otter, racoon-dog and grey wolf.).

PRIPYATSKY NATIONAL PARK

Some of the forests and marshes which cover much of southern Belarus lie within this 940-km² park, which is about 280 km south of Minsk. Although some areas have been drained and turned over to agriculture, the vast majority remains a virtual wilderness where around 260 species have been recorded and 195 have been known to breed. During a week or so here in mid-May it is possible to see around 120 species, including Pallid Harrier* and Azure Tit.

The species listed below occur during the summer unless otherwise indicated.

Localised Specialities
Aquatic Warbler*.

Other Localised Species
Greater Spotted Eagle*, Terek Sandpiper.

Others
Ferruginous Duck*, Black and White Storks, White-tailed Eagle*, Pallid Harrier*, Lesser Spotted Eagle, Common Crane, White-winged Tern, White-backed Woodpecker, Collared Flycatcher, Barred Warbler, Azure Tit.

(Other species recorded here include Lesser White-fronted Goose*— 119 in spring 1995 near Turov.)

Other Wildlife
Eurasian beaver, European bison, elk, lynx, Eurasian otter, racoon-dog, grey wolf.

The park is accessible via roads, river cruisers and smaller boats, from the small town of Turov. The floods alongside the River Pripyat just outside Turov are the best place to look for Terek Sandpiper.

Accommodation: Turov.

Great Egret bred for the first time in Belarus in 1994 and by 1997 there were eight pairs breeding in the district of **Luninets** in the southwest, where the Polesskaya area is also exceptionally good for waterbirds.

There are also important wetlands in north Belarus, which are crucial resting and refuelling stations for hundreds of thousands of migrant waterbirds. These include **Karachevskoye Boloto**, which also supports large numbers of breeding ducks, and **Lake Osveyskoye**, which also supports large numbers of breeding grebes and White-tailed Eagle*.

ADDITIONAL INFORMATION

Addresses
Please send records of rarities to the Ornitho-Faunistic Comission, Institute of Zoology, Ul.F. Skoriny St. 27, 220072—Minsk, Belarus.

BELGIUM

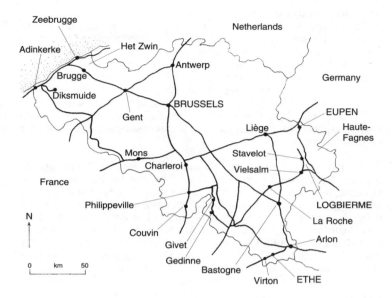

INTRODUCTION

Most birders who visit Belgium are British. They are unable to resist the close proximity of birds such as Eurasian Eagle-Owl, Tengmalm's Owl, Black Woodpecker and Eurasian Nutcracker, which are either very rare or absent altogether on the north side of the English Channel, and yet fairly common and widespread across much of mainland Europe and Russia.

At 30,520 km², this small country is less than a quarter the size of England and 5% the size of Texas. Zeebrugge, on the north coast, is accessible via vehicular ferry from Harwich, England, but birders without vehicles could use the extensive bus and rail networks to reach the best birding sites, and bicycles can be hired at some railway stations. There are plenty of relatively expensive hotels and guesthouses, as well as 400 or so much cheaper campsites, although the majority of these are rather basic. The local cuisine, including soups, meats and 'mussels and chips' (classified by some as the national dish), is also rather expensive, but beer, including Stella Artois, and wine, predominantly French, is cheaper than in many other European countries.

The climate is relatively mild maritime with warmish summers and fairly mild winters. The best time to look for owls and woodpeckers is at the end of March when many trees are still without leaves and birds are establishing their breeding territories.

The primarily flat fertile plains of Flanders in the north rise gradually to a low plateau in the middle of the country and this in turn rises to the steep wooded hills and valleys of the Ardennes, reaching 694 m (2277 ft) at Signal de Botrange in southern Belgium. Habitat loss and degradation, agricultural intensification and hunting are the main problems facing the three threatened species as well the relatively common and widespread birds which occur in Belgium.

Notable species for British birders include Eurasian Eagle-Owl (a few pairs, which represent an overspill from the reintroduced population in Germany), Tengmalm's Owl, Middle Spotted, Black and Grey-headed Woodpeckers, Eurasian Nutcracker and Bluethroat ('White-spotted' *cyanecula*). Belgium lies at the extreme western edge of the range of Hazel Grouse and this species is usually present only after the main population to the east has experienced a successful breeding season.

Birders hoping to see the woodpeckers and, especially, Tengmalm's Owl, on a short trip are most likely to be successful with the assistance of local birders.

Snowy Plover and Crested Lark (in the docks) occur at **Zeebrugge** on the northwest coast. To the south, Black Woodpecker has attempted to colonise the parks and woodlands in and around **Brugge** and Europe's largest woodpecker occurs around **Beernam**, south of Brugge. In the extreme northwest of Belgium two pairs of European Bee-eater bred near **Adinkerke** in 1996. The wetlands and woodlands in the **Blankaart Reserve**, about 8 km south of Diksmuide, just west of the N369, attract Little Bittern, which, along with Great Reed-Warbler has bred along the east bank of the River Ijzer near Woumen.

In northeast Belgium the internationally important coastal reserve of **Het Zwin**, adjacent to the border with The Netherlands east of Zeebrugge, supports large numbers of wintering wildfowl, including Smew, breeding shorebirds such as Snowy Plover, Icterine Warbler, and wintering Horned Lark, and Lapland and Snow Buntings. This reserve also houses a wildfowl collection and a free-flying feral colony of White Storks. To reach it from Brugge head north on Route 67 and turn off to Knokke-Heist, from where a minor road leads east to the reserve. One to two pairs of Cattle Egret bred in the area from 1997 to 1999. In the **Antwerp** area a singing male Zitting Cisticola was present near Mechelen in 1996 and during late June and early July in 1998, and a pair built a nest at Oostmalle in July 1998. Bluethroat ('White-spotted' *cyanecula*) breeds near Herentals, Geel and Kasterlee, in the region known as the Campine where there are several small reserves, and near Lier. One of the best places to look for this beauty is at the private Zegge Reserve, which is situated about 35 km east of Antwerp near Geel. For details of access contact the warden at Groene Wandeling 9, 2232 Gravenwezel, Belgium. Black Woodpecker is most likely to be seen near Antwerp at the Kalmthoutse Heide Reserve, which is situated about 15 km north of Antwerp, and in the Stiemerbeck Valley Reserve near Genk.

ARDENNES

The steep wooded hills and valleys of the Ardennes, which rise to 694 m (2277 ft) at Signal de Botrange in southern Belgium, support Tengmalm's Owl and Black Woodpecker, as well as a few pairs of Hazel Grouse in some years.

The species listed below occur during the spring and summer unless otherwise indicated.

Notable Species

Red and Black (summer) Kites, Black Grouse, Common Crane (spring passage), Eurasian Eagle-Owl, Tengmalm's Owl, Middle Spotted, Black and Grey-headed Woodpeckers, Eurasian Nutcracker.
(Other species recorded here include Hazel Grouse.)

Grey-headed Woodpecker occurs around **Lac D'Eupen** near the border with Germany in eastern Belgium. To reach here head east from Liège to Eupen, then head southwest from there on Route 67, fork left in response to the 'Barrage de la Vesdre' signpost and follow this road past the dam (ignoring the left turn on to the road across the dam) to the road barrier. Park here, even if the barrier is up, and continue on foot to the beech and oak woods on the steep slopes above the opposite side of the reservoir where Black Woodpecker has also been recorded. Another good site for Grey-headed Woodpecker is **Hertogenwald Forest** to the south of Eupen. The **Hautes-Fagnes** (High Fens), the largest reserve area in Belgium, south of Hertogenwald, was established to protect a small population of Black Grouse, but Tengmalm's Owl also occurs here and their small numbers are maintained with the aid of a successful nest-box scheme. There are a number of marked trails, running from the N68, through the area. The **Schwalm Valley**, southeast of Hautes-Fagnes, is another good site for Tengmalm's Owl as well as Black Woodpecker, both of which occur in old beech woods where there is also a chance of seeing Eurasian Nutcracker, especially during the winter. To the west of the Schwalm Valley the extensive conifer plantations and old beech woods around **Logbierme**, near the village of Wanne, also support several pairs of Tengmalm's Owls (which make use of nest boxes), as well as Black Woodpecker and a few Eurasian Nutcrackers, which, again, are most likely to be seen during the winter. To reach the best area head south out of Stavelot on the minor road to the village of Logbierme, and continue east through the village to the end of the road and on to a track into the forest. Hazel Grouse and Black Woodpecker have been recorded in the **Rouge Ponce Reserve** near the village of Tenneville southwest of La Roche.

Near Virton in the extreme south of Belgium both Middle Spotted and Black Woodpeckers occur in the mature woods around the village of **Ethe**, five hours by road from Calais, France. If Hazel Grouse are present in the country this is one of the most likely places to find them, although they have also been recorded around **Croix-Scaille** near Gedinne to the northwest, along with Eurasian Nutcracker.

The two best places to look for Eurasian Eagle-Owl are both at the western end of the Ardennes. They are: (i) the cliffs alongside the river near the village of **Chooz**, south of Givet, which can be viewed from the northern part of the river loop, accessible via the west bank of the river; and (ii) the **Frasnes-les-Couvin Quarry**, reached by heading south from Philippeville towards Couvin. Look out for the quarry ('Carriere du Nord') on the west side of this road near Couvin and view it from the sewage works. If the birds are roosting elsewhere they often fly in at dusk, or to the woods on the other side of the valley.

Accommodation: Barrage de la Gileppe (for the Eupen area)—Hotel du Lion. Malmedy (for the Logbierme area)—Hotel St Gereon. There are also hotels and a campsite in Stavelot. La Roche—Hotel de Liège.

ADDITIONAL INFORMATION

Addresses
Please send records of rarities to the Belgische Avifaunistische Homologatie Commissie, c/o Gunter de Smet, E. Blockstraat 7, 9050 Gentbrugge, Belgium (Flemmish), or the Commission D'homologation, Hugues Dufourny, 20 Rue du Rambaix, 7387 Honelles, Belgium (Walloon).

Birdline
Information and hotline (tel: 03 4880194).

Books and papers
Where to watch birds in Holland, Belgium and Northern France. Van den Berg A and Lafontaine D, 1996. Hamlyn.
Naamlijst van de Vogels van Belgie/Liste des Oiseaux de Belgique 1901–1995. Herroelen P, 1998. This checklist details the status of birds in Belgium and is available for $4 from Paul Herroelen, Leuvensesteenweg 347, B-3370 Boutersem, Belgium.

BOSNIA-HERZEGOVINA

Few birders have visited this former Yugoslavian republic, before or after the ethnic wars of the mid-1990s, and few are likely to visit in the future, as long as the birds which still occur in Bosnia, from Pygmy Cormorant* to Ural Owl, remain easier to see elsewhere, and so long as the countryside is strewn with land mines. However, by the late 1990s some ski resorts had re-opened, enabling access to at least some areas.

At 51,130 km², Bosnia is a quarter the size of England and 8% the size of Texas. Birding is likely to be difficult away from the ski-resort areas due to access restrictions relating to land mines and a lack of accommodation, although staying with local people is always one option worth exploring. Immunisation against hepatitis, polio and typhoid is recommended. The climate is Mediterranean along the Adriatic coast, with hot summers, but it is cooler inland where the winters can be very harsh. The best time to visit Bosnia would be during late May and June when most of the summer visitors have arrived.

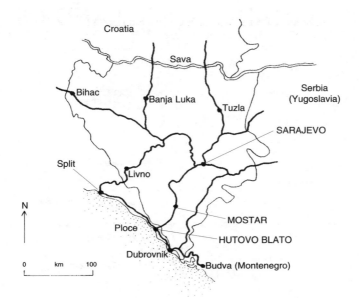

Apart from the extreme north along the border with Croatia, where there may still be remnant unimproved flood-meadows, marshes, lakes, fishponds and riverine woods along the River Sava and its tributaries, Bosnia is a mainly mountainous country with extensive forests, as well as garrigue and maquis near the Adriatic coast in the southwest. Burning, drainage, hunting, overgrazing and timber loss through such activities as clearance for cultivation were all major problems before the war, since when pollution associated with the industrial restart has added to the woes of the two threatened species, as well as the relatively common and widespread birds which occur in Bosnia.

Any wetlands and woods which remain along the River Sava in northern Bosnia may still support breeding species such as Ferruginous Duck*, Squacco Heron, Glossy Ibis, Corn Crake* and Whiskered Tern. This wide valley may also still be an important resting and refuelling station for passage migrants which used to include White Stork and White-tailed Eagle*.

Any marshes, meadows and riverine poplar and willow woods which remain at **Hutovo blato**, an Ornithological Reserve south of Mostar in southern Bosnia and contiguous with the Neretva Delta in adjacent Croatia (p. 146), may still support breeding waterbirds such as Pygmy Cormorant*, Ferruginous Duck* and Squacco Heron. To the north of Mostar the deciduous forests on the steep mountain slopes above the lake in the valley known as **Boracko jezero** may still support Ural Owl and White-backed Woodpecker. Another area which may be worth birding in southern Bosnia is the 173 km^2 **Sutjeska National Park**, where the mountains rise to 2386 m (7828 ft) at Maglic and support lakes, extensive woodland (including 14 km^2 of reputedly virgin forest at Perucica) and montane pastures. With mammals such as brown bear and grey wolf still believed to be present, the birdlife is likely to be just as exciting.

BRITAIN AND IRELAND

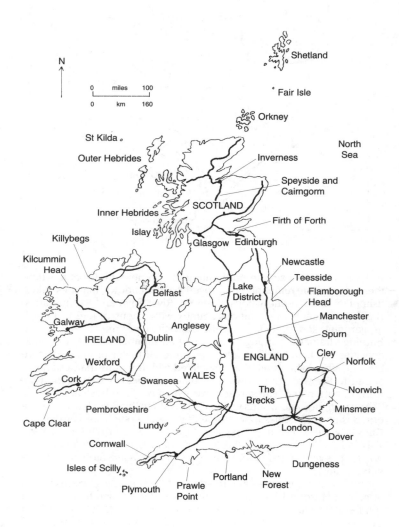

INTRODUCTION

Summary
Mainland Britain and Ireland together with their numerous offshore islands, particularly those in the north, are the best places for seabirds in Europe, both during the breeding season when many spectacular cliffs pulsate with the crammed masses, and during the early autumn when non-breeding species move into the northeast Atlantic and North Sea, and can be seen from most coasts in favourable weather condi-

tions, especially in the southwest. Seeing all these wonderful birds will involve a considerable amount of travel, but the rewards will more than offset the costs for such birds complete some of the most beautiful scenery in the region.

Size
At 299,500 km², Britain and Ireland is about half the size of France and just under half the size of Texas.

Getting Around
Travelling around Britain and Ireland on public transport is, in European terms at least, relatively expensive (especially via rail), and although the air, bus and rail networks are fairly extensive a lot of time and effort will be required to reach all of the best birding sites, primarily because services in rural areas are thin on the ground. Birders with little time to spare may therefore be better off with a vehicle.

Accommodation and Food
Hotels are much more expensive than guesthouses, which in turn, are much more expensive than youth hostels and campsites. All these types of accommodation can be found throughout Britain and Ireland where the tourist infrastructure is well established. In many guesthouses 'British Breakfast' is included in the price and a plate full of bacon, eggs, sausages, beans, mushrooms and tomatoes with fried bread and/or bread-and-butter, washed down with tea or coffee, is usually enough to fuel even the most ravenous birder for a whole day in the field. Such a stomach full is also available in the ubiquitous, usually basic, 'greasy spoon' cafes and motorway service stations. The other, slightly more healthy but far less tasty 'national dish' is 'fish and chips' which ranges from rank to surprisingly delightful. Many public houses (pubs), where the local people meet up for a drink and a chat, also serve excellent food. However, as is the case with beer, wine and spirit selections, pubs are highly variable and a matter of taste. Many pubs, or inns as some are called, also provide accommodation, hence birders travelling around Britain and Ireland who like a decent beer and tasty meal at the end of a hard day in the field, as well as a roof over their heads, may wish to add *The Good Pub Guide*, published annually by Ebury Press, to their pile of bird books.

Health and Safety
Never leave any valuables, especially optical equipment, in vehicles, even out of sight, and be sure to lock all vehicles securely, even in nature reserve car parks.

Climate and Timing
Britain and Ireland has a relative mild and wet maritime climate with warmish summers and fairly mild winters, although it is relatively colder in the north during the winter. The west is the wettest, especially Ireland where as much as 1400 mm (4.6 ft) has been recorded in a single year. Birding in Britain and Ireland can be good at any time of the year, with large numbers of a wide variety of waterbirds present during the winter, millions of breeding seabirds during the summer, often excellent sea-watching during the late summer and early autumn, and regular rarities during the spring and, especially, autumn passage periods.

Habitats

The lowlands of southeast, central and northern England, south Wales and south-central Scotland are densely populated and industrialised, and most of the remaining lowland areas are intensively cultivated, hence only a minuscule amount of almost natural habitat remains in Britain and Ireland. However, 48 million of the 61.6 million people (78%) who inhabit these islands are crammed into England, where most of the 225,000 miles (362,000 km) of roads which connect the numerous towns and cities are also situated, so there are plenty of open spaces in the hills and mountains of far north England, north Wales, Scotland and Ireland, which rise to 1344 m (4410 ft) at Ben Nevis in Scotland. Although much of this open space is forested or grazed there are also large areas of heather moorland and peatlands such as the 'Flow Country' in northern Scotland. Large stretches of the coastline around the whole of Britain and Ireland are also relatively wild, with spectacular seabird cliffs, especially in the north, and numerous large estuaries which support internationally important numbers of water-birds, particularly in the south. Elsewhere, remnant heathlands, wet-lands and woodlands also exist, although many of these are island reserves amidst a sea of concrete, tarmac and barren farmland.

Conservation

Many habitats were destroyed or degraded long ago, and since the end of World War II in 1945 there has been a cataclysmic intensification of land use, resulting in some shocking statistics: 95% of lowland neutral grasslands damaged or gone; 50% of lowland fens and mires gone; 40% of southern heathlands gone; 30–50% of ancient lowland broadleaved woodlands gone; 30% of upland bogs, grasslands and heathlands gone; and 150,000 miles of hedgerows removed. This mass destruction of what little was left after the war combined with the increasingly inten-sive use of farmland has had a disastrous impact on the birdlife of Britain and Ireland. The 1997 Common Birds Census indicated that even the populations of once common and widespread species such as Eurasian Blackbird (down over a million between 1988 and 1997), Song Thrush (down 66% on farmland between 1972 and 1996), Common Starling (down one million between the mid-1970s and mid-1990s) and Sky Lark (down four million between the mid-1970s and mid-1990s) plummeted to their lowest levels since the census was established in the early 1960s. Birds occupy every habitat and sit at the top of the food chain in Britain and Ireland, hence they are excellent indicators of the quality of the 'countryside'. The fact that numbers of familiar birds are in freefall, despite the rising number of reserves, says it all: agricultural intensification = avian decimation.

It's a good job the birds of Britain and Ireland have been served by the County Wildlife Trusts, the Royal Society for the Protection of Birds (RSPB) and other non-governmental organisations for many years. Without this protection, there would be even fewer birds. The members of these organisations—the RSPB alone has over a million—provide the funds to buy land which is then managed specifically for wildlife, but it is beyond these reserves where once common and widespread species are declining so fast. And yet the government let the people of Britain and Ireland down again at the end of the 20th century when they failed to negotiate the necessary reforms to the archaic Common Agricultural Policy (CAP). They had a chance to ensure a future where farmers would be able to make a better living out of farming in an environ-mentally sustainable way than by meeting production quotas, but they refused to take it, despite all the evidence provided by rare success sto-ries such as 'The Corn Crake* comeback'. Since farmers in the Hebrides have been paid to manage their land appropriately, the numbers of call-ing male Corn Crakes* on those islands off the west coast of Scotland have increased from 446 in 1993 to 637 in 1997. Economic encourage-ment may be better than direct payment, but the danger with either is that the few small, sustainable, mixed farms (the best for birds) which remain in Britain and Ireland will be lost in the mad sea of monoculture much of the countryside already resembles, for the only way to farm profitably at the beginning of the 21st century is to farm big.

Bird Species
The number of species recorded in an apparently natural state between 1950 and 1999 in Britain and Ireland was about 535 (about 425 in Ireland). This list does not include 16 species which may not have occurred in a natural state (for example, Mugimaki Flycatcher), 13 species which have not been recorded since the end of 1949, and eight feral species. Notable breeding species include Manx Shearwater, European and Leach's Storm-Petrels, Willow Ptarmigan ('Red Grouse' *scoticus*), Rock Ptarmigan, Corn Crake*, Red-necked Phalarope, Eur-asian Dotterel, Great Skua, Black Guillemot and Atlantic Puffin. Notable seabirds possible during the late summer and autumn include Cory's (*borealis*), Great, Sooty and Mediterranean ('Balearic' *mauretanicus*) Shearwaters, Sabine's Gull, and Pomarine and Long-tailed Skuas.

Endemics
Scottish Crossbill* is endemic to central Scotland where the population of 300-1250 birds is more or less confined to Caledonian pine forests.

Expectations
It is possible to see as many as 200 species during a three-week trip in spring to England, Wales and Scotland, and 150 species on a two-week trip in spring to southern England and Wales, or Scotland.

ENGLAND

ISLES OF SCILLY

During the spring and, especially, the autumn, birders from all over Britain, and some from the rest of Europe, make their first, or, in the case of many, their annual pilgrimages to this beautiful archipelago 28 miles southwest of the mainland, to scour the white-sand beaches, rocky bays, heather moorlands, flower fields, hedges, pools and pock-ets of woodland for passage migrants which regularly include rarities, and to revel in birding tales with old and new friends in the cafes and pubs. The number of visiting birders peaked during October 1987 when nearly 1,000 made the trip to Tresco to see a Philadelphia Vireo, and hundreds still stay on the islands at that time of year so be prepared to put up with the crowds.

Over 400 species have been recorded on these islands, including some of the rarest birds ever to have reached Europe. During April and May, and from mid-September to early November, virtually anything can turn up, from North America, 3000 miles to the west, to Siberia, 3000 miles to the east. Sights such as Pallas's Warbler and Scarlet Tanager in the same area of trees and Red-throated Pipit and Blackpoll Warbler in the same field are not unusual, and on 12 October 1985 the presence of Black-billed and Yellow-billed Cuckoos, Red-eyed Vireo, Northern Parula, Yellow-rumped Warbler, Rose-breasted Grosbeak and Bobolink meant it was possible to see seven Nearctic landbirds in a single day on the wrong side of the Atlantic. Furthermore, during the following week it was possible to see European Bee-eater, Booted, Olivaceous, Dusky and Radde's Warblers, Olive-backed and Red-throated Pipits, and Little and Rustic Buntings. It has arguably never been that good since, but in 1998 Common Nighthawk, Pallid Swift, American Robin, and Olivaceous and Radde's Warblers all made it to just one of the islands, St Agnes, and in early October 1999 Siberian Thrush, White's Thrush and Short-toed Eagle turned up on consecutive days.

Regular Spring Passage Migrants
Eurasian Dotterel, Eurasian Hoopoe, Eurasian Golden-Oriole, Wood-chat Shrike.

Regular Autumn Passage Migrants
Jack Snipe, Pectoral Sandpiper, American Golden-Plover, Eurasian Dotterel, Eurasian Wryneck, Red-backed Shrike, Rosy Starling, Red-breasted Flycatcher, Firecrest, Melodious, Icterine, Pallas's and Yellow-browed Warblers, Greater Short-toed Lark, Richard's, Tawny and Red-throated Pipits, Common Rosefinch, Ortolan, Little, Rustic, Lapland and Snow Buntings.

Regular Summer Visitors
Manx Shearwater, Common Guillemot, Razorbill, Atlantic Puffin.

Other Wildlife
Harbour porpoise, grey seal.

(Other regularly recorded species include a wide selection of seabirds in late summer and early autumn, at which time Wilson's Storm-Petrel may be seen on shark-fishing trips. Rarities not mentioned above have included (American) Purple Gallinule, Solitary Sandpiper, Caspian Plover, Chimney Swift, Blue-cheeked Bee-eater, Yellow-bellied Sapsucker, Wood Thrush, Tree and Cliff Swallows, Blue Rock-Thrush, Orphean Warbler, Bimaculated Lark, Spanish Sparrow, Magnolia and Black-and-white Warblers, Northern Waterthrush, Common Yellowthroat, Yellow-browed Bunting and Baltimore Oriole.)

The islands are accessible by air via light planes which fly from Land's End and helicopters which fly from Penzance, both of which take 15–20 minutes; and by sea, via the *MV Scillonian III* from Penzance, which takes 2.5 hours. To book the plane or boat in advance contact the Isles of Scilly Travel Centre (tel: 0345 105555) or the Isles of Scilly Steamship Company, Quay Street, Penzance, Cornwall, TR18 4BD, UK (tel: 01736 362009; fax: 01736 351223; website: www.islesofscilly-travel.co.uk). To book the helicopter in advance contact the British International Helicopter Travel Service, The Heliport, Penzance, Cornwall, TR18 4AP, UK (tel: 01736 363871; fax: 01736 332253). Most birders base themselves on St Mary's, the main island, but others, usually those who have been visiting the islands for many years, stay on the far less crowded off-islands of St Agnes and Tresco. Only a few care for Bryher despite its long list of rarities, and hardly anyone ever stays on St Martin's which is probably why so few rarities have been found there. Regular daily boat services connect all the off-islands with St Mary's. News of birds spreads fast, via pagers, CB radios, word-of-mouth, blackboards and the local birdline (tel: 0891 700243), and if the latest rarity turns up on an off-island the inter-island boats usually respond very quickly to the panic and, weather permitting, it is usually possible to get to that island before nightfall as long as the bird is found early enough in the day. If there is no time to get there the same day it is usually possible to be on site by dawn the following morning, no matter what island the bird is on. When not chasing rarities the best places to find them include the following: **St Mary's**—Lower Moors Nature Trail, Porthellick Pool (close-up views of Jack Snipe possible in October from the hides at these two sites), Holy Vale Nature Trail, the Golf Course, the Garrison and Peninnis Head; **Tresco**—Great Pool, the adjacent Abbey Pool and the Borough Farm area; **Bryher** and **St Agnes**—both small enough to cover in a day; and, finally, poor neglected **St Martin's**, a large island which is very difficult to cover in a day and so underwatched there are no known hot-spots. During mid-October there is a nightly log call in the Porthcressa Restaurant basement on St Mary's, where there is also usually a selection of stalls, some of which sell photos of the birds which may have turned up earlier in the day.

Accommodation: is in short supply, especially on the off-islands, so it is wise to book well in advance. For a complete list of what is available contact the Isles of Scilly Tourist Office, St Mary's, Isles of Scilly, TR21 0JL, UK (tel: 01720 422536).

From late July to early November many British birders head for **West Cornwall**, either to seawatch (mainly from late July to mid-September) or to look for passage migrants and rarities, especially Nearctic vagrants (mainly from mid-September to early November). During strong south-

The annual pelagic trips to the northeast Atlantic from England present the best chance of seeing Wilson's Storm-Petrel in Europe

WEST CORNWALL

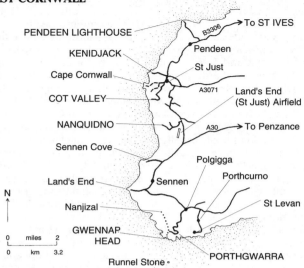

westerly winds most seawatchers sit on Gwennap Head, next to **Porth-gwarra**, especially if the wind is south of west, or, if the wind veers north, either by the lighthouse at **Pendeen** or in the coastguard look-out on the island at **St Ives**. Cory's (*borealis*), Great and Mediterranean ('Balearic' *mauretanicus*) Shearwaters are much more likely to be seen at Porthgwarra, while European and Leach's Storm-Petrels, and Sabine's Gull are more likely to be seen off Pendeen or St Ives. All three sites are good for Sooty and Manx Shearwaters, and all four skuas. All these sea-birds as well as Wilson's Storm-Petrel can also be seen on annual pelagic trips from Penzance to the **Southwest Approaches** on the *MV Scillonian III*, which usually take place in mid-August. To book a place contact the Isles of Scilly Travel Centre or the Isles of Scilly Steamship Company (addresses above). Seabird numbers usually drop dramatically by the end of September, by which time low-pressure systems sweeping east across the North Atlantic promise all sorts of goodies, for the amazing list of birds recorded in the sheltered valleys of the west Cornwall coast already include Veery (St Levan), Chimney Swift (Porthgwarra), Varied Thrush and Scarlet Tanager (Nanquidno), Northern Parula (Cot Valley), and Yellow-throated Vireo and American Redstart (Kenidjack).

The steep cliffs on the island of **Lundy**, 10 miles off the north Devon coast, support breeding seabirds which include a few Atlantic Puffins, and the overgrown coastal gullies together with the wooded Millcombe Valley and boggy inland moors attract a wide range of passage migrants and rarities which have included Baillon's Crake, Ancient Murrelet, Eastern Phoebe, Veery and Rüppell's Warbler. The island is accessible via regular ferries throughout the year (tel: 01237 470422) and boats can be chartered at Ilfracombe. It is possible to stay in a bed & breakfast, or camp on the island.

Prawle Point, the southernmost point of Devon, south of Kings-bridge, is one of the best places in Britain to see Cirl Bunting, which is fairly easy to find on the hillside by the car park, along nearby lanes, along the coastal path to East Prawle, and in nearby Pig's Nose Valley. This is also an excellent area to look for passage migrants, and rarities have included Chestnut-sided and Black-and-white Warblers. The highest concentration of Britain's Cirl Bunting population (450 pairs in 1998) occurs around the village of **Bishopsteignton**, in Devon.

PORTLAND

The island of Portland, which is connected to the mainland by a fragile spit known as Chesil Beach, sticks out 6 miles into the English Channel, and is therefore a top spot for passage migrants and rarities. Nearly 350 species have been recorded on the island, including 290 or so in (or from) the Bird Observatory garden. In suitable conditions the bill, at the southern tip of the island, is also a good seawatching site. Together with the mudflats at Ferrybridge, the large sheltered harbour between the island and the mainland, and the nearby RSPB wetland nature reserves at Lodmoor and Radipole on the outskirts of Weymouth, it is possible to see a wide range of species here in a single day, especially during spring, autumn and winter.

Regular Spring Passage Migrants
Garganey, Pomarine Skua, Eurasian Hoopoe, European Serin.

Regular Autumn Passage Migrants
Eurasian Wryneck, Melodious and Icterine Warblers, Richard's and Tawny Pipits.

Others
Little Egret, Mediterranean Gull, Atlantic Puffin (Apr–Aug), Cetti's Warbler, Reedling.

PORTLAND

87

(Rarities recorded here include Forster's Tern, Egyptian Nightjar, Pallas's Grasshopper Warbler, Lesser Short-toed Lark and Northern Waterthrush.)

If approaching Weymouth from the east call in at the RSPB **Lodmoor** nature reserve, which is an excellent site for shorebirds, gulls and terns. The gulls at the RSPB **Radipole** nature reserve (tel: 01305 778313), which is virtually in the town itself, are always worth grilling, and this is a reliable site for Cetti's Warbler and Reedling. Just to the south of Weymouth, **Portland Harbour** can be viewed from the grounds of Sandsfoot Castle. The harbour can also be viewed from **Ferrybridge** on the raised road between the mainland and Portland. There is a car park here which also overlooks the mudflats at the east end of The Fleet, which at low tide are excellent for shorebirds, gulls and terns. The best areas for passage migrants on **Portland** include the area around the Bird Observatory, the Top Fields, the Eight Kings Quarry (behind the Eight Kings pub in Southwell) and the patch of bushes at Culverwell.

Accommodation: Portland Bird Observatory, Old Lower Light, Portland Bill, Dorset, DT5 2JT, UK.

Little Egret bred for the first time in Britain in 1996 on **Brownsea Island** in Poole Harbour, west of Bournemouth. One pair raised three young that year, then five pairs raised 12 young in 1997. The island and the surrounding mudflats are also an excellent site for passage and wintering waterbirds, including Pied Avocet, the wintering numbers of which exceeded 500 in late 1999. The island is accessible by boat from Poole Quay and Sandbanks between April and September. The nearby RSPB **Arne** nature reserve supports Dartford Warbler. Further east this species is widespread in the **New Forest** where there were about 600 pairs in the late 1990s (compared to just six in 1963). The area around Beaulieu Road railway station is particularly good for this little beauty as well as wintering Northern Shrike ('Great Grey' *excubitor*). Up to eight pairs of European Honey-buzzard also breed in the New Forest and this British rarity is most likely to be seen from Acres Down, accessible from Stoney Cross on the A31, between 1000 and 1300 hours. Little Egrets colonised much of southern England during the 1990s and small numbers can be seen on most estuaries along the south coast, but the largest numbers occur on **Thorney Island** in West Sussex (the record count, 281, was made on 24th August 1999).

One of the best birding sites in southeast England is **Dungeness**, a huge shingle promontory with gravel pits, marshes, scrub and a cooling water outlet known as 'The Patch' next to the nuclear power station which dominates the flat landscape. About 330 species have been recorded here, thanks to the wide variety of habitats and the site's position so close to continental Europe, which means it attracts a wide variety of passage migrants. Hence, it is possible to see over 100 species in a day, especially during April and May. At this time of the year, and especially in early May, many local and visiting birders start the day by seawatching, for this is the best place to observe the spring passage of Pomarine Skuas in England (133 in 1997), as well as plenty of divers, ducks, shorebirds and terns. Keep one eye on 'The Patch' too for it attracts passing gulls, terns and skuas, especially during the autumn, when rarities such as White-winged Tern are almost regular. After about

1000 hours it is time to head inland to the moat around the nearby Bird Observatory and the scrub northeast of there in search of passerine migrants such as Eurasian Golden-Oriole and Firecrest, then the RSPB Dungeness nature reserve (tel: 01797 320588) and the adjacent gravel pits for breeding gulls and terns which include a few pairs of Mediterranean Gull, as well as Garganey, Cetti's Warbler and Reedling. During the winter the gravel pits in and around the reserve are some of the best waters in Britain for Greater Scaup (especially Scotney Pit alongside the Lydd–Camber road) and Smew (53 in January 1997). Rarities recorded in the area include several Short-toed Treecreepers and Eurasian Penduline-Tit, which was a regular winter visitor to the RSPB reserve during the second half of the 1990s. It is possible to stay at Dungeness Bird Observatory, 11 RNSSS Cottages, Dungeness, Romney Marsh, Kent, UK (tel: 01797 321309) which also produces an annual bird report, available by post from there. Further east along the coast large numbers of Mediterranean Gulls (over 200 at times) roost at **Copt Point**, Folkestone.

Two sites in Kent which came to the fore in the late 1990s are **Grove Ferry**, an extension to Stodmarsh National Nature Reserve south of the A28 east of Canterbury, where Baillon's Crake, Slender-billed Gull and over 30 Eurasian Hobbies in the air together were recorded in 1999, and **Oare Marshes**, bisected by the road leading to the Swale Estuary near Faversham, which attract a wide variety of shorebirds, often in large numbers.

During the autumn, crisp juvenile Little Gulls from the Baltic often grace sites in southeast England, including Dungeness, Minsmere and Norfolk

MINSMERE

This wonderful RSPB reserve on the Suffolk coast supports the widest diversity of breeding species found at any one site in Britain. Over 330 species have been recorded here and about 95 breed on a regular basis, thanks to the stack of habitats, from the sea shore through shallow lagoons and reedbeds to some fine heathland and deciduous woods. In one long day during the spring it is possible on foot to see over 100 species (the day-list record is 127), as well as, unfortunately, well over 100 birders, for this is one of the most popular birding sites in Britain and tens of thousands of birders pass through here during the course of a year.

The species listed below occur during the summer unless otherwise indicated.

Regular Summer Visitors and Resident Species

Great Bittern, Western Marsh-Harrier, Pied Avocet, Black Redstart (nearby), Cetti's Warbler, Reedling.

(Other species recorded on a regular basis here in spring include Garganey, Eurasian Spoonbill (19 were present during summer 1996) and Mediterranean Gull. During the spring and autumn numerous passage shorebirds have included rarities such as Greater Yellowlegs, Stilt Sandpiper and Wilson's Phalarope.)

Minsmere is open daily from 0900 hours except Tuesdays. To reach the reserve, complete with visitor centre and numerous hides, turn east off the A12 just north of Yoxford to Westleton, from where it is signposted. To reach the public hide which overlooks the reserve from the seaward side head for the car park at Dunwich Cliffs and walk south. Black Redstart breeds on Sizewell nuclear power station to the south of the reserve.

THE BRECKS

The farmland, grassy heaths, and conifer and poplar plantations in central East Anglia support rare British breeding birds such as Eurasian Thick-knee (142 pairs in 1998) and Eurasian Golden-Oriole.

The species listed below occur during the summer unless otherwise indicated.

EAST ANGLIA

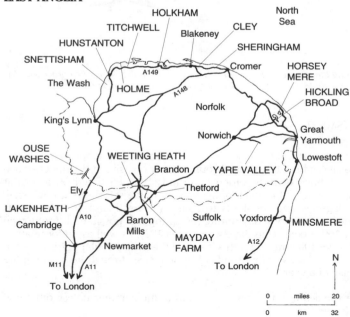

90

Regular Summer Visitors and Resident Species
Northern Goshawk, Eurasian Thick-knee, Eurasian Golden-Oriole, Wood Lark.

Fewer than 20 pairs of Eurasian Golden-Oriole breed in Britain, most of them in the Brecks, and at secret locations. The easiest place to see Eurasian Thick-knee in Britain, as well as Wood Lark, is the well known Norfolk Wildlife Trust **Weeting Heath** nature reserve, complete with visitor centre and hides which are open from late March to the end of August. It lies a mile west of Weeting, which is north of Brandon, alongside the minor road to Hockwold-cum-Wilton. Do not stop along the road near the car park. One of the best places to look for Northern Goshawk in Britain is **Mayday Farm** which lies alongside the B1106 south of Brandon. Walk along the main track here to the large clearing and look out for the goshawks, which along with Wood Larks, are most likely to be seen on crisp sunny days in February and March when they are displaying.

Around 1,000 Whooper Swans and 4,000–5,000 Bewick's Swans winter on the **Ouse Washes**, north of Cambridge, and they can be seen at close range from the WWT Welney nature reserve hides (best light conditions in the morning), accessible via Outwell or Littleport, and the RSPB Ouse Washes nature reserve hides (best light conditions in the afternoon), accessible via Chatteris and Manea. During the summer several pairs of Garganey and Black-tailed Godwit (up to 1,500 of the *islandica* race pass through in the early spring) breed, and a few calling male Spotted Crakes are usually heard.

NORFOLK

Believed by many to be Britain's finest birding area, the wetlands, scrub, deciduous woods and pine plantations of Norfolk support a superb variety of breeding and wintering birds, and during the spring and autumn attract more passage migrants and rarities than many other parts of mainland Britain. Hence, an amazing 362 species have been recorded in the Cley 10-kilometre square alone. Much of the land near the coast lies within nature reserves, some of which have visitor centres, shops, hides and other paraphernalia, and most of these are often crammed with birders, especially at weekends.

Regular Spring Passage Migrants
Garganey, Eurasian Spoonbill, Little Gull, Bluethroat ('Red-spotted' *svecica*).

Regular Autumn Passage Migrants
Arctic Skua, Eurasian Wryneck, Red-backed Shrike, Red-breasted Flycatcher, Firecrest, Icterine, Pallas's, Yellow-browed and Barred Warblers.

Regular Winter Visitors
Pink-footed, Bean ('Taiga' *fabalis*) and Greater White-fronted Geese, Greater Scaup, Long-tailed Duck, Velvet Scoter, Red-throated Diver, Horned Lark, Twite, Snow Bunting.

Regular Summer Visitors and Resident Species
Great Bittern, European Honey-buzzard, Western Marsh-Harrier, Montagu's Harrier, Common Crane, Pied Avocet, Arctic Tern, Barn Owl, Cetti's Warbler, Reedling.

Other Wildlife
Common seal.

(Other regularly recorded species include: during the autumn—Leach's Storm-Petrel, Sabine's Gull, Long-tailed Skua, and Dusky and Greenish (*trochiloides*) Warblers; and during the winter—Brent Goose ('Black Brant' *nigricans*), Little Auk, Bohemian Waxwing and Lapland Bunting. Rarities have included Little Curlew, Red-necked Stint, Collared Pratincole (a single bird each summer from 1994), Slender-billed and Ross's Gulls, Siberian Thrush, Red-breasted Nuthatch, and Desert and Rüppell's Warblers. Introduced species include Egyptian Goose and Golden Pheasant.)

The following sites are all accessible via the A149 coast road between King's Lynn in the west and Cromer in the east. The farmland near **Wolferton**, north of King's Lynn, supports breeding Montagu's Harrier, as well as Western Marsh-Harrier. A little further north follow signs to the RSPB **Snettisham** nature reserve where the old gravel pits are good for stray sea-ducks during the winter and, because they lie just over the sea-wall from the huge intertidal areas of The Wash, they regularly attract masses of roosting shorebirds, including as many as 120,000 Red Knot, which can be seen from the four hides which look over the most southerly pit. North from Snettisham one of the best places to look for wintering grebes and sea-ducks is from the cliff-top at **Hunstanton**. To the east of here, along the north Norfolk coast, the saltmarshes, lagoons and pine plantations at **Holme**, where there is a Bird Observatory, visitor centre and several hides, support breeding Pied Avocet and attract numerous passage migrants, especially during the autumn.

The RSPB **Titchwell** nature reserve (tel: 01485 210779), signposted east of Thornham, supports Western Marsh-Harrier and Reedling and, during the winter, this is a good place for Horned Lark and Snow Bunting. This reserve, which has a visitor centre, shop, snackbar and hides is the most popular in Britain. A total of 135,000 people visited it during 1998, hence it is usually overcrowded, especially at weekends. However, it is still a great place to see many birds and it attracts regular rarities which, in May 1998, included both Laughing and Franklin's Gulls on the same day. The pine plantations behind the beautiful beach at **Holkham**, east to Wells, are a good place to look for passage migrants, especially during the autumn, and rarities here have included Red-breasted Nuthatch. Bird from Holkham Gap, accessible via Lady Anne's Drive opposite Holkham Hall, or from the car park at the eastern end, directly north of Wells. During the winter Lady Anne's Drive is an excellent place from which to watch geese (over 70,000 Pink-feet winter in north-west Norfolk) and the grounds of Holkham Hall are worth checking for Hawfinch.

Titchwell is a brilliant place for birds and it seems to get better and better, but it still can't beat the Norfolk Wildlife Trust **Cley** nature reserve. This is the most famous birding site in Britain because not only does it support rare British breeding birds such as Great Bittern, but it has also been attracting great rarities since the 1950s, when places such as Fair Isle and the Isles of Scilly were still making names for themselves. The original 'birdwatchers'—there was no such thing as 'birders' in those days—used to spend hours at a time on the East Bank scanning for incoming migrants. To this day this legendary bank separates Arnold's Marsh to the east from the lagoons and reedbeds of the reserve to the west, two tip-top birding spots. The reserve is open daily except Mondays (unless they are bank holidays) and from April to December permits can be obtained from the visitor centre (tel: 01263 740008) just east of Cley village. From January to March permits can be obtained from the nearby warden's house. Cley was battered by severe winter storms in February 1996 when high spring tides combined with force-ten northeasterlies, smashed the shingle bank built to protect the reserve from the sea and flooded the reserve with several metres of sea-water, after which some village residents were able to seawatch from their lounge windows. Three hides were destroyed and two more damaged, but swift repair work meant that the infrastructure was soon back in place. It is a long hard slog (or a murderous jog for those chasing rarities) west from Cley beach along the 3.5-mile-long shingle spit to **Blakeney Point**, but this spit is a superb place to hunt down passage migrants during the spring and autumn. A spell of east to northeasterly winds with drizzle beckons the local and not so local birders out to Blakeney where Bluethroats are expected in such conditions during the spring and almost anything can turn up in the autumn, amongst what often amounts to substantial falls of commoner migrant passerines. The best spots to concentrate on are from Halfway (Watch) House to The Hood and on to Long Hills and Yankee Ridge. At the point, accessible by boat from Morston Quay, there is an impressive ternery with Sandwich (2,000 pairs), Common (200 pairs), Arctic (25 pairs) and Little (100 pairs) Terns viewable from hides.

From 1992 European Honey-buzzards bred in the **Swanton Novers** area and this rare raptor can be looked for between May and September from the Raptor Viewpoint reached by taking the B1110 southwest out of Holt for about 8 miles. Turn off here on to a minor road, signposted to Fulmodeston, and continue for half a mile to reach the viewpoint car park.

East of Cley as far as Cromer, virtually anywhere accessible along the coast is worth birding. In northerly gales during the autumn and winter, seawatching can be very productive anywhere along the coast, but especially at Cley and **Sheringham**, just west of Cromer, where the old hands gather in the beach-level shelter below the toilet block at the extreme western end of the esplanade.

The **Norfolk Broads**, to the south of Cromer, support a few Great Bitterns, up to 20 nests of Western Marsh-Harrier, a few resident Common Cranes and about 50 singing male Cetti's Warblers. All but the cranes can usually be seen around Hickling Broad, accessible from Potter Heigham church (walk north), where Savi's Warbler and swallowtail butterflies also occur. The best chance of seeing the elusive cranes is to head for Horsey Mere in the late afternoon, since they usually roost there, along with harriers. South of the broads, between Norwich and Lowestoft, up to a few hundred Bean Geese winter in the **Yare Valley** near Buckenham, especially on the carefully managed, seasonally flooded grazing meadows in the RSPB Mid-Yare nature reserve. Some can usually be seen from hides, reached from Brundall, near the A47 Norwich–Great Yarmouth road, by heading southeast from there, under the railway bridge and then turning right on to Low Road, along which there is a car park and trail to the hides, although directions change according to contemporary RSPB guideposts in order to avoid disturbance. The best time to see them is during November and December.

Norfolk is the most popular birding area in Britain and Ireland, thanks to its wide range of wintering birds, passage migrants and breeding species which include Pied Avocet

European Honey-buzzards are often present during the summer in and around **Welbeck and Clumber Parks**, between Ollerton and Worksop in Nottinghamshire. There are many exciting birding areas along England's northeast coast, not least the **Spurn Peninsula**, accessible via Kilnsea east of Hull, where over 330 species have been recorded. The first Bird Observatory on mainland Britain was established here in 1946 because even then it was known as a great place for passage migrants. To this day huge numbers of commoner passerine passage migrants occasionally fall out of the sky here, especially after being pushed west across the North Sea during the autumn. Sometimes birders almost have to wade through thrushes and Goldcrests to get to the regular rarities. Bluethroats ('Red-spotted' *svecica*) are regular during easterly winds in spring, and during similar conditions in the autumn regular visitors include Eurasian Wryneck, Red-backed Shrike, Red-breasted Flycatcher, Firecrest, and Icterine, Yellow-browed and Barred Warblers. Star rarities have included Tengmalm's Owl, Cliff Swallow and Marmora's Warbler. There is a network of trails with hides overlooking pools, although most birders concentrate on The Warren, Kilnsea, Beacon Lane, and, at Easington, the cemetery on Seaside Lane and Sammy's Point. **Stone Creek**, near Cherry Cobb Sands on the River Humber northwest of Spurn, is another migrant hotspot where two major rarities have been discovered: Green Heron and Mugimaki Flycatcher.

The next major promontory up the northeast coast, **Flamborough Head**, is just as good as Spurn for passage migrants and rarities, and over 320 species have been recorded here. It extends for six miles out into the North Sea and is therefore also one of the top seawatching sites in Britain. In addition the headland also supports 200,000 breeding seabirds, most of which are crammed on to the cliffs at the RSPB Bempton Cliffs nature reserve. Easterly winds regularly push Bluethroats ('Red-spotted' *svecica*) west on to the headland during the spring, but it is the autumn when birding really hots up here. For example, in 1988 an 'Eastern' Black Redstart (*phoenicuroides*), five 'Eastern' Common Redstarts

FLAMBOROUGH HEAD

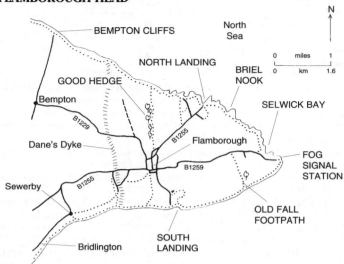

(*samamisicus*), a Pied Wheatear, a Dusky, two Radde's, eight Pallas's, 70 Yellow-browed and two Greenish (*trochiloides*) Warblers, an Olive-backed Pipit and a Pine Bunting were recorded. The long list of rarities ranges from Desert to Blackpoll Warblers and the best places to look for such birds are Dane's Dyke, south of the B1255 west of Flamborough village, the wooded ravine at South Landing, the footpath which runs close to the private Old Fall Plantation, Selwick Bay, Briel Nook, North Landing and the wooded gulley by the Bempton Cliffs car park. Northerly based winds with poor visibilty from late July to October are the best conditions for seawatching when regular species include Sooty Shearwater (several hundred in a single day), and Pomarine (up to 330 in a single day), Arctic (over 1,000 in a single day) and Long-tailed (352 in autumn 1988) Skuas. In strong northeasterlies at the end of October Little Auks pass the headland, and on 29 October 1983 a single-day record of 6,337 went by. Rare seabirds have included Black-browed Albatross, Fea's Petrel types and Little Shearwater. To reach the best seawatching spot, park at the lighthouse, walk down the road to the Fog Signal Station, then clamber carefully down to the cliff-top below the fence. For details of 'Seabird Cruises' from Bridlington to Bempton Cliffs between June and September send a stamped addressed envelope to the RSPB North of England Regional Office, 4 Benton Terrace, Sandyford Road, Newcastle-upon-Tyne, NE2 1QU, UK (tel: 0191 281 3366). To obtain a copy of the Flamborough Ornithological Group's annual Bird Report contact the Honorary Secretary, 4 Silver Birch Drive, Wyke, West Yorkshire. Filey North Cliff Country Park at **Filey Brigg**, at the base of the headland, is equally attractive to passage migrants which have included major rarities such as Lanceolated and Spectacled Warblers, Pechora Pipit and Yellow-breasted Bunting.

The next major birding site along the northeast coast is in and around the national nature reserve at **Teesside** near Middlesbrough. The mud-flats, marshes and pools here are surrounded by power stations and the greatest concentration of chemical factories in Britain, hence this is a far from pretty, but extremely productive and popular birding site. It acts as a resting and refuelling stop for internationally important numbers of passage and wintering shorebirds, and regular rarities have included the likes of Short-billed Dowitcher and Great Knot (Seal Sands), Long-toed Stint (Saltholme Pools) and Sharp-tailed Sandpiper (Long Drag). To bird Greatham Creek, where shorebirds usually roost at high tide, and Seal Sands, where many shorebirds feed at low tide, park in the car park alongside the A178 just south of the creek roadbridge at Cowpen Marsh, from where there is a trail to a hide overlooking the creek, and walk east along the south side of the creek to another hide overlooking Seal Sands. The Long Drag is a raised bank which runs between Seal Sands and Dorman's, Reclamation and Saltholme Pools, the latter two of which are also accessible via the private North Tees Road which runs from the A178 about a mile north of Port Clarence. For more details of access, restricted in some cases, contact the Cleveland Wildlife Trust, Bellamy Pavillion, Kirkleatham Old Hall, Kirkleatham, Redcar, TS10 5NW, UK. For more information on other good birding sites in the area and annual bird reports for the area contact the Teesmouth Bird Club, 63 Stokesley Crescent, Billingham, Cleveland, TS23 1NF, UK.

The **Wheldrake Ings-Lower Derwent Valley** area in north Yorkshire supports about 100 breeding species, including important British populations of Black-necked Grebe, Garganey (30 pairs in 1998), Common Quail (32 calling males in 1999), and Corn* (eight calling males in 1998) and Spotted (up to 24 calling males in 1998) Crakes. The valley is accessible via Wheldrake village in the north, and Bubwith and North Duffield villages in the south. Probably over 75% of the English Black Grouse population is now confined to the Yorkshire and Durham Dales and the best place to look for these birds is **Upper Teesdale**, west of Barnard Castle. Cruising along the Eggleston–Stanhope road and others in the area is the best way to locate the birds.

One of the best birding sites in northwest England is the RSPB **Leighton Moss** nature reserve (tel: 01524 701601), thanks to, in 1998, three to four pairs of Great Bittern, three nests of Western Marsh-Harrier and 45 pairs of Reedling, as well as Eurasian otter. To reach here leave the M6 at junction 35A, head north on the A6 and follow the signposts. The best place to look for birds in the beautiful **Lake District** is the RSPB Haweswater nature reserve, the only regular breeding site of Golden Eagle in England. Between April and August there is an observation post for viewing the eagles, accessible via the path which leads from the car park at the south end of the reservoir. For more details on this site contact The Warden, RSPB Haweswater Nature Reserve, 7 Naddlegate, Burn Banks, Haweswater, Cumbria, CA10 2RL, UK.

SCOTLAND

The vast majority of the Barnacle Geese which breed on Spitsbergen (p. 363), about 19,000 of them, winter on and around the WWT **Caerlaverock** nature reserve next to the Solway Firth in southwest Scotland. Numbers peak in mid-November but they are numerous throughout the winter when they are joined by up to 15,000 Pink-footed Geese, plenty of Whooper and Bewick's Swans, and over 2,000 Greater Scaup (over 50% of the British wintering population occur on the firth). The reserve, complete with a mile of screened walkways, 20 hides and a few observation towers, is situated 8 miles southeast of Dumfries and signposted from the A75. The Solway can also be a good place to observe overland spring skua passage, particularly at Bowness.

ISLAY

The shallow sea lochs, low hills and fields of this lovely island, off the west coast of Scotland, support a superb range of birds during the winter months, including many of the Greenland breeding population of Greater White-fronted (up to nearly 13,000) and Barnacle (usually around 30,000 but up to 45,000) Geese, Golden Eagle and Red-billed Chough.

The species listed below occur during the winter unless otherwise indicated.

Regular Winter Visitors and Resident Species
Pink-footed, Greater White-fronted ('Greenland' *flavirostris*) and Barnacle Geese, Greater Scaup, Long-tailed Duck, Golden Eagle, Willow Ptarmigan ('Red Grouse' *scoticus*), Purple Sandpiper, Black Guillemot, Red-throated, Black-throated and Great Northern Divers, Rock Dove, Barn Owl, Red-billed Chough, Twite.

Other Wildlife
Eurasian otter, common and grey seals.

(Other species recorded here during the winter include Snow and Canada ('Lesser' *hutchinsii*) Geese, White-tailed Eagle*, Glaucous and Iceland Gulls, and Snow Bunting. Other summer visitors include Corn Crake*, and during the autumn it is possible to see European and Leach's Storm-Petrels in suitable weather.)

Islay (pronounced Eye-la) is accessible by air and sea. A vehicular ferry (two hours) connects Port Askaig and Port Ellen with Kennacraig on the mainland. To book a seat on one of the daily flights from Glasgow contact Loganair (tel: 0141 889 1311). To book the ferry contact Caledonian MacBrayne, The Ferry Terminal, Gourock, PA19 1QP, UK (tel: 01475 650000). When the Barnacle Geese arrive in late October most of them concentrate on the RSPB **Loch Gruinart** nature reserve. They disperse afterwards but this is still one of the best areas to see them throughout the winter, along with **Bridgend Bay**, over which they fly to roost. To look for Golden Eagle and Red-billed Chough walk from the 131-m (430 ft) high sea cliffs at **Mull of Oa** to Beinn Mhor Cairn, at the southwest corner of the island. The sheltered waters of **Loch Indaal**, best viewed from the pier in Bowmore, are excellent for wintering seaduck, including as many as 1,000 Greater Scaup in some years, and all three divers, while the rubbish tip south of Bowmore is worth checking for Glaucous and Iceland Gulls. **Rubha Na Faing**, at the western end of the island, is the best seawatching site and in northwesterlies to southwesterlies from August to October it is possible to see European and Leach's Storm-Petrels.

Accommodation: for details contact the Islay Tourist Office, The Square, Bowmore, Isle of Islay, Strathclyde, UK (tel: 01496 810254).

INNER HEBRIDES

The Inner Hebridean islands of Mull, Coll, Tiree, Eigg, Rhum and Skye, off the west coast of Scotland, support White-tailed* and Golden Eagles, as well as breeding Corn Crake*.

The species listed below occur during the summer unless otherwise indicated.

Localised Specialities
White-tailed Eagle*, Corn Crake*.

Others
Manx Shearwater (summer), Greater White-fronted ('Greenland' *flavirostris*/winter) and Barnacle (winter) Geese, Golden Eagle, Black Guillemot (summer), Atlantic Puffin (summer).

Other Wildlife
Eurasian otter, minke whale.

The islands of Mull, Coll and Tiree are accessible by ferry from Oban and Lochaline on mainland Scotland, with an onward connection to the island of Barra at the southern end of the Outer Hebrides (p. 99). The ferry's first stop is at mountainous **Mull** which supports one of the highest concentrations of Golden Eagle in Europe, as well as a few White-tailed Eagles* which are most likely to be seen around Loch Spelve. From Ulva on Mull it is possible to visit the **Treshnish Isles** of Staffa (where Fingal's Cave is situated) and Lunga, the latter of which is reputed to host Britain's tamest Atlantic Puffins. The next ferry stop after Mull is **Coll**, where the RSPB nature reserve at the western end of the island supports breeding Corn Crake* and wintering geese. The third stop is **Tiree**, another good island for breeding Corn Crake* and wintering geese. When at sea around these islands look out for minke whales.

The ferry between Mallaig on mainland Scotland and Lochboisdale on South Uist in the Outer Hebrides calls in at **Rhum**, famous for being the centre of a long-running White-tailed Eagle* reintroduction programme. This species became extinct as a British breeding bird by 1916, but a total of 83 wild-bred Norwegian birds were introduced between 1975 and 1985, with a further 59 since, and in 1996 the first youngster to be raised by a wild-bred British pair fledged successfully, followed by the first double-figure count of wild fledglings in 1998 (when 17 pairs laid eggs). Many of the previously released birds and the more recently raised youngsters have dispersed widely throughout northwest Scotland and they can now be seen at a number of locations. However, there are few better settings than mountainous Rhum in which to see this huge raptor, where they share the air with Golden Eagles and give it up at night to about 100,000 pairs of Manx Shearwaters—one of the largest colonies of this species on earth. The beautiful island of **Skye**, accessible by road bridge from Kyle of Lochalsh, is reputed to support

INNER and OUTER HEBRIDES

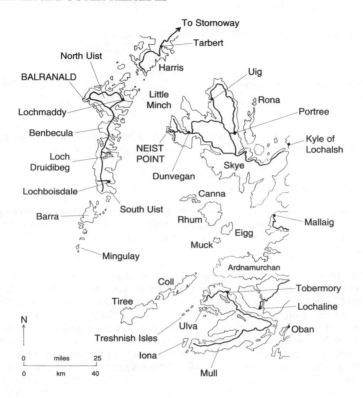

the highest density of Golden Eagles in Europe. It is certainly one of the easiest places to see this magnificent raptor and those who look for it here may well see one in the air with a White-tailed Eagle*, for this species also breeds on the island. The best places to see them hunting together are west of Dunvegan, especially in the Neist Point area at the western tip of the island, and along the coast road north of Portree.

One of the easiest places to see Rock Ptarmigan in Scotland is on the mainland near Kyle of Lochalsh. Park at the high point of the highest road in Scotland, that which connects **Applecross** with the A896 between Strathcarron, northeast of Kyle of Lochalsh, and Torridon, and explore on foot from there. Head northeast from Torridon to reach **Gruinard Bay**, a top site for White-tailed Eagle*.

OUTER HEDBRIDES

The Outer Hebrides are some of the wildest and most beautiful islands on earth. The low rocky headlands, long white shell-sand beaches, dunes, machair, lochs, bogs, rough pasture and craggy hills all form a wonderful wilderness which is completed by birds such as White-tailed Eagle*, Corn Crake* and Red-necked Phalarope.

The species listed below occur during the summer unless otherwise indicated.

Localised Specialities
White-tailed Eagle* (reintroduced), Corn Crake*, Red-necked Phalarope.

Others
Golden Eagle, Willow Ptarmigan ('Red Grouse' *scoticus*), Common Greenshank, Arctic Tern, Red-throated Diver, Rock Dove, Twite.

Other Wildlife
Eurasian otter, common seal.

(Other species recorded here include European and Leach's Storm-Petrels, and Pomarine and Long-tailed Skuas. Rarities have included a drake Steller's Eider* (1972–1984), Mourning Dove, White's Thrush and Veery.)

The three major southern islands, North Uist, Benbecula and South Uist, all of which are connected by roads on causeways, are the best for birds. Benbecula is accessible by air (tel: British Airways 0181 897 4000) and both North Uist and South Uist are accessible by vehicular ferries from Uig (on Skye), and Mallaig and Oban (on the mainland) respectively, hence it is possible to travel to Lochboisdale on South Uist, drive up through the islands and return to the mainland from Lochmaddy on North Uist, or vice versa. To book the ferries contact Caledonian Mac-Brayne, The Ferry Terminal, Gourock, PA19 1QP, UK (tel: 01475 650000). During the spring, especially in May, seabirds, including European Storm-Petrel, and Pomarine and Long-tailed Skuas, may be seen from the ferries. Virtually anywhere on the islands is worth birding, although the best spots are, arguably, the RSPB **Loch Druidibeg** nature reserve and **Loch Eynort** (White-tailed Eagle*) on South Uist, the areas of machair on **Benbecula**, and, best of all, the RSPB **Balranald** nature reserve on North Uist, which supports one of the highest breeding densities of shorebirds in Europe, including a few Red-necked Phalaropes, as well as Corn Crake* (18 calling males in 1997). It is fairly easy to hear *Crex crex* on the south side of the approach road to the reserve centre at Goular Cottage, but seeing even the head of one of these super skulkers is another matter altogether. Most of the time they stick to thick cover, and after June, when the vegetation is much taller, they can be virtually impossible to see. In May and early June, however, bold birds have been known to break cover, especially when walking from one iris bed to the next. Like most crakes, once out in the open they seem to forget that they are not supposed to be there and allow splendid, often remarkably close, views. Aird an Runair, the rocky headland at the west end of the reserve is an excellent seawatching site, especially following wet weather fronts and a change of wind direction from south or southwest to west, northwest or north, during the middle of May, when Pomarine (1,716 between 11 and 28 May 1986, 372 on 7 May 1997) and Long-tailed (1,340 between 12 and 21 May 1991, including 540 on the

19th and a single flock of 180 on the 21st) Skuas have been recorded in large numbers. To reach Balranald turn off the A865 3 miles north of Bayhead to Hougharry and follow signposts from there.

Accommodation: for details contact the North Uist Tourist Office, Pier Road, Lochmaddy, North Uist, Outer Hebrides, UK (tel: 01876 500321).

Britain's remotest archipelago, **St Kilda**, is situated about 41 miles west-northwest of the Outer Hebrides. The highest sea cliffs in Britain, which rise to 376 m (1234 ft) at Conachair on the north side of Hirta, the main island, and some of the most amazing sea stacks on earth, support breeding Manx Shearwater, European (the largest colony in Britain) and Leach's (the largest colony in the east Atlantic) Storm-Petrels, Northern Gannet, Great Skua (200 pairs), Black Guillemot, Atlantic Puffin (the largest colony in Britain—about 100,000 pairs) and the en-demic *hirtinis* subspecies of Winter Wren, which is about one third larg-er than the mainland form (about 125 pairs). In addition, killer, minke and pilot whales are regularly recorded *en route* to and from, and around the archipelago, which is accessible by sea only (and during the summer only), when weather conditions permit. There are no regu-lar services but companies offering trips in 1999 included the following: Kylebhan Charters, 3 Barclay Court, Old Kilpatrick, G60 5HX, UK (tel: 01389 877028) and Northern Light, Ben Buie Cottage, Lochbuie, Isle of Mull, Argyll, PA62 6AA, UK (tel: 01680 814260). It can take up to two days to reach the islands from mainland Scotland and once there visi-tors must sleep on the boat. However, there is an army missile-tracking station on Hirta, and the commanding officer of the troops present has been known to invite visitors for a drink in the officers' mess, a sort of pub called the Puff Inn. It is also possible to join conservation work par-ties, which camp on Hirta, organised by The Secretary, St Kilda Club, National Trust for Scotland, 5 Charlotte Square, Edinburgh, EH2 4DU, UK. If the islands were accessible via a regular ferry and/or public air service, they would no doubt receive more visitors, including twitchers who currently have to cry into their beer when news of Nearctic vagrants such as Tennessee and Hooded Warblers filters out.

St Kilda supports over 60,000 pairs of Northern Gannets, nearly a quarter of the world total, in what is believed to be the largest colony on earth

In southeast Scotland the **Firth of Forth** is the best site in Europe for Surf Scoter and one of the best places for wintering grebes and other sea-ducks in Britain. There were up to four drake Surf Scoters present during the winters throughout most of the 1990s, to early 1999 at least, as well as extra birds at various times in **St Andrews Bay**, another regular site, to the north. The best place in the firth to look for them is **Largo Bay**, on the north side, where Methil power station and Ruddon's Point are the best places to start. On **Bass Rock**, an island at the mouth of the firth, it is possible to walk through a Northern Gannet colony. The rock is accessible on regular boat trips out of North Berwick, 20 miles east of Edinburgh, between late June and late September (tel: 01620 893863 for details of departures). Black-necked Grebe breeds at the RSPB **Loch of Kinnordy** nature reserve, a mile west of Kirriemuir on the B951, about 20 miles north of Dundee.

Further north along the east coast of Scotland a drake King Eider was a regular summer visitor to the **Ythan Estuary**, 12 miles north of Aberdeen, from 1983 to at least autumn 1999. To reach the estuary mouth where this lovely duck is most often found, amongst the hundreds of Common Eiders, turn east just south of Newburgh towards the golf course and continue past the car park on the track to the river. North of Newburgh the A975 crosses the river at Waterside Bridge; a good place to scan for Eurasian otter. During the autumn and winter, **Fraserburgh** and the nearby Kinnairds Head are two of the top spots in Britain for rare gulls; Ivory and Ross's were both recorded in 1997 for example.

SPEYSIDE AND CAIRNGORM

The ancient Caledonian pine forests, lochs, rivers and mountains, which rise to 1310 m (4298 ft) at Ben Macdui, in central Scotland, support the endemic Scottish Crossbill*, as well as Eurasian Capercaillie and Crested Tit, which are also restricted to this region within Britain. Up until the end of the 1990s, this was still one of the most scenically beautiful large areas of Britain to go birding in and one of the few parts of mainland Britain which still resembled a wilderness. However, in 1998 the government decided to allow a funicular railway to be built, in order to transport as many as 220,000 lazy visitors to the top of Cairngorm every year. Anyone who has been here and seen the likes of Eurasian Dotterel gracing the wild high tops can only shake their heads in despair.

The species listed below occur during the summer unless otherwise indicated.

Scottish Endemics
Scottish Crossbill*.

Regular Summer Visitors and Resident Species
Slavonian Grebe, Osprey, Rock Ptarmigan, Eurasian Capercaillie (reintroduced since 1837), Eurasian Dotterel, Crested Tit, Snow Bunting.

Others
Golden Eagle, Willow Ptarmigan ('Red Grouse' *scoticus*), Twite.

Other Wildlife
Pine marten, red squirrel, reindeer (introduced), wild cat.

(Some ornithologists believe Scottish Crossbill* is most closely related to/or a form of Parrot Crossbill and that at the end of the 1990s many of the large-billed crossbills in Speyside were in fact Parrot Crossbills rather than Scottish Crossbills*. Other species recorded here include Black Grouse, Spotted Crake (9 at Insh Marshes in May 1999), Wood Sandpiper and the occasional Snowy Owl (usually around Ben Macdui).)

The best base is Aviemore, southeast of Inverness. The three Caledonian pine forest specialites, Eurasian Capercaillie, Crested Tit and Scottish Crossbill*, occur at the RSPB **Loch Garten** nature reserve, signposted from the A9 a few miles north of Aviemore and open daily from 1000 to 1800 hours between late April and late August. The best way to see the huge but elusive capercaillie is to visit the area at dawn in April and May when the males lek in forest clearings and the birds feed for long periods in the tops of the pine trees. Walk the two tracks which lead from Forest Lodge and the tracks which lead to Loch Mallachie. These three species also occur in the forest adjacent to the golf course at **Grantown-on-Spey** and in **Rothiemurchus Forest**, southeast of Aviemore. Loch Garten is a reliable place to see Osprey but anyone spending a few days in Speyside will almost certainly see at least one elsewhere and thus avoid the crush and CCTVs at the famous loch. However, if none have been seen at Loch Garten or elsewhere there is always **Inverdruie Fish Farm**, just outside Aviemore along the road to Coylumbridge, where there is a hide overlooking a well-stocked fishpond which is deliberately left uncovered so Ospreys can plunge in to

SPEYSIDE, CAIRNGORM AND DEESIDE

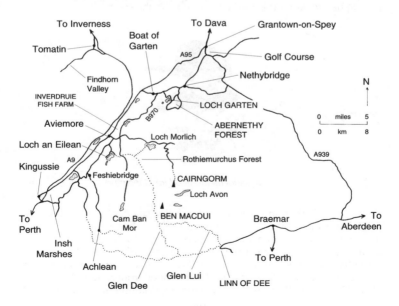

pick up their daily fish. The farm is also visible across the railway line from the tourist information centre car park in Aviemore. The three **Cairngorm** specialities: Rock Ptarmigan, Eurasian Dotterel and Snow Bunting, can usually be found by following the ridge towards Ben Macdui from the top of Cairngorm, accessible via the ski-lifts at the end of the road beyond Coylumbridge, or on foot. Snow Buntings are rare on the barren plateau tops during the summer but in winter they occur around the Ptarmigan Restaurant just below the Cairngorm summit and the car parks at the base of the ski-lifts. Rock Ptarmigan and Eurasian Dotterel also occur on the less disturbed **Carn Ban Mor** which lies south of Cairngorm and is accessible from Achlean, 5 miles south of Feshiebridge. Golden Eagles hunt regularly over Cairngorm and Carn Ban Mor, but are more likely to be seen in the upper **Findhorn Valley**, reached by turning southwest off the A9 near Tomatin 15 miles south of Inverness. Slavonian Grebe breeds on the RSPB **Loch Ruthven** nature reserve (13 pairs in 1997), reached by turning west off the A9 6 miles south of Inverness on to the B851. At East Croachy fork right to the car park from where there is a trail to a hide which overlooks a sheltered bay where a few pairs nest.

Accommodation: Aviemore etc.

In **Deeside**, to the east of Cairngorm, it is possible to see all four species of grouse which occur in Britain, as well as Golden Eagle and Scottish Crossbill*, before mid-morning on a good day in April and May. Head west from Braemar before dawn in order to be in the woods between Inverey and Linn of Dee at first light (Golden Eagle, Black Grouse, Eurasian Capercaillie, Scottish Crossbill*), then return to Braemar and head south 6 miles on the A93 to the car park at the Glen Shee Ski Centre, from where Rock Ptarmigan can often be seen feeding in the rocky outcrops and scree just below the high tops with a telescope. During bad weather this bird even occurs in the car park.

Some Scottish lochs are good for Goosanders

The **Moray Firth**, north of Inverness, is full of sea-ducks (including over 5,000 Long-tailed) and divers during the winter, but is more famous for its resident population of about 130 bottlenose dolphins. Birds and dolphins can be seen from Chanonry Point near Fortrose. Take the A9 north from Inverness and cross the bridge to reach the information centre in the rest area, a mile or so further on; open from April to November, 1000–1700 hours (tel: 01463 731866; email: dolphinchaz@yahoo.com).

Red Kites have been reintroduced into northern Scotland since 1989 (and the farmland around the firth is a good place to see them).

The islands of **Orkney** are rather flat except for Hoy, some of which is composed of rugged moorland which supports about 1,500 pairs of Great Skua. The islands may not be mountainous but along some parts of their coasts there are towering sea cliffs which rise to 300 m (984 ft) and are crammed with breeding seabirds, notably those which adjoin the giant sea stack known as the Old Man of Hoy, which rises to 150 m (492 ft). During the winter, Orkney's lochs, such as Harray and Stenness, and sheltered inlets support large numbers of sea-ducks and divers. For example, over 1,000 Long-tailed Ducks and 644 Great Northern Divers (January 1999—the record count for Britain) have been recorded at any one time in Scapa Flow alone. Twitchers may argue that Orkney is at its most exciting during the spring and autumn when the islands, notably Stronsay and North Ronaldsay at the extreme northeast end of the archipelago, regularly receive large falls of passage migrants, including Bluethroat ('Red-spotted' *svecica*), and rarities, which have included White-throated Needletail, Siberian Thrush, Pallas's Grasshopper Warbler, Yellow Warbler, and Cretzschmar's and Yellow-browed Buntings. Mainland also receives its share of goodies and these have included the likes of Western Sandpiper. Orkney is accessible via vehicular ferries from Aberdeen and Shetland (tel: 01856 850655); from Scrabster (Thurso) on the Scottish mainland to Stromness on the Orkney island of Mainland (two hours); and by foot ferry, during the summer, from John O'Groats to South Ronaldsay (tel: 01955 81353), as well as by air. North Ronaldsay is accessible by air (tel: 01856 872494) and sea (tel: 01856 872044), and it is possible to stay at the Bird Observatory there (tel: 01857 633200). For more details contact the Orkney Tourist Board, 6 Broad Street, Kirkwall, Orkney KW15 1NX, UK (tel: 01856 872856; fax: 01856 875056).

FAIR ISLE

This isolated, rugged island, which is about 3 miles long and 1.5 miles wide, lies about halfway between Orkney and Shetland. Its lofty sea cliffs, which rise to 198 m (650 ft) at the north end of the island, support 250,000 breeding seabirds, but the vast majority of birders visit Fair Isle to search for an amazing variety of passage migrants which arrive *en masse* on a regular basis, especially during periods of southeasterly winds during the autumn. Experiencing a fall on Fair Isle is one of the highlights of birding, especially if it contains one or more of the island's five main specialities: Lanceolated (over 40 records and present in all but one of the autumns since 1984), Pallas's Grasshopper (over 11 records) and Paddyfield (annual 1992 to 1997) Warblers, Pechora Pipit (annual 1991 to 1998) and Yellow-breasted Bunting (annual), all of which are virtually guaranteed here in mid- to late September, but very rarely seen on mainland Britain.

Birders with a particular interest in seeing scarce migrants and rarities will do well to find a place more exciting than Fair Isle. Take 1997 for example, when between 20th and 28th September there were two Lanceolated, one Pallas's Grasshopper and two Paddyfield Warblers, one Pechora Pipit and two Yellow-breasted Buntings, as well as two Olive-backed Pipits (more individuals of this species have been recorded here than anywhere else in Europe) on the island. One of the best autumn falls on the island ever took place on 14 September 1995 when a Great Snipe*, a Rosy Starling, a Black-eared Wheatear, single Paddyfield, Icterine, Arctic and Barred Warblers, a Pechora Pipit, and five Ortolan, two Little and a Yellow-breasted Bunting arrived. Spring is less exciting but one of the best falls at that time of year was on 13 May 1985 when 70 Bluethroats ('Red-spotted' *svecica*) and 18 Red-backed Shrikes were present. Over 350 species have been recorded in total (only 34 breed regularly), about 50 fewer than the Isles of Scilly, but rarities here can be watched in relative peace, in crowds which rarely exceed 25, compared to the Isles of Scilly where nearly 1,000 birders have been known to descend upon one spot.

The best time to visit during the spring is in May and early June, while the peak autumn period is mid-September to mid-October, particularly the middle and second half of September for eastern vagrants.

Regular Spring Migrants
Eurasian Wryneck, Eurasian Golden-Oriole, Red-backed and Woodchat Shrikes, Bluethroat ('Red-spotted' *svecica*), Thrush Nightingale, Icterine Warbler.

Regular Autumn Migrants
Great Snipe*, Eurasian Wryneck, Red-backed Shrike, Red-breasted Flycatcher, Bluethroat (*svecica*), Lanceolated, Pallas's Grasshopper, Paddyfield, Icterine, Pallas's, Yellow-browed and Barred Warblers, Greater Short-toed Lark, Citrine Wagtail, Richard's, Olive-backed, Pechora and Red-throated Pipits, Little, Rustic and Yellow-breasted Buntings.

Regular Summer Visitors and Resident Species
European Storm-Petrel, Arctic Tern, Great and Arctic Skuas, Black Guillemot, Atlantic Puffin, Rock Dove, Winter Wren (endemic *fridariensis* subspecies), Twite.

Other Wildlife
Risso's and white-beaked dolphins, Eurasian otter, killer, minke and pilot whales.

(Rarities have included Lesser* and American Kestrels, Sandhill Crane, White's Thrush, Siberian Rubythroat, Thick-billed Warbler, Bimaculated Lark, Tennessee and Blackburnian Warblers, Cretzschmar's, Yellow-browed and Pallas's Buntings, Song, White-crowned and Savannah Sparrows, and Yellow-headed Blackbird.)

The island is accessible by air (tel: Loganair 01595 840246) or sea, on the *MV Good Shepherd IV* mailboat (tel: 01595 760222). Bird everywhere at least once and the south end at least twice, per day.

Accommodation: most people stay at the Bird Observatory (open mid-April to late October), which must be booked well in advance by contacting The Administrator, Fair Isle Bird Observatory, Fair Isle, Shetland, ZE2 9JU, UK (tel: 01595 760258; email: fairisle.birdobs@zetnet.co.uk).

SHETLAND

This remote, rugged, virtually treeless archipelago, which lies closer to Bergen in southern Norway than Aberdeen in northern Scotland and spans 75 miles from north to south, supports vast numbers of seabirds and attracts a wide variety of passage migrants and rarities. The seabirds adorn spectacular cliffs and, inland, the lochans and moorlands support about 50% of the world population of Great Skuas, as well as, on the island of Fetlar, the British stronghold of Red-necked Phalarope. So many rarities have been recorded that the list for the archipelago is about 363, which isn't bad considering how barren the islands are, how far north they are situated (it is possible to bird for almost 24 hours a day in midsummer) and how many 'common' mainland species are absent (there have been more records of Little Bunting than Goldfinch).

The best time to visit during the spring is mid-May to early June, while in autumn the peak time for scarce migrants and rarities is mid-September to mid-October.

Localised Specialities
Red-necked Phalarope (summer).

Regular Spring Migrants
Eurasian Wryneck, Red-backed Shrike, Bluethroat ('Red-spotted' *svecica*), Icterine Warbler, Common Rosefinch, Ortolan Bunting.

Regular Autumn Migrants
Eurasian Wryneck, Red-breasted Flycatcher, Icterine, Yellow-browed and Barred Warblers, Greater Short-toed Lark, Richard's, Pechora and Red-throated Pipits, Common Rosefinch, Little and Rustic Buntings.

Regular Summer Visitors and Resident Species
European and Leach's Storm-Petrels, Arctic Tern, Great and Arctic Skuas, Black Guillemot, Atlantic Puffin, Red-throated and Great Northern Divers, Rock Dove, Winter Wren (endemic *zetlandicus* subspecies), Twite.

Other Wildlife
Risso's, white-beaked and white-sided dolphins, Eurasian otter, common and grey seals, humpback, killer, minke and pilot whales.

(Rarities have included Black-browed Albatross (a single bird returned to Herma Ness every summer between 1972 and 1995 except for 1988 and 1989), King Eider (regular), Harlequin Duck, Little Bustard*, Great Knot, Caspian Plover, Ivory and Ross's Gulls, White-billed Diver, Pallas's Sandgrouse, Snowy Owl (present 1962 to 1995—bred 1967–1975—then again, on Fetlar, in March–April 1997), Northern Hawk Owl, White-throated Needletail, Brown Shrike, White's Thrush, Lanceolated, Pallas's Grasshopper, Thick-billed and Rüppell's Warblers, Yellow and Chestnut-sided Warblers, Ovenbird, Common Yellowthroat and Pine Grosbeak.)

The islands are accessible by air (tel: British Airways 0345 222111, or Business Air Freephone 0500 340146, or 01382 566345) and sea from Aberdeen (tel: P&0 01224 572615). Loganair operates several inter-

SHETLAND

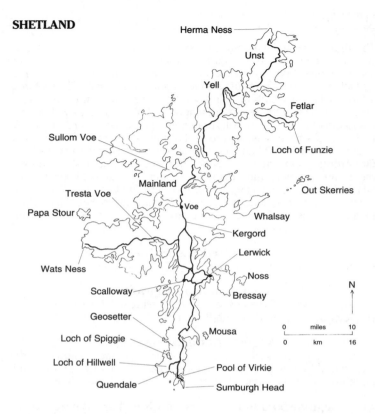

Herma Ness

Unst

Yell

Fetlar

Sullom Voe

Loch of Funzie

Mainland

Out Skerries

Tresta Voe

Voe

Papa Stour

Whalsay

Kergord

Lerwick

Wats Ness

Noss

Scalloway

Bressay

Geosetter

Mousa

Loch of Spiggie

N

Loch of Hillwell

Pool of Virkie

Quendale

Sumburgh Head

| 0 | miles | 10 |
| 0 | km | 16 |

island flights a week to Fetlar, Foula, Out Skerries, Unst and Whalsay. There are regular vehicular ferries (tel: 01957 722259) between the main islands of Mainland, Bressay, Whalsay, Yell, Unst and Fetlar, and two to three per week to Foula and Out Skerries (both of which are best booked in advance). For more information contact the Shetland Tourist Office, Market Cross, Lerwick, Shetland, ZE1 0LU, UK (tel: 01595 693434).

On the island known as Mainland there are many top birding spots, but the best is arguably the **Sumburgh Head** area at the southernmost point of the island. The head is adorned with puffins in summer, but the main reason why birders scour this area is to search for passage migrants and rarities. In addition, up to six species of cetacean have been seen off here in a single day, hence its always worth seawatching, especially in June. A little way to the north is the **Pool of Virkie** (Great Knot) which is best viewed from the minor road which runs along the north side, and the **Loch of Hillwell** area which has been graced by the likes of Pallas's Sandgrouse and White-throated Needletail. Passage migrants can and do turn up almost anywhere, although other previously productive spots on Mainland include **Geosetter**, a 200-m-long overgrown burn (warblers), the trees and gardens in and around **Lerwick** (Northern Hawk Owl, Yellow Warbler, Pine Grosbeak), the trees and bushes in the small fishing town of **Scalloway**, the largest areas of trees in Shetland in the plantations at **Kergord**, and the gardens on the B9071 at **Voe**. During the spring, seawatchers head for

Wats Ness, the most westerly point of Mainland, where 2,093 Pomarine Skuas passed on a single day in May 1992 and where Long-tailed Skuas are also regularly seen, especially after wet weather fronts and a change in the wind direction, from south or southwest to west, northwest or north. At the north end of Mainland the **Tresta Voe** area tends to be best for King Eider (one drake to the end of 1997 at least).

During the summer there are regular boat trips from Sandwick, at the southern end of Mainland, to the island of **Mousa**, where, around midnight, European Storm-Petrels can be seen returning to their nest-holes in the walls of the Iron Age broch. For details of these boat trips contact the tourist office (address above). From Lerwick, the main town on Mainland and the 'capital' of Shetland, it is a short ferry journey to the island of **Bressay**. The crofts on its west side are good for passage migrants but most visiting birders just pass through *en route* to the island of **Noss**, accessible via a five-minute boat trip from the east side of Bressay. Once on Noss it is a long, hard slog up to the Noup, at the top of the cliffs which rise to a staggering 180 m (591 ft), but the walk is worth it for these cliffs are a seabird city, with over 200,000 inhabitants, including some very tame Atlantic Puffins and over 5,200 pairs of Northern Gannets. Over 400 pairs of Great Skuas also nest on Noss which can also be reached on organised boat trips out of Lerwick. For details of boat trips contact the tourist office (address above). Off northeast Mainland more migrant hot-spots can be found on the islands of **Whalsay** (Thick-billed Warbler) and **Out Skerries** (Ovenbird).

From the barren island of **Yell**, where the many lochs are favoured by Red-throated Divers, there is a regular vehicular ferry to **Fetlar**, the smallest but greenest of the main islands, famous amongst birders for being the British stronghold of Red-necked Phalarope (29 pairs bred in 1997, about 90% of the British population), for the Snowy Owls which bred here from 1967 to 1975 (non-breeding birds remained until 1995, and after a blank year in 1996, another was seen in March–April 1997) and for great rarities which have included Common Yellowthroat in spring and Chestnut-sided Warbler in autumn. The RSPB warden, based at Bealance (tel: 01957 733246), is usually happy to let visitors know 'what's about' and where to look for the best birds. Otherwise head for the Loch of Funzie at the eastern end of the island to look for Red-necked Phalarope, the area around Oddsta where the ferry docks for Eurasian otter, the Head of Lambhoga at nightfall for European Storm-Petrel and just about anywhere for Snowy Owl and rarities, although the latter tend to favour the islanders' gardens so ask permission before checking them.

The most northerly main island is **Unst**. It is three hours by road from Lerwick via two ferries to Burrafirth at the north end of the island then a 40-minute walk from there to Herma Ness where the dangerous 198 m (650 ft) high sea cliffs and stacks support one of the largest seabird colonies in Britain. From 1972 to 1995 the Northern Gannets were joined almost every summer by a solitary Black-browed Albatross which actually built a nest on Saito Outcrop. To reach here walk north from the car park at the end of the B9086, north of Burrafirth, then turn west along the Burn of Winnaswarra. At this point prepare to be bombarded by 'Bonxies', the local name for Great Skua, which deserves embracing by the worldwide ornithological community. If they have young to protect they will dive bomb any intruders mercilessly, sometimes even striking the most stubborn invaders with their bills, wingtips or feet. Once across the moor turn left at the cliff-top and walk south about half a mile to the gannetry at Saito. Some of the Atlantic Puffins here are very tame. Otherwise walk north to the tip of Herma Ness which overlooks the large gannetry on the rock stacks around Muckle Flugga, the most northerly point in Britain. Keep to the paths and take great care along the cliff edge for at least one birder saw their last bird here.

Atlantic Puffins are often tame and those which breed at the top of the danger-ous cliffs of Herma Ness, at the northern tip of Shetland, are no exception

Some of the most spectacular sea cliffs in Britain can be seen on **Foula**, which lies 14 miles west of Mainland. They rise to 369 m (1210 ft) and, along with the rest of the island, support massive seabird colonies which include Britain's greatest concentration of Great Skuas, as well as small numbers of Leach's Storm-Petrel. The island, especially Ham Burn, also attracts many passage migrants and rarities which have included White's Thrush and several Pechora Pipits.

WALES

PEMBROKESHIRE COAST NATIONAL PARK

This scenically splendid part of southwest Wales includes 168 miles of coastline and four offshore islands which support some important seabird colonies and Red-billed Chough.

The species listed below occur during the summer unless otherwise indicated.

Regular Summer Visitors and Resident Species
Manx Shearwater, European Storm-Petrel, Northern Gannet, Atlantic Puffin, Red-billed Chough.

Other Wildlife
Risso's dolphin (May–Oct), harbour porpoise, grey seal.

(Rarities have included Little Shearwater and Wilson's Storm-Petrel (both off Strumble Head), White-throated Robin (Skokholm), Moussier's Redstart (Dinas Head), Blackburnian and Black-and-white Warblers (both on Skomer), and Yellow-rumped Warbler and Indigo Bunting (both on Ramsey.)

The most easily accessible offshore island, a little over a mile from the mainland, is **Skomer**, which supports about 1,000 pairs of European Storm-Petrel, about 6,000 pairs of Atlantic Puffins and an amazing 100,000 pairs of Manx Shearwaters—possibly the largest colony of this species on the planet—as well as Red-billed Chough. Between easter or the beginning of April and mid-September there are regular boat trips to the island everyday, except Mondays, from Martin's Haven near Marloes, from about 1000 hours onwards (tel: Dale Sailing Company 01646 601636). The island of **Skokholm** also supports large numbers of breeding seabirds, including over 40,000 pairs of Manx Shearwaters, as many as 7,000 pairs of European Storm-Petrel and plenty of puffins. For details of visiting Skokholm contact the Dyfed Wildlife Trust (address below). The island of **Ramsey**, which is a RSPB reserve and supports far fewer seabirds and Red-billed Chough, is accessible every day, except Tuesdays, from April to October via boats which sail from St Justinian's Lifeboat Station west of St David's from about 1000 hours onwards (tel: 01437 720285 for details). All three of these islands attract large numbers of passage migrants with a few major rarities thrown in (finders of new birds on Skokholm can paint them on the toilet wall in the Bird Observatory). The island of **Grassholm**, another RSPB reserve, is little more than a huge rock half-covered in 30,000 pairs of Northern Gannets during the summer. For details of the infrequent boat trips to Grassholm contact the Dale Sailing Company or the RSPB Welsh Regional Office (tel: 01686 626678). On mainland Pembrokeshire Red-billed Chough can be see on **Strumble Head**, which is also an excellent seawatching site during the autumn, especially when strong northwesterlies follow southwesterlies. There is a sheltered look-out below the car park just before the lighthouse. Walk east for chough if they are not seen while seawatching.

Manx Shearwaters are usually easy to see from the headlands of the Pembroke-shire coast during the summer, especially during the late afternoon before they return to their huge breeding colonies on the nearby offshore islands

Accommodation: to stay at the hostel on Skomer and experience the nightly invasion of shearwaters, and to book full-board accommodation in the Bird Observatory on Skokholm contact the Dyfed Wildlife Trust, 7 Market Street, Haverfordwest, Dyfed, DA61 1NF, UK (tel: 01437 765462).

On boat trips out of Neyland harbour, Milford Haven, to the **Celtic Deep**, it is possible to see many seabirds, including Wilson's Storm-Petrel, during July and August. For details contact Celtic Bird Tours, 1 Hensol Road, Miskin, Pontyclun, CF72 8JT, Wales, UK (tel: 01443 228148; email: celtictours@dial.pipex.com).

Mid-Wales is a very beautiful part of the world and the stronghold of Red Kite in Britain. In 1998 over 160 pairs raised over 170 young here, the most successful breeding season for over a century. Virtually any road in the area enclosed by the roads between Devil's Bridge (10 miles east of Aberystwyth), Rhayader, Llanwrtyd Wells and Tregaron are worth cruising in search of kites, especially the B4343 north of Tregaron and east from the B4343 or Devil's Bridge to Rhayader via the Camddwr Valley. However, to ensure seeing up to 80 kites in a day head for Gigrin Farm, South Street, Rhayader, Powys, LD6 5BL, Wales, UK (tel: 01597 810243; email: kites@gigrin.ndirect.co.uk; website: www.gigrin.ndirect. co.uk), just south of Rhayader on the A470, where, from three large hides, the birds can be seen swooping in to pick up the food put out for them from 1400 hours every day between November and April. North of Devil's Bridge, it is possible to watch kites hunting along the Melindwr Valley from the cafe at the Nant yr Arian Forest Centre, which is open from easter to September. It is only a short distance west from kite country to Llangranog, a good site for Red-billed Chough, and the Cardigan Bay Marine Wildlife Centre in New Quay, where details of the latest sightings of the bay's resident bottlenose dolphins can be obtained.

NORTHERN IRELAND

The mudflats and large freshwater lagoon in the RSPB **Belfast Lough** nature reserve (closed Mondays/tel: 01232 479009) at the entrance to the busy Belfast Harbour, support a wide variety of waterbirds, including as many as 1,000 migrant 'Icelandic' Black-tailed Godwits *(islandica)* during the autumn. During the winter Glaucous and Iceland Gulls are often present in the area. The reserve is located within Belfast Harbour Estate, into which there are two main access points, both of which are signposted from the Belfast–Holywood road (A2). **Copeland Island**, near the mouth of Belfast Lough, supports Northern Ireland's largest colony of Manx Shearwaters and has hosted several rarities including Fox Sparrow and Scarlet Tanager. To stay at the Bird Observatory contact The Bookings Secretary, 67 Temple Rise, Templepatrick, BT39 0AG, UK (tel: 01849 433068).

The 400-km² **Lough Neagh**, the largest freshwater lake in Ireland, lies 20 miles west of Belfast. It is shallow and reedy, and reaches a maximum width of over 15 miles, hence it is not surprising that more wildfowl (60,000–80,000 birds) winter here than at any other site in Ireland. Common Pochard and Tufted Duck dominate with a combined total regularly reaching 40,000, but over 1,000 each of several other species are also present, including up to 3,000 Greater Scaup (off Ballyronan at the northwest end of the lake). During the summer about 750 pairs of Great

Crested Grebe are present. Birding such a huge body of water is difficult so most birders concentrate on Oxford Island, which is actually a peninsula just north of Lurgan at the southeast corner of the lake, complete with the full range of visitor facilities. It is signposted from junction 10 on the M1. Almost 1,000 Whooper Swans, as well as Bewick's Swans, winter along the southern shore of the lake and at **Lough Beg**, a smaller, shallower lake 2 miles northwest of Lough Neagh. To reach here turn north off the A6 on to Deerpark Road (signposted to Bellaghy) 2 miles west of Toome.

For more information on birding in Northern Ireland contact Birdwatch Northern Ireland, Freepost BE2304, Belfast, BT8 4BR, UK (tel: 01232 693232; fax: 01232 644681; email: birdwatch@dnet.co.uk; website: www.d-n-a.net/users/birdwatch).

EIRE

During the early spring, gulls including counts of up to 14 Ring-billed 'Gulls in the late 1990s, and during the autumn, thousands of terns including Roseate, gather around the strand at Sandymount near **Dublin**. In September 1999 an 'American Black Tern' (*surinamensis*) was also seen here. Many of the terns breed on the tiny island of **Rockabill**, 4 miles off the coast northeast of Dublin, where the main Roseate Tern colony in Eire is situated (598 pairs in 1997).

Up to 10,000 Greater White-fronted Geese, about half of the world population of the Greenland *flavirostris* form, winter on the 10 km^2 of empoldered farmland known as **North Slob**, a reserve on the north side of Wexford harbour in southeast Ireland, along with Brent Geese ('Lightbellied' *hrota*) and occasional rarities which have included Lesser White-fronted*, Snow, Canada ('Lesser' *hutchinsii*) and Red-breasted* Geese.

SOUTHERN IRELAND

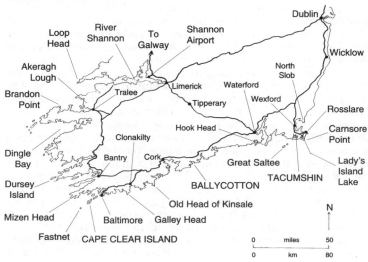

TACUMSHIN

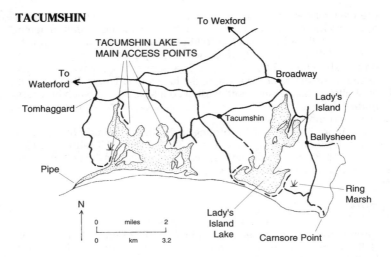

To reach the reserve (tel: 53 23129) head north out of Wexford to Gorey then follow the signposts.

Most British and many other European birders have heard of **Tacumshin**, a large coastal lagoon with extensive sandflats in the southeast corner of Ireland which has hosted virtually every shorebird on the British list. Some nearctic species are not only almost annual visitors but they have also turned up in flocks. For example, there were eight Buff-breasted Sandpipers present at one time in autumn 1999 and six White-rumped Sandpipers together in autumn 1996. The best time to look for such birds and other rarities is from mid-August to October. The lagoon lies south of Wexford and there are three main access points: (i) the northeast shore, accessible from the village of Tacumshin; (ii) the northwest shore, accessible by turning south at the 'cul-de-sac' sign about half a mile east of Tomhaggard; and (iii) the southwest corner (the area known as the White Hole), also accessible from Tomhaggard. Up to 70 pairs of Roseate Tern have bred on **Lady's Island Lake**, a couple of miles to the east of Tacumshin, on a small island off Lady's Island which is connected to the mainland by a causeway. During some springs large numbers of skuas move north through the Irish Sea and these may be observed from **Carnsore Point**, to the east of Tacumshin, and **Hook Head**, to the west. In 1986 a total of 566 Pomarine Skuas were seen passing the former between May 3rd and 18th.

Ballycotton, about halfway along the south coast of Ireland, is another name which rolls off the tongues of birders when they are discussing the best sites in Britain for rare shorebirds. Yet, the Ballycotton banter does not stop at the 11 Nearctic species (including up to three Semi-palmated Sandpipers together, and Stilt Sandpiper) which it has managed to attract, for this amazing place has also hosted Red-necked and Long-toed Stints. The mudflats of Ballycotton Bay, together with the adjacent Ballycotton Lake and Shanagarry Pools, all deserve the utmost attention, especially from mid-August to October, and they are all accessible on foot from the car park at Ballynamona Strand, reached by turning east off the Cork–Ballycotton road about half a mile south of Shanagarry.

While the eastern half of Ireland's south coast is famous for shore-birds, the western half's claim to fame is passing seabirds and the first major headland west of Cork, the **Old Head of Kinsale**, is as good a place to start seawatching as any. In strong southwesterlies during the autumn it is possible to see hundreds of large shearwaters. Fea's Petrel types have also been seen off here, although the *Pterodroma* has been seen more frequently than anywhere else in Britain and Ireland from **Galley Head**, further west along the coast near Clonakilty, along with Black-browed Albatross and Wilson's Storm-Petrel in autumn 1999. This headland is also renowned for attracting Nearctic vagrants, since the gardens, hedges and trees leading up to it have been adorned by such great rarities as Philadelphia Vireo and American Redstart. Resident species include Rock Dove and Red-billed Chough, and between Clonakilty and the headland it is also worth looking out for Eurasian otter.

CAPE CLEAR ISLAND

Long recognised as a good place to see passage migrants a Bird Observatory was established on this island, which lies between the southwest coast of Ireland and Fastnet Rock, in 1959, after which it was also discovered that Cape Clear was one of the top seawatching sites in the world. Over 20,000 Manx Shearwaters per hour have been seen shearing their way past, and hundreds, sometimes thousands, of large shearwaters are recorded from late July to September, with peak daily counts of 10,940 Cory's on 16 August 1980 and 5,508 Greats on 14 September 1965. More recently, 5,285 Greats passed by on 26 August 1997, at a rate of about 800 per hour. The third week of August is the peak time for these birds, but the best period for passage migrants is during September and October.

The species listed below occur during the autumn unless otherwise indicated.

Seabirds
European and Leach's Storm-Petrels, Cory's (*borealis*), Great, Sooty and Manx Shearwaters, Great, Pomarine and Arctic Skuas, Black Guillemot, Atlantic Puffin (scarce).

Others
Rock Dove, Red-billed Chough.
(Rarities have included Black-browed Albatross, Fea's Petrel types, Bulwer's Petrel, Little Shearwater, Yellow-bellied Sapsucker, Grey Catbird, Zitting Cisticola and Black-and-white Warbler.).

To reach this 3-mile-long, mile-wide island head southwest from Cork to Baltimore, from where the mail boat crosses Roaringwater Bay to the island on a daily basis. For details contact the Cape Clear Cooperative (tel: 28 39102). The whole island is worth birding but the most productive places for passage migrants are usually: (i) Cotter's Garden, just south of the Bird Observatory, especially around the pub (sitting in the garden with a pint is a good way to find birds—the Yellow-bellied Sapsucker spent the last part of its stay here); (ii) the Coastguards (Grey

Catbird), Escalonia, Youth Hostel and Post Office gardens; (iii) Lough Errul; and (iv) Hidden Valley, north of the church at Knockannamaurnagh. At the south end of the island is Point a'Bullaun and the jagged rocks of Blananarragaun—one of the most famous seawatching sites in the world. Check to see if Manx Shearwaters are on the move from the point, and if they are, scramble carefully over the rocks, especially when crossing the blow-hole, to the tip of 'Blanan' where seabirds other than Manx which were invisible from the point usually materialise. Wear warm, wet-weather gear, take a hot drink, make yourself as comfortable as possible and settle down to enjoy what even seasoned seawatchers often describe as the best birding possible. Weather permitting, boat trips from Cape Clear out past Fastnet Rock are occasionally arranged, in order to look for more pelagic species such as Wilson's Storm-Petrel. For details ask at the Bird Observatory.

Accommodation: to stay at the Bird Observatory book well in advance via Sean Farrell, 81 Ferndale Avenue, Dublin 11, Eire (tel: 1 834 3620). There are also two guesthouses, a youth hostel and a campsite on the island.

Birding rarely gets more exciting than when watching masses of Cory's and Great Shearwaters twisting and turning their way over the waves off the tip of 'Blanan' at the southern end of Cape Clear

Mizen Head, at the tip of the peninsula west of Cape Clear, is another excellent seawatching site, from where Fea's Petrel types have been seen. Watch from the lighthouse, reached via a narrow suspension bridge over a chasm. If the winds are northwesterly try nearby Brandon Head instead. Off the next major peninsula (Beara) to the west is **Dursey Island**, accessible via cable-car, where Nearctic vagrants have included Ovenbird. **Brandon Point**, west of Tralee Bay in County Kerry is another top seawatching site, where 347 Sabine's Gulls passed by on 29 August 1997. **Akeragh Lough**, to the north, used to attract more Nearctic shorebirds than it did in the 1990s, including, in September 1971, no fewer than 11 Pectoral Sandpipers at once. Western and Least Sandpipers have also been recorded here, along with ducks from 'the other side of the pond', including a flock of 13 American Wigeon in October 1968.

On the north side of the Shannon, on Ireland's west coast, **Loop Head** is another excellent seawatching site which is particularly good in autumnal west to northwesterly winds when the likes of Leach's Storm-Petrel, Grey Phalarope and Sabine's Gull are regularly seen. Seawatch from the head or the Bridges of Ross, on the north coast about 2 miles before the lighthouse. From Doolin or Galway it is possible to visit the **Aran Isles**, where Red-billed Chough and Eurasian otter occur, and the 198 m (650 ft) high **Cliffs of Moher**, 4 miles to the south of Doolin, where 1,000 pairs of Atlantic Puffin (on Goat Island) breed, as well as Rock Dove, Red-billed Chough and Twite. The visitor centre lies off the R478. Inland from Galway, south from Athlone to Shannonbridge, the low-lying meadows, known as the **Shannon Callows**, support over 50 calling male Corn Crakes*, which can be looked for by walking along the banks of the River Shannon, accessible at a number of points via minor roads in the area. The other Irish strongholds of Corn Crake* are **West Connaught** (over 20 calling males in the mid-1990s) and the **Tory Island** area of coastal Donegal in the far northwest of Ireland (over 100 calling males in the mid-1990s). It is possible to hear *Crex crex* before the boat docks on tiny Tory Island, where Atlantic Puffin and Red-billed Chough also breed, and where rare passage migrants have included Paddyfield Warbler. Look out for European Storm-Petrel and minke whale on the 10-mile crossing from Port-na-blagh.

On the north coast of County Mayo in northwest Ireland there is yet another superb seawatching site. **Kilcummin Head**, the promontory north of Ballina, is good in less than favourable conditions, but after onshore autumnal northwesterly winds, especially from late August to early October, Donegal Bay fills to the brim with seabirds, which, when the wind backs westerly, then make their elegant way out of the bay, almost underneath the undercut headland. Over 3,600 Sooty Shearwaters, over 1,000 Leach's Petrels and over 60 Sabine's Gulls flew past the observer's noses here on 10 September 1998, and on the best days those birders who make it here also expect to see masses of Manx Shearwaters, European Storm-Petrels and all four skuas. Birders who wish to celebrate a sensational seawatch with a stiff drink and yet more seabirds, can do so in Bessie's Bar which overlooks the pier at Ballinlena, a little over a mile south of Kilcummin. To reach here (and the headland) head north from Ballina to Killala, turn right there towards Ballycastle, then right again after a couple of miles in response to 'The Kerryman's Inn' banners. This inn is near Bessie's, from where continue

Seabirds, such as Sabine's Gulls, pass remarkably close to Kilcummin Head during suitable conditions in the autumn

north, take the second left and then turn right at the T-junction on to the track to a small car park at the headland. Get out of the car, step over the wall of the car park, sit down and enjoy what are arguably the best views possible of seabirds in Europe.

Larid lovers head for **Newport Dump**, County Mayo ('Kumlien's' *kumlieni*, Thayer's (*thayeri*) and 'American Herring' *smithsonianus* Gulls, as well as Ivory Gull all turned up here in winter 1998–1999), or the small fishing town of **Killybegs** on the southern Donegal coastline, especially during the second half of winter. Fishing boats up to factory-ship size arrive here from as far away as the waters around Iceland and Norway, pulling in their wake such taxonomically challenging birds as 'Kumlien's', Thayer's and 'American Herring' Gulls, amongst the regular Glaucous and Iceland Gulls. All these birds were present in early 1998, including about 25 each of Glaucous and Iceland.

For more information on birding in Eire contact Birdwatch Ireland, Ruttledge House, 8 Longford Place, Monkstown, Dublin, Eire (tel: 1 280 4322; email: bird@indigo.ie).

ADDITIONAL INFORMATION

Addresses

Please send records of rarities in England, Scotland and Wales to M J Rogers, Secretary, *British Birds* Rarities Committee, 2 Churchtown Cottages, Towednack, Cornwall, TR26 3AZ, UK. The annual rarities report is published in *British Birds*.

Please send records of rarities in Northern Ireland to G Gordon, 2 Brooklyn Avenue, Bangor, County Down, BT20 5RB, UK.

Please send records of rarities in Eire to P Milne, 62 The Village, Bettyglen, Raheny, Dublin 5, Eire. The annual rarities report is published in *Irish Birds*.

The **Royal Society for the Protection of Birds (RSPB)**, The Lodge, Sandy, Bedfordshire, SG19 2DL, UK (tel: 01767 680551; website: www.rspb.org.uk). This is the largest conservation organisation in Europe (the one millionth member joined in September 1997) and the society owns and runs numerous important reserves.

The **British Ornithologists' Union (BOU)**, c/o The Natural History Museum, Tring, Hertfordshire, HP23 6AP, UK (tel: 01442 890080; fax: 01442 890693; website: www.bou.org.uk), publishes the quarterly *Ibis* journal.

The **British Trust for Ornithology (BTO)**, National Centre for Ornithology, The Nunnery, Thetford, Norfolk, IP24 2PU, UK (tel: 01842 750050).

The **Wildfowl and Wetlands Trust (WWT)**, Slimbridge, Gloucester, GL2 7BT, UK (tel: 01453 890333).

The **Northern Ireland Birdwatchers' Association**, 12 Belvoir Close, Belfast, BT8 4PL, UK, publishes the annual *Northern Ireland Bird Report*.

Birdlines and Pagers

Birding World (Birdlines), Stonerunner, Coast Road, Cley next the Sea, Holt, Norfolk, NR25 7RZ, UK: Information—0891 700222. Hotline—01263 741140. Enquiries—01263 741139 (also runs regional lines for England, Scotland & Wales).

Birdnet Limited (Birdline and Pagers), 5 Trenchard Drive, Harpur Hill, Buxton, Derbyshire, XK17 9JY, England, UK. Information—number given to subscribers only. Hotline—01298 73052. Enquiries—01298 25513.

Rare Bird Alert Pagers, 17 Keswick Close, Norwich, NR4 6UW, UK (tel: 01603 456789; fax: 01603 456700). Hotline—01426 952952.

Northern Ireland (Birdline): Information and hotline—01247 467408.

Eire (Birdline): Information—1550 111700 (0891 700800 from UK). Hotline—Dublin 348917.

Bird books

'Where to watch birds in ...' almost every square inch of Britain and Ireland, covered by 15 guide books published by Helm.

Collins Top Birding Spots in Britain and Ireland. Tipling D, 1996. Harper-Collins. (*Collins Top British Birding Spots*—1999 reprint.)

Birdwatching in Britain: A Site by Site Guide. Redman N and Harrap S, 1987. Helm.

Finding Birds in Britain—A Site Guide. Speight G, 1995. Privately published but available through most specialist book clubs.

The Ultimate Site Guide to Scarcer British Birds (slightly updated edition). Evans L, 1999. Privately published but available through most specialist book clubs.

Where to Photograph Wildlife in Britain. Lane M, 1998. Available from Mike Lane, 36 Berkeley Road, Solihull, West Midlands, B90 2HS, UK (tel: 0121 744 7988).

The New Atlas of Breeding Birds in Britain and Ireland: 1988–1991. Gibbons D *et al.*, 1993. Poyser.

The Atlas of Wintering Birds in Britain and Ireland. Lack D, 1986. Poyser.

A Checklist of Birds of Britain and Ireland (sixth edition). Knox A, 1992. BOU.

Rare Birds in Britain and Ireland: A Photographic Record. Cottridge D and Vinicombe K, 1996. HarperCollins.

Rare Birds in Britain and Ireland. Dymond J N *et al.*, 1989. Poyser.

Rare Birds Day by Day. Dudley S *et al*, 1996. Poyser.

The Cley Year: A Birders' Guide. Golley M, 1997. Hill House Press.

The State of the Nation's Birds. Mead C, due 1999. Whittet.

Books on other wildlife

A Guide to the Dragonflies of Great Britain. Powell D, 1999. Arlequin Press.

Butterflies and Dragonflies: A Site Guide (second edition). Hill P and Twist C, 1997. Arlequin Press.

Field Guide to the Dragonflies and Damselflies of Great Britain and Ireland. Brooks S and Lewington R, 1997. British Wildlife Publishing.

Where to watch Mammals in Britain. Bright P, 1991. Mammal Society.

Journals and Magazines

Birding World, aimed primarily at twitchers, is published monthly and available by subscription only from the Circulation Manager, *Birding World*, Stonerunner, Coast Road, Cley next the Sea, Holt, Norfolk, NR25 7RZ, UK (tel: 01263 741139; email: sales@birdingworld.co.uk; website: www.birdingworld.co.uk).

British Birds is published monthly and available by subscription only from British Birds, The Banks, Mountfield, Robertsbridge, East Sussex,

TN32 5JY, UK (tel: 01580 882039; fax: 01580 880541; email: design@britishbirds.co.uk).

Birdwatch is published monthly and available in newsagents or by subscription from Birdwatch Subscriptions Office, The Mailing House Limited, Unit 1, Northumberland Park Industrial Estate, 76–78 Willoughby Lane, London, N17 0SN, UK (tel: 020 8885 2447; fax: 020 8365 0145).

Bird Watching is published monthly and available in newsagents or by subscription from Bird Watching Subscriptions, FREEPOST (LE 6400), Leicester, LE87 4BS, UK (tel: FREEPHONE 0800 018 0373).

Yorkshire Birding is published quarterly and available by subscription only from 14 Hoober View, Wombwell, Barnsley, South Yorkshire, S73 0SH, UK.

Birding Scotland is published quarterly and available by subscription only from H Scott, c/o Pica Design, 259 Union Grove, Aberdeen, AB10 6SX, UK.

CD-ROMs and Videos

A wide range of CD-ROMS and videos is available from Bird Images, BirdGuides and WildSounds (addresses, p. 395).

Rare Birds in Britain 1994–1998 (five videos). Shaw A. Available from most specialist booksellers.

Bird Sounds

Teach Yourself Bird Sounds (ten cassettes covering 241 species). Compilation.

British Bird Sounds (two CDs covering 175 species). National Sound Archive.

Collins Field Guide to Bird Songs and Calls (two CDs covering 152 species). Sample G.

BULGARIA

INTRODUCTION

Summary

Bulgaria arguably offers the best birding in the Balkans: a wealth of waterbirds, a wide range of raptors, high-altitude specialities such as Wallcreeper and rare European breeding species such as Pied Wheatear and Paddyfield Warbler. Distances are not huge and there are cheap package holiday resorts in the mountains and along the Black Sea coasts, hence the popularity of Bulgaria has increased rapidly during the 1990s and seems set to continue.

Size

At 110,910 km², Bulgaria is a little smaller than England and about one sixth the size of Texas.

Getting Around

Most visitors arrive by air in Sofia, the gateway to montane package holiday ski resorts such as Borovets and Pamporovo, or at one of the Black Sea coastal towns and resorts such as Albena, its neighbour Golden Sands, Burgas and Varna, which are ideally situated for birding the rich lowland wetlands. Marked trails and ski-lifts make getting around the mountains fairly easy.

Apart from hiring a vehicle most birding sites can be reached easily via reasonably priced taxis and the extremely cheap but rather slow bus and train services. It cost just £5/US$8 to travel by train between Sofia and Burgas (on the Black Sea coast) in the mid-1990s. but the journey does take 6–8 hours. In Sofia and the Black Sea resorts most people speak a little English or German, and elsewhere they speak French and Russian.

Accommodation and Food

Most large hotels are rather basic and confined to Sofia, ski-resorts and Black Sea coastal resorts. Tourists are charged two to three times the rate for Bulgarians to stay in such hotels, but prices are still cheap compared with much of the rest of Europe. There are also 'villas' on the coast, and campsites, some of which have chalets. Many places can be booked in advance through Neophron Limited, c/o Bulgarian Society for the Protection of Birds (BSPB) Varna Branch, PO Box 492, BG-9000, Varna, Bulgaria. The food, based on grilled meats, stews, fresh fruit and vegetables, and wine, are, on the whole, excellent.

Health and Safety

Immunisation against hepatitis, polio and typhoid is recommended. Take plenty of insect repellent, especially if visiting the Black Sea coast during the summer.

Climate and Timing

Bulgaria has a continental climate with warm summers and cold winters. During the spring and summer it is usually hot in the lowlands with occasional heavy downpours, especially along the Black Sea coast. Winters are often very cold, especially inland, and during January and February one should expect snow and icy winds, even along the Black Sea coast. The best times to visit Bulgaria are during spring (April for peak passage, late May to early June for breeding species and some passage migrants), autumn (best from late August to late September), and winter when Red-breasted Geese* are often present in large numbers, especially in January and February.

Habitats

Central and southern Bulgaria is mainly mountainous and on the rolling foothills and higher slopes of the Stara Planina, which extend for 600 km across the middle of the country and rise to 2376 m (7795 ft) at Botev, and the Rodopi Planina, which range across the southwest and rise to 2925 m (9597 ft) at Musala, there are extensive deciduous woodlands, coniferous forest and mostly overgrazed alpine grasslands. Along the fertile Danube Plain, which runs along the country's northern border with Romania, and on the Black Sea coastal plain at the east end of the country there are remnant wetlands, mainly in the form of lagoons and lakes. There is also some remnant steppe amongst the extensive open farmland along the Black Sea coast, mainly in the extreme northeast, in the region known as Dobrudja which extends north into Romania. Steep cliffs and sandy beaches alternate along the coast.

Conservation

One of Bulgaria's most threatened habitats is its natural wetlands. At the beginning of the 20th century these covered over 2000 km² but by the mid-1990s nearly 95% were gone, leaving just 110 km². Other conservation problems include habitat loss and degradation, hunting (Italian hunters take a large toll here), overgrazing and pollution, all of which need to be solved if the 13 threatened and near-threatened species as well as the relatively common and widespread birds which occur in Bulgaria are to survive.

Bird Species

Around 400 species have been recorded in Bulgaria. Notable birds include Pygmy Cormorant*, Great White and Dalmatian* Pelicans, Red-breasted Goose*, Ruddy Shelduck, Cinereous Vulture*, Levant Sparrowhawk, Long-legged Buzzard, Imperial Eagle*, Rock Partridge, Chukar, Little Crake, all ten European woodpeckers, Masked Shrike, Semicollared Flycatcher, Pied and Isabelline Wheatears, Rock Nuthatch, Wallcreeper, Paddyfield and Olive-tree Warblers, Sombre Tit, Alpine Accentor and Black-headed Bunting.

Expectations

It is possible to see 220–240 species, a very good total for Europe, including over 20 raptors, on a trip lasting two weeks during the spring. On shorter trips of a week or so it is possible to see 170–200 species during the spring and 130-160 during the autumn.

Some excellent birds occur in and around **Sofia**, especially in Vitosa National Park, which rises to 2290 m (7513 ft) at Cherni Vruh (Black Peak), just to the south of the capital and supports Black Woodpecker, Eurasian Nutcracker, Rufous-tailed Rock-Thrush, Horned Lark and Alpine Accentor. The latter two species occur on the boulder-strewn slopes around the summit.

WESTERN RODOPI PLANINA

The Rila Mountains, at the northwest end of the Rodopi Planina, are the highest in Bulgaria, rising to 2925 m (9597 ft) at Musala, about 70 km south of Sofia, and lofty enough to support the likes of Rock Partridge and Wallcreeper.

The species listed below occur during the summer unless otherwise indicated.

Localised Specialities
Rock Partridge.

Other Localised Species
Wallcreeper.

Others
Short-toed, Lesser Spotted, Golden and Booted Eagles, Hazel Grouse, Alpine Swift, Syrian and Black Woodpeckers, Eurasian Nutcracker, Yellow-billed Chough, Lesser Grey Shrike, Rufous-tailed Rock-Thrush, Rock Nuthatch, Eurasian Crag-Martin, Red-rumped Swallow, Sombre Tit, Horned Lark, Alpine Accentor, Rock Bunting.

Other Wildlife
Brown bear, chamois.

These mountains are accessible from several ski resorts, from where trails and ski-lifts enable easy access to the high tops. Wallcreepers have been seen feeding on chalet walls in the ski resort of **Maljovice** (Maljovica). If the walls are bare walk up through the woods above the chalets to reach the crags where the beauty breeds. To reach here from Sofia head south along Route 2 then turn east at Stanke Dimitrov to Samokov. From there head for Govedarci and Maljovice. Wallcreeper, as well as Horned Lark and Alpine Accentor, also occurs around the ski resort of **Borovets** (Borovec) near Samokov. The areas around Musala Hut, accessible via a ski-lift, and alongside the quiet road west to Beli-iskar and Samokov, are arguably the best. Rock Partridge, Rock Nut-hatch, Sombre Tit and Horned Lark occur above **Rila Monastery**, a popular tourist attraction also accessible from Route 2 south of Sofia (turn east on Route 164 to Kocerinovo, from where the monastery is signposted).

Accommodation: Maljovice—hotels and campsite. Borovets—hotels. Rila—hotel and campsite.

The scrubby hillsides between the Rila Mountains and the **Pirin Mountains** to the south support Masked Shrike (here at the northern edge of its range and therefore rather scarce), Orphean Warbler and Black-headed Bunting.

CENTRAL RODOPI PLANINA

These mountains are not so high as those to the west but they still support a wide range of montane specialities as well as Levant Sparrowhawk.

The species listed below occur during the summer unless otherwise indicated.

Localised Specialities
Rock Partridge.

Other Localised Species
Levant Sparrowhawk, Wallcreeper.

Others
Black Stork, Short-toed, Lesser Spotted and Booted Eagles, Hazel Grouse, Alpine Swift, White-backed (*lilfordi*) and Black Woodpeckers, Eurasian Nutcracker, Yellow-billed Chough, Lesser Grey Shrike, Rufous-tailed Rock-Thrush, Eurasian Crag-Martin, Red-rumped Swallow, Sombre Tit, Rock Bunting.

The extensive forest around the ski-resort of **Pamporovo**, four hours by road southeast of Sofia, supports Hazel Grouse, and European Scops-Owl is usually easy to see along the main road through the resort. To reach here, head from Plovdiv (where one to two pairs of Levant Sparrowhawk breed in the main park) on Route 36 to Progled, from where it is signposted. About one hour by road from Pamporovo, Rock Partridge and Wallcreeper occur in the **Trigradski Gorge**, near the border with Greece. The gorge is accessible via organised weekly excursions, complete with guides who know the best spots, but these allow very little time at the site, so it may be better to visit the site alone, either in a hire vehicle or by local taxi.

EASTERN RODOPI PLANINA

The rolling hills of the eastern Rodopi Planina are the best in Bulgaria and some of the best in Europe for raptors. The BSPB runs some raptor feeding stations here, in order to provide a poison-free food supply and supplement the low levels of carrion available, and up to 12 Egyptian Vultures, 40 Eurasian Griffons and five Cinereous Vultures* have been seen at once, at the station most frequently visited by birders.

The species listed below occur during the summer unless otherwise indicated.

Localised Specialities
Chukar.

Other Localised Species
Cinereous Vulture*, Levant Sparrowhawk.

Others
Black Stork, Egyptian Vulture, Eurasian Griffon, White-tailed* and Short-toed Eagles, Long-legged Buzzard, Lesser Spotted, Imperial*, Golden and Booted Eagles, Lesser Kestrel*, European Bee-eater, European Roller, Lesser Grey Shrike, Rufous-tailed and Blue Rock-Thrushes, Rock Nuthatch, Olivaceous, Barred, Sardinian and Subalpine Warblers, Sombre Tit, Spanish Sparrow, Rock Bunting.

(Other species recorded here include Isabelline Wheatear and Orphean Warbler.)

To reach the **Studen Kladenets** reserve, which surrounds the Studen Kladenec reservoir and is a good area for raptors, head east from Plovdiv to Khaskovo then turn south to Kŭrdzhali. Turn east at the first roundabout here in response to the 'OU3' signpost, then after about 5 km turn south on to the track opposite a KAT checkpoint which leads to a village and the wooded hillsides beyond where most raptors occur. To reach the **Krumovica Valley**, where one of the raptor feeding stations is situated, from Studen Kladenets, head east to the village of Potochnitza, turn right by the school in the middle of village (left if arriving at the village from Krumovgrad) on to a road which becomes a track, and continue for 3–4 km to reach the feeding station. To find out the best time to visit contact the BSPB a couple of months in advance.

Accommodation: Madzharevo—lodge (bookable via BSPB).

Between the Rodopi Planina and the Black Sea coast it is worth taking time out to scour suitable looking habitats for localised species such as Masked Shrike and Olive-tree Warbler.

BURGAS

The western Black Sea coast, on which Burgas is situated, is a major flyway for passage migrant pelicans, storks, raptors and shorebirds, especially during the autumn when birds are heading south to the Bosphorus from eastern Europe and as many as 5,000 White Storks have been seen soaring over the area around the city at once. Annual average counts for the autumn period elsewhere in the area include 15,000 Great White Pelicans and 5,700 Lesser Spotted Eagles. This heavily industrialised large port also lies near a number of lagoons and salinas which together support a fine selection of waterbirds, which in early January 1999 included over 1,300 Pygmy Cormorants* and 230 Dalmatian Pelicans*, while in March 1999 a record count of 2,000 or so White-headed Ducks* was made.

The species listed below occur during the summer unless otherwise indicated.

Localised Specialities
Ruddy Shelduck.

Other Localised Species
Pygmy Cormorant*, Dalmatian Pelican* (Sep–Apr), White-headed Duck* (winter), Levant Sparrowhawk (passage migrant and summer visitor).

Regular Passage Migrants
Great White Pelican, Black and White Storks, Short-toed and Booted Eagles, Red-footed Falcon, Marsh Sandpiper, Whiskered and White-winged Terns.

Others
Ferruginous Duck*, Squacco Heron, Black-crowned Night-Heron, Glossy Ibis, Long-legged Buzzard, Lesser Spotted Eagle (passage and summer visitor), Little Crake, Collared Pratincole, Gull-billed Tern, European Roller, Syrian Woodpecker, Lesser Grey Shrike, Spanish Sparrow, Yellow Wagtail ('Black-headed' *feldegg*), Black-headed Bunting.

(Other species recorded here include Pallid Harrier* (passage), Steppe Eagle (passage), Saker Falcon, Common Crane (passage), Slender-billed Curlew*, Broad-billed Sandpiper, Great Black-headed and Slender-billed Gulls, and Moustached and Olive-tree Warblers.)

Burgas is accessible by air, rail and road from Sofia. Concentrate on the following: (i) the brackish **Lake Mandra** and its adjacent marshes, to the west of the E87 main coast road south of Burgas; (ii) the small **Poda Lagoon** reserve, with a visitor centre, hide and nature trail, at the coastal end of Lake Mandra, where about 240 species have been recorded, including rarities such as Slender-billed Curlew*; (iii) the freshwater **Lake Burgas**, visible from the road west and north of Gorno Ezerovo village, reached by turning west off the E87 south of Burgas. This is a particularly good place for passage shorebirds, including Broad-billed Sandpiper (17 in late June 1998). The road along the north shore runs through a massive industrial complex which is best avoided; (iv) the marshes and salinas at **Atanassovo**, a protected area which lies either side of the E87 north of Burgas. Over 200 species have been recorded here, including Little Crake, and this site is arguably Bulgaria's best for observing the visible migration of pelicans, storks and raptors during the autumn, as well as the passage of shorebirds and gulls; (v) **Pomorie Salinas**, which lie east of the E87 north of Burgas are also worth checking for passage shorebirds, gulls and terns; and (vi) the **Ajtos Hills**, inland from Burgas to the northwest, are a good place to look for summering and passage raptors.

Accommodation: Burgas—many hotels.

The wet woodland and pools in **Ropotamo National Park** south of Burgas support Ferruginous Duck*, Levant Sparrowhawk, Little Crake, Semicollared Flycatcher and Olivaceous Warbler. It is possible to take boat trips along the River Ropotamo, just south of Sozopol, through the riverine woods in search of such birds, although Semicollared Flycatcher is most likely to be seen around the car park.

About 30 km north of Burgas it is worth checking the valley, on the inland side of the E87 main coast road, just south of the resort at **Sunny Beach**, for Olive-tree Warbler. At Sunny Beach follow the stream, at the south end of the resort, inland to look for waterbirds, as well as Olivaceous Warbler, Spanish Sparrow and Black-headed Bunting. Further north along the E87, 66 km south of Varna, turn east then south after 1.5 km to reach the headland known as **Nos Emine** where Olive-tree Warbler breeds, along with Barred Warbler and, occasionally, Isabelline Wheatear. This headland lies at the eastern end of the Stara Planina mountain range and acts as a bottleneck for huge numbers of migrating Great White Pelicans, Black Storks, and Short-toed and Lesser Spotted Eagles during the autumn, while its scrubby hillsides provide food and shelter for passerine passage migrants. The marsh known as **Staro Orjahovo** attracts a wide variety of waterbirds, including Ruddy Shelduck and Glossy Ibis, and is excellent for passage shorebirds. To reach it turn east just north of Staro Orjahovo on to the road signposted Skorpilovci then take the track left. Back on the E87 head north again then turn east about 20 km south of Varna to **Kamcija** and park by the River Kamcija where the woods around and to the west of the jetty support Semicollared Flycatcher.

ALBENA

This resort, about 25 km north of Varna, is an ideal base for tracking down the east Mediterranean passerine specialities of the Black Sea coast, including Semicollared Flycatcher, Pied Wheatear and Olive-tree Warbler, and an excellent site for observing the visible migration of pelicans, storks and raptors along the western Black Sea coast on which it is situated.

The species listed below occur during the summer unless otherwise indicated.

Localised Specialities
Semicollared Flycatcher, Pied Wheatear, Olive-tree Warbler.

Regular Passage Migrants
Pygmy Cormorant*, Great White Pelican, Black and White Storks, Short-toed and Booted Eagles, Red-footed Falcon.

Others
Squacco Heron, Black-crowned Night-Heron, Long-legged Buzzard (passage and summer visitor), Lesser Spotted Eagle (passage and summer visitor), Lesser Kestrel*, Eurasian Eagle-Owl, Alpine Swift, European Bee-eater, Syrian and Black Woodpeckers, Lesser Grey Shrike, Red-rumped Swallow, Spanish Sparrow, Yellow Wagtail ('Black-headed' *feldegg*), Rock and Black-headed Buntings.

Concentrate on the following areas: (i) the woodland in the Baltava Reserve west of the resort, and between there and the River Batova, for Black Woodpecker and Semicollared Flycatcher; (ii) alongside the River Batova at the western edge of the Baltava Reserve (best early in the morning in order to avoid causing a stir at the nudist beach at the rivermouth); (iii) the escarpment to the east of the resort, for Pied Wheatear; (iv) the escarpment further east, just south of Balchik, for Lesser Kestrel* and Eurasian Eagle-Owl. To reach here head north out of Albena and turn right at the third exit at the roundabout. Eurasian Eagle-Owl occurs on the cliffs to the left of this road after 6 km; and (v) the escarpment reached by taking the second exit (north) at the above roundabout and continuing for 11 km, after which the road reaches a disused airfield (look out for the three old MIG fighter jets). Head along the track, which leads left just before the entrance to the airfield, to look for soaring raptors which may include Lesser Kestrel*. **Golden Sands**, the neighbouring resort, is not so good for birding although Pied Wheatear has been recorded along the harbour wall.

Accommodation: Albena—ask for a room on the top floor of the Hotel Dobrudza, an excellent place for observing visible migration and directly opposite a small park which attracts passerine migrants such as shrikes and flycatchers. Golden Sands, the next resort along, is not so ideally situated.

Pied Wheatear just makes it into Europe as a breeding species and the Black Sea coast of Bulgaria is the best place to see this cracking bird

NOS KALIAKRA

The arid remnant steppe on the plateau above the 70-m (230 ft)-high limestone cliffs of this headland on the Black Sea coast supports breeding Pied and Isabelline Wheatears, and the promontory is an excellent place to observe the visible migration of pelicans, storks and raptors, especially during the autumn.

The species listed below occur during the summer unless otherwise indicated.

Localised Specialities
Pied Wheatear.

Other Localised Species
Pygmy Cormorant*, Levant Sparrowhawk (passage and summer visitor), Isabelline Wheatear.

Regular Passage Migrants
Great White Pelican, Black and White Storks, Short-toed and Booted Eagles.

Others
Mediterranean Shearwater ('Yelkouan' *yelkouan*), European Shag ('Mediterranean' *desmarestii*), Long-legged Buzzard (passage and summer visitor), Lesser Spotted Eagle (passage and summer visitor), Red-footed Falcon (passage and summer visitor), Eurasian Eagle-Owl, Alpine Swift, European Bee-eater, European Roller, Lesser Grey Shrike, Olivaceous and Barred Warblers, Calandra Lark, Spanish Sparrow, Black-headed Bunting.

Other Wildlife
Bottlenose dolphin, European souslik.

(Other species recorded here include Pallid Harrier*, Rosy Starling, Collared (passage) and Semicollared Flycatchers, wheatears resembling Finsch's (otherwise unknown outside Europe, although some observers consider the birds involved to be hybrid Pied/Black-eared), and Eurasian River (passage) and Olive-tree Warblers.)

NOS KALIAKRA

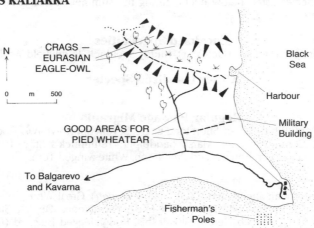

The headland is just over an hour by road north from Albena. Follow the signposts from just north of Kavarna (ignore the signs to the south of this town) which is about 35 km north of Varna on the E87. Most of the area can be worked from the road to the headland, but take care not to arouse too many suspicions amongst the military personnel in the area, although most are friendly enough. Pied Wheatear occurs around the buildings at the tip of the headland and either side of the road which leads inland about 1 km before the tip of the headland is reached. This road leads to a ravine where Pygmy Cormorant* (roosting in poplars), Eurasian Eagle-Owl and Barred Warbler occur. Four km back along the main road from the tip of the headland take the track inland to reach a steppe-like area where the possibilities include Pallid Harrier*. The best place to look for Isabelline Wheatear is alongside the road 500 m west of Balgaravo.

LAKES DURANKULAK AND SHABLA

The Black Sea coastal plain in northeast Bulgaria, known as the Dobrudja, which extends north into southeast Romania (p. 294), is the most important wintering area on earth for Red-breasted Goose*. Most of the world population, which breeds on the Taimyr Peninsula in Arctic Russia (p. 305), spends the winter in Romania unless the weather is bad enough to force them further south into Bulgaria, which it frequently is. For example, in January 1997 a total of 62,653 were present, and together with about 100,000 Greater White-fronted Geese such numbers make quite a spectacle when they fly in from the surrounding cereal fields to bathe and rest on the coastal lagoons. The Dobrudja is just as exciting during the summer, thanks to the presence of Ruddy Shelduck, Little Crake and Paddyfield Warbler, here at one of its few known localities in Europe, and during passage periods, especially the autumn when many migrant pelicans, storks, raptors and shorebirds pass through.

The species listed below occur during the summer unless otherwise indicated.

Localised Specialities
Red-breasted Goose* (Oct–Mar), Ruddy Shelduck, Paddyfield Warbler.

Other Localised Species
Pygmy Cormorant*.

Regular Passage Migrants
Black and White Storks, Short-toed Eagle, Levant Sparrowhawk, Booted Eagle, Common Crane, Marsh Sandpiper, Temminck's Stint, Broad-billed Sandpiper, Red-necked Phalarope, White-winged Tern.

Others
Mediterranean Shearwater ('Yelkouan' *yelkouan*), Great White Pelican, Greater White-fronted Goose (Oct–Mar), Ferruginous Duck*, Smew (Oct–Mar), Squacco Heron, Glossy Ibis, Rough-legged Buzzard (Oct–Mar), Red-footed Falcon (passage and summer visitor), Little Crake, Collared Pratincole, Whiskered and Gull-billed Terns, European Bee-eater, Lesser Grey Shrike, Spanish Sparrow, Yellow Wagtail ('Black-headed' *feldegg*).
(Other species recorded here include Dalmatian Pelican* (passage), Lesser White-fronted Goose* (Oct–Mar), Black-winged Pratincole* and Rosy Starling.)

To reach the **Lake Shabla** area from Varna head north on the E87 and fork right in Shabla village, stay left and after about 1.5 km turn east to reach a campsite on the coast. Bird: (i) the marshy areas and rough ground to the west of the road before and after the turn-off to the campsite; (ii) any small pools to the north of the campsite which attract

LAKE SHABLA

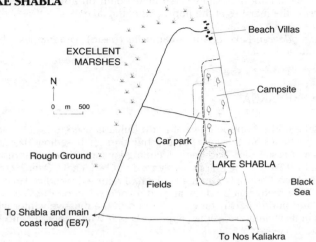

passerines such as Spanish Sparrow to bathe and drink; (iii) Lake Shabla to the south of the campsite, which is an excellent place to observe visible migration, attracts numerous passage shorebirds and, in winter, is used by Red-breasted Geese* for bathing, drinking and roosting; and (iv) the steppe-like area by the coast reached by continuing directly east from Shabla village, then heading south towards Nos Kaliakra. **Lake Durankulak**, about 22 km north of Shabla and visible from the road just to the south of Durankulak town, is also a favoured bathing, drinking and roosting site of Red-breasted Geese*. During the summer, Little Crake and Paddyfield Warbler occur here. To reach the best area turn northeast in response to the 'Kocmoc' signpost just north

LAKE DURANKULAK

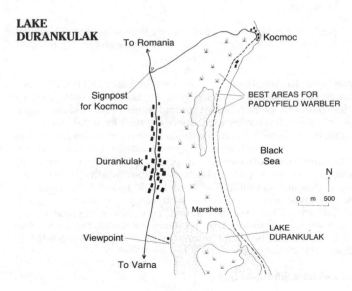

of the town. Park at Kocmoc then head south on a track which runs alongside the marshes at the north end of the lake.

Accommodation: Lake Shabla—campsite (basic). Durankulak—basic campsite at Kocmoc.

LAKE SREBARNA

This lake in the Danube Plain of north Bulgaria used to be one of the finest wetlands in Europe, but the numbers of breeding Dalmatian Pelican*, its star bird, had been declining for some time when disaster struck in 1994 and the colony was wiped out by jackals. Over 100 pairs used to breed but only about 40 pairs had returned by 1998. However, this 600-ha reedy lagoon does support a good selection of other water-birds and during harsh winters further north the massive winter wheat fields in its vicinity occasionally attract Lesser White-fronted* and Red-breasted* Geese.

The species listed below occur during the summer unless otherwise indicated.

Localised Species
Pygmy Cormorant*, Dalmatian Pelican*, Levant Sparrowhawk.

Others
Great White Pelican, Ferruginous Duck*, Squacco Heron, Black-crowned Night-Heron, Glossy Ibis, Whiskered Tern, European Bee-eater, European Roller.

Other Wildlife
Wild boar, jackal.

(Other species recorded here include Lesser White-fronted* (Oct–Mar) and Red-breasted* (Oct–Mar) Geese, Ruddy Shelduck, White-tailed Eagle*, Little Crake and White-winged Tern.)

The lake is two to three hours by road from the Black Sea coast. About 12 km west of Silistra stop in the lay-by on the north side of the road to scan the southwest corner, before turning north to the reserve visitor centre a couple of km further west. There is a path from the centre to a viewpoint, from where it is possible to see the pelican colony as well as many other waterbirds and Levant Sparrowhawk over the nearby wood-ed escarpment. The **Zafirovo Lagoons**, alongside the road about 20 km west of the turning to Srebarna, are also worth checking for Dalmatian Pelican* as well as Ruddy Shelduck. To reach the lagoon at **Malak Preslavec** which is also worth checking, turn north at the vil-lage of Zafirovo, 22 km west of Srebarna. Turn right at the next T-junc-tion, then after 7 km turn left in the village of Malak Preslavec. The lagoon is 5 km along here and attracts many of the birds recorded at Lake Srebarna, including breeding Whiskered Tern.

Accommodation: Silistra—hotel.

ADDITIONAL INFORMATION

Addresses

Gerard Gorman, Budapest 1511, Pf:4, Hungary (tel/fax: 1 319 9689; email: ggbirder@elender.hu; website: www.elender.hu/~ggbirder/), is a prolific author and professional birding guide with a wealth of experience in eastern Europe (he has led well over 100 tours) who caters for tour companies as well as individuals and teams, and specialises in target birds.

Please send records of rarities to the Bulgarian Society for the Protection of Birds (BSPB), 2 Gagarin St., 1113 Sofia, Bulgaria. The HQ for the BSPB is at PO Box 114, BG 1172 Sofia, Bulgaria (tel/fax: 2 689413; email: bspb_hg@main.infotel.bg) and more details of the organisation can also be obtained from The Secretary of BSPB (UK), 8 Woodlands, St Neots, Cambridgeshire, PE19 1UE, UK.

Permits to visit protected areas may be obtained with some difficulty from the Ministry of Environment, 67 William Gladstone Str., BG-1000 Sofia, Bulgaria.

Books and papers

Where to watch birds in Bulgaria. Jankov P, 1996. Pensoft, Bulgaria.

Finding Birds in Bulgaria (revised edition). Gosney D, 1993. Available from BirdGuides (address, p. 395).

Important Bird Areas in Bulgaria (in Bulgarian with short English summaries). Jankov P *et al.* (eds.), 1997. BirdLife.

CHANNEL ISLANDS

INTRODUCTION

The Channel Islands are about 80 miles south of England but under 12 miles from northwest France, hence one species which does not normally occur in Britain and Ireland is found here: Short-toed Treecreeper.

The four main islands, Jersey, Guernsey, Alderney and Sark, cover just 194 km^2. Jersey is accessible by air and sea from England, and by sea from St Malo in France. An internal air network connects all the islands. There are 500 miles of roads on Jersey, which is just 116 km^2, and traffic is a major problem, but cars are forbidden on the 5-km^2 island of Sark. There is a wide range of accommodation on all the islands and many public houses (pubs) which serve excellent food.

The climate is rather mild and the best time of year to visit is arguably the late autumn when the passage of Little Gulls is in full swing and rarities such as Siberian Blue Robin have turned up.

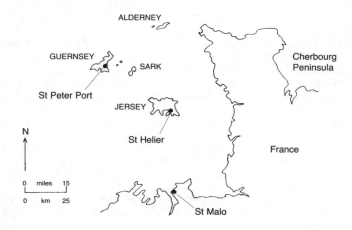

The coastlines are a mixture of rocky headlands and sandy beaches, while inland there are extensive areas of farmland covered in glasshouses, remnant heathlands and wetlands, high hedges and wooded valleys. Habitat loss and degradation (most coastal grassland and sand dune habitat, as well as the majority of marshes, have been lost to built development and conversion to farmland), hunting and natural disasters (half a million trees on Jersey alone were lost during the Great Storm of 1987) are the major problems facing the birds of the Channel Islands.

Regular Summer Visitors and Resident Species
European Storm-Petrel, Northern Gannet, Atlantic Puffin, Short-toed Treecreeper, Cetti's and Dartford Warblers, Reedling, Cirl Bunting.

Regular Autumn Passage Migrants
Sooty, Manx and Mediterranean ('Balearic' *mauretanicus*) Shearwaters, Little Gull, Great, Pomarine and Arctic Skuas.

Regular Winter Visitors
Red-throated and Great Northern Divers, Snow Bunting (also occurs on autumn passage).

(Rarities have included Green Heron, Upland Sandpiper, Siberian Blue Robin, Red-flanked Bluetail, Aquatic Warbler*, Northern Waterthrush and Rose-breasted Grosbeak.)

Cetti's Warbler bred for the first time in the Channel Islands in 1973 and by 1996 there were 17–19 singing males present on **Jersey**, where the best place to hear this species' explosive song is around St Ouen's Pond, the largest stretch of natural fresh water in the archipelago. Situated on the west coast, it also supports one or two pairs of Reedling and, during the autumn, regularly attracts the extremely elusive Aquatic Warbler*. Jersey's most extensive area of heathland is situated at Les Landes, north of St Ouen's Bay, and this supports Dartford Warbler (24 singing males were present on Jersey in 1996). During strong autumnal westerlies or northwesterlies, local birders head for Grosnez Point near here to seawatch. Small numbers of Atlantic Puffins breed at Piemont and they can usually be seen from the cliff-top path below Pontin's Holiday Camp. The Great Storm of 1987 seriously depleted the island's Cirl Bunting population and only nine pairs were present on Jersey in 1998. The storm caused particularly serious damage at Point le Grouin, one of this species' former strongholds. It may still occur here and in Pont Marquet Country Park but the best place on the island for this bird is probably along the Railway Walk which runs from St Aubin's Bay to Corbiere, especially between La Moye Golf Course and Corbiere.

Another good place to look for Dartford Warbler is Ouaisne Common, which is over the headland from Point le Grouin. On the eastern side of Jersey Aquatic Warbler* has been recorded in the wet meadows at Rue des Pres and at Grouville Marsh, where Northern Waterthrush has also turned up. Between late October and late November thousands of Little Gulls (the majority of the Baltic population) usually pass through the Channel Islands and St Catherine's Breakwater, at the north end of Jersey's east coast is one of the best places to witness this spectacular passage, although 10,000 appeared in the Bay of St Marlowe one Boxing Day.

The small island of **Guernsey** supports several pairs of Short-toed Treecreeper and is renowned amongst local birders for its falls of passage passerine migrants, especially on the Chouet and Pleinmont headlands, which have included rarities such as Rose-breasted Grosbeak. The former stronghold of Dartford Warbler, decimated by cold winters in the late 1980s, was the maritime heathland at the top of the sea-cliffs of the south coast.

The sheltered wooded valleys on the island of **Alderney** are also good for passage passerine migrants and Dartford Warbler breeds in the heathlands along the south coast. From Braye at the southwestern tip of the island it is possible to take a boat trip a mile or so out to the Northern Gannet colony (1,600 pairs) on the islet of Ortac. Boats pass Burhou *en route* where European Storm-Petrel and Atlantic Puffin breed.

On 27 October 1975 the island of **Sark** was printed in red ink on the birding map of Europe when a first-winter female Siberian Blue Robin was trapped in the Banquette Valley. 25 years later it remains the sole European record. The following year (1976), when they were still extremely rare in western Europe, a Red-flanked Bluetail was trapped in the same valley on 31 October.

ADDITIONAL INFORMATION

For full details see Britain and Ireland (p. 118).

Addresses

Please send records of rarities to the M J Rogers, Secretary, *British Birds* Rarities Committee, 2 Churchtown Cottages, Towednack, Cornwall, TR26 3AZ, UK. The annual rarities report is published in *British Birds*.

Books and papers

Important Sites for Birds in the Channel Islands. Veron P K (ed.), 1997. Societe Guernesaise, Channel Islands.
Important Bird Areas in the UK including the Channel Islands and the Isle of Man. Pritchard D *et al.* (eds.), 1992. RSPB.

CORSICA

Cap Corse   Isola di Capraia
L'île-Rousse   Bastia
Calvi
Étang di Biguglia
VALLE DE ASCO
RÉSERVE
NATURELLE   Corté   VIZZAVONA
DE SCANDOLA   Porto
Evisa
Cargese
Aléria
GORGES DE LA RESTONICA
Ajaccio
N
Bonifacio
île Cavallo
0   km   50
Sardinia

INTRODUCTION

Summary

Very few birders visit this Mediterranean island, mainly because accommodation and food are more expensive than Mallorca, and the distances between the best sites are greater, but this sparsely populated largely unspoilt and scenically splendid island, which has thankfully managed to evade mass tourism, supports similar birds and an endemic nuthatch, so it may be worth the extra expense involved.

Size

The 8800-km^2 island measures about 180 km from north to south and 80 km from west to east at its widest point.

Getting Around

Most visitors arrive by air at Ajaccio and the relatively few package holiday resorts such as Cargese and L'Île-Rousse. There are also regular daily vehicular ferries from Italy, the French mainland and Sardinia. The easiest way to bird the island is to hire a vehicle, therefore booking a package fly-drive holiday is arguably the cheapest and most convenient way to see the birds of Corsica using a vehicle. However, there are also good bus and rail networks so it is possible to see all of the island's top birds in a short time using public transport. Some of the roads are very steep and narrow, especially in the mountains where there are

136

numerous hairpin bends and heart-stopping drop-offs, hence birding drivers are advised to concentrate on the road ahead. Although politically part of France, Corsica is culturally more akin to Italy, which is situated just 80 km to the east, hence the majority of people speak Corsican, which is an Italian dialect.

Accommodation and Food
Good hotels are expensive, but there are a few package holiday resorts, and other, even cheaper, places to stay. Beyond the few large supermarkets food is fairly expensive. Island specialities include cured ham, sausages, blackbird paté and wild boar.

Climate and Timing
The peak times to visit Corsica are during April and early May, when spring passage migrants are moving through and it is possible to see around 80 species in a week, and early summer when early July is particularly good for butterflies. It is usually baking hot during midsummer, although humidity is often low and the heat is offset somewhat by cool sea breezes. During the autumn and winter it can be very wet, especially in the mountains.

Habitats
Corsica is a mainly mountainous island with several snow-capped peaks over 2500 m (8202 ft), and it reaches a maximum height of 2710 m (8891 ft) at Monte Cinto in the northwest. The 1000-km-long coastline is mainly rugged with some spectacular cliffs, particularly in the northwest, and beautiful beaches. Inland, the cultivated lowlands soon give way to maquis-strewn slopes, holm oak and beech woods, Corsican pine forest, subalpine grasslands, gorges, rocky crags and peaks. The largest expanses of flat lowland are primarily confined to the east coast where there is a series of lagoons, most of which are little more than intensively managed fish farms and therefore of little ornithological value.

Conservation
Habitat loss and degradation, mainly as a result of drainage and residential and tourist developments, as well as disturbance, hunting and pollution are the major problems facing the two threatened and near-threatened species, as well as the relatively common and widespread birds which occur on Corsica.

Bird Species
The species listed below occur during the summer unless otherwise indicated.

Corsican Endemics
Corsican Nuthatch*.

Localised Specialities
Lammergeier (rare), Audouin's Gull*, Marmora's Warbler.

Other Localised Species
Spotless Starling, Citril Finch ('Mediterranean' *corsicanus*).

Others

Cory's ('Scopoli's' *diomedea*) and Mediterranean Shearwaters, European Shag ('Mediterranean' *desmarestii*), Black-crowned Night-Heron, Osprey, Red Kite, Short-toed and Golden Eagles, Red-legged Partridge, Alpine and Pallid Swifts, European Bee-eater, Yellow-billed Chough, Woodchat Shrike, Blue Rock-Thrush, Eurasian Crag-Martin, Zitting Cisticola, Moustached, Sardinian, Subalpine and Dartford Warblers, Greater Short-toed Lark, House Sparrow ('Italian' *italiae*), Rock Petronia, Alpine Accentor (rare), Red Crossbill ('Corsican' *corsicana*).

Other Wildlife

Mouflon, monk seal and 58 species of butterfly.

(Other species recorded here include Eleonora's Falcon, Slender-billed Gull and European Roller (spring passage).)

The last population census of Corsican Nuthatch* estimated that there were about 2,000 pairs on the island in 1981–1984. It is widespread on inland ridges with the greatest densities present in mature Corsican pine forest. One of the best places to look for it is near **Vizzavona** which is situated alongside the main N193 road in the middle of the island between Ajaccio and Corté. Take the trail opposite the Office National des Forêts a little way south of the signpost to 'La Gare de Vizzavona'. This starts besides a hut, passes over a bridge and alongside a picnic site before crossing another bridge and zigzagging up into the pine forest where Citril Finch and Red Crossbill also occur. Citril Finch is also seen regularly around Vizzavona railway station.

The Lammergeier population appears to have stabilised around eight pairs since 1983, but there were believed to be 15 pairs in 1981 and the national park authorities have initiated a supplementary feeding programme in an effort to increase numbers. The best place to look for this huge vulture is the **Gorges de la Restonica**, reached via a rough road southwest from Corté. Walk from Bergerie de la Grotelle at the end of the road at the tree-line towards Lac de Melo and Lac de Goria, where Golden Eagle, Yellow-billed Chough, Alpine Accentor (around Lac de Melo) and Citril Finch also occur. Lammergeier, as well as Alpine and

Four of the seven species endemic to Europe can be seen on Corsica, including Corsican Nuthatch* which occurs only on this small island

Pallid Swifts, Corsican Nuthatch*, Alpine Accentor and Citril Finch may also be seen in the **Valle de Asco**, which can be reached by heading towards Bastia from Corté then turning west at Ponte Leccia on to the N197. After 25 km turn left on to the D47 towards Asco. Look out for Lammergeiers along the gorges before the village, over the woods beyond, and from the ski station car park at Haut Asco at the head of the valley. The pine forest at **Forêt de Aitone**, which is situated near the village of Evisa, by the side of the D84 about 25 km east of Porto, is another good site for the nuthatch and Citril Finch.

Corsica supports about 25% of the Mediterranean's breeding Ospreys and these are mainly confined to the island's spectacular northwestern coast where about 15 pairs breed along the 100-km stretch between Calvi and Cargese. There are regular 3-hour hydrofoil trips (mostly for tourists wishing to view the sea cliffs) to the **Réserve Naturelle de Scandola** which protects part of the coast about 16 km northwest of Porto, from Calvi, Cargese and Porto, on which it is possible to see the Ospreys, together with Cory's and Mediterranean Shearwaters (both at close range), Audouin's Gull*, Alpine and Pallid Swifts, and Blue Rock-Thrush, as well as monk seal. For more information on these boat trips visit the Syndicate d'Initiative offices in Cargese or Sagone. Audouin's Gull* also occurs at **Pointe de Cargese** (along with Dartford and Marmora's Warblers) and at the mouth of the **River Liamone**, south of Sagone (along with Alpine and Pallid Swifts).

The package holiday resort of **L'Île-Rousse** on the northwest coast lies close to the maquis-covered slopes around Monticello, and Île de la Pietra, a good seawatching site, hence it is possible to see birds such as shearwaters, Spotless Starling and Marmora's Warbler with some ease in the vicinity of the resort. **Cap Corse**, the mountainous headland at the extreme north end of the island is one of the best places to look for spring passage migrants and there is a temporary ringing station in operation here during April and early May. Both Dartford and Marmora's Warblers are resident on the headland.

The best wetlands on Corsica are the east coast lagoons known as **Étang de Biguglia** and **Étang de Palo**. Minor roads run around Étang de Biguglia, which lies to the east of the N198 near the airport south of Bastia. Its northeast corner is a fairly reliable place to see Audouin's Gull* (perched on posts), which may also be found in Bastia harbour. The south end is the best for Moustached Warbler. During the spring the general area of both étangs attracts passage migrants such as European Roller.

Cory's and Mediterranean Shearwaters, European Storm-Petrel and Audouin's Gull* breed on some of the islands off the southeast coast and, weather permitting, it is possible to reach some of them by boat from the busy port of **Bonifacio**. The cliffs, well-vegetated valleys and maquis-covered slopes near here support Alpine and Pallid Swifts, Blue Rock-Thrush, Spotless Starling, Marmora's Warbler, Rock Petronia and Citril Finch. Passage migrants recorded here have included Eleonora's Falcon. Seabirds can be seen from shore by descending the cliffs to a point opposite the island of Grain de Sable.

Accommodation: Porto—Hotel Kalliste. Bastia—Hotel Lido de la Marana. Corté—Hotel de la Paix. Gorges de la Restonica—Hotel Dominique Colonna.

ADDITIONAL INFORMATION

For more details see France (p. 193).

Addresses

Please send records of rarities to CHN, La Corderie Royale, BP 263, 17305 Rochefort cedex, France. The annual rarities report is published in *Ornithos* (in French with an English summary).

Club Ornithologie, Immeuble Petra Marina, 20220 Toga, Corse, France (tel: 95 327163).

Books and papers

Where to watch birds in France. La Ligue Française pour la Protection des Oiseaux, 1989. Helm.

The Birds of Corsica: BOU Checklist No. 17. Thibault J C and Bonaccorsi G, 1999. BOU.

Les Oiseaux de la Corse. Thibault J-C, 1983. Parc Naturel Regional de la Corse, BP 417, 20184 Ajaccio cedex, Corse, France. Out of print but sometimes available in Ajaccio.

CRETE

INTRODUCTION

This 250-km-long, narrow mountainous island in the eastern Mediterranean is a popular birding destination, thanks mainly to the presence of cheap package holiday resorts and some high quality localised birds, including Lammergeier, and Eleonora's and Lanner Falcons.

Most visitors take advantage of the many cheap package holidays available and arrive by air at Khaniá (Chania) or Iráklion (Heraklion) on the north coast. The island is also accessible via daily ferries from the Greek mainland. It is fairly easy to get around via the fairly cheap and efficient bus network but fly-drive package deals enable greater flexibility and the opportunity to venture further afield. The main road, the 197-km-long dual-carriageway between Khaniá and Ayios Nikólaos on the north coast is excellent, but those running south off it to the middle and southern parts of the island are often rough. Most visitors stay on the north coast but the Plakias resort on the south coast is arguably the best base for birders. Western European food is available at the package holiday resorts, whereas the tavernas throughout the island serve a wide range of Greek dishes.

The best time to visit Crete is during April when spring passage migrants are moving through and it is possible to see 110–120 species in a week, and during mid-May when breeding summer visitors such as Eleonora's Falcon and Olive-tree Warbler have arrived. August and September is also a good time to visit, although there are fewer passge migrants at this time of year.

This rugged, mountainous island is dominated by three main ranges: the Levka Ori (White Mountains) in the west; the Idhi Oros in the middle, which rises to 2456 m (8058 ft) at Psiloritis, the highest peak on the island; and the Dhikti Ori in the east, all of which are renowned for their deep gorges and upland plateaux, known as *poljes*, which support a very rich flora. Many mountainous areas are grazed, but there is also plenty of mainly coastal maquis. In the lowlands there are numerous orchards and the northern coastal plain is heavily cultivated. The extensive forest which once covered most of the island was felled long ago. There was just one 'protected' area, at Samaria Gorge, in the late 1990s, despite conservationists working hard to save other sites such as Almyros Marsh at Ayios Nikólaos and the River Aposelemis at Gouves. Meanwhile the conservationists are also trying to persuade some local people to stop ignoring 'No Hunting' signs and convince many more that blasting birds out of the sky is just not on when so many species are in decline.

Bird Species

The species listed below occur during the summer unless otherwise indicated.

Localised Specialities

Lammergeier, Chukar, Olive-tree and Rüppell's Warblers.

Other Localised Species

Eleonora's and Lanner Falcons.

Others

Cory's Shearwater ('Scopoli's' *diomedea*), Eurasian Griffon, Golden and Bonelli's Eagles, Alpine and Pallid Swifts, European Bee-eater, Red-billed Chough, Blue Rock-Thrush, Eurasian Crag-Martin, Moustached, Orphean, Sardinian and Subalpine Warblers, Spanish Sparrow, Black-headed Bunting.

(Spring passage migrants have included Squacco Heron, Glossy Ibis, Little Crake, Collared Flycatcher and Red-throated Pipit.)

Falasarna, at the extreme northwestern end of the island is a good place for Eurasian Griffon, Bonelli's Eagle and Eleonora's Falcon (which breeds on offshore islands). Inland from Khaniá the **Ayia Reservoir** is a good place to look for Moustached Warbler and passage waterbirds, especially crakes. The **Akrotíri Peninsula**, east of Khaniá, is one the best places to look for passage migrants on the island. Concentrate on the areas around the Ayia Triada, Katholiko (where Chukar occurs) and Gouvernetou Monasteries, and the Souda Bay Cemetery, where birds such as Collared Flycatcher are more or less annual during the spring.

The cultivated **Omalos Plateau**, which is situated at about 1000 m (3281 ft) in the snow-capped Levka Ori range south of Khaniá, is an excellent area for Lammergeier as well as other raptors, Alpine Swift, Red-billed Chough and Blue Rock-Thrush, all of which also occur in the **Samaria Gorge**, which is situated in White Mountains National Park to the south. This spectacular 19-km-long limestone chasm is reputed to be the longest fissure in Europe and at its foot (the Sidheresportes) it is just 3 m (10 ft) wide but almost 305 m (1000 ft) high. No vehicles are allowed but there is a trail through the chasm which descends from Omalos (accessible by bus from Khaniá) to Ayia Roumeli (accessible by bus and boat from Khaniá). Allow 6–8 hours for the one-way trek and take food and drink, although there are plenty of cafes (and places to stay) in Omalos and at the beach below Ayia Roumeli.

The area around the south coast resort of **Plakias** is another good place to look for passage migrants and the maquis below Moni Prevelli monastery, to the east, supports Rüppell's Warbler. Inland, Lammergeier occurs in the Kotsiphos and Kourtaliotiko gorges.

The harbour at **Iráklion**, one of the major tourist centres, is always worth checking for Cory's Shearwater, gulls and terns, and the island of Día offshore from here supports what is believed to be the world's densest concentration of Eleonora's Falcons, estimated at 180–230 pairs. The **River Aposelemis and Gouves Lagoon**, 21 km east of Iráklion, attract passage waterbirds (Slender-billed Curlew* was reported from here in early April 1999) and this is a good place to look for Cory's Shearwater offshore. Along the north coast to the east, the small river, marsh and surrounding fields at **Mállia** are worth checking for passage migrants such as Red-throated Pipit. The cliffs above the old road between Mállia and Ayios Nikólaos in the **Selinari Gorge** are used as a roost-site by Eurasian Griffons.

Along with the Omalos Plateau and Samaria Gorge at the west end of the island the fertile **Lasíthi Plateau** in the Dhikti Ori range at the east end of the island is one of the most reliable places on Crete to see Lammergeier as well as other raptors including Lanner Falcon. The plateau is accessible from Iráklion to the north and Ayios Nikólaos to the east. From Ayios Nikólaos head inland and look for raptors on the steep ascent into the mountains, especially on the south side of the road. Also bird the track leading south from the village of Kaminakion, 2 km west of Avrakontes, and along the Seli Ambelous Pass road which winds its way into the mountains from the north.

The **Dionisides Islands**, off the northeast coast of Crete, support about 290 pairs of Eleonora's Falcon. Small flocks of these birds visit the **Skopi Valley** on the main island on most days, and they may also be seen along the coast between Sitia and Piskikefalon, especially during the evening. At the extreme eastern end of the island, Lanner Falcon occurs in the gorge south of **Palaiókastrou**. The Marina Village Hotel near here is an excellent base and a number of raptors including Bonelli's Eagle have been seen from its balcony.

ADDITIONAL INFORMATION

For more details see Greece (p. 219).

Addresses
Please send records of rarities to George Handrinos, 44 El Venizelou St., 16675 Glyfada, Greece.

Books and papers
A Birdwatching Guide to Crete. Goghlan S, 1996. Arlequin Press.
Crete Bird Report. Townsend D & Coghlan S (annual).

CROATIA

INTRODUCTION

Before the terrible ethnic wars of the 1990s, this former republic of Yugoslavia was a popular tourist destination, and since the cessation of major conflicts, the number of foreign visitors has started to rise again.

With a rich mixture of wetland and mountain birds, including Lanner Falcon and Rock Partridge, the increasing number of visitors is sure to include some birders.

At 56,540 km², Croatia is less than half the size of England and one twelfth the size of Texas. The capital, Zagreb, is situated in the northern interior, hence package tour participants usually fly directly to Dubrovnik on the Dalmatian Coast and/or the island of Korcula in the Adriatic. For the latest information on travelling to Croatia and the situation regarding the restoration of the tourist infrastructure contact the nearest Croatian National Tourist Board (tel. in Britain: 0181 563 7979). There are hotels, village apartments and rooms available, but it is best to contact your local travel agent for further details as they emerge. One specialist company offering trips to Croatia is Bond Tours, 49 The Broadway, Stoneleigh, Epsom, Surrey, KT17 2JE, UK (tel: 0181 786 8511; fax: 0181 394 0962). Immunisation against hepatitis, polio and typhoid is recommended. The horrendous ethnic war between the Croats and Serbs, which began in 1991, appeared to have been resolved by the late 1990s, although some areas were still under the supervision of the United Nations, and before planning a trip here it may be wise to contact the relevant foreign office for the latest details on whether or not it is safe to visit.

The best times to visit Croatia are during the peak spring passage period in April, during late May and early June when some birds are still moving through and most summer visitors have arrived, and during the autumn passage period which peaks in late August to early September. The climate is Mediterranean along the coast, with hot summers and cool winters, and continental inland, with warm summers and very cold winters.

The fertile lowlands of northern Croatia are intensively farmed, but they may still support riverine woodlands, oak woods, unimproved flood-meadows, marshes, lakes and large fishponds. The high mountains which lie parallel to the 1800-km-long Dalmatian Coast along the western arm of the country, support numerous citrus and olive orchards, garrigue, maquis and some mixed woods, and along the narrow coastal plain which lies between the mountains and the Adriatic, there are some small deltas and saltmarshes. Offshore there are numerous rocky limestone islands, and at Dundo on the island of Rab, there may still be a rare stand of mature evergreen oak woodland. The effects of the war in the 1990s have yet to be evaluated, but even before then agricultural intensification was damaging and destroying valuable lowland habitats, and in montane areas natural evergreen oak woods were being reduced, by burning and grazing, to garrigue and maquis. The war must have affected the numbers of the four threatened species, as well as the relatively common and widespread birds which occur in Croatia, despite the presence of several national parks, and one can only hope that a modern nation, one in which the conservation of natural resources is regarded as paramount, emerges from the troubled times gone by.

Notable species include Pygmy Cormorant*, Levant Sparrowhawk, Lanner and Saker Falcons, Rock Partridge and Wallcreeper.

The large fishponds, grasslands and deciduous forests in the **Pokupsko Depression** near Zagreb may still support breeding species such as Ferruginous Duck*, Black Stork, White-tailed* and Lesser Spotted Eagles, and Corn Crake*. This also used to be an important resting and refuelling station for spring and autumn passage migrants, notably Ferruginous Duck*, which, in days gone by, numbered as many as 5,000 during the autumn. The only part of this area under some form of protection before the 1990s was at **Crna Mlaka**, a special ornithological reserve in the middle of the depression.

The farmland, large fishponds, marshes and woods on the **Sava Floodplain**, together with those along the Rivers Lonja and Strug, may still support breeding Squacco Heron, Black and White Storks, White-tailed* and Lesser Spotted Eagles, Corn Crake*, Whiskered Tern and Collared Flycatcher. Before the 1990s Krapje Dol, Rakita and Vrazje Blato in the western floodplain were protected as bird sanctuaries. The floodplain also used to be an important resting and refuelling site for passage migrants which have included Slender-billed Curlew*.

In the extreme northeast corner of Croatia, near the borders with Hungary and Yugoslavia, the marshes, meadows and woods of **Kopacki rit**, together with Lake Kopacki and fishponds along the Rivers Danube and Drava, used to be an immensely important breeding ground for herons with up to 1,450 pairs present between 1968 and 1985. The area may also still support breeding Pygmy Cormorant*, Ferruginous Duck*, White-tailed Eagle*, Saker Falcon and Whiskered Tern, as well as passage migrants such as Common Crane. Part of the area was protected in a 108-km^2 nature park and a 62-km^2 zoological reserve before the 1990s.

Ural Owl has been recorded in **Risnjak National Park**, about 40 km northeast of Rijeka in extreme northwest Croatia, but the most frequently visited forested mountain area in the former Yugoslavia was **Plitvice National Park**, a World Heritage Site. The string of lakes, linked by beautiful waterfalls, was the major attraction and the lakes may still form a fine backdrop to some excellent birding.

The farmland, marshes, salinas and forested canyons along the **Dalmatian Coast**, together with the largest natural lake in the country, may still support localised species such as Lanner Falcon, Rock Partridge and Wallcreeper, as well as Squacco Heron, Glossy Ibis, Egyptian Vulture, Eurasian Griffon, Lesser Kestrel*, European Roller, Lesser Grey Shrike, Blue Rock-Thrush and Moustached Warbler. The two forested limestone canyons in **Paklenica National Park**, near Zadar, may still be good places to find Rock Partridge and Wallcreeper, the 30-km^2 **Lake Vrana** (Vransko jezero) near Sibenik may still support breeding herons and ibises, including Squacco Heron, as well as Moustached Warbler (part of it was protected within an ornithological reserve before the 1990s), and the wooded gorges in **Krka National Park**, which runs alongside the River Krka for 75 km inland from Sibenik, could still support Lanner Falcon and Rock Partridge.

The high sea cliffs, garrigue, forested canyons and stony grasslands on the **Adriatic Islands** of Cres, Krk and Prvic, off the northwest coast of Croatia, may still support Rock Partridge, while offshore it should still be possible to see Cory's ('Scopoli's' *diomedea*) and Mediterranean Shearwaters, and European Storm-Petrel. Before the 1990s there were two ornithological reserves on Cres, one on Krk (protecting canyons and high sea cliffs at the northeast end where Rock Partridge occurs), and a botanical and zoological reserve on Prvic. The archipelago of several hundred karst limestone islands in the central Adriatic, which lie within **Kornat National Park**, probably still support breeding Eleonora's Falcon, as well as shearwaters and European Storm-Petrel.

Inland from Split, the wet meadows known as **Pasko polje** at the head of the River Cetina, may still attract passage migrants such as Squacco Heron and Black Stork, and the forested **Dinara Mountain** nearby may still support Hazel Grouse. South from Split along the Dalmatian Coast lies the **Neretva Delta** which was partly protected before the 1990s in four ornithological reserves (Orepak, Pod Gredon, Prud and the southeast). This delta, which is contiguous with Hutovo blato in Bosnia-Herzegovina (p. 79), has long been degraded by drainage and agricultural encroachment but it may still support breeding species such as Baillon's Crake. The popular tourist destination of **Dubrovnik**, to the south of the delta, is a good place to see Alpine and Pallid Swifts, both of which may be seen whizzing along the streets at head-height!

CZECH REPUBLIC

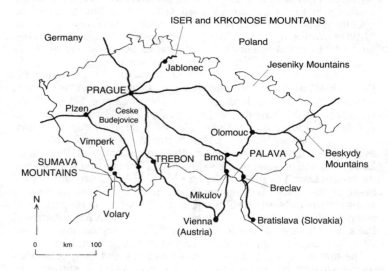

INTRODUCTION

Summary

Since the bloodless revolution of 1989, the Czech Republic has become quite a popular birding destination, thanks to the presence of typical central-European forest species such as Eurasian Pygmy-Owl, Tengmalm's Owl and all ten European woodpeckers.

Size

At 78,864 km², this country is almost half the size of England and just under 10% the size of Texas.

Getting Around

Prague is the gateway to the country and the hub for the internal air network but Vienna, Austria, is arguably a better starting point for birding the south. It is easy to get around by car, on predominantly traffic-free roads, and by using public transport (cheap and extensive), although more time will be required if using the latter. It is courteous to ask for permission to wander around private fishponds and this is usually granted with glee by the friendly owners. English is not usually spoken outside Prague and the large hotels elsewhere, so a little German, the widest used second language, would be useful.

Accommodation and Food

There are some large hotels in Prague and elsewhere, and plenty of small hotels, but both types are relatively expensive because prices are hiked up for tourists. There are few youth hostels away from Prague but in most rural areas it is possible to track down a 'Bed and Breakfast' (*Zimmer frei*) or a campsite (*autokemp*), some of which have chalets (*chata*). To book accommodation in advance contact the Czechbook Agency, 52 St John's Park, Blackheath, London, SE3 7JP, UK (tel/fax: 0181 853 1168). Food and drink is cheap, especially away from Prague. Meat plays a large part in the Czech diet and is often served up with dumplings and lashings of gravy, although it is also possible to get cheesy snacks. The beer (*pivo*) is of an exceptionally high quality, which explains why the Czechs consume more of it than any other country in the world. The original Pils is brewed in Plzen (Pilsen) in west Bohemia and the original Budweiser, called Budvar, is brewed in Ceske Budejovice in south Bohemia. The wines, especially from south Moravia, are also pretty good.

Health and Safety

Immunisation against hepatitis, polio and typhoid is recommended. Most visitors and many Czechs drink bottled water. Crime increased throughout the 1990s so beware of theft from accommodation and vehicles, and carry your passport at all times.

Climate and Timing

The climate is, on the whole, temperate, with wet springs and autumns, warm summers and cold winters. The best time to visit the Czech Republic is during March and April when Hazel Grouse, owls and woodpeckers, the country's major avian attractions, are easier to find. However, snow can prevent access to many areas at this time of year so it is probably best to leave a visit until as late as possible. Owls are also rather vocal from October to December.

Habitats

Although the Czech Republic is a land-locked country, it has a wide variety of habitats, including mountains with remnant primeval beech and coniferous forests and upland peat bogs, and lowlands with remnant riverine woodlands, reservoirs, lakes and extensive areas of fishponds, noted for a wide range of wetland species. However, much of these lowland areas are heavily cultivated or industrialised. During the

Warsaw Pact (eastern Europe and Russia's answer to NATO, lasting from 1955 to 1991) most of the country's borders were out-of-bounds and this is where the vast majority of the Czech Republic's best birding areas are today.

Conservation

An extensive network of protected areas was established after World War II and two areas (Podyji and Sumava) behind the iron curtain which were closed between 1955 and 1990 and thus free from agricultural or built development, have since been declared national parks. All this is very well, but much of north Bohemia (the western half of the country) and southeast Moravia (the eastern half of the country) is heavily industrialised and the Czech Republic is one of the most heavily polluted countries in Europe, with sulphur dioxide levels particularly high over Prague and large tracts of forest damaged by acid rain. Hunting is another major problem facing the six threatened and near-threatened species as well as the relatively common and widespread birds which occur in the Czech Republic. In 1996, for example, the Ministry of Agriculture did their best to reduce the numbers of water-fowl in the country by extending the goose-hunting season by two months and increasing the number of days per week when waterfowl could be shot from one to seven.

Bird Species

About 390 species, of which 210 have been known to breed, have been recorded in the Czech Republic. Notable species include Saker Falcon, Hazel Grouse, Little Crake, Eurasian Pygmy-Owl, Tengmalm's Owl, all ten European woodpeckers and Collared Flycatcher.

Expectations

It is possible to see 120–150 (perhaps 170) species on a trip lasting one to two weeks during the spring.

BOHEMIA

Despite acid rain damage the beech woods, coniferous forest, blanket bogs and alpine grasslands in the **Iser and Krkonose Mountains**, which rise over 1600 m (5249 ft) alongside the border with Poland, about 130 km northeast of Prague, support a typical central-European forest avifauna, including Black Stork, Black Grouse, Eurasian Caper-caillie, Corn Crake*, Eurasian Pygmy-Owl, Tengmalm's Owl, White-backed (rare), Three-toed and Black Woodpeckers, Eurasian Nutcrack-er, Bluethroat ('White-spotted' *cyanecula*), Greenish Warbler (*trochil-oides*, first proved to breed in Krkonose National Park in 1998) and Alpine Accentor. To reach Krkonose National Park from Prague head northeast on the N10 to 10 km beyond Jablonec then turn east to Vrchlabi, the gateway to the area, which is accessible via Routes 295 and 296. For more information contact Krkonose National Park, 54301 Vrchlabi-Zamek, Czech Republic (tel: 438 28511). To reach the Iser Mountains head for Liberec, west of Jablonec. The whole area is a very popular walking region, complete with chair-lifts to the high tops.

The numerous fishponds surrounded by farmland and floodplain woods and plantations in the 700-km^2 **Trebon Basin**, a biosphere reserve in southern Bohemia, support a wide range of breeding water and woodland birds, from Little Crake to Collared Flycatcher, and during the autumn when many of the ponds are usually drained, they attract passage shorebirds. Nesting White Storks adorn the town of Trebon, which is just three hours by road north of Vienna, Austria, and lies at the centre of the area which is easy to bird via a network of roads. There are over 500 fishponds, some of which date back to the 15th century, ranging in size from tiny hatchery ponds to the 450-ha Rozmberk, just north of Trebon, which takes a whole day to walk around. The pond known as Svet, just south of Trebon, is usually good for ducks and the parkland around the church on its far side supports several species of woodpecker. For more information on the area contact Biospheric Reserve Trebonsko, 379 OL Trebon-Zamek, Czech Republic (tel: 333 721248).

The extensive beech and coniferous forests of the **Sumava Mountains**, which rise to 1378 m (4521 ft) at Plockenstein in southern Bohemia, support a typical central-European forest avifauna, although, unlike many such places there is a fairly good chance of finding Eurasian Pygmy-Owl, Tengmalm's Owl and White-backed Woodpecker here. The Boubinsky Prales Reserve southeast of Vimperk is the best place to look for these three, as well as Hazel Grouse, while, huge numbers of Brambling have been known to congregate here during the spring. The forests to the southeast are also good for woodpeckers and they can be reached by heading west out of Volary for 1 or 2 km, then turning north on to a track which runs through good forest for 4 km or so. Further west the forests around Modrava ski-resort are worth checking for Eurasian Pygmy-Owl. Other breeding species include Black and White Storks, Lesser Spotted Eagle, Corn Crake*, Ural Owl (reintroduced into Sumava National Park since 1996), Black Woodpecker, Eurasian Nutcracker and Bluethroat ('White-spotted' *cyanecula*). The Pension IDA, Zaton 66, Lenora (tel: 339 436214) is a good place to stay. For further information contact Sumava National Park, 38501 Vimperk-zamek, Czech Republic (tel: 339 21355).

MORAVIA

The fishponds, reservoirs and marshes at the confluence of the Rivers Dyje and Morava, near the border with Austria in the **Palava** area of the southeast Czech Republic, support Saker Falcon as well as breeding birds such as Ferruginous Duck*, Black-crowned Night-Heron, Black and White Storks, European Bee-eater, Syrian Woodpecker, Collared Flycatcher, Bluethroat ('White-spotted' *cyanecula*), Eurasian River and Barred Warblers, and a large wintering population of White-tailed Eagles*. Another possiblity is Imperial Eagle* since two were present here in January 1997 and January 1998 and a pair bred for the first time in 1998. Mikulov, arguably the best base for birding this area, is one to two hours by road north of Vienna, Austria. The best place to look for Saker Falcon is the Soutok Reserve, southeast of Breclav. The fishponds around Lednice (where Collared Flycatcher occurs in the grounds of

Zamecky Chateau) and Pohorelicke rybniky, together with the Nove Mlyny Reservoirs, support a fine range of waterbirds which have included up to 54 wintering White-tailed Eagles*, one of which took a Red-breasted Goose* in January 1998. The craggy, limestone Palava Hills, just northeast of Mikulov, occasionally attract Wallcreepers in winter. Recommended accommodation includes the Hotel Rohaty Krokdyl in Mikulov and the Hotel Harlekin in Lednice. For more information on the whole area contact Palava Protected Landscape, Namesti 32, 69201 Mikulov, Czech Republic (tel: 625 2585).

The beech woods and coniferous forest on the **Beskydy Mountains** at the eastern end of the Czech Republic support a typical central-European forest avifauna, including over a hundred pairs of White-backed Woodpecker as well as Black Stork, Lesser Spotted Eagle, Ural Owl, Eurasian Pygmy-Owl and Tengmalm's Owl. Ruznov p. Radh is the gateway to the area but the best accommodation is the Hotel Lanterna in Velke Karlovice-Leskove. For more information contact Beskydy Protected Landscape Area, Nadrazni 36, 75661 Roznov p. Radh, Czech Republic (tel: 651 55592).

ADDITIONAL INFORMATION

Addresses

Gerard Gorman, Budapest 1511, Pf:4, Hungary (tel/fax: 1 319 9689; email: ggbirder@elender.hu; website: www.elender.hu/~ggbirder/), is a prolific author and professional birding guide with a wealth of experience in eastern Europe (he has led well over 100 tours) who caters for tour companies as well as independent individuals and teams, and specialises in target birds.

ATYPUS Travel Company Limited, PO Box 190, CZ-601 00 Brno, Czech Republic (tel/fax: 5 4124 1121; email: atypus@sky.cz; website: www.czechia.com/atypus), is a local travel company with experienced guides which specialises in trips to the Czech Republic and Slovakia.

Please send records of rarities to the Czech Faunistic Comittee, Laboratory of Ornithology, Palacky University, trida Svobody 26, CZ-771 46 Olomouc, Czech Republic.

Czech Ornithological Society, Hornomecholupska 34, CZ-100 10 Prague 10-Hostivar, Czech Republic.

Moravska Ornitologicka Stanice (Moravian Ornithological Station), Museum Komenskeho, CZ-751 52 Prerov, Horni namesti c 1, Czech Republic.

Books and papers

Important Bird Areas in Europe: Czechoslovakia. Hora J *et al.* (eds.), 1992. BirdLife International.

The Atlas of Wintering Birds in the Czech Republic 1982–1985. Bejcek V *et al.*, 1995.

The Atlas of Breeding Birds in the Czech Republic 1985–1989. (In Czech). Stastny K *et al.*, 1996.

DENMARK

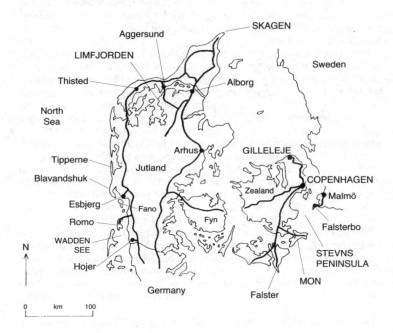

INTRODUCTION

This small country, which occupies much of the peninsula between the Baltic Sea to the east and the North Sea to the west, supports a wide variety of waterbirds and lies on a major migration route, hence its coastal wetlands in particular are important resting and refuelling stations for masses of migrant waterbirds, especially during the autumn.

At 43,075 km², Denmark is a third the size of England and about 6% the size of Texas. Regular ferries link the country to Britain, Germany and the Scandinavian countries. The extremely well integrated internal bus, train and ferry services make travelling by public transport almost a pleasure, and since bicycles are available for hire at some railway stations, tourist offices and youth hostels, there is little point in hiring a vehicle, except to keep warm during the winter. Accommodation costs are a major expense in Denmark, although hotels do usually include all-you-can-eat breakfasts in their prices, a morning feast of cereals, bread, cheese, eggs, milk and juice which should be enough to keep most birders going for a day. Guesthouses are slightly cheaper than hotels and may still include breakfast, but the cheapest form of indoor accommodation available is that old saviour, the youth hostel, some of which have private rooms. True budget birders will find plenty of campsites, many of which have chalets. Food and drink is also relatively expensive in Denmark, even the staples such as fish, meat, potatoes and beer.

151

The climate is temperate with warm summers and cool winters. The best times of year to visit Denmark are during April and May when raptors are passing through, waterbirds are breeding and summer visitors are arriving, during September, which is also a good time for passage raptors and passerines, and during the winter when there are often high numbers of wildfowl and, in some years, rare visitors from Scandinavia and Siberia.

Denmark is a low-lying country, rising to just 173 m (568 ft), and much of it is primarily rolling, fertile farmland (over 70% of the land is agricultural), although there are also beech and oak woods, coniferous plantations and a long, largely unspoilt coastline with extensive intertidal areas, sandy beaches, dunes, and marshes which support the bulk of the country's birds. At least 90% of the land has been modified in some way, mostly for conversion to agriculture, and much of the formerly extensive heathlands and peatlands have been drained and ploughed, hence habitat loss and degradation are the major problems facing the three threatened and near-threatened species, and relatively common and widespread birds which occur in Denmark. Fortunately, most of the best habitats lie within natural parks, and private and state reserves.

Notable species include Great Bittern (192–231 booming males in 1995), White-tailed Eagle* (at least two pairs bred in 1996, the first since 1980, and three to four pairs were present in 1998) and Eurasian Eagle-Owl (about 25 pairs). Due to fluctuations in food supplies in northern Scandinavia and Russia, the country is occasionally invaded by birds such as Northern Hawk Owl, Eurasian Nutcracker (3,676 were recorded in 1985 and 1,493 in 1995), Pine Grosbeak (at least 73 in Skagen in November 1998, the largest influx for over 100 years) and Parrot Crossbill.

There are several good birding sites in and around **Copenhagen**, Denmark's capital city, including: (i) Utterslev Mose, a public park northwest of the city centre, where Red-necked Grebe and Thrush Nightingale have bred; (ii) the lakes at Ishoj Strand where up to 600 Greater Scaup and 100 Smew have been recorded during the winter. When the lakes freeze over the birds usually move to Copenhagen harbour which can be viewed from Sjaellandsbroen, at the southern end; (iii) Gronjordssoen, a small lake at Amager Faelled just north of Sjaellandsbroen, where Red-necked Grebe and Thrush Nightingale also occur; (iv) Vestermager, a large partly open ex-military area southeast of Sjaellandsbroen, which during the winter and spring attracts raptors which may include White-tailed Eagle* and Rough-legged Buzzard. After a massive influx of White-winged Terns into Denmark during the spring of 1997, a pair attempted to breed here, but were unsuccessful; and (v) the mixed woodland at Kongelunden south of Vestermager, where Thrush Nightingale occurs and during some winters Tengmalm's Owl frequents the pine belts. This is also one of the best sites for passage migrants in and around Copenhagen (a spring record of 2,315 Common Cranes passed over on 9 May 1998), along with Utterslev Mose and Ishoj Strand.

The best area to look for Black Woodpecker in Denmark is in the beech woods and coniferous forests north of Copenhagen, especially in: (i) the largest area of forest in the country at **Gribskov**, north of Hillerod; (ii) the pines at **Tisvilde Hegn** along the coast southwest of Tisvildeleje; and (iii) **Jaegerspris Nordskov**, to the northwest of Tisvilde Hegn. Other breeding species present in northern Zealand, the island on which Copenhagen is situated, include a few pairs of Green

Sandpiper, Red-backed Shrike, Thrush Nightingale and Icterine Warbler, the latter three of which breed in **Dyrehaven**, a royal park accessible from Tarbaek near Copenhagen. **Gilbjerg Hoved** or the northern tip of Zealand 2 km west of Gilleleje is a good place to witness the strong spring and autumn raptor passage through Denmark. Most birds fly over here between March and May during southerlies or south-easterlies. In westerlies or northerlies watch from Gribskov or Hellebaek Avlsgard, 5 km west of Helsingor. Average totals of 9,000 birds pass during the spring and 14,000 birds during autumn, mostly Eurasian Sparrowhawks and Common Buzzards, but also including good numbers of Rough-legged Buzzards. The passage of Common Cranes can also be impressive and in early April 1996 a total of 1,193 were observed passing over Gilleleje in a single day.

Denmark's premier autumn raptor migration watchpoint lies in southern Zealand, at Stevns Klint, a steep cliff at the eastern end of the **Stevns Peninsula**. This site is 25 km southwest of Falsterbo in Sweden (p. 367) and 75% of the raptors which pass over there reach here 40 minutes later. An average of about 20,000 birds pass over each autumn, mainly from the end of August to mid-October, and up to a few thousand may be seen on a single day, a total which could comprise up to 15 species. European Honey-buzzard, Eurasian Sparrowhawk and Common Buzzard are the commonest species but annual totals also include 400–500 Red Kites, 400–500 Western Marsh-Harriers and up to 1,000 Rough-legged Buzzards. To reach the south end of the cliff head out of Koge on Route 261 to Store Heddinge then continue to Hojerup and park by the church. The best site in south Zealand for shorebirds is **Olsemagle Strand**, about 4 km north of Koge. The wetlands here attract several thousand passage shorebirds, mainly during the autumn when on a good day it is possible to see 25 species.

The small island of **Mon**, just two hours by road south of Copenhagen, is where many Danish birders head for in the spring, in search of Barred Warblers (which occasionally breed here) and passage migrants. The best sites for passage migrants are Nyord, Ulvshale and Ostmon. Mon's neighbouring island, **Falster**, is also good for passage migrants. During the autumn its southernmost point, Gedser, is another good place to look for raptors (during northerlies or north-westerlies) or to seawatch from (during strong easterlies).

Up to six Tengmalm's Owls were calling during early March 1996 on the island of **Bornholm**, in the Baltic Sea near Sweden to the east of Denmark's main islands. This island is also a good place to observe the passage of Common Cranes (on a single day in mid-October 1996 a record 3,350 passed over Gudhjem) and to look for rarities which have included Siberian Rubythroat and an amazing 55 or more Pallas's Warblers in the Christianso area alone on 19 October 1996. The island is accessible by ferry from Denmark, Sweden and Germany.

WADDEN SEE

The most important intertidal area in Europe extends east from The Netherlands (p. 262) through northwest Germany (p. 200) to southwest Jutland, the mainland part of Denmark, where it also supports masses of waterbirds.

Regular Summer Visitors and Resident Species
Red-necked Grebe, White Stork, Pied Avocet, Black Tern.

Regular Winter Visitors
Whooper and Bewick's Swans, Pink-footed and Barnacle Geese.

(Other species recorded here during the summer include Snowy Plover and White-winged Tern (after a massive influx of this species into Denmark during the spring of 1997, 16–18 pairs attempted to breed at Tondermarsken, but were unsuccessful).)

One of the best places to look for the birds of the Wadden See is from the causeway to the island of **Romo**, south of Esbjerg. During the autumn Pied Avocets are abundant off here and over 7,000 may be present in a single flock. The wetlands on the island of Romo itself support breeding waterbirds. Snowy Plover, a rare bird in Denmark, is most likely to be seen on **Fano**, to the north of Romo, but this island is more renowned as a place to observe the visible migration of what often amounts to thousands of passerines, especially during September and October, and the best place to look for them is Sonderho at the island's southern tip. **Tondermarsken**, the marsh to the east of Saltvandssoen, supports White Stork (at Rudbol) and Black Tern. It can be viewed from minor roads between Hojer and Rudbol. During late winter and early spring thousands of geese usually roost at **Ballum Enge**, south of Hojer (view from the sluice), after feeding on the marshes southeast of Hojer.

Accommodation: Romo—several hotels and campsites.

Another top site for passage migrants is **Blavandshuk**, a sandy peninsula west of Esbjerg complete with a bird observatory and lighthouse. During or after strong westerlies in the autumn, there is often a good passage of skuas off here, and an outside chance of seeing European Storm-Petrel or even Sabine's Gull. The marshes at **Tipperne**, a reserve 40 km north of Blavandshuk (open only from 0500 to 1000 on Sundays from April to August and 1000 to 1200 on Sundays from September to March), support breeding Great Bittern and Pied Avocet, and attract a wide variety of passage waterbirds, particularly shorebirds during the autumn (for example, 272 Curlew Sandpipers on 20 July 1998). Thousands of geese, mainly Pink-feet, usually roost at **Filso**, a small lake between Oksbol and Norre Nebel at this time.

Limfjorden, the large shallow inlet in northern Jutland, supports the country's largest breeding populations of Great Bittern, Black-tailed Godwit, Black Tern and Reedling, and other species present during the summer include Red-necked Grebe, Garganey, White Stork (breeding in Veslos village) and Pied Avocet, and other possibilities include Little Gull, Gull-billed Tern and Great Reed-Warbler. The best birding areas are along the north shore between Thisted and Aggersund Bridge, and at the two wetland reserves here: Ostlige Vejler and Vestlige Vejler. Ostlige is viewable from the dam at Bygholm, east of Oslos, and Vestlige can be viewed from minor roads around Arup, south of Osterlid. Twenty km to the northwest of this outstanding area a few pairs of Common Crane breed at **Hantsholm Vildtreservat** (they are well protected and very difficult to see) and Wood Sandpiper breeds at nearby **Vigso**.

The sandy peninsula known as **Skagen**, at the extreme northern tip of Jutland, is one of the most popular spring birding sites in the country because it attracts so many passage migrants, especially raptors such as Pallid Harrier* and Rough-legged Buzzard, and passerines, as well as rarities which have included White-billed Diver. The best time to be here is from April to early June, especially during easterlies. The best seawatching spot and a good place for passage passerine migrants is just east of the lighthouse at Nordstrande. Another migrant hotspot, especially in the mornings, is Grenen at the tip of the peninsula, including the bushes and trees north of the road just before it enters the town. After scouring this area many birders move on to Flagbakken, a hill just west of Skagen town along the road south of the railway, and other hills in the area. Many birders stay at the campsite just northeast of Skagen, or in the youth hostel west of the town.

ADDITIONAL INFORMATION

Addresses
Please send records of rarities to the Danish Rarities Committee, Dansk Ornitologisk Forening, Vesterbrogade 140, 1620 Kobenhavn V, Denmark (tel: 31 31 8563). The annual rarities report is published in *Dansk Ornitologisk Forenings Tidsskrift*, in Danish with an English summary.

Birdline
Information (tel: 90 232400). Hotline (tel: 33 255300).

ESTONIA

INTRODUCTION

This small former Russian state, independent since 1991, lies on the major migration highway at the eastern edge of the Baltic Sea and huge numbers of birds, mainly waterfowl, pass through Estonia, especially during the autumn. Otherwise the avifauna is similar to that of nearby southern Finland.

At 45,100 km², Estonia is nearly one third the size of England and 7% the size of Texas. Most visitors arrive in Tallinn, the capital, by air or via the regular ferries from other Baltic ports. It is possible to reach most of the best birding sites, including Matsalu Bay, on public transport or long-distance taxis, but as usual, the most convenient way to get around is to hire a vehicle. Hotel prices are slightly lower than in most of western Europe, and most towns have one or two budget hotels, guesthous-

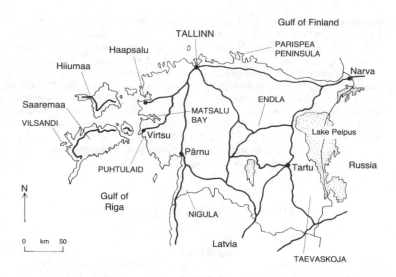

es and youth hostels. There are also some campsites, complete with chalets in some cases. Major foods include fish, pig products, soups and sour cream, washed down with copious amounts of beer (*olu*) and vodka by the locals.

The climate is temperate with warm summers and cold winters when there can be plenty of snow. The best times to visit are during late winter for Hazel Grouse, Ural Owl and woodpeckers, and in mid-May and between mid-September and mid-October for passage migrants.

Estonia is a generally flat, low-lying lakeland which rises to just 318 m (1043 ft) at Surr-Munamagi in the southeast. It has a long coastline with numerous offshore islands and islets, bordering the Gulf of Finland to the north and the Baltic Sea to the west. This coastline is mainly rocky but there are also extensive saltmarshes, reedbeds and seasonally flooded meadows. Inland, there are numerous marshes which cover about 20% of the country and large tracts of predominantly birch and coniferous forest which accounts for nearly 40% of the land surface. During Russian 'rule', Estonia suffered extensive environmental damage due to uncontrolled industrialisation. However, large areas still remain free of such horrors and traditional farming methods have prevailed in many places up until the end of the 1990s at least. If agricultural intensification can be resisted and the large number of 'protected' areas (which amounted to about 10% of the land surface at the end of the 20th century) maintained and increased, the four threatened and near-threatened species as well as the relatively common and widespread birds which occur in the country, may still be around by the end of the 21st century.

About 328 species have been recorded in Estonia, of which 222 have been known to breed. Notable species include Steller's Eider*, Great Snipe*, Caspian Tern and Greenish Warbler (*trochiloides*). It is possible to see up to 180–200 species on a trip lasting two to three weeks during the spring and ten to 20 fewer in the autumn. A team of four birders set the record for the number of species recorded in a single day within Europe, when they notched up 190 species in Estonia on 25th May 1998.

The **Parispea Peninsula** in the Gulf of Finland, about 60 km east of Tallinn, is a good place to observe the summer moult-migration of Common Scoters. Up to 10,000 have been seen passing in a single day, and nearly 150,000 during a single season. The autumn migration of waterfowl, which peaks between mid-September and mid-October, is also impressive and usually involves thousands of Barnacle Geese, Greater Scaups and Long-tailed Ducks. To reach here from Tallinn head east along the M1 towards Narva then turn north to Loksa at the base of the peninsula. The best places to seawatch from are to the south of Viinistu and north of Parispea.

BALTIC COAST

The northwest coast of Estonia is situated on the major migration route at the eastern edge of the Baltic Sea and during the spring and autumn up to 350,000 waterfowl have been recorded passing through here, including a few of the Steller's Eiders* which winter in the Baltic. Spring migrants include as many as 100,000 Barnacle Geese and several hundred thousand Long-tailed Ducks, and during the autumn up to 20,000 Common Cranes pass through.

Regular Passage Migrants
Whooper and Bewick's Swans, Greater White-fronted and Barnacle (mainly in May/also breeds) Geese, Greater Scaup, Steller's Eider*, Long-tailed Duck (mainly in May), Velvet Scoter, Smew, Common Crane (autumn).

Regular Summer Visitors
Corn Crake*, Great Snipe*, Black and Arctic Terns, Thrush Nightingale, Eurasian River Warbler.

(Other rare breeding species include White Stork, White-tailed Eagle*, Little Crake, Caspian Tern and Blyth's Reed-Warbler, rare spring passage migrants include Lesser White-fronted Goose*, and uncommon breeding and wintering species include Ural Owl and Eurasian Pygmy-Owl.)

The large **Matsalu Bay**, part of which is a nature reserve, is about 110 km (two hours) by road southwest of Tallinn, just to the west of the M30 to Virtsu. About 260 species have been recorded in the shallow bay and its surrounding marshes and woods, of which 170 have been known to breed. In order to arrange the permits necessary to visit the reserve, and possible boat trips and guided walks contact the reserve office at Penijoe (tel: 47 78413). **Puhtulaid**, a 1.5-km-long and 500-m wide wooded island connected to the mainland via a dam, 3 km south of Virtsu and about 130 km (two hours) via the M30 southwest of Tallinn, is an excellent place to observe the visible migration of waterfowl. The best place to seawatch from is the observation tower at the southern tip of the peninsula. About 230 species have been recorded here, 137 of which have been known to breed. The north-facing promontory known as **Spitami**, about an hour by road north of Haapsalu, is also a top seawatching site, especially during the autumn.

Accommodation: Haapsalu—Paeva Villa (tel/fax: 47 45484), as well as a hotel and a guesthouse. For more information contact Haapsalu Tourist Office (tel: 47 33248; fax: 47 33464). Virtsu—hostel. Puhtulaid—Puhtu Bird Station (tel: 52 40862).

Thousands of Tufted Ducks migrate along the Baltic Coast of Estonia during the spring and autumn, and many stop off in Matsalu Bay

There is a small colony of Caspian Terns on the island of **Vilsandi**, which is situated a few km off the west coast of the island of Saaremaa. Visitors must contact the national park office in Kihelkonna (tel: 45 76604/76624) beforehand in order to arrange the necessary permits, boat trips and, if required, accommodation. Saaremaa is accessible by vehicular ferry from Virtsu (130 km southwest of Tallinn via the M30). From Kuivastu, where the ferry from the mainland docks, head for Papisaare, from where boats to Vilsandi depart. Papisaare is about 250 km (five hours) by road southwest of Tallinn in total and the boat journey across to Vilsandi takes about 30 minutes. The island lies within Vilsandi National Park where about 247 species have been recorded, 114 of which have been known to breed, including Barnacle Goose and Barred Warbler. During the spring up to 10,000 Barnacle Geese have been present at any one time before continuing their journey northwards.

The best place to look for Ural Owl in Estonia is at the **Nigula** reserve near Vanajarve, about 50 km south of Pärnu, which is about 100 km south of Tallinn via the M4 and about 60 km southeast of Matsalu Bay. It is necessary to contact the reserve office prior to arrival (tel: 44 92470). Once there, bird along the walking track which leads west about a km south of Vanajarve. Take plenty of insect repellent. Other species which occur here include Black Stork, Lesser Spotted Eagle, Eurasian Capercaillie, Common Crane, Wood Sandpiper, Eurasian Eagle-Owl, Eurasian Pygmy-Owl, Tengmalm's Owl, White-backed and Black Woodpeckers, and Eurasian Nutcracker. There is a guesthouse in Vanajarve.

The best place to look for Hazel Grouse is the **Endla** reserve near Tooma, which is about 130 km southeast of Tallinn and 70 km northwest of Tartu. Contact the reserve office (tel: 77 45359/46429) before arrival and once there walk the trail from Tooma to Lake Endla. Over 170 species have been recorded, of which 145 have been known to breed, including Black Stork, White-tailed*, Lesser Spotted and Golden Eagles, Black Grouse, Eurasian Capercaillie, Common Crane, Wood

Sandpiper and Black Woodpecker. The nearest accommodation is in Tartu but it is possible to camp at Tooma.

Hazel Grouse also occurs near **Taevaskoja** in southeast Estonia, along with Tengmalm's Owl, White-backed, Three-toed and Black Woodpeckers, and Greenish Warbler (*trochiloides*). Taevaskoja is about 30 km southeast of Tartu (176 km southeast of Tallinn) via the M61 Polva–Voru road or about 50 minutes by train from Tartu. From Taevaskoja continue northeast to Saesaare, then turn east to reach the Saesaare Pavilion from where walking tracks start. The nearest accommodation is in Tartu but it is possible to camp at Saesaare. The floodplain of the **River Emajõgi** near Tartu supports Greater Spotted Eagle* and Great Snipe* during the summer.

ADDITIONAL INFORMATION

Addresses

Please send records of rarities to the Eesti Linnuharulduste Komisjon (Estonian Ornithological Society/EOS), Eestimaa Loodhuse Fond, 2 Struwe Str., 2400 Tartu, Estonia.

Books and papers

Bird-watching Localities in Estonia (second revised edition). Leito A, 1996. Available from the author at Roomu tee 18-10, EE2400 Tartu, Estonia.

Birds of Estonia: status, distribution and numbers. Leiback E, Lilleleht V & Veromann H (eds.), 1994. EOS.

Eesti Linnuatlas (Atlas of Breeding Birds of Estonia). Estonian Academy, 1993. Estonian Academy.

FAROES

This archipelago of rocky islands, rising to 882 m (2894 ft), is situated between Shetland and Iceland. Apart from a few stunted maples and willows, the islands, away from the vertical coastal cliffs, are composed of windswept, sparsely vegetated moors, and yet about 45,000 people live here, alongside some of Europe's most impressive seabird colonies, including the largest known colony of European Storm-Petrels on earth.

The species listed below occur during the summer (June is the best time to visit) unless otherwise indicated.

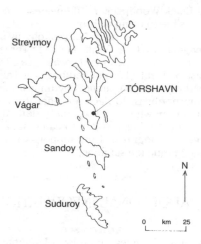

Regular Summer Visitors and Resident Species

Manx Shearwater, European and Leach's Storm-Petrels, Northern Gannet, Purple Sandpiper, Red-necked Phalarope, Arctic Tern, Great and Arctic Skuas, Black Guillemot, Atlantic Puffin, Red-throated Diver, Rock Dove, Redwing, Northern Wheatear, Winter Wren, Snow Bunting.

The Faroes are accessible by air from Denmark, Iceland and Scotland, and by boat, during the summer, from Denmark and Norway. Regular boats and helicopters link most of the 18 inhabited islands, and boats, hire-vehicles, taxis and buses are available to get around these islands. European and Leach's Storm-Petrels breed on **Mykines**, accessible by boat from Vágar, and the largest European Storm-Petrel colony in the world is on **Nolsoy**, along the coast southeast of the village. There are several boats per day to Nolsoy from Tórshavn, the capital, which is situated on the island of Streymoy, and it is necessary to stay overnight on Nolsoy in order to look for the birds returning to the colony late at night.

Accommodation: Large hotels are confined to Tórshavn, but other forms of accommodation, including guesthouses, youth hostels and campsites are available on most islands. For more information contact the Faroe Tourist Board, Kunningarstovan, Vaglid, FR-100 Tórshavn, The Faroes (tel: 15877; fax: 14883).

ADDITIONAL INFORMATION

Addresses

Please send records of rarities to the Danish Rarities Committee, Dansk Ornitologisk Forening, Vesterbrogade 140, 1620 Kobenhavn V, Denmark (tel: 31 31 8563). The annual rarities report is published in *Dansk Ornitologisk Forenings Tidsskrift*, in Danish with an English summary.

FINLAND

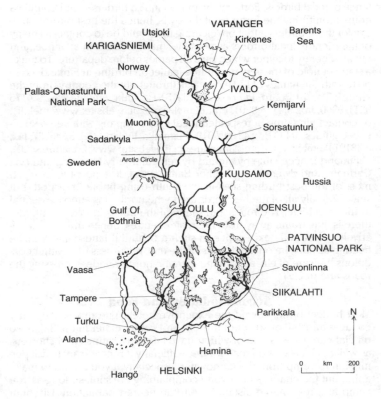

VARANGER
Utsjoki
KARIGASNIEMI
Kirkenes
Barents
Sea
Norway
Pallas-Ounastunturi
National Park
IVALO
Kemijarvi
Muonio
Sorsatunturi
Sadankyla
Sweden
Arctic Circle
KUUSAMO
Russia
Gulf Of
Bothnia
OULU
JOENSUU
PATVINSUO
NATIONAL PARK
Vaasa
Savonlinna
Tampere
SIIKALAHTI
Turku
Parikkala
N
Aland
Hamina
Hangö
HELSINKI
0   km   200

INTRODUCTION

Summary

Most birders who visit Finland do so to see owls, for it is possible with local assistance to see up to nine species here, more than in any other European country, as well as some high-arctic specialities such as Siberian Jay and Pine Grosbeak, and a few species at the edge of their mainly Siberian breeding ranges, including Red-flanked Bluetail and Yellow-breasted Bunting. In addition, many visitors move on to Varanger in north Norway where there is a chance of adding Snowy Owl, as well King and Steller's* Eiders, and plenty of breeding shorebirds. Such a trip is likely to prove expansive and expensive, but to see so many wonderful birds in some of the wildest country on earth would surely be one of the highlights of any birder's life.

Size

At 337,030 km², Finland is 2.6 times larger than England and half the size of Texas.

161

Getting Around

In order to achieve anything near a 100% success rate with the owls and many of the other specialities, it is absolutely essential to enlist the assistance of local birders. Fortunately, many Finnish birders spend countless hours monitoring the fortunes of the owls, hence the best birding strategy for those birders intent on 'clearing up' would be to contact as many of the friendly local birders as possible, many months in advance, and put an itinerary together which suits all parties before departure. To make a start get hold of the very useful free leaflet on birding in Finland, complete with the names of local contacts throughout the country, from the Finnish Tourist Board, PO Box 249, 00131 Helsinki, Finland (tel: 9 4176 9211/9300; fax: 9 4176 9301; email: mek@mek.fi; website: www.mek.fi), or contact Finnature, a respected local tour company with very experienced guides, at PO Box 42, FIN-91901 Liminka, Finland (tel: 8 345737; fax: 8 381914; email: finnature@finnature.sci.fi; website: www.finnature.sci.fi).

Finland is accessible by air and by vehicular ferry from England (via Germany and Sweden) and other Baltic states. It is possible to reach most of the best birding sites in the south using public transport, but since virtually all of the best birds are in the north, it is almost essential to hire a vehicle. The roads and many of the tracks are excellent, and there is little traffic away from the major centres, hence driving is a relatively pleasurable experience in such a beautiful landscape. Vehicle headlights must be on at all times of the day, regardless of weather conditions. Beware of elk, and, in the extreme north, reindeer, crossing the roads and tracks.

Accommodation and Food

Most budget birders avoid the expensive hotels, guesthouses, country cottages and 140 or so youth hostels, and camp, either in the 350 or so official campsites, some of which have kitchens, saunas and showers, as well as chalets, or off-road for free. Officially it is necessary to ask permission to camp from the landowner, especially if you intend to make a fire, but the chances of anyone complaining are slim, so long as you camp at a reasonable distance from the nearest habitation. Discount schemes can take away the sting of hotel prices and they seem even cheaper when one considers the price usually includes an all-you-can-eat breakfast, usually composed of bread, cereals, cheese, eggs, herring and salami. Lunchtime and evening menus are dominated by elk, reindeer, fish such as salmon, and pork and cabbage casseroles. Most roadside service stations have restaurants. The sale of alcohol is subject to strict licensing laws, but beer (*olut*), vodka and other alcoholic drinks can be purchased in the widespread *Alko* stores.

Health and Safety

Much of Finland, especially the north, is damp, cold, wild, remote and, during the summer, swarming with midges and mosquitoes, hence it is best to bird with a detailed map, a compass, plenty of food and drink, wellies, warm and waterproof clothing, top camping gear and the best insect repellent money can buy.

Climate and Timing

Late May to mid-June is the best time to visit Finland, for this coincides with spring migration, it is the beginning of the breeding season for many forest species, the owls are usually feeding young and it is early enough to avoid the billions of biting insects which usually start to build up after mid-June and soon start to spoil the birding. However, Yellow-breasted Buntings sometimes fail to arrive until mid-June. During the summer the temperature may rise to 81°F in the south, but during the extremely cold winters thermometers fall as low as −50°C in the north. The midnight sun can be seen in the far north between mid-May and the end of July, when the best time of day to start birding is midnight. The Aurora Borealis (Northern Lights) are at their best on cold, clear nights in February–March and September–October.

Habitats

Southern Finland is predominantly flat lowland, rarely rising above 200 m (656 ft). Most of the 188,000 or so lakes in the country, which account for about 10% of the 'land' surface, are situated here, in between farm-land and extensive areas of mainly commercial boreal (*taiga*) forest. About 70% of the country is forested, including much of the lowlands which extend into northern Finland, but where the ground rises to the fells and high plateaux of Lapland in the far north, the coniferous forest, where birds are thin on the ground, give way to the tundra, which is alive with breeding birds during the short summer season.

Conservation

Much of the country, especially the 30% or so which lies within the Arc-tic Circle, is very sparsely populated and despite the fact that Finland is well over twice the size of England, where 48.2 million people live, only just over five million people populate this land, and only 8% is cultivat-ed, hence there is plenty of room for birds. Although the major habitat, boreal forest, supports few bird species at very low densities, it covers large enough areas to be important as a whole, hence maintaining the extent of these forests as well as the other habitats is of paramount im-portance in conserving the six threatened and near-threatened species, as well as the relatively common and widespread birds which occur in Finland. There are numerous reserves, mostly under state ownership, but problems such as habitat loss and degradation, disturbance and hunting are ongoing.

Bird Species

About 430 species have been recorded in Finland. Notable species in-clude Lesser White-fronted Goose* (143 were released near the breed-ing sites of the few remaining wild birds in Lapland between 1989 and 1997), Terek and Broad-billed Sandpipers, Red-necked Phalarope, Casp-ian Tern, Long-tailed Skua, Eurasian Eagle-Owl, Snowy (regular winter visitor to the south), Ural, Great Grey and Northern Hawk Owls, Eur-asian Pygmy-Owl, Tengmalm's Owl, Siberian Jay, Eurasian Nutcracker, Bohemian Waxwing, Red-flanked Bluetail (numbers vary, with about 25 singing males in 1998, compared to 35–38 in 1997, which was regarded as an exceptional year), Lanceolated (seven singing males in 1998) and Eurasian River Warblers, Blyth's Reed-Warbler, Arctic and Greenish (*trochiloides*) Warblers, Siberian Tit, Pine Grosbeak, Parrot and Two-barred Crossbills, and Little, Rustic and Yellow-breasted Buntings.

Expectations

With local assistance it is possible to see over 200 species on a ten to 14 day trip during the late spring and early summer which includes

Varanger in nearby north Norway. Great Grey Owl, which was almost wiped out by the severe late frosts in spring 1997 (and hence very difficult to locate in 1998) and Northern Hawk Owl, which was scarce throughout the 1990s, are the most difficult owls to see, whereas Eurasian Eagle-Owl, Ural Owl (4,500 nest boxes are checked annually), Eurasian Pygmy-Owl (about 10,000 pairs breed in central and southern Finland) and Tengmalm's Owl (over 10,000 nest boxes are checked annually) are almost guaranteed. The remaining three regularly seen species are Tawny, Long-eared and Short-eared Owls. In Finland and Norway, Snowy Owl is an irregular breeder, although it does winter on a regular basis in southern Finland.

NORTHERN FINLAND

OULU

The wetlands near Oulu, at the north end of the Gulf of Bothnia on Finland's west coast are an important resting and refuelling stop for a wide range of passage migrants, especially waterfowl and shorebirds, and they support a few pairs of Terek Sandpiper and Yellow-breasted Bunting, here at the western outposts of their main breeding ranges. In addition, with local assistance it is also possible to see Ural and Great Grey Owls in the nearby forests and over 100 species in a day at the end of May and in early June.

The species listed below occur during late May to early June unless otherwise indicated.

Localised Specialities
Terek Sandpiper, Great Grey Owl, Yellow-breasted Bunting.

Others
Bean Goose ('Taiga' *fabalis*), Velvet Scoter, Smew, Rough-legged Buzzard, Eurasian Capercaillie, Hazel Grouse, Common Crane, Wood Sandpiper, Temminck's Stint, Broad-billed Sandpiper, Red-necked Phalarope, Little Gull, Ural and Tengmalm's Owls, Bluethroat ('Redspotted' *svecica*), Reedling, Brambling, Parrot Crossbill.

(Other species recorded here include Lesser White-fronted Goose*, Jack Snipe, Caspian Tern, White-billed Diver (30 or so in mid-May 1998), Eurasian Eagle-Owl, Northern Hawk Owl, Eurasian Pygmy-Owl, Three-toed and Black Woodpeckers, Blyth's Reed-Warbler, Greenish Warbler (*trochiloides*) and Rustic Bunting.)

Oulu is accessible by air and road from Helsinki, 611 km to the south. The top site is **Liminganlahti** where there is a visitor centre and observation towers. To reach here turn west off Route 4 south of Oulu on to Route 8 and then take Route 813 through Liminka. Then turn north in response to the 'Liminganlahti opastuskeskus' signpost. The path to the tower at Virkkula, where the visitor centre is located, is usually the best for Yellow-breasted Bunting. Ask at the visitor centre where the best places to look for Terek Sandpiper are.

Accommodation: Ala-Temmes (tel: 8 38 4643) and camping at Limingan-lahti.

Finland is the best country in Europe for owls, including the magnificent Great Grey.

KUUSAMO

The forests which grow on the rugged hills around Kuusamo in north-central Finland, near the border with Russia, are the best place in Europe to look for Red-flanked Bluetail, which first bred in Finland, at the western edge of its range, in 1969. About 15 singing males were present here in 1999, and this little beauty is ably supported by Siberian Jay, Arctic Warbler, Siberian Tit, Little and Rustic Buntings, and a whole lot more besides, hence many Finnish birders believe this is probably the best birding area in the country and every year many take part in the Kuusamo Bird Race. Thirty or more teams have been known to enter the race, which usually takes place in mid-June, and between them they notched up 207 species between 1984 and 1998. The total number of species seen in 1998 was 153. To take part contact Heikki Seppanen, Uivelontie 2, FIN-93600 Kuusamo, Finland (mobile: 400 582058; email: heikki.seppanen@nls.fi) or Olli Lamminsalo (mobile: 500 501706; email: inaria.studio@pp.kolumbus.fi).

The species listed below occur from mid-May to late July unless otherwise indicated.

Localised Specialities
Red-flanked Bluetail, Arctic Warbler.

Other Localised European Specialities
Siberian Jay, Siberian Tit, Parrot Crossbill.

Others
Bean Goose ('Taiga' *fabalis*), Velvet Scoter, Smew, Osprey, Rough-legged Buzzard, Golden Eagle, Willow Ptarmigan, Eurasian Capercaillie, Hazel Grouse, Common Crane, Jack Snipe, Broad-billed Sandpiper, Red-necked Phalarope, Red-throated and Black-throated Divers, Tengmalm's Owl, Three-toed and Black Woodpeckers, Bohemian Waxwing, Bluethroat ('Red-spotted' *svecica*), Greenish Warbler (*trochiloides*), Brambling, Little and Rustic Buntings.

(Other species recorded here include White-tailed Eagle*, Ural, Great Grey and Northern Hawk Owls, Common Stonechat (a pair of 'Siberian' *maura* bred here in 1997), Pine Grosbeak and Two-barred Crossbill.)

Kuusamo is 800 km north of Helsinki and 212 km northeast of Oulu. On arrival the best thing to do is to ask fellow birders where the best spots are, since these vary from year to year. Otherwise, the best place to look for 'bluetails' is the **Valtavarra Ridge**, particularly on the slope above the car park at Konttainen. To reach the ridge head for Ruka ski centre 25 km to the north of Kuusamo via Route 5 and Route 8694 to the east. In good years a 'bluetail' sings from the tree-tops in front of the observation tower, which is an hour's walk up hill from **Saavivaara**. Another site worth trying is the **Ristikallio Gorge**. To reach here continue north on Route 5, then take the right fork on to Route 950 to Kayla. Continue to the Oulankajoki, a river just beyond Kayla, and walk downstream. If all else fails try **Oulanka National Park**, about 45 km north of Kuusamo, where there is an excellent network of trails.

The best place to look for Arctic Warbler is usually **Naatikkavaara** which can be reached by heading north out of Kuusamo on Route 5 then turning west on to Route 81 towards Posio. Two km west of the 'Vasarapera' signpost turn north, keep right at the fork following signs to 'Lentama', and 2.5 km up from the fork start looking for the warbler singing from the spruce tops.

Jack Snipe and Broad-billed Sandpiper breed in the bogs at **Isosuo**, about 30 km southeast of Kuusamo, and this is also a particularly good spot for Bohemian Waxwing. In the general area around Kuusamo look out for Hazel Grouse drinking at roadside pools and Siberian Jays visiting picnic tables.

Accommodation: Kuusamo—three hotels, Taskula Farm (tel/fax: 8 868 5318), holiday apartments (tel: 8 850 6777) and a campsite. Ruka—Viipus Campsite. Oulanka National Park HQ, east of Kayla at Kintakongas—campsite.

The beautiful Black-throated Diver breeds throughout Finland and the rest of Scandinavia

One of the best areas for Northern Hawk Owl in Finland is **Sorsatunturi**, reached by heading north from Kuusamo to Salla then turning northeast on to Route 82 to Kotala. A few km northwest of Kotala turn northeast on to a track which after about 40 km finally reaches suitable hawk-owl terrain, between Hietaniemi and Tunsta. Other species which occur here include Pine Grosbeak, which also occurs in: (i) **Pyhatunturi National Park**, which is about 50 km north of Kemijarvi, just inside the Arctic Circle. Head for the visitor centre alongside the road to Pelkosenniemi, where a number of trails radiate from and there is a chair-lift to the higher areas; and (ii) in the relatively bird-rich valley south of **Luosto**, which is northwest of Pyhatunturi and about 45 km southeast of Sadankyla. The trail which leads west through this valley starts at the car park just after the first stream past the ski centre. The town of **Sadankyla**, 250 km northwest of Kuusamo, is surrounded by fine forests and marshes which support most of the species associated with the Arctic, including Pine Grosbeak and Parrot Crossbill, as well as Three-toed Woodpecker (along the east side of the river 10 km south of Sadankyla). The bog at **Petkula**, north of Sadankyla, supports Broad-billed Sandpiper, and to the north of here White-tailed Eagle*, Common Crane and Bohemian Waxwing occur around the lake known as **Tekojarvi**, north of Madetkoski. The holiday village and campsite called Peurasuvannon siltamajat, about 45 km north of Sadankyla, is a good base for birding this area and can be booked in advance by contacting PPA 1, 99600 Sadankyla, Finland (tel: 16 63 6711; fax: 16 63 6721).

The small lakes, marshes, fjells and forests around **Ivalo** in Finnish Lapland support most of the high-arctic specialities, including Long-tailed Skua and Arctic Redpoll, as well as Rough-legged Buzzard, Rock Ptarmigan, Jack Snipe, Wood Sandpiper, Temminck's Stint, Broad-billed Sandpiper, Red-necked Phalarope, Eurasian Dotterel, Three-toed Woodpecker, Siberian Jay, Bohemian Waxwing, Siberian Tit, Pine Grosbeak, Parrot Crossbill, and Little, Rustic, Lapland and Snow Buntings. Outside possibilities in this area include White-tailed Eagle*, Gyrfalcon, Northern Hawk Owl, Arctic Warbler and Two-barred Crossbill. Ivalo, 159 km north of Sadankyla, is accessible by air. Arctic Redpoll visits town gardens and the feeding station in the local woods is one of the most reliable places to catch up with Siberian Tit, which feeds out of the hand there. This somewhat elusive species also occurs along the road to Veskoniemi, reached by heading northeast from Ivalo on routes 968 and 9681 towards Nellim, then turning north. Back on Route 9681 continue northeast towards Nellim, then turn east towards Kontosjarvi on to a good stretch of road for Pine Grosbeak, as well as Three-toed Woodpecker, Siberian Jay and Parrot Crossbill.

From Ivalo northwards look out for the elegant Long-tailed Skua

Between Ivalo and Varanger in north Norway (p. 268) it is worth stopping at the marsh about 10 km north of **Utsjoki**, 125 km north of Inari.

In the **Karigasniemi** area northwest of Inari: (i) Broad-billed Sandpiper, Red-necked Phalarope and Long-tailed Skua breed on the marsh 13 km to the east; (ii) Bohemian Waxwing, Arctic Warbler and Arctic Redpoll occur in the Tenojoki Valley to the north; (iii) Long-tailed Skua and Horned Lark occur on Ailigas, a 620-m (2034 ft) peak to the northeast; and (iv) other species to look out for include White-tailed Eagle*, Gyrfalcon (along the road to Utsjoki), Eurasian Dotterel, Siberian Tit and Pine Grosbeak. There are a couple of hotels, a youth hostel and a campsite at Karigasniemi. Food and fuel are much cheaper in Finland than in Norway, hence it is prudent to stock up on both before or after crossing the border.

The huge **Pallas-Ounastunturi National Park** in northwest Finland near the border with Sweden supports a typical *taiga* and tundra avifauna highlighted by Gyrfalcon, Long-tailed Skua, Great Grey and Northern Hawk Owls, Siberian Jay, Siberian Tit and Pine Grosbeak, as well as brown bear, elk, grey wolf and wolverine. Mafkmaja, where the Tourist Hotel is situated, is a good starting point. This is accessible from Route 957 east of Muonio. Bird alongside the road, around the hotel and along the trail to Pallasjarvi, or, if time allows, along the 60-km-long trail north from the hotel to the Lapp village of Enontekio, complete with huts for overnight stays.

SOUTHERN FINLAND

The lakes, marshes, farmland and woods in and around **Helsinki** support an impressive variety of birds, including Eurasian Eagle-Owl, a few of which regularly winter within the city limits. However, this species, as well as forest species such as Hazel Grouse, Eurasian Pygmy-Owl, Tengmalm's Owl and Three-toed Woodpecker, which also occur near Finland's capital city, are only likely to be seen with local assistance. During the spring there is an impressive passage of wildfowl along the south coast of Finland which peaks during the second half of May. Seventy thousand Barnacle Geese, over 150,000 Brent Geese and 10,000 divers have been recorded on single days, with other possibilities including Lesser White-fronted* and Red-breasted* Geese, King and Steller's* Eiders, and White-billed Diver. In addition, the spring Common Crane passage included an exceptional 10,000 or so in the Helsinki area between 21 and 28 April 1997. Other species which occur in the Helsinki area during the spring and summer include Red-necked Grebe, Long-tailed Duck, Velvet Scoter, Smew, Corn Crake*, Caspian Tern, Black Woodpecker, Thrush Nightingale, Eurasian River Warbler, Blyth's Reed-Warbler and Barred Warbler. The best birding sites in and around the capital include: (i) **Vanhankaupunkilahti**, the bay of the old town also known as Viikki; (ii) **Grontrask**, a reedy lake in the northwest suburbs, where Red-necked Grebe breeds and regular visitors include Caspian Tern; and (iii) the peninsula known as **Porkkalanniemi**, about 30 km southwest of the city, which is a good place to observe the spring passage of wildfowl and divers, especially in southerlies or southwesterlies during the early morning or late afternoon. Much further afield, **Hangö**, 100 km southwest of Helsinki, is another good place to observe the spring passage of wildfowl and divers, especially during southeasterlies in the early morning and late afternoon. The large island known as **Kimito**, northwest of Hangö, is a good place to observe migrating Common Cranes (the peak spring count in the Dragsfjard part of the island in 1998 was 2,654 in mid-April).

The beautiful white-headed caudatus *race of Long-tailed Tit occurs throughout southern Scandinavia and from northeast Europe through Siberia to Ussuriland*

The wetland reserve at **Siikalahti** near the border with Russia, 280 km northeast of Helsinki, is one of the most important in Finland, both for breeding species, which include Red-necked Grebe, Smew, Common Crane, Wood Sandpiper, Eurasian River Warbler and Blyth's Reed-Warbler (most likely in gardens between Parikkala and the reserve), and passage migrants. In the surrounding willow scrub and forest it is also possible to see White-backed Woodpecker, and other species recorded in the area include Lanceolated Warbler. The reserve, which has a visitor centre, a nature trail and an observation tower, is just to the east of Parikkala and signposted from the E3. Accommodation in the area includes the Pistoniemi Holiday Cottages, Pistoniementie 189, 59100 Parikkala, Finland (tel: 5 449 103 or 49 751 767) and Muikkulahti Farm, Muikkulahdentie 16, 59210 Melkoniemi, Finland (tel: 5 447 104; fax: 5 447 118). It is also possible to camp at the reserve.

Eurasian Nutcracker occurs in the forest around the research station at **Punkaharju**, 30 km northwest of Parikkala. The densest population of Ospreys in Europe and 40 pairs of White-backed Woodpecker, as well as 'Saimaa' ringed seal, breed in **Linnansaari National Park**, further northwest still, near Savonlinna. The wooded islands in this park, which comprises primarily water, are accessible by boat from Rantasalmi on Haukivesi Lake or Oravi on the opposite shore.

Joensuu, 438 km northeast of Helsinki, lies in an area which is good for Three-toed Woodpecker (at Kitsi), Greenish Warbler (*trochiloides* at Kolvanan Uuro) and Rustic Bunting (in woods around the observation tower, reached by heading east out of Joensuu to Kulho and turning east there, from where the tower is signposted). To reach **Kitsi**, one of the best areas in Finland for Three-toed Woodpecker, head north from Joensuu on Route 5202 to Kitsi, continue on Route 5223 and take the second track on the left (keep left) which after a few km reaches a large area of burnt and dead trees, the favoured feeding ground of the woodpeckers. To reach the deep valley known as **Kolvanan Uuro** head north out of Joensuu on Route 18 and after passing the village of Uuro take the minor road to the right which is signposted 'Kolvanan Uuro'.

Jack Snipe, Three-toed Woodpecker, Bohemian Waxwing, Parrot Crossbill and Rustic Bunting, as well as brown bear and Eurasian beaver, occur in **Patvinsuo National Park** near Lieksa (where there was an Oriental Cuckoo in June 1998 and 1999. Another was present at Karstula during both summers). The best birding areas include the old forest on the north side of the main road, the forest to the east of the park, the lakeside forest around the campsite and the bog to the south. Look out for Ural Owl, Red-flanked Bluetail and Greenish Warbler (*trochiloides*) as well.

At the **Martinselkonen Wilderness Preserve** on the border with Russia there are hides for viewing brown bears, which are most likely to be seen between late June and early July.

At **Kangasala**, just east of Tampere (173 km north of Helsinki) in southwest Finland, there is a pond which was built specifically to feed wild Ospreys and they can be seen fishing from a hide and shelter between May and mid-September. The fields of **Soderfjarden**, 7 km south of Vaasa (420 km northwest of Helsinki) on Finland's west coast adjacent to the Gulf of Bothnia, are the country's most important autumn staging post for Common Crane. Numbers usually peak during the last week of September when as many as 2,700 have been present. The birds roost on offshore islands and make a splendid sight as they fly in at dawn to feed in the fields. Also during the autumn thousands of passerines pass through here, including regular Red-throated Pipits, and rarities have included Pallid Harrier*, Gyrfalcon, Snowy and Northern Hawk Owls, Arctic Redpoll and even Oriental Turtle-Dove. During the spring migration period, which peaks during the second half of April, this is a good area for geese, White-tailed Eagle*, Rough-legged Buzzard, Eurasian Dotterel and Snow Bunting (a flock of 7,000 has been recorded). During the summer Corn Crake*, Eurasian River Warbler and Blyth's Reed-Warbler have bred in the area. The **Vaasa Archipelago** is just as good for rarities, having seen the likes of Siberian Rubythroat and Thick-billed Warbler, and during the spring over 1,000 Rough-legged Buzzards have been recorded passing over in a single day. Breeding species include White-tailed Eagle* and Caspian Tern.

ADDITIONAL INFORMATION

Addresses

Please send records of rarities to Tom Lindroos, Uudentuvankatu 6 A 29, FIN-20740, Turku, Finland (email: rvyaopet@nett.fi). The annual rarities report is published in *Linnut*, in Finnish with an English summary.

The website www.birdlife.fi contains more details of birding in Finland. Still need help? Then email annika.forsten@iki.fi.

Books and papers

Finding Birds in Finland. Gosney D. Available from BirdGuides (address, p. 395).

Magazines

Alula, an excellent quarterly birding magazine published in English, is available via Knappa, FIN-10160 Degerby, Finland.

FRANCE

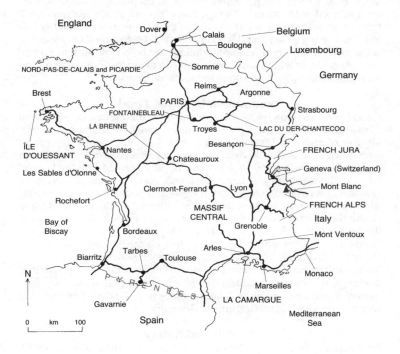

England
Dover
Calais
Boulogne
Belgium
Luxembourg
NORD-PAS-DE-CALAIS and PICARDIE
Somme
Germany
Brest
Reims
Argonne
PARIS
FONTAINEBLEAU
Strasbourg
LA BRENNE
Troyes
LAC DU DER-CHANTECOQ
ÎLE D'OUESSANT
Nantes
Besançon
FRENCH JURA
Chateauroux
Geneva (Switzerland)
Les Sables d'Olonne
Mont Blanc
Rochefort
Clermont-Ferrand
Lyon
MASSIF CENTRAL
FRENCH ALPS
Bay of Biscay
Italy
Grenoble
Bordeaux
Mont Ventoux
Biarritz
Tarbes
Arles
Toulouse
N
Monaco
Marseilles
Gavarnie
LA CAMARGUE
0 km 100
Spain
Mediterranean Sea

INTRODUCTION

Summary

While northern France has little to tempt birders, there are few better birding experiences than a trip to La Camargue and Pyrenées in the south of France, particularly for birders yet to travel beyond Europe. From flamingos and flocks of bee-eaters to Lammergeiers and Wallcreepers, such a trip is a must for anyone with a keen interest in European birds. To top it all there is so much more to France than the birds themselves, for, in the Pyrenées especially, they inhabit some fantastic landscapes, and, at the end of a long day in the field it is possible to absorb it all over fine food and wine without breaking the bank.

Size

At 535,265 km², mainland France, the largest country in Europe, is over four times larger than England and a little smaller than Texas.

Getting Around

The very efficient bus and rail services make travelling through France easy. Europe's most extensive rail network includes the flying *Trains a*

171

Grande Vitesse (TGVs) which are more expensive than other trains and must be booked in advance at peak times. Train journeys can be broken anywhere, any time, any place, for up to 24 hours, and bicycles can be hired at most railway stations and returned to any participating stations. Where there are no trains, mainly in mountainous terrain, they are replaced with buses, although these do not reach everywhere a birder may want to go, so, as usual, budget birders in search of big lists in a short space of time, and who are likely to be camping because that is the cheapest form of accommodation, are better off birding France with a vehicle. In which case it is possible to avoid the expensive motorway (*autoroute*) tolls by sticking to the 'N' or 'D' roads.

Accommodation and Food

Good hotels are expensive. *Chambres d'hôte*, the French equivalent of 'Bed and Breakfast', can be found almost anywhere, but they are usually as expensive as 2-star hotels. 'Formule 1' hotels, situated near most large towns, are slightly less expensive, but to keep costs to a minimum budget birders will need to make use of *gites* (rented holiday homes, often in the form of rural farm buildings), youth hostels (*auberges de jeunesse*) and the ubiquitous, often well-equipped campsites. All forms of accommodation are best booked in advance by those intending to stay in them between mid-July and mid-August. French food is arguably the best in the world and, fortunately, it is possible to dine out relatively cheaply. Birders who prefer even cheaper take-aways should head for the *charcuteries* (delicatessens) or better still the supermarkets. Many birding crews have survived two weeks in France on baguettes, cheese and tomatoes, washed down with wine, and spent very little money in the process. Wine is far, far more popular than beer, most of which is imported from Belgium or Germany.

Health and Safety

French police have the power to stop anyone at anytime to see their ID, so carry your passport with you at all times, especially when in a vehicle.

Climate and Timing

France is such a large country that the climate varies considerably. Generally speaking, the north has warm summers and cool winters, whereas the south has a Mediterranean climate with hot, dry summers and mild, wet winters. Early May is the peak time during spring to visit La Camargue, when passage migrants mix with resident species and summer visitors. Unfortunately many high-altitude roads in the French Alps and Pyrenées usually remain blocked by snow until mid-May and even early June so many birders who visit La Camargue and the Pyrenées on the same trip do so in late August and early September, when autumn passage peaks in La Camargue, the high mountain roads are still passable and birds such as Wallcreeper are easier to find.

Habitats

Anyone who has travelled through north-central France will know that large areas are intensively farmed and depressingly devoid of hedges, woods and, consequently, birds. However, despite the fact that 60% of the land in France is used for agriculture, it still supports a great range of other high-quality habitats, especially in the south. Basically, the north and west is low-lying country, bordered by a very long coastline with alternate beaches, rocky coasts and, especially by the Bay of Biscay, extensive intertidal areas. The east is hilly in the north and mountainous in the south, rising to 4808 m (15,774 ft) at Mont Blanc on the border with Italy. The Rhône Valley, to the west of the French Alps, separates these mountains from the sparsely populated Massif Central, a huge upland plateau which rises to 1886 m (6188 ft) at Puy de Sancy, and this in turn is separated from the 400-km-long French Pyrenées, to the south, which rise to 3298 m (10,820 ft) at Vignemale on the border with Spain.

It is thanks mainly to the presence of upland areas that about 25% of France remains forested. Above the deciduous and coniferous zones there are alpine grasslands, scree slopes, boulder fields, glaciers and jagged snow-capped peaks. The hills along the Mediterranean also support garrigue, maquis and pine forest. A number of large rivers flow off the hills and mountains throughout the country, and along some of them there are a number of fishpond and lake complexes. One of the largest rivers, the Rhône, forms a huge delta at the Mediterranean, part of which is known as La Camargue, an immensely rich wetland and one of Europe's most important areas for birds. To the east of here are the stony plains of La Crau, an arid enough area to be classified as a semi-desert.

Conservation

All of the country's natural habitats have more or less been degraded by human activities, and contemporary problems include habitat loss and degradation, through drainage, tourist developments and urbanisation, as well as hunting, disturbance and pollution. Conservation is still a relatively new concept in France and the membership of the Ligue Française pour la Protection des Oiseaux (LPO) reached just 25,000 by the end of 1997. LPO deserve credit for recruiting this many supporters, but considering the British equivalent amassed a million members by the same time, the membership of LPO is still a sad reflection on the general public's attitude towards the environment in France. Much work needs to be done to ensure a future for the eight threatened and near-threatened species, as well as the relatively common and widespread birds which occur on mainland France. Dealing with the hunting problem would be a good place to start, for numerous species are persecuted beyond belief by the massed ranks of khaki-clad *chasseurs*. There are more 'hunters' in France than any other European country and nowhere in Europe is the problem of pollution from discharged lead shot so accute as it is in La Camargue, one of the region's most important places for birds. This archaic activity should have been stopped decades ago and yet the French Parliament continued to flout the European Union's Directive on the Conservation of Wild Birds, under pressure from the hunting lobby, up to the end of the 1990s and even passed a law in July 1998 which extended the hunting season.

Bird Species

About 400 bird species are recorded on an almost annual basis in France, of which over 250 have been known to breed. Notable species include Greater Flamingo, Lammergeier, Cinereous Vulture*, Little Bustard*, Slender-billed Gull, Pin-tailed Sandgrouse, Great Spotted Cuckoo, Wallcreeper, Moustached and Spectacled Warblers, White-winged Snowfinch, Alpine Accentor and Citril Finch.

Expectations

During the spring and summer it is possible to see about 160 species in a week on a trip to the La Camargue area, and a visit to the same area during the winter is likely to produce about 110 species. During early September it is possible to see 160–180 species in a week to ten days on a trip which combines the La Camargue area with the Pyrenées. Only up to 100 species are possible in a week based solely in the Pyrenées at this time.

NORD-PAS-DE-CALAIS AND PICARDIE

These two regions in extreme northern France do not support a great wealth of birdlife compared the south, but many British birders often nip across the Straits of Dover for a day or a weekend in order to look for a number of species which are rare on the north side of the English Channel, just 21 miles (34 km) away. Such birds include Black Woodpecker, Zitting Cisticola and Crested Lark, as well as occasional European Bee-eaters.

Regular Summer Visitors and Resident Species

European Honey-buzzard, Pied Avocet, Snowy Plover, Mediterranean Gull, Black Woodpecker, Eurasian Golden-Oriole, Bluethroat ('White-spotted' *cyanecula*), Short-toed Treecreeper, Zitting Cisticola, Melodious and Icterine Warblers, Crested Tit, Crested Lark, European Serin.

(Other species regularly recorded here include seabirds (see below), Cattle Egret, Little Bittern, Eurasian Spoonbill, Black-winged Stilt, European Bee-eater, Savi's Warbler, Great Reed-Warbler, Horned Lark, Common Rosefinch and Snow Bunting. Rarities have included Red-necked Stint, Buff-breasted Sandpiper and Audouin's Gull*. Feral species include White Stork.)

There are regular vehicular ferries between Dover and Calais but by travelling through the Channel Tunnel on *le Shuttle* it is possible to gain about two hours birding time in France. Seawatching can be spectacular at **Le Clipon**, the end of the harbour wall at Dunkerque (Nord), especially during northerly to northwesterly gales, when 236 Leach's Storm-Petrels, 455 Pomarine Skuas and 28 Sabine's Gulls have all been seen on different single days. At **Calais** Eurasian Golden-Oriole, Short-toed Treecreeper and Icterine Warbler occur in the small wood behind the Tioxide factory which is situated off the first roundabout from the ferry terminal, and Crested Lark occurs around the car parks at the hover and ferry ports. In 1997 two pairs of Zitting Cisticola bred around the pools near **Les Hemmes de Marck**, which can be reached by heading east from Calais along the coastal track. The best site for Snowy Plover near Calais is **Platier d'Oye**, a reserve with three hides and a nature trail which has also attracted rarities such as Red-necked Stint and Buff-breasted Sandpiper. To reach here head east from Calais for 16 km to Oye-Plage then turn off to les Dunes d'Oye and head towards the coast, from where the reserve is signposted. Bluethroat breeds at **Marais de Guines**, a reserve about 10 km south of Calais on the east side of the D127. To reach here, just before Guines turn southeast on to the D248E and take the path beyond the gate just west of St Joseph's Hospice. Bluethroat also breeds at **Romelaere**, another reserve near St-Omer,

NORD-PAS-DE-CALAIS and PICARDIE

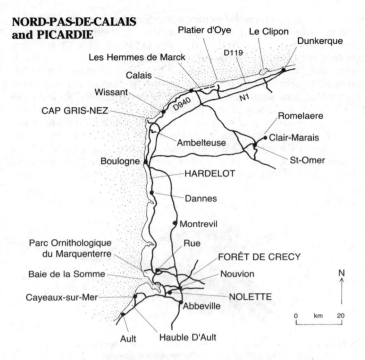

about 40 km southeast of Calais, where other species recorded include Little Bittern (three pairs in 1995) and Great Reed-Warbler. To reach here head northeast from St-Omer towards Clair-Marais and look for the reserve visitor centre 400 m past St Bernard's church.

Other sites worth visiting to the west and south of Calais, and accessible from the D940, include: (i) **Cap Blanc Nez**, 11 km southwest of Calais, where Common Rosefinch has bred along the north side of the road to the monument; (ii) **Wissant Marsh**, a reserve about 20 km southwest of Calais, reached by turning northwest south of Wissant. Bluethroat and Savi's Warbler occur here; (iii) **Cap Gris-Nez**, about 30 km southwest of Calais, is a good place to look for passage migrants and to seawatch from; (iv) **Ambelteuse**, about 40 km southwest of Calais, reached by turning inland on to a narrow lane just south of a small World War II museum, just north of Ambelteuse. One hundred and fifty m along here check the area around the stream for European Bee-eaters, two to three pairs of which bred in this area in 1996–98 (but not in 1999); (v) **Boulogne**, where the harbour and le Portel beach on the south side of the port are excellent for gulls (an Audouin's Gull* was present here from mid-June to late July 1995) and Crested Lark (on the beach); (vi) **Hardelot**, about 50 km southwest of Calais, where the area around the golf course clubhouse and nearby houses is excellent for Crested Tit and European Serin, and the Dunes de Mont St Frieux, a few km further south, is worth checking for Black Woodpecker; (vii) **Parc Ornithologique du Marquenterre**, a reserve which is signposted from Rue, about 90 km southwest of Calais. The lagoons here are worth checking for Snowy Plover, and the surrounding woods seem set to be colonised by Black Woodpecker. Feral White Storks are also present; (viii) to the south of Marquenterre the estuary of the **Somme** is best viewed from le Crotoy. Cattle Egret and Great Reed-Warbler are both possible in the La Basee marshes alongside the D4, a few km north of le Crotoy; (ix) **Forêt de Crecy**, about 90 km southwest of Calais, which supports Black Woodpecker, Short-toed Treecreeper and Melodious Warbler. A network of roads and tracks enables easy access to this fine wood which lies east of Forest Montiers, southeast of Rue; (x) **Nolette**, accessible from the N1 via Nouvion and Sailly Bray, where about 14 pairs of Bluethroat bred in 1997, mostly in the marshy area near Pont-le-Dien picnic site, 1 km northwest of Nolette; and, finally (xi) **Hauble D'Ault**, a series of coastal pools between Cayeaux-sur-Mer and Ault, south of the Somme, where Great Reed-Warbler has been recorded. Turn west off the D940 at Haute-but to reach the pools, most of which lie to the north towards Cayeaux.

The imposing Black Woodpecker, one of the world's largest woodpeckers, is widespread throughout mainland Europe

There is a small breeding colony of Collared Flycatchers in the **Argonne**, a ridge of forested hills 70 km east of Reims in northeast France. Black Stork, Red and Black Kites, Booted Eagle, and Middle Spotted, Black and Grey-headed Woodpeckers also occur here. One place worth checking for Collared Flycatcher is in the forest on the east side of the D20 about 3 km south of Thiaucourt (30 km northwest of Bar-le-Duc) and around the playground on the west side of the D20 about 2 km south of Thiaucourt. For close-up views of Crested Larks head for the Aire Champs Roland Service Station on the A26, 20 km north of Reims, where they feed on hand-outs.

The mainly mixed forests in the 170-km^2 **Forêt de Fontainebleau**, 60 km southeast of Paris, supports six species of woodpecker, including Middle Spotted, Black and Grey-headed (as well as a feral population of Reeves's Pheasant, left over from the days when this was a hunting reserve). Any of the woodpeckers could be seen virtually anywhere here, but the best previously productive areas are all within the 'Route Ronde' south of the town and less than 5 km from the centre of Fontainebleau. They include: (i) the track south from alongside the N152 where it passes under the Aqueduc de la Vanne near the show-jumping arena; (ii) the area just north of where the Aqueduc de la Vanne crosses the N7; (iii) head west along the D63E, a small turning just south of where the Aqueduc de la Vanne crosses the N7, for 1 km, to an area of pines and bird both sides of the road; and (iv) walk south from the cottage situated on the south side of the road about halfway between the D63E and N7 along the ring road.

LAC DU DER-CHANTECOQ

Almost all of the Common Cranes which breed in Scandanavia and northwest Russia, and winter in Spain, up to 30,000 of them, use this reservoir and the farmland which surrounds it as a staging site, and especially from late February to early March and late October to mid-November bugling flocks of these birds can be seen flying in from the fields, where food is put out for them, to roost on the islands in the largest artificial waterbody in France. A few thousand are also usually present during the winter when there are also a few White-tailed Eagles* present.

Regular Winter Visitors and Resident Species
Red-necked Grebe, Whooper and Bewick's Swans, Bean Goose ('Taiga' *fabalis*), Smew, Red Kite, White-tailed Eagle*, Common Crane, Middle Spotted, Black and Grey-headed Woodpeckers, Crested Tit.

(Other species recorded here include Great Egret and Rough-legged Buzzard)

The best places to watch Common Cranes coming in to roost at **Lac du Der-Chantecoq** are usually at the northern end of the Digue de Nord, the marina east of Giffaumont-Champaubert and in the area across the bay accessible via the D55. The latter area is also good for White-tailed Eagle*, as is **Lac du Temple**, where small numbers of Great Egrets have also wintered, **Lac de la Forêt d'Orient,** which is situated about 17 km east of Troyes alongside the N19 (the northeastern end, where there is

FRENCH JURA

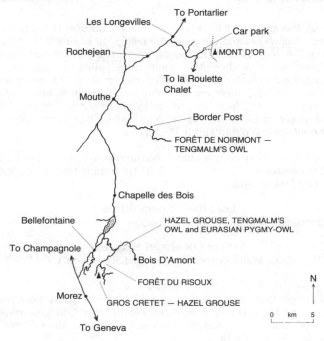

177

a hide, is the best), and **Lac Amance**, further east, where up to three eagles have been present at any one time. The woods near **Trois Fontaine**, north of St Dizier, support six species of woodpecker, as do the woods surrounding the **Étang de Lindre**, east of St Dizier, but Black Woodpecker may be easier to find in the woods north of **Frampas**.

Accommodation: St Dizier (near Lac du Der-Chantecoq). Giffaumont-Champaubert.

The **French Jura**, the mountain massif north of the French Alps, supports Hazel Grouse, Eurasian Pygmy-Owl, Tengmalm's Owl, Wallcreeper and Citril Finch. To look for Wallcreeper, as well as Hazel Grouse and Citril Finch bird the slopes of **Mont D'Or**, south of Pontarlier. To look for all of the above except Wallcreeper head for the **Forêt du Risoux** next to the border with Switzerland, south of Mont D'Or, and bird the 2–3 km stretch of forest at the top of the steep road out of Bois D'Amont, and around Gros Cretet.

In 1989 European Bee-eaters colonised the valleys of the **Allier** and middle **Loire**, northwest of Lyon in central France, and subsequently increased in numbers so spectacularly that by 1996 there were 239 pairs in the area. Northeast of Lyon, the hundreds of lakes between the valleys of the Rhône and Saone, around **Villars-les-Dombes**, support a fine selection of breeding waterbirds, including Squacco Heron and Whiskered Tern.

FRENCH ALPS

Although the alpine avifauna includes Rock Partridge, Hazel Grouse, Eurasian Pygmy-Owl and Eurasian Nutcracker, all of which are absent from the Pyrenées (p. 188), the mountains of central Europe are devoid of vultures, although attempts to reintroduce Lammergeier started to meet with success in the late 1990s. Many birders have avoided this area in the past because there are no vultures and because birds are so much harder to find here than in the Pyrenées but the return of the 'bone-breaker' to the birdlife of the Alps could tempt more birders to visit these beautiful mountains in the future.

The birds listed below occur during the summer unless otherwise indicated. All routes above 2000 m (6562 ft) are usually blocked by snow until early June at least.

Localised Specialities
Rock Partridge.

Other Localised Species
Rock Ptarmigan, Wallcreeper, White-winged Snowfinch, Citril Finch.

Others
Golden Eagle, Black and Hazel Grouse, Alpine Swift, Black Woodpecker, Eurasian Nutcracker, Red-billed and Yellow-billed Choughs, Rufous-tailed and Blue Rock-Thrushes, Eurasian Crag-Martin, Rock Petronia, Alpine Accentor, Rock Bunting.

Other Wildlife

Wild boar, chamois, ibex (reintroduced), Alpine marmot, mouflon. The
alpine meadows between La Grave and Col du Lautaret on the N91
southeast of Grenoble lie at the heart of the richest botanical area in
France.

(Other species recorded here include Lammergeier (a pair of reintroduced birds bred successfully from 1997 to 1999, in the Aravis-Mont
Blanc area in the Haute-Savoie region) and Common Rosefinch, which
bred for the first time in 1997, in the Giffre Valley, also in the Haute-
Savoie region.)

There are numerous marked trails in the French Alps, most of which
connect up with *gites* and refuge huts. Many of the species listed above
occur throughout this huge area and could be encountered almost anywhere there is suitable habitat. However, certain parts may be better
than others and these are outlined, roughly from north the south, as follows:

(i) the **Haute-Savoie** region, around the famous ski-resort of Cham-
onix and Mont Blanc, is a good area to look for reintroduced Lammergeiers and Rock Partridge; (ii) **Vanoise National Park**, south of Bourg-
St-Maurice, is a high-altitude region which rises to 3852 m (12,638 ft) at
La Grande Casse and supports Wallcreeper and White-winged
Snowfinch. The Col de L'Iseran at 2270 m (7448 ft) on the D902 south of
Val D'Isere is the best place to start; (iii) the **Col du Coq**, where Wallcreeper and Citril Finch occur. To reach here turn east off the D512
about 1.5 km south of La Diat, north of Grenoble. At the ski-resort take
the upper of the two tracks on the left and continue for about 300 m,
forking right at the junction. Pass through the 1434 m (4705 ft) col and
descend for about 500 m on the road to the parking space on the left
before the first major bend by the 'Chiens Interdit' signpost. About 100
m down the road from the parking space take the trail on the left up to
an area of large rocks (to the right of the path) where Alpine Accentor
and Citril Finch occur. Further on, follow the signpost to 'Trou de Glaz'
along a trail which leads to a rock face (about 45 minutes walk) where
Wallcreeper may be seen. About 100 m beyond the large cave along
this path there is a wire 'ladder' sunk into the rock face which enables
access to the limestone plateau above, known as Dent de Crolles,
where White-winged Snowfinch, Alpine Accentor and Rock Bunting
occur. Allow a full day if birding this area thoroughly; (iv) **Le Som**, a
good area for Hazel Grouse. Take the D520 from St-Pierre-de-Chartreuse
to La Correrie (musée du Monastere) and park in the car park on the
left. From here it is a three-hour walk to near the summit of Le Som
through extensive woods where the grouse occurs. Local maps are
available free from the Office de Tourisme in the square of St-Pierre-de-
Chartreuse; (v) the area near the village of **St-Christophe**, which is a
particularly good place to look for Rock Partridge. To reach the village
turn south off the N91 Grenoble-Briancon road 8 km east of Le Bourg-
d'Oisans on to the D530. Once out of the village turn left to reach a car
park. Walk up the track which runs alongside the torrent du Diable from
here then turn left on to a trail which crosses a ridge before reaching
rocky outcrops and scree slopes below a radio mast—the best area for
the partridge; (vi) the **Col du Lautaret**, on the N91 between Grenoble
and Briancon, where White-winged Snowfinch and Alpine Accentor

FRENCH ALPS

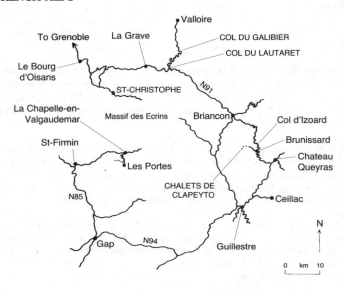

occur; (vii) the **Col du Galibier**, at 2545 m (8350 ft) on the D902 north of Col du Lautaret, where White-winged Snowfinch occurs in the cafe car park; (viii) the **Chalets de Clapeyto**, which can be reached from Col du Lautaret by heading southeast to Briancon. Continue on the D902 to the village of Brunissard then turn west in response to the 'Les Esquirousses' signpost and continue past the Du Planet campsite to the car park at the end of the track where Citril Finch occurs. Proceed from here on foot to the Chalets de Clapeyto, checking the rock-faces for Wallcreeper, and climb above the chalets to look for Rock Ptarmigan and White-winged Snowfinch; (ix) **Les Portes**, another good site for Rock Partridge. Between Grenoble and Gap turn east off the N85 on to the D985a to St-Firmin and continue to the village of La Chapelle-en-Valgaudemar. Turn south out of the village, just past Hotel du Mont Olan, and a couple of km up the road park in the parking space on the right-hand side of the road just before Les Portes. Walk into Les Portes and turn right on to a footpath (with an obscured signpost) which leads up the hillside. Follow this to just above the tree-line then turn left on to a smaller path which ascends Chatelard Belvedere where Rock Part-ridge occurs on the higher slopes, along with Black Grouse and Rufous-tailed Rock-Thrush; and (x) **Vercors Regional Natural Park**, south-west of Grenoble, which rises to 2341 m (7681 ft) at Grand Veymont, high enough to support Rock Ptarmigan and Wallcreeper.

In the Maritime Alps, 1.5 hours by road north of Nice, Lammergeier is also being reintroduced to **Mercantour National Park**, where Eurasian Nutcracker, White-winged Snowfinch and Citril Finch also occur. Boreon, which is situated at 1524 m (5000 ft), is a good base, and the Col du Lombardie, a high road pass at 2286 m (7500 ft) straddling the border with Italy, is one of the best birding areas.

Rock Partridge is one of Europe's few endemic birds, and, arguably, the hardest to find, for it primarily inhabits the remotest high tops

MASSIF CENTRAL

This sparsely populated upland in south-central France, which rises to 1886 m (6188 ft) at Puy de Sancy, and is characterised by spectacular deep, forested gorges, supports a superb range of raptors, including Eurasian Griffon and Cinereous Vulture*, both of which have been successfully reintroduced. Eurasian Griffons have been reintroduced since the 1970s and by the end of the 1990s at least 75 pairs were present. Cinereous Vultures* have been reintroduced since 1992 and by the end of the decade at least six pairs were present.

The species listed below occur during the summer unless otherwise indicated.

Localised Species
Cinereous Vulture* (reintroduced).

Others
Red Kite, Egyptian Vulture, Eurasian Griffon (reintroduced), Short-toed, Golden, Bonelli's and Booted Eagles, Eurasian Eagle-Owl, Alpine Swift, Black Woodpecker, Red-billed Chough, Rufous-tailed and Blue Rock-Thrushes, Eurasian Crag-Martin, Orphean Warbler, Rock Petronia, Alpine Accentor, Rock Bunting.

Many of the species listed above occur throughout this huge area but the best sites are as follows: (i) the area northeast (along the D10 and D12) and south of the town of **St-Flour**, about 70 km south of Clermont-Ferrand, is excellent for raptors; (ii) **Cevennes National Park**, between Mende and Ales, is also a top spot for raptors, particularly the Corniche des Cevennes, a 50-km-long ridge famous for the dinosaur footprints near St Laurent and traversed by a road, and the Sentier des Botanistes walk just below the summit of Mont Aigoual which is a great place to see Egyptian Vulture. The slopes of Mont Lozere, accessible via the road through Col de Finiels, support Alpine Accentor and Rock Bunting; (iii) arguably, the best birding area within the Massif Central, especially for Eurasian Griffons, is the 30-km-long and up to 600 m (1969 ft) deep **Gorges du Tarn**, which is traversed by the D907 northeast of Millau towards Florac; (iv) Eurasian Griffons and Cinereous Vultures* occur in

MASSIF CENTRAL

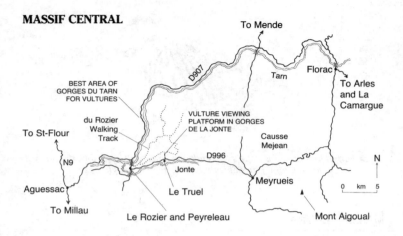

the **Gorges de la Jonte**, which joins the Gorges du Tarn at Le Rozier, and there is a vulture viewing platform near Le Truel, about 10 km east of Le Rozier on the D996 known as Belvedere des Vantures. There is also a visitor centre here which is open from 1000 to 1800 hours daily from mid-March to mid-November (tel: 0565 626969); and (v) the **Millau Causses**, three limestone plateaus just east of Millau on the N9/E11, where Orphean Warbler occurs.

Accommodation: Cocures. Pont du Montvert—Hotel la Source du Tarn. St Enimie.

LA CAMARGUE

The 750-km^2 Rhône Delta on the Mediterranean coast of southern France is without doubt one of top five birding sites in Europe. Although much of the northern half of the delta has been turned over to agriculture, the beaches, dunes, marshes, salinas, scrub and woods in the southern half support over 100 breeding species, including Greater Flamingo (between 6,000 and 13,000 pairs, about a quarter of which remain throughout the year), Glossy Ibis (four pairs in 1996, the first time this species bred successfully in the 20th century), Collared Pratincole (at its only breeding site in France, but just six pairs were present in 1997), Slender-billed Gull (500–900 pairs have bred annually since 1993), Great Spotted Cuckoo, and Moustached and Spectacled Warblers. La Camargue is also a major resting and refuelling site for masses of passage migrants (up to 3,500 Snowy Plovers have been recorded during the autumn) and a wintering site for tens of thousands of waterbirds, including 12,000 Gadwall, 50,000 Common Teals, 16,000 Northern Shovelers, up to 6,000 Red-crested Pochards, and about 200 Great Egrets, hence around 340 species have been recorded in total.

The species listed below occur during the summer unless otherwise indicated. The *mistral*, a cold, dry wind from the north, which can reach speeds of up to 90 mph (145 kph), occasionally spoils the birding experience, especially during the winter.

Localised Specialities
Slender-billed Gull.

Other Localised Species
Greater Flamingo, Great Spotted Cuckoo.

Others
Cory's ('Scopoli's' *diomedea*) and Mediterranean Shearwaters, Red-crested Pochard, Great and Cattle Egrets, Squacco Heron, Black-crowned Night-Heron, Glossy Ibis, Red Kite (winter), Short-toed Eagle, Black-winged Stilt, Pied Avocet, Collared Pratincole, Snowy Plover, Mediterranean Gull, Whiskered and Gull-billed Terns, European Bee-eater, European Roller (scarce), Moustached and Spectacled Warblers, Calandra Lark, Yellow Wagtail ('Spanish' *iberiae*).

(Other species recorded here on a fairly regular basis include Ferruginous Duck* (winter), Western Reef-Egret (summers 1988–1998, including one to two dark morphs in 1998), White Stork, White-tailed Eagle* (winter), Long-legged Buzzard (winter), Greater Spotted* (two to three in winters 1997–98 and 1998–99) and Booted (about ten in winter 1997–98) Eagles, Marsh (regular on passage in small numbers—32 in August 1999 is the record), Terek and Broad-billed Sandpipers, White-winged and Caspian Terns, Alpine and Pallid Swifts, and Pine Bunting (four in early 1999, several in early 1998 and up to eight in early 1997 at Albaron and elsewhere/wintering here has probably been regular since at least the 1960s when five were ringed during the winter of 1965–66). Rarities have included Spanish Eagle*, Slender-billed Curlew*, Audouin's Gull* and Marmora's Warbler (three to four in mid-April 1997, part of a small influx into southern France).)

Arles is the gateway to La Camargue. Follow signposts for Saintes-Maries-de-la-Mer to start birding in the western half, signposts for Salin-de-Giraud to start birding in the eastern half, and signposts for Gallician, west of St-Gilles, to start at the Petit Camargue. *En route* to Saintes-Maries-de-la-Mer on the D570 look out for Collared Pratincole north of Albaron, although the best place in La Camargue for this species is along the track which leads southeast from **Paty de la Trinite** to Domaine de Mejanes. The seafront at **Saintes-Maries-de-la-Mer** is good for gulls and, during strong onshore winds, shearwaters. Head east from here along **La Digue** (the embankment built in 1867 to keep the sea out) to look for migrant passerines (especially by the lighthouse) and Spectacled Warblers in the *salicornia* scrub which surrounds the small salinas where Slender-billed Gull is possible. Back at Domaine de Mejanes or Albaron head for the D37 which passes by some of the best marshes in La Camargue, along the north side of **Étang de Vaccares**. The marshes at the northwest end of the étang, where there is an observation tower, are particularly good for Glossy Ibis. Further east along the D37 turn north to reach the small settlement of **Mas D'Agon**, 1 km beyond which the roadside marshes are usually full of herons and terns, and the reedbeds support Moustached Warbler. A little further north, just past the canal, scan for pratincoles. Further east along the D37 turn south to reach **La Capelliere**, the main reserve visitor centre which is situated at the east side of Étang du Vaccares and is open 0900–1200 and 1400–1700 hours, Monday to Saturday. There is a nature reserve here where Western Reef-Egret is a regular visitor to the pools in front of

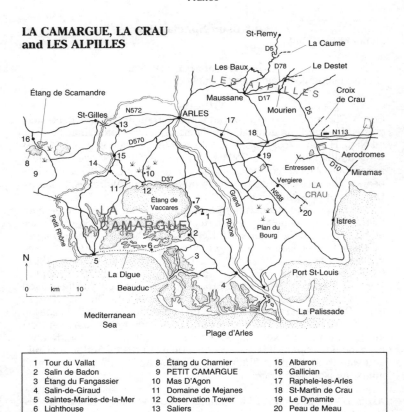

LA CAMARGUE, LA CRAU and LES ALPILLES

1	Tour du Vallat	8	Étang du Charnier	15	Albaron
2	Salin de Badon	9	PETIT CAMARGUE	16	Gallician
3	Étang du Fangassier	10	Mas D'Agon	17	Raphele-les-Arles
4	Salin-de-Giraud	11	Domaine de Mejanes	18	St-Martin de Crau
5	Saintes-Maries-de-la-Mer	12	Observation Tower	19	Le Dynamite
6	Lighthouse	13	Saliers	20	Peau de Meau
7	La Capelliere	14	Paty de la Trinite		

the hides. South of La Capelliere turn east towards the Tour du Vallat research centre and scan the marshes to the north of the road for marsh terns which may be present in large numbers, along with plenty of bee-eaters. The area south of Tour du Vallat is good for Greater Spotted Eagle* during the winter.

Back on the road south from La Capelliere there is another visitor centre known as **Salin de Badon** where the nature trail passes several pools worth checking for crakes and shorebirds such as migrant Marsh Sandpipers. South of here turn west to reach the **Étang du Fangassier** where there is an observation point for viewing the flamingo colony, although they are what seems to be miles away. From the car park at the north end of the etang it is possible to walk west along La Digue, past the lighthouse, to the southern end of Étang de Vaccares. Together with **Étang du Galabert** the Étang du Fangassier area is arguably the best in La Camargue for migrant shorebirds. Slender-billed Gull occurs alongside the road southwest from here to Beauduc but the best place in La Camargue to see this strange bird is at the pools southwest of **La Palissade** in the far southeast corner of the delta, beyond Salin-de-Giraud.

The best place to look for European Roller in La Camargue (this species is more likely to be seen in nearby La Crau, p. 185) is at **Marais**

des Saliers, a few km south along the east bank of Petit Rhône, east of St-Gilles. Further west, the extensive reedbeds between the Étangs du Charnier and Scamandre in the **Petit Camargue** support most of the species which occur in La Camargue proper. From Gallician look out for a reed-cutters car park on the right after crossing the raised bridge. Park here and walk south.

Accommodation: Arles area—plenty to choose from, including six campsites. Saintes-Maries-de-la-Mer—Dauphin Bleu (hotel with seaview). Beaucaire—Hotel Robinson.

LA CRAU

The semi-arid stony plains of the 500-km² La Crau, much of which has been destroyed or degraded by continuing agricultural intensification, still supports several hundred Little Bustards*, up to 300 Eurasian Thick-knees, an isolated population of about 170 pairs of Pin-tailed Sandgrouse, and a few Great Spotted Cuckoos and European Rollers.

The species listed below occur during the summer unless otherwise indicated. Despite the presence of so many Little Bustards* they can be very difficult to locate and the best time to look for them is in early May when the males are displaying.

Localised Specialities
Pin-tailed Sandgrouse.

Other Localised Species
Little Bustard*, Great Spotted Cuckoo.

Others
Red-crested Pochard, Red (winter) and Black Kites, Egyptian Vulture, Lesser Kestrel* (48 pairs in 1997), Red-legged Partridge, Eurasian Thick-knee, European Bee-eater, European Roller, Calandra Lark.

(Other species recorded here include Short-toed Eagle, Collared Pratincole, Lesser Grey Shrike, Orphean Warbler and Richard's Pipit (up to 16 at Entressen in early 1998, with one Blyth's Pipit, and four in early 1999).)

La Crau is about 25 km southeast of Arles. During the summer, birding is at its best here early in the day, before the heat-haze spoils viewing conditions. To reach the **Croix de Crau**, which is arguably the top area, at the east end of La Crau, turn north on to the D5 at its intersection with the N113, then take the track east, or take the track north from the long building (ask for permission) on the north side of the N113 about 1.5 km east of the D5 intersection. This area, which is particularly good for Little Bustard* and Pin-tailed Sandgrouse, especially during the winter, is being viewed as a potential reserve, so, ironically, access may be restricted in the future, making it more difficult to see the specialities. The Aerodrome de Salon-Eyguieres, reached by turning north off the N113 on to the D569, east of Croix de Crau, is another good place for Little Bustard*. The disused aerodrome known as **Piste de Vallon**, which is situated to the east of the D5 about 1 km south of the N113, is also a good site for the bustard and sandgrouse, but, as is the case with a number of areas within La Crau, this is a military zone where access is restricted and trespassing birders have been harshly dealt with in the past. However, there is an old tower here which makes an excellent viewpoint. Four km south of the N113 along the D5 turn west to reach the large rubbish tip at **Entressen** which attracts numerous Black Kites, as well as a few Red Kites and the occasional Egyptian Vulture.

Away from Spain, La Crau is the only place in Europe where the beautiful Pin-tailed Sandgrouse occurs

To bird the west end of La Crau turn south at Raphele-les-Arles on to the D83d. Once across the dual-carriageway stop at the farm after about 1.5 km along here and check the pylons along the farm entrance road for a White Stork's nest. Continue along the D83d through an excellent area for European Roller then head east towards Le Dynamite, then south on the N568 to the extensive marshes of the **Plan du Bourg**, worth checking for Collared Pratincole, or south to Vergiere and the **Peau de Meau** reserve where Little Bustard* occurs. It may be necessary to obtain a permit to visit this reserve from the Ecomuseum in St-Martin de Crau. Naturally, throughout La Crau, it is worth exploring any potentially good areas so long as the military zones are avoided.

LES ALPILLES

These limestone hills east of Arles, which rise to 387 m (1270 ft), support a number of species which are unlikely to be seen elsewhere in the Camargue area, including Eurasian Eagle-Owl and Blue Rock-Thrush, and, during the winter, even Wallcreeper is possible.

The species listed below occur during the summer unless otherwise indicated.

Localised Species
Wallcreeper (winter).

Others
Short-toed and Bonelli's Eagles, Eurasian Eagle-Owl, Alpine Swift, Blue Rock-Thrush, Eurasian Crag-Martin, Sardinian and Subalpine Warblers.
  (Other species recorded here include Egyptian Vulture, Rock Petronia (winter), Alpine Accentor (winter) and Rock Bunting.)

In the northern outskirts of Arles turn east off the N570 on to the D17, then turn north to **Les Baux**, where, during the winter, Wallcreepers sometimes grace the steep rock-faces below the ruined Roman rock fortress. The number of these birds wintering in Les Alpilles varies from year to year but at least four were present in February 1998. During the summer the area below the fortress is a good place to see Alpine Swift, Blue Rock-Thrush and Sardinian Warbler. To reach here park at the south side of town and take the trail along the hillside by the fortress. Other good spots for Wallcreeper include the road which runs along the Val d'Enfer to the west, the route from the castle to the cathedral, and **La Caume**, a prominent mountain with a TV relay station stuck on top, northeast of Les Baux, where Egyptian Vulture and Bonelli's Eagle are most likely to be seen. To reach La Caume head east from Les Baux on the D27A then turn north on to the D5 and park just north of the highest point of the road. From here it is a 3-km walk through maquis full of Subalpine Warblers, along the relay station service road to the wardened viewpoint at the southern edge of the summit. Eurasian Eagle-Owl has also been recorded here, in the gully northeast of the relay station, and, during the winter, Alpine Accentor is possible. There may be over 30 pairs of eagle-owls in Les Alpilles but, despite its size, this massive owl is still an extremely difficult bird to see. The best two places to try are: (i) along the road between **Maussane** and Le Destet. Head east out of Maussane and turn north immediately on to the D78 towards Le Destet. After about 1.5 km where there are cliffs on both sides of the road park carefully and listen for the owls at dusk; and (ii) north of **Le Destet**, where about 300 m north of the few buildings which make up Le Destet, there is a track which leads east to a chateau (marked by a giant wine barrel). Park carefully about 800 m along here, just after the remains of an iron gate, and scan the cliffs to the south. The best time to try is during February when the owls are at their most vocal. Once *Bubo bubo* has been heard, scan the cliffs it calls from (returning in daylight if necessary, in the hope that it is roosting on an open crag), but remember the deep call can be heard up to 5 km away.

The nearest reliable site to La Camargue for Citril Finch is **Mont Ventoux**, a 1909-m (6263 ft) high outlier of the French Alps, where there is a major ski-resort, about 100 km northeast of Arles. During the

Alpine Swifts are not confined to high mountains. They also occur in towns and cities down to sea level, and in hills such as Les Alpilles, and can even be seen feeding over nearby wetlands such as, in this case, La Camargue

winter, Wallcreeper, White-winged Snowfinch (especially around juniper bushes on the ski slopes) and Alpine Accentor are also possible. To reach here head for Carpentras, northeast of Avignon, then take the D974 (to the right) to Bedoin and continue to reach the road to the summit (usually closed until mid-May at least) where the best places for Citril Finch are around the chalets at Chalet Reynard, 6 km below the summit, and up from there. Other species recorded here include Tengmalm's Owl, Black Woodpecker, Rufous-tailed Rock-Thrush and Rock Bunting.

The wooded Gorge du Gardon at **Pont du Gard**, about 20 km west of Avignon on the D981, is a good place to look for Alpine Swift, Eurasian Crag-Martin and Rock Petronia, all of which breed on the Roman aqueduct (which, during the winter, is worth checking for Wallcreeper).

Birders travelling between La Camargue and the Pyrenées may wish to consider a detour to the **Roussennae** area in Aveyron, where a pair of Black-shouldered Kites bred in 1998, and **Etang du Canet** about 12 km southeast of Perpignan, where three pairs of Purple Swamphen ('Western' *porphyrio*) bred in 1996, the first time this species bred in France.

FRENCH PYRENÉES

The Pyrenées extend for about 400 km from the Bay of Biscay in the west to the Mediterranean in the east, along the border between France and Spain, rising to 3298 m (10,820 ft) at Vignemale on the border west of Gavarnie, and to 3404 m (11,168 ft) at Pic de Aneto in Spain. The north-facing slopes of France are, for the most part, wetter than those facing south in Spain, and the lush pastures of the French foothills give way to deciduous woodland, pine forest and montane meadows at the foot of spectacular rock walls, scree slopes and jagged snow-capped peaks. The fantastic scenery is completed by such brilliant birds as Lammergeier and Wallcreeper, making this one of the most exhilarating birding areas in Europe.

The species listed below occur during the summer unless otherwise indicated. Most high-altitude roads are blocked by snow until May at least, and Gavarnie is very busy during its summer festival which takes place in early July.

Localised Specialities
Lammergeier.

Other Localised Species
Wallcreeper, White-winged Snowfinch, Citril Finch.

Others
Egyptian Vulture, Eurasian Griffon, Short-toed, Golden and Bonelli's Eagles, Black Woodpecker, Red-billed and Yellow-billed Choughs, Rufous-tailed Rock-Thrush, Eurasian Crag-Martin, Alpine Accentor, Rock Bunting.

Other Wildlife
Chamois, Alpine marmot, beech and pine martens. Late June–early July is the best time for plants and butterflies, when it is possible to see many

of the 50 or so endemic plants and 70–80 species of butterfly (out of 100 or so), including over 40 species in single large meadows.

(Other species recorded here include passage migrants (mainly in September) such as Black and White Storks, Red and Black Kites, Booted Eagle, Eleonora's Falcon and European Bee-eater. Rare residents include Rock Ptarmigan, Eurasian Capercaillie and White-backed Woodpecker (probably fewer than 100 pairs in the whole Pyrenées).

All of the top birds occur around the small town of **Gavarnie**, nestled below the awesome rock walls of the Cirque de Gavarnie, at 1350 m (4429 ft), and accessible from Toulouse via Tarbes. On the way up look out for Bonelli's Eagle above Luz-St Sauveur and once at Gavarnie watch out for Lammergeiers drifting over the town. Don't fret if you haven't seen any before leaving town for there are plenty nearby. At Gavarnie turn right to head for Port de Gavarnie and the Valle de Oussoue, or left to reach the car parks where the trails up to the Cirque de Gavarnie and Espagnuettes begin. The road to **Port de Gavarnie**, which is usually open only from mid-June to late September, ascends to a ski centre (where White-winged Snowfinch and Alpine Accentor occur along the ski-lifts) and the Port de Gavarnie car park at 2270 m (7448 ft) where Alpine Accentors are virtually guaranteed. Look for them hiding under the cars. Lammergeiers have been seen dropping bones on to the hilltop adjacent to the car park, which is also a good place to look for small flocks of snowfinches. There are great birds everywhere here, including plenty of Eurasian Griffons, but the *piece de resistance* lies at the end of the rough trail which leads from the car park across the scree slopes and a cascade to the cafe at the Refuge Sarradets (where Yellow-billed Choughs, snowfinches and Alpine Accentors are all very tame), then up over a glacier to a monumental gap in the mountain wall above, known as **Breche de Roland**, at 2807 m (9209 ft), where Alpine Swifts zoom through, and onwards, to the right, up to a pinnacle known as La Doigt, on the Spanish side of the Pyrenées, where the rock walls alongside the trail may be adorned with Wallcreepers. If present, the 'butterfly-bird' may be seen down to just a few paces here. If the road to Port de Gavarnie is closed it may be possible to proceed on foot, although before June an ice-axe and crampons may be needed to reach Wallcreeper country.

The sheer cliffs above Gavarnie in the French Pyrenées are inhabited by the unique Wallcreeper, a highly elusive but truly stunning bird

GAVARNIE

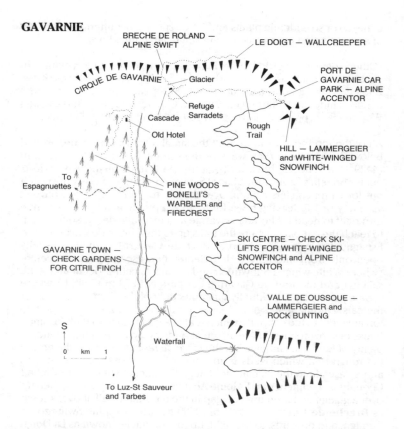

BRECHE DE ROLAND — ALPINE SWIFT

LE DOIGT — WALLCREEPER

CIRQUE DE GAVARNIE

Glacier

PORT DE GAVARNIE CAR PARK — ALPINE ACCENTOR

Refuge Sarradets

Cascade

Rough Trail

Old Hotel

HILL — LAMMERGEIER and WHITE-WINGED SNOWFINCH

To Espagnuettes

PINE WOODS — BONELLI'S WARBLER and FIRECREST

GAVARNIE TOWN — CHECK GARDENS FOR CITRIL FINCH

SKI CENTRE — CHECK SKI-LIFTS FOR WHITE-WINGED SNOWFINCH and ALPINE ACCENTOR

VALLE DE OUSSOUE — LAMMERGEIER and ROCK BUNTING

S

0   km   1

Waterfall

To Luz-St Sauveur and Tarbes

Another fairly good place to look for Wallcreeper is in the **Valle de Oussoue**, to the west of Gavarnie. Try the cliff face directly above the small lay-by on the right-hand side of the road just beyond the village (coming from Gavarnie) where the 'Chaussee Otfoncee' signpost is, and anywhere else which looks suitable. Wallcreeper is a difficult bird to see here, but one bird which is virtually guaranteed is Lammergeier, and anyone who spends at least half a day here is almost certain to see the 'bonebreaker', as well as Eurasian Griffon and Golden Eagle. Other, harder birds to find, include Rufous-tailed Rock-Thrush, Alpine Accentor and Rock Bunting. Wallcreeper also occurs at the **Cirque de Gavarnie** and **Espagnuettes**, along with Lammergeier, Alpine Accentor, Citril Finch (which also occurs in the gardens in Gavarnie) and Rock Bunting.

There are a number of other sites worth visiting in the Gavarnie region. The **Cirque de Troumouse**, high above the tree-line southeast of Gédre, is another good site for raptors, as well as Alpine Accentor. The forest alongside the road up to **Col du Tourmalet** supports Black Woodpecker, and at the col, which is usually accessible via Luz-St Sauveur after mid-June, it is possible to see Rufous-tailed Rock-Thrush and White-winged Snowfinch, which nests in the ski-cable pylons at La Mongie ski-village. The snowfinch and Alpine Accentor also occur alongside the highest road in Europe, that which winds up to the summit of **Pic du Midi** and reaches 2865 m (9400 ft). If they are absent from

FRENCH PYRENÉES

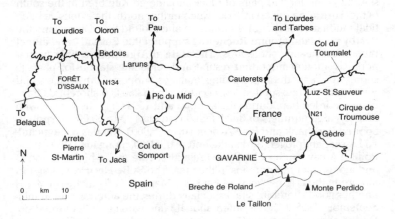

the roadside scour the car park and observatory walls at the peak. In the La Falaise aux Vautours Nature and Raptor Centre area near **Laruns**, west of Luz-St Sauveur, there are plenty of vultures and the centre has remote-control video cameras set up on the cliffs used as a roost site by Eurasian Griffons.

Further west, the small, isolated Pyrenean population of White-backed Woodpecker is centred on the **Forêt d'Issaux**, about 90 km west of Gavarnie in Bearn country. To reach here head south along the N134 which follows the Vallée d'Aspe from Oloron to Col du Somport and turn west at Bedous (where there is a campsite) in response to the 'Osse-en-Aspe' signpost. Pass through Osse and look for the birds on the wooded slopes alongside the road just west of the bridge over a small stream, about 20 minutes by vehicle from Bedous. Black Woodpecker and Citril Finch also occur here, and the high meadows and scree slopes near Arrete also support the finch, as well as Alpine Accentor. To look for Rock Ptarmigan and White-winged Snowfinch turn west off the N134 to **Lescun** and continue to the west end of the loop road beyond this village, where there is a forest track up through woods to Poure Lamary. Park there then continue on foot for about two hours to the Col O'Ansabere where the birds occur on the boulder slopes. Citril Finch also occurs around the tree-line crossed by the roads to **Col de Belagua**, west of the White-backed Woodpecker site, and to **Col du Somport** further south along the N134. The latter is the main entry point to Spain, since it is usually snow-free, and the route to Jaca, the gateway to the Spanish Pyrenées (p. 354). The **Col d'Orgambideska** is the most important valley in the west Pyrenées for migrating raptors. Hundreds of birds, including Red and Black Kites, and Short-toed Eagles, may fly through this low-lying pass in a day during early September, and they are often accompanied by smaller numbers of Black and White Storks.

Accommodation: plenty to choose from, including some excellent campsites.

Birders interested in a wide selection of possible goodies and the chance to find a rarity or two may wish to spend a week or so along the

Biscay Coast. The extreme southwest corner of France would be a good starting point, for two pairs of Black-shouldered Kite bred in the south of the **Aquitaine** region in 1996. Much further north, the extensive intertidal mudflats, marshes and salinas on and around Île d'Oleron and the nearby mainland around **Rochefort** support Little Bustard* and attract numerous passage shorebirds. The **Baie d'Aiguillon**, a little further north, is another important resting and refuelling station for passage shorebirds, and the surrounding marshes support Corn Crake* and Bluethroat ('White-spotted' *cyanecula*). Up to 250,000 shorebirds have been recorded here during the autumn and 150,000 in the winter, with notably large numbers of Black-tailed Godwits (up to 50,000 in spring), Spotted Redshank and Pied Avocet (up to 6,000). Rarities have included Lesser Sandplover. Bird at the end of the D60, along the D46A, at the Point d'Arcay south of La Faute-l'Aiguillon (the major high-tide roost) and along other minor roads in the area. The **Belle-Henriette Lagoon** alongside the D46 between La Faute-sur-Mer and La Tranche-sur-Mer is another good shorebird site, especially during the autumn, and in mid-September 1998 it shot to international fame when a Willet turned up. During strong westerly gales in September as many as 850 or more Sabine's Gulls (7 September 1995) have been seen in the harbour at **Les Sables d'Olonne**, a little further north. The large intertidal **Baie de Bourgneuf**, about 35 km southwest of Nantes, is yet another very important site for passage shorebirds and the surrounding marshes support several hundred pairs of Bluethroat ('White-spotted' *cyanecula*). At Nantes why not turn inland and head for the **Maine-et-Loire** near Angers, the most important breeding area for Corn Crake* in western Europe. A total of 527–549 calling males were present in summer 1998, 400 of which were in the Basses Vallees Angevilles. **La Brenne**, an area of many man-made reedy fishponds and lakes, southeast of Angers via Tours, used to support over 500 pairs of Whiskered Tern, making it the most important area in the country for this species. However, the population crashed and by 1998 only 52 pairs were present (on Étang de la Touche and Étang Masse). Little and Baillon's Crakes, both of which are almost impossible to see, also occur here. La Brenne is about 80 km southeast of Tours midway between Chatellerault and Chateauroux. The best ponds and lakes lie between Rosnay and Mezieres-en-Brenne although which waters are the best varies from year to year. One of the most reliable sites is the Réserve Naturelle de Chérine, about 4 km south of Mezieres by the D17. Baillon's Crake also breeds in the **Sologne**, an extensive area of numerous lakes south of Orleans which is traversed by the N20, D922 and many other minor roads. Back at the Biscay coast, northwest of Nantes, an incredible 1,220 Sabine's Gulls have been recorded in mid-September on the estuary of the **Vilaine**, accessible via La Roche-Bernard and Penestin to the southwest.

The best place to look for scarce migrants and rarities in France is **Île d'Ouessant** (Ushant), an 8-km-long and 3-km-wide island which is situated about 20 km off the northwestern tip of Brittany. Falls have included over 20 Red-breasted Flycatchers, over 200 Firecrests and over 30 Yellow-browed Warblers, and star rarities have included Great Blue Heron, Solitary Sandpiper, Common Nighthawk, Gray's Warbler (Septembers 1913 and 1933) and Northern Parula. On one occasion a Grey-cheeked Thrush was seen feeding alongside an Eyebrowed Thrush while a Pallas's Warbler hovered above. The island also supports breeding Red-billed Chough (about ten pairs) and Dartford Warbler (a few pairs), and Zitting Cisticola is a regular early autumn migrant from the nearby mainland colonies. Seawatching can also be very exciting, especially during northwesterlies in the autumn when species such as Bulwer's Petrel, Little Shearwater and Sabine's Gull have been seen. The best place to seawatch from is below the largest lighthouse, known as Phare de Creac'h. The best way to get to the island from Britain is to take the ferry from Plymouth to Roscoff, then drive to Brest, from where there are flights and a regular ferry service to the island. Most visiting birders—only 30 are usually present at any one time—hire bicycles to get around, but there are also buses and taxis. There are several hotels, a couple of lodges, an excellent campsite at Laimpaul in the centre of the island, and a Bird Observatory with self-catering accommodation. To arrange a stay at the observatory or to purchase the annual bird report (in French) contact The Warden, Centre Ornithologique, F-29242 Île d'Ouessant, Finistere, France (tel: 9848 8265). During the late 1990s birders started to find rarities on **Île de Sein**, a smaller island to the south of Île de O'uessant.

On mainland **Brittany** Zitting Cisticola breeds around pools at the tip of Cap Sizun and the best place to look for Nearctic shorebirds (and Snowy Plover) is the Baie d'Audierne between Pointe du Raz and Pointe de Penmarc'h.

ADDITIONAL INFORMATION

Addresses

Ligue Française pour la Protection des Oiseaux (LPO—the French Association for the Protection of Birds), BP 263, F-17305 Rochefort cedex, France (tel: 4682 1234) publishes the quarterly *Ornithos* magazine. The organisation can also be contacted via LPO (UK), The Anchorage, The Chalks, Chew Magna, Bristol, BS40 8SN, UK.

Please send records of rarities to the CHN, La Corderie Royale, BP 263, F-17305 Rochefort cedex, France. The annual rarities report is published in *Ornithos*, in French with an English summary.

Birdline

Information and hotline (tel: 4379 8188).

Books and papers

Where to watch Birds in Holland, Belgium and Northern France. Van den Berg A and Lafontaine D, 1996. Hamlyn.

A Birdwatching Guide to France South of the Loire. Crozier J, due 2000. Arlequin Press.

A Birdwatching Guide to the Pyrenées. Crozier J, 1998. Arlequin Press.

Finding Birds in Northern France. Gosney D, 1994. Available from BirdGuides (address, p. 395).

Finding Birds in Southern France. Gosney D, 1994. Available from BirdGuides (address, p. 395).

Where to watch birds in France. Ligue Française pour la Protection des Oiseaux, 1992. Helm.

Les Oiseaux Rares en France (Rare Birds in France). Dubois P and Yesou P, 1992. LPO, Chabaud, France.

Les Oiseaux de Camargue. Boutin J, 1993. Lynx Edicions.

GEORGIA

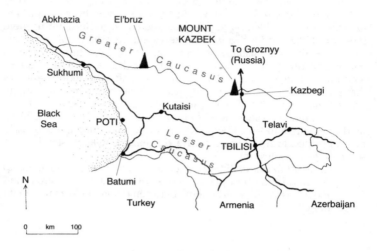

INTRODUCTION

This small former Russian republic, independent since 1991, relatively free from armed conflict since the mid-1990s and safe to visit by the end of the 1990s, is dominated by the Greater and Lesser Caucasus mountain ranges, which support the endemic Caucasian Snowcock, restricted to the Greater Caucasus of Georgia, Azerbaijan and adjacent southern Russia, and the nearly endemic Caucasian Grouse*, which has a distribution extending south from Georgia into Armenia, Azerbaijan, Iran and Turkey. These two star birds can be seen fairly easily in Georgia, along with other regional rarities such as Guldenstadt's Redstart and Great Rosefinch, both of which have isolated populations in the Caucasus.

At 69,700 km^2, Georgia is just over half the size of England and one tenth the size of Texas. It is accessible by air, and by road from northeast Turkey. Tourism is in its infancy hence it is probably best to join one of the tours organised by the Georgian Centre for the Conservation of Wildlife (GCCW), Ambrolauri Str. 4/2, GE-380060, Tbilisi, Georgia (tel: 32 373894; email: gccw@ip.osgf.ge), or enlist the help of a local travel agent to arrange transport and accommodation, in which case try Caucasus Travel Limited, PO Box 160, GE-380008, Tbilisi, Georgia (tel: 32 987400; email: saba@comp.ge). Either way be sure to make use of experienced local guides for they will help to arrange accommodation in private houses or choose suitable campsites, the only forms of accommodation available at most birding sites, and help to minimise possible problems with bandits who still roam some remote parts of the country. Public transport is unreliable and it does not reach many of the best birding areas, hence independent birders will need to hire an expensive vehicle, with a driver. There should be at least one, very expensive, hotel and a couple of guesthouses available in Tbilisi and some basic places elsewhere, but at most birding sites it will be necessary to ask for accommodation with the local people and/or camp. Fresh fruit and vegetables, chicken and wine are usually in good supply in Tbilisi and other large towns, but food can be hard to find in remoter areas where it is best to take all your own supplies to most birding sites. Immunisation against hepatitis, polio and typhoid is recommended. Since the civil war ended in the mid-1990s Georgia has become a friendly and safe country to visit, although as recently as the summer of 1998 a reported 35,000 people were forced to flee the northwestern province of Abkhazia, which is run by a rebel regime. The potential for further conflicts between other rebels and the government remains so it is best to contact the relevant foreign office for information on the latest situation before setting off to Georgia.

The best times to visit are during May or June, after which the high-altitude specialities such as the snowcock and grouse become much more difficult to locate, or September and early October when many waterbirds and raptors migrate south through the country. On the whole, Georgia has warm to hot summers and cold winters.

Inland, the two rugged, snow-capped mountain ranges are separated by the narrow upper Kura Valley, but this widens to form a broad valley in the western lowlands and where the River Kura reaches the Black Sea coast it forms one of a series of small deltas, in between some long sandy beaches. The mountains rise to 5642 m (18,510 ft) at El'bruz on the border with Russia—the highest peak in Europe and Russia—in the Greater Caucasus. It is thanks to the country's mainly mountainous terrain that 30% of the land is still forested. Habitat loss and degradation, and hunting and pollution are the major problems facing the ten threatened and near-threatened species as well as the relatively common and widespread birds which occur in Georgia.

About 360 species have been recorded, of which over 250 have been known to breed. Notable species include Ruddy Shelduck, Lammergeier, Cinereous Vulture*, Pallid Harrier*, Levant Sparrowhawk, Steppe Eagle, Caucasian and Caspian Snowcocks, Chukar, Black Francolin, Caucasian Grouse*, Black-winged Pratincole*, Great Black-headed Gull, White-throated Robin, Guldenstadt's Redstart, Krüper's, Rock and Persian Nuthatches, Wallcreeper, Upcher's Warbler, Chiffchaff ('Caucasian' *lorenzii*), Greenish Warbler ('Green Warbler' *nitidus*), White-winged Snowfinch, Radde's Accentor, Fire-fronted Serin, Crimson-winged Finch, Great Rosefinch and Grey-necked Bunting.

MOUNT KAZBEK

All of Georgia's high-altitude specialities occur on this mountain, which rises to 5041 m (16,539 ft) and is just three hours by road from the Georgian capital, Tbilisi.

The species listed below occur during the summer unless otherwise indicated.

Localised Specialities
Caucasian Snowcock, Caucasian Grouse*, Guldenstadt's Redstart, Fire-fronted Serin, Great Rosefinch.

Other Localised Species
Lammergeier, Wallcreeper, White-winged Snowfinch.

Others
Eurasian Griffon, Golden Eagle, Chukar, Tengmalm's Owl, Alpine Swift, European Bee-eater, Red-billed and Yellow-billed Choughs, Lesser Grey Shrike, Rufous-tailed Rock-Thrush, Isabelline Wheatear, Chiffchaff ('Caucasian' *lorenzii*), Greenish Warbler ('Green Warbler' *nitidus*), Horned Lark, Alpine Accentor, Twite, Rock Bunting.

Other Wildlife
The Greater Caucasus flora is amongst the most diverse on earth.

Mount Kazbek is accessible from the village of Gergeti which is on the opposite side of the River Tergi to the village of Kazbegi, which is situated on the Old Georgian Military Highway three hours by road north of Tbilisi. In 1998 the taxi journey from Tbilisi cost US$10–20. There is little food available in the area so it is best to stock up in Tbilisi. From Gergeti it is a tough 10.5-km (3-hour) hike up to a 2950-m (9679-ft) pass at the southern end of the Gergeti Glacier, beyond which the high-altitude specialities occur, and it is therefore best to camp here for the night in order to be in the right habitat at dawn. Caucasian Snowcock is locally common on steep, stony slopes in the highest reaches. Caucasian Grouse* tends to occur on moderately grazed slopes with juniper and rhododendron scrub. Guldenstadt's Redstart is very scarce just below the snowline.

Accommodation: Gergeti—Bed and Breakfast. Lower down—Gudauri (Hotel).

The arid semi-desert, steppe, savanna-like woodlands and riparian forest in the hills of the David Gareji and Vashlovani areas in the **Iori** upland, in east Georgia, support a wide diversity of breeding species, including Cinereous Vulture*, Pallid Harrier*, Imperial Eagle*, Chukar, Black Francolin, Common Pheasant, European Bee-eater, European Roller, Semicollared Flycatcher, White-throated Robin, Rufous-tailed Scrub-Robin, Finsch's and Isabelline Wheatears, Rock Nuthatch, Spanish Sparrow and Black-headed Bunting. Beware of the poisonous Levantine viper here.

The almost treeless **Javakheti** plateau is an excellent place to visit during September and early October when species recorded have included Pygmy Cormorant*, Great White and Dalmatian* Pelicans, Lesser White-fronted Goose*, Ruddy Shelduck, Ferruginous Duck*, Squacco Heron, Glossy Ibis, Black and White Storks, Pallid Harrier*, Common Crane, Great Snipe*, Marsh and Terek Sandpipers, Red-necked Phalarope, Black-winged Pratincole* and Great Black-headed Gull. In addition, the dormant volcanoes which rise above the lakes and sparsely populated mountain steppe, support Caspian Snowcock, Radde's Accentor and Crimson-winged Finch. The best areas of the plateau are around Lake Khanchali (near Ninotsminda), Lake Burnasheni (near Gorelovka), Lake Madatapa and Mount Madatapa (near Kalinino), and Khidmagala fishponds and Lake Paliastomi (near Poti). The latter lake and nearby town of **Poti** are particularly good places to look for the thousands of migrant raptors which pass along the Black

Sea coast during September and early October. Most of these birds are Black Kites and Common Buzzards, but they also include all four 'European' harriers, Levant Sparrowhawk, eagles such as Greater Spotted*, Steppe and Imperial*, and Red-footed Falcon.

The wetlands and woodlands of the **Kolkheti** region, in the densely populated Black Sea coastal lowlands, also attract numerous migrant waterbirds and raptors.

GERMANY

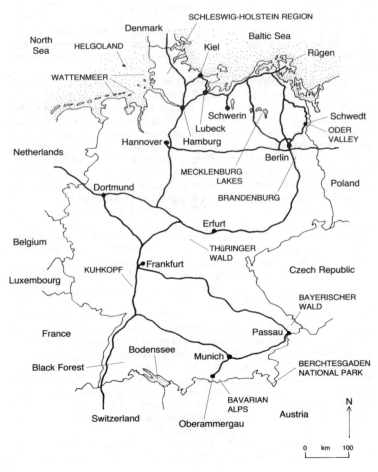

INTRODUCTION

Few foreign birders visit Germany, probably because its notable birds are easier to see in smaller countries where they are also supported by a wider variety of other birds. However, the large areas of relatively pristine habitat which remain in the east may tempt more birders to venture here in the future.

At 356,840 km², Germany is nearly three times larger than England and about half the size of Texas. Germany's integrated public transport system is efficient, fast and far-reaching, but expensive. Bicycles can be hired at some railway stations and returned to any other stations participating in the scheme. Accommodation includes hotels, inns, guesthouses, 'Bed and Breakfast' (*Zimmer frei*), numerous youth hostels (*jugendherberge*) and campsites. Food is good value in European terms, especially staples such as 'meat and two veg.'. There are over 1,500 breweries in the country, about 40% of the world total, so there are a few beers to choose from and the Germans consume almost as much of it as the Czechs. The wines can also be good, especially those made from Riesling grapes.

The climate is, on the whole, continental, with warm summers and cold winters. The best time to visit Germany depends on the target species; for example, woodpeckers are easier to locate in March, but to see high-altitude specialities it is necessary to wait until the summer (many high tops remain inaccessible until mid-June at least) or autumn when the mountain roads are open.

The north coast abuts the North Sea in the west and the Baltic Sea in the east. There are huge areas of intertidal mud along both of these coasts, especially at Wattenmeer, the German section of the Wadden See in the northwest, which is one of the most important areas for birds in Europe. The lowland farmland, marshes, lakes, remnant riverine woodland, and forest of the Northern Plain, from the border with The Netherlands in the west to the River Oder on the border with Poland in the east, give way to the forested hills of the Central Uplands which include the Thüringer Wald in central Germany and the Erzgebirge along the border with the Czech Republic in the east. A huge area of rolling lakeland separates these uplands from the Black Forest (Schwarzwald) region, which rises to 1493 m (4905 ft) in the southwest, and the Bavarian Alps which straddle the southern border with Austria and Switzerland in the south and rise to 2966 m (9731 ft) at Zugspitze. These 'southern uplands' support substantial areas of coniferous forest and alpine pastures. Virtually all of the natural habitats in western Germany have been degraded by human activities, notably agriculture, forestry and industry, whereas in eastern Germany large areas of relatively pristine habitat remain intact, including extensive marshes, steppe-like open country and forest. Habitat-rich indicator species such as Osprey, Red Kite, Eurasian beaver and Eurasian otter are still seen regularly less than an hour's train ride from Berlin. How long this will last remains to be seen. What is for sure is that the situation could be maintained if the contemporary problems facing the six threatened and near-threatened species, as well as the relatively common and widespread birds which occur in Germany, are tackled. These problems include habitat loss and degradation, hunting and pollution (over 50% of forests have been damaged by acid rain).

Notable species include Little Crake, Great Bustard*, Great Snipe*, Wallcreeper, Aquatic Warbler*, White-winged Snowfinch and Citril Finch.

NORTHERN GERMANY

In the Rhein Valley between Frankfurt and Mannheim in west-central Germany the large oxbow lake and oak woods in the reserve at **Kuhkopf** (pronounced 'Kookof') combine to support over 100 breeding species, including Red-necked Grebe, Corn Crake*, Black Woodpecker and Bluethroat ('White-spotted' *cyanecula*). This is also an excellent place to look for passage shorebirds and other species recorded include Little Crake. To reach the reserve turn west off the autobahn to Gernsheim, then turn north on to Route 44 towards Riedstadt. The gravel pits on the south side of the minor road which leads west just north of Biebesheim are worth checking for grebes, but otherwise continue north from Biebesheim to Stockstadt. North of here take the first road west and on entering the village of Riedstadt-Erfelden park in the car park on the east side of the road. From here walk over the bridge on the opposite side of the road in to the reserve where there is a loop-trail around the oxbow lake.

In central Germany there are two excellent forest reserves in the hilly **Thüringer Wald**, which rises to 982 m (3222 ft) southwest of Erfurt. These reserves support Eurasian Capercaillie (in the 18-km^2 Vessertal Biosphere Reserve), Eurasian Eagle-Owl (in the 6-km^2 Schwarzatal Reserve), Eurasian Pygmy-Owl, Tengmalm's Owl, Black Woodpecker and Eurasian Nutcracker (Vessertal). To reach Vessertal head north on Route 247 from Schleusingen towards Suhl for 2 km then turn east to the village of Breitenbach. Park at the north end of the village then walk upstream alongside the River Vesser for 6 km until reaching the village of Vesser, birding along the way. To reach Schwarzatal head out of Schleusingen on Route 4 to Ilmenau then take Route 88 to Bad Blankenburg 63 km away. Turn south in town here to keep to the west side of the River Schwarza. Once out of town bird both valley sides for about 5 km on the walking trails which run parallel to the road.

The extensive marshes, grasslands and forests around Berlin, in an area of northeast Germany known as **Brandenburg**, support White-tailed Eagle*, Great Bustard* and Great Snipe* (in the internationally important wetlands of Spreewald, along the floodplain of the River Spree from Lubben to Cottbus). Lubben, a short drive south from Berlin, is a good base from which to bird this area. Northeast of Berlin the floodplain in the **Oder Valley**, which runs along the border between Germany and Poland for 180 km, supports Corn Crake*, who knows how many Little Crakes and 10–20 pairs of Aquatic Warblers*, as well as Black and White Storks, White-tailed* and Lesser Spotted Eagles, and Common Crane. During the winter there may be as many as 200 Smew present, as well as Whooper and Bewick's Swans, and Rough-legged Buzzard. Schwedt, situated halfway along the valley about 100 km northeast of Berlin, is a good base for birding the area.

The **Mecklenburg Lakes** area in the lowlands between Berlin and Rostock, on the Baltic Coast to the north, supports about 150 breeding species, including White-tailed* and Lesser Spotted Eagles, and Common Crane. One of the best birding areas is Lewitzer Teiche and the grasslands surrounding this reserve, east of Parchim. Also, Common Cranes roost on the two lakes by the Goldberg–Crivitz road near Langenhagen, east of Parchim. To the northwest of the Mecklenburg Lakes a few Ferruginous Ducks* occur on the two shallow lakes of

Dambecker See, reached by heading north out of Schwerin on Route 106 then turning west to the village of Wendisch Rambow after 16 km, and then walking north from the village. Most of the estuaries and marshes along the **Baltic Coast** in northeast Germany are good for birds, but birders with little time to spare may wish to concentrate their efforts on the mouth of the Flensburger Forde north of Gelting, the mouth of the Schlei (Schleimunde) to the south (approach from Olpenitz), and the island of Rügen where it is possible to see over a hundred species in a day during September including White-tailed Eagle* and passage migrants such as Broad-billed Sandpiper, Caspian Tern and Aquatic Warbler*. Also during the autumn up to 40,000 Common Cranes pass through, stopping at traditional sites such as Udarser Wiek, visible from the east side of Ummanz, a relatively quiet off-island which is also accessible via Gingst.

The two islands which make up **Helgoland** off the North Sea coast of Germany are well known to European birders because they have attracted some of the rarest birds ever to have reached Europe, including the only Eastern Crowned-Warbler, which was collected here on 4 October 1843, and the constant procession of rarities has pushed Helgoland's list to the 400 mark. Regular passage migrants include Thrush Nightingale during the spring, and Yellow-browed Warbler, Richard's Pipit, and Little and Rustic Buntings during the autumn. Exceptional periods have included autumn 1988 when a White's Thrush, a Dark-(Black) throated Thrush, a Radde's Warbler, at least 20 Yellow-browed Warblers and three Olive-backed Pipits occurred, autumn 1995 when a White's Thrush, a Siberian Rubythroat and a Pine Bunting occurred, and spring 1996 when a record 135 species were seen on a single day in May, including Thrush Nightingale and Little Bunting, as well as over 200 Common Redstarts, nearly 600 Northern Wheatears, 370 Garden Warblers and 400 (Greater) Whitethroats. There is a bird observatory on the island of Oberland which attracts the majority of migrants. The other island, known as Dune, is a major tourist resort with fine beaches and tax-free goods, but it also attracts plenty of passage shorebirds. Take care not to upset the nude sunseekers when birding here.

The German section of the Wadden See coastline, which extends from The Netherlands in the west (p. 262) to Denmark in the north (p. 153), is known as **Wattenmeer**. The Wadden See is one of the most important areas for birds in Europe, especially during the autumn passage period when up to 1.8 million waterfowl and shorebirds may be present, including up to 100,000 Common Shelducks which spend mid-July to September moulting in the German section at Schleswig-Holsteinisches Wattenmeer National Park, which stretches north from the Elbe Estuary to the border with Denmark. This is one of the three national parks which cover most of the Wattenmeer coast and its offshore islands. The **Schleswig-Holstein Region** is a staging area for Lesser White-fronted Geese* from the Lapland reintroduction scheme (try Eidersperrwerk in Katinger Watt) and for shorebirds such as Broad-billed Sandpiper.

Altwarmbuchener See, near Hannover in north-central Germany, is a great place for gulls, with its most famous visitor up until the end of the 1990s being the first juvenile Great Black-headed Gull in western Europe, in early September 1998.

SOUTHERN GERMANY

The beech and coniferous forests in the 130-km² **Bayerischer Wald National Park** near the border with the Czech Republic in Bavaria, southeast Germany, support Hazel Grouse, Eurasian Pygmy-Owl, Tengmalm's Owl, and White-backed (scarce), Three-toed and Black Woodpeckers. The park visitor centre is at Neuschonau, east of Speigelau which is situated at the southwest corner of the park about 40 km north of Passau, and arguably the best base. The top areas are Gfall, about 6 km north of Speigelau *en route* to Rachel (Eurasian Pygmy-Owl and Three-toed Woodpecker), Flanitzbene, north of Spiegelau via Althutte (Eurasian Pygmy-Owl) and Zwieslerwaldhaus, 15 km north of Zwiesel, beyond the park boundary near the border with the Czech Republic (White-backed Woodpecker).

South of Bayerischer Wald the lower reaches of the **River Inn**, alternatively known as the Inn Lakes Region due to a series of dams, alongside the road between Passau and Simbach, support Red-crested Pochard, Black-crowned Night-Heron and Eurasian River Warbler. In extreme southeast Germany the **Berchtesgaden National Park** is a beautiful alpine area which rises to 2713 m (8901 ft) at Watzmann and supports Rock Ptarmigan, Eurasian Pygmy-Owl (above Hintersee, southwest of the village of Ramsau about 20 km southwest of Salzburg), Tengmalm's Owl, White-backed, Three-toed and Black Woodpeckers, and Yellow-billed Chough. There are visitor centres at Berchtesgaden and Konigssee.

The best birding area close to **Munich** is Ismaninger Teichgebiet, about 5 km northeast of the city, where the Mittlerer-Isar Canal, the adjacent reservoir known as Speichersee and the associated wetlands support a good selection of waterbirds, including Red-crested Pochard and Black-crowned Night-Heron. Germany's highest peaks, which rise to 2966 m (9731 ft) at Zugspitze, lie in the **Bavarian Alps** to the south of Munich near the border with Austria. These mountains support a typical alpine avifauna, although some high-altitude specialities are much scarcer here than elsewhere in the Alps. The high tops, where most of the goodies occur, are easily accessible via Oberammergau which is situated in the Ammer Valley 72 km southwest of Munich, and the olympic ski-resort of Garmisch-Partenkirchen which is 90 km south of Munich via Autobahn 95. To look for woodpeckers such as White-backed, head for the reserve at **Karwendel** near Oberammergau. To look for Rock Ptarmigan and White-winged Snowfinch, as well as Yellow-billed Choughs which feed out of the hand, head for **Zugspitze** which is accessible via cable-car or rack-railway from near Garmisch. Another good spot near here is **Hochalm**, accessible via a cable-car from the Alpspitze valley station at Osterfelderkopf, which reaches 1700 m (5577 ft), high enough for Alpine Accentor and Citril Finch. The best place to look for Wallcreeper is probably the walls of **Neuschwanstein Castle** and the nearby gorge, about 60 km west of Garmisch.

The waters of the **German Bodenssee** (Lake Constance) which is situated on the borders with Austria (p. 59) and Switzerland (p. 379) in southwest Germany, together with the surrounding marshes and woods, support breeding Red-crested Pochard and White Stork. The best area to concentrate on is the west end of the lake where almost 100 species breed around **Mindelsee**, a small lake just northeast of Radolfzell. Bird along the walking track which begins at Moggingen. A few pairs of White Stork nest on the walls of Wasser Schloss, the castle just west of Moggingen which also hosts the Radolfzell Bird Observatory. **Wollmatinger Ried**, a wetland reserve to the east of Mindelsee and just west of Konstanz, supports Red-crested Pochard. The reserve is accessible only on guided tours which can be booked in advance by contacting NABU, Naturschutzzentrum Wollmatinger Ried, D-78479 Konstanz, Germany (tel: 7531 78870), but part of the reserve can be seen from the causeway which leads from the mainland to Insel Reichenau, and the village of Moos, 2 km southwest of Radolfzell, is a good place from which to scan the lake. During the winter, Wallcreeper has been recorded on the walls of the **Hohentwiel** ruined castle near Singen, west of the lake, and on the castle at **Meersburg**, accessible via ferry from Konstanz. Birders interested in orchids may wish to visit the reserves with 'orchid trails' alongside Route 31 southwest of Donaueschingen and **Hufingen**, northwest of Mindelsee.

ADDITIONAL INFORMATION

Addresses
Please send records of rarities to the Deutsche Seltenheitenkommission, Dokumentationsstelle fur seltene Vogelarten, Uber dem Salzgraben 11, D-37574 Einbeck-Druber, Germany. The annual rarities report is published in *Limicola*, in German with an English summary.
Deutscher Bund fur Vogelschutz, Achalmstrasse 33a, D-7014 Kornwestheim, Germany.

GREECE

INTRODUCTION

Summary
With so many species, including Spur-winged Plover, Masked Shrike and Rüppell's Warbler, which within Europe occur only in the southeast, a wealth of waterbirds and more raptors than any other country in the region, most of which can be seen in a relatively small area of the north, surprisingly few birders visit Greece, despite its long-established reasonably priced tourist infrastructure and sun-drenched spectacular scenery.

Size
At 131,985 km², Greece is slightly larger than England and one fifth the size of Texas.

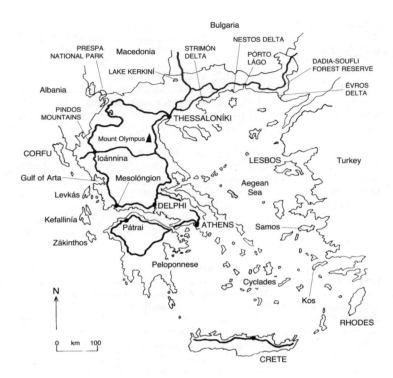

Getting Around

There are international airports near Athens in the south and Thessaloníki in the north, and it is also possible to fly directly into a number of package holiday resorts from abroad. Since many of the best birding sites are situated in relatively remote areas the best way to get around is by hiring a vehicle, in which case it is wise to remember that, despite the relatively light traffic, Greece has the second highest road accident rate in Europe. A good road map is essential because road-signs are few and far between in some areas. Birders who prefer using public transport will be pleased to know that there is a very efficient train service on the major tourist routes and a fairly extensive bus service. In many places, notably on the offshore islands, it is also possible to hire bicycles, mopeds and motorcycles in order to reach the quietest corners.

Accommodation and Food

Reasonably priced hotels, guest houses, youth hostels and campsites are available almost everywhere, but many of these places are almost overflowing in July and August so it is best to book in advance if you intend to visit during this period. Camping outside authorised sites is frowned upon and the police have been known to crack down hard on anyone attempting it. Food and drink is also good value. The Greeks prefer light breakfasts such as bread, jam and yogurt, but snacks are usually readily available and include cheese pies, doner kebabs and pretzels, while estiatorias and tavernas (the cheapest) serve up Greek classics such as moussaka and tzatziki. The local people chat and drink in kafenios which serve coffee, tea and alcoholic drinks such as beer, brandy and the local firewater known as ouzo.

Health and Safety
Immunisation against yellow fever is compulsory if arriving from an infected country. Near the borders with Albania, Bulgaria, Macedonia and Turkey it is wise not to point any optics at anything the military might consider to be 'sensitive'.

Climate and Timing
The climate is basically Mediterranean with an average summer temperature of 82°F and fairly mild winters. It can snow a lot in the mountains during the winter but even then, clear, sunny skies are more or less the norm in the lowlands. The best times to visit are during April and May, and the second half of August, when many passage migrants pass through the country, although some summer visitors don't arrive until late May.

Habitats
Few if any other European countries support such a diverse range of habitats as Greece. True, it is predominantly mountainous, rising to 2917 m (9570 ft) at Mount Olympus, and many a foothill, especially in the south, is rather bare, but the rugged mountains also support garrigue, maquis, deciduous woodland, coniferous forest (mostly in the north), natural lakes and alpine grassland. However, the country's most important habitats are its wetlands, including the mountain lakes and the lowland deltas, lagoons and salinas, nearly half of which are now confined to the northeast. About 30% of the land has been turned over to agriculture and about a third of this is composed of almond, citrus, fig and olive groves, although cotton, grain and tobacco are cultivated on the plain of Thessaly in the east. Numerous islands lie offshore from the 15,000-km-long coastline, including those along the west (Mediterranean) coast known as the Ionian Islands (including Corfu), those sprinkled across the Aegean known as the Cyclades, those along the Turkish coast known as the Dodecanese (including Lesbos and Rhodes) and Crete (which is dealt with in a separate section (see p. 140)).

Conservation
Just over ten million people populate Greece, about half of whom live in the three major cities of Athens, Pátrai and Thessaloníki, hence the 'countryside' is relatively sparsely populated when one considers that over 48 million people smother similar-sized England. However, centuries of forest clearance and overgrazing have left large areas almost devoid of vegetation, and this combined with increasing human encroachment leading to further habitat loss and degradation, the continuing popularity of blasting anything with feathers out of the sky, and pollution (acid rain and other airborne pollutants are not only damaging archaeological ruins, but forests as well) all present major obstacles to the continued survival of the 15 threatened and near-threatened species (the equal highest total for a European country) as well as the relatively common and widespread birds which occur in Greece.

Bird Species

About 422 species have been recorded in Greece. Notable species include Pygmy Cormorant*, Great White and Dalmatian* Pelicans, White-headed Duck*, Ruddy Shelduck, Greater Flamingo, Cinereous Vulture*, Levant Sparrowhawk, Long-legged Buzzard, Greater Spotted* and Imperial* Eagles, Eleonora's and Lanner Falcons, Rock Partridge, Chukar, Spur-winged Plover, Audouin's* and Slender-billed Gulls, Caspian Tern, Masked Shrike, Semicollared Flycatcher, Rufous-tailed Scrub-Robin, Isabelline Wheatear, Rock Nuthatch, Wallcreeper, Olive-tree, Orphean and Rüppell's Warblers, Sombre Tit, White-winged Snowfinch, Alpine Accentor, and Cretzschmar's and Black-headed Buntings.

In addition, the island of Lesbos, near the west coast of Turkey, supports the only European populations of Krüper's Nuthatch and Cinereous Bunting*.

Expectations

It is possible to see 150–180, exceptionally 200, species, including 20 raptors and 30 shorebirds, on a trip lasting one to two weeks to northern Greece during the spring. On the island of Lesbos it is possible to see 130–150 species in a week during the peak spring passage period of late April-early May.

Rüppell's Warbler occurs near **Athens** (where there is a colony of Pallid Swifts at the airport), in Parnitha National Park just to the north, and Alpine Swifts add an extra dimension to the Acropolis. To the west of Athens, Agamemnon's citadel, another major tourist attraction at **Mycenae** on the large island known as Peloponnese, is graced by Blue Rock-Thrush and Rock Nuthatch, as are many archaelogical sites throughout Greece. At the southern end of Peloponnese, Rock Partridge occurs above the abandoned Byzantine city of **Mystra** on the slopes of the Taygetos Mountains and four Slender-billed Curlews* were reported from the **Evrotas Delta** near Kalamata in early April 1999.

The southern Ionian Islands of **Zákinthos** (Zante) and **Keffalinía** (Cephalonia) are accessible by ferries from Peloponnese. Zákinthos, also accessible by air, supports Cretzschmar's Bunting, as well as one of the few remaining breeding beaches of loggerhead turtle. There is a Turtle Information Centre, open during the summer, east of Laganas on the south coast. White-backed Woodpecker (*lilfordi*) occurs in the fir forest on Mount Aenos (Enos), which rises to 1632 m (5354 ft), on Kefallinía. The other southern Ionian Island is **Levkás**, accessible from mainland Greece via a bridge and causeway, which supports summer visitors such as Rufous-tailed Scrub-Robin, Olive-tree Warbler and Cretzschmar's Bunting, and attracts passage shorebirds and terns (on the lagoons and salinas at the north and east ends of the island).

The ruined city of **Delphi**, 150 km northwest of Athens, was constructed on the southern slopes of Mount Parnassus and lies beneath an imposing 305-m (1000-ft)-high crag. The Temple of Apollo is situated here and it is one the most popular archaeological sites in Greece, hence birders more interested in the site's avian inhabitants should be the first through the gate in the morning. The city itself, and the nearby Temple of Athene, are excellent places to look for Blue Rock-Thrush and Rock Nuthatch, while the surrounding olive groves and scrubby hillsides support Olive-tree and Rüppell's Warblers, and Cretzschmar's and Black-headed Buntings. The area above the arena, which is above the Temple of Apollo, is particularly good, and other possibilities include Orphean Warbler and Sombre Tit. Once the tourists arrive in force head for the track which descends in a southwesterly direction below the entrance to the ruins and leads to another, larger, track south of the town, along which it is possible to see Rock Partridge and Cretzschmar's Bunting. The olive groves a km or so east of **Itea**, southwest of Delphi, support Olivaceous and Olive-tree Warblers. East from the ruined city along the N48 to Arahova a road ascends **Mount Parnassus**, which rises to 2457 m (8061 ft). Species recorded here include Lammergeier (one pair may still be present), Egyptian Vulture, Eurasian Griffon, Short-toed and Booted Eagles, Lanner Falcon, Rock Partridge, White-backed Woodpecker (*lilfordi*), Rufous-tailed Rock-Thrush, Horned Lark, Rock Petronia and Alpine Accentor.

Although northern Greece is the top birding region within the country,
Rüppell's Warbler is restricted to the extreme south

The marshes, lagoons and salinas south of the N48 near **Mesolóngion** are usually at their best during the winter and the spring passage period, particularly mid-April to May. The causeway south of town is the place to be, with the lagoons to the west and the salinas to the east. Grill any shorebirds carefully, for they have included Slender-billed Curlew*, as well as Marsh, Terek and Broad-billed Sandpipers, and other possibilities include Dalmatian Pelican* and Glossy Ibis.

The intertidal mudflats, saltmarshes, lagoons, marshes, extensive reedbeds and olive groves around the **Gulf of Arta** on the west coast, support Dalmatian Pelican*, Semicollared Flycatcher and Olive-tree Warbler, as well as other summer visitors and resident species such as Ferruginous Duck*, Squacco Heron, Glossy Ibis, White-tailed* and Lesser Spotted Eagles, Collared Pratincole, European Bee-eater, European Roller and Lesser Grey Shrike. The north shore is the best, especially: (i) Logarou Lagoon (Dalmatian Pelican*), accessible via the road south from Arta to Koronisia; (ii) Tsoukalio Lagoon (Dalmatian Pelican*), accessible via a sandy track west of the same road; (iii) the olive groves around Strongili (Semicollared Flycatcher and Olive-tree Warbler), accessible via the road which leads south 20 km west of Arta, through Petra; (iv) Strongili Lagoon, to the south; and (v) the lagoon northeast of Michaelitsi. Along the southern side of the bay the mudflats at Amfilokhia are particularly good for passage shorebirds and Lake Voulkaria occasionally attracts Dalmatian Pelican*.

CORFU

This large island, off the west coast of mainland Greece, has more package holiday resorts than any other Greek island, but it is still an excellent place for a cheap but exciting birding trip, thanks to the presence of resident species such as Rock Partridge, summer visitors which include Cretzschmar's Bunting and a wide range of spring passage migrants. The island, which rises to over 900 m (2953 ft) at Pandokrator in the north but is predominantly low-lying, receives more rainfall than the mainland hence its meadows, lagoons, maquis and woods are relatively lush.

The species listed below occur during the spring and summer unless otherwise indicated. Spring passage peaks during early May.

Localised Specialities
Rock Partridge, Semicollared Flycatcher (spring migrant), Cretzschmar's Bunting.

Regular Spring Passage Migrants
Red-footed Falcon, Temminck's Stint, White-winged Tern, Collared Flycatcher.

Others
Squacco Heron, Golden Eagle, Collared Pratincole, Gull-billed Tern, Alpine and Pallid Swifts, European Bee-eater, European Roller, Blue Rock-Thrush, Rock Nuthatch, Red-rumped Swallow, Moustached, Orphean, Sardinian and Subalpine Warblers, Spanish Sparrow, Rock Petronia, Black-headed Bunting.

Other Wildlife
Hermann's tortoise, nose-horned viper. The rich flora includes at least 44 orchids (best late March to early April).

(Other species recorded here, mainly on passage, include Pygmy Cormorant*, Dalmatian Pelican*, Ferruginous Duck*, Glossy Ibis, White-tailed Eagle*, Pallid Harrier*, Lesser Kestrel*, Saker Falcon, Little Crake, Great Snipe*, Marsh Sandpiper, Slender-billed Gull, Rufous-tailed Scrub-Robin, Olive-tree Warbler and Red-throated Pipit.)

Corfu is accessible by air from many European countries and by ferry from Igoumenitsa on the Greek mainland. The majority of the beach resorts are situated along the east coast. It is worth birding almost anywhere but the most previously productive sites are as follows: (i) **Antinioti Lagoon**, which lies alongside the north coast road west of Kassiopi at the northeast end of the island. This is a good spot for waterbirds, raptors, Rufous-tailed Scrub-Robin and Olive-tree Warbler; (ii) the top few km of the road which ascends **Mount Pantor Krator** is good for Rock Partridge and Cretzschmar's Bunting; (iii) the **Sidari** area where migrants have included Collared Flycatcher and Red-throated Pipit; (iv) the **Ropa Plain** in the centre of the island. Walk alongside the river, reached by driving along the track to Yiannadhes, for Moustached Warbler and passage raptors; (v) the **Korission Lagoon** at the southwest end of the island, reached by walking along the track through the fields from the cafe-petrol station at Linia; (vi) the junipers at nearby

Aghios Georgios Beach, which are good for passage migrants; and (vii) **Alikes Salinas**, north of Lefkimmi at the extreme south end of the island. These are a must for migrant waterbirds which have included Little Crake, although the area may seem to be devoid of avian life on quiet days. Botanising birders may wish to visit the cemetery in Corfu town (Kerkira) where orchids are carefully protected.

Accommodation: North—Roda Beach Hotel. South—Hotel Delfinakia in Moraitika. Also numerous package holiday resorts.

The extensive forests, rocky gorges and lakes in the **Pindos Mountains**, which rise to 2633 m (8639 ft) at Mount Smolikas, in northwest Greece near the border with Albania, are off the beaten birding track but they could prove tempting to those birders who prefer such places, for the avifauna comprises an enticing mixture of high-altitude and southeast European specialities, which include Lammergeier, Lanner Falcon, Rock Partridge, Wallcreeper, White-winged Snowfinch and Cretzschmar's Bunting. Ioánnina is the gateway to these mountains. The Lesser Kestrel* colony in this town is one of several in the area and Lake Pamvotis, just to the east, is worth checking for passage migrants such as Pygmy Cormorant* and pelicans, as well as breeding species such as Moustached Warbler. The south shore is the best and can be reached by turning east off the E19 south of town on to a rough track. Look for Lanner Falcon at the 1690-m (5545-ft)-high Kataras Pass, about 40 km east of Ioánnina along the E92, near Metsovo. About 35 km north of Ioánnina via the E20, Lammergeier, Rock Partridge, Wallcreeper and Cretzschmar's Bunting occur in Vikos-Aoos National Park. The Vikos Gorge, with walls nearly 1000 m (3281 ft) high in places, within the park, is accessible from the village of Monodendri which is perched on its southern rim. From the church here there is a trail to Papingo, about eight hours away, where there is accommodation available. Rock Partridge, White-winged Snowfinch and Alpine Accentor are most likely to be seen above Papingo, along the mule trail to Mount Astaka. All of the aforementioned high-altitude specialities are also present around Mount Smolikas and Mount Grammos, further north still, but the greater the distance from Ioánnina the fewer the facilities, and marked trails and villages are few and far between near the border with Albania.

In north-central Greece near Kalabaka the cliffs and pinnacles at **Meteora** support several precariously placed medieval monasteries, as well as Egyptian Vulture, Bonelli's Eagle, Alpine Swift, Blue Rock-Thrush and Rock Nuthatch. Near the east coast, the sheer cliffs, mixed forests and barren, rocky summit of **Mount Olympus**, the mythical seat of the gods and highest peak in Greece at 2917 m (9570 ft), support White-backed Woodpecker (*lilfordi*) and Wallcreeper, as well as Egyptian Vulture, Eurasian Griffon, Eurasian Eagle-Owl, Black Woodpecker and Rock Bunting. However, these birds are all hard to find at this popular tourist attraction.

PRESPA NATIONAL PARK

The two huge shallow lakes in this park, which extend across the borders with Albania and Macedonia in northwest Greece, about 160 km west of Thessaloníki, support important numbers of breeding water-birds, notably the world's largest known Dalmatian Pelican* colony, which contained about 250 pairs before 200 nests were abandoned when a mad fisherman with a gun paid a visit in April 1998, and about 50 pairs of Great White Pelican.

The species listed below occur during the summer unless otherwise indicated.

Localised Species
Pygmy Cormorant*, Great White and Dalmatian* Pelicans.

Regular Spring Passage Migrants
Red-footed Falcon, Collared Pratincole, Whiskered and White-winged Terns.

Others
Great Egret, Squacco Heron, Glossy Ibis, White Stork, Egyptian Vulture, Short-toed, Golden and Booted Eagles, Lesser Kestrel*, Eurasian Eagle-Owl, Alpine Swift, European Bee-eater, European Roller, Syrian and Black Woodpeckers, Lesser Grey Shrike, Rufous-tailed Rock-Thrush, Rock Nuthatch, Eurasian Crag-Martin, Moustached, Olivaceous, Orphean and Subalpine Warblers, Sombre Tit, Rock Petronia, Rock and Black-headed Buntings.
    (Other species recorded here include Ferruginous Duck*, Rock Partridge, and Little and Baillon's Crakes.)

PRESPA NP

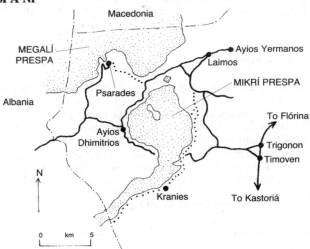

From Thessaloníki head west to Flórina and on to Trigonon, then turn west towards Ayios Yermanos, then west again to reach the sandy isthmus between the two lakes; Mikrí (lesser) Prespa to the south and Megalí (greater) Prespa to the north. The isthmus is the best birding area (although the observation tower is not very useful) and both species of pelican often fly over here. The rest of the shoreline around Mikrí Prespa, the best lake, is accessible via minor roads, tracks and trails.

Many birding visitors to Greece choose to fly directly to **Thessaloníki** in the north because it is much closer to the best birding sites in the country than Athens, and before dashing off to Prespa National Park to the west or the numerous top sites to the east it is worth spending a day or so in the Thessaloníki area. Start off by looking out for Pallid Swifts over the city, then head a little way south to the **Axios Delta** where two Slender-billed Curlews* were recorded on 30 March 1997, and where more regular summer visitors and passage migrants include Pygmy Cormorant*, Greater Flamingo, Collared Pratincole, White-winged and Caspian Terns, and Red-throated Pipit. To the south of the Axios Delta, about 30 km southwest of Thessaloníki east of the N1, is the **Aliakmon Delta**, which is also suffering from agricultural encroachment but still attracts Little Crake, Collared Pratincole and Spur-winged Plover. To reach here from the N1 head for the old main road and Nea Agathoupolis, then turn on to any track leading north. The **Kitros (Alykí) Salinas**, about 20 km south of Aliakmon, support the only Slender-billed Gull colony and the largest Mediterranean Gull colony in Greece, and often attract large numbers of Greater Flamingo, as well as Caspian Tern. This is also the only regular site in Greece for Cattle Egret, and as good a place as any to look for Greater Spotted Eagle* and Saker Falcon during the winter. To reach here turn off the old Athens–Thessaloníki road south of Metonia in response to the 'Salt Works Port of Pidna' signpost. Finally, Slender-billed Curlew* has also been recorded around the lagoon and salinas on the promontory of **Angelohori** across the Thermaikos Kolpos (Gulf of Thermaikos).

LAKE KERKINÍ

This dammed ox-bow lake in the River Strimón floodplain, about 75 km north of Thessaloníki, supports the greatest diversity and the highest numbers of waterbirds in Greece. There are large breeding colonies of Pygmy Cormorant* (about 50 pairs) and Whiskered Tern, while during the winter as many as 50,000 waterbirds may be present, including up to 4,000 Pygmy Cormorants*, 300 Dalmatian Pelicans* and 1,000 Great Egrets. During the spring and autumn, masses of birds use the lake as a resting and refuelling site, including as many as 300 Great White Pelicans. If that isn't enough, the lake is surrounded by wooded limestone valleys which support a fine range of raptors.

The species listed below occur during the summer unless otherwise indicated.

Localised Species
Pygmy Cormorant*, Great White (most in spring and autumn) and Dalmatian* (most in winter) Pelicans, Levant Sparrowhawk, Eleonora's Falcon.

Others

Ferruginous Duck*, Great Egret (Aug–Apr), Squacco Heron, Glossy Ibis, Black and White Storks, Short-toed Eagle, Long-legged Buzzard, Lesser Spotted, Golden and Booted Eagles, Collared Pratincole, Whiskered and Gull-billed Terns, European Bee-eater, European Roller, Syrian Woodpecker, Lesser Grey Shrike, Blue Rock-Thrush, Rock Nuthatch, Eurasian Crag-Martin, Sombre Tit, Spanish Sparrow, Yellow Wagtail ('Black-headed' *feldegg*), Rock Bunting.

(Other species recorded here include White-headed Duck* (Jan), Lesser White-fronted Goose* (up to 44 in October 1995), White-tailed* (one pair), Greater Spotted* (Oct–Mar) and Imperial* Eagles, Marsh Sandpiper (passage), Caspian Tern and Eurasian Eagle-Owl.)

LAKE KERKINÍ

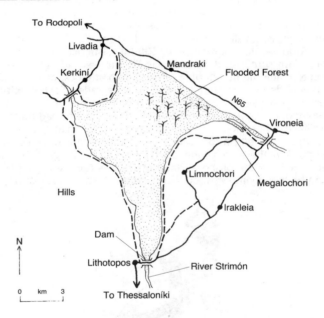

Head northeast from Thessaloníki towards Serrai (Serres) then turn west after about 60 km. From here it is 14 km to the dam and the village of Lithotopos at the southern end of the lake. Take the track northwest from Lithotopos to bird the western shoreline where the adjacent hills are good for raptors. This track reaches the road to Kerkiní after 17 km. Turn north here, cross the creek, then turn east to continue along the northwestern shoreline where the extensive areas of water lilies support breeding Whiskered Terns. From Livadia at the northwest corner of the lake head east to Vironeia. Turn south here and after crossing the river turn west to bird the northeast corner of the lake where the flooded forest supports the cormorant colony and a large heronry. This is also the best area for pelicans. From here it is then possible to return south to Lithotopos along the eastern shoreline. Levant Sparrowhawk occurs in the Strimón valley upstream from the lake and the limestone valley behind the town of Sidhirokastro supports Eurasian Eagle-Owl, Rock Nuthatch, Sombre Tit and Rock Bunting.

Accommodation: Serrai. Sidhirokastro.

The **Kerkiní Mountains** north and east of the lake support Rock Partridge (drive to 1524 m (5000 ft) and scour scree slopes), as well as Collared Flycatcher. **Lake Koronia**, east of Thessaloníki, is an excellent place to look for passage waterbirds and passerines (including Red-throated Pipit). The east end of **Lake Volvi**, further east near Rentina, is also worth birding. The main road east then passes through the wooded **Rentina Gorge**, a good place to stop and scan the skies for soaring raptors. The **Strimón Delta** further to the east is a good place to sea-watch from, since Cory's ('Scopoli's' *diomedea*) and Mediterranean ('Yelkouan' *yelkouan*) Shearwaters, and Audouin's* and Slender-billed Gulls are often offshore, and other possibilities in the area include Levant Sparrowhawk, Red-footed (passage) and Eleonora's (around the village of Asprovalta in the evening) Falcons, Pallid Swift, Masked Shrike, Rufous-tailed Scrub-Robin, Zitting Cisticola and Orphean Warbler. Turn south off the main road on the east side of the River Strimón to reach the mouth of the River Limin, the best place for passage shorebirds, gulls and terns. The severely degraded **Nestos Delta** to the east of Kavala (where Pallid Swift occurs) is the most reliable site in Europe for Spur-winged Plover. To reach the best area head north out of the village of Keramoti, pass the lagoons, fork left and after a few hundred metres turn left on to a sandy track which leads to some small buildings. Bird the area to the north of these buildings. Eleonora's Falcon breeds on the offshore island of Thassos (accessible by ferry) and can be seen flying between there and the delta near Keramoti.

Northern Greece is the only region within Europe where the striking Spur-winged Plover occurs

PÓRTO LÁGO

The shallow brackish lagoons, reedy freshwater lakes, salinas and extensive areas of tamarisk near the small village of Pórto Lágo in north-east Greece combine to produce one the best birding sites in the country. During the summer Pygmy Cormorant* and Spur-winged Plover breed here, during the autumn numerous passage shorebirds have included Slender-billed Curlew* (this site is second only to the Évros Delta for records of this species in Greece), and during the winter there are usually plenty of Dalmatian Pelicans* and White-headed Ducks*. About 2,300 of the latter were present on Lake Vistonis in January 1997, in what was believed to be the largest ever concentration in Europe. However, the numbers of this duck fluctuate wildly and in January 1998 only 687 were present.

This area is worth visiting at almost any time of the year, but the species listed below occur during the summer unless otherwise indicated.

Localised Specialities
White-headed Duck* (winter), Spur-winged Plover, Slender-billed Gull, Caspian Tern (mostly in winter).

Other Localised Species
Pygmy Cormorant*, Great White (passage) and Dalmatian* (Aug–Mar) Pelicans.

Regular Passage Migrants
Marsh and Broad-billed Sandpipers, Whiskered and White-winged Terns, Thrush Nightingale (autumn), Eurasian River Warbler (autumn).

Others
Red-necked Grebe, Ferruginous Duck*, Great Egret, Squacco Heron, Glossy Ibis, White Stork, Collared Pratincole, European Bee-eater, European Roller, Syrian Woodpecker, Lesser Grey Shrike, Sardinian and Subalpine Warblers, Calandra Lark, Spanish Sparrow, Yellow Wagtail ('Black-headed' *feldegg*), Black-headed Bunting.

(Other species recorded here include Greater Flamingo, Red-footed Falcon, Slender-billed Curlew* (recent records: three on 16 April and two on 6 April 1998, and one on 27 June 1996), Terek Sandpiper, Red-necked Phalarope and Rufous-tailed Scrub-Robin.)

PÓRTO LÁGO

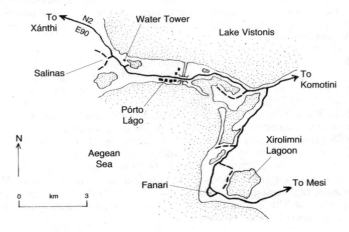

213

The village of Pórto Lágo is situated on a narrow sand spit between the Aegean Sea and a large lagoon known as Lake Vistonis. This lagoon is good for birds such as Pygmy Cormorant*, White-headed Duck* and Caspian Tern, but the salinas, shoreline and smaller lagoons on its south side are arguably better. Concentrate on the lagoon north of the N2 (E90) at the west end of the spit next to a water tower (Spur-winged Plover), the grassy areas east of here (Slender-billed Curlew*), the lagoon west of the road south to Fanari (Dalmatian Pelican* and Greater Flamingo) and Xirolimni Lagoon east of Fanari. Hundreds of Spanish Sparrows breed in the pine plantation in the middle of Sapes village.

Accommodation: Fanari—hotel and campsite.

One of the best places in Greece to look for Ruddy Shelduck is **Lake Mitrikou** (also known as Limni Ismarida), east of Pórto Lágo. This is also an excellent place for passage waterbirds, especially during the autumn, when both Little and Baillon's Crakes have been recorded. During the winter, Lesser White-fronted Goose* is possible in the surrounding fields. To reach the lake head south from Pagouria village towards Molivoti Beach, hang left, cross a bridge and turn right on to a rough raised track which leads to the lagoon and the small pools near its east shore.

ÉVROS DELTA

This delta in the extreme northeast corner of Greece on the border with European Turkey has been so badly degraded since the 1960s that its status as one of the most important wetlands in Europe is under serious threat. However, it is still a major wintering ground for waterfowl, when about 100,000 birds may be present at any one time, including up to 27,000 Pygmy Cormorants*, and during spring and autumn it attracts numerous Great White Pelicans, waterfowl, raptors such as Pallid Harrier* and Red-footed Falcon (hundreds have occurred in single spring seasons) and shorebirds, including occasional Slender-billed Curlews*. During the summer it is also one of the handful of places in Europe where Ruddy Shelduck, Spur-winged Plover and Isabelline Wheatear breed.

Due to its position on the border with Turkey, access to some parts of the delta is occasionally restricted, so enjoy birding freely if that is the case, but prepare for the worst and obtain what may turn out to be the crucial permits by contacting, a few months in advance, Charioteer Limited, PO Box 400, 10 Agias Sophias Street, Thessaloníki (tel: 31 284373; fax: 31 228968). Try to get permits ready stamped and delivered to your accommodation, or it will be necessary to collect them from the police office opposite the theatre in Alexandroúpolis, then take them to the white military building a few blocks west for stamping.

The Évros Delta is a good place to be at most times of the year, but one of the very best periods to be here is in late April and early May when spring passage is usually in full swing and the first summer visitors are arriving. The species listed below occur during the spring and summer unless otherwise indicated.

Localised Specialities

Ruddy Shelduck, Spur-winged Plover, Masked Shrike, Rufous-tailed Scrub-Robin, Isabelline Wheatear, Olive-tree Warbler.

Other Localised Species

Pygmy Cormorant* (winter), Great White and Dalmatian* (winter) Pelicans, Levant Sparrowhawk.

Regular Passage Migrants

Black Stork (also occurs in summer), Pallid Harrier* (spring), Long-legged Buzzard (also occurs in summer), Greater Spotted Eagle* (also occurs in winter), Red-footed Falcon (spring), Marsh and Broad-billed Sandpipers.

Others

Squacco Heron, Glossy Ibis, White Stork, White-tailed*, Short-toed and Lesser Spotted Eagles, Collared Pratincole, Gull-billed Tern, European Bee-eater, European Roller, Lesser Grey Shrike, Orphean Warbler, Spanish Sparrow, Sombre Tit, Yellow Wagtail ('Black-headed' *feldegg*), Black-headed Bunting.

(Other species recorded here include Lesser White-fronted* (winter) and Red-breasted* (winter) Geese, Ferruginous Duck*, Steppe Eagle, Lanner and Saker (winter) Falcons, Chukar, Little and Baillon's Crakes, Slender-billed Curlew* (see below), Terek Sandpiper, Greater Sand-plover, Caspian Plover, Sociable* and White-tailed (recent records: one in late April 1999, one in May 1998 and five in late July 1997) Lapwings, Great Black-headed and Slender-billed Gulls, Caspian Tern, Collared Flycatcher and Red-throated Pipit.)

Recent reports of Slender-billed Curlew* in the Évros Delta: 5 April 1995 (one), 1–3 April 1996 (one), 13 April 1996 (two), late November or early December 1996 to 21 March 1997 (one), 10–18 April 1997 (two), 27 November 1997 (one).

The delta is situated about 25 km east of Alexandroúpolis, which is accessible by air from Athens and where vehicles are available for hire. Good birding areas, usually accessible without a permit, can be reached by turning south off the road through Loutros, either: (i) to the west of the River Evros, south to some marshes and pools where Spur-winged

The superb Masked Shrike is one of several species which reaches the north-western edge of its breeding range in extreme southeast Europe and can therefore be seen in northern Greece

ÉVROS DELTA

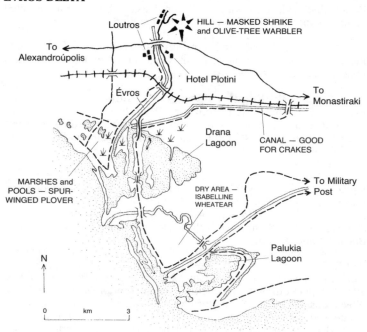

Plover is most likely to be seen; or (ii) to the east of the River Evros, on to what becomes a track which runs by Drana Lagoon (the saltmarsh around which is the best place to look for Lesser White-fronted Goose* and Slender-billed Curlew* (south side)), then a dry, open area where Rufous-tailed Scrub-Robin and Isabelline Wheatear occur, and on to a military post, where, by turning left it is possible to complete a circuit alongside a drainage canal (worth checking for crakes) back to the River Evros. Birders with permits are usually allowed to continue east and south from the military post to Lake Nymfon and Palukia Lagoon. On the steep hill with a white chapel on top, north of the delta, it is possible to see Masked Shrike (south side), Isabelline Wheatear, and Olive-tree and Orphean Warblers.

Accommodation: Loutros—Hotel Plotini.

DADIA-SOUFLI FOREST RESERVE

The open oak woods and pine forests of the Évros Mountains in extreme northeast Greece support the greatest diversity of raptors in Europe and one of the most impressive selections in the world. At least 20 species have been known to breed, including a high density of Cinereous Vultures* (over 100), and 32 species are recorded on an almost annual basis. In addition, this is one of the few sites in Europe where Chukar occurs.

The species listed below occur during the summer unless otherwise indicated.

Localised Specialities
Chukar, Masked Shrike.

Other Localised Species
Cinereous Vulture*, Levant Sparrowhawk, Imperial Eagle*, Lanner Falcon.

Others
Black and White Storks, Egyptian Vulture, Eurasian Griffon, White-tailed* (most in winter), Short-toed Eagle, Long-legged Buzzard, Lesser Spotted, Golden and Booted Eagles, European Bee-eater, European Roller, Syrian Woodpecker, Blue Rock-Thrush, Eurasian Crag-Martin, Sombre Tit, Spanish Sparrow, Black-headed Bunting.

(Other species recorded here include Lammergeier (one bird), Greater Spotted* (winter) and Steppe Eagles, Red-footed and Eleonora's Falcons, Semicollared Flycatcher, Olive-tree, Barred and Orphean Warblers, and Rock Bunting.)

DADIA-SOUFLI FOREST RESERVE

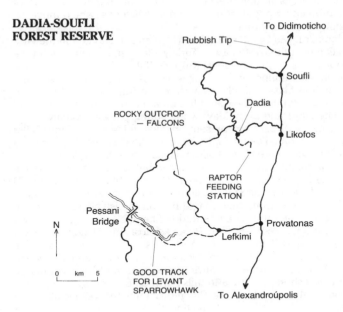

Head north from Alexandroúpolis for 47 km then turn west at Provatonas to reach **Lefkimi**. The open areas around this village are a good place to look for Masked Shrike. From here it is possible to continue west on a track through excellent forest for Levant Sparrowhawk to Pessani Bridge or northwest on the steep road to a rocky outcrop where Eleonora's and Lanner Falcons occur. North of Provatonas turn west just north of Likofos to reach the village of **Dadia** and the visitor centre 1 km south of there. Vultures can usually be seen soaring from the roads and tracks throughout the Dadia area but to get views on the ground, at 150 m, visit the Raptor Feeding Station, where there is a hide for watching the vultures feed on dead cows, a mini-bus ride or 40-minute walk from the visitor centre. The best time of day to be at the feeding station is usually the late afternoon when as many as 25–30 Cinereous Vultures*, 15–20 Eurasian Griffons and 10–15 Egyptian Vultures have been present. They are often accompanied by Black Stork, Golden Eagle and Lanner Falcon. Continue north of Dadia into good forest for Lesser Spotted Eagle. For more details of the Raptor Feeding Station contact the Community of Dadia (tel: 554 32208) or the Forestry Department (tel: 554 22221).

Accommodation: Dadia—Visitor Centre Guesthouse.

Due to the lack of nutrients and resulting low levels of plankton the eastern Mediterranean is not rich in seabirds. However, the **Aegean Sea** between Greece and Turkey still supports most of the 5,000 pairs of Cory's Shearwaters ('Scopoli's' *diomedea*) estimated to be present around Greece, Mediterranean Shearwater ('Yelkouan' *yelkouan*), small numbers of European Storm-Petrel, Audouin's Gull* (200–250 pairs breed on tiny islets around Greece) and, most importantly, up to 65% of the world breeding population of Eleonora's Falcons, which thrive on the uninhabited rocky islets.

The large, rugged island of **Lesbos** (Mytilene) is situated in the eastern Aegean near the west coast of Turkey, close enough to support the only populations of (the resident) Krüper's Nuthatch and (the summering) Cinereous Bunting* in Europe, as well as other breeding summer visitors such as Masked Shrike, Olive-tree and Rüppell's Warblers, and Cretzschmar's Bunting. The island lies on a major migration route and during late April and early May, when spring passage usually peaks (and plenty of birders are present) regular migrants include Pallid Harrier*, Red-footed Falcon, Little Crake and Marsh Sandpiper, and rarities have included the likes of Spur-winged Plover and White-throated Robin. Autumn passage is less pronounced but still impressive, particularly in late September–early October. The best birding areas are: (i) around the best base at Skala Kalloni, where there are rivers, salinas and olive groves surrounding a large bay on the island's south coast, which attract waterbirds such as Ruddy Shelduck, Greater Flamingo, Squacco Heron, Glossy Ibis, Little Crake (almost annual along the River Kalloni), Collared Pratincole and Audouin's Gull*, passage passerine migrants such as Red-throated Pipit, and breeding species which include Olive-tree Warbler (in olive groves near the River Potamia on the northwest shore; (ii) the arid hills between Eressos and Sigri at the west end of the island, where Cinereous Bunting* (especially near Antissa), as well as Chukar, Isabelline Wheatear and Cretzschmar's Bunting, occur; (iii) Plomari, north of Agiassos, where the pine forests support Krüper's Nuthatch; and (iv) the rugged north coast, where Eleonora's Falcon's, which breed on offshore islands, can be seen. Lesbos is accessible by air from most European countries, and by ferries from Kavala and Thessaloníki.

The large, mainly mountainous island of **Rhodes**, 19 km off the southwest coast of Turkey, rises to 1215 m (3986 ft) at Mount Attaviros. Its vineyards, olive groves and pine woods support breeding species such as Long-legged Buzzard, Eleonora's and Lanner Falcons, Chukar, Pallid

Swift and European Bee-eater, and during the autumn there can be a strong movement of passage migrants through the island, especially passerines. These birds may appear anywhere, even around resorts such as Lindos where up to 58 Red-backed Shrikes have been seen in a single day. However, the island is more renowned amongst naturalists for its flora and the millions of Jersey tiger moths which gather in a narrow gorge, known as 'Butterfly Valley', near Petaloudhes, to aestivate during July and August.

ADDITIONAL INFORMATION

Addresses
Please send records of rarities to George Handrinos, 44 El Venizelou St., 16675 Glyfada, Greece.

Books and papers
Where to watch birds in Turkey, Greece and Cyprus. Welch H *et al.*, 1996. Hamlyn.

Finding Birds in Northern Greece. Gosney D, 1993. Available from Bird-Guides (address, p. 395).

The Birds of Greece. Handrinos G and Akriotis T, 1997. Helm.

Birding on the Greek Island of Lesvos. Brooks R, 1998. Brookside Publishing.

Lesvos Update: Spring 1999. Brooks R, 1999. Brookside Publishing.

A Revised Checklist of the Birds of Lesvos. Brooks R, 1999. Brookside Publishing.

HUNGARY

INTRODUCTION

Summary
Hungary is a very popular birding destination, thanks mainly to the steppe-grasslands and wetlands in a small area of the Great Hungarian Plain where, during the spring and early summer, it is possible to see plenty of waterbirds, lots of Red-footed Falcons, Saker Falcon, Great Bustard* and Aquatic Warbler*. In addition, the same area supports Europe's largest autumnal gathering of Common Cranes.

Size
At 93,030 km², Hungary is 60% the size of England and 14% the size of Texas.

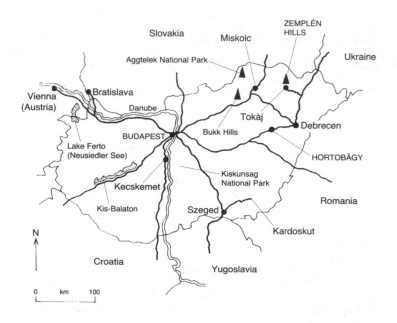

Getting Around

Most visitors arrive by air in Budapest, three hours by road west of the Hortobâgy, the country's most popular birding site in the Great Hungarian Plain. Hiring a vehicle is expensive but unfortunately this is the most efficient way of getting around, at least for birders with little time available, because the bus and rail networks are limited. English is not widely spoken beyond Budapest, hence a little German would be useful.

Accommodation and Food

The majority of places to stay outside Budapest are reasonably priced 3-star inns and pensions which resemble motels, 'Bed and Breakfast' establishments (*Zimmer frei*), youth hostels and campsites (*kemping*), some of which have chalets (*fahaz*). The campsites are the cheapest but they are busy between late May and September. Traditional foods such as goulash (meat and potato soup with paprika), strudels and stuffed pancakes are cheap in European terms, and this is also the case with beer, local spirits such as *palinka* (apricot brandy) and wine.

Health and Safety

During the summer be sure to take plenty of insect repellent. It is arguably best to drink bottled water only.

Climate and Timing

As is the case with most land-locked continental countries Hungary experiences warm summers, when the temperature can rise above 85°F, and harsh winters, when temperatures often fall well below freezing. The peak times to visit are February to May (best for owls and woodpeckers, as well as displaying Great Bustards* in first half of May), the second half of August (peak shorebird passage), and September–October (spectacular autumn passage of Common Cranes, Great Bustards* forming flocks and the chance of Lesser White-fronted Goose* in late September–early October).

Habitats

Nearly 60% of the land in low-lying Hungary has been converted to farmland, much of which is given over to vast fields of maize and sunflowers, but at least the left over stubble provides food for tens of thousands of migrating geese and Common Cranes. The most extensive areas of the country's most notable habitat, the unique dry steppe-grassland known as *puszta*, which has been created by the felling and burning of steppe-woodlands over the centuries, and is maintained by grazing, are situated in the eastern half of the country, on the Great Hungarian Plain. Various wetlands, including huge fishponds, marshes and shallow saline lakes are also present throughout the plain. Remnant riverine poplar and willow woods survive along the Rivers Danube (Duna) and Tisza which run roughly north to south across the middle of the country, as well as along several other rivers. The only land above 500 m (1640 ft) is in the north near the border with Slovakia, where it rises to 1015 m (3330 ft) at Kekes in the Matra Hills. These karst-limestone uplands, riddled with huge caves, support scrub, deciduous woods and coniferous forest.

Conservation

Over the centuries many marshes have been turned over to fishponds, but since many of these ponds would be better described as casually managed lakes they still support plenty of wetland species. The post World War II agricultural policy led to the further degradation and destruction of large areas of grassland and marshes, but some areas have been spared and are protected in a network of reserves and national parks. The country also has a very effective raptor conservation programme, but the (relatively) good news ends there. The government and non-governmental conservation organisations will need to address many issues, not least agricultural intensification and hunting, if the ten threatened and near-threatened species as well as the relatively common and widespread birds which occur in Hungary, are to survive.

Bird Species

About 368 species have been recorded in Hungary. Notable species include Pygmy Cormorant*, Lesser White-fronted Goose*, Imperial Eagle*, Red-footed and Saker (over 100 pairs—Europe's largest population) Falcons, Little Crake, Great Bustard* (over 1,000 birds), Ural Owl, nine out of the ten European woodpeckers (only Three-toed is absent), Collared Flycatcher and Aquatic Warbler* (over 600 singing males in 1998).

Expectations

It is possible to see 130–160 species on trips lasting seven to ten days during the spring and autumn, and up to 200 species when the lowlands of eastern Hungary are combined with the Tatry Mountains in adjacent Slovakia.

HORTOBÁGY NATIONAL PARK

The Hortobágy (pronounced Hortobarge) is the great wide open: a huge area of farmland, dry steppe-grassland (*puszta*), marshes, fish-ponds (*halasto*) and saline lakes under the big skies of the Great Hungarian Plain. Due to the variety of habitats it is possible to see over 100 species in a day here during the spring, including Pygmy Cormorant* (about 100 pairs in 1999), Red-footed and Saker Falcons, Little Crake, Great Bustard*, passage shorebirds, White-winged Tern (about 1,200 pairs in 1999) and Aquatic Warbler*. During the late summer and early autumn it is not unusual to see over 100 Red-footed Falcons hunting together in huge, loose flocks, and throughout the autumn the Hortobágy is the setting for Europe's most spectacular autumnal gathering of Common Cranes. Their numbers usually peak at the end of October when up to 72,000 have been present and it is possible to watch as many as 20,000 at a time flying into roost. This is one of the wonders of the natural world and a fitting finale to a day's birding in the autumn, when 100 species in a day is also possible. The place is even worth visiting during the winter when up to 28 White-tailed Eagles* have been present.

It is necessary to obtain permits to visit most areas in the Hortobágy and without them this site could prove to be rather disappointing. They can be obtained, well in advance, from Hortobágyi Nemzeti Park, 4015 Debrecen, Boszormenyi ut 138, Hungary (tel: 52 19206).

The species listed below occur during the spring and summer unless otherwise indicated.

Localised Specialities
Saker Falcon, Great Bustard*, Aquatic Warbler*.

Other Localised Species
Pygmy Cormorant*.

Regular Passage Migrants
Bean ('Taiga' *fabalis*), Greater White-fronted and Lesser White-fronted* Geese, Marsh Sandpiper, Temminck's Stint, Broad-billed Sandpiper, Red-necked Phalarope, Eurasian Dotterel (autumn).

Others
Ferruginous Duck*, Great Egret, Squacco Heron, Glossy Ibis, Little Crake, White-tailed* (most in winter) and Short-toed Eagles, Long-legged and Rough-legged (winter) Buzzards, Red-footed Falcon, Common Crane (most in autumn), Collared Pratincole, Whiskered and White-winged Terns, European Bee-eater, European Roller, Lesser Grey Shrike, Bluethroat ('White-spotted' *cyanecula*), Moustached and Barred Warblers.

Other Wildlife
European souslik.

(Other species recorded here include Red-breasted Goose* (Mar–Apr and Oct–Nov), Pallid Harrier*, Lesser Spotted and Booted Eagles, Baillon's Crake, Slender-billed Curlew* (mainly Aug–Nov), Black-winged

Pratincole* (amongst breeding colonies of Collared Pratincole in 1995 and 1996), Sociable Lapwing*, Great Black-headed Gull, Caspian Tern, Rosy Starling and Red-throated Pipit.)

The large fishpond complex with hides and observation towers to the north of Route 33, about three hours by road east of Budapest airport, supports a mixed breeding colony of herons and ibises, as well as Pygmy Cormorant*, which can be seen from one of the hides. During the spring and autumn this complex attracts a wide variety of passage shorebirds and gulls which should be grilled for Great Black-headed Gull and, especially during the second half of August, Slender-billed Curlew*. The first Common Cranes of the autumn usually arrive in early September and by the end of the month flocks of hundreds and thousands pour in on an almost daily basis. During the day they feed on the stubble left over after the maize harvest in fields within 10–30 km of the fishponds, and at night they roost on the fishponds, some of which are drained specifically to provide a secure roost site for them. They fly into the fields surrounding the ponds one to two hours before dusk and then, as darkness falls, they take to the air in wave after wave to move on to the roosts, one of which contained 50,000 birds in late October 1998. During the summer, when 200–500 are usually present, the best place to look for cranes is at the constructed wetland known as Kis-Kecskes. In addition to the cranes, large flocks of Greater White-fronted Geese also roost on the ponds and they are always worth checking for Lesser White-fronted* and Red-breasted* Geese. During the early 1900s up to 150,000 Lesser White-fronted Geese* passed through Hungary, but recent counts have only reached 35 (April 1999) and 28 (September 1999). The recent peak counts of Red-breasted Goose* have been up to 21 (March 1997) and 49 (November 1996).

Saker Falcon may be seen alongside Route 33, which runs through the middle of the park, especially on the pylons east of Hortobâgy village, but the best area for this large falcon and other raptors is Darassa in the northern Hortobâgy. Great Bustard* and Aquatic Warbler* are more or less restricted to the southern Hortobâgy, where the best places are accessible only with park wardens. Up to 150 Eurasian Dotterels were seen during the autumns of the late 1990s (the record count is 224, in October 1993), mainly on the flat, heavily grazed puszta at Angyal-háza which is near Nagyivan (the top spot for bustards).

Accommodation: near Tiszafured, at the western edge of the Hortobâgy—Patkos Motel. Hajduszoboszlo—Hotel Liget. Epona Riding Village. Also several pensions and campsites in the area.

There are some excellent birding sites in southeast Hungary where it is possible to see Lesser White-fronted Goose*, Ferruginous Duck*, and passage shorebirds, gulls and terns, which have included several Slender-billed Curlews*, mainly between August and November. These include: (i) the shallow soda lake and surrounding puszta at **Kardos-kut**, east of Szeged; (ii) the puszta at **Pitvarosi**; (iii) the fishponds at **Csajto** (the best for shorebirds): and (iv) the lake known as **Szegedi Feherto**, which supports a large colony of Mediterranean Gulls and has attracted several Great Black-headed Gulls. During late August over a hundred Collared Pratincoles often gather on the rice paddies near **Karcas** and they are always worth checking for the odd Black-winged

Pratincole*. A few pairs of Levant Sparrowhawk were discovered near **Sarkad** in the late 1990s.

The **Debrecen Forest**, near the university on the outskirts of Debrecen, 193 km east of Budapest and 30 km east of the Hortobâgy via Route 33, supports Black Woodpecker and Collared Flycatcher. Between the Hortobâgy and the Zemplén Hills it is worth looking out for Black Stork, and Eurasian River and Barred Warblers along the **River Tisza Floodplain**.

Male Collared Flycatchers stop most birders in their tracks

ZEMPLÉN HILLS

The deciduous woods and coniferous forests in the Tokàj wine-producing region of the Carpathian foothills near the border with Slovakia, just 150 km north of the Hortobâgy, support 12 species of raptor, including Imperial Eagle* and Saker Falcon, as well as Ural Owl (over 100 pairs in good years) and nine of the ten European woodpeckers (only Three-toed is absent).

The species listed below occur during the summer unless otherwise indicated.

Localised Specialities
Saker Falcon.

Other Localised Species
Imperial Eagle* (eight pairs), Ural Owl.

Others
Black Stork, Short-toed Eagle, Rough-legged Buzzard (winter), Lesser Spotted (16 pairs) and Golden Eagles, Corn Crake*, Eurasian Eagle-Owl, European Bee-eater, White-backed (scarce), Syrian and Black Woodpeckers, Rufous-tailed Rock-Thrush, Collared Flycatcher, Barred Warbler.

(Other species recorded here include Tengmalm's Owl—two pairs in 1997 represented the first breeding record for the hills.)

Sarospatak, near Tokàj, is situated on the **River Bodrog Floodplain** which supports the largest population of Corn Crakes* in Hungary (about 300 calling males in some years), as well as Black Stork and Barred Warbler. A good area is accessible via the ferry from Bodrogkeresztur. Abandoned quarries near **Tokàj** support Eurasian Eagle-Owl, European Bee-eater and Rufous-tailed Rock-Thrush. The best way to see Ural Owl is to hire one of the local guides, for they will know where the 50 or so nest boxes scattered throughout the area are situated. Otherwise try around the numerous large clearings, and during the winter, in the local parks where they have been known to hunt during the day.

Accommodation: Sarospatak—Hotel Bodrog.

West of the Zemplén Hills, Imperial Eagle*, Hazel Grouse, Ural Owl, Collared Flycatcher and Rock Bunting (around the ruined castle on the summit of Szadvar, accessible from Szogliget) occur in **Aggtelek National Park**, famous for the longest cave system in Europe which lies deep under the karst limestone hills here, about 35 km north of Miskolc. The forested **Bukk Hills**, just west of Miskolc, support Imperial Eagle* (which favours the southern slopes east of Eger), White-backed and Syrian (in Eger) Woodpeckers, and Collared Flycatcher.

No fewer than seven species of woodpecker occur in and around **Budapest**, including Syrian which can be found in the city parks and the gardens near the Buda Hills. These hills are just 15 minutes by taxi from the city centre and support Black Woodpecker, as well as Collared Flycatcher. A network of trails through the woods branches out from Normafa.

At the southwest end of **Lake Balaton**, one of the largest lakes in Europe and Hungary's major resort area, there is an excellent nature reserve called **Kis-Balaton**, just south of Keszthely (where there is a hotel). This reserve does not support any species which cannot be seen elsewhere in Hungary and this coupled with its location well off the beaten birding track means few birders make it here to enjoy its birds, which include Squacco Heron, Little Crake and Moustached Warbler. It is necessary to obtain a permit to visit here (in advance from Nyu-Kovizig, 9700 Szombathely, Vorosmarty U2, Hungary), although many species occur outside the reserve, between there and Lake Balaton.

European Roller and Moustached Warbler occur in the Danube Valley, within the landscape protection area at **Ocsa**, about 25 km southeast of Budapest. There is a permanent ringing station here and the participants, and/or the staff at the visitor centre in Ocsa, may be able to lead visitors to the best spots for these species. Lesser White-fronted* and Red-breasted* Geese, and Slender-billed Curlew* (mainly Aug–Nov) have been recorded on the saline lake and surrounding puszta at Kelemen Szek in **Kiskunsag National Park** about 30 km south of Budapest. Other species recorded here include White-tailed Eagle*, Saker Falcon (at Bugac sand dunes), Great Bustard* (on Apaj puszta), Collared Pratincole and European Roller. There is a visitor centre at Liszt Ferenc in Kecskemet where it may be possible to hire a guide.

Finally, it is worth remembering while in Hungary that Baillon's Crake has been recorded at several wetlands (for example, in the wet meadows south of **Csakvar** village in Fejer County) but is rarely reported by visiting birders.

ADDITIONAL INFORMATION
Addresses
Gerard Gorman, Budapest 1511, Pf:4, Hungary (tel/fax: 1 319 9689; email: ggbirder@elender.hu; website: www.elender.hu/~ggbirder/), is a prolific author and professional birding guide with a wealth of experience in eastern Europe (he has led well over 100 tours) who caters for tour companies as well as independent individuals and teams, and specialises in target birds.

Sakertour (a tour company which specialises in organising birding trips to Hungary and Slovakia with experienced guides), Tarjan ut 6, H-4032 Debrecen, Hungary (tel/fax: 52 350306).

Please send records of rarities to the Hungarian Rarities Committee, c/o the Hungarian Ornithological and Nature Conservation Society (MME), Budapest 1121, Kolto U. 21, Hungary. The annual rarities report is published in *Tuzok*, in Hungarian with an English summary.

Books and papers
Finding Birds in Hungary. Gosney D, 1993. Available from BirdGuides (address, p. 395).

A guide to birdwatching in Hungary. Gorman G, 1991. Corvina.

The Birds of Hungary. Gorman G, 1996. Helm.

ICELAND

INTRODUCTION
Summary
The isolated island of Iceland supports two birds which do not usually occur elsewhere in Europe: the superb Harlequin Duck and Barrow's Goldeneye, as well as huge numbers of other waterfowl, Red-necked and Grey Phalaropes, and some of the largest seabird colonies in Europe. In addition, its surrounding waters are some of the best in the world for cetaceans, including blue whale. It is a relatively expensive place to visit but getting around the small area in which these species occur is easy and the costs involved seem a small price to pay for seeing such wonderful birds and whales in an appropriately spectacular setting.

Size
At 102,820 km^2, Iceland is just smaller than England and about 15% the size of Texas.

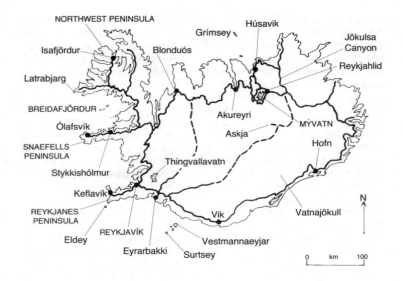

Getting Around

Most people arrive in Iceland by air, but it is also accessible during the summer by vehicular ferry from Aberdeen in Scotland, via the Faroes (p. 159). There is a good internal air network and an excellent bus service which reaches most birding sites, but hiring a vehicle, a very expensive outlay in Iceland, is arguably the best mode of transport for birders short of time. The 1453-km-long 'Ring Road' (Route 1) circumnavigates the island, enabling easy access to all the major birding sites. It is mostly surfaced, as are a number of narrower minor roads, traffic is light and it is open all year round. However, some minor roads and tracks, mainly those in the mountains which are 4WD-only anyway, are usually open only during the short summer season, from mid-July or even later to early September.

Accommodation and Food

The full range of accommodation is available, from expensive hotels and less expensive guesthouses to youth hostels, campsites and even mountain refuge huts. Food and drink, with the exception of coffee, is expensive, since virtually everything has to be imported.

Health and Safety

Even in summer it is necessary to take warm, waterproof clothing and a four-season sleeping-bag, as well as sunglasses, a sunhat, sunscreen, wellies and, last but by no means least, the best insect repellent money can buy. In June and August particularly the millions of midges and biting blackflies can seriously hamper birding.

Climate and Timing

Iceland has a cool temperate maritime climate with an average summer temperature of just 49°F. The weather is changeable to say the least, so be prepared for those days when it seems like all four seasons have passed in just 24 hours. Birders intending to visit Mývatn, arguably the island's foremost birding site, are advised to do so in the second half of July, when breeding activity is at its peak and the numbers of biting insects are relatively low. It is possible to bird for 24 hours from mid-May to late July, but only for a few hours between November and January. The best period to see the Aurora Borealis ('Northern Lights') is between late August and March.

Habitats

This scenically spectacular island, which rises to 2119 m (6952 ft) at Oraefajokull in the southeast, is far enough north to support the largest permanent icecaps away from Antarctica and Greenland, the most extensive of which is the 8400-km² Vatnajökull where the ice is 1000 m (3281 ft) thick in places. Much of the rest of the island is composed of glaciers, together with their associated outwash plains, rivers and numerous beautiful waterfalls. Iceland is also a relatively young and growing volcanic landmass, with lava fields and most, if not all, of the other features associated with volcanic activity, including more hot springs than any other country in the world, geysers, steam vents, sulphur pits and boiling mud pools. Amidst all this action lie some wonderful wetlands which support huge numbers of breeding waterbirds. In addition, the wild and rugged coastline with numerous fjords and towering cliffs supports plenty of breeding seabirds. While Iceland's limited range of habitats supports large numbers of a few bird species, all the land mammals except Arctic fox have been introduced, there are no amphibians or reptiles, no resident butterflies or dragonflies, and only 520 species of flowering plants.

Conservation

Iceland's habitats have been degraded by agricultural intensification, drainage, grazing, industrialisation and energy development projects. These problems continue to raise doubts about the future of the Icelandic avifauna, which includes one near-threatened species. For example, in 1996 there were just 45 pairs of Gyrfalcon present on the island, only 75% of the population which had been present in 1989, a decline which is believed to be linked to the falling numbers of Rock Ptarmigan.

Bird Species

Over 240 species have been recorded in Iceland, of which 70 or so have been known to breed. Notable species include Harlequin Duck, Barrow's Goldeneye, White-tailed Eagle*, Gyrfalcon, Red-necked and Grey Phalaropes, Great Skua, Little Auk, Brünnich's and Black Guillemots, Atlantic Puffin, and Snow Bunting.

Iceland is ideally placed to receive Nearctic vagrants and these have included various waterfowl, Mourning Dove, Belted Kingfisher, Ruby-crowned Kinglet and, up to the end of 1997, a mouthwatering list of 12 New World warblers (numbers of records up to 1997 in parentheses) which includes Tennessee Warbler (1), Northern Parula (7), Magnolia (2), Black-throated Blue (1), Yellow-rumped (10), Palm (1), Blackpoll (7), Cerulean (1) and Black-and-white (2) Warblers, American Redstart (1), Common Yellowthroat (1) and Canada Warbler (1).

Expectations

It is possible to see 60–70 species on a trip lasting a week during the summer.

During the summer all small pools around **Reykjavík** are worth checking for the cracking little Red-necked and Grey (rare) Phalaropes, while Lake Tjörnin in town supports a small colony of Arctic Terns, as well as breeding Greater Scaup and Common Eider. Glaucous Gulls are usually present all year round along the nearby coast and they are joined by Iceland Gulls (including 'Kumlien's' *kumlieni*—13 in late 1998) during the winter, when Lake Tjörnin attracts almost regular American Wigeons (two in early 1999) and Barrow's Goldeneye, and the great rafts of Common Eiders in the harbour often contain King Eider (two in early 1999). During the autumn the Botanical Gardens have attracted Nearctic vagrants such as Swainson's Thrush. The pools at the golf course on the Seltjarnar Peninsula support breeding Red-necked Phalarope and a colony of Arctic Terns. Other species present in and around Reykjavík all year round include Whooper Swan and Common Redpoll ('Icelandic' *islandica*).

From the capital it is only a short trip across the lava flows to the **Reykjanes Peninsula** where the towering cliffs of Hafnarberg and Krisuvikurberg support numerous breeding auks. The cape north of Keflavík, site of the international airport 45 minutes by road from Reykjavík, is a good place to look for Nearctic vagrants, which have included such delights as Common Yellowthroat (at Garoskagi). Whalewatching trips run from Keflavík, in search of humpback, killer and minke whales, and white-beaked dolphin, while avian possibilities include Manx Shearwater and European Storm-Petrel. Boats can also be chartered to sail around the island of **Eldey** where the last Great Auk was reputedly recorded in 1844. It now supports over 16,000 pairs of Northern Gannets.

One or two pairs of Grey Phalarope occasionally breed at Floi, in the area from the mouth of the River Olfusa east to the River Thjorsa close to the villages of **Eyrarbakki** and **Stokkseyri**, in the southwestern lowlands of Iceland, about 50 km southeast of Reykjavík. During early October 1997 this area shot to ornithological fame when a Cerulean Warbler, the first to be seen on the eastern side of the Atlantic, was found at Eyrarbakki on 1 October, and a Palm Warbler, the first live record for Europe, turned up at Stokkseyri, 5 km east of Eyrarbakki, on 5 October. During the same period there were also three Red-eyed Vireos within a 12 km radius of Eyrarbakki. Harlequin Duck and Barrow's Goldeneye also occur in this part of Iceland, on the River Sog, a few minute's drive from Selfoss, the main town in the region, and other species present during the summer include Black-tailed Godwit (the greatest breeding density of the *islandica* race occurs on the Olfusforir and Kaldadharnes Wetlands), Red-necked Phalarope, Great Skua, Redwing and Snow Bunting.

The **Vestmannaeyjar** (Westmann Islands) archipelago, off the south coast, supports breeding colonies of Manx Shearwater, European Storm-Petrel, Leach's Storm-Petrel (one of Europe's largest colonies is on the outer island of Ellidhaey), Northern Gannet, Glaucous Gull, Great Skua, Black Guillemot and Atlantic Puffin. **Heimaey**, the largest and only inhabited island in the group, is accessible via a daily ferry from Thorlakshofn (accessible by bus from Reykjavík) or via several daily flights from Reykjavík. Look out for all the aforementioned species from the ferry, as well as northern bottlenose whale. On arrival at the island, where there is accommodation, it is possible to hire a boat to visit some of the seabird colonies. Heimaey is also a good place to look for Nearctic vagrants during the autumn, having already hosted Ruby-crowned Kinglet and Black-throated Blue Warbler. The second largest island in the archipelago is Surtsey which emerged from under the sea between 1963 and 1967 during a period of violent volcanic activity.

BREIDAFJÖRDUR

The huge shallow bay known as Breidafjördur and its surrounding cliffs, on Iceland's west coast, support most of the country's White-tailed Eagles* (over 50 pairs) and Grey Phalaropes (a few pairs), as well as some large seabird colonies, but it is possible to beat the lot with blue whale, the largest animal on earth and just one of several which can be seen on cetacean whale-watching trips out from the bay.

The species listed below occur during the summer unless otherwise indicated.

Localised Specialities
Harlequin Duck, Gyrfalcon, Grey Phalarope, Brünnich's Guillemot.

Other Localised Species
Rock Ptarmigan.

Others
Greater Scaup, Long-tailed Duck, White-tailed Eagle*, Black-tailed Godwit (islandica), Purple Sandpiper, Red-necked Phalarope, Glaucous and Iceland (winter) Gulls, Arctic Tern, Great and Arctic Skuas, Black Guillemot, Atlantic Puffin, Red-throated and Great Northern Divers, Snow Bunting.

Other Wildlife
White-beaked dolphin, common and grey seals, blue, fin, humpback, killer, minke, pilot, sei and sperm whales.

Auks breed on the cliffs 70 km west of **Arnastapi** on the south side of the Snaefells Peninsula, at the south end of the bay. Harlequin Duck occurs along the coast south of Arnastapi and around **Ólafsvík** on the north side of the peninsula, where up to 900 Red-necked Phalaropes have been seen in a day. Ólafsvík is the departure point for long whale-watching trips, on which it is possible to see blue whale (most likely during second half of July). It is also possible to go on boat trips out from **Stykkishólmur**, to look for smaller cetaceans and White-tailed Eagles* which nest on a nearby cliff. There is also a ferry between Stykkishólmur and Brjanslaekur, on the Northwest Peninsula, which stops at a couple of the many islands in the bay, including **Flatey** where Grey Phalarope breeds.

Accommodation: there is a wide variety of accommodation in the area (best booked in advance), in Borganes and Stykkishólmur for example, and camping is possible at Ólafsvík.

NORTHWEST PENINSULA

The remote Northwest Peninsula is another stronghold of White-tailed Eagle*, as well as Gyrfalcon, and the three colossal cliffs at Haelavikurgbjarg, Hornbjarg and Latrabjarg, which tower 500 m (1640 ft) above the sea, support masses of auks. Latrabjarg alone is reputed to be Europe's and the north Atlantic's largest seabird colony, thanks to the presence of about a million birds, including 400,000 pairs of Razorbills—the largest concentration of this species on earth.

Localised Specialities
Harlequin Duck, Gyrfalcon, Brünnich's Guillemot.

Other Localised Species
Rock Ptarmigan.

Others
Whooper Swan, Long-tailed Duck, White-tailed Eagle*, Merlin (endemic breeding *subaesalon* race), Purple Sandpiper, Red-necked Phalarope, Glaucous Gull, Arctic Tern, Arctic Skua, Razorbill, Black Guillemot, Red-throated and Great Northern Divers, Redwing, Snow Bunting.

Other Wildlife
Arctic fox.

From Brjanslaekur bird alongside the roads to Isafjördur, taking in the 12-km-long and up to 440 m (1444 ft) high cliffs at **Latrabjarg** where thousands of Brünnich's Guillemots and Atlantic Puffins breed alongside the hundreds of thousands of Razorbills. To reach these cliffs park at Bjargtangar Lighthouse, accessible via a risky drive along a beach, or in Hvallatur, which is a 5-km walk away, or take the Brjanslaekur–Breidavik Youth Hostel bus which runs three times per week. Haelavikurgbjarg and Hornbjarg can only be reached by boat. **Lake Vatnsdalsvatn**, 6 km east of Brjanslaekur in Vatnsfjördur National Park, is a good site for Harlequin Duck, White-tailed Eagle*, Gyrfalcon and Rock Ptarmigan.

Accommodation: Brjanslaekur, Isafjördur or other fishing villages, accessible by road, in the western part of the peninsula. Campsites include those near Bjargtangar Lighthouse, on the shore of Lake Vatnsdalsvatn and at Breidavik Youth Hostel.

Between the Northwest Peninsula and Blonduós on Iceland's north coast look out for Harlequin Ducks on fast-flowing rivers and for Iceland Gull amongst the Glaucous Gulls at the mouth of the River Blanda at **Blonduós**. Between Blonduós and Mývatn there are plenty of places to stay in **Akureyri**, which is a good place to see the endemic *islandicus* race of Winter Wren, and nearby the main ring road reaches its maximum height of 540 m (1772 ft) in the valley of **Oxnadalur** where Rock Ptarmigan occurs. During the summer there are daily air and ferry tours from Akureyri to the small offshore island of **Grímsey**, which lies on the Arctic Circle and supports a few pairs of Little Auk, the only ones left in Iceland. From the ferry it is possible to see fin, killer and minke whales. Accommodation on the island includes a guesthouse and campsite.

MÝVATN

Mývatn is Icelandic for 'Lake of Midges', an apt name for the country's fourth largest lake, which measures 37 km² and has a maximum depth of just 4 m (13 ft). Midges and blackflies abound, but so do birds, and birders prefer to call Mývatn the 'Lake of Ducks', for more ducks breed here than anywhere else in Europe; tens of thousands (perhaps 50,000 pairs) of 15 species in fact, including about 200 pairs of Harlequin Duck and about 800 pairs of Barrow's Goldeneye.

Biting blackflies, which are more or less restricted to the running waters of the River Laxa, and midges have two main flight periods, during June and August. Birders should avoid these times like the plague they resemble and try to visit Mývatn during the second half of July when breeding activity is at its peak. The species listed below occur during this time unless otherwise indicated.

Localised Specialities
Harlequin Duck, Barrow's Goldeneye.

Other Localised Species
Rock Ptarmigan.

Others
Slavonian Grebe, Whooper Swan, Eurasian Wigeon, Gadwall, Common Teal, Mallard, Northern Pintail, Northern Shoveler, Common Pochard, Tufted Duck, Greater Scaup, Long-tailed Duck, Common Scoter, Red-breasted Merganser, Merlin (endemic breeding *subaesalon* race), Black-tailed Godwit (*islandica*), Purple Sandpiper, Red-necked Phalarope, Arctic Tern, Red-throated and Great Northern Divers, Redwing, Winter Wren (*islandicus*), Snow Bunting.

Other Wildlife
Arctic fox (scarce).

(Other species recorded here include Ruddy Duck, Pink-footed Goose, American Wigeon (up to three long-staying birds were still present in summer 1999), Ring-necked Duck, Steller's Eider* (a drake from 20th May to 1st June 1997), Common Goldeneye, Goosander and Gyrfalcon.)

Mývatn is accessible by air (one hour) and bus (eight hours) from Reykjavík several times daily. Cars, motorbikes and bicycles can be hired in Reykjahlid. Harlequin Ducks are particularly numerous along the River Laxa at the western end of the lake where the beautiful drakes grace the turbulent waters and provide the highlight of a birding trip to Iceland for most visitors. Bird from the bridge over the river near the lake and alongside the road northwards. Gyrfalcon is most likely to be seen to the south of the lake at Vindbelgjarfjall.

Accommodation: two hotels, including Hotel Reynihlid, a wide variety of other accommodation including guesthouses in the village of Reykjah-lid, farmhouses, and campsites at Vogar (with toilets and hot showers).

Europe's most powerful waterfall, Dettifoss, which is 44 m (144 ft) high, lies in the **Jökulsa Canyon**, northeast of Mývatn. This is a good place to

*Fifteen species of duck breed at Mývatn and the beautiful Harlequin is
arguably the best*

look for Gyrfalcon and Snow Bunting, particularly around the horseshoe-
shaped canyon of Asbyrgi where there is a good campsite. A long way
south of here, via 4WD-only tracks, in the remote interior of Iceland at
the highland area of **Askja**, there is a slim possibility of finding Snowy
Owl. To the north of Dettifoss the road follows the coast around the
Tjörnes Peninsula where almost every year since 1987 a Broad-billed
Sandpiper has appeared at Hóll during the spring, with its recent visits
falling between 20th May and 1st June 1998, and 18 May and 27 May
1997. The road around this peninsula passes through the fishing town of
Húsavik, from where there are whale-watching trips in search of regular
white-beaked dolphin and minke whale, and more unusual humpback
and sei whales. Húsavik harbour is a good place to look for Iceland Gull.

The fishing town of **Hofn** (pronounced 'Hupp') in southeast Iceland,
accessible by air from Reykjavík, is another whale-watching base.
Minke whale, as well as white-beaked dolphin are seen on a regular
basis, while fin, humpback and killer whales are also possible. The best
time to go is in August and September. Iceland's main icecap, Vatnajökull, and a vast sand-plain, lie partly within the 500-km^2 **Skaftafell National Park**, near Hofn, where breeding birds include Rock Ptarmigan,
Red-necked Phalarope, Great and Arctic Skuas, Red-throated Diver,
Redwing and Winter Wren (*islandicus*). Along the coast southwest of
Hofn lies **Jokulsarlon**, which together with two other vast areas of silt,
sand and gravel deposits resulting from glacial erosion, known as *san-
durs*, at Breidamerkur and Skeidarar, support between 2,000 and 3,000
pairs of Great Skua, the largest breeding concentration of this species in
the world.

ADDITIONAL INFORMATION

Addresses

The travel company, Arctic Experience Limited, 29 Nork Way,
Banstead, Surrey, SM7 1PB, UK (tel: 01737 218800; fax: 01737 362341;
email: sales@arctic-discover.co.uk; website: www.arctic-discover.
co.uk), specialises in Iceland and offers an incredible variety of organised tours and independent self-drive packages.
Please send records of rarities to the Icelandic Rarities Committee,
Melbae 40, IS-110 Reykjavík, Iceland. The annual rarities report is
published in *Bliki*, in Icelandic with an English summary.

Books and papers

Guide to the Birds of Iceland. Einarsson P, 1991. Iceland.

Birds of Iceland (second edition). Bardarson H, 1987.

Sjaldgaefir fuglar a Islandi fyrir 1981 (Rare Birds in Iceland Before 1981 —brief English summaries for 226 species). Petursson G and Brainsson G, 1999. Available from Icelandic Institute of Natural History, PO Box 5320, IS-125 Reykjavík, Iceland.

Three excellent books: *Iceland: Nature's Meeting Place*, Cawardine M; *Iceland: The Traveller's Guide*, Escritt T; and *The Key to Iceland*, are available from Arctic Experience Limited (address above).

ITALY

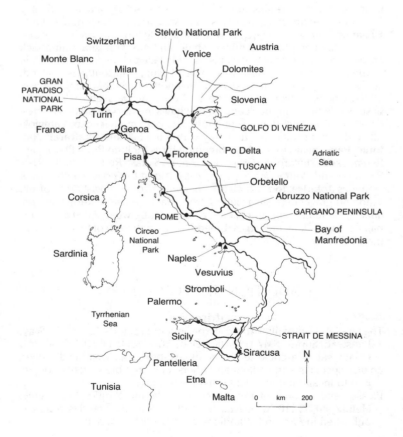

INTRODUCTION

Summary

Despite the presence of birds such as Lanner Falcon and Rock Partridge, as well plenty of waterbirds, a spectacular raptor passage and high-altitude specialities, very few birders make it to Italy, which is a shame because, although it is a large country, relatively expensive to visit and riddled with hunters, Italy's wide range of habitats and birds really do deserve more attention.

Size

At 301,245 km^2, Italy (not including Sardinia which is dealt with in a separate section, p. 321) is 2.3 times larger than England and 40% the size of Texas.

Getting Around

Travelling around Italy on public transport is fairly straightforward, especially on the relatively cheap trains in the north, but buses don't operate in many rural areas, especially in the south, so, as usual, the best way for birders on a tight schedule to get around is to hire a vehicle, although the costs of hire and petrol are amongst the highest in Europe and most highways (*autostrada*) are toll roads.

Accommodation and Food

Built accommodation is expensive, but there are about 50 youth hostels and plenty of campsites. Food and drink are relatively cheap and include pizza, pasta, *panini* (substantial sandwiches), beer, wine and lots of liqueurs such as Amaretto and Sambuca.

Health and Safety

Theft from vehicles is a problem in major cities and throughout the south.

Climate and Timing

Northern Italy has a temperate climate with warm to hot summers and often very cold winters, whereas the south has a Mediterranean climate with very dry and hot summers and cool winters. Italy is a good place to visit at most times of the year, although spring is arguably the best, what with the raptor passage over the Strait de Messina, between the mainland and Sicily, and a strong northward movement of other passage migrants, especially waterbirds.

Habitats

Extreme northern Italy is mountainous, with the Alps in the northwest rising to 4808 m (15,774 ft) at Monte Blanc on the border with France, and the Dolomites in the northeast rising to 3342 m (10,965 ft) at Marmolada. These ranges support mixed and coniferous forests, and alpine pastures. To their south lie the Po Lowlands, the largest low-lying area in the country, which is densely populated, heavily industrialised, intensively cultivated and badly polluted. To the south of here the land rises again, to the Appennines, which reach a maximum height of 2914 m (9564 ft) at Gran Sasso d'Italia and form the spine of peninsular Italy. This range and its outliers which include the active volcano, Vesuvius, support garrigue, maquis and deciduous forest. Coastal plains of varying width lie either side of the Appennines and they contain some very important wetlands, ranging from seasonally flooded *salicornia* flats to reedy lagoons. There is also plenty of farmland in southern Italy, but in stark contrast to much of the northern lowlands the south is predominantly rugged and rural. The island of Sicily rises to 3323 m (10,902 ft) at Etna, the highest volcano in Europe. The last major eruption of Etna took place in 1971 but it came briefly to life again in 1985, threatening devastation throughout the densely populated lower slopes.

Conservation
Habitat loss and degradation, primarily due to agricultural intensification, built development and industrialisation, as well as hunting, pollution and tourism are the major problems facing the ten threatened and near-threatened species as well as the relatively common and widespread birds which occur in Italy. These problems, especially hunting, became so severe in the early 1990s that the non-governmental conservation movement finally took off and the Lega Italian per la Protezione degli Uccelli (LIPU) have since managed to establish numerous reserves, recruit 30,000 members and, most importantly, successfullly curb the slaughter of raptors and trapping of migrant passerines, all no mean feats in the Mediterranean.

Perhaps primarily due to the efforts of LIPU in enlightening people, the Italian public's distaste for shooting and trapping appears to be growing, but despite a 50% fall in the number of 'official' hunters between 1980 and 1996 (1.8 million to 0.9 million) hunting is still very popular. Hence, even though no fewer than 18 million people (over 30% of the population) voted for the complete abolition of this so-called sport during the mid-1990s the government didn't take a blind bit of notice. However, government ministers must know that even though many hunters are now taking their terrible toll beyond the country's borders in eastern Europe, and the problem, at least in part, seems to be moving elsewhere, the shame remains with Italy.

Bird Species
About 482 species have been recorded in Italy. Notable species include Greater Flamingo, Eleonora's and Lanner Falcons, Rock Partridge, Audouin's* and Slender-billed Gulls, Great Spotted Cuckoo, Wallcreeper, White-winged Snowfinch, Alpine Accentor, Citril Finch and Black-headed Bunting.

GRAN PARADISO NATIONAL PARK

The coniferous forest, montane pastures and spectacular mountains which rise to 4061 m (13,324 ft) at Gran Paradiso in this Alpine park in northwest Italy support an impressive high-altitude avifauna which includes Rock Partridge and Wallcreeper.

Localised Specialities
Rock Partridge.

Other Localised Species
Rock Ptarmigan, Wallcreeper, White-winged Snowfinch, Citril Finch.

Others

Golden Eagle, Hazel Grouse, Eurasian Pygmy-Owl, Tengmalm's Owl, Alpine Swift, Three-toed and Black Woodpeckers, Eurasian Nutcracker, Red-billed and Yellow-billed Choughs, Eurasian Crag-Martin, House Sparrow ('Italian' *italiae*), Rock Petronia, Alpine Accentor, Rock Bunting.

Other Wildlife

Chamois, ibex, Alpine marmot.

The species listed above occur in the park, which is located about 15 km south of Aosta, but one of the best place to look for Rock Partridge is north of here near **Valpelline**. A km or so east of the hamlet of Thoulles-Dessus turn south over a bridge and continue for about 800 m to a small parking area on the north side of the minor road. Walk south from here up the steep trail opposite, through alpine pastures for about two hours, to reach the rocky slopes suitable for the partridge. To look for Wall-creeper head west from Aosta towards the 11.5-km-long Monte Blanc Tunnel and turn south into the **Val Savarenche**. Where the road reaches a small hotel and campsite at Pont there is a well signposted trail up to Vittorio Emmanuel II Refuge at 2732 m (8963 ft), about three hours away. Wallcreeper has been recorded around this refuge, one of a number in the park where there are small shops and overnight accommodation facilities, perfect for birders in search of high-altitude specialities.

Accommodation; Aosta. Rhemes Notre Dame—Camping La Marmotta.

Elsewhere in the Alps Lammergeier has been reintroduced into **Alpi Maritime Nature Park**, on the border with France adjacent to Mercantour National Park (p. 180), and **Stelvio National Park**, where Rock Partridge also occurs, on the border with Switzerland.

The shores of the **Golfo di Venézia** (Gulf of Venice) at the north end of the Adriatic are lined by lagoons and marshes. Most of these are worth birding, although the best previously productive spots include: (i) **Foci dell'Isonzo** (the mouth of the River Isonzo), just southwest of Monfalcone near the border with Slovenia, where breeding waterbirds include Little Bittern. There is a visitor centre, observation post, hide and ringing station at the Isola Cona Nature Reserve and a LIPU reserve near Punta Spigolo at the rivermouth; (ii) the **Laguna di Venézia** around Venice (which is situated on islands at the inland edge of this huge coastal lagoon), most of which can be viewed from surrounding roads. A dark morph Western Reef-Egret was present around the lagoon from 1994 to March 1997 at least, and the best area is Lio Piccolo to the east; and (iii) the **Po Delta**, which extends south from Venice to Ravenna and is skirted on its west side by the SS309. This is an important wetland for breeding birds (such as Collared Pratincole and Gull-billed Tern, and three pairs of Pygmy Cormorant* bred here in 1994), a major resting and refuelling station for passage waterbirds (which have included Marsh and Terek Sandpipers) and passerines (including Aquatic Warbler*), and one of the most important wildfowl wintering grounds in Europe (with species such as Ferruginous Duck* present). At the north end of the delta Collared Pratincole breeds on the huge brackish lagoon known as Valli di Comacchio, where Lesser Crested-Tern also bred in 1997 and a dark morph Western Reef-Egret was present in the Little Egret colony, also in 1997. Valli di Comacchio is visible from the roads between Ostellato and Porto Garibaldi, and Spina and Alfonsine. At the south end of the delta the WWF Punte Alberete nature reserve, which lies either side of the River Lamone 13 km north of Ravenna, supports breeding Black-crowned Night-Heron and, occasionally, Glossy Ibis. For more information contact Delta 2000, Via G. Garibaldi, 29/31, 1-44020 Ostellato (Fe), Italy (tel: 0533 680515; email: delta.2000@galactica.it).

TUSCANY

The rolling hills with olive groves and vineyards lying below the ancient hilltop towns of northwest peninsular Italy support few notable birds, but it is a different matter along the coast where the dunes, scrub, lagoons and marshes support a fine range of waterbirds, and in wooded limestone hills, where Lanner Falcon, here at the northern edge of its range, occurs. In addition, Pine Bunting is an occasional winter visitor to the coastal scrub of this region, a remarkable phenomenon considering this species' normal wintering range is in northeastern China and from Afghanistan to northwest India.

The species listed below occur during the summer unless otherwise indicated. The searing heat can be a problem in summer, but in winter it is often very cold.

Localised Species
Greater Flamingo, Lanner Falcon.

Others
Cory's ('Scopoli's' *diomedea*) and Mediterranean Shearwaters, Great Egret, Squacco Heron, Black-crowned Night-Heron, Little Bittern, Red Kite, Short-toed Eagle, Black-winged Stilt, Snowy Plover, Eurasian Eagle-Owl, European Bee-eater, European Roller, Lesser Grey Shrike, Moustached and Sardinian Warblers.

Other Wildlife
Eurasian otter.

(Other species recorded here include Ferruginous Duck*, Smew (winter), Cattle Egret, Common Crane, Slender-billed Curlew* (three to four were reported from Diaccia Botrona Marsa in April 1997), Marsh Sandpiper, Red-necked Phalarope, Audouin's Gull*, Whiskered and White-winged Terns, and Pine Bunting (between November and February 1995–1996 an unprecedented flock of 45–50 were present in the *salicornia* and tamarisk scrub on the inland side of the dunes near the rivermouth at Bocca di Serchio on the west coast near Pisa. Five returned here in November 1996 and one was present in late January 1998. Another three were present about 60 km to the south, at Montecatini, in 1995–96).

About 250 species, including 50 which have been known to breed, have been recorded at the LIPU **Lago di Massaciuccoli** nature reserve, about 20 km north of Pisa near Lucca, including Moustached Warbler. The wildlife refuge at **Bolgheri**, near the coast south of Cécina, sup-

TUSCANY

ports similar species and is a particularly good place to see Eurasian otter. South of Florence and Figline Valdarno, the lakes at the LIPU **Montepulciano** nature reserve and **Trasimeno** also support a wide range of waterbirds. The wooded hills of the **Valle del Farma** about 35 km south of Siena near Lamalesa are excellent for raptors, including Lanner Falcon as well as Eurasian Eagle-Owl. The low hills and marshes in the natural park at **Maremma**, on the coast about 15 km south of Grosseta, support European Roller and Lesser Grey Shrike. The roller, as well as Cattle Egret, are most likely to be seen in the vicinity of the Ombrone Rivermouth, just north of Marina di Alberese which is a good place from which to look for shearwaters. The **Laguna di Orbetello**, 2600 ha of which is managed as a WWF reserve (open on Thursdays and Sundays only), just to the south of Maremma (148 km northwest of Rome), supports Greater Flamingo, Great Egret (at least 290 were present here and at Lago di Burano, a few km to the southeast, in late December 1997) and Moustached Warbler, and attracts a wide variety of passage waterbirds. This lagoon is one of two which are visible from the road on the isthmus which links Monte Argentario, a rocky promontory, to the mainland. Similar species occur at **Diaccia Botrona Marsa**, a large marsh near Castiglion della Pescaia. The WWF **Bosco Rocconi** nature reserve near Roccalbegna is another good site for Lanner Falcon.

Accommodation: During the summer, tourists outnumber the locals two to one in Tuscany so accommodation can be in short supply.

The **Macchiatonda Nature Reserve** near Rome is an excellent site for passage shorebirds, which have included rarities such as Baird's Sandpiper and Pacific Golden-Plover. In addition a Pine Bunting was present here during winter 1997–98.

Over 230 species have been recorded in **Circeo National Park**, around Sabaudia about 90 km south of Rome, including breeding Great Spotted Cuckoo and Moustached Warbler, and passage migrants such as Glossy Ibis, Greater Spotted Eagle*, Red-footed Falcon, Common Crane, Great Snipe*, Marsh Sandpiper, Collared Pratincole, Audouin's Gull* and Caspian Tern. During the winter Ferruginous Duck* and Wallcreeper have been recorded. Head south from Rome on the main coastal road to reach the main lagoons which lie alongside the road between Latina and Sabaudia.

The wild wooded mountains in **Abruzzo National Park**, arguably one of the finest in Italy and Europe, are situated about 110 km east of Rome in the high Appenines and they support Golden Eagle and White-backed Woodpecker (*lilfordi*), as well as 'Marsican' brown bear (only about 80 left in the wild), 'Abruzzo' chamois and 'Appennine' grey wolf (only about 30 left in the wild). The small town of Civitella Alfadena would make a good base from which to hike a variety of trails, most of which are only open between April and September. Rufous-tailed Rock-Thrush occurs around the summit crater of **Vesuvius** which is situated at 1277 m (4190 ft) just east of Naples (Napoli) and Blue Rock-Thrush occurs in the limestone mountains of the **Sorrento Peninsula**, an hour by road south of Naples. From the town of Sorrento it is possible to take a ferry to the small island of **Capri** where Cory's ('Scopoli's' *diomedea*) and Mediterranean Shearwaters breed. These birds can be seen from this ferry or the one from Naples.

GARGANO PENINSULA

The variety of habitats on and around this peninsula which protrudes into the Adriatic on the east coast help to make this one of the best birding areas in Italy and Europe. The south side of the peninsula lies alongside the Bay of Manfredonia, which came to the attention of the birding world with a bang in early 1995 when up to 19 Slender-billed Curlews* were found wintering there. There used to be a 40-km stretch of prime saltmarsh along this bay, but due to agricultural intensification throughout the 20th century only pockets of wetland remain amongst the vegetable and wheat fields. However, these wetlands, which also include freshwater marshes and salinas, still support Italy's largest population of Pied Avocets (6,000), large colonies of Slender-billed (500 pairs) and Mediterranean (1,000 pairs) Gulls, and as many as 10,000 Black-tailed Godwits and 25,000 Ruff during passage periods. In addition, the two huge lakes, Lesina and Varano, on the northern side of the peninsula attract thousands of wintering wildfowl and the forested limestone mountains of the peninsula support White-backed Woodpecker.

The species listed below occur during the summer unless otherwise indicated.

Localised Specialities
Slender-billed Gull.

Other Localised Species
Lanner Falcon.

Others
Cory's ('Scopoli's' *diomedea*) and Mediterranean Shearwaters, Short-toed Eagle, Common Crane (passage), Pied Avocet, Mediterranean Gull, Alpine Swift, European Roller, White-backed (*lilfordi*) and Black Wood-peckers, Lesser Grey Shrike, Calandra Lark, Rock and Black-headed Buntings.

(Other species recorded here include Squacco Heron, Glossy Ibis, Egyptian Vulture and Slender-billed Curlew*.)

Records of Slender-billed Curlew since 1988*
Between 1876 and 1938 a total of 18 specimens were collected, between 1988 and 1993 there were six records, and between 21st January and 28 March 1995 up to 19 were present.

August 1988	two at Margherita di Savoia.
January 1989	two at Lago di Lesina.
March 1989	one at Frattarolo Nature Reserve.
December 1992	two at Margherita di Savoia.
January 1993	one at Margherita di Savoia.
May 1993	one at Margherita di Savoia.
Jan–Mar 1995	up to 19.

The early 1995 birds foraged mainly in partially flooded *salicornia* and *suaeda* scrub. When looking for Slender-billed Curlews* beware of pale-looking Eurasian Curlews of the eastern *orientalis* race and be extremely careful not to disturb any birds, particularly during the offi-cial hunting season (between the third week of September and the end of January), or they may fly within range of the indiscriminate shooters.

There are four major birding areas on the peninsula: (i) **Lago di Varano** and **Lago di Lesina**, which are separated by a rocky headland at the northwestern end of the peninsula. Reedy Lesina is the most acc-essible and there is a reserve at its eastern end; (ii) the **Foresta d'Umbra** at the east end of the peninsula, where White-backed Woodpecker occurs; and (iii) the **Margherita di Savoia** area, to the south of the peninsula between Manfredonia and Barletta, and viewable from the SS159 which runs along the coast. This huge area of salinas, saltmarsh-es and grazing land supports breeding shorebirds and large numbers of wintering and passage birds. There are extensive areas of *salicornia* in the WWF Frattarolo nature reserve at the Candelaro rivermouth, 9 km south of Manfredonia. Permits are required to visit some sensitive areas and these can be obtained from the Forester's Office in Trinitapoli (tel: 88 373 2160). Finally, shearwaters breed on the **Isole Tremiti**, a group of islands to the north of the peninsula which are accessible via regular ferries from Termoli and Rodi Garganico.

Accommodation: Peschici.

The small town of **Matera** in southern Italy hosts one of the wonders of the ornithological world—a colony of 1,000–1,200 pairs of Lesser Kestrels*, and in the evening they roost in just one or two nearby pine trees!

STRAIT DE MESSINA

Every spring 30,000–40,000 raptors, including as many as several thousand in a single day, cross this narrow 3.5-km-long channel between mainland Italy and Sicily. An amazing 36 different species of raptor have been recorded here, of which about 25 are recorded annually. The vast majority of birds are European Honey-buzzards (up to 22,000 including as many as 3,000 in a single day), and most of the rest are Black Kites, Western Marsh-Harriers (1,100 in 1998, 3,200 in 1997) and Red-footed Falcons (the spring average is 300–400 but up to over 6,900 have been recorded), but regular migrants also include the likes of Pallid Harrier* (over 100 in spring 1998, 35 in 1999). All of these birds are accompanied by other passage migrants such as storks, and if few birds are on the move it is always worth seawatching.

Unfortunately, one of the best birding experiences Europe has to offer is spoiled, at least on the mainland side of the strait, by ranks of stupid shooters who line up each spring to try and shoot down as many of these birds as possible. LIPU hosts an annual research and surveillance camp to record the movements of birds and the actions of the hunters, and birders who think they can face the prospect of watching these idiots, and perhaps, ultimately, help end the carnage, can gain more information from Andrea Corso, via Camastra 10, 96100 Siracusa, Italy, or David Lingard, Fernwood, Doddington Road, Whisby, Lincoln, LN6 9BX, UK.

The species listed below occur during the spring (the majority of birds pass through in April) unless otherwise indicated.

Localised Specialities
Rock Partridge.

Regular Spring Passage Migrants
Cory's ('Scopoli's' *diomedea*) and Mediterranean Shearwaters, Black and White Storks, European Honey-buzzard, Red (scarce) and Black Kites, Egyptian Vulture, Western Marsh-Harrier, Pallid* and Montagu's Harriers, Long-legged Buzzard (scarce), Bonelli's and Booted (scarce) Eagles, Lesser Kestrel*, Red-footed and Eleonora's Falcons, European Bee-eater.

Others
Pallid Swift, Red-billed Chough, Blue Rock-Thrush.

(Other species recorded here include Black-shouldered Kite, Short-toed Eagle, Levant Sparrowhawk (one in spring 1999 was the third record), Lesser Spotted, Greater Spotted*, Steppe, Imperial* and Golden Eagles, Amur (two on 15th May 1999, singles on 7th and 19th May 1998, 4th May 1997 and 29th April 1995), Lanner, Saker and Barbary Falcons, Common Crane and Audouin's Gull*.)

When the north wind blows, the top places from which to observe raptors are on the mainland, especially at Portella di Castanea or Torre Faro. Otherwise, it is best to be on Sicily, where the coast road north and south of Messina at the northeast end of the island enables access to the best viewing areas, which are as follows: (i) Santa Rosalia, near the village of Castanea, especially during southerly or southeasterly winds; (ii) the 1100 m (3609 ft) high Mount Dinnammare, especially on windless days; and (iii) Pilone di Cannitello. The scrubby cliffs above Messina support Rock Partridge, which also occurs on Etna.

SICILY

This rugged, mountainous island with holm-oak woods and pine forest supports localised species such as Rock Partridge, but it is the salinas and other coastal wetlands of southeast Sicily which offer the most exciting birding, for they attract impressive numbers of a wide range of passage migrant and wintering waterbirds, including Glossy Ibis (over 150 in March 1998), Marsh Sandpiper (about 100 in August 1998), Little Stint (over 2,000 in August 1998), Curlew Sandpiper (over 4,000 in August 1998), Black-winged Stilt (about 2,000 in August 1998) and Mediterranean Gull (over 4,000 in March 1998).

The species listed below occur during the summer unless otherwise indicated.

Localised Specialities
Eleonora's Falcon, Rock Partridge.

Regular Passage Migrants
Greater Flamingo, Squacco Heron, Glossy Ibis, Marsh Sandpiper, Little Stint, Curlew Sandpiper, Black-winged Stilt, Mediterranean Gull, Gull-billed Tern, European Bee-eater.

Others
Cory's ('Scopoli's' *diomedea*) and Mediterrean Shearwaters, Pallid Swift, European Roller, Red-billed Chough, Rufous-tailed and Blue Rock-Thrushes, Zitting Cisticola, Sardinian and Subalpine Warblers, Calandra Lark.

(Other species recorded here include Ferruginous Duck* (autumn and winter), Western Reef-Egret (Longarini), Egyptian Vulture (two pairs in 1999), Slender-billed Curlew* (one on 31st March 1996 at Lago di Lentini), Terek Sandpiper, Sociable Lapwing*, Audouin's*, Great Black-headed (up to three during winters 1996–1997 to 1998–1999) and Slender-billed Gulls, Caspian Tern, Richard's Pipit (3–4 in the Siracusa area during winter 1998–1999 and four at Lago di Lentini, with a Blyth's Pipit, in December 1997) and Red-throated Pipit).

Sites worth visiting in the southeast include Lago di Lentini, Siracusa Salinas, Longarini, Pantani di Capo Passero, the Priolo Salinas, the mouth of the River Simeto and the lower reaches of the River Tellaro. The **Isole Eolie o Lipari**, a group of small islands and rock stacks off the north coast of Sicily, which include the active volcano of Stromboli, support Cory's Shearwater and small numbers of Eleonora's Falcon. Some islands are accessible by boat from Messina and Milazzo.

ADDITIONAL INFORMATION

Addresses

Please send records of rarities to the Comitato di Ohologazione Italiano (COI), via A. Tommosi, 21-57124 Livorno, Italy. The annual rarities report is published in *Riv. Ital. Om.* (in Italian with an English summary).

The Lega Italiana per la Protezione degli Uccelli (LIPU), via Trento 49, 43100 Parma, Italy (fax: 521 273419; email: lipusede@tin.it), publishes *The Hoopoe* newsletter. This vital organisation can also be contacted via LIPU (UK), c/o 6 Butlers Close, Broomfield, Chelmsford, Essex, CM1 5BE, UK.

Books and papers

Where to watch birds in Italy. LIPU, 1994. Helm.

The Birds of Sicily: An Annotated Checklist. Iapichino C and Massa B, 1989. BOU Checklist No. 11.

Check-list Degli Uccelli Italiani. Brichetti P and Massa B, 1993. *Riv. Ital. di Birdwatching* 1: (2) 61–73 and (3) 20–26.

LATVIA

INTRODUCTION

Few birders visit this small country on the eastern side of the Baltic Sea, but the presence of a good visitor infrastructure, extensive areas of largely unspoilt countryside and birds such as Marsh Sandpiper, here at the western extremity of its breeding range, in an avifauna which is otherwise similar to Poland, may tempt birders further east in the future.

At 64,000 km², Latvia is about half the size of England and just under 10% the size of Texas. The capital, Riga, is accessible by air from most European capitals and by ferry from many Baltic ports. From here it is possible to reach most birding sites via public transport. Buses are more expensive but more frequent and quicker than the trains, and journeys on both must be booked in advance. The country has only one major highway but the roads which connect other towns are fine. Minor roads are bad, however, and the driving standards leave something to be desired. Away from Riga and Jurmala, a little way along the coast to the west, where there is a good range of accommodation, including hotels (which are either expensive rundown relics from better times or cheap and nasty), guesthouses and youth hostels, the choice is limited to a few hotels, pensions and campsites, some of which have chalets. Food is relatively expensive, even staples such as cabbage soup, dairy products, fish, meat and potatoes. Beer (*alus*), vodka and wine are readily

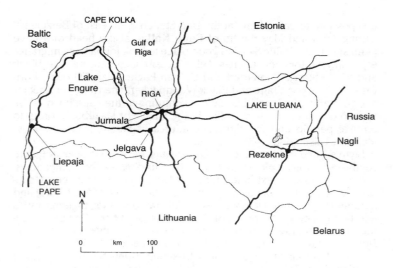

available. Riga has a major organised crime problem but theft from accommodation is of more concern to visitors. There have been problems with tap water so it is best to avoid drinking this straight.

Latvia's avifauna is, arguably, highlighted by its breeding species, hence the best time to visit this country is during the summer, from mid-May to August. However it is rather wet in June and July. The long winters are also very cold.

Away from the long Baltic coastline, which is littered with wrecks of Russian ships but otherwise largely unspoilt, Latvia is a low-lying forested lakeland which rises to just 312 m (1024 ft). During the Russian occupation there was considerable localised environmental damage, but large areas of Latvia remain relatively unscathed. If it remains that way there should be few problems for the seven near-threatened and threatened species as well as the relatively common and widespread birds which occur in the country.

About 322 species have been recorded in Latvia, including Greater Spotted Eagle*, Hazel Grouse, Little Crake, Marsh Sandpiper, White-winged Tern, Ural Owl and Aquatic Warbler* (10–50 pairs).

It is possible to enjoy some excellent birding between Riga, Latvia's capital, and Cape Kolka to the northwest. **Lake Babite**, just to the west of Riga, is an important resting and refuelling station for passage waterbirds and a pair of Marsh Sandpipers was present near here during the summer of 1997, perhaps indicating that this species may continue to expand its breeding range westwards. Further west along the coast of the Gulf of Riga the lakes, raised bogs and forest in **Kemeri National Park** support breeding Little Bittern, Black Stork, Lesser Spotted Eagle, Common Crane, Wood Sandpiper, Three-toed Woodpecker (rare) and Greenish Warbler (*trochiloides*). **Lake Kanieris**, to the north, supports White-tailed Eagle*. The shallow, well-vegetated **Lake Engure**, which is situated on the coast about halfway between Riga and Cape Kolka, supports breeding Little Crake, as well as all five European grebes, Little Bittern and Little Gull, while Black Stork, Lesser Spotted Eagle, Black and Hazel Grouse, and Tengmalm's Owl inhabit the surrounding woods.

It is possible to camp here, at the Bird Station 2 km east of Berzciems. During April and May the tip of **Cape Kolka**, at the head of a large peninsula in the Baltic Sea, is a good place to look for passage migrants, especially raptors and finches. Other possibilities here include Black and White Storks, Short-toed and Golden Eagles, Hazel Grouse, Corn Crake*, Common Crane and Black Woodpecker. The village of Kolka is accessible by bus from Riga. Before venturing to the cape it would be wise to contact the reserve office in the village of Mazirbe, in order to arrange permits and camping. The address is Slitere Nature Reserve, Mazirbe, Talsu raj. LV—3273, Latvia.

Blyth's Reed-Warbler and Citrine Wagtail have bred near **Jelgava**, southwest of Riga. **Lake Pape** and its surrounding reedbeds, meadows, scrub and pines, in extreme southwest Latvia on the Baltic coast, supports large numbers of passage migrants in both spring (April–May) and autumn (September–October), especially raptors, owls, pigeons, pipits and finches, hence there is a Bird Station situated here. Regular breeding species include Common Crane, while recent rarities have included Northern Hawk Owl and a breeding pair of Paddyfield Warblers, way northwest of this species' normal breeding range by the Black and Caspian Seas. To reach the lake, head for the village of Pape from Rucava, 12 km to the east, then continue north for 3 km to the Bird Observatory where permits, possible guided walks and camping may be arranged.

The bogs, 30 km² of fishponds, marshes, meadows and woods surrounding **Lake Lubana** in east Latvia support a fine range of breeding birds, including Greater Spotted Eagle*, Little Crake, a few pairs of Marsh Sandpipers and the occasional pair of Terek Sandpipers, as well as Black Stork, White-tailed* and Lesser Spotted Eagles, Little Gull, White-winged Tern, White-backed and Black Woodpeckers, and Eurasian Nutcracker. The best birding areas are as follows: (i) alongside the road south and east of Lubana to Grigalava, which skirts the north shore of Lake Lubana; (ii) continue south and east along this road to bird one of the three fishpond complexes; and (iii) then turn south to bird the other two fishpond complexes which lie either side of Nagli. In order to arrange access to the fishponds visit the Orenisi Bird Station in the fishpond complex east of Nagli, or the local fishfarmer's offices in Nagli.

The largest raised bog in Latvia, which is situated within the 190-km² **Teychu Nature Reserve**, to the west of Nagli, supports Lesser Spotted and Greater Spotted* Eagles, Hazel Grouse, and White-backed, Three-toed and Black Woodpeckers. For more information on this huge area contact Teychu Nature Reserve, Laudona, Madonas raj. LV—4862, Latvia.

ADDITIONAL INFORMATION

Addresses

Please send records of rarities to the Latvijas Ornithofaunistikas Komisijas, Laboratory of Ornithology, Miera 3, LV-2169 Salaspils, Latvia. The annual rarities report is published in *Putni Daba*, in Latvian with an English summary.

Books and papers

List of Latvian Bird Species 1992. Celmins A, 1992. Eastbird.

LIECHTENSTEIN

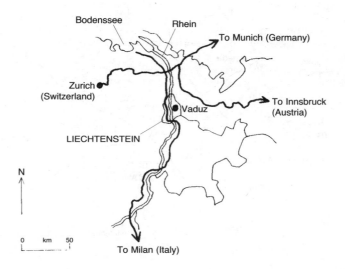

Few birders have been to this tiny principality (160 km²) in the central Alps between Austria and Switzerland, although the forest and alpine pastures on its mountains, which rise to 2599 m (8527 ft), support the likes of Hazel Grouse and Eurasian Pygmy-Owl, albeit in low numbers, and the cultivated Rhein Valley with tiny remnant marshes and woods, which accounts for the remaining third or so of the principality, supports Corn Crake*. Many wetlands in the Rhein Valley were destroyed long ago and the native deciduous woods on the slopes above have largely been replaced with conifer plantations. There are several nature reserves but problems such as agricultural intensification need to be solved if the one threatened species as well as the relatively common and widespread birds which occur in Liechtenstein are to survive.

Liechtenstein is a modern part of the world with a good visitor infrastructure. The official language is German. The best times to visit are between February and May for owls and woodpeckers, and during late May and early June when breeding activity is at its peak and spring passage migrants are still moving through.

The best birding sites are: (i) the lowland nature reserve known as **Ruggeller Riet**, in north Liechtenstein near Feldkirch in west Austria, which supports the only population of Corn Crakes* in the principality; and (ii) the mountains of **Garselii-Zigerberg**, east of the capital, Vaduz, in central Liechtenstein, which support small numbers of Black Grouse, Eurasian Capercaillie, Hazel Grouse, Eurasian Pygmy-Owl, Tengmalm's Owl, and White-backed, Three-toed and Black Woodpeckers.

LITHUANIA

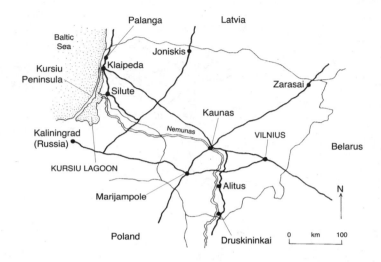

INTRODUCTION

Although this small country supports a similar avifauna to nearby north-east Poland it looks set to become a popular birding destination in the 21st century thanks to the impressive numbers of passage migrants which move along the Baltic Coast, the extensive areas of largely unspoilt countryside and a continuing improvement in visitor facilities.

At 65,200 km², Lithuania is half the size of England and about a tenth the size of Texas. Most visitors arrive by air in the capital, Vilnius, from where it is possible to get to some birding sites via public transport. Buses are generally quicker but more expensive than trains and it is best to book both in advance. As usual the best way to get around if time is short is to hire a vehicle. There is only one major highway, between Vilnius and Kaunas, to the northwest, but the largely traffic-free main roads which connect other towns are fine. Minor roads are bad, however, and there are few petrol stations in rural areas so it is wise to fill up whenever possible. Good hotels, spartan budget hotels, guesthouses, the few youth hostels and campsites (*kempingas*), some of which have chalets, are all cheaper than in most of the countries of western Europe. Staple foods include herring, meat, pickled salads, potatoes, sausages and stuffed dumplings. Beer (*alus*) and vodka are readily available. Organised crime is a problem in Vilnius but this rarely affects visitors.

The best times to visit Lithuania are during mid-March, when the passage of Steller's Eiders* along the Baltic Coast can be spectacular, mid-May, when a greater variety of migrants mix with breeding species such as Greater Spotted Eagle* and Little Crake, and the autumn when thousands of passage migrants are moving south through the country, even though it is often wet inland during the summer and on the coast during the autumn.

Inland from the short stretch of sandy Baltic coast Lithuania is a low-lying lakeland with extensive traditionally managed meadows, marshes and forest, all of which need to be protected if the six threatened and near-threatened species as well as the relatively common and widespread birds which occur in the country are to survive.

Notable species include Steller's Eider*, Greater Spotted Eagle*, Hazel Grouse, Little Crake, Great Snipe*, White-winged Tern and Aquatic Warbler*. It is possible to see 120–150 species on a trip lasting one week during mid-May.

Nature reserves with forested lakeland and fishponds about three hours by road southwest and west of the capital, Vilnius, include: (i) the 85-km² **Cepkeliai Nature Reserve**, near Druskininkai (where there is accommodation) in the extreme south of the country, which supports White-backed and Black Woodpeckers, Greenish Warbler (*trochiloides*) and Citrine Wagtail; and (ii) the 54-km² **Zuvintas Reserve**, 45 minutes by road from Marijampole (where there is accommodation), which supports Aquatic Warbler*. Birds likely to be seen at one or both of these reserves include Black Stork, White-tailed Eagle*, Little Gull and White-winged Tern. The River Nemunas flows north and west from this region of Lithuania for 224 km before forming a delta where Little Bittern and passage waterbirds occur. The delta lies in **Kursiu Lagoon** which, together with the nearby fishponds, marshes and woods, supports breeding species such as Osprey, White-tailed Eagle*, Corn* and Little Crakes, Great Snipe*, Black Woodpecker, and Eurasian River and Aquatic* Warblers. The lagoon lies on a major migration route for thousands of waterbirds and passerines, and a ringing station has been operating on the tip of the 99-km-long Kursiu Peninsula, which all but separates the lagoon from the Baltic Sea, for many years. It is known as **Ventes Ragas** and it is particularly good here during the autumn when regular migrants include Tengmalm's Owl and Barred Warbler, and rarities have included Azure Tit and Siberian Accentor. The peninsula lies within Kursiu Nerija National Park and is accessible by ferry from Klaipeda. To the northeast of here Black Stork and Common Crane breed around **Lakes Birzulis and Styrvas**, and Black and White Storks, Hazel Grouse, Common Crane and Black Woodpecker breed on and around the 37-km² reserve at **Kamanos Bog**. During mid-March 1998 a total of 1,246 Steller's Eiders* were recorded in the **Palanga** region along the west coast. In northeast Lithuania the freshwater **Lake Kretuonas**, together with its surrounding marshes, meadows and woods, support small breeding populations of Lesser Spotted Eagle, Corn Crake*, Black Woodpecker, European Roller, and, possibly, Great Snipe*.

ADDITIONAL INFORMATION

Addresses
Please send records of rarities to Petras Kurlavicius, Institute of Ecology, Academijos St. 2, 2600 Vilnius, Lithuania. The annual rarities report is published in *Aita Ornithologica Lituanica*, with an English summary.

LUXEMBOURG

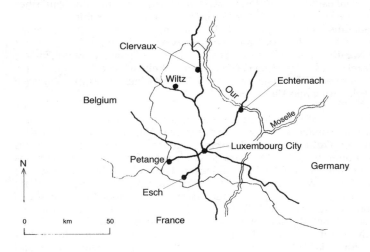

INTRODUCTION

This very small country (2585 km²) between Belgium, France and Germany, is largely neglected by birders because its best birds can be seen elsewhere along with a whole host of other goodies.

Travelling around Luxembourg on public transport is fairly straightforward since the bus service makes up for the poor rail network and bicycles are available for hire in many places. Hiring a vehicle on the other hand is relatively expensive, as are rooms in hotels and guesthouses, hence budget birders will need to use youth hostels and campsites. Food is also relatively expensive, but beer and wine are reasonably priced.

The climate is temperate with warmish summers and cool winters. The best time to visit is between mid-March and May when Hazel Grouse and woodpeckers are most likely to be seen.

The steep wooded valleys of the Ardennes extend eastward from Belgium into northern Luxembourg. Much of the rest of the country comprises a cultivated plateau with remnant marshes and woods, although there are also intensively cultivated lowland floodplains along the Rivers Our and Moselle along the border with Germany in the east. In total, over 50% of the land is used for arable farming, the fields having replaced once extensive wetlands, and about 30% is forested, conifer plantations having replaced most of the native woods, so the avifauna of Luxembourg, which includes one threatened species, has been severely depleted during the 20th century. Hopefully further habitat loss and degradation will be stopped and hunting brought under control in the near future.

The deep wooded valleys and remnant bogs and marshes of the **Ardenne Plateau** in northern Luxembourg support breeding Black Stork, Red and Black Kites, Hazel Grouse, and Black and Grey-headed Woodpeckers. One of the best places to look for Hazel Grouse and woodpeckers is in some of Europe's oldest deciduous woodland near Echternach. There is also an impressive spring and autumn passage of Common Cranes through this area. The small wetland reserves, seasonally flooded meadows and woods alongside the **River Alzette** in southwest Luxembourg support Red Kite, Corn Crake* and Black Woodpecker. In the southeast, the farmland, gravel-pits, vineyards and woods support Black Stork (a few on passage), Red Kite, Common Crane (up to 5,000 on passage), Eurasian Eagle-Owl and Black Woodpecker. The area around **Remerschen** adjacent to the River Moselle in the extreme southeast is the best.

ADDITIONAL INFORMATION

Addresses

Please send records of rarities to the Luxemburger Homologations Kommission, 38 Kiischtewee, L-6113 Junglinster, Luxembourg. The annual rarities report is published in *Regulus*, in German with and English summary.

MACEDONIA

INTRODUCTION

This small, landlocked, mountainous Balkan republic supports a wide range of raptors, Rock Partridge and some species which are confined to southeast Europe during the breeding season, including Olive-tree Warbler and Cretzschmar's Bunting, hence it was a popular birding destination before the wars in former Yugoslavia and the Kosovo crisis which erupted during spring 1999. It is therefore advisable to check with the relevant foreign office whether or not it is safe to travel to and around the country before planning a trip. If it becomes a safe place to visit and the rudimentary tourist infrastructure, which was in place before the wars, is maintained and improved this country will almost certainly regain its status as one of the best places for a cheap and exciting birding holiday in Europe.

At 25,715 km², Macedonia is one fifth the size of England and 4% the size of Texas. Most visitors arrive by air in the capital Skopje, from where

the best way to get around is to hire a vehicle. There are hotels and guesthouses in most large towns. Immunisation against hepatitis, polio and typhoid is recommended.

The climate is continental with fine hot summers and very cold winters. The summer, when breeding species such as Olive-tree Warbler and Cretzschmar's Bunting are present, is, arguably, the peak time to visit.

Macedonia is a land-locked country dominated by predominantly rugged mountains which support largely natural deciduous woods, pine forest and montane pastures. One major river, the Vardar, runs northwest to southeast across the middle of the country, and the lowlands which surround it support fruit orchards, vegetable fields and a little remnant steppe. In the southwest corner of the country there are two huge lakes, Ohrid and Megalí Prespa, which are shared with Albania and Greece. Hunting, poisoning, trapping, overgrazing and timber loss are the main problems facing the nine threatened and near-threatened species as well as the relatively common and widespread birds which occur in Macedonia.

Notable species include Pygmy Cormorant*, Levant Sparrowhawk, Long-legged Buzzard, Imperial Eagle*, Lanner Falcon, Rock Partridge, Rufous-tailed Scrub-Robin, Wallcreeper, Olive-tree Warbler, and Cretzschmar's and Black-headed Buntings.

Rock Partridge, as well as Eurasian Griffon, Golden Eagle and Hazel Grouse have all been recorded in the rocky, forested gorges and montane pastures of the **Sar Planina**, west of Skopje in northwest Macedonia, while other species which may occur here include Tengmalm's Owl and White-backed Woodpecker.

The deciduous woods, coniferous forest and montane pastures in and around the 730-km² **Mavrovo National Park**, with more than 50 peaks over 2000 m (6562 ft), in northwest Macedonia, support Egyptian Vulture, Eurasian Griffon, Lesser Spotted, Imperial*, Golden and Booted Eagles, Lanner Falcon, Hazel Grouse, White-backed Woodpecker (*lilfordi*) and Wallcreeper. The park is about 65 km southwest of

Skopje near the border with Albania. The wooded Radika Gorge and the mountain slopes of Korab above, parts of which lie within the park, are the best areas.

Lakes Ohrid and Megalí Prespa, the two huge freshwater lakes situated at about 914 m (3000 ft) in southwest Macedonia and shared with Albania (p. 47) and Greece (p. 208), support important numbers of breeding, wintering and passage waterbirds, including Pygmy Cormorant*, Ferruginous Duck*, Squacco Heron and Moustached Warbler. Rock Partridge, European Bee-eater, European Roller, Syrian Woodpecker, Olivaceous, Olive-tree and Orphean Warblers, and Cretzschmar's and Black-headed Buntings inhabit the surrounding farmland, orchards, scrub and mountains (which rise to 2601 m (8534 ft) and support largely natural deciduous woods, Macedonian pine forest and montane pastures). Other species recorded in this area include Great White and Dalmatian* Pelicans, and Little and Baillon's Crakes. The best base is, arguably, the small town of Struga on the shore of Lake Ohrid. Bird the lakes and their surrounds, including the 230-km² **Galicica National Park**, which lies at the south end of the Dinaric Mountains between the two lakes, and the 104-km² **Pelister National Park**, which lies northeast of Megalí Prespa, between there and Bitola. The Crni Drim Valley is particularly good for European Bee-eater and European Roller.

The deep **Babuna, Topolka and Vardar Gorges**, with their associated riverine vegetation and scrub-strewn slopes, south of Titov Veles in central Macedonia, support Black and White Storks, Egyptian Vulture, Long-legged Buzzard, Lesser Kestrel*, Lanner Falcon, Rock Partridge, European Roller, Rufous-tailed Rock-Thrush, Rock Nuthatch and Wallcreeper. Concentrate on the area around the confluence of the Rivers Babuna and Vardar, and also look out for Lammergeier, Eurasian Griffon, Cinereous Vulture*, Imperial* and Golden Eagles, and Isabelline Wheatear.

The damp woodland and remnant steppe in the **Bregalnica Valley** near Titov Veles in central Macedonia support Egyptian Vulture, Eurasian Griffon, Short-toed, Imperial* and Golden Eagles, and European Roller, while other species which may be present here include Long-legged Buzzard and Little Bustard*.

Long-legged Buzzard, Lanner Falcon and Rock Partridge, as well as Black Stork, Egyptian Vulture, Eurasian Griffon, Short-toed, Golden, Bonelli's and Booted Eagles, Lesser Kestrel* and European Roller, have been recorded in the **Crna Gorge** in southeast Macedonia. Other species which may occur here include Lammergeier, Cinereous Vulture* and Imperial Eagle*. To the southeast, Lammergeier and Rock Partridge have been recorded around the mountain of **Kozuf**.

The wooded gorges and remnant steppe in the remote **Demir Kapija** region of southeast Macedonia support Black Stork, Egyptian Vulture, Eurasian Griffon, Levant Sparrowhawk, Long-legged Buzzard, Imperial Eagle*, Lesser Kestrel*, Lanner Falcon, Rock Partridge, European Roller and Rufous-tailed Scrub-Robin. Bird the Krastavec Ridge, along the River Celevecka and the remnant steppe in the Vardar Valley, and also look out for Lammergeier and Cinereous Vulture*.

Pygmy Cormorant*, Great White Pelican and White-headed Duck* have been recorded on the shallow **Lake Dojransko**, which extends eastwards into Greece, in extreme southeast Macedonia.

MALTA

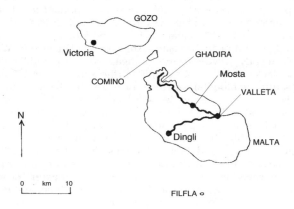

This tiny archipelago, which is situated about 100 km south of Sicily in the middle of the Mediterranean Sea, supports important numbers of breeding seabirds but has a very poor wetland and terrestrial avifauna due to the extremely high human population and the Maltese obsession with hunting anything with feathers. Birding here has long been a depressing experience, but the wall-to-wall shooting and trapping appears to be on the wane and a visit during the peak passage periods may prove to be very rewarding in the 21st century.

There are three main islands: Comino (2.6 km^2); Gozo (70 km^2); and Malta (249 km^2), and a number of smaller islands. Malta is quite a popular tourist destination, hence a wide range of accommodation and food is available. Immunisation against yellow fever is recommended/compulsory if arriving from an infected country.

The best times to visit are during the spring and autumn when the depauperate avifauna is augmented by passage migrants, although the variety and numbers of birds depend greatly on the weather. It is very hot in midsummer and usually mild during the winter.

Malta's excessive human population (3.7 million) means very little natural habitat remains. Most terrestrial species have to make do with terraced fields although in northern and western parts of the main island, and on Gozo, there are some steep rocky ridges with garrigue, separating the fertile valleys. The only area of trees which could reasonably be described as a 'wood' is the belt of conifers at Buskett, although the Wied il-Luq, the valley below there, has some deciduous trees. The only wetlands worth mentioning are the irrigation dams present in many of the valleys and the brackish pool at Ghadira on the main island. Hence the most important habitat in Malta is the sea cliffs which support important colonies of seabirds. The lack of terrestrial habitats is a major limiting factor on the numbers and diversity of bird species in Malta, but this, arguably, has less impact on the avifauna than hunting. A large proportion of the Maltese population shoot birds and they are so obsessed with killing as many birds as possible that when strict bird protection laws were passed in the early 1990s, largely due to the courageous efforts of the Malta Ornithological Society (MOS), some shooters sent death threats to some MOS members. However, the passage of time, together with a decreasing amount of public sympathy for the shooters, seems to have calmed these maniacs down and by the mid-1990s there appeared to be a growing acceptance of the new laws. The rigid enforcement of the law, followed, in time, by the introduction of a law banning shooting outright, is the way forward, and coupled with strict controls over unplanned development, which leads to habitat loss and degradation, as well as pollution, such measures may help to save the many migrants, the two threatened species and the other birds which occur in Malta.

About 360 species have been recorded, of which over 100 are regular migrants, 52 are winter visitors, 13 are resident and five are summer visitors.

On the main island the **Buskett** (the most extensive belt of conifers in the archipelago) and **Wied il-Luq** (a valley with deciduous trees) areas are particularly good for wintering and passage passerines, and migrant raptors including Eleonora's Falcon have been recorded roosting there. The brackish pool at **Ghadira**, a 6-ha nature reserve with a visitor centre and hides, on Mellieha Bay at the northeast end of the island, is a good place to look for wintering and passage waterbirds, which have included Great Snipe* and Slender-billed Gull. The sea cliffs at **Rdum Tal-Madonna**, at the northern tip of the island, support about 500 pairs of Mediterranean Shearwater ('Yelkouan' *yelkouan*), as well as Blue Rock-Thrush, Spectacled Warbler and Greater Short-toed Lark. The 6-ha islet known as **Filfla**, which is situated about 8 km off the south coast of the main island and accessible only with a permit from the Environment Ministry in Valletta, has been known to support up to 200 pairs of Cory's Shearwater ('Scopoli's' *diomedea*) and as many as 10,000 pairs of European Storm-Petrel.

The 135-m (443 ft) high Ta'Cenc Cliffs on the south-central coast of **Gozo** support up to 1,000 pairs of Cory's Shearwater ('Scopoli's' *diomedea*), as well as unknown numbers of Mediterranean Shearwater ('Yelkouan' *yelkouan*), European Storm-Petrel, Blue Rock-Thrush, Spectacled Warbler and Greater Short-toed Lark. Gozo is accessible by ferry from Marfa Point on the main island.

ADDITIONAL INFORMATION

Addresses

Please send records of rarities to the Malta Ornithological Society/BirdLife Malta, PO Box 498, Valletta CMR01, Malta (tel: 230684/250229; fax: 225665).

Books and papers

Fatal Flight: The Maltese obssession with killing birds. Fenech N, 1992. Quiller.

MOLDOVA

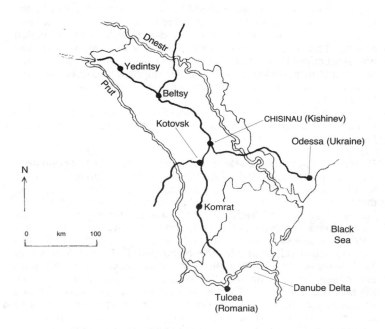

Very little is known about the avifauna of this small, landlocked country, and its main attraction lies in what might be there, bearing in mind its position between Romania and the Ukraine, both of which are very 'birdy'. At 33,700 km², Moldova is one quarter the size of England and 5% the size of Texas. It is only about 320 km from north to south and 160 km from west to east and thanks to the bus and rail networks getting around from the capital Chisinau (Kishinev) without a vehicle is not too difficult. Birders who do hire a vehicle to save time will find that some roads are in poor condition. There are a few hotels, most of which are basic but expensive, as well as guesthouses and campsites to stay in. The few restaurants tend to stick to goulash, spicy soups and stuffed cabbage leaves, all of which can be washed down with fairly good local wines. Immunisation against hepatitis, polio and typhoid is recommended. Ethnic clashes between Moldavians and Russians, which broke out in 1989, were ended by a ceasefire in 1993.

The climate is dry and warm for the most part, although temperatures drop to an average of 6°C during the winter. The best times to visit are probably during the spring and, especially, the autumn when many birds are moving along the nearby Black Sea coast.

Moldova is a land of sparsely populated hills and steppe plains which lie between the Rivers Prut and Dnestr, although the narrow province of Transdnestr, east of the River Dnestr, which declared independence in 1992, is industrialised. Habitat loss and degradation, hunting and pollution are the major problems facing the ten threatened and near-threatened species as well as the relatively common and widespread birds which occur in Moldova. For example, Ferruginous Duck* has undergone a serious decline from up to 1,300 pairs to just 100 pairs in the mid-1990s. Other notable species which have been recorded breeding here include Pygmy Cormorant*, White-tailed Eagle*, Pallid Harrier*, Lesser Kestrel*, Corn Crake*, Great Bustard*, Black-winged Pratincole*, Eurasian Eagle-Owl, and Lesser Spotted, Greater Spotted*, Imperial*, Golden and Booted Eagles, all five of which occur in the **Kapriyanovsko-Lozovo Forest**, northwest of the capital.

NETHERLANDS

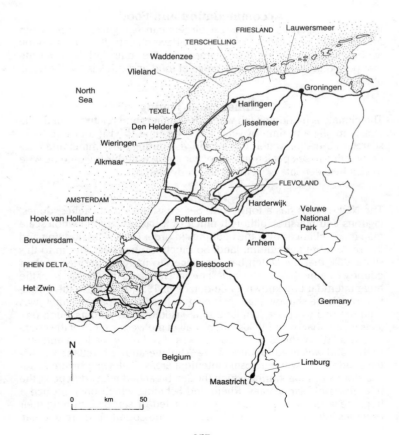

INTRODUCTION

Summary

This small country supports important breeding, passage and wintering populations of waterbirds, and during the winter it is possible to see one of the best selections of swans, geese and ducks in Europe.

Size

At 41,160 km², the Netherlands is about one third the size of England and 6% the size of Texas.

Getting Around

Most visitors arrive by air at Schiphol airport, Amsterdam, although the Netherlands is also accessible via vehicular ferries from nearby countries. One such ferry, from Harwich, England, takes about four hours and docks at Hoek van Holland. The highly integrated, cheap and efficient public transport system includes one of the best rail networks in Europe, and since this is a small country where petrol is expensive but bicycles can be hired at all main railway stations and then used on the excellent nationwide cycle path system, the cheapest, but still efficient, way to bird the Netherlands is by using public transport—and a bicycle!

Accommodation and Food

Hotels are expensive but budget birders can use guesthouses, youth hostels and campsites, some of which have chalets. It is best to book accommodation during the summer and the main holidays outside that period in advance. A wide range of food and drink is readily available.

Climate and Timing

The climate is maritime with warmish summers and relatively mild winters. Virtually any time of year is a good time to visit, but birders in search of breeding waterbirds should visit during the summer and birders wanting to see peak numbers of wintering waterbirds would be wise to visit between late November and early March.

Habitats

The Netherlands has a long North Sea coastline with beaches, dunes, lagoons and marshes, although much of it has undergone wholescale man-made changes over the centuries in order to provent flooding and to create more agricultural land. So much toil has been put in to this since 1200 that the Dutch have managed to increase the size of their country by almost 20%. The largest project involved the enclosure of the huge intertidal bay known as Zuiderzee in 1932, leading to the formation of a huge shallow lagoon known as Ijsselmeer, part of which was then drained to create farmland in areas known as polders. Such projects meant that by the 1990s virtually all of the western side of the country (over 30% of the total land area) was at or below sea level and 60% of the land was used for agriculture. The alteration of wetland ecosystems didn't end with enclosing intertidal areas. Following severe North Sea storms in 1953, during which the sea breached many defences, the tidal flows of Rivers Maas, Rhein and Schelde, which once formed a huge delta in the southwest, were restricted or stopped, turning their estuaries into lagoons. The eastern side of the country is more undulating, with remnant pockets of heathland, small birch and oak woods, and some conifer plantations.

Conservation

The people of the Netherlands have created more and more land over the centuries in order to grow the food necessary to sustain what by the mid-1990s was the densest human population in Europe (about 372 people per km^2), and in the process some important habitats were lost and some were created. With so many people to feed and house in such a small country there is bound to be enormous pressure on land, hence Dutch farmers contribute to the serious pollution of the Rivers Maas, Rhein and Schelde, as well as the country's other waterbodies, including those within reserves, by using the highest concentration of nitrogen-based fertiliser per hectare per year in the world. The seemingly endless cycle of creating more land to feed more people, which also involves the constant need to modernise the country's complicated drainage system, putting even more pressure on reserves, surely needs to be broken if the three threatened species as well as the relatively common and widespread birds which occur in the Netherlands are to survive.

Bird Species

About 448 species have been recorded in the Netherlands, not including ten feral species and 19 'splits'. Notable species include Lesser White-fronted* (the wintering population of reintroduced birds from Lapland, which became established in the 1990s, reached 61 by 1997–98) and Red-breasted* (a rare but regular winter visitor) Geese. On very rare occasions large numbers of northern species turn up during the winter (for example, about 150 Two-barred Crossbills were reported during 1997–98).

Expectations

During the winter it is possible to see as many as 130–140 species on a week-long trip, including up to 11 species of goose.

There are some good birding sites near **Amsterdam**, including: (i) the reserve at **Naardermeer**, 16 km east of the city, where Purple Heron and Black Tern breed. It is accessible by permit only, obtainable from Natuurmonumenten, Schaep en Burgh, NL-1243 JJ Graveland, Netherlands (tel: 35 655 9933; fax: 35 656 3174). To reach the reserve head east on the A1, take the exit to Muiderberg, continue on the road to the right which runs parallel to the A1 and turn right after 1 km to 'Visserij'; (ii) the **Zaanstreek** area, north of the city via the A7 and Westzaan, where Spotted Crake, Black Tern and Bluethroat ('White-spotted' *cyanecula*) occur.

FLEVOLAND

This large area east of Amsterdam consists primarily of three polders which have been created in what was once the intertidal bay known as Zuiderzee. It is, for the most part, flat and fertile, and, in some places, still full of birds, despite the continued loss of marshes, reedbeds and scattered willows. Over 325 species have been recorded here and during mid-May it is possible to see 120 species or so during a weekend. However, Flevoland is, arguably, even more exciting during the winter when it is has attracted as many as 10,000 Smew, one or two White-tailed Eagles*, about 500 Common Buzzards and a few Rough-legged Buzzards.

Regular Winter Visitors
Red-necked Grebe, Smew, Rough-legged Buzzard, Twite, Snow Bunting.

Regular Summer Visitors
Eurasian Spoonbill, Spotted Crake, Mediterranean Gull, Black Tern, Bluethroat ('White-spotted' *cyanecula*), Savi's and Icterine Warblers, Eurasian Penduline-Tit, Common Rosefinch.

Resident Species
Pied Avocet, Black Woodpecker, Crested Tit.

(Other species recorded here on a more or less regular basis include White-tailed Eagle* (winter), Great Egret (has bred), Snowy Plover (summer), Eurasian Dotterel (passage), White-winged (passage) and Caspian (passage) Terns, Eurasian Golden-Oriole (summer), Great Reed-Warbler (summer) and Yellow Wagtail ('Grey-headed' *thunbergi/* passage). Rarities have included Pygmy Cormorant*, Little and Baillon's Crakes, Great Knot, Pallas's and Yellow-browed Warblers, and Red-throated Pipit.)

FLEVOLAND

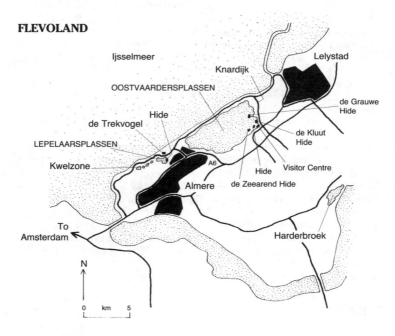

From Amsterdam head to **de Trekvogel**, via Almere, where there is a car park and a trail to a hide overlooking a Great Cormorant colony. Bluethroat, Icterine Warbler and Common Rosefinch occur alongside this trail and along the obscure path to the willow wood known as **het Wilgenbos**. Southwest of here there is a small parking area from where it is possible to view a pool in the reserve at **Lepelaarsplassen**, which is good for shorebirds. The light is best in the early morning and late afternoon. Walk along the reserve to look for Bluethroat, Savi's Warbler and Eurasian Penduline-Tit. The pools alongside the dyke southwest of Lepelaarsplassen, known as **Kwelzone**, are also excellent for shorebirds (Black-winged Stilt bred here in 1994).

During the spring and autumn, easterly winds bring passage passerine migrants and rarities to the bushes along **Oostvaardersdijk**, the dyke which forms the western boundary of Flevoland, especially around Blocq van Kuffeler near de Trekvogel and along the road to Almere-de Vaart, and from the end of July to September it is possible to see thousands of Black Terns gathering to roost along here, with the odd White-winged Tern.

From de Trekvogel head northeast along Oostvaardersdijk to reach what is arguably the best birding area in Flevoland. If water levels are low during the spring, summer and autumn (the place can look deserted when water levels are high) the reserve at **Oostvaardersplassen** can be full of birds. It supports the largest colony of Great Cormorants in Europe (8,000 pairs), the largest colony of Eurasian Spoonbills in the Netherlands (310 pairs in 1994—up to 800 may be present during July and August), and good numbers of Bluethroat (most easily seen during the second half of April, singing from the tops of reeds). The reserve can be viewed from Oostvaardersdijk, which runs along the northwest side, and hides at the east end, near the dyke known as Knardijk and the visitor centre. These hides include: (i) de Grauwe. Bluethroat, Savi's Warbler, Eurasian Penduline-Tit and Common Rosefinch may be seen alongside the path to this hide or on the dry patch in front of it; and (ii) de Kluut, to the south, which is a good place to look for Eurasian Spoonbill and Spotted Crake, especially during the early morning.

During the winter the best places to look for the great rafts of ducks on **Ijsselmeer**, the huge lagoon created by the enclosure of Zuiderzee, lie to the north (where power station water outlets concentrate some species) and west of Lelystad. Near Harderwijk, about 80 km east of Amsterdam, the reedy **Harderbroek** area (turn left immediately after crossing the Harderhaven bridge) is an excellent place to hear, but rarely see, crakes. For woodland birds try the area just east of **Harderwijk**, where Black Woodpecker and Crested Tit occur.

Accommodation: Lelystad—het Oppertje campsite, just south of Lelystad and within walking distance of Knardijk.

Between Alkmaar and Den Helder, north of Amsterdam, the wet bulb fields at **Wieringen** attract numerous shorebirds and roosting Gull-billed Terns during August and September. Huge numbers of Black Terns also gather along the coast near here at this time of year, when their roosts often contain 10,000 birds, and have exceeded over 90,000. There are usually a few White-winged Terns amongst them. Up to 27 Lesser White-fronted Geese* also visited this region during the winters 1997–1998 and 1998–1999, when areas worth checking included **Abtskolk**, **Burgervlotburg** and **Petten**.

The island of **Texel** (pronounced 'Tessel') is the largest and most southerly of the Frisian Islands, which form a chain parallel to the north

Thousands of Smews grace the waters of the Netherlands during the winter

coast of the Netherlands. The wetlands, many of which are reserves, on this island support large numbers of breeding, passage and wintering waterbirds, especially shorebirds. There is a frequent ferry service (20 minutes) to the island from Den Helder, on the mainland one hour by road north of Amsterdam. The many reserves are run by various organisations, from which permits must be obtained in advance. For details contact the Texel Birdwatching Centre (TBWC), Vuurtorenweg 94, NL-1795 LM De Cocksdorp, Texel, Netherlands (tel: 222 316416; fax: 222 316688) or the Tourist Office, VVV Texel, Den Burg, Texel, Netherlands.

To the north of Texel the Frisian Island of **Terschelling** (30 km x 5 km), a popular tourist resort during the summer, supports breeding Eurasian Spoonbill (115 pairs), Spotted Crake, Bluethroat ('White-spotted' *cyanecula*) and Common Rosefinch (11 pairs in 1996), and during the winter Rough-legged Buzzard is a regular visitor. However, this island and its neighbour, **Vlieland**, are more famous amongst Dutch birders for spectacular falls of passage passerine migrants, which often include rarities, especially during easterly winds through September and October. Yellow-browed Warbler and Richard's Pipit are more or less regular visitors, while star rarities have included Blue-cheeked Bee-eater, Dusky and Radde's Warblers, and Pine and Yellow-breasted Buntings. There is a birders logbook in the Cafe de Boschplaat in Oosterend. The island is accessible by ferry (two hours) from Harlingen and there are plenty of places to stay, including a youth hostel and campsites. To book a vehicle on the ferry contact Rederij Doeksen, Postbus 40, 8880 AA Terschelling, Netherlands (tel: 562 442141; fax: 562 443241).

FRIESLAND

The coast of the northern Netherlands lies alongside the Waddenzee, the most important intertidal area in Europe for waterfowl and shorebirds which extends east through north Germany (p. 200) to Denmark (p. 153). Hundreds of pairs of Black-tailed Godwit and Pied Avocet breed here, thousands of birds pass through on migration, and during the winter it supports masses of waterfowl, including up to 20,000 Barnacle Geese and regular rare geese such as Lesser White-fronted*.

Regular Winter Visitors

Whooper and Bewick's Swans, Pink-footed, Bean ('Tundra' *rossicus*), Greater White-fronted, Lesser White-fronted* and Barnacle Geese, Rough-legged Buzzard, Horned Lark, Snow Bunting.

Regular Summer Visitors

Black-tailed Godwit, Pied Avocet, Black and Caspian (late summer) Terns.

(Other species recorded here during the winter include Snow, Brent ('Black Brant' *nigricans*) and Red-breasted* Geese, and White-tailed Eagle*.)

Lesser White-fronted Goose* became a regular winter visitor to the **Lauwersmeer** area during the 1990s, when Red-breasted Geese* also made frequent appearances. This large dammed estuary with remnant saltmarshes about 40 km northwest of Groningen, is accessible via the N361 which runs along the seaward side, and the minor roads off it which allow access southwards. Cruise roads south of Anjum, Bakhnizen and Bant polder to look for geese.

Accommodation: Groningen.

The construction of several major dams in the **Rhein Delta** (Zeeland) at the southwest end of the Netherlands has upset the complex ecosystem but the remaining lakes and marshes still support up to 500,000 wintering waterfowl, including one of highest concentrations of Great Crested Grebes on earth (tens of thousands winter by **Brouwersdam** along with a few Red-necked Grebes and masses of sea-ducks). During the summer, Pied Avocet, Snowy Plover and Bluethroat ('White-spotted' *cyanecula*) breed. About 1,000 pairs of Bluethroat breed in the 180-km^2 **Biesbosch** area where there are several reserves southeast of Dordrecht, between the Waal and Bergse-Maas branches of the Rhein. Also in Zeeland, up to ten pairs of Zitting Cisticola were present in 1999, eight of which were at **Verdronken Land var Saeftinghe**. At **Hoek van Holland**, where most ferries from England dock, west of Rotterdam, a pair of House Crows (which probably arrived on warships returning from the Gulf War in 1994) bred from 1997 to 1999.

In 1999 there were 11 territories of Middle Spotted Woodpecker in the southern province of **Limburg**, the first since 1962. In 1998 three pairs were present at Ambt Montfort and Margraten, and in March 1999 11 birds were heard in the province. Also in Limburg, a pair of Eurasian Eagle-Owls bred near Maastricht in 1997–99 (with a senond pair present in 1999).

ADDITIONAL INFORMATION

Addresses

The Dutch Society for the Protection of Birds (Vogelbescherming), Driebergseweg 16C, NL-3708 JB Zeist, Netherlands.

Please send records of rarities to the Commissie Dwaalgasten Nederlandse Avifauna (CDNA), Postbus 45, NL-2080 AA Santpoort-Zuid, Netherlands (email: cdna@dutchbirding.nl). The annual rarities report is published in *Dutch Birding*, in English.

SOVON (bird censuses), Postbus 81, NL-6573 ZH Beek-Ubbergen, Netherlands, publishes in the quarterly *Limosa* journal.

BINS (Birdwatching in the Netherlands), Sandenburglaan 38, NL-3571 BC Utrecht, Netherlands (tel/fax: 30 272 2182; email: BINS_tours@ yahoo.com; website: www.gjvandenberg.demon.nl/binsmain.html), helps to arrange trips to the Netherlands.

Birdline

Information (tel: 0900 203 2128). Hotline (tel: 010 428 1212).

Books and papers

Where to watch birds in Holland, Belgium and Northern France. Van den Berg A and Lafontaine D, 1996. Hamlyn.

Rare birds of the Netherlands: avifauna van Nederland I. Van den Berg A & Bosman C A W, 1999. Haarlem.

Atlas van de Nederlandse vogels. SOVON, 1987. Arnhem.

Magazines

The top class bimonthly *Dutch Birding* magazine, in Dutch and English, is published by the Dutch Birding Association (DBA), Postbus 75611, NL-1070 AP Amsterdam, Netherlands (email: dba@dutchbirding.nl), and subscription details can be obtained from Jeannette Admiraal, Iepenlaan 11, NL-1901 ST Castricum, Netherlands (email: circulation@ dutchbirding.nl). The magazine also has a website at www. dutchbirding.nl.

NORWAY

INTRODUCTION

Summary

Norway cannot compete with Finland as far as owls go, but it does have Varanger, where, well inside the Arctic Circle, it is possible to see a superb selection of Arctic specialities including King and Steller's* Eiders, White-billed Diver and a whole host of breeding shorebirds, hence many birders who visit Finland also include the nearby northern tip of Norway in their itinerary.

Size

At 323,895 km², mainland Norway is 2.5 times larger than England and about half the size of Texas.

Getting Around

In southern Norway it is fairly easy to get around on the reliable public transport system, but in the north a vehicle is essential to reach most of the best birding sites. It is possible to get near to Varanger by train (to Fauske) and bus (a daily, all year round 48-hour service from Fauske to Kirkenes), or by air (from Oslo to Kirkenes) but getting to the best spots once there could be very difficult without private transport. Vehicles can be hired at Kirkenes which is two hours by road from Varangerbotn, the major starting point for birding Varanger. Most birders usually approach Varanger by road from Finland, in which case it is best to stock up on food and petrol before entering Norway because these products are much cheaper in Finland. Some birders also drive there from the ferry ports of Stavanger (Norway), Oslo (Norway) and Göteborg (Sweden), all of which are at least 24 hours away.

Accommodation and Food

Norway is the most expensive Scandinavian country, hence hotels and guesthouses are very expensive, so budget birders usually camp in the hundreds of official campsites, some complete with chalets, or off-road for free. There are also plenty of youth hostels. In most national parks, even those in the remotest areas, refuge huts, linked by well-marked tracks and trails, have been specifically built to provide overnight accommodation for trekkers. Food is also expensive and in the north during the winter grocery stores open only for a few hours a day, so stock up whenever possible. Staple food items include elk, fish and reindeer, although fast food and sandwiches are usually available in and near the large towns. Alcoholic drinks are very expensive.

Health and Safety

Much of Norway, especially the north, is damp, cold, wild and remote. Even during the summer it is wise to bird such areas with a detailed map, a compass, plenty of food and drink, a sunhat, sunscreen, wellies, warm and waterproof clothing, a four-season sleeping bag, top camping gear, and the best insect repellent available.

Climate and Timing

The best time to visit Norway, especially the far north, is during late May and early June, before the millions of midges emerge. From mid-May to late July in the far north there is enough light to bird 24 hours a day, but the peak time for birding is during the first few hours after midnight. The brief warmish summers contrast starkly with bleak, very cold winters, and even though the west coast is relatively mild all year round it is very wet, receiving as much as 1960 mm (6.6 ft) in a single year. The Aurora Borealis (Northern Lights) are at their best on cold, clear nights in February–March and September–October.

Habitats

Inland from the scenically stunning fjords of the lengthy west coast, Norway is predominantly a land of mountainous tundra (fjells) which rises to 2470 m (8104 ft) at Glittertind, the highest point in Scandinavia. The western and southern slopes of these mountains support birch and rowan woods, as well as boreal (*taiga*) forest, although only about 25% of the country is forested. In the extreme south and southwest there is a narrow coastal plain, most of which is agricultural land.

Conservation

Vast areas of the country, especially in the north and east, are so sparsely populated it is possible to drive for hours with only the odd band of *Same* tribes people, with their reindeer, and birds for company. Hence, the Norwegian avifauna, which includes five threatened and near-threatened species, is relatively safe from agricultural intensification and pollution, although these problems, as well as poor forestry practices, do exist, and an estimated 80% of the waterbodies in the southern half of the country have been severely damaged by acid rain.

Bird Species

Notable species include King and Steller's* Eiders, Gyrfalcon, Great Snipe*, Red-necked Phalarope, Eurasian Dotterel, Long-tailed Skua, Brünnich's Guillemot, Atlantic Puffin, White-billed Diver, Snowy Owl, Northern Hawk Owl, Siberian Jay, Bohemian Waxwing, Siberian Tit, Arctic Redpoll and Parrot Crossbill. In some years certain Arctic specialities move into southern Norway in large numbers, as was the case with Pine Grosbeaks during the winter of 1998–1999 when about 570 were recorded.

Expectations

It is possible to see about 130 species on a trip lasting two weeks during the summer, but fewer than 40 on a similar trip during the winter, to Arctic Norway, based around Varanger. On a ten-day spring trip to Varanger and Finland it is possible to see over 200 species.

The forested mountain plateau, which rises to 1719 m (5640 ft) at Sandflot, in the 3420-km² **Hardangervidda National Park**, about 160 km west of Oslo, is a very popular birding area thanks to the presence of Osprey, Golden Eagle, Temminck's Stint, Eurasian Dotterel, Eurasian Pygmy-Owl, Tengmalm's Owl, Three-toed and Black Woodpeckers, Bluethroat ('Red-spotted' *svecica*) and Brambling, as well as (wild) reindeer. There are many marked trails and refuge huts, and the best birding areas are the Bjoreidal Valley (accessible from Dyranut on the Bergen–Oslo road), Randhellern on Lake Langesjoen to the south, Sandhang on Lake Normannslagen, and Hadlasker.

The island of **Utsira**, about 17 km off Karmoy, just south of Haugesund in southwest Norway, attracts a wide range of passage migrants and rarities which have included Yellow-rumped Warbler and Rose-breasted Grosbeak, hence over 300 species have been recorded here, despite the island being no more than 3 km wide. It is accessible via daily ferries from Haugesund and it is possible to stay at the Bird Observatory. For details of the accommodation there, and its annual report, contact Utsira Fuglestasjon, Postboks 23, 5515 Utsira, Norway (tel: 5274 9204; website: www.home.sol.no/~bhoeylan/utsira). There is another Bird Observatory in southern Norway at **Lista** where during the autumn 1996 invasion of Tengmalm's Owls a total of 310 were ringed, and during the winter 1998–1999 invasion of Pine Grosbeaks 220 were recorded. The regular drake Surf Scoter also returned here during winter 1998–1999.

The 580-km² **Rondane National Park**, east of the E6 about 20 km southeast of Dombas, which is about 300 km north of Oslo, supports Gyrfalcon, Rock Ptarmigan, Red-necked Phalarope, Eurasian Dotterel and Snow Bunting, as well as elk, Eurasian otter and (wild) reindeer. The bogs, lakes, birch and rowan woods, snowfields and mountains, which rise to 2286 m (7500 ft), in **Dovrefjell National Park**, which lies either side of the E6 about 130 km south of Trondheim, support breeding Great Snipe*, as well as Rough-legged Buzzard, Common Crane, Temminck's Stint, Red-necked Phalarope, Eurasian Dotterel, Red-throated Diver, Horned Lark, Brambling, and Lapland and Snow Buntings. A number of trails lead off the E6, especially near Kongsvoll where there is a visitor centre. Also bird in and around the 7.5-km² bird reserve at **Fokstumyra**, about 20 km to the south. To visit this reserve it is necessary to obtain a permit from the warden who is based near the railway station.

Lofoten Vesterålen, a large archipelago off the northwest coast of Norway inside the Arctic Circle, supports over a million breeding seabirds, including European and Leach's Storm-Petrels, Black Guillemot and Atlantic Puffin, as well as White-tailed Eagle*, and during the winter thousands of King Eiders, Gyrfalcon and White-billed Diver occur. The best islands are Rost and Vaeroy, at the southern end of the archipelago, and Vedoy (where White-tailed Eagles* gather in spring). There are regular flights to Rost from Bodo on the mainland and regular ferry services to Rost from Bodo and Moskenesoy (via Vaeroy). Accommodation and trips can be arranged via Destination Lofoten AS, Postboks 210, 8301 Svolvaer, Loften, Norway (tel: 088 73000). During the summer the archipelago is also a good place to see killer, minke and sperm whales, and regular whale-watching trips run from Andenes on the northernmost island of Andoeya, accessible by road from Narvik and Tromso. Outside possibilities include white-beaked and white-sided dolphins, and fin, humpback, killer (hundreds, in pursuit of herring, pass within varying distances of the archipelago, usually between October and January) and pilot whales. For more information contact The Whale Centre, Postboks 8480, Andenes, Norway (tel: 761 42611; fax: 761 42377).

VARANGER

This peninsula is situated near mainland Europe's northernmost point, 400 km north of the Arctic Circle. The terrain is rather bleak and cold, even during the summer, but what a wonderful place this is for any bird-ers interested in seeing such stunning high-arctic specialities as King and Steller's* Eiders, Long-tailed Skua and White-billed Diver, as well as a superb selection of breeding shorebirds, including rust-red Bar-tailed Godwits, black Spotted Redshanks and Red-necked Phalaropes. Some of these birds occur in phenomenal numbers. For example, during late March 1996 there were 3,500 King Eiders and 5,300 Steller's Eiders* between Varangerbotn and Vardo, and, in May 1996, a joint RAF/WWT survey recorded 381 King Eiders (24% of which were adult drakes) and 9,586 Steller's Eiders* (54% of which were adult drakes). In mid-May 1999 over a thousand White-billed Divers moved east along the coast, along with 1,700 Pomarine and 300 Long-tailed Skuas.

During the short summer season it is possible to see more than 100 species over a period of several days, an amazing total for somewhere so close to the North Pole, but during the winter, when late March is the best time to visit despite temperatures as low as minus −20°C inland, don't expect to see more than 40 species, even in a week. The species listed below occur during the summer unless otherwise indicated.

Localised Specialities
King and Steller's* Eiders, Gyrfalcon, Brünnich's Guillemot, White-billed Diver, Red-throated Pipit, Arctic Redpoll.

Other Localised Species
Rock Ptarmigan.

Others
Northern Fulmar (blue form), Bean Goose ('Tundra' *rossicus*), Greater Scaup, Long-tailed Duck, Velvet Scoter, White-tailed Eagle*, Rough-legged Buzzard, Willow Ptarmigan, Bar-tailed Godwit, Spotted Redshank,

Varanger is the best place in Europe to look for White-billed Diver

Wood Sandpiper, Ruddy Turnstone, Little and Temminck's Stints, Purple Sandpiper, Ruff, Red-necked Phalarope, Eurasian Dotterel, Glaucous Gull, Arctic Tern, Arctic and Long-tailed Skuas, Black Guillemot, Atlantic Puffin, Red-throated and Black-throated Divers, Siberian Jay, Bluethroat ('Red-spotted' *svecica*), Siberian Tit, Horned Lark, Brambling, Twite, Eurasian Bullfinch (*pyrrhula*), Lapland and Snow Buntings.

Other Wildlife

Risso's dolphin, Arctic fox, Eurasian otter, reindeer, grey and harp seals, killer whale.

(Other species recorded here include Lesser White-fronted Goose*, Jack Snipe, Broad-billed Sandpiper, Ivory Gull, Pomarine Skua (passage), Little Auk (3,500 at Nesseby in October 1998, with 11,000 Atlantic Puffins), Snowy Owl and Arctic Warbler (four singing males in Sor-Varanger in 1998).)

From **Varangerbotn**, at the head of Varangerfjord, travel east along the north shore on Route 98 to reach **Nesseby**. Turn south here to the church and continue on the path south from there to a small pool which is usually graced by Red-necked Phalaropes. The bay to the west is worth checking for Steller's Eiders*. East of Nesseby check the birch scrub for Siberian Tit (breeding in nest boxes) and Arctic Redpoll, then continue to **Vadso** (which is far enough east along the fjord to be free from ice during the winter) where up to 900 Steller's Eiders* have been seen together in the harbour. The best viewpoint over the harbour is from the stinking fish oil factory on the south side, reached via a bridge south of the Shell petrol station. Temminck's Stints trill from street lights and feed on the lawns in Vadso and there is another excellent pool for Red-necked Phalaropes on Vadso Island (Vadsoya), where over 100 are often present and an incredible 560 were seen together in early July 1998. To the east of Vadso the small harbour at **Store Ekkeroya** is

VARANGER

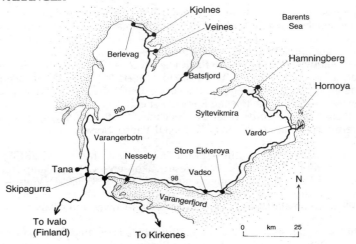

269

worth checking for White-billed Diver, and the cliffs 500 m to the east support large numbers of seabirds which in turn attract White-tailed Eagle* and Gyrfalcon. Inland from here there is a Ruff lek at **Salttjern**, and Snowy Owl is possible on the highest slopes of **Falkefjell**, where Bluethroat and Arctic Redpoll also occur. At the extreme eastern end of the peninsula on the north side of the fjord is **Vardo**, a small town situated on two offshore islands connected to the mainland via a tunnel. It is surrounded by yet another exceptional area for birds, with King and Steller's* Eiders alongside rusty Russian fishing ships in the harbour, and auk colonies complete with Brünnich's Guillemots on the offshore island of Hornoya, accessible via regular boat trips (tickets are available from the harbour office). On Hornoya's neighbour, Reinoya, it is possible to walk below the bird-filled cliffs. To the north of Vardo is **Hamningberg** where there is snow at sea level throughout the year and a good headland for seawatching. Look out for White-billed Diver from here and in the harbours and bays along the coast to the north and west. A little way south of Hamningberg there is a steep, narrow track which leads west to **Syltevikmira**, a good area for Gyrfalcon.

Steller's Eiders occur in large numbers throughout the year at Varanger*

There is more birding to be done north and inland from Varangerbotn, although this is a remote region so it is sometimes necessary to join convoys which, when organised, usually leave about every three hours (the times are normally put up where Route 890 begins, north of Skipagurra). Otherwise, follow signs to **Berlevag** which is 135 km north of Skipagurra. Alongside Route 890 look out for Long-tailed Duck, White-tailed Eagle*, Gyrfalcon, Red-necked Phalarope, Long-tailed Skua and Snowy Owl, as well as Arctic fox and Eurasian otter.

Please send records of unusual sightings in the Varanger area to Sverre Asmar Nilsen, PO Box 247, N-9801 Vadso, Norway.

Accommodation: Tana Bru—Tourist Hotel (expensive, tel: 85 28198). Varangerbotn—expensive hotel. Vestre Jakobselv—Cottage Camp (relatively cheap cottages, dormitory and campsite, tel: 85 56064). Vadso—two expensive hotels. Vardo—one expensive hotel. Otherwise it is possible to camp almost anywhere away from the towns and villages.

The mixed forests in the **Pasvik Valley**, which is situated in the narrow strip of Norway between Finland and Russia south of Kirkenes, support

Copper-topped Ruddy Turnstones are one of the many shorebirds breeding on the Varanger Peninsula

small numbers of elusive species such as Eurasian Capercaillie, Northern Hawk Owl, Three-toed Woodpecker, Bohemian Waxwing, Siberian Tit and Parrot Crossbill.

If travelling between Varanger in north Norway and Ivalo in north Finland (p. 167) it is worth checking the bogs (about 10 km north of **Utsjoki** for example) and roadside barren mountain tops for Rough-legged Buzzard, Gyrfalcon, Broad-billed Sandpiper, Red-necked Phalarope, Long-tailed Skua, Horned Lark and Lapland Bunting.

ADDITIONAL INFORMATION

Addresses
Please send records of rarities to the NSKF, Norsk Ornitologisk Forening, Seminarplassen 5, N-7054 Klaebu, Norway. The annual rarities report is published in *Var Fuglefauna*, in Norwegian with an English summary.

Birdline
Information (tel: 820 55050). Hotline (tel: 383 97588).

POLAND

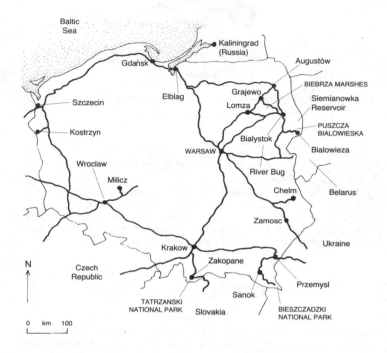

INTRODUCTION

Summary

Poland is a large country but it is only necessary to visit the extensive marshes and forests in a relatively small area of the east to see its major avian attractions: Great Snipes* lekking, all ten European woodpeckers and Aquatic Warbler*.

Size

At 312,685 km², Poland is 2.4 times larger than England and almost half the size of Texas.

Getting Around

Most visitors arrive in Warsaw by air or via the rail network which has good connections with Austria, the Czech Republic and Germany. The extensive, cheap, but crowded and slow internal bus and rail networks could be used to get to most birding sites, but birders with little time to spare will, as usual, be better off hiring a vehicle.

Accommodation and Food

A wide range of accommodation is available in most areas, including hotels, 'Bed and Breakfasts' (*Zimmer frei*), some small pensions, some youth and tourist hostels, and campsites, many of which have basic chalets. Most of these are cheaper than in many other European countries. Eating out in Poland is also relatively cheap, especially when the size of the portions are taken into account. 'Snacks' here would be feasts almost anywhere else, and they include chips, hot dogs and pancakes. The huge meals served up in cafes and restaurants are based on cabbage, dumplings, fish and meat, and the Poles like to wash their food down with equally awesome amounts of beer (*piwo*) and vodka.

Health and Safety
Stick to bottled water, use plenty of insect repellent (especially at dawn and dusk in the Biebrza Marshes) and beware of theft from accommodation and vehicles in most areas.

Climate and Timing
The climate is continental with short, warm summers, when most of the rain falls, and long, harsh winters. Mid-May is the peak time to visit Poland, because Great Snipes* are lekking, Aquatic Warblers* are singing and virtually all of the summer visitors have arrived.

Habitats
Poland is predominantly a lowland country, from the 524-km-long Baltic coast in the north to the foothills of the Carpathian Mountains, which rise to 2499 m (8199 ft) at Rysy, on the southern borders with the Czech Republic and Slovakia. The major habitats are traditionally managed farmland, wetlands and forest, all of which combine to support a rich avifauna. The numerous wetlands include coastal lagoons, hundreds of lakes, reservoirs and fishponds, and most importantly of all, floodplains, including the one along the River Biebrza in the northeast, which is reputed to be the most natural inland wetland in Europe. Forests cover about 28% of the land. The vast majority are conifer plantations, although one major exception is Bialowieska, which is the only substantial tract of untouched lowland temperate mixed forest left in Europe.

Conservation
Traditional 19th-century farming practices were still widespread at the end of the 20th century, maintaining the value of Poland's agricultural land to birds. However, it seems almost inevitable that the 21st century will see the arrival of agricultural intensification, and that this, along with pollution and the continuing degradation and destruction of other habitats, including the forest at Bialowieska, will seriously deplete the numbers of the seven threatened and near-threatened species as well as the relatively common and widespread birds which occur in Poland. For example, despite the fact that Bialowieska is a World Heritage Site only a tenth of the 560 km² of this forest which lies within Poland (the remaining 690 km² (55%) lies within Belarus) remains virtually untouched and only half of that is within a national park. The remaining 80% has been logged for the past 80 years and if this senseless destruction, and the subsequent replacement with conifer plantations, continues, one of the world's few remaining truly natural habitats will be gone shortly after the dawn of the 21st century. Unless that is the government realises the value of this and its other natural resources, and decides that they are worth preserving.

Bird Species

Over 400 species have been recorded in Poland. Notable species include Greater Spotted Eagle*, Great Snipe*, Little Crake, White-winged Tern, Ural Owl, all ten European woodpeckers, Collared Flycatcher, Wallcreeper, Aquatic Warbler*, Citrine Wagtail and Alpine Accentor.

Expectations

It is possible to see about 170, and exceptionally up to 200 species, on a trip (to east Poland during the spring) lasting a week to ten days.

Huge numbers of birds migrate along Poland's **Baltic Coast** and during the spring and autumn a ringing station operates near **Chalupy** on the Mierzeja Helska Peninsula near Gdańsk. Regular spring passage migrants include Red-throated Pipit, while, during the autumn, Broad-billed Sandpiper and Richard's Pipit are more or less regular visitors. Many Polish rarities are found here and at nearby **Jastarnia**, and in March 1997 two immature Steller's Eiders* were present at Gdańsk. In the mid-1990s a few pairs of Citrine Wagtail started breeding in Poland and in 1996 most of them (five pairs) were present around the mouth of the **River Reda**, north of Rewa, north of Gdańsk. The best site in Poland for shorebirds, gulls and terns, including regular Terek and Broad-billed Sandpipers, Red-necked Phalarope (about 140 in September 1998) and Caspian Tern, is the mouth of the **River Vistula**, east of Gdańsk. Inland from here, near Elblag, lies the shallow **Lake Druzno** which supports breeding Ferruginous Duck*, Little Gull and Black Tern. For more details of birding in the Gdańsk area contact the Ornithological Station, ul. Nadwislanska 108, 80-680 Gdańsk 40, Poland.

In extreme northeast Poland it is possible to look for lynx and grey wolf in the forests of **Puszcza Romincka**, based at the forester's lodge in Zytkiejmy. The best time to track these elusive animals down is during the harsh winter months when birds present in the area may include White-tailed Eagle*, Hazel Grouse, Black Woodpecker, Eurasian Nutcracker and Bohemian Waxwing. For more details contact Marek Borkowski (address, p. 279).

BIEBRZA MARSHES

The floodplain of the River Biebrza (pronounced Bee-ebja) in northeast Poland is believed to be the most natural inland wetland in Europe. It is certainly full of birds. Over 262 species have been recorded, 178 of which have been known to breed, including up to nine pairs of Greater Spotted Eagle*, over 1,000 calling male Corn Crakes*, 50 calling male Little Crakes, over 400 displaying male Great Snipes*, over 1,000 pairs of White-winged Tern and up to 3,500 singing male Aquatic Warblers*.

The species listed below occur during the summer unless otherwise indicated.

Localised Specialities

Greater Spotted Eagle*, Great Snipe*, Aquatic Warbler*.

Others

Red-necked Grebe, Little Bittern, Black and White Storks, Red Kite, White-tailed*, Short-toed and Lesser Spotted Eagles, Corn* and Little Crakes, Common Crane, Whiskered, White-winged and Black Terns, Tengmalm's Owl, White-backed and Black Woodpeckers, Eurasian Nutcracker, Thrush Nightingale, Bluethroat ('White-spotted' *cyanecula*), Eurasian River Warbler, Common Rosefinch.

(Other species recorded here include Great Egret (three pairs were present in 1997, the first since 1863), Jack Snipe, Marsh Sandpiper (has bred), Red-necked Phalarope (spring), Caspian Tern, Bohemian Waxwing (winter), Collared Flycatcher, and Greenish (*trochiloides*) and Barred Warblers.)

BIEBRZA MARSHES and PUSZCZA BIALOWIESKA

There is a raised platform overlooking a Great Snipe* lekking area near **Dobarz**, which is accessible from: (i) Route 669 between Grajewo and Bialystok; and (ii) from Route 64 between Lomza and Bialystok. Just

NORTHERN BIEBRZA MARSHES

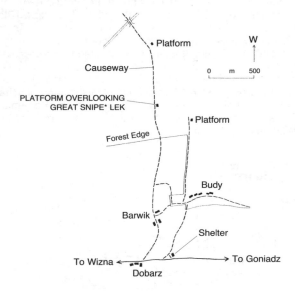

north of Dobarz take the sandy track west, stay left through the forest and park at the edge of the forest. From here there is a trail across the marsh to the lek, which the snipes usually visit only at dusk. This lekking area is in a private nature reserve which belongs to the well-known Polish ornithologist Marek Borkowski, who put a great deal of time, effort and money into purchasing the land in order to safeguard the birds from disturbance, so please watch from the platform only and by no means encroach upon the lekking area, as a number of photographers have done in the past. This is an extremely popular site with birders and in order to avoid 'crowd trouble' Marek would appreciate knowing about all visits in advance (see address, p. 279). Aquatic Warblers*, which sing mostly after sunset, are also present here, and some fortunate observers have seen Great*, Common and Jack Snipes, as well as Eurasian Woodcock, in the same evening. Further along the 'Great Snipe*' trail there is another raised platform, which is good for scanning over the marshes in search of Black Stork, raptors and Common Crane, as well as elk (at dusk). Back on the sandy track in the forest near Dobarz turn north to reach Budy where there is another good observation platform.

One of the best places for Aquatic Warbler* is a few km along the track which leads west from the road south of Dobarz (towards Wizna). Turn north just east of Wizna to reach the village of **Brzostowa** which lies next to an excellent area for marsh terns, as well as White-tailed Eagle*. The best place to scan the marshes from near here is the small hillock just north of the village. North of Dobarz, the **Osowiec** and **Goniadz** areas are good for Greater Spotted Eagle*. For more information and detailed maps of the Biebrza Marshes area contact OTOP.

Accommodation: Budy and Kuligi—traditional farmhouses owned by Marek Borkowski.

Brilliant White-winged Terns brighten up even the dullest days in the extensive marshes of eastern Poland

Little Crake and Aquatic Warbler* occur along the River Narew backwaters near the village of **Waniewo** (pronounced Vanni-ayvo) between the Biebrza Marshes and Bialystok. Walk to the eastern end of the village where there is a track north to the edge of the marshes, which are also accessible by punt.

PUSZCZA BIALOWIESKA

The temperate mixed forest which sprung up over much of the northern European lowlands after the last ice age ended 10,000 years ago was all cut down a long, long time ago. All that is except for a few pockets, the largest of which is present in part of Puszcza Bialowieska (pronounced Pooshta Bi-ow-veeayska), the 1250-km² area of forest on the border between Poland and Belarus. The 50 km² of virtually untouched forest, together with the managed forests which surround it and the associated grassy clearings and riverine marshes, support 159 breeding species, a massive total for the temperate zone, including 15 raptors, eight owls, nine of the ten European woodpeckers (Syrian is the only one missing) and 18 warblers. However, while walking amongst the giant oaks and other mature trees is a wonderful experience in itself, finding its avian treasures requires maximum patience and persistence.

Regular Summer Visitors and Resident Species
Black and White Storks, Lesser Spotted Eagle, Hazel Grouse, Corn Crake*, Eurasian Pygmy-Owl, Tengmalm's Owl, White-backed, Three-toed and Black Woodpeckers, Eurasian Nutcracker, Collared Flycatcher, Thrush Nightingale, Eurasian River and Barred Warblers, Common Rosefinch.

Other Wildlife
European bison (reintroduced), wild boar, elk, beech and pine martens, Eurasian otter, racoon-dog.

(Other species recorded here include Short-toed and Booted Eagles, Bohemian Waxwing (winter) and Greenish Warbler (*trochiloides*).)

The best base for birding Puszcza Bialowieska is the small town of Bialowieza. It is only possible to enter the virtually untouched forest in

PUSZCZA BIALOWIESKA AREA

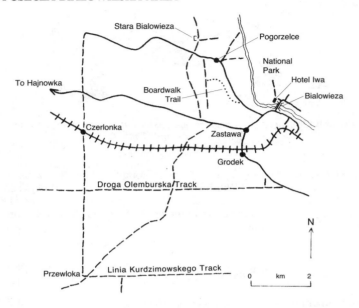

the national park to the north with a permit and official guide, both of which can be organised at the tourist office in the Hotel Iwa which is situated in Palacowy Park on the northwest outskirts of Bialowieza. Most guides spend the early spring locating woodpecker nest-holes so it would be wise to ask for their help in locating the elusive members of this family. Although some parts of the forest outside the national park are fenced off it is possible to bird most of the area without permits, via the numerous tracks and paths shown on maps available from Hotel Iwa. There are no particular hotspots but the following places may be worth concentrating on: (i) the boardwalk trail by the road between Bialowieza and **Pogorzelce** to the northwest (Hazel Grouse, and White-backed and Three-toed Woodpeckers); (ii) the tracks northeast of Pogorzelce; (iii) the track east from the car park at Stara Bialoweiza (White-backed Woodpecker and European Bison); (iv) the area around **Grodek** (Eurasian Pygmy-Owl); and (v) the area around the deserted building at **Przewloka**, to the southwest of Bialowieza (Eurasian Nutcracker). Remember that the amount of time spent in the forest is usually more important than the amount of ground covered.

Accommodation: Bialowieza—Hotel Iwa, Hotel Hunter House.

Citrine Wagtail breeds along the south shore of **Siemianowka Reservoir**, which is situated next to the border with Belarus, 20 km north of Bialowieza. The area surrounding this large reservoir is also a good place to look for other scarce breeding species in Poland, such as European Roller and Lesser Grey Shrike, as well as passage migrants which have included Marsh Sandpiper and Caspian Tern. To bird the south shore head for the village of Siemianowka, then continue east out of the village, keep left, and use the tracks leading north to reach the shore. Species recorded at the northern end of the reservoir include White-tailed* and Lesser Spotted Eagles. To reach here head west out of Siemianowka to Tarnopol and Juszkowy Grod. Turn east here to Szymki, south there to Cisowka and continue straight on.

Southwest of Bialowieza, the valley of the **River Bug** is a good place to look for passage shorebirds which have included Marsh and Terek Sandpipers. The best place is probably along the track from Wyszkow–Rybno–Dreszew–Kuligow.

The marshy peatlands between **Chelm** and Zwierzyniec support Little Crake, Great Snipe* and a high density of Aquatic Warblers*, as well as Black Stork, and Whiskered and White-winged Terns (near Dorohusk). To bird this area head towards the border with the Ukraine from Chelm and near Brzezno take the track north towards Zalin or, better still, the track south towards Plawanice and Babarowka. To reach the Gotowka Marshes, which are part of the Chelm Marshes and also support Great Snipe* and Aquatic Warbler*, head from Chelm towards Okszow–Nowiny–Zarudnia then take the first right to Gotowka 5 km after Nowiny. Birders who have managed to see nine woodpeckers at Bialowieza, could complete the European set with Syrian Woodpecker in the parks and gardens around **Zamosc**, south of Chelm.

The forested Carpathian Mountains in extreme southeast Poland, on the borders with Slovakia and the Ukraine, support Greater Spotted Eagle* and Ural Owl. Bird in and around **Przemysl** where Ural Owl occurs in the town park, as well as on the nearby uplands where it breeds in nest boxes. From Przemysl head southwest to Sanok, then southeast into **Bieszczadzki National Park** to look for Greater Spotted Eagle*. It is also possible to track wolves here, under the guidance of the researchers at the Nature Protection Institute Krakow (Wojcieh Smietana), Zatwarnica-Suche Rzeki, PL-38-715 Dwernik, Poland. For more details contact Marek Borkowski.

The Tatra Mountains in **Tatrzanski National Park** along Poland's southern border with Slovakia (p. 327) are high enough to support Wallcreeper, Yellow-billed Chough and Alpine Accentor, as well as more widespread species such as Eurasian Pygmy-Owl, Tengmalm's Owl, White-backed and Three-toed Woodpeckers, and Eurasian Nutcracker. To reach here head south from Krakow to Zakopane where there are a number of valleys (*dolinas*) with walking tracks south of the road which runs along the northern border of the park either side of Zakopane. The walking track which connects the tops of most these valleys is best for Eurasian Pygmy-Owl and Tengmalm's Owl, although both are highly elusive. To look for Wallcreeper and Alpine Accentor take the cable-car from the hamlet of Kuznice (reached via the road from Bystre, east of Zakopane) to the high tops of Kasprowy Wierch on the border with Slovakia at 1985 m (6513 ft). Some of the walking tracks and trails in the park have refuge huts which serve food.

ADDITIONAL INFORMATION

Addresses

Marek Borkowski, who founded the Biebrza Wildlife Trust and runs the Wildlife Poland tour company, has over 20-years' experience of leading wildlife trips in Poland, and can be contacted at his Warsaw office: Jablonowskiego 23, PL-02-956 Warszawa, Poland (tel: 862 733666; fax: 862 733667; email: marek.borkowski@wildlife.pl; website: www.wildlife.pl); or at home in the Biebrza Marshes, at Kuligi— Gradziki, 19–205 Woznawies, Poland.

Please send records of rarities to the Komisja Faunistyczna, Museum of Natural History, Sienkiewicza 21, PL-50-335 Wroclaw, Poland (tel: 71 225041; fax: 71 222817). The annual rarities report is published in *Notatki Ornitologiczne*, in Polish with an English summary.

The Polish Society for the Protection of Birds (OTOP), ul. J Hallera 4/2, 80-401 Gdańsk, Poland (tel/fax: 58 341 2693; email: office@otop.most. org.pl).

The North Podlasie Society for Bird Protection (PTOP), PO Box 32, PL-17-230 Bialowieza, Poland.

Books and papers

Finding Birds in Eastern Poland. Gosney D, 1993. Available from Bird-Guides (address, p. 395).

Ostoje ptakow w Polsce (Important Bird Areas of Poland). Gromadzki M *et al.*, 1994. Ogolnopolskie Towarzystwo Ochrony Ptakow, Gdańsk.

Portrait of a Living Marsh: 32 International Artists Visit Northeast Poland. Shillcock R D, 1993. Wildlife Art Gallery.

PORTUGAL

INTRODUCTION

Summary

Although something of a shadow of Spain as far as birding is concerned, it is possible to see some of the Iberian specialities, including Purple Swamphen, White-rumped Swift and Azure-winged Magpie, as well as Great Bustard* and many more Mediterranean species in a relatively compact area of southern Portugal. It is therefore a good country to visit for birders who prefer to use just one or two bases and this together with the wide variety of birds and the availability of cheap package holidays makes Portugal a very attractive birding destination.

Size

At 91,630 km^2, Portugal is 70% the size of England and about 12% the size of Texas.

Getting Around

Virtually all of the best birds in Portugal occur in the south, in the coastal Algarve and the Baixo Alentejo, a short distance inland, in an area about 150 km x 200 km, hence, package holidays which include

Portugal

flights to Faro, the main resort area in the Algarve, accommodation and a hire-car, present a perfect opportunity for some of the best birding in Europe with the minimum of expenditure. In addition, a new highway means it is just three to four hours from Faro to the Coto Doñana (p. 344) in Spain, where most of the Iberian specialities missing from southern Portugal can be seen. Birders intending to attempt the 'clean-up' should check that their hire-car agreement allows them to drive to Spain. It is possible to get around the Algarve via public transport, but a vehicle will definitely be required to bird the Alentejo. Unfortunately, many roads and the local driving standards are poor, and Portugal has by far the worst road accident rate in Europe, so birders are strongly advised to keep at least one eye on the road and to remember that the local police do not look favourably on speeding.

Accommodation and Food

A wide range of accommodation is available almost everywhere. Birders intending to use a package holiday to bird Portugal may be wise to miss out on half-board or full-board accommodation since set meals decrease flexibility and food is just as cheap outside the resorts. As an alternative to the resorts, budget birders may wish to use the equally cheap guesthouses, pensions (*pensoes*), youth hostels and campsites. Food is excellent value because the portions are usually very generous, especially staples such as chips, fish, sandwiches and soups. Beer (*cerveja*), local spirits and wine are all cheaper in bars.

Health and Safety
Beware of theft from campsites and vehicles.

Climate and Timing
The climate is mild to warm or hot all year round, becoming increasingly more arid and hotter towards the south where, especially inland, it is usually sizzling in midsummer. A good time to visit Portugal is between the last week of March and the third week of April, when resident species and many summer visitors are already breeding, bustards are displaying and spring migration is in full swing. However, this is too early for some summer migrants, including White-rumped Swift, which does not usually return until late May, hence June would also be a good time to visit. Forget July and August, its far too hot. The autumn migration period is also a good time to be in the country, especially during late September and October.

Habitats
The coastal cliffs, beaches, dunes, estuaries, lagoons, salinas, stone pine woods, olive and orange groves, and hillsides covered with garrigue and maquis, are scarred with development only in the vicinity of Lisbon and along the Algarve. Inland, some Portuguese believe they live in the Third World of Europe, since the place has barely changed for centuries, especially south of the Río Tejo (Tagus), which effectively divides the country in two. Apart from cultivated and grazed areas, the Alentejo, south of the Río Tejo, is characterised by undulating steppe grasslands dotted with natural and planted cork-oaks (Portugal produces almost half of the world's cork); a landscape known as *dehesa* in Spain, but *montado* in Portugal. There are limestone outcrops in the montado but real highlands are confined to north of the Río Tejo where most of the land lies above 400 m (1312 ft) and reaches a maximum height of 1256 m (4121 ft) at Cabreira in the northwest. These hills and mountains support some deciduous forest, heathland and coniferous plantations.

Conservation
The natural deciduous and coniferous forests have largely been cleared over the centuries to make room for agriculture and so-called reafforestation, which, in many cases, has involved the planting of alien *Eucalyptus* species which are quick-growing and thus ideal for the thriving pulp-mill industry. Coastal development, linked mainly to tourism, is mostly confined to the Algarve and Lisbon area, but has played its part in the decline of the Osprey, which failed to breed in Portugal in 1997. There were 14 pairs in the country in 1950, but it now seems destined to become extinct there, at least as a breeding species. Inland, the countryside has changed slowly since medieval times but the scale of mechanised farming is increasing and a proposal to build a dam on the Río Guadiana, helped by a £134 million grant from the EU, which will provide enough water to irrigate 1100 km^2, is a serious threat to the steppe grasslands of the Alentejo where large populations of bustards still survive. And this is just the tip of the iceberg, since EEC/EU funding could catalyse numerous other projects involving agricultural intensification, industrialisation and reafforestation, all of which spell doom as far as birds are concerned. These massive problems, together with the increasing use of plastic corks, threatening the sustainable harvest of

cork from the important cork-oak woodlands, as well as hunting and pollution, need tackling now in order to ensure the continued survival of the relatively common and widespread birds of Portugal, and most importantly, the seven threatened and near-threatened species which occur in the country.

Bird Species
Notable species include Greater Flamingo, Black-shouldered Kite, Purple Swamphen ('Western' *porphyrio*), Little* and Great* Bustards, Collared Pratincole, Great Spotted Cuckoo, Red-necked Nightjar, White-rumped Swift, Azure-winged Magpie, Spotless Starling, Rufous-tailed Scrub-Robin, Black Wheatear, Spectacled Warbler, Thekla Lark, Spanish Sparrow and Alpine Accentor.

The last confirmed record of Small Buttonquail (Andalusian Hemipode) concerned two birds which were flushed south of Lisbon in June 1973, although there is a report of one being shot in the southern Alentejo during November 1997.

Near-endemics
Spanish Eagle*, which has bred in Portugal, is now very rare.

Expectations
It is possible to see 150–170 species during a visit lasting one to two weeks in late March and early April.

ALGARVE

The Algarve, alias the south coast of Portugal, extends about 150 km from Cabo de São Vicente in the west to the border with Spain in the east. Amongst and inland from the tourist resorts there is a fine diversity of habitats, including long beaches, picturesque coves, estuaries, lagoons, dry heathlands and stands of stone pines, as well as plenty of well-watered golf courses and cultivated valleys. Many migrant species moving north in spring land on this south-facing coast, but the avian highlights are arguably the resident breeding species such as Purple Swamphen.

The species listed below occur during the summer unless otherwise indicated.

Localised Specialities
Purple Swamphen ('Western' *porphyrio*).

Other Localised Species
Greater Flamingo, Little Bustard*, Great Spotted Cuckoo, Azure-winged Magpie, Spotless Starling, Lesser Short-toed and Thekla Larks.

Others
Cory's ('Scopoli's' *diomedea*) and Mediterranean Shearwaters, Red-crested Pochard, Purple Heron, Cattle Egret, Black-crowned Night-Heron, Little Bittern, White Stork, Osprey, Short-toed and Booted Eagles, Lesser Kestrel*, Red-legged Partridge, Eurasian Thick-knee, Collared

Pratincole, Alpine and Pallid Swifts, European Bee-eater, Red-billed Chough, Blue Rock-Thrush, Bluethroat ('White-spotted' *cyanecula*, Oct–Mar), Eurasian Crag-Martin, Red-rumped Swallow, Zitting Cisticola, Sardinian, Subalpine and Spectacled Warblers, Calandra Lark, Alpine Accentor (Oct-Mar), Rock Bunting.

(Other species recorded here include White-headed Duck*, Marbled Teal*, Squacco Heron, Little Crake, Audouin's* and Slender-billed Gulls, Gull-billed and Caspian Terns, European Roller, Rufous-tailed Scrub-Robin and Orphean Warbler. During the autumn Black Storks may be seen passing over in favourable conditions, along with raptors. Introduced species include Common Waxbill. Seabirds recorded from the headlands and at sea primarily during the late summer and autumn have included Great and Little Shearwaters, Wilson's, European and Band-rumped Storm-Petrels, Grey Phalarope, Sabine's Gull and Long-tailed Skua.)

MARSHES NEAR FARO

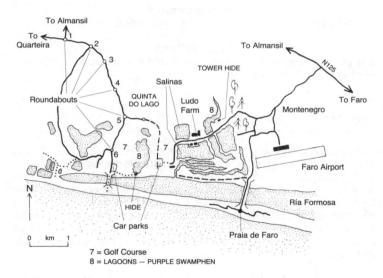

7 = Golf Course
8 = LAGOONS — PURPLE SWAMPHEN

The large town of **Faro** and its associated resorts, including Albufeira, lie close to some of the best birding sites in the Algarve. Birders flying into Faro may notice the marshes to the west of the airport before they land, and on seeing them may start hoping that they pass through customs as quickly as possible so that they can get out there, because the many birds to be seen there include Purple Swamphen and Azure-winged Magpie. To reach these marshes head west from the Montenegro district near the airport through the stone pine woods inhabited by Azure-winged Magpies. Just east of Ludo Farm check the freshwater lagoon north of the track for Purple Swamphens. If they fail to show don't despair, because the best place to see them in the Algarve is not far away. They are usually easy to find at the **São Lourenco Golf Course**, one of four golf courses in the Quinta do Lago area. To reach here head west from Faro for about 10 km to Almansil, then turn south

ALGARVE and BAIXO ALENTEJO

and continue to the car park south of roundabout number six, next to a footbridge over the Ría Formosa (worth walking over to check for gulls and terns on the tidal mudflats). From the car park walk east to a hide at the south end of a large reedy lake where ten swamphens were present in October 1998. It is also possible to walk around this lake, where White-headed Duck*, Red-crested Pochard and Little Crake have also been recorded.

West of Faro the next area worth birding is the mountainous area around **Monchique**, about 25 km north of Portimao, which rises to 902 m (2959 ft) at Foia and is traversed by the N265, from which it is possible to see Blue Rock-Thrush, Eurasian Crag-Martin. Alpine Accentor (winter) and Rock Bunting. To reach the Odelouca Valley where Eurasian Eagle-Owl and Azure-winged Magpie occur head inland from Portimao then turn right on to the N124 towards Silves, then left just before the bridge over the River Odelouca on to what becomes a rough track through the valley. This track eventually reaches a road which ascends to Monchique.

Back at the coast, about 275 species have been recorded in the area between the mouths of the Rivers Alvor and Odiaxere, known as **Quinta da Rocha**, just west of Portimao. To reach here turn south off the N125 west of the Alvor Estuary, opposite the road to Mexilhoeira Grande, on to a track which descends to some salinas, worth checking in late summer for Audouin's Gull*, and the A Rocha Reserve, Cruzinha, Mexilhoeira Grande, 8500 Portimao (open on Thursdays only), run by the A Rocha Trust, c/o 13 West Drive, Upton, Wirral, Merseyside, UK. Further west along the N125 turn north at Odiaxere and follow signs to Barragem to reach the **Bravura Reservoir** where Red-rumped Swallow and Rock Bunting breed.

At the extreme southwest end of Portugal and Europe is **Cabo de São Vicente**, the spectacular southwestern extremity of the Sagres Peninsula where the limestone cliffs reach a height of 150 m (492 ft). The cape is an excellent place for Alpine Swift, Blue Rock-Thrush and Spectacled Warbler, while the dry heathland inland supports a few Lesser Kestrels*

The striking Eurasian Hoopoe is a frequent sight in the Algarve

and Little Bustards* (especially alongside the Cabo–Ponta de Sagres road), as well as Spotless Starling and Thekla Lark. During the winter up to 15 Alpine Accentors have been recorded around the lighthouse at the cape, and this species also occurs in the rocky area inland. During the autumn, especially between mid-September and mid-October, there can be a strong raptor passage over the peninsula, and seawatching from the cape, **Ponta de Sagres** or **Ponta da Piedade** (1.5 km south of Lagos) at this time of year can also be fairly good, especially in southwesterlies with rain. Possibilities from the mainland include shearwaters and Audouin's Gull*, but more pelagic species such as Wilson's and Band-rumped Storm-Petrels are much more likely to be seen on boat trips out from Sagres or Portimao during late summer and early autumn (at least 70 Wilson's Storm-Petrels were present at sea 11 km south of Sagres in mid-September 1998, and during late June and early July 1998 single Band-rumped and Swinhoe's Storm-Petrels were tapelured into Ponta da Almadena).

East of Faro the first place worth stopping at is the **Olhao Salinas**, which are situated near a radio mast visible from the N125 between

Faro and Olhao. This used to be the only breeding site of Collared Pratincoles in Portugal but there were few, if any, birds left by the end of the 1990s. At the extreme east end of the Algarve near the border with Spain on the west side of the Río Guadiana the reserve at **Castro Marim**, north and west of Vila Real de St Antonio, supports White Stork, Little Bustard* (in dry saltmarsh but difficult to see due to disturbance), Collared Pratincole, Spectacled Warbler and Lesser Short-toed Lark, while other species recorded here, mainly on passage, include Greater Flamingo (over 1,000 have occurred at any one time, on the salinas southwest of Castro Marim), shorebirds, Slender-billed Gull, Caspian Tern and Rufous-tailed Scrub-Robin. To reach the salinas, scrub and dry areas east of Castro Marim it is necessary to head north from the town, under the autopista, then east in response to the 'transito local' signpost, and back under the autopista. This a particularly good area for Collared Pratincole, Little Bustard*, Spectacled Warbler and Lesser Short-toed Lark.

BAIXO ALENTEJO

The rolling steppe grasslands, rocky limestone outcrops, olive groves, extensive cork-oak woods and plantations, and river gorges of the southern (Baixo) Alentejo, known by the locals as the Campo Branco ('White Country') because of the spectacular showing of white spring flowers, support a lot of birds which do not occur in the Algrave, just 75 km to the south. So, with birds such as Great Bustard*, Red-necked Nightjar and White-rumped Swift present it would be daft not to spend at least a day here, although it may take longer to find the bustards.

The species listed below occur during the summer unless otherwise indicated.

Localised Specialities
Great Bustard*, White-rumped Swift, Rufous-tailed Scrub-Robin, Spanish Sparrow.

Other Localised Species
Great Spotted Cuckoo, Red-necked Nightjar, Azure-winged Magpie, Spotless Starling, Thekla Lark.

Others
Cattle Egret, Black and White Storks, Egyptian Vulture, Eurasian Griffon, Short-toed, Bonelli's and Booted Eagles, Lesser Kestrel*, Red-legged Partridge, Little Bustard*, Eurasian Thick-knee, Alpine Swift, European Bee-eater, European Roller, Blue Rock-Thrush, Eurasian Crag-Martin, Red-rumped Swallow, Calandra Lark, Rock Petronia, Rock Bunting.
    (Other species recorded here include Black-shouldered Kite, Cinereous Vulture*, Black-bellied Sandgrouse and Black Wheatear. If the report of a Small Buttonquail (Andalusian Hemipode) being shot here in November 1997 is true, it will be the first record in Portugal for 24 years.)

There are two ways of reaching the southern Alentejo from the Algarve: (i) head north from Faro on the N2 to Almodovar then turn east on to the N267 to Mértola; and (ii) head north from Albufeira on the longer but faster (1–2 hours) route to Ourique then turn east to Castro Verde and continue to Mertola. Virtually any likely looking grasslands east of **Almodovar** and **Castro Verde** are worth checking for bustards and other steppe specialists, but particularly productive spots in the past have included the following: (i) alongside the tracks leading off the N123 2–3 east of Castro Verde; (ii) alongside the tracks which lead north and south, about 12 km east of Almodovar; and (iii) alongside the road which leads north just west of São Joao dos Caldeireiros to Penilhos. Black-bellied Sandgrouse, Rufous-tailed Scrub-Robin and Spanish Sparrow have been recorded alongside this road. Check the base of White Stork's nests, most of which are situated on the tops of telegraph poles, for the sparrow squatters.

The largest colony of Lesser Kestrels* in Portugal and a few pairs of White-rumped Swift (at Mina de São Domingos, just to the east) breed in and around the medieval hilltop town of **Mértola**, perched high above the Río Guadiana at the eastern edge of the southern Alentejo. From Mértola head northeast on the N265, looking out for Great Spotted Cuckoo and European Roller, to **Serpa**. To the north of here Black-shouldered Kite has been recorded in the following areas: (i) within the triangle of roads between Serpa, Brinches and Pias; (ii) in the area between Moura and Safara (along with bustards); and (iii) between Moura and Barrancos (along with Cinereous Vulture*). The Castle of Noudar near Barrancos provides an excellent vantage point from which to scan the surrounding hills for raptors. Also check the Granja rubbish tip just north of the village. East of Moura it is possible to cross into Spain, where on turning left after about 500 m the track reaches a small reservoir surrounded by a stony plain where both bustards, Black-bellied Sandgrouse and European Roller occur. West of Moura on the N256, Rufous-tailed Scrub-Robin has been recorded around the Río Guadiana crossing. Black Stork and Bonelli's Eagle breed at **Pulo do Lobo**, a spectacular gorge with a waterfall in the Río Guadiana valley, also north of Mértola.

Accommodation: Castro Verde—Castro Aparthotel. Moura—Hotel de Moura.

The **Alto Alentejo** (Northern Alentejo), which forms the western extension of Extremadura in Spain (p. 347), supports the same species as the southern Alentejo, but this is a better place to look for Black-shouldered Kite. The best area is between Évora, Elvas and Montforte, east to the border with Spain, particularly east of Évora and Montforte.

Cabo de Sines, on the southwest coast of Portugal, is arguably the best seawatching site in the country, especially in wet southwesterlies during the autumn. Cory's ('Cory's' *borealis*/'Scopoli's' *diomedea*) and Mediterranean ('Balearic' *mauretanicus*) Shearwaters, Wilson's Storm-Petrel and Sabine's Gull have all been recorded from here.

The brackish **Lagoa de Santo Andre**, on the coast about 20 km north of Cabo de Sines, together with the surrounding reedbeds, dunes and woods, support breeding Black-shouldered Kite, Baillon's Crake and Great Spotted Cuckoo. This is also a well known hot-spot for passerine passage migrants which have included a few rarities from the far east, hence a ringing station operates here every autumn and reports of five Richard's Pipits during early and late 1995, a Little Bunting in

February 1996 and a Pallas's (Reed) Bunting on three dates in early 1997 all beg the questions: could it be that 'reverse migrants' from Siberia reach the end of the line here, or elsewhere in Portugal; or, did these birds travel even further southwest the previous autumns and then drop in here on their staggered journeys back to Siberia? Whatever the answers, any birder interested in rarities who visits Portugal during the autumn or winter should seriously consider spending at least a couple of days at this site. It can be reached by turning west off the N120 on to the N261–2 to Melides, which is situated near the lagoon, as well as its neighbouring lagoons to the north (Lagoa de Melides) and south (Lagoa de Sancha), which are also worth birding.

SADO AND TEJO ESTUARIES

Despite much destruction and degradation these two large estuaries near Lisbon are still two of the most important intertidal areas in Iberia, since they support a wide range of breeding species and attract high numbers of passage and wintering shorebirds. During passage periods up to 12,000 Black-tailed Godwits and 1,000 Curlew Sandpipers, and during the winter up to 18,000 Pied Avocets, have been recorded on the Tejo alone. Furthermore, the adjacent farmland, paddies, salinas and cork-oak woods support Black-shouldered Kite and Little Bustard*.

The species listed below occur during the summer unless otherwise indicated.

Localised Specialities
Black-shouldered Kite.

Other Localised Species
Greater Flamingo (winter), Red-necked Nightjar, Azure-winged Magpie, Spotless Starling, Thekla Lark.

Others
White Stork, Bonelli's and Booted Eagles, Little Bustard*, Collared Pratincole, Alpine and Pallid Swifts, European Bee-eater, European Roller, Bluethroat ('White-spotted' *cyanecula*, winter), Zitting Cisticola, Rock Petronia.

Other Wildlife
Bottlenose dolphin, Eurasian otter.

(Before the 1970s at least 20 pairs of Spanish Eagle* bred in the cork-oak woodlands of the Tejo and Sado valleys, but they now appear to be extinct. Other species recorded here include Squacco Heron. Introduced species include Common Waxbill.)

The south side of the **Sado Estuary**, 230 km^2 of which lies within a reserve, is the best for Black-shouldered Kite, Red-necked Nightjar and Azure-winged Magpie. The north side is accessible directly by road via Alcácer do Sal and via a vehicular ferry from Troia to Setubal (look out for bottlenose dolphin on the crossing). Head east out of Setubal (where Pallid Swift occurs) on the N10 for about 14 km then turn south on to a track which leads to various wetlands where there are usually plenty of birds.

To reach the 145-km² reserve at the **Tejo Estuary** turn south at Porto Alto, which is on the N10 east of Vila Franca da Xira, on to the N118 and after 10 km turn west on to a track which reaches the gate at the reserve entrance after 4 km. From here it is 1.5 km on foot to salinas which are full of shorebirds at the right time of year. The cork-oak woods to the south of the reserve entrance support Black-shouldered Kite, Red-necked Nightjar and Azure-winged Magpie. Also around the Tejo Estuary bird the Lezirias Land between the Río Tejo and Río Sorraia, the salinas at Alcochete and Montijo, and, to the south, beyond Pancas, the farmland, for Little Bustard*. To reach Lezirias turn south on to a large track (signposted to a Sailing Centre) just east of the N10 road bridge over the Tejo at Vila Franca da Xira.

Accommodation: Alcochete—Montijo Parque Hotel.

Marbled Teal* and Red-knobbed Coot have been recorded on the small roadside lake about 5 km north of **Alcacovas**, which is east of Alcácer do Sal at the inland end of the Sado Estuary, between there and Évora in the Alto Alentejo (p. 288). **Cabo Espichel**, west of Setubal on the Sado Estuary, can be good for seawatching in wet southwesterlies during the autumn, and it attracts passage migrants and rarities which have included Richard's Pipit and Yellow-breasted Bunting.

The only known colonies of *borealis* Cory's Shearwater and Band-rumped Storm-Petrel in continental Europe are present on the **Berlenga and Farilhoe Islands**, which lie offshore from Cabo Carvoeiro, about 70 km northwest of Lisbon. There are regular boat trips to the Berlenga Islands from Peniche during the summer, on which it is possible to see these two species, as well as other seabirds. Getting to the Farilhoe Islands, 35 km offshore, where the 50 pairs of Band-rumped Storm-Petrel breed on Farilhoe Grande, is more difficult.

Portugal's most important inland freshwater wetland, the **Paul do Boquilobo Nature Reserve**, supports the country's largest and most diverse colony of egrets and herons, containing about 500 pairs of Little Egret, 1,500 pairs of Cattle Egret, 100 pairs of Black-crowned Night-Heron and smaller numbers of other species. The reserve is situated about 20 km northeast of Santarem, just west of the Tejo Valley, and is accessible from Golega to the north.

East of **Castelo Branco** in east-central Portugal it is possible to see a number of species which are scarce or difficult to see in Portugal but relatively common just across the border in Spain. These include Black Stork, Egyptian Vulture, Eurasian Griffon, Cinereous Vulture* (rare), Golden and Bonelli's Eagles, Pin-tailed (rare) and Black-bellied Sandgrouse, Black Wheatear, Spanish Sparrow (at Ladoeiro) and Rock Bunting, as well as Little* and Great* (rare around Idanha-a-Nova) Bustards. Many of these species occur along the Upper Río Tejo, about 20 km southeast of Castelo Branco, along the border with Spain. Across the border in Spain, south of Segura, the extensive grasslands between Brozas and Membrío (p. 349) support 800–1,000 Great Bustards*, plus both species of sandgrouse.

The valley of the upper **Río Douro** in northeast Portugal on the border with Spain, supports Black Stork, important numbers of raptors,

Great Spotted Cuckoo, Red-necked Nightjar, European Roller, Black Wheatear, Orphean Warbler, Thekla Lark, Rock Petronia and Rock Bunting. Bird south of the town of Miranda do Douro, especially where the river turns west.

ADDITIONAL INFORMATION

Addresses

Please send records of rarities to the Comite Portugues de Raridades, Sociedade Portuguesa para o Estudo das Aves (Portugese Society for the Study of Birds), Rua da Vitoria 53, 2° Dto, 1100 Lisboa, Portugal. The annual rarities report was published in *Airo* up until the end of 1994, and then in *Pardela*, in Portuguese with an English summary.

Books and papers

A Birdwatchers' Guide to Portugal and Madeira. Moore C *et al.*, 1998. Prion.

Where to watch birds in Spain and Portugal. Rose L, 1995. Hamlyn.

A Birdwatching Guide to the Algarve. Carlson K and C, 1995. Arlequin Press.

Finding Birds in Southern Portugal. Gosney D. Available from Bird-Guides (address, p. 395).

Breeding birds of the Algarve. Vowles, G and R, 1994. Privately published.

An Atlas of wintering birds in the western Algarve. Bolton B, 1987. A Rocha Trust.

ROMANIA

INTRODUCTION

Summary

Since the end of the communist dictatorship in 1989 Romania has become a very popular birding destination, mainly because cheap package holidays, with one week based on the Black Sea coast and one week based in the Carpathian Mountains, offer a great opportunity to see one of the widest ranges of species possible on a trip to Europe, from pelicans and Paddyfield Warblers in the Danube Delta area and Wallcreepers in Transylvania through numerous passage migrants to huge numbers of wintering Red-breasted Geese*.

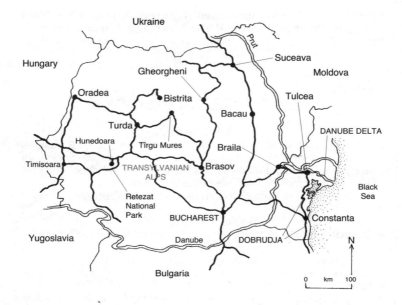

Size
At 237,500 km², Romania is 1.8 times larger than England and one third the size of Texas.

Getting Around
Some visitors arrive in Bucharest by air, from where it is a few hours by road or an overnight train ride to the Black Sea coast beach resorts or Tulcea, the gateways to the Danube Delta and Dobrudja, the two major lowland birding sites in the country. Other people fly directly to the Black Sea coast on the extremely cheap package tours, some of which also include a week based at ski-resorts in the Carpathian Mountains of Transylvania, the major highland birding area in the country. Once at base camp, be it on the coast or in the mountains, it is best to hire a vehicle to get around, although some areas, including the delta, are accessible via the cheap public transport system.

Accommodation and Food
A wide range of built accommodation is available, most of which is much cheaper when booked as part of a package holiday. There are also plenty of basic campsites, some with chalets. The wide variety of food is also excellent value and includes such delights as cabbage stuffed with herbs, meat and rice, and topped with sour cream (*samarle*), as well as meatballs, omelettes and sausages. Imported German beers are more widespread than national brews, the local spirits are fearsome and wine is also generally available.

Health and Safety
Immunisation against hepatitis, polio and typhoid is recommended, as are precautions against rabies. Mosquitoes can be a serious problem in places like the Danube Delta so take plenty of repellent. Avoid

uncooked food, wash unpeeled fruit and vegetables carefully, and drink bottled water. Do not point optics at airports, large factories and large bridges, and be discreet when birding in the border areas. The increasingly enlightened officials are not likely to throw offenders in jail, but taking such precautions may save hours explaining the finer details of birding.

Climate and Timing

The climate is continental with hot summers and cold, wet winters. It can be rather chilly in the Danube Delta when it is windy, even during the summer, and during the winter it can be extremely cold here and on the nearby Dobrudja due to freezing temperatures and the wind-chill factor. The best times to visit Romania are: during the peak spring migration period between April and mid-May; in late May and early June when some migrants are still passing through and most of the summer visitors have arrived; from late August to mid-September when the autumn migration is in full swing; and from mid-November to mid-December when the numbers of Red-breasted Geese* usually reach their peak.

Habitats

Northern and western Romania is dominated by the Carpathian Mountains, which rise to 2543 m (8343 ft) at Moldoveanu in the Transylvanian Alps. The beech woods, coniferous forest, gorges and alpine pastures on the slopes of these wild, spooky, snow-capped mountains, are still in good enough condition to support plenty of birds, as well as 6,000 brown bears and 2,000 grey wolves. The River Danube flows eastwards to the south of these mountains along the border with Bulgaria, through lowland farmland with fishponds, lakes, marshes, oak woods and remnant steppe-woodland, before reaching the 200-km-long Black Sea coast where it forms the massive Danube Delta, one of Europe's top five most important wetland sites for birds. On the Black Sea coastal plain there are yet more excellent habitats full of birds, including coastal lagoons, and, in the extreme southeast corner of the country, some remnant steppe-grassland amongst vast cereal fields, in the region known as Dobrudja.

Conservation

During Ceausescu's regime non-governmental conservation organisations were outlawed. Fortunately, as soon as he was thrown out in December 1989, conservation-minded Romanians wasted no time in setting up the Societatea Ornitologica Romana (SOR—Romanian Ornithological Society) which soon began a vigorous and successful public awareness campaign. However, the 15 threatened and near-threatened species (the equal highest total for a European country) as well as the relatively common and widespread birds which occur in Romania still face a mountain of problems, which include habitat loss and degradation, hunting (the Italians take their toll here as well) and pollution. Even the Danube Delta is not sacred. Proposals to construct fishponds never seem to go away and although the delta covers some 4400 km^2, an area greater than that covered by the Camargue and Coto Doñana combined, only 560 km^2, including part of the Danube Valley and some adjacent lagoons, actually lies within the boundaries of a biosphere reserve.

Bird Species

Over 350 species have been recorded in Romania. Notable species include Pygmy Cormorant*, Great White and Dalmatian* Pelicans, Red-breasted Goose*, Levant Sparrowhawk, Long-legged Buzzard, Imperial Eagle*, Little Crake, Marsh and Broad-billed Sandpipers, Pied Wheatear, Wallcreeper, Paddyfield Warbler, Sombre Tit and Alpine Accentor.

Expectations

It is possible to see 160–190 species on a trip to the Black Sea coast and Carpathian Mountains lasting a week to ten days during the spring or autumn.

Birders with time to spare around **Bucharest** may wish to visit Laculs Floreasca and Herastrau which are good for waterbirds and occasionally attract a few over-wintering Pygmy Cormorants*. Between Bucharest and the Black Sea Coast it may be worth stopping at **Canuraua Fetei** where the low limestone cliffs support occasional wintering Wallcreepers, and resident Eurasian Eagle-Owl and Rock Bunting.

DOBRUDJA

Many birding visitors to Romania head straight for the Danube Delta, but although the numbers of breeding birds are much more impressive there than in the Dobrudja, the variety is far less impressive, and all in all the Dobrudja is probably the best birding area in Romania and one of the very best in Europe.

Some species which can be difficult to find in the delta are much easier to see here, including Paddyfield Warbler, which breeds here along with Marsh Sandpiper and Pied Wheatear. The Black Sea coast lies on a major migration route and during the autumn especially, visible migration over the Dobrudja can be spectacular. For example, over 1,000 Purple Herons have been observed passing over in just one evening. Many birds also stop to rest and refuel, particularly shorebirds, and this is probably the best place in Europe to see Broad-billed Sandpiper, up to 300 of which have been seen on a single autumn day. During the early winter the vast fields of winter wheat and ice-free saline lagoons in the southern Dobrudja support up to 130,000 Greater White-fronted Geese and 40,000 Red-breasted Geese*—virtually the entire world population—but these birds are usually forced by bad weather to move south into neighbouring north Bulgaria by midwinter (p. 130).

The species listed below occur during the summer unless otherwise indicated.

Localised Specialities

Pied Wheatear, Paddyfield Warbler.

Other Localised Species

Pygmy Cormorant*, Great White and Dalmatian* Pelicans, Levant Sparrowhawk, Imperial Eagle*, Marsh Sandpiper.

Airborne Great White Pelicans make a splendid sight

Regular Passage Migrants
Black Stork, Temminck's Stint, Broad-billed Sandpiper (most in Sep), Red-necked Phalarope (most in Sep), Little Gull, Collared Flycatcher (most in Sep).

Regular Winter Visitors
Greater White-fronted and Red-breasted Geese*, Smew, Rough-legged Buzzard.

Others
Ferruginous Duck*, Great Egret, Squacco Heron, Black-crowned Night-Heron, Glossy Ibis, White Stork, White-tailed Eagle*, Long-legged Buzzard, Lesser Spotted and Booted Eagles, Red-footed Falcon, Little Crake, Collared Pratincole, Whiskered, White-winged and Gull-billed Terns, European Bee-eater, European Roller, White-backed (*lilfordi*), Syrian and Black Woodpeckers, Lesser Grey Shrike, Rufous-tailed Rock-Thrush, Eurasian River, Moustached, Olivaceous and Barred Warblers, Sombre Tit, Calandra Lark, Spanish Sparrow, Yellow Wagtail ('Black-headed' *feldegg*).

(Other species recorded here include White-headed Duck*, Lesser White-fronted Goose* (winter), Ruddy Shelduck, Pallid Harrier* (rare breeder), Saker Falcon (rare breeder), Slender-billed Curlew* (several records), Terek Sandpiper, Black-winged Pratincole*, Great Black-headed (up to three around Plopul in September 1999) and Slender-billed Gulls, Caspian Tern and Rosy Starling (at least 100 pairs bred at Enisala in 1997).)

There are a number of suitable bases for birding the Dobrudja, including Tulcea, which is also the gateway to the Danube Delta, and Black Sea resorts such as Mamaia. The first place to head for is the **Lacul Histria** area, one of the finest birding sites in Europe. To reach it turn east off the Tulcea–Constanta road 3.5 km south of Istria (7.5 km north of Sacele) in response to the 'Cetatae Histria' signpost and head towards the museum. The marshes alongside the road to the museum support most of the waterbirds listed above, including Little Crake (in channels on the south side of the road east of Lacul Nuntasi), Collared Pratincole and Paddyfield Warbler (in small marshes and lake fringes, especially at Lacul Nuntasi where 400 have been ringed during a single autumn). Beyond the museum thousands of birds can often be seen at **Lacul Sinoie** during the autumn, when up to 750 Garganey, 50 Marsh and 300 Broad-billed Sandpipers, and over 250 Collared Pratincoles have been recorded, as well as other migrants such as Red-necked Phalarope and

DOBRUDJA and DANUBE DELTA

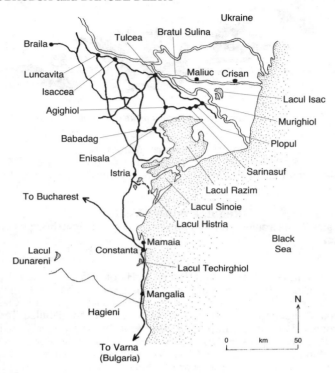

rarities which have included Slender-billed Curlew*. The **Cheia Dobrogea Valley**, inland from Istria, is the best place for Pied Wheatear.

The wooded hills to the west of the Tulcea–Constanta road several km south of **Babadag** support Levant Sparrowhawk, Lesser Spotted and Imperial* Eagles, White-backed Woodpecker (scarce) and Sombre Tit. The fishponds (3 km to the east towards Unirea), reedy pools (4 km to the north towards Tulcea) and sewage works around **Enisala**, about 10 km east of Babadag, support Ferruginous Duck*, Little Crake and European Bee-eater (at a colony below the ruined castle). Little Crake also occurs in the pools along the west side of **Lacul Razim**, east of Enisala. Northeast of here (southeast of Tulcea) take any track north out of the village of Plopul to reach **Lacul Beibugeac** which is usually good for passage shorebirds, and continue northeast from Plopul to reach **Lacul Saraturii** which supports Red-necked Grebe. East of here is Murighiol (Independenta) which lies within the Danube Delta (opposite).

Wintering Red-breasted Geese* are highly mobile, moving between the huge fields of winter wheat and barley, the ice-free saline lagoons such as Razim and Sinoie and offshore sandbanks. However, a tour of the area between Constanta Airport, Istria, the key roosting sites of Laculs Sinoie and Razim (where birds also feed in the fields near Sarinasuf at the northern end), Enisala, Lacul Beibugeac (a favoured bathing and drinking site, especially around midday) and Mahmudia should end up trumps.

Lacul Techirghiol, at the southern end of the Dobrudja south of Constanta, is a good place to look for White-headed Ducks* during the winter (about 400 were present in late November 1998). The parks and gardens in and around the Black Sea resorts here in the southeast corner of the Dobrudja are the best places to look for Olive-tree Warbler, which may be expanding its breeding range north from Greece along the Black Sea coast, and Spanish Sparrow. The **Hagieni Reserve**, a small wooded valley with marshes inland from Mangalia, supports Ferruginous Duck*, Levant Sparrowhawk and Imperial Eagle*.

Accommodation: Constanta. Eforie. Mamaia—Hotel Jupiter-Juona. Mangalia. Nuntasi Bay—campsite. Navodari—campsite.

DANUBE DELTA

The River Danube, the longest river in Europe, rises in the Black Forest region of southern Germany and flows 2850 km from there across eastern Europe to the Black Sea where it spreads out to form a massive 90-km-wide delta, which covers 4400 km², an area greater than that covered by the Camargue and Coto Doñana combined. It is quite simply the largest and one of the most natural, richest and important wetlands in Europe. Over 160 species have been recording breeding amongst the labyrinth of lily-covered lakes and channels, the largest expanse of reeds in Europe, floating islands of vegetation (*plaur*) and wooded dunes and embankments, many of them in phenomenal numbers, such as up to 2,500 pairs of Pygmy Cormorants*, 2,000 pairs of Squacco Herons, 1,500 pairs of Glossy Ibises and 20,000 pairs of Whiskered Terns. The delta also supports the largest breeding population of Great White Pelicans in Europe and up to 40 pairs of Dalmatian Pelicans*, and during the autumn over 1,500 Ferruginous Ducks*, about 13,000 Mediterranean Gulls and over 250 Caspian Terns have been recorded.

Although the delta has been badly degraded by fish farming, drainage, pollution and the construction of numerous navigable channels it is still relatively unblemished by development and the only way of getting around is by boat. Once aboard, birders should prepare themselves for a trip back in time, to the days when birds were everywhere.

The species listed below occur during the summer unless otherwise indicated.

Localised Species
Pygmy Cormorant*, Great White and Dalmatian* Pelicans.

Regular Passage Migrants
Black Stork, Marsh Sandpiper, Temminck's Stint, Broad-billed Sandpiper (most in Sep), Red-necked Phalarope (most in Sep), Caspian Tern.

Others
Ferruginous Duck*, Smew (winter), Great Egret, Squacco Heron, Black-crowned Night-Heron, Glossy Ibis, White Stork, White-tailed Eagle*, Rough-legged Buzzard (winter), Red-footed Falcon, Little Crake,

Collared Pratincole, Whiskered, White-winged and Gull-billed Terns, European Bee-eater, European Roller, Syrian and Black Woodpeckers, Lesser Grey Shrike, Eurasian River, Moustached and Barred Warblers.

(Other species recorded here include Ruddy Shelduck, Pallid Harrier*, Greater Spotted Eagle* (four were present in December 1998), Saker Falcon and Paddyfield Warbler.)

There is a regional SOR office in Tulcea, the main gateway to the delta. The only way to bird the delta thoroughly is by boat, but even then many areas, especially the northern half of the delta near the border with the Ukraine where most of the pelicans breed, are virtually impossible to reach, thanks to variable water levels, the constantly changing position of the *plaur* (floating vegetation), seemingly endless dense reedbeds, and the considerable bureaucratic hurdles which need to be overcome in order visit strictly protected areas. Nevertheless, the southern part of the delta is usually easy to access, on boats which run from Tulcea, as well as other waterside villages to the east, including Maliuc, Crisan (where there is a visitor centre), Sulina and Murighiol. Most of the regular ferries, motorboat day-trips, tourist boats and floatels (*pontons*)—high enough to allow viewing over the reedbeds which, in places, grow to 4 m (13 ft)—tend to stick to the Bratul Sulina, the delta's central channel, although some reach as far as Laculs Baclanestii, Furtuna and Nebuna, which are all excellent for birds, and some take along smaller boats to enable access to other backwaters such as Lacul Martin. Book all boat trips at least a day before departure to ensure an early start on the big day, and make sure they take along smaller boats, in order to gain access to the quietest corners.

Just outside the delta, **Lacul Cisla** near Mineri west of Tulcea, and **Lacul Somova** (1,514 Ferruginous Ducks* in autumn 1998), west of Mineri near Somova, are also worth birding.

Accommodation: Tulcea—Hotel Europolis. Crisan—Hotel Lebada. Murighiol—Hotel Pelican. It is also possible to stay on the floatels, most of which are based in Tulcea.

TRANSYLVANIAN ALPS

These snow-capped mountains at the southern end of the Carpathians rise to 2543 m (8343 ft) at Moldoveanu and the beech woods, coniferous forest, cliffs and alpine grasslands on their slopes combine to support such high quality birds as Ural Owl and Wallcreeper, as well as more brown bears than the whole of the rest of Europe, which together provide the perfect complement to the hoardes of lowland birds which occur along the Black Sea coastal plain.

The species listed below occur during the summer unless otherwise indicated.

Localised Species
Ural Owl, Wallcreeper.

Others

Booted Eagle, Alpine Swift, White-backed (*lilfordi*), Three-toed and Black Woodpeckers, Eurasian Nutcracker, Collared Flycatcher, Sombre Tit, Horned Lark, Alpine Accentor, Rock Bunting.

Other Wildlife

Brown bear, wild boar, chamois, lynx, grey wolf.

The best bases for birding the Transylvanian Alps are Brasov, Sinaia and Zarnesti, all of which are about five hours by road west of Tulcea at the Danube Delta. For Ural Owl and Wallcreeper try above the **Poiana Brasov** ski-resort (look out for brown bears which are attracted to the rubbish at the resort) or the **Prahova Valley** in the beautiful Bucegi Mountains south of Brasov. At the nearby mountain resort of **Sinaia** it is possible to take a cable-car up the Jepii Gully to the eastern ridge of these mountains, well above the tree-line, where Horned Lark and Alpine Accentor occur. It is best to look for brown bears, which forage amongst the rubbish in the suburbs of Brasov or in the quarry (now a rubbish tip) ten minutes' drive from Sinaia, under the guidance of the the Carpathian Large Carnivore Project (fax: 68 311205), which has established an ecotourism programme in order to show visitors the bears and to demonstrate to the local community that these animals could be just as valuable to them as livestock farming, forestry and hunting. The project also radiotracks the wolves in the area and they have cabins and hides from which there is a slim chance of actually seeing these elusive beauties, as well as bears. For more details contact Ibis Birdwatching Tours (address below).

Accommodation: Brasov, Sinaia and Zarnesti.

The semi-natural steppe-grasslands of the Hungarian *puszta* extend eastwards in extreme western Romania and here they support a small population of Great Bustards*. This is a difficult bird to see in Romania but anywhere west-northwest of Timisoara is worth trying. There are also some remnant marshes in this area, some of which lie within a reserve south of **Satchinez**, about 25 km northwest of Timisoara, which supports Ferruginous Duck* and Little Crake.

ADDITIONAL INFORMATION

Addresses

Gerard Gorman, Budapest 1511, Pf:4, Hungary (tel/fax: 1 319 9689; email: ggbirder@elender.hu; website: www.elender.hu/~ggbirder/), is a prolific author and professional birding guide with a wealth of experience in eastern Europe (he has led well over 100 tours) who caters for tour companies as well as independent individuals and teams, and specialises in target birds.

Ibis Birdwatching Tours, str. Grivitei nr. 1, Bl. C1, Ap. 9, Tulcea 8800 (tel/fax: 40 511261; mobile: 92 381398; email: ibis@tlx.ssitl.ro; website: www.netcolony.com/members/ibis/) arrange trips for visiting birders.

Please send records of rarities to the Societatea Ornitologica Romana (SOR), Str Republicii 48, RO-3400 Cluj, Romania.

Books and papers

A Birdwatching Guide to Romania. Roberts J, due 1999. Arlequin Press.
Finding Birds in Romania. Gosney D, 1992. Available from BirdGuides (address, p. 395).
The Status of Birds in Romania. Munteanu D, 1998. SOR. Available from the International Division, RSPB, The Lodge, Sandy, Bedfordshire, SG19 2DL, UK.

RUSSIA

INTRODUCTION

Summary

Many western European birders regard Russia as something special, because the vast, wild bogs, boreal forests and tundra of Siberia support so many birds which are great rarities west of the Urals. However, while these birds may fulfil many dreams, there is so much more to Russia, what with the islands of the far east and the mixed forests of Ussuriland which support huge numbers of seabirds and such brilliant birds as Steller's Sea-Eagle* and Red-crowned Crane*. Unfortunately however, wide-ranging birding trips to Russia are amongst the most expensive in the world because most of the special birds inhabit the remotest terrain, far beyond the roads and railways, and getting to see many of them is virtually impossible without joining organised tours or enlisting the help of local travel agents who use chartered helicopters and organise camping expeditions in order to cover what amounts to a huge amount of ground.

Size

At just over 17 million km^2, Russia is over 130 times larger than England and 25 times larger than Texas, and accounts for a sixth of the planet's landmass. It is 11,250 km (twelve time zones) from the Baltic Sea in the west to the Bering Strait in the east and up to 3500 km from north to south.

Getting Around

While getting around is fraught with problems the first hurdle which needs to be cleared is getting in, for independent travellers still needed to provide details of itineraries, including proof of booking accommodation, at the end of the 1990s, before even being considered for a visa. While European Russia has a cheap, fairly extensive and efficient public transport system, there are no birds here which can not be seen elsewhere in the region with considerably more ease. The best birding is east of the Urals and it is virtually impossible to get around most of this vast area without joining an organised tour or enlisting the help of local travel agents. Either way, getting around Russia east of the Urals will cost an awful lot of money. It is possible to get across Siberia, rather than around it, on the 8700-km-long Trans-Siberian Railway which runs from St Petersburg in the west to Vladivostok in the east, the gateway to Ussuriland and Amurland where it is possible to get around on roads and railways, although even here it may be best to enlist the help of a local travel agent which arranges camping trips, often with a cook, a driver, a guide and a translator, throughout Ussuriland, and elsewhere in the Russian Far East. In conclusion therefore, Russia east of the Urals is, on the whole, one of the few parts of the world where in order to see the top birds, birders need to seriously consider joining an expedition, an organised tour or a scientific exchange programme.

Accommodation and Food

Hotels where tourists are allowed to stay are very expensive, but on most birding trips to Russia it will only be necessary to use these when passing through the major cities. In rural areas it is usually possible to stay in basic guesthouses or with local people, in which case being able to speak a little Russian would be extremely useful. Some of the best birding areas, especially in Arctic Siberia, are well away from any kind of human habitation, hence in order to visit these it is necessary to take camping gear and stock up on all supplies before leaving the nearest town. Naturally, the simplest way to sort out accommodation and food is to employ a local travel agent, who will usually be able to arrange both, at a price. In large cities such as Moscow and St Petersburg most types of food are available, but elsewhere—that is, the vast majority of the country—the choice is more limited, usually to staples such as beetroot soup (*borshch*), cabbage soup with sour cream (*shchi*), meat (the main part of most diets), salted fish, porridge and pancakes. If there are shops they may have biscuits, bread, jam, pasta and rice, but in rural areas it is usually necessary to ask at farms for eggs, milk and vegetables. The average Russian drinks more than a litre of vodka a week and many reckon the best cure for the inevitable hangovers is beer (*pivo*).

Health and Safety

Take all possible precautions to avoid contracting diptheria, encephalitis (carried by ticks in Amurland and Ussuriland), polio and tetanus. Anyone intending to visit Siberia during the summer, especially the Arctic and Far East areas, should prepare to meet masses of midges, mosquitoes and other biting and piercing insects. Take a hat with netting, light but impenetrable clothes, including gloves, and the best insect repellent on the market. Other essentials, especially for the Arctic, include wellies, or, better still, waist-high waders, warm and waterproof clothing, the full range of camping gear, sunglasses, sun hat and sunscreen. Organised crime has been a major problem in Russia since the demise of communism and the daily murder rate in major cities often reaches double figures. While this rarely affects tourists, petty crime is also a problem in major towns and cities, so photocopy tickets, traveller's cheques, cash, credit cards, visas, passports and anything else possible, and leave it all in the hotel safe when passing through these places. At the end of 1999 the Russian army was at war with the breakaway republic of Chechnya in the Caucasus region of the south, hence this part of the country is likely to be too dangerous to visit well into the 21st Century. Away from so-called civilisation in the best birding areas such problems will seem light years away, for the vast majority of rural Russians are amongst the friendliest people on the planet.

Climate and Timing

Russia is a vast country where the climate varies from the extremely hot summers in the semi-deserts of the extreme south to Verkhoyansk in northeast Siberia which is the second coldest place on the planet after Antarctica. The temperature here falls to minus 68°C during January, and the winter lasts for seven months. Despite the great range of temperatures and the considerable climatic variation, many parts of Russia, including the Arctic, the far east, the Lake Baikal area and the Caspian Sea area, are all at their best for birding between mid-May and the end of June.

Habitats

European Russia, which extends eastwards as far as the Urals, over 1000 km east of Moscow, is dominated by wet lowlands, although there are some hills and, at the north end of the Caspian Sea, semi-desert and dry steppe. Apart from the broadleaved and mixed forests here, and those in the extreme southeast of Russia, in Amurland and Ussuriland, where the avifauna is very distinct from that in the rest of the country, there are three major east-west habitat zones east of the 2000-km-long forested Urals, which rise to 1894 m (6214 ft) at Narodnaya: (i) in the south—semi-desert and steppe, with mountainous regions in the southeast and east which rise to 4506 m (14,784 ft) at Mount Belukha in the Altai; (ii) in the middle—the bogs, innumerable rivers and dark coniferous boreal forests of the taiga, which extend for some 10,000 km from west to east, cover almost 40% of the country and form the greatest swathe of forested land on earth; and (iii) in the north—the often wet tundra, which covers almost 20% of the country. To the north of the tundra the Arctic coast and its offshore islands such as Novaya Zemlya and Wrangel are virtually lifeless ice-locked shields. Kamchatka, a large peninsula on the north side of the Sea of Okhotsk in extreme east Russia, supports jagged mountains and numerous volcanoes, some of which are still active.

Conservation

Agricultural intensification (especially in the southern steppes), drainage, illegal and indiscriminate logging, overgrazing, overfishing, hunting, oil and gas exploration, and pollution (western and southern Russia is liberally sprinkled with areas of critical environmental degradation) are all responsible for habitat loss and degradation in Russia, and the 56 threatened and near-threatened species as well as the relatively common and widespread birds which occur in the country all face a tough time in the 21st century, despite the relatively low human population, the fact that only 17% of the country is used for agriculture and the presence of numerous nature reserves.

Bird Species

About 740 species have been recorded in Russia. Notable species include: (i) those widespread in Siberia, such as Great Grey Owl, Siberian Jay, Siberian, White's and Dusky Thrushes, Siberian Rubythroat, Siberian Blue Robin, Azure Tit, Siberian Accentor and several buntings; (ii) those which occur in Arctic Siberia, such as Red-breasted Goose*, King, Spectacled* and Steller's* Eiders, Gyrfalcon, Siberian Crane*, a superb selection of shorebirds including Spoonbill Sandpiper*, and Ross's and Sabine's Gulls; (iii) those which occur in the coastal far east, including Steller's Sea-Eagle*, Latham's Snipe*, Aleutian Tern and a wide range of auks; (iv) those which occur inland in the extreme southeast, in Amurland and Ussuriland, including Mandarin Duck*, Scaly-sided Merganser*, Oriental Stork*, Pied Harrier, Hooded*, Red-crowned* and White-naped* Cranes, Blakiston's Fish-Owl*, Japanese Waxwing*, White-throated Rock-Thrush, several flycatchers and warblers, Reed Parrotbill* and Japanese Grosbeak; (v) those which occur in the Lake Baikal area, such as Daurian Partridge; (vi) those which occur in the Altai, such as Altai Snowcock, Solitary Snipe, Pallas's Sandgrouse and Eversmann's Redstart; and (vii) those which occur in the Caspian Sea region, including Dalmatian Pelican*, Demoiselle Crane, Great Black-headed Gull, Blue-cheeked Bee-eater and Ménétries's Warbler.

Near-Endemic Species
Species with ranges more or less restricted to Russia include Siberian Grouse* and Black-billed Capercaillie.

Expectations
During the summer it is possible to see around 225 species on a trip to Ussuriland lasting one to two weeks, and over 300 species, including over 20 ducks, over 40 shorebirds, over 30 warblers and over ten buntings, on a three-week trip to Ussuriland, the island of Sakhalin and Kamchatka.

The major sites are shown on the map on page 300.

The hills, parks and pools in and around **Moscow** support White-backed Woodpecker (around the national airport), Eurasian Nutcracker, Bohemian Waxwing (scarce during winter in the Botanical Gardens), Thrush Nightingale (in the Sparrow Hills), Bluethroat ('White-spotted' *cyanecula*, at the sewage works), Blyth's Reed-Warbler (in the Botanical Gardens and Sparrow Hills), Greenish Warbler (*trochiloides*, along the upper walkway in The Secret Garden which lies along the south wall of the Kremlin, and in the Sparrow Hills) and Citrine Wagtail (at the sewage works). The Hotel Ismailova, with nearby woods, is as good a place as any to stay.

The 99-km-long Kursiu Peninsula in the isolated Russian province of **Kaliningrad**, between Lithuania and Poland in the southeast corner of the Baltic Sea, lies on a major migration route and often provides refuge for impressive numbers of passage migrants, hence the Rossitten Bird Observatory has been up and running here for some time. Part of the spit lies within Lithuania where there is another ringing station (p. 249).

The sea, sea cliffs and tundra on and around the **Kola Peninsula**, east of Finland, support King and Steller's* Eiders, Gyrfalcon, Red-necked Phalarope, Herring Gull ('Heuglin's' *heuglini*), Long-tailed Skua and Brünnich's Guillemot. From Murmansk on the north coast of the peninsula it is possible to travel to the North Pole on six-feet-thick, state-of-the-art, nuclear Russian icebreakers, via the Barents Sea and the Arctic archipelago of **Franz Josef Land** (Zemlya Frantsa Josifa), where Ivory Gull and Little Auk, as well as polar bear and walrus occur. Three days out of Murmansk the ships reach the polar ice cap and after a week the pole is usually in sight. Once amongst the ice the only birds likely to be seen are flocks of Black-legged Kittiwakes and Brünnich's Guillemots following the ship, although a few Ivory Gulls, as well as polar bears, may also turn up. However, once north of 88°N, about 150 miles (240 km) from the pole, the only species likely to be seen, indeed the only species recorded actually at the **North Pole**, is Black-legged Kittiwake.

A few species reach the western limits of their breeding ranges around the **Polar Urals**, with Pintail Snipe and Pallas's (Reed) Bunting reaching as far west as the Bolshezemelskaya Reserve, just west of the mountains in Europe, and Siberian and Black-throated Accentors reaching the northern tip of the range. To bird the Polar Urals head for Salichard (where there are a few hotels), which is connected by air and rail to Moscow, 2000 km to the southwest. From there walk up the mountains along a tributary of the River Ob for Siberian Accentor, and bird around Labytnangi (where there is one hotel) on the opposite side of the Ob to Salichard for Black-throated Accentor. Other species which have been recorded here include Gyrfalcon, Red-necked Phalarope, Eurasian Dotterel, Pomarine and Long-tailed Skuas, Arctic Redpoll and Pine Grosbeak. The high Arctic tundra on the **Yamal Peninsula** to the north, accessible by chartering a boat or a helicopter at Salichard, supports Red-breasted Goose*, Gyrfalcon, Pacific Golden-Plover, White-billed Diver and Snowy Owl.

Red-necked Stint and Pectoral Sandpiper reach the western limits of their breeding ranges on the massive **Taimyr Peninsula**, which forms the northernmost part of central Siberia. The large numbers of breeding waterfowl and shorebirds here also include Red-breasted Goose*, King Eider, Pintail Snipe, Curlew Sandpiper, Red-necked and Grey Phalaropes, Pacific Golden-Plover and Grey Plover, as well as Herring Gull ('Siberian' *birulai*), Pomarine and Long-tailed Skuas, Snowy Owl, Dusky Thrush ('Dusky' *eunomus*), Siberian Accentor and Pallas's (Reed) Bunting. The only time it is usually possible to visit the peninsula is during June and July, and the best two birding areas, accessible from Khatanga are: (i) the Novaya Valley, about 60 km northwest of Khatanga, where Siberian Accentor occurs alongside the stream which runs through the world's most northerly (larch) wood, to the south of the River Novaya, and Red-necked Stint and Pectoral Sandpiper breed on the flat tundra north of the river; and (ii) the Logata Valley, about 300 km northwest of Khatanga, where there are several colonies of up to six or seven pairs of Red-breasted Geese*.

KOLYMA DELTA

This vast Arctic delta at the mouth of the 2500-km-long River Kolymå in northeast Siberia supports a superb range of high-arctic breeding species, including Spectacled Eider*, Sandhill Crane, most of the world breeding population of Siberian Cranes*, Little Curlew, Great Knot, Sharp-tailed Sandpiper and up to 100,000 Ross's Gulls.

The species listed below occur during June unless otherwise indicated.

Localised Specialities
Spectacled Eider*, Siberian Crane*, Ross's Gull.

Others
King and Steller's* Eiders, Gyrfalcon (grey and white phases), Sandhill Crane, Pintail Snipe, Little Curlew, Terek Sandpiper, Long-billed Dowitcher, Great Knot, Pectoral and Sharp-tailed Sandpipers, Red-necked and Grey Phalaropes, Eurasian Dotterel, Herring Gull ('Vega' *vegae*), Pomarine and Long-tailed Skuas, White-billed Diver, Great Grey Owl, Northern Hawk Owl, Three-toed Woodpecker, Siberian Jay, Bohemian Waxwing, Dusky Thrush ('Dusky' *eunomus*), Siberian Tit, Pechora and Buff-bellied Pipits, Arctic Redpoll, Pine Grosbeak, Pallas's (Reed) Bunting.

From the small settlement of Cherskiy, accessible by charter flights from St Petersburg, it is possible to travel by chartered helicopter to the following areas: (i) a remote guard post at the southern edge of the Kolyma Reserve where the forest-tundra supports Little Curlew, Great

Grey Owl, Northern Hawk Owl and Pechora Pipit; (ii) nearby low mountains where Great Knot breeds; (iii) several areas in the northern Kolyma where localised breeding species such as Siberian Crane* and Sharp-tailed Sandpiper occur; and (iv) a remote guard post in the northern Kolyma where Ross's Gull breeds.

Accommodation: Cherskiy—guesthouse (basic). Kolyma—camping.

Sabine's Gull, as well as the only regular breeding populations of Snow Goose and Buff-breasted Sandpiper west of the Bering Strait, breed on the desolate **Wrangel Island** where the rugged snow-capped mountains rise to 1096 m (3596 ft). Other species present here during June, the best time to visit the island, include Sandhill Crane, Baird's Sandpiper and Snowy Owl, while major mammalian attractions include polar bear and walrus, both of which occur in higher densities here than anywhere else on Earth. Wrangel is accessible by chartered helicopter (90 minutes) from Mys Shmidta on the north coast of the Chukotka Peninsula, and such transportation will also be required to get around the island from the reserve HQ which is situated at Ushakovskiy, the only permanent settlement, on the south coast. There is a very basic guesthouse in Mys Shmidta but it will be necessary to camp on the island.

CHUKOTKA PENINSULA

The extreme northeastern tip of Siberia is one of the most difficult parts of the world to get to, but it is also the most accessible place on the planet to see the unique Spoonbill Sandpiper* in full summer plumage. This brilliant little bird, which only breeds here and on the even remoter isthmus of the Kamchatka Peninsula to the south, is just one of several shorebirds which breed here, including Western, Baird's and Rock Sandpipers.

The species listed below occur during June unless otherwise indicated.

Localised Specialities
Emperor Goose, Rock and Spoonbill* Sandpipers.

Others
King and Steller's* Eiders, Harlequin Duck, Sandhill Crane, Long-billed Dowitcher, Western Sandpiper, Red-necked Stint, Baird's and Pectoral Sandpipers, Red-necked and Grey Phalaropes, Pacific Golden-Plover, Lesser Sandplover, Herring Gull ('Vega' *vegae*), Pomarine and Long-tailed Skuas, Brünnich's and Pigeon Guillemots, Kittlitz's Murrelet, Parakeet, Crested and Least Auklets, Horned and Tufted Puffins, White-billed Diver, Grey-cheeked and Dusky ('Dusky' *eunomus*) Thrushes, Dusky Warbler, Yellow Wagtail ('Green-headed' *taivana*), Arctic Redpoll, Pallas's (Reed) Bunting.

Other Wildlife
Brown bear, ringed seal, Arctic souslik, walrus, grey whale.

(Other species recorded here include Gyrfalcon (white phase), Wandering Tattler, Semipalmated Sandpiper, Ivory and Sabine's Gulls, and Savannah Sparrow.)

From Mys Shmidta on the north coast of the peninsula, accessible only by chartered helicopter, bird the following sites, with the same helicopter: (i) the wet coastal tundra to the southeast where Spoonbill Sandpiper* occurs, as well as Emperor Goose, and Western and Rock Sandpipers; (ii) the river valley between Mys Shmidta and Egvekinot on the southern coast, which supports Harlequin Duck and Dusky Thrush; and (iii) the tundra around Egvekinot at the head of Zaliv Kresta (Cross Bay), where Spoonbill Sandpiper* also breeds. The Anadyr Delta, south of Egvekinot, is the last place in Russia where Eskimo Curlew* was recorded, back in the 1800s.

Accommodation: Mys Shmidta—guesthouse (very basic). Egvekinot—guesthouse (very basic). Elsewhere—camping.

KAMCHATKA

The 1000-km (or so) long peninsula, known as Kamchatka, which separates the Sea of Okhotsk to the west from the Bering Sea to the east, is dominated by snow-capped mountains and volcanoes, about 30 of which are still active, rising to over 4267 m (14,000 ft) at Klyushevskaya Sopka. The river valleys, stone birch forest and rugged coastline which lie below these icy and fiery heights support over 1,000 breeding pairs of Steller's Sea-Eagles*, about half of the world breeding population, and during the winter about 4,000 of these massive raptors are believed to be present on the peninsula. However, most birders visit Kamchatka during the brief summer when many other great birds are present, including Aleutian Tern and Tufted Puffin.

The species listed below occur during June unless otherwise indicated.

Localised Specialities
Steller's Sea-Eagle*, Long-billed Murrelet*.

Other Localised Species
Red-faced Cormorant, Slaty-backed Gull, Aleutian Tern, Spectacled Guillemot, Brown-headed Thrush, Middendorff's Warbler, Black-backed Wagtail, Grey Bunting.

Others
Pelagic Cormorant, Harlequin Duck, White-tailed* and Golden Eagles, Grey-tailed Tattler, Long-toed Stint, Pectoral Sandpiper, Glaucous-winged and Common ('Kamchatka' *kamtschatschensis*) Gulls, Pigeon Guillemot, Ancient Murrelet, Horned and Tufted Puffins, Oriental Cuckoo, Three-toed Woodpecker, Eyebrowed Thrush, Dark-sided Flycatcher, Rufous-tailed Robin, Siberian Rubythroat, Lanceolated Warbler, Yellow Wagtail ('Green-headed' *taivana*), Pechora and Buff-bellied Pipits, Grey-capped Greenfinch.

Other Wildlife

Brown bear, Siberian bighorn, Arctic fox, sea otter, Steller's sea lion, harbour and northern fur seals, killer whale.

(Other species recorded here include Spoonbill Sandpiper* (which breeds on the isthmus at the remote base of the peninsula), as well as walrus.)

Kamchatka is over 11,000 km and nine time zones east of Moscow. Petropavlovsk, the largest city on the peninsula is accessible by air from there, from Khabarovsk (2.5 hours) and from Anchorage, Alaska. Around **Petropavlovsk** bird Avacha Bay, where Red-faced Cormorant and Steller's Sea-Eagle* occur, and the nearby stone birch forest, where birds such as Siberian Rubythroat occur. Over 200 species, including Steller's Sea-Eagle* and Brown-headed Thrush, have been recorded in the **Kronotskiy Reserve**, a World Heritage Site on the east coast of the central peninsula, dominated by the classic white cone of Kronotskaya which rises to over 3528 m (11,575 ft). Off the mouth of the **River Zhupanova** here, look out for Long-billed Murrelet*.

From Petropavlovsk it is possible to fly to the small town of **Ossora** on the isthmus at the northern end of the peninsula where Spoonbill Sandpiper* breeds, but very few foreigners have made it here, hence it is necessary to report to the Immigration Office on arrival, before asking if it is possible to hire the local government's 4WD in order to search for the sandpiper and other goodies. There are only about 15 km of dirt roads in the area but the compulsory driver will no doubt make up for this, especially on request. Otherwise, it is possible to charter small fishing boats to cover the coast.

Accommodation: Petropavlovsk—although about 250,000 people live here, there is only one hotel with a restaurant and hot water, and this is situated well outside the city. Ossora—hotel (basic).

Red-legged Kittiwake* and Whiskered Auklet both occur on the **Komandor Islands**, which lie to the east of Kamchatka, while the nearby deep waters attract summering Black-footed* and Laysan Albatrosses, Mottled Petrel, Short-tailed Shearwater, Leach's and Fork-tailed Storm-Petrels, and Aleutian Tern. From the settlement of Nikolskoye on Bering Island, where the Danish explorer of that name died of scurvy after being shipwrecked in 1741, there is a rough track through the inland tundra where Rock Sandpiper, Rock Ptarmigan and Snowy Owl occur. The nearby headland supports breeding seabirds such as Red-faced Cormorant, Pigeon Guillemot and Tufted Puffin, while the adjacent sandy beach supports a northern fur seal rookery. The dramatic cliffs of Mednyy Island support masses of seabirds, including Whiskered Auklet, and Horned and Tufted Puffins, as well as Asian Rosy-Finch (*brunneonucha*). Sea mammals around this island include hundreds of sea otters.

Masses of seabirds breed on the grassy, boulder-strewn slopes of the island of **Talan**, accessible via charter boat from Magadan on the north coast of the Sea of Okhotsk, including hundreds of thousands of Crested Auklets, tens of thousands of Ancient Murrelets, smaller numbers of Parakeet Auklets and a few Least Auklets, with Horned and Tufted Puffins thrown in, as well as two pairs of Steller's Sea-Eagles* and Siberian

Rubythroats. It is possible to camp overnight on the island, next to the small research station, above which many of the aforementioned birds can be seen. The steep, rugged coast around **Magadan** also supports Steller's Sea-Eagle*, as well as Marbled Murrelet*, which nests in trees up to tens of km inland. There is a basic hotel in Magadan which is accessible by air from Moscow and Anchorage, Alaska.

Tens of thousands of seabirds, as well as hundreds of sea otters frequent the strait between Kamchatka and the Kuril Islands. The 1000-km (or so) long **Kuril Islands**, a series of forested snow-capped mountains and volcanoes strung out in a line from the southern tip of Kamchatka to the northern tip of Hokkaido, Japan, support millions of seabirds, as well as a number of species which reach their northern outposts here, including White-bellied Pigeon*, Blakiston's Fish-Owl*, Crested Kingfisher, Narcissus Flycatcher (*narcissina*), Japanese Robin, Brown-eared Bulbul, Japanese White-eye, Varied Tit, Japanese Sky Lark and Japanese Accentor. Most of these species are restricted to the southern islands such as Iturup, Kunashir and Shikotan. Other species recorded in these islands include Leach's (350,000 pairs) and Fork-tailed (over 200,000 pairs) Storm-Petrels, Japanese and Red-faced Cormorants, Steller's Sea-Eagle*, Gyrfalcon, Long-toed Stint, Black-tailed and Slaty-backed Gulls, Crested and Whiskered Auklets, Tufted Puffin, Bull-headed Shrike, Pale and Brown-headed Thrushes, Japanese Bush-Warbler, Sakhalin Warbler, Sakhalin Leaf-Warbler, Russet Sparrow and Grey Bunting, as well as brown bear, Dall's porpoise, sea otter, Steller's sea lion, harbour seal and killer whale.

Over 800 Laysan Albatrosses and 5,000 Whiskered Auklets, as well as Short-tailed Shearwater, Fork-tailed Storm-Petrel, Ancient Murrelet, Parakeet Auklet, hundreds of thousands of Crested Auklets, and Horned and Tufted Puffins, plus Pacific white-sided dolphin, Dall's porpoise and minke whale, have been recorded on single boat trips between the Kuril Islands and the island of Sakhalin, across the southern **Sea of Okhotsk**.

SAKHALIN

The coastal waters, marshes and mostly mixed taiga forest on and around this 950-km-long and 100-km-wide island, which rises to 1600 m (5249 ft), support a heady mixture of Far East specialities, from Steller's Sea-Eagle* and Blakiston's Fish-Owl* through seabirds and passage shorebirds which include Nordmann's Greenshank* and Spoonbill Sandpiper* to a fine selection of passerines which includes two near-endemic breeding species: Sakhalin Warbler and Sakhalin Leaf-Warbler. The total of 355 species recorded on the island also includes breeding Nordmann's Greenshank*, although unfortunately the only known breeding area of this great rarity in the world is confined to the remote northern end of the island.

The species listed below occur during the spring (late May to mid-June) unless otherwise indicated.

Localised Specialities
Steller's Sea-Eagle*, Nordmann's Greenshank*, Blakiston's Fish-Owl*, Sakhalin Warbler, Sakhalin Leaf-Warbler, Japanese Accentor.

Other Localised Species

Japanese Cormorant, Latham's Snipe*, Black-tailed and Slaty-backed Gulls, Brünnich's and Spectacled Guillemots, Marbled Murrelet*, Brown-headed Thrush, Narcissus Flycatcher (*narcissina*), Japanese Robin, Middendorff's Warbler, Russet Sparrow, Black-backed Wagtail, Grey Bunting.

Regular Passage Migrants

Far Eastern Curlew*, Terek Sandpiper, Grey-tailed Tattler, Great Knot, Red-necked and Long-toed Stints, Sharp-tailed, Spoonbill* and Broad-billed Sandpipers, Red-necked Phalarope, Lesser Sandplover, Eyebrowed Thrush.

Others

Short-tailed Shearwater, Pelagic Cormorant, Harlequin Duck, Herring Gull ('Vega' *vegae*), Ancient Murrelet, Crested and Rhinoceros Auklets, Tufted Puffin, Ural Owl, Pygmy Woodpecker, Eurasian Nutcracker, Brown Dipper, Siberian Thrush, Mugimaki Flycatcher, Rufous-tailed Robin, Siberian Rubythroat, Siberian Blue Robin, Asian Stubtail, Japanese Bush-Warbler, Yellow Wagtail ('Green-headed' *taivana*), Buff-bellied Pipit, Grey-capped Greenfinch, Long-tailed Rosefinch, Black-faced Bunting.
(Other species recorded here include Japanese Night-Heron*, Ruddy-breasted Crake, Pectoral Sandpiper, Aleutian Tern, Grey-headed Lapwing*, Ruddy Kingfisher and Bull-headed Shrike.)

The grim, sprawling town of Yuzhno-Sakhalinsk at the southern end of the island is accessible by air from Moscow (11 hours) and nearby Korsakov is accessible by ferry from Hokkaido, Japan. The best base for birding is Aniva, a short distance away by road, where **Aniva Bay** is a great place to look for passage shorebirds, especially during the spring, when they include Nordmann's Greenshank* and Spoonbill Sandpiper* (at least eight have been seen on single days, amongst flocks of Red-necked Stints which have exceeded 1,000). This bay is also good for auks, which, weather permitting, can be looked for by boat. Sakhalin Warbler favours bushy areas along river valleys and Japanese Accentor occurs in bushy areas above the tree-line.

Accommodation: Aniva.

Brilliant male Siberian Blue Robins skulk in Sakhalin's forests

The River Amur, which at 4416 km is the tenth longest river on the planet, is 16 km wide where it meets the Sea of Okhotsk in the 50-km-wide **Amur Delta**, where one of the world's highest breeding concentrations of Steller's Sea-Eagles* is situated. The delta is accessible from Khabarovsk, 650 km to the southwest, via a 14-hour hydrofoil journey, or by air to **Komosomolsk** (where Siberian Grouse* and Japanese Waxwing* occur) then a 60-km boat trip down river to **Lake Udyl** where about 50 pairs of Steller's Sea-Eagle* nest, along with Swan Goose*, White-tailed Eagle*, Swinhoe's Snipe and Slaty-backed Gull. It is possible to stay in the delta at Bogorodskoye, where there is a basic hotel, and charter a boat from there to Lake Udyl.

White-throated Needletails are supreme flyers—they have been recorded flying at over 100 miles (160 km) per hour—and a delight to watch

USSURILAND

This region in extreme southeast Russia, where the Sikhote-Alin Mountains rise over 1829 m (6000 ft), supports the greatest diversity of fauna and flora in the country. Over 400 bird species have been recorded, over 250 of which have been known to breed, and during a week to ten days here in the spring it is possible to see around 225 species. The offshore islands, coastal mudflats and marshes, a large inland lake surrounded by extensive marshes, clear-water mountain rivers and rich mixed forests (which cover over 70% of the area) support some very rare and localised birds, not least Scaly-sided Merganser*, Oriental Stork*, Band-bellied Crake*, Hooded*, Red-crowned* and White-naped* Cranes, Blakiston's Fish-Owl*, Pleske's Warbler, Reed Parrotbill* and the isolated *menzbieri* race of Pechora Pipit. In addition, many Siberian shorebirds stop off along the coast during spring passage and numerous species are near their northern limits here, including Schrenck's Bittern*, Pied Harrier, Yellow-rumped Flycatcher, Forest Wagtail, Japanese Grosbeak and Ochre-rumped Bunting*. The list is simply amazing and Ussuriland is without doubt one of the best birding areas in the world.

The species listed below occur during the spring (mid-May to mid-June) unless otherwise indicated.

Localised Specialities

Scaly-sided Merganser*, Band-bellied Crake*, Hooded*, Red-crowned* and White-naped* Cranes, Blakiston's Fish-Owl*, Pleske's Warbler, Reed Parrotbill*.

Other Localised Species

Swinhoe's Storm-Petrel, Japanese Cormorant, Swan Goose*, Mandarin Duck*, Oriental Stork*, Latham's* and Swinhoe's Snipes, Asian Dowitcher*, Black-tailed and Slaty-backed Gulls, Spectacled Guillemot, White-throated Rock-Thrush, Manchurian Reed-Warbler*, Black-backed Wagtail, Pechora Pipit (*menzbieri*), Japanese Grosbeak, Ochre-rumped Bunting*.

Regular Spring Passage Migrants

Pintail Snipe, Grey-tailed Tattler, Great Knot, Red-necked and Long-toed Stints, Sharp-tailed and Broad-billed Sandpipers, Pacific Golden-Plover, Lesser Sandplover, Eyebrowed and Dusky ('Dusky' *eunomus*) Thrushes, Dark-sided Flycatcher, Rufous-tailed Robin, Dusky Warbler.

Others

Streaked Shearwater, Pelagic Cormorant, Falcated, Spot-billed and Harlequin (winter) Ducks, Striated Heron, Schrenck's Bittern*, Oriental Honey-buzzard, Pied Harrier, Japanese Sparrowhawk, Grey-faced Buzzard, Amur Falcon, Japanese Quail, Common Pheasant, Yellow-legged Buttonquail, Far Eastern Curlew*, Herring ('Vega' *vegae*, winter) and Yellow-legged (*mongolicus*, winter) Gulls, Ancient Murrelet, Rhinoceros Auklet, Oriental Turtle-Dove, Hodgson's Hawk-Cuckoo, Indian, Oriental and Lesser Cuckoos, Oriental Scops-Owl, Ural Owl, Brown Hawk-Owl, Jungle Nightjar, White-throated Needletail, Fort-tailed Swift, Dollarbird, Pygmy, White-backed and Black Woodpeckers, Asian Paradise-Flycatcher, Azure-winged Magpie, Daurian Jackdaw, Black-naped Oriole, Ashy Minivet, Bull-headed (scarce), Brown and Chinese Grey (scarce) Shrikes, Brown Dipper, Blue Rock-Thrush (*philippensis*), Siberian, White's, Grey-backed and Pale Thrushes, Daurian and White-cheeked Starlings, Grey-streaked, Asian Brown, Yellow-rumped, Mugimaki and Blue-and-white Flycatchers, Siberian Rubythroat, Siberian Blue Robin, Daurian Redstart, Red-rumped Swallow, Asian Martin, Chestnut-flanked White-eye, Asian Stubtail, Japanese Bush Warbler, Lanceolated, Pallas's Grasshopper and Gray's Warblers, Black-browed and Oriental Reed-Warblers, Thick-billed and Radde's Warblers, Pale-legged Leaf-Warbler, Eastern Crowned-Warbler, Vinous-throated Parrotbill, Azure Tit, Forest, White (*leucopsis* and *ocularis*), and Yellow (*macronyx*, 'Kamchatka' *simillima* and 'Green-headed' *taivana*) Wagtails, Olive-backed and Buff-bellied Pipits, Grey-capped Greenfinch, Long-tailed Rosefinch, Yellow-billed Grosbeak, Meadow, Tristam's, Chestnut-eared, Yellow-browed, Yellow-throated, Yellow-breasted, Chestnut and Black-faced Buntings.

Other Wildlife

Asian black bear, Siberian chipmunk, muskrat, racoon-dog, Steller's sea lion, harbour seal, tassle-eared squirrel, Eurasian flying squirrel.

(Other species recorded here include Baer's Pochard*, Intermediate Egret, Japanese Night-Heron*, Yellow Bittern, Swinhoe's Rail*, Baillon's

Crake, Greater Painted-snipe, Spoonbill Sandpiper*, Oriental Pratincole, Long-billed Plover*, Collared Scops-Owl, Black-capped Kingfisher, Grey-capped and Rufous-bellied Woodpeckers, Black and Hair-crested Drongos, Tiger Shrike, Japanese Waxwing*, Chestnut-cheeked Starling* (occasionally breeds on islands in Bay of Peter the Great), Snowy-browed Nuthatch* (Chuguevskiy and Ussuriyskiy districts in extreme south), Marsh Grassbird* (Lake Khanka), Japanese Wagtail and Rufous-backed Bunting* (formerly in the extreme south), as well as 'Amur' leopard (Kedrovaya Pad reserve) and Siberian tiger (Lazovsky reserve). There are about 250 Siberian tigers left on the planet, between the River Amur and Pacific coast, and although anti-poaching units have slowed down the carnage caused by illegal hunting, the tigers are now threatened by habitat loss through illegal and indiscriminate logging.)

The dashing Amur Falcon can be seen hunting flying insects around Lake Khanka

Ussuriland can be approached from **Vladivostok** at the southern end or **Khabarovsk** at the northern end. Both are accessible by air from Moscow (nine hours) and Anchorage, Alaska, and by rail from Moscow via the Trans-Siberian Railway (one week), and Vladivostok is also accessible by air and ferry (Jun–Oct) from Japan. The sites outlined below run south to north, from Vladivostok to Khabarovsk. **De Vries Bay** is an excellent place to look for passage shorebirds, which have included Spoonbill Sandpiper*, while the damp meadows and woods inland support Latham's Snipe* and Ochre-rumped Bunting* (in bushy damp meadows). The islands offshore from Vladivostok in the **Bay of Peter the Great** support Pleske's Warbler, which is unknown from the mainland, and during the boat trips to and from these islands it is possible to see Streaked Shearwater, Swinhoe's Storm-Petrel and Spectacled Guillemot. The excellent forest in the **Kedrovaya Pad** reserve, where 250 or so species have been recorded, near Vladivostok, supports Tristram's Bunting. One of the top areas here is Gryanya Valley where the best birding strategy is to take a truck up the valley for 10 km or so and then walk back down. The meadows and woods in the Elduga Valley, in the **Barachny Hills** southwest of Lake Khanka near the border with China, support four species at the northern edge of their world ranges: Lesser Cuckoo, Bull-headed Shrike, Japanese Bush-Warbler and Vinous-throated Parrotbill, as well as Schrenck's Bittern*, Yellow-legged Buttonquail and, around the small lake near the fishing lodge near Vinevitino, Band-bellied Crake*. The huge, shallow **Lake Khanka** and

USSURILAND

the marshes and meadows which surround it support a wide range of waterbirds including Oriental Stork*, Pied Harrier, Red-crowned* and White-naped* Cranes, Asian Dowitcher* and Reed Parrotbill*, as well as Pechora Pipit. The best base is Guyvaron, which translated into English means 'village of the Rook', an appropriate name because there is indeed a rookery here, in which Amur Falcon and Daurian Starling also breed. The lake is situated in a treeless plain, hence the narrow belt of woodland (up to 200 m wide) along its eastern edge attracts numerous passage passerine migrants and on good days hundreds of birds pass through here, notably a wide variety of thrushes, flycatchers and warblers.

The **Bikin Valley**, accessible from Luchegorsk north of Lake Khanka, supports Mandarin Duck*, Scaly-sided Merganser* (both up to eight hours downriver from the town of Verkhny Pereval), Band-bellied Crake*, Hooded Crane* (in the vast marsh beyond the wet woods across the river from Verkhny Pereval), Long-billed Plover*, Blakiston's Fish-Owl* and White-throated Rock-Thrush. Similar species occur in the **Iman Valley**, in northern Ussuriland. Bird up and downstream from the villages of Meteoritny and Vostretsovo by boat and road. Mandarin Duck*, Scaly-sided Merganser*, Hooded Crane* and Long-billed Plover* have been recorded in the **Khor Valley**, in north Ussuriland near Khabarovsk.

Other good birding sites near Khabarovsk include: (i) the taiga in the **Bolshe-Khekhtsir** reserve, southeast of Khabarovsk, which is good for

*The clear-water rivers and streams of Ussuriland support the
rare Scaly-sided Merganser**

Hodgson's Hawk-Cuckoo, thrushes including White-throated Rock-
Thrush, Rufous-tailed Robin and Japanese Grosbeak; (ii) the island of
Salmaki, where Thick-billed Warbler occurs; (iii) **Lake Katar**, where
Oriental Stork*, Swinhoe's Snipe and Jungle Nightjar occur; and (iv)
the wet meadows and pools across the river from Khabarovsk, accessible via a short train journey, where Schrenck's Bittern* and Pied Harrier
occur. In the city itself the arboretum and other gardens are also worth
birding if there is time to spare.

Accommodation: Barachny Hills—small, basic fishing lodge near Vinevitino. Lake Khanka—village houses in Guyvaron. Iman Valley—village
houses in Meteoritny and Vostretsovo. Khabarovsk—Hotel Amur, Hotel
Voskhod.

The dark-billed Oriental Stork breeds only in the Amur and Ussuri regions in
Russia, and in northeast China*

LAKE BAIKAL

The 'Sacred Sea of Siberia' is the earth's deepest, most voluminous and
eighth largest lake, extending for 636 km from north to south, up to 87
km from west to east, and reaching a maximum depth of 1741 m (5712
ft). It is fed by over 300 rivers, but drained by one, the Lower Angara,
and is believed to hold some 20% of the planet's freshwater, some of
which turns to ice between January and May. However, it is not Baikal's
waters, badly polluted by industry, which support the best birds, it is the
surrounding marshes and forested mountains, where the likes of Swinhoe's Snipe, Asian Dowitcher* and Yellow-browed Bunting occur.

The species listed below occur during the spring (mid-May to mid-June) unless otherwise indicated.

Localised Species
Swinhoe's Snipe, Asian Dowitcher*, Great Grey Owl, Siberian Accentor.

Regular Passage Migrants
Terek Sandpiper, Grey-tailed Tattler, Pacific Golden-Plover, Dusky Thrush ('Naumann's' *naumanni*), Pechora and Buff-bellied Pipits, Little and Pallas's (Reed) Buntings.

Others
Ruddy Shelduck, Falcated Duck, Greater Spotted* and Imperial* Eagles, Marsh Sandpiper, Yellow-legged Gull (*mongolicus*), White-winged and Caspian Terns, Hill Pigeon, Oriental Cuckoo, Ural Owl, White-throated Needletail, Fork-tailed Swift, Three-toed Woodpecker, Azure-winged Magpie, Eurasian Nutcracker, Daurian Jackdaw, Brown Shrike, Rufous-tailed Rock-Thrush, Siberian, White's and Eyebrowed Thrushes, Dark-sided, Asian Brown and Mugimaki Flycatchers, Rufous-tailed Robin, Siberian Rubythroat, Siberian Blue Robin, Daurian Redstart, Pied Wheatear, Spotted and Chinese Bush-Warblers, Lanceolated, Pallas's Grasshopper, Gray's, Thick-billed, Dusky, Radde's and Greenish ('Two-barred' *plumbeitarsus*) Warblers, Citrine Wagtail, Olive-backed Pipit, Two-barred Crossbill, Pine, Godlewski's, Meadow, Rustic, Yellow-browed, Yellow-breasted, Chestnut and Black-faced Buntings.

Other Wildlife
Brown bear (scarce), Baikal seal (scarce), sturgeon.

Irkutsk, the gateway to the Lake Baikal area, is accessible by air from Moscow and via the Trans-Siberian Railway. The nearby marshes support Swinhoe's Snipe, and Imperial Eagle* occurs on the Buryat Steppes to the north. At Lake Baikal, 65 km southeast of Irkutsk, bird the following areas: (i) the area a few km south of the village of **Listvianka** (accessible by road and hydrofoil (in summer) from Irkutsk), where the wooded hills support Siberian, White's and Eyebrowed Thrushes, and Spotted and Chinese Bush-Warblers, and the valley below the Baikal Hotel is a good place to look for passage passerine migrants such as warblers and buntings. Azure-winged Magpie, Pied Wheatear and Godlewski's Bunting occur on the opposite side of the River Angara, accessible by boat; (ii) the **Selenga Delta**, on the opposite shore of the lake to Listvianka, in the southeast corner, where Asian Dowitcher* breeds; and (iii) around the small town of **Baikal'sk**, also on the lakes southern shores, about 150 km by road from Irkutsk, where Swinhoe's Snipe, Great Grey Owl and Siberian Accentor occur.

Accommodation: Irkutsk—Intourist Hotel. Listvianka—Intourist Baikal Hotel. Selenga Delta—fishing lodge (very basic). Baikal'sk—town houses.

The dry steppe, lakes and rocky hills southeast of Lake Baikal in **Transbaikalia** support Ruddy Shelduck, Upland Buzzard, Steppe Eagle, Saker Falcon, Daurian Partridge, Demoiselle Crane, Relict Gull*, Hill Pigeon, White-throated Needletail, Isabelline Shrike ('Daurian' *speculigerus*),

*Several 'dream-birds' for Europeans, including Siberian Thrush,
can be seen around Lake Baikal*

Mongolian and Asian Short-toed Larks, Blyth's Pipit, Long-tailed and
Pallas's Rosefinches, and Godlewski's and Meadow Buntings. From Ulan
Ude, accessible by road from Irkutsk and by air from Moscow (seven
hours), bird the following areas: (i) alongside the River Selenga and in
the hills near **Bayangol Skayabaza**, southwest of Ulan Ude, where Up-
land Buzzard, Saker Falcon and Mongolian Lark occur; (ii) by the river
near **Temnstk** railway station, southwest of Bayangol, where Daurian
Partridge occurs; (iii) around **Ayrestui**, further southwest, where Steppe
Eagle, Daurian Partridge and Mongolian Lark occur; and (iv) Lake
Barun-Torey where Relict Gull* occurs.

The marshes and forested mountains in **Zabajkalian National Park**
on the eastern side of Lake Baikal support Ruddy Shelduck, Spot-billed
Duck, Upland Buzzard, Baillon's Crake, Swinhoe's Snipe, Long-toed
Stint, White-winged and Caspian Terns, Hill Pigeon, Ural and Great Grey
Owls, Siberian Jay, Brown Shrike, Grey-streaked and Dark-sided
Flycatchers, Siberian Rubythroat, Lanceolated, Thick-billed, Dusky and
Greenish ('Two-barred' *plumbeitarsus*) Warblers, Brown Accentor,
Asian Rosy-Finch, Pine Grosbeak, Two-barred Crossbill, and Yellow-
browed and Chestnut Buntings. From the HQ at Ust-Barguzin a single
dirt road traverses the park, enabling access to the marshes at Kulst-
nnoe, but birds such as Brown Accentor and Asian Rosy-Finch are
restricted to the high tops which are accessible only on foot. For more
information write to Kontora Zabajkalskogo Gosudarstvenogo Nacion-
alnogo Parka, Bolnicnyj pereulok, Ust-Barguzin 671 623, Russia (tel:
92575 or 92578).

RUSSIAN ALTAI

Between Barnaul and the border with Mongolia in south-central Russia
the montane wooded valleys and mountain semi-desert steppe in the
Russian Altai, which rises to 4506 m (14,784 ft) at Belukha, support
some superb birds, not least Altai Snowcock, Solitary Snipe, Pallas's
Sandgrouse and Eversmann's Redstart.

The species listed below occur during the summer unless otherwise
indicated.

Localised Specialities
Altai Falcon, Altai Snowcock, Solitary Snipe, Pallas's Sandgrouse, Eversmann's Redstart, Père David's Snowfinch, Himalayan and Black-throated Accentors, Plain and Black-headed Mountain-Finches, Mongolian Finch.

Other Localised Species
Cinereous Vulture*, Steppe and Imperial* Eagles, Demoiselle Crane, Asian Rosy-Finch.

Others
Ruddy Shelduck, Upland Buzzard, Greater Sandplover, Eurasian Dotterel, Yellow-legged Gull (*mongolicus*), Rufous-tailed Robin, Siberian Rubythroat, Bluethroat (*pallidogularis*), Yellow-browed Warbler ('Hume's' *humei*), Small Whitethroat, Siberian and Azure Tits, Pale Rockfinch, White-winged Snowfinch, Blyth's Pipit, Brown Accentor, Pallas's Rosefinch, Pine Bunting.

Novosibirsk, about 250 km northwest of Barnaul, the gateway to the Altai, has an international airport. From Barnaul follow the Chuya Trakt, the ancient route between Russia and Mongolia, which passes through the 2000-m (6562 ft) wooded Seminsky Pass and the Kosh Agach area in the Chuya Steppe near the border with Mongolia, both of which are worth birding, and enables access to: (i) the **South Chuya Range** where Altai Falcon, Altai Snowcock and Black-headed Mountain-Finch occur; (ii) the **Kuray Range** where the high semi-desert supports Pallas's Sandgrouse and Père David's Snowfinch; and (iii) the Lake Akkem area situated at 2100 m (6890 ft) below Belukha in the **Katun Range** where Altai Snowcock, Solitary Snipe, Eversmann's Redstart, and Himalayan and Black-throated Accentors occur.

Accommodation: Barnaul. Ak Tash.

The only known breeding area of Slender-billed Curlew* (the last nests (14) were found in 1924) lies near **Tara**, northwest of Novosibirsk and north of Omsk, although only a single bird was recorded on a single day here over a period of several decades during the second half of the 20th century.

VOLGA DELTA

The longest river in European Russia flows 3688 km before reaching the north end of the Caspian Sea where it forms one of the largest deltas on earth, and its 6500 km² support a suitably impressive avifauna. Over 250 species have been recorded, of which at least 100 have been known to breed, including 200 pairs of Dalmatian Pelicans*, 200 pairs of White-tailed Eagles*, up to 10,000 pairs of Great Black-headed Gulls (the world's largest breeding population), and over 100,000 pairs of marsh terns. With other breeding birds such as Pallid Harrier* and Ménétries's Warbler, a summer birding trip which combines the delta with the adjacent Kalmykian Steppe (see next site) would almost certainly be one of the most potentially exciting trips west of the Urals. It is also possible to see Siberian Crane* during the spring (up to nine were recorded at this time of year during the 1990s, mainly from late March to mid-April) and autumn (up to 13 during the 1990s in October) as the tiny west Siberian breeding population migrates to and from its wintering grounds in northern Iran.

It is necessary to arrange accommodation and permission to visit the best areas of the delta well in advance, and this can be done by contacting the National Biosphere Reserve of Astrakhan, Nabereshnaja r. Zarew Street 119, RU-414021 Astrakhan, Russia, and the Commission of Ecology and Natural Resources of the Administrative District of Astrakhan, Bakinskaja Street 113, RU-414000, Astrakhan, Russia.

The best times to visit the Volga Delta are from mid-April to mid-June, especially during mid-May, and from mid-August to mid-October. The species listed below occur during mid-April to mid-June unless otherwise indicated.

Localised Specialities
Siberian Crane* (spring and autumn), Great Black-headed Gull.

Other Localised Species
Pygmy Cormorant*, Dalmatian Pelican*, Pallid Harrier*, Saker Falcon, Baillon's Crake, Paddyfield and Ménétries's Warblers.

Regular Passage Migrants
Marsh, Terek and Broad-billed Sandpipers, Red-necked Phalarope.

Others
Ruddy Shelduck, Squacco Heron, Black-crowned Night-Heron, Glossy Ibis, White-tailed Eagle*, Red-footed Falcon, Little Crake, Yellow-legged Gull ('Caspian'/'Pontic' *cachinnans*), Whiskered, White-winged, Gull-billed and Caspian Terns, European Bee-eater, European Roller, Lesser Grey Shrike, Moustached and Desert Warblers.

Other Wildlife
Caspian seal, sturgeon.

(Other species recorded here include Great White Pelican, Ferruginous Duck*, Black-winged Pratincole*, White-tailed Lapwing and Black Lark (winter).)

The city of Astrakhan, which is situated at the north end of the delta 88 km from the Caspian Sea, is accessible by air from Moscow (two hours). The base for birding the delta is the small village of Damchik, which is 60 km south of Astrakhan and accessible by road and boat (five hours) from there. The cost of staying in one of the two guesthouses here includes daily excursions led by experienced ornithologists.

KALMYKIAN STEPPE

The semi-desert, rolling sandy hills, saline and freshwater lakes, tamarisk stands and steppe north of the Volga Delta support a wide range of top birds, including Demoiselle Crane (6,000–8,000 pairs breed in the lower Volga region and Kalmykian steppe—the world strong-hold), Red-footed Falcon (it is possible to see up to 400 in a day here during August), Black-winged Pratincole* and Blue-cheeked Bee-eater.

The species listed below occur during mid-April to mid-June unless otherwise indicated.

Localised Specialities
Black-winged Pratincole*.

Other Localised Species
Pallid Harrier*, Steppe Eagle, Saker Falcon, Demoiselle Crane, Black-bellied Sandgrouse, Blue-cheeked Bee-eater, Menetries's Warbler, Red-headed Bunting.

Regular Passage Migrants
Marsh, Terek and Broad-billed Sandpipers, Red-necked Phalarope.

Others
Long-legged Buzzard, Red-footed Falcon, Little Bustard*, Gull-billed Tern, European Bee-eater, European Roller, Lesser Grey and Northern ('Steppe' *pallidirostris*) Shrikes, Rosy Starling, Pied and Isabelline Wheatears, Desert Warbler, Black-headed Bunting.

(Other species recorded here include Ferruginous Duck*, Great Bustard*, Caspian Plover, White-tailed Lapwing, Pallas's Sandgrouse and Egyptian Nightjar.)

From Astrakhan bird: (i) alongside the main road to Elista, starting a few km west of Astrakhan. This is the best area for Black-winged Pratincole*; (ii) around the small town of Liman, southwest of Astrakhan. This is the best area for Steppe Eagle which nests on roadside pylons; and (iii) the sandy semi-desert with numerous dunes by the road to Volgograd north of Astrakhan, where Black-bellied Sandgrouse and Desert Warbler occur.

Accommodation: Astrakhan—Hotel Lotos.

The large saline **Lake Baskunchak**, the rocky **Bolshoe Bogdo** region and the remnant steppe they are situated in, a day's drive across the Volga-Akhtuba floodplain (Red-headed Bunting) about 350 km north of Astrakhan, support White-winged Lark, as well as Imperial Eagle*, Little Bustard* and Pied Wheatear, and the Saiga antelope. It is necessary to obtain permission to visit this area in advance, via the Commission of Ecology and Natural Resources of the Administrative District of Astrakhan, Bakinskaja Street 113, RU-414000, Astrakhan. There are guesthouses in the villages of Verkhny and Nishny Baskunchak near Lake Baskunchak.

In the **Russian Caucasus** it is possible to see Caucasian Snowcock and Caucasian Grouse* as well as Lammergeier, Semicollared Fly-catcher, Krüper's Nuthatch, Chiffchaff ('Caucasian' *lorenzii*), Greenish Warbler ('Green' *nitidus*) and Great Rosefinch above the village of Teberda (where there is a hotel), about 250 km west of Minervalnye Vody. Travelling east of here, in the Chechnya area, was inpossible at the end of 1999 due to the war between the Chechen guerrillas and the Russian army.

ADDITIONAL INFORMATION

Books and papers

Strict Nature Reserves (Zapovedniki) of Russia. Volkov A E (ed.), 1996. Russia.

The Natural History of the USSR. Knystautas A, 1987. Century Hutchinson.

A Field Guide to the Birds of Russia and Adjacent Territories (the former USSR). Flint V *et al.*, 1983. Princeton University Press.

Collins Guide to the Birds of Russia (photographic). Knystautas A, 1993. HarperCollins.

Birds of the Southern Kuril Islands (in Japanese and Russian). Nechaev V A and Fujimaki Y, 1994. Hokkaido UP.

Birds of Sakhalin Island (in Russian). Nechaev V A, 1991. Amur-Ussuri Centre, Russia.

Birds of the Wetlands of the Southern Russian Far-East and their Protection (with English summaries). Litvinenko N M (ed.), 1996. Amur-Ussuri Centre, Russia.

The Birds of Siberia: To the Petchora Valley and *The Yenesei.* Seebohm H, 1901. Two excellent reading books published by Alan Sutton Publishing Limited, 30 Brunswick Road, Gloucester GL1 1JJ, UK.

SARDINIA

INTRODUCTION

Despite the presence of large numbers of elegant Eleonora's Falcons, Barbary Partridge, which only occurs elsewhere in Europe on Gibraltar, Purple Swamphen, Audouin's Gull*, Marmora's Warbler and a wide range of other birds, few birders visit this large Mediterranean island, probably because the birds are persecuted mercilessly by many hunters, and because the costs of hiring a vehicle and staying in built accommodation are higher than in much of the rest of Europe.

At 24,090 km², Sardinia is about 20% the size of England and about 3% the size of Texas. Cágliari, at the south end of the island, is the air gateway to Sardinia, even though most of the recent tourist developments have taken place in the northeast. The island is also accessible by ferry from Corsica and mainland Italy. There is a fairly good public transport system but the best way to bird the island thoroughly is to hire a vehicle, even though the costs of hire and petrol are amongst the highest in Europe. Apart from expensive built accommodation there are campsites available for budget birders. Food and drink are relatively cheap and include *panini* (substantial sandwiches), pasta, pizza, beer and wine.

Sardinia has a Mediterranean climate with very hot and dry summers and cool winters. Early June onwards, after the first Eleonora's Falcons have arrived, is the best time to visit.

The offshore islands and predominantly rugged coastline support important breeding colonies of shearwaters, Eleonora's Falcon and Audouin's Gull*, while some of the best lagoons left in the Mediterranean light up the coastal plain, and together with their associated marshes and some salinas, they support internationally important numbers of waterbirds, especially during the passage and winter periods. Inland, most of the lowland plains and upland plateaux on this sparsely populated island have been turned over to agriculture, although the more rugged mountains, which rise to to 1835 m (6020 ft) at Gennargentu, are still rather wild and support remnant cork-oak and pine woods, garrigue, maquis and grasslands. Contemporary conservation problems facing the four threatened and near-threatened species as well as the relatively common and widespread birds which occur on Sardinia include habitat loss and degradation, primarily due to agricultural intensification, but also as result of built development and industrialisation, and hunting, which is as popular here as it is on mainland Italy.

The species listed below occur during the summer unless otherwise indicated.

Localised Specialities
Barbary Partridge, Purple Swamphen ('Western' *porphyrio*), Audouin's*
and Slender-billed Gulls, Marmora's Warbler.

Other Localised Species
Greater Flamingo (over 2,000 pairs in 1997), Eleonora's Falcon (320
pairs in 1996), Spotless Starling, Citril Finch ('Mediterranean' *corsicanus*).

Others
Cory's ('Scopoli's' *diomedea*) and Mediterranean Shearwaters, Euro-
pean Storm-Petrel, European Shag ('Mediterranean' *desmarestii*), Glossy
Ibis, Eurasian Griffon (42 pairs in 1996), Golden and Bonelli's Eagles,
Lesser Kestrel*, Little Bustard*, Collared Pratincole, Gull-billed Tern,
Alpine and Pallid Swifts, European Bee-eater, European Roller, Blue
Rock-Thrush, Zitting Cisticola, Sardinian, Subalpine, Spectacled and
Dartford Warblers, Calandra Lark, Spanish Sparrow (this is one of few
places in Europe where there are no House Sparrows), Rock Petronia.
   (Other species recorded here include Western Reef-Egret (singles at
Golfo di Oristano in August 1997 and in a Little Egret colony in June
1996), Greater Spotted Eagle* (winter), Marsh Sandpiper and Caspian
Tern.)

There are two excellent birding sites near the island's capital, **Cágliari**,
at the south end of the island: (i) the extensive **Quartu Salinas** a few
km to the west, visible from the main coast road to Pula; and (ii) **Stagno
di Molentargius**, a 500-ha wetland of international importance, a few
km to the east, which supports Greater Flamingo, Glossy Ibis, Purple
Swamphen, Slender-billed Gull (about 1,000 pairs, also occurs in
Cágliari harbour) and Gull-billed Tern. During the winter, Greater Spotted Eagle* has also been recorded here. To view the lake walk along
the trail which begins at the IP petrol station in Cágliari, or along the
canal next to Quartu S. Elena. Monte Arcosu and Monte Caravius in the
Iglesiente Massif, to the west of Cágliari, are good places to look for
raptors, and Marmora's Warbler and Citril Finch occur in and around
the forest reserve on Monte Arcosu.
   Most of the Eleonora's Falcons which breed on Sardinia are confined
to two major sites: (i) around **Capo di M. Santu** on the east coast; and
(ii) on **Isola di San Pietro**, which is accessible via ferries from Porto-
scuso, on the mainland, and Calasetta on Isola di San Antioco. Look out
for Audouin's Gull* on the crossings. A colony of over 100 pairs of
Eleonora's Falcon is present in the LIPU reserve around Cala Fico and
Capo Sandalo, complete with telescopes for observing these superb
raptors. Isola di San Pietro also supports Greater Flamingo, Audouin's*
and Slender-billed Gulls (both on Saline di Carloforte), Blue Rock-
Thrush and Marmora's Warbler.
   Barbary Partridge and Little Bustard* are thin on the ground in the
boulder-strewn grasslands on the plateau known as **Giara de Gesturi**,
which is situated about 30 km southeast of Oristano in west Sardinia.
Try the area west of the village of Gesturi, which is a few km north of
Barumini on the SS197, to begin with, then explore elsewhere.
   The lagoons and salinas on the Sinis Peninsula and elsewhere around
the **Golfo di Oristano**, on the the west coast about 90 km northwest of
Cágliari via the N131, attract internationally important numbers of

waterbirds, including thousands of Greater Flamingo, as well as Purple Swamphen. Concentrate on the following areas: (i) the large lagoons of Stagno di Cábras and Stagno di Mistras, northwest of Oristano; (ii) the LIPU reserve at Stagno Sale Porcus, a lake northwest of Stagno di Cábras; (iii) Stagno di Santa Giusta, just south of Oristano; and (iv) other wetlands further south to Arborea and Punta Corru Mannu.

The best place to see Eurasian Griffon on Sardinia is at **Capo Marargiu**, just north of Bosa, where they breed. At the extreme northeast end of the island, the partly inhabited **Maddalena Archipelago**, accessible by ferry from Palau, supports Cory's and Mediterranean Shearwaters, Audouin's Gull* and Marmora's Warbler. Finally, there are more seabird colonies at **Isola Asinara**, at the island's northwestern tip.

ADDITIONAL INFORMATION

Addresses

Please send records of rarities to the Comitato di Ohologazione Italiano (COI), via A. Tommosi, 21-57124 Livorno, Italy. The annual Italian rarities report is published in *Riv. Ital. Orn.*, in Italian with an English summary.

Lega Italiana per la Protezione degli Uccelli (LIPU), via Trento 49, 43100 Parma, Italy (fax: 521 273419; email: lipusede@tin.it), publishes *The Hoopoe* newsletter. This important organisation can also be contacted via LIPU UK, c/o 6 Butlers Close, Broomfield, Chelmsford, Essex, CM1 5BE, UK.

Books and papers

Where to watch birds in Italy. LIPU, 1994. Helm.
Check-list Degli Uccelli Italiani. Brichetti P and Massa B, 1993. *Riv. Ital. di Birdwatching* 1: (2) 61–73 and (3) 20–26.

The elegant Eleonora's Falcon was named after a medieval princess who put a protection order on Sardinia's birds of prey. About 25% of the population which breeds throughout the Mediterranean is represented by the dark phase

SLOVAKIA

INTRODUCTION

Summary

While the Slovakian avifauna is not as enticing as that of its southern neighbour, Hungary, a birding trip which combines the high-altitude highlights of Slovakia with the lowland grassland and wetland specialities of Hungary would rank amongst the best possible in inland eastern Europe. However, while this is a small country with a good infrastructure the major avian attractions, which include all ten European woodpeckers and Wallcreeper, may prove difficult to track down without local assistance.

Size

At 49,035 km², Slovakia is about 40% the size of England and about 7% the size of Texas.

Getting Around

Many birders combine a visit to Slovakia with Hungary, from where they enter the country, although some opt for a cheap package tour to the Tatry Mountains, where all of the best birds occur. The resorts at the feet of these mountains are accessible by road and the cheap rail network from the capital, Bratislava, and the high tops can be reached via cable-cars, chair-lifts, ski-lifts and trails. Some of the top birds, as well as brown bear, are only likely to be seen with the assistance of experienced guides, most of whom work for two local travel companies (see Additional Information).

Accommodation and Food

Most of the hill and mountain ranges have expensive resort accommodation, where the prices are hiked up for tourists, but in nearby towns and villages it is usually possible to find cheaper 'Bed and Breakfast' places (*Zimmer frei*) and campsites, some of which have chalets. The most popular foods are a sort of macaroni cheese (*bryndzove halusky*) and goulash. Slovakians are great beer drinkers, although they also like their local brandies and wines.

Health and Safety

Immunisation against hepatitis, polio and typhoid is recommended. Crime rates rose steadily during the 1990s, so beware of theft from accommodation and vehicles.

Climate and Timing

The climate is continental, with warm summers and cold winters (the average winter temperature is 0°C, even in the lowlands). The best time of year to look for Hazel Grouse, owls and woodpeckers is during March and April, but snow may restrict access to some areas at this time so it is best to leave a trip until as late as possible if these are the birds at the top of the hit-list. Mid-April–mid-May, when some owls and woodpeckers are still calling, summer visitors are arriving and brown bears are emerging from their winter hibernation, is arguably the peak time to visit, although it can still be cold and wet at high-altitude at this time.

Habitats

Apart from the lowland plains alongside the River Danube in the southwest and the River Ondava in the southeast, where, amongst the extensive areas of cultivated land, there are large fishponds, reservoirs, remnant riverine forests and remnant steppe grasslands, this land-locked country is dominated by hills and mountains. These highlands are dissected by deep valleys and limestone gorges with scrubby hillsides, and fine beech, oak and coniferous forests which give way to alpine pastures and snow-capped peaks at higher altitudes. The highest mountains, the Tatry, which lie at the western end of the Carpathians along the northern border with Poland, rise to 2655 m (8711 ft) at Gerlachovsky Stit.

Conservation

Slovakia has some large parks and reserves which, together with special protection measures for individual species, including the placement of artifical nests for Imperial Eagles*, go some way to ensuring a future for the four threatened and near-threatened species as well as the relatively common and widespread birds which occur in the country. However, ongoing problems include habitat loss and degradation, hunting and pollution (some of the country's forests have been severely damaged by acid rain).

Bird Species

About 336 species have been recorded in Slovakia. Notable species include Imperial Eagle* (up to 35 pairs), Saker Falcon, Little Crake, Great Bustard*, Ural Owl, all ten European woodpeckers, Collared Flycatcher, Wallcreeper and Alpine Accentor.

Expectations

It is possible to see about 150 species on a trip lasting a week to ten days which covers the whole country during the spring, and up to 200 when a visit to the Tatry Mountains is combined with the lowlands of eastern Hungary.

The floodplain of the **River Danube** in southwest Slovakia supports a small population of Great Bustard*, as well as Ferruginous Duck*, Black Stork and Little Crake. This area extends southeast from Bratislava to Komarno and it is accessible via Routes 63 and 506, as well as numerous minor roads, although it is only possible to reach some areas by boat. At the eastern end the river splits into two, forming a large low-lying island which is where most of the Great Bustards* in the area survive. They are most likely to be seen in the reserve at Zlatna na Ostrove, about 12 km west of Komarno. Ferruginous Duck* occurs on Cicovske Mrtve rameno, an ox-bow lake, and at Parizske mociare, a reserve near Gbelce, northeast of Komarno, which also supports Little Crake and occasional breeding pairs of Moustached Warbler.

The limestone hills of the **Male Karpaty**, about 40 km northeast of Bratislava, support plenty of raptors, including Imperial Eagle* and Saker Falcon. There are numerous roads and trails in this popular walking region where Modra would make a good base. White-backed Woodpecker occurs in the beech woods around the spa town of **Trencianska Teplice**, a few km northwest of Trencin, which is about 100 km northeast of Bratislava by road or rail. The best place to look for this elusive woodpecker is where there is plenty of dead wood, above Zelena Zaba or 'Green Frog' spa. **Mala Fatra National Park**, where the limestone mountains reach nearly 1829 m (6000 ft), about 180 km northeast of Bratislava (15 km east of Zilina), supports Lesser Spotted Eagle, Hazel Grouse, Eurasian Pygmy-Owl, Tengmalm's Owl, Three-toed Woodpecker, Collared Flycatcher and Wallcreeper, as well as brown bear.

TATRY MOUNTAINS

This often overcrowded but nevertheless beautiful and important isolated high-altitude area in the snow-capped Slovakian Carpathians rises to 2655 m (8711 ft) at Gerlachovsky Stit, near the border with Poland. The extensive forest, steep rocky outcrops and alpine pastures support a more or less typical central European upland fauna, topped by Wallcreeper, although some species are only likely to be seen with the help of local guides who know which nest boxes the owls are using. These guides also know where the carefully sited screens used for observing bears are.

The species listed below occur during the summer unless otherwise indicated.

Localised Species
Wallcreeper.

Others
White Stork, Lesser Spotted and Golden Eagles, Eurasian Capercaillie, Hazel Grouse, Eurasian Eagle-Owl, Eurasian Pygmy-Owl, Tengmalm's

Owl, White-backed, Three-toed and Black Woodpeckers, Eurasian Nutcracker, Rufous-tailed Rock-Thrush, Alpine Accentor.

Other Wildlife

Brown bear, chamois, lynx, Alpine marmot, Eurasian otter, grey wolf, many butterflies and a rich flora which includes 25 endemics.

The **High Tatras National Park** covers much of the area. There are a string of resorts at the base of the mountains, all of which are connected by a frequent train service, and within four to five hours by road from Vienna in Austria and the Zemplen Hills in Hungary. The high tops are easily accessible via cable-cars, chair-lifts, ski-lifts and trails, and some of the best birding can be had around the ski-resorts, where Wallcreepers have been seen on the ski-lift buildings. Due to the waves of walkers in summer, it is crucial to arrive at the crack of dawn at **Tatranska Lomnica** to board the cable-cars to Lomnicke at 2190 m (7185 ft) and Lomnicky Stit at 2632 m (8635 ft), in order to stand a chance of seeing Alpine Accentor, which also occurs at the top of **Dumbier**, which is accessible via a ski-lift. It is also possible to reach Lomnicke via the funicular railway from Stary Smokovec, one of the major resorts. Three-toed Woodpecker and Eurasian Nutcracker occur along the Strbske Pleso-Popradske Pleso Track (allow about an hour to walk this), one of several walking tracks worth birding around **Strbske Pleso**. From here it is also possible to reach Predne Solisko (via chair-lift and ski-lift to Solisko, then a hard climb) where Alpine Accentors are usually quite easy to see. From the mountain hotel and lake at Popradske Pleso there is a walking track which ascends to Chata Pod Rysmi and **Rysy** (allow about three hours to walk this), with a refuge hut at 2250 m (7382 ft) where it is possible to eat and stay the night. This is also a good area for Alpine Accentor, especially around Chata during the early morning and evening. There are plenty of other well-stocked refuge huts in the mountains for the more adventurous.

Accommodation: Hotel Bobrovnik, on the shores of Liptovska Mara Reservoir. Tatranska Lomnica. Stary Smokovec. Strbske Pleso. Pod Lesom campsite.

The 360-km^2 limestone karst plateau known as **Slovensky Kras**, by the border with Hungary in eastern Slovakia, supports Imperial Eagle*, Saker Falcon, Eurasian Eagle-Owl, Ural Owl, Rufous-tailed Rock-Thrush and an isolated population of Rock Bunting. Zlata Idka, 30 km west of Kosice, is an hour away from the plateau, to the east, but arguably the best base. Route 50/E571 passes through the area and several minor roads and marked trails lead off it. Eurasian Eagle-Owl, Rufous-tailed Rock-Thrush and Rock Bunting are most likely to be seen in the Zadielska Dolina gorge near the village of Zadielske Dvorniky. The whole area between Plesivec in the west to Bodvou and Moldava in the east is worth birding.

Slovakia's top range of hills for raptors is the **Slanske**, which extend from Presov in the north to the Kosice–Trebisov road in the south and are accessible via several minor roads and marked trails. There are five species of eagle here: Short-toed, Lesser Spotted, Imperial*, Golden and Booted Eagles, as well as Ural Owl and White-backed Woodpecker, and Saker Falcon is an outside possibility.

The large reservoir, known as **Zemplinska Sirava**, just east of Michalovce in extreme eastern Slovakia supports a good range of water-birds, especially during the spring and autumn when passage migrants are moving through the area. Species recorded here during these peri-ods include Ferruginous Duck*, Black and White Storks, Whiskered Tern, European Bee-eater, European Roller and Lesser Grey Shrike, while winter visitors include Smew and White-tailed Eagle*. Bird the north and east shores and the small ponds and their surrounding thick-ets around the village of Jovsa on the reservoir's east side. Eurasian Eagle-Owl occurs in the quarries by the road along the north shore of the reservoir.

It is possible to see over 100 species in a single day during late April and early May around the fishponds at **Senne**, south of Zemplinska Sirava, including, during the summer, Black and White Storks, Corn Crake*, Whiskered Tern, Lesser Grey Shrike and Bluethroat ('White-spotted' *cyanecula*), while Common Crane is a regular passage migrant and more unusual visitors have included Pygmy Cormorant* (has bred), Ferruginous Duck*, Glossy Ibis, Red-footed and Saker Falcons, Little Crake, Great Snipe*, Marsh Sandpiper, White-winged Tern and Aquatic Warbler* (has bred).

Many of the species listed for the two previous wetland sites also occur on the **Bodrog-Latorica Floodplain**, which runs along the bor-ders with Hungary and the Ukraine in extreme southeast Slovakia. It also supports the country's only regular Red-footed Falcons and Black-winged Stilts, as well as European Roller. Concentrate on the Zatinske mociare and Tabja reserves. The largest peat-bog in the country, **Gbelce**, also in southeast Slovakia, supports Little Crake and Moustach-ed Warbler.

ADDITIONAL INFORMATION

Addresses
Please send records of rarities to the Slovenska Ornithologicka Spolocnost (SOS/The Slovakian Society for the Protection of Birds), Zapadoslovenske muzeum Trnava, Muzejne namestie 3, 91809 Trnava, Slovakia.

For help with locating owls, other birds and bears contact either: (i) Atypus Travel Company Limited, PO Box 190, 601 00 Brno, Czech Republic (tel/fax: 5 4124 1121; email: atypus@sky.cz; website: www.czechia.com/atypus); or (ii) Sakertour, Tarjan ut 6, H-4032 Debrecen, Hungary (tel/fax: 52 350306), which specialises in organ-ising tours to Slovakia and Hungary.

Books and papers
Important Bird Areas in Europe: Czechoslovakia. Hora J & Kanuch P (eds.), 1992. BirdLife International.

SLOVENIA

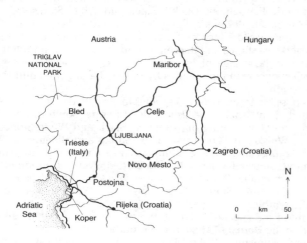

INTRODUCTION

This country is situated at the eastern end of the Alps where the mountains are high and rugged enough to support such localised species as Rock Partridge, and due to the country's small size and fairly modern infrastructure it is easy to look for lowland birds such as Little Crake on the same day.

At 20,254 km², Slovenia is about 15% the size of England and 3% the size of Texas. The cheap, efficient public transport system and fairly good road network makes getting around fairly easy, and there is a wide range of accommodation to choose from, including high-rise hotels, guesthouses, small pensions, a few youth hostels, plenty of modern campsites and mountain refuge huts. Slovenians like to eat goulash, grilled meats, hot dogs, pasta, pastries, pizza, ravioli and strudels, washed down with their excellent beer (*pivo*) and wine. Immunisation against hepatitis, polio and typhoid is recommended.

The climate inland is continental, with warm summers and cold snowy winters, but along the Adriatic coast it is relatively mild all year round. The best time to visit Slovenia is during the summer when summer visitors join resident species such as Rock Partridge.

Over half of the country comprises sparsely populated forested and grazed limestone karst hills and mountains, rising to 2864 m (9396 ft) at Triglav in the Julijske Alps, in the northwest near the borders with Austria and Italy. There are also three major river valleys, one of which runs through the middle of the country, carved out by the River Sava, and a short stretch of coastal plain adjacent to the Adriatic, where there are remnant riverine forests, seasonally flooded meadows and some saltmarsh. Agricultural intensification, overgrazing and timber loss are the main problems facing the three threatened species as well as the relatively common and widespread birds which occur in Slovenia.

Over 350 species have been recorded in Slovenia, including 210 which have been known to breed and 192 which regularly occur during the winter. Notable species include Rock Partridge, Little Crake, Ural Owl, Collared Flycatcher, Wallcreeper, White-winged Snowfinch and Alpine Accentor. It is possible to see up to about 150 species on a visit lasting one to two weeks during the late spring and early summer.

The remnant peat bogs, farmland and seasonally flooded meadows in the area known as Ljubljansko barje, which lies either side of the Rivers Ljubljanica and Iscica on the edge of Slovenia's capital, **Ljubljana**, support Black Stork, Corn Crake* and Barred Warbler. Southwest from the capital, Corn Crake* also occurs in the seasonally flooded meadows around the large, eutrophic **Lake Cerknica**, where a few Ferruginous Ducks* and Little Crake breed, and spring passage migrants have included White-winged Tern. Further southwest, the salinas at Secovlje, and the small area of reedbeds (Moustached Warbler), intertidal mud and saltmarsh at the mouth of the **River Dragonja**, are well worth prolonged attention. West of Bled in extreme northwest Slovenia, Golden Eagle, Rock Partridge, Rock Ptarmigan, Black Grouse and Three-toed Woodpecker occur in the limestone mountains of the 840-km^2 **Triglav National Park**, along with chamois, ibex, Alpine marmot and mouflon.

East from the capital, Black Stork and Collared Flycatcher occur in the reserve at **Krakovski Forest** in central Slovenia. The rivers, wet meadows, marshes, ponds, deciduous and coniferous forests, and increasingly intensified farmland in northeast Slovenia—an area known as **Krakovski gozd**—support summer visitors such as White Stork, European Roller, Collared Flycatcher and Eurasian River Warbler, and large numbers of wintering waterbirds. The best areas are as follows: (i) along the River Drava between Maribor and Zavrc where the Ormoz and Ptuj reservoirs support up to 20,000 wintering waterbirds; (ii) part of the hilly region known as Slovenskih Goric, through which the Rivers Globovnica and Velka flow (European Roller); (iii) along the River Mura between Gibina and Verzej (Eurasian River Warbler); and (iv) the forest along the River Ledava, which is reputed to be the most extensive alder forest in central Europe (Collared Flycatcher). The best base for birding this part of Slovenia is Maribor. The extensive forests in the **Gorjanci Mountains**, in southeast Slovenia by the border with Croatia, support Ural Owl and White-backed Woodpecker.

ADDITIONAL INFORMATION

Addresses
Please send records of rarities to the Bird Watching and Bird Study Association of Slovenia, Langusova 10, SI-1000 Ljubljana, Slovenia (website: www.mobitel.si/eng/mbird_e.html). The annual rarities report is published in *Acrocephalus* with an English summary.

Books and papers
The Atlas of Breeding Birds in Slovenia. Geister I, 1995. Dravna zaloba Slovenije, Llubljana.
The Atlas of Wintering Birds in Slovenia. Sovinc A, 1994. Tehnika zaloba Slovenije, Llubljana.

SPAIN

INTRODUCTION

Summary

Spain is the most popular birding destination in Europe, thanks to its wealth of waterbirds, raptors, bustards, sandgrouse, high-altitude specialities and rare European breeding species, some of the region's most beautiful terrain and the wonderful weather, all of which can be soaked up without breaking the bank.

Size

At 504,880 km², Spain is Europe's second largest country. It is nearly four times the size of England and just over 75% the size of Texas.

Getting Around

The major air gateways to southern Spain are Alicante, Almería and Málaga, all of which are accessible on very cheap flights from many European countries. By using one of these or the nearby package holiday resorts as a base it is possible to see a great range of species, but they are all too far away from the top birding areas for comfortable daytrips, hence the best approach for birding Spain cheaply is to fly into one of the above resorts, hire a car, then head along the Costa del Sol and/or inland to the Coto Doñana and Extremadura, before returning to the point of arrival via the Pyrenées, the Zaragoza area and the Ebro Delta. Hiring a car is without doubt the best way to get around, since many of the best birding sites are in relatively remote areas, which are otherwise accessible only on a skeletal bus service, and the hire costs are, arguably, the cheapest in Europe, especially if booked in advance from outside the country. However, local driving standards are poor and a high percentage of birding crews return home with terrible tales of narrow escapes from nasty road accidents.

Accommodation and Food
Accommodation, listed here more or less in order of decreasing cost, includes paradores (state-run conversions of castles and other historic buildings), hotels, pensiones, guesthouses (*casas de huespedes*), youth hostels (*albergues juveniles*) and campsites. In addition, it is possible to camp off-road almost anywhere so long as the chosen site is at a reasonable distance from tourist beaches and habitations. The cheapest places to eat out are cafeterias, comedores and restaurants, although most bars offer a range of snacks including bocadillos (sandwiches) and tapas (a few chunks of fish or meat). Beer is more expensive than wine. Evening meals are rarely served before 2100 hours in many places.

Health and Safety
During the spring and summer lowland southern Spain is more often than not very, very hot, hence it is wise to take sunglasses, a sun hat and sunscreen, as well as insect repellent.

Climate and Timing
The climate in Spain is highly variable, ranging from the very wet mountains in the northwest to the driest area in Europe, at Cabo de Gata near Almería, on the southeast coast. However, apart from the Pyrenées, which experiences short warm summers and long cold winters, and some other mountain ranges, Spain is, on the whole, very dry, and has long, very hot summers and cool winters. Spring, especially late March to mid-April, is the best time for displaying bustards and singing Dupont's Larks (although this species may sing until early June), late April to early May is the peak time for passage migrants, and late May to early June is the best time for late summer visitors such as White-rumped Swift and a few more passage migrants. From mid-June to mid-August it is usually too hot, with temperatures rising regularly above 100°F, to enjoy birding all day, but by late August–early September it is usually cool enough again to visit the Pyrenées and this is one of the best times of the year to look for the high-altitude specialities of these mountains, since most high-altitude roads are usually blocked by snow until mid-May or even early June, preventing access to many of the best areas earlier in the year.

Habitats
Due to the presence of the Pyrenées, which rise to 3404 m (11,168 ft) at Pic de Aneto and extend for about 400 km from the Atlantic in the west to the Mediterranean in the east, along Spain's northern border with France, and the even higher Sierra Nevada, which rises to 3482 m (11,424 ft) at Mulhacen in the southeast, as well as extensive high interior plateaux, Spain has an average altitude of 660 m (2165 ft), the second highest in Europe, after Switzerland. Below the snow-capped peaks

of the Pyrénées there are glaciers, snowfields, scree and boulder-strewn slopes above the alpine pastures, coniferous forest, deciduous woods, scrubby hillsides and olive groves. Plateau and sierra slopes elsewhere in the country are primarily covered in Mediterranean vegetation such as garrigue, maquis and pine forest. Otherwise, much of interior Spain is rather arid and open with huge cereal fields and sparsely populated rolling steppe grasslands with open cork-oak woods (*dehesa*). Despite the presence of so many uplands there are few large rivers or natural lakes, and yet Spain has some immensely important wetlands, not least the Ebro Delta in the northeast and the Guadalquivir Delta, better known as the Coto Doñana, in the southwest. There are also some excellent wetlands, such as salinas, along the mainly narrow but densely populated, fertile eastern coastal plain, where the long beaches are lined by numerous tourist resorts.

Conservation

Spain is Europe's most important country for birds. It supports all of the region's Spanish Eagles*, 75% of the region's Bonelli's and Booted Eagles, 50% of the region's Egyptian Vultures, Eurasian Griffons and Cinereous Vultures*, and 33% of the region's Red Kites and Montagu's Harriers. It also probably supports more Little* and Great* Bustards than any other European country, and is the only country in Europe where White-headed Duck* and Marbled Teal* breed on a regular basis. All of these birds, some of which are included in the eleven threatened and near-threatened species which occur in the country, as well as the relatively common and widespread species, are under threat from habitat loss and degradation (especially through agricultural intensification), the invention of plastic corks which threatens the sustainable harvest of cork from the cork-oak woods (where birds such as Spanish Eagle* breed), hunting (empty shot-gun cartridges litter the countryside), disturbance, poisoning (78% of all Spanish Eagles* found dead since 1993 died from poisons), pollution and trapping (millions of birds are still caught using lime and sold abroad to be used in pâtés).

Bird Species

Notable species include (in southern Spain): White-headed Duck*, Marbled Teal*, Greater Flamingo, Black-shouldered Kite, Cinereous Vulture*, Purple Swamphen ('Western' *porphyrio*), Red-knobbed Coot, Little* and Great* Bustards, Audouin's* and Slender-billed Gulls, Pin-tailed and Black-bellied Sandgrouse, Great Spotted Cuckoo, Red-necked Nightjar, White-rumped Swift, Azure-winged Magpie, Spotless Starling, Rufous-tailed Scrub-Robin, Black Wheatear, Orphean and Spectacled Warblers, Lesser Short-toed, Dupont's and Thekla Larks, Spanish Sparrow, Alpine Accentor, Citril and Trumpeter Finches, and Rock Bunting, and in northern Spain, additional localised species such as; Lammergeier, Wallcreeper and White-winged Snowfinch.

Small Buttonquail (Andalusian Hemipode) used to be recorded from Málaga along the coast to Cádiz, as well as around Huelva (in coastal scrub between the Río Guadiana and the Río Odiel), and Seville, and a few may still remain in these areas.

Endemics

Spain is the only mainland European country with an endemic species. There are about 120 pairs of Spanish Eagle* (down from 150 in mid-

1990s), most of which are confined to the south and west of the country, and a few of which can be seen fairly easily.

Expectations

On a trip to the Coto Doñana and Extremadura which lasts a week or two during the spring it is possible to see 150–180 species. In northern Spain it is possible to see up to 200 species on a trip lasting a week or two during late May and early June, but fewer during the autumn. On a spring trip to the whole of Spain which lasts at least two weeks it is possible to see over 220 species.

ANDALUCÍA (SOUTHERN SPAIN)

ALMERÍA

Despite the fact that Almería is situated between the Costa del Sol and the Costa Blanca in southeast Spain this area of coastal salinas and semi-desert remains relatively free from mass tourism, and thanks to the presence of birds such as Audouin's Gull*, Dupont's Lark and Trumpeter Finch, which despite colonising the area in 1971 has yet to spread elsewhere in Europe, is an excellent place to go birding, as well as an ideal starting point for a trip to the rest of Spain.

The species listed below occur during the spring and early summer unless otherwise indicated.

Localised Specialities

White-headed Duck*, Marbled Teal*, Audouin's Gull*, Rufous-tailed Scrub-Robin, Dupont's Lark, Trumpeter Finch.

Other Localised Species

Greater Flamingo, Black-bellied Sandgrouse, Great Spotted Cuckoo, Spotless Starling, Black Wheatear, Lesser Short-toed and Thekla Larks.

Others

Cory's ('Scopoli's' *diomedea*) and Mediterranean (mainly 'Balearic' *mauretanicus*) Shearwaters, Cattle Egret, Squacco Heron, Black-crowned Night-Heron, Short-toed and Bonelli's Eagles, Lesser Kestrel*, Red-legged Partridge, Eurasian Thick-knee, Black-winged Stilt, Collared Pratincole, Snowy Plover, Whiskered (passage) and Gull-billed (passage) Terns, Eurasian Eagle-Owl, Alpine and Pallid Swifts, European Bee-eater, European Roller, Blue Rock-Thrush, Eurasian Crag-Martin, Red-rumped Swallow, Zitting Cisticola, Olivaceous, Orphean, Sardinian, Spectacled and Dartford Warblers, Calandra and Greater Short-toed Larks, Rock Petronia, Rock Bunting.
   (Other species recorded here include Small Buttonquail, Baillon's Crake (suitable habitat for this species can be found between Mojácar and Vera, north of Almería), Slender-billed Gull and Red-necked Nightjar.)

ALMERÍA

Almería is accessible by air from a number of European countries. Black-bellied Sandgrouse, Great Spotted Cuckoo, Rufous-tailed Scrub-Robin, Dupont's Lark and Trumpeter Finch occur in the arid 'spaghetti western' country of Campo de Níjar, Sierra Alhamilla and Sierra de Filabres, to the northeast of Almería. There are no stake-outs as such, but the following areas are worth concentrating on: (i) the **Tabernas** badlands, 25 km north of Almería, where Trumpeter Finch is occasionally seen on the hills reached by taking the track east of the entrance to 'Mini Hollywood', a popular tourist attraction; (ii) the **Campo de Níjar**, to the south of Níjar, is a large area which will probably need prolonged investigation; and (iii) the (usually) dry riverbed just south of **Rambla Honda**, north of Níjar towards Lucainena de las Torres, which is a particularly good place to look for Rufous-tailed Scrub-Robin.

The **Salinas de Cabo de Gata**, about 25 km southeast of Almería, regularly support up to 2,000 Greater Flamingos (breeding has been attempted), hundreds of Black-winged Stilts and Audouin's Gulls* (mostly in April), as well as occasional Slender-billed Gulls, while Spectacled Warbler (especially at the western end), and Lesser Short-toed and Thekla Larks occur around them. The salinas, which extend for several km, begin just south of the town of El Cabo de Gata, and they can be viewed from some excellent hides, the road to the cape, or via a track which runs along their northern edge. To look for Black-bellied Sandgrouse, Dupont's Lark and Trumpeter Finch near here turn east off the road between Retamar and El Cabo de Gata, between two bridges about 4 km north of El Cabo de Gata, on to a road leading to an airport beacon. Where this road bends north after about a km take the track leading straight on to the **Plain de Cabo de Gata** and start birding in earnest. The sandgrouse also occurs at the **Las Amoladeras** reserve, signposted inland from the salinas. South of the salinas the road reaches the **Cabo de Gata** which is a good place for seawatching (from the shelter by the lighthouse), Black Wheatear (in the rocky valley by the lighthouse) and Trumpeter Finch (at dawn), as well as passerine migrants. White-headed Duck* (up to 70 in winter), Greater Flamingo, shorebirds such as Collared Pratincole, roosting gulls, including Audouin's*, and Lesser Short-toed Lark occur in the saltmarshes, salinas and reedy lagoons along the coast between the small holiday resort of **Roquetas de Mar**, about 20 km southwest of Almería, and Punta Entinas. During the summer White-headed Duck* and Marbled Teal* are most likely to be found on the sunken pits at Canada de las Norias, alongside the road between Mojonera and Las Norias, and in July 1997 there were nearly 50 White-headed Ducks* on the **Lagunas de Adra** about 50 km west of Almería.

Accommodation: Roquetas de Mar—Hotel Sabinal (tel: 950 333600; fax: 950 333533). Mojácar—La Parata (bookable in advance through Kenneth Ward Resorts, The White House, Portsmouth Road, Thames Ditton, Surrey KT7 0SY, UK (tel: 0181 339 0010; fax: 0181 339 0444).

The isolated **Sierra Nevada** rises steeply from near the Costa del Sol to the highest point in Spain: 3482 m (11,424 ft) at Mulhacen, which is roughly halfway between Almería and Málaga. Its sparsely vegetated mountain slopes support Rufous-tailed Rock-Thrush, Black Wheatear and Alpine Accentor, as well as Golden and Bonelli's Eagles, Red-legged Partridge, Alpine Swift, Blue Rock-Thrush and Rock Bunting. To look for these birds head inland on the N323 from Motril towards Granada, then turn east on to the C333 to Orgiva. Bird alongside the minor road, which becomes a very rough track, from here to the viewpoint at Pico Veleta, beyond which the track becomes a road again as it descends to Granada.

Fifteen minutes before landing at Málaga on the Costa del Sol it is sometimes possible to see the pink shimmer of a Greater Flamingo colony from the aeroplane window. In the late 1990s around 16,000

SITES NEAR MÁLAGA

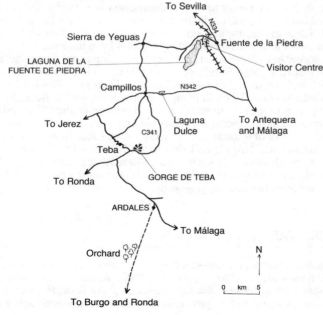

pairs were breeding on **Laguna de la Fuente de Piedra**, 24 km north-west of Antequera along the N334, which is just over an hour by road inland from the major tourist resort of Málaga, and this excellent reserve also supports breeding White-headed Duck* and up to 200 pairs of Gull-billed Tern, while several hundred Eurasian Thick-knees and small numbers of Slender-billed Gull occur during the winter, and the nearby marshes have attracted as many as 2,000 Black Terns during the spring. The large saline lake covers 14,000 ha when full, but even then it is very shallow and by midsummer much of it is usually a dazzling white salt-pan. Following a wet autumn and early winter period several thousand flamingos may be present by Christmas, when courting gets under way, and in good years such as 1998 a total of 13,387 chicks were counted in July. Breeding may also take place in dry years, but the adults have to feed elsewhere during such conditions. To reach the reserve visitor centre and hides head north from Antequera to the small town of Fuente de la Piedra, and once through the town turn west.

The **Gorge de Teba**, southwest of Fuente de la Piedra via Sierra de Yeguas and Campillos, supports Egyptian Vulture, Eurasian Griffon, Bonelli's Eagle, Alpine Swift, Black Wheatear and Rock Petronia. To look for such birds park by the bridge and walk up the steep side of the gorge until it is viewable from the west. From here head for **El Chorro** in the Embalse del Guadalteba-Guadalhorce where the pine woods alongside the road at the top of the valley west of town support Red-necked Nightjar. Near **Ardales**, south of Teba, Eurasian Eagle-Owl and Orphean Warbler have been recorded alongside the rough road to Burgo. Park by the deserted buildings about 7 km south of Ardales, check the crags for Eurasian Eagle-Owl, and scour the general area for Orphean Warbler. The town of **Ronda**, west of Burgo and about 35 km northwest of Marbella, is a popular tourist destination because it is situated on the edge of a 130-m (427 ft)-deep limestone chasm, an excellent place to see Lesser Kestrel*, Alpine and Pallid Swifts, and Eurasian Crag-Martin. Have a drink in the gorge-top garden at the Reina Christina and, while absorbing the remarkable scene, Lesser Kestrels* may be seen down to a few metres. Otherwise bird from the main bridge over the gorge, the gardens just north of the bullring and along the paths down into the gorge. Ronda is surrounded by some splendid mountains which support plenty of raptors, Eurasian Eagle-Owl, Black Wheatear, Orphean Warbler, Rock Bunting, and, in winter, Alpine Accentor. The best places to look for these birds are: (i) alongside the C339 west to El Bosque, including the minor roads leading south from it; (ii) the C341 southwest out of Ronda, including the minor roads to its west, such as the MA549 and MA511; and (iii) around Grazalema. Turn northwest here to reach Puerto de los Palomas where Alpine Accentor and Rock Bunting are usually easy to see in the car park during the winter. White-rumped Swift has also been recorded in this area.

GIBRALTAR

Gibraltar is an overcrowded 6.5-km² spectacular giant limestone rock which rises 427 m (1400 ft) out of the Mediterranean off the southern tip of Spain. Many birders visit here to see Barbary Partridge, which only occurs elsewhere in Europe on Sardinia, and to experience at least a little of the heaviest raptor passage in Europe. Such an experience may not just involve views of 'soaring dots' either, for in favourable weather conditions on Gibraltar it is possible to look many birds in the eye.

During the autumn almost twice as many birds pass over here than its nearest rival, the Bosphorus, including 100,000 more European Honey-buzzards, ten times as many Egyptian Vultures, five times as many Short-toed Eagles and 30 times as many Booted Eagles. In total, 25 species of raptor have been recorded making the 25-km crossing between Europe and Africa, the most numerous of which are European Honey-buzzard and Black Kite, which can often be seen in flocks containing hundreds of birds. During March, Black Kite is the dominant species (4,500–6,500 have been recorded between March and May), although this is also the best month for Osprey, Short-toed Eagle and Lesser Kestrel*. Species diversity usually reaches a peak in late March, when 15 species may be seen in a single day, but the quantity of birds rises in April when as many as 1,000 may pass over in a single day. By May most migrants are European Honey-buzzards. Numbers are even higher during the autumn when the greatest diversity of species passes through in late September.

Localised Specialities
Barbary Partridge (introduced).

Regular Passage Migrants
Cory's ('Scopoli's' *diomedea*) and Mediterranean (mainly 'Balearic' *mauretanicus*) Shearwaters, Black and White Storks, Osprey, European Honey-buzzard, Red and Black Kites, Egyptian Vulture, Eurasian Griffon, Short-toed and Booted Eagles, Lesser Kestrel*.

Regular Summer Visitors
Alpine and Pallid Swifts.

Resident Species
Blue Rock Thrush, Sardinian Warbler.

Other Wildlife
Barbary ape (introduced), bottlenose, common and striped dolphins, harbour porpoise, pilot whale.

(Other species recorded here include Greater Spotted Eagle*, Audouin's Gull*, Great Spotted Cuckoo, Rufous-tailed Scrub-Robin and Orphean Warbler.)

Westerly winds are the best for observing raptor migration and one of the top spots to scan from is the **Upper Rock Reserve**, with a visitor centre and a nature trail leading to the south-facing cliffs which, in favourable conditions, afford wonderful views of migrating raptors. Barbary Partridge has been recorded on the bushy hillsides by the reserve car park, but the best place for this species is around St Bernard's Chapel, especially during the evening. The best place to seawatch from is **Europa Point**, and apart from possibilities such as Audouin's Gull*, common dolphins may be present in schools up to 100 strong, especially between May and September when they breed around the rock. There are regular boat trips to see them at close quarters. For details contact

FIRMM, Pedro Cortés 3, near San Mateo church, Tarifa, Spain (tel: 95 662 7008).

The Strait of Gibraltar Bird Observatory (SGBO), established by the Gibraltar Ornithological and Natural History Society (GONHS, PO Box 843, Gibraltar (tel: 72639; fax: 74022; email: gonhs@gibnet.gi)) in 1987, welcomes volunteers willing to help them monitor passage. To help, contact Programa MIGRES, Sociedad Espanola de Ornitologia (SEO), C/Miguel Bravo Ferrer, 25 bajo, E-41005, Sevilla, Spain (tel/fax: 95 464 4294; email: migres@seo.org). Free accommodation and food is provided.

Birders determined to avoid the terrible traffic on Gibraltar may wish to look for raptors and seabirds from **Punta de Carnero** on the opposite side of Algeciras Bay to the rock, especially during westerly winds. Whatever the wind direction thousands of storks and raptors pass over the coast near **Tarifa** during the autumn and the best place to scan the skies here is the Mirador de Estrecho, a popular viewpoint with a large car park and cafe about 7 km east of Tarifa. Birders who prefer more peaceful surroundings should take the track north from the main road 100 m towards Tarifa. The beach north of Tarifa, reached via the car park next to the stadium, 1 km north of town, and then by walking north and west, attracts Audouin's Gull*.

COSTA DE LA LUZ

The cliffs, beaches, estuaries, salinas, farmland, wooded valleys and rocky ridges along the Andalucian coast between Algeciras and Cádiz at the southern tip of Spain support the highly localised White-rumped Swift, as well as many other typical southern Iberian species. The swifts are summer visitors which rarely arrive before the end of May or the beginning of June, and the species listed below occur during the summer period after this time of year, unless otherwise indicated.

Localised Specialities
Audouin's Gull*, White-rumped Swift.

Other Localised Species
Red-necked Nightjar, Spotless Starling, Lesser Short-toed and Thekla Larks.

Others
Cory's ('Scopoli's' *diomedea*) and Mediterranean (mainly 'Balearic' *mauretanicus*) Shearwaters, Cattle Egret, White Stork, Egyptian Vulture, Eurasian Griffon, Short-toed, Golden, Bonelli's and Booted Eagles, Lesser Kestrel*, Common Crane (winter), Collared Pratincole, Alpine and Pallid Swifts, European Bee-eater, European Roller, Blue Rock-Thrush, Red-rumped Swallow, Olivaceous, Orphean and Sardinian Warblers, Calandra and Greater Short-toed Larks, Rock Bunting.

(Other species recorded here include passage and rare wintering raptors such as Black-shouldered Kite, Greater Spotted* and Spanish* Eagles, as well as Cinereous Vulture*, Little* and Great* Bustards, Pintailed Sandgrouse, Caspian Tern and Little Swift, up to five of which were recorded in the Sierra de la Plata near Bolonia during summers 1996–98.)

SIERRA DE LA PLATA

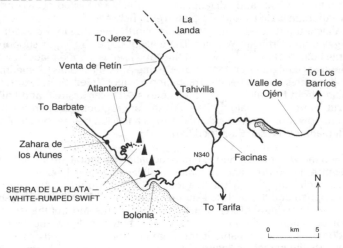

The **Valle de Ojén**, which is traversed by the very poor minor road (CA221) between Facinas and Los Barríos, west of Algeciras, is excellent for raptors and a good place to look for White-rumped Swift (especially around the KM 22 marker). The farmland east of the N340 north of Facinas, known as **La Janda**, supports a few highly elusive bustards, Pin-tailed Sandgrouse and, in winter, a few hundred Common Cranes and rare wandering raptors. In 1964 the first breeding colony of White-rumped Swifts in Europe was located in the **Sierra de la Plata**, a rocky ridge east of Zahara, and this European rarity still breeds here, in old nests of Red-rumped Swallows, at the end of the narrow, winding road up from Zahara to the villa complex known as Atlanterra. Park carefully at the end of this road where there is a gate and walk up the track. The best time of day to look for them is during the evening when they tend to feed lower down. Alpine and Pallid Swifts, and Rock Bunting also occur here. White-rumped Swifts have also been seen at the southern end of the Sierra de la Plata near Bolonia, as well as Pallid and Little (see above) Swifts.

White-rumped Swift is one of Europe's rarest birds, but it can usually be seen from late May until September in the Sierra de la Plata in southernmost Spain

From the bridge over the estuary just south of **Barbate** it is possible to scan the mudflats and adjacent salinas which are visited occasionally by Audouin's Gull* and Caspian Tern. Between Barbate and Cape Trafalgar the roadside pine woods are worth checking for Red-necked Nightjar and Orphean Warbler. The cliffs of **Cape Trafalgar** support a large colony of Cattle Egrets and the cape itself is a good place to look for passage migrants and seabirds. Passing Audouin's Gulls* sometimes stop for a rest on the beach. The hilltop town of **Vejer de la Frontera**, inland from Barbate, is a good place to see Lesser Kestrel* and Pallid Swift. Further north along the coast the open ground around a white round tower on the west side of the road a few km before **Puerto Real** often attracts Lesser Short-toed Lark.

When the water levels and extent of aquatic vegetation are suitable the **Laguna de Medina** and the other small lagunas near Jerez in western Andalucía support White-headed Duck*, Marbled Teal*, Purple Swamphen and the odd Red-knobbed Coot, as well as Collared Pratincole and passing Whiskered and Gull-billed Terns. Most of the lagunas can be reached via the new C440 road between Jerez and Medina Sidonia. The most reliable is the Laguna de Medina, together with its tiny satellite known as Laguna Istata, which is signposted 10 km southeast of Jerez (30 km northwest of Medina Sidonia). Scan the lagoon from the trail which runs along the south shore from the car park, looking out for Red-knobbed Coots, which don't usually associate closely

ALGAIDA AREA

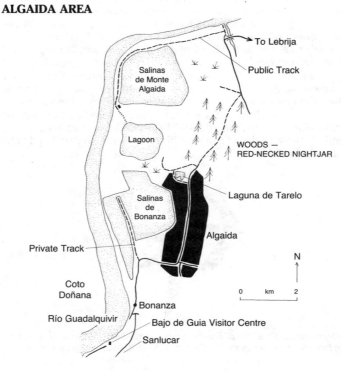

with the masses of Eurasian Coots, especially at the western end. Laguna Istata, which is usually a better place to look for Purple Swamphen, is on the west side of the C440 about 1 km further north, beyond a cement plant. One of the most reliable sites for Red-knobbed Coot is the **Lagunas de Espera**, reached by turning east off the N4 onto the C447 towards Espera. Keep left at the fork 3 km after leaving the N4, turn right at the first crossroads after the 2 km post (in Cadiz Province), then right again at the next crossroads, from where it is 4.6 km to the warden's hut. Continue past here and park by the gate, then walk past the gate and view the two lagoons on the right, where White-headed Duck* and Marbled Teal* also occur.

Northwest of Jerez, White-headed Duck*, Audouin's* and Slender-billed Gulls, Caspian Tern, Red-necked Nightjar and Lesser Short-toed Lark all occur in the **Algaida Area**, on the east side of the Río Guadal-quivir and the Coto Doñana. This can be a superb birding area but getting on-the-spot permission to cover the place thoroughly is not guaranteed, so it is best to arrange a visit in advance by contacting Aprove-chamientos Marinos SA, Apartado de Carreos 111, 11540 Sanlucar de Barrameda, Cádiz, Spain. Otherwise, call in at the director's office at the Salinas de Bonanza and turn on maximum persuasive powers. Fortunately, many birds can be seen from the public track (at the bottom of, not on top of, the embankment) which runs along the northern and western edges of the Salinas de Monte Algaida, north of the Salinas de Bonanza, and it is even possible to see Spanish Eagle* from here, soaring over the Coto Doñana to the west of the Río Guadalquivir. There are also organised boat trips from Bajo de Guia, south of Bonanza on the outskirts of Sanlucar, into the Coto Doñana which call in at some of the salinas.

BRAZO DEL ESTE

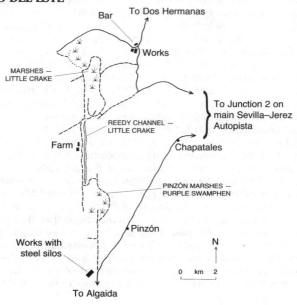

One of the few known Spanish sites for Little Crake is **Brazo del Este** which is accessible via Los Palacios y Villafranca and nearby Pinzón, accessible from Junction 2 of the Jerez–Sevilla autopista. To reach the Pinzón Marshes take the track north, signposted 'Izquierda del Este', 3 km southwest of Pinzón. A couple of km along here the track runs along an embankment above a marsh which when wet may be full of Purple Swamphens, and graced with smaller numbers of Glossy Ibis and Black Stork. To the north the track runs along a reedy channel, worth checking for crakes, before reaching another marsh which when wet supports Little Crake, as well as Squacco Heron, Black Stork, Spotted Crake, Purple Swamphen and Collared Pratincole. This marsh is also accessible from the north, via the road to Isla Mayor.

COTO DOÑANA

The beaches, dunes, scrub, cork-oak and stone pine woods, and marshes and lagoons of the 2300-km² Coto Doñana, alias the Guadalquivir Delta (Europe's second largest), or Las Marismas, form what is arguably the richest area for birds in Europe. Over 340 species, including 140 residents, have been recorded, although it is the sheer quantity of breeding, wintering and passage waterbirds which make the Coto Doñana such a special place. In normal circumstances seasonal flooding during the late autumn and winter leads to the formation of extensive areas of shallow water, known as marismas, which gradually dry out during the course of spring and summer, leaving plenty of pools and lots of mud which provide an incredibly rich food source for breeding species such as Purple Swamphen, hundreds of pairs of Little Egrets and Purple Herons, 350 pairs of Eurasian Spoonbills, over 1,000 pairs of Black-winged Stilts, 350 pairs of Pied Avocets, hundreds of pairs of Collared Pratincoles and Snowy Plovers, and one of Europe's greatest concentrations of raptors, including nine pairs of Spanish Eagle*. During the winter almost half a million waterbirds may be present, including 69,000 Greylag Geese, 126,000 Common Teals, 40,000 Northern Pintails, up to 600 Marbled Teals*, up to 10,000 Greater Flamingos and 20,000 Black-tailed Godwits. In addition, masses of migrants pass through during the spring and autumn, hence part of the area has been designated as a biosphere reserve, a national park and a world heritage site.

These afford little protection, however, in a country where the government consistently fails to absorb what conservationists have been telling them for decades. The Coto Doñana is one of, if not *the*, most important wetland in Europe, and yet problems such as pollution, proposed roads and the over-exploitation of the groundwater supplies, through the intensification of agriculture on reclaimed marismas and tourist resort developments such as those at adjacent Matalascanas, continually raise their ugly heads out of the marismas, only to be totally ignored by the authorities. Birders can only hope that the toxic mudslide which flowed across part of the area from a waste reservoir 40 km upstream in April 1998 will convince the government that they must address this potentially catastrophic cock-up and all the other aforementioned issues with the appropriate amount of vigour, in order to ensure that the Coto Doñana remains a paradise for birds and birders.

The species listed below occur during the spring and summer unless otherwise indicated.

Spanish Endemics

Spanish Eagle*.

Localised Specialities

Marbled Teal*, Purple Swamphen, Audouin's* and Slender-billed Gulls.

Other Localised Species

Greater Flamingo, Pin-tailed Sandgrouse, Great Spotted Cuckoo, Red-necked Nightjar, Azure-winged Magpie, Spotless Starling, Lesser Short-toed and Thekla Larks.

Others

Ferruginous Duck*, Cattle Egret, Squacco Heron, Black-crowned Night-Heron, Little Bittern, Eurasian Spoonbill, Glossy Ibis, White Stork, Egyptian Vulture, Eurasian Griffon, Short-toed and Booted Eagles, Black-winged Stilt, Pied Avocet, Collared Pratincole, Snowy Plover, Whiskered and Gull-billed Terns, Pallid Swift, European Bee-eater, Red-rumped Swallow, Zitting Cisticola, Moustached, Olivaceous, Orphean, Sardinian, Subalpine and Spectacled Warblers, Calandra and Greater Short-toed Larks.

(Other species recorded here include White-headed Duck*, Western Reef-Egret (dark morph still present in August 1999), Black-shouldered Kite, Cinereous Vulture*, Greater Spotted Eagle* (winter), Lesser Kestrel*, Little Crake, Red-knobbed Coot, Marsh Sandpiper, European Roller and Rufous-tailed Scrub-Robin. Captive waterfowl, prone to escaping, include Marbled Teal*, Red-crested Pochard and Ferruginous Duck*. Other wildlife present but rarely seen include small-spotted genet, pardel lynx, Egyptian mongoose and Lataste's viper.)

The national park HQ and main visitor centre are at **El Acebuche**, reached by turning south off the Sevilla–Huelva autopista to El Rocio, then continuing further south towards Matalascanas for 10 km. There are hides overlooking prime Purple Swamphen habitat here (especially Laguna de los Pajaros), and other birds present include Red-necked Nightjar (on nearby tracks at dusk) and Azure-winged Magpie (at picnic tables next to the car park), while Audouin's* and Slender-billed Gulls are possible along the coast at **Matalascanas**, a tourist resort 6 km south of El Acebuche. However, most birders begin their Coto experience at the whitewashed 'wild west' town of **El Rocio** where the marismas to the south can be scanned from the town or from the nearby bridge on the C435. Nearby, Purple Swamphen may be seen from the hides overlooking the well-vegetated marismas alongside the 2.5-km nature trail which begins at the **La Rocina** visitor centre. One of the top birding areas is the **Coto del Rey** to the east of El Rocio. The easiest way to reach here is to head north from El Rocio on the main road for about 2.5 km then turn east, just after KM Post 13, towards Villamanrique. After 16 km along here take the east fork in response to the 'Bar Polideportivo' signpost, then follow the map on p. 346. This whole area is a good place to look for Marbled Teal* (especially on Lucio Cerrado Garrido in front of the visitor centre, which also has a large heronry and a colony of Glossy Ibis), Squacco Heron, Purple Swamphen, Collared

**COTO
DOÑANA**

Pratincole, Pin-tailed Sandgrouse, Azure-winged Magpie and Lesser Short-toed Lark. Other, remoter, possibilities include Spanish Eagle* and Red-knobbed Coot (has bred on Lucio Cerrado Garrido). Beware of soft sand when cruising around this area. Since it is possible to see virtually all of the Coto birds outside the core of the **Parque Nacional de Doñana**, which is accessible only on expensive, breakneck, four-hour, 4WD, official excursions around an 80-km-long loop, geared towards tourists rather than birders, there is not much point going there, although it is where the main colonies of egrets and herons are, and the most reliable part of the Coto for Spanish Eagle*. For details ask at El Acebuche or, better still, book in advance through the Reserva Biologica de Doñana, Crta. de Matalascanas s/n, Apartado de correos No. 4, 21760 Matalascanas, Almonte, Huelva (tel: 959 440032; fax: 959 440033).

Accommodation: El Rocio. Matalascanas—Hotel Tierra Mar (complete with beach and swimming pool) and Torre de la Higuera Campsite, 1 km west of the resort crossroads (complete with Red-necked Nightjar).

Birders *en route* between the Coto Doñana and the Algarve in Portugal may wish to stop at the fortified hilltop of **Niebla**, northeast of Huelva, where there is a Lesser Kestrel* colony, and at **las Marismas del Odiel y su Entorno**, just southwest of Huelva, where 293 species have been recorded. The area supports Greater Flamingo and a large colony of Eurasian Spoonbills (300 pairs in good years), while it is worth seawatching for Audouin's Gull* and Caspian Tern.

346

Northeast of the Coto Doñana *en route* to Madrid, White-headed Duck*, Greater Flamingo and Purple Swamphen occur on the series of artificial and natural freshwater and saline lakes about 45 km south of Cordoba, accessible via the C329. They include the reserves at **Laguna de Zonar**, where there is a visitor centre, and **Laguna de Rincón**, where there is a hide, which, when wet, are two of the most important breeding sites in Spain for White-headed Duck*. Laguna de Zonar lies near the C329 about 4 km southwest of Aguilar. To scan it turn west opposite the visitor centre on to a track which runs along part of the north shore. The tiny Laguna de Rincón can be reached by turning south off the N331 between Monturque and Aguilar towards Moriles. Five km along here turn west to the reserve.

EXTREMADURA (WEST-CENTRAL SPAIN)

The sparsely populated rolling farmland, steppe grassland and open cork-oak woods with granite outcrops of Extremadura, about 250 km west of Madrid and 300 km north of Sevilla, is the most important area in the country for Black-shouldered Kite, Little Bustard* (an estimated 20,000 birds, which occur in loose flocks of up to 1,000), Great Bustard* (over 500 birds, which occur in loose flocks of up to 70), Pin-tailed Sandgrouse (thousands) and Black-bellied Sandgrouse (hundreds). During the winter the area also supports what is probably the largest concentration of Common Cranes in western Europe (up to 25,000 birds). Along with Kori Bustard of Africa the male Great Bustard*, which is twice the size of the female and can weigh up to 18 kg, is the heaviest flying bird in the world. They look particularly impressive when displaying, usually during early spring mornings in March and April, when they transform themselves into a mass of silky white plumes. Together with the birds already mentioned and the likes of bee-eaters and rollers adorning the wooded streamcourses, the big bustards complete what is delightful birding country.

The birds listed below occur during the summer unless otherwise indicated.

Localised Specialities
Black-shouldered Kite, Great Bustard*.

Other Localised Species
Pin-tailed and Black-bellied Sandgrouse, Great Spotted Cuckoo, Azure-winged Magpie, Spotless Starling.

Others
Cattle Egret, Black-crowned Night-Heron, Black and White Storks, Egyptian Vulture, Eurasian Griffon, Short-toed, Golden and Booted Eagles, Lesser Kestrel*, Common Crane (winter), Little Bustard*, Eurasian Thick-knee, Collared Pratincole, Pallid Swift, European Bee-eater, European Roller, Red-rumped Swallow, Calandra Lark.
(Other species recorded here include Spanish Sparrow.)

EXTREMADURA

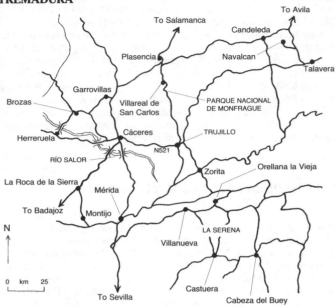

One of the best ways to bird the Spanish steppes is to cruise the smaller roads and tracks, some of which are very rough and barely passable in a 2WD. At Mérida (where Pallid Swift may be seen from the roman bridge) turn east to reach the 1000-km² upland plain known as **La Serena** where the best area for bustards and sandgrouse is the 'triangle' formed by Castuera, Cabeza del Buey and Orellana la Vieja. The northern shore of the reservoir near Orellana is good for raptors and wintering cranes and the roads north from Orellana to Trujillo via Madrigalejo and Zorita pass through good Black-shouldered Kite country. Over 100 Lesser Kestrels* have been recorded at one time over the small town of **Trujillo** where White Stork and Pallid Swift also breed around the square in the old town. To look for bustards near here head towards Madrid on the old main road for 3 km then turn right, 200 m east of the Hotel Peru, to the village of **Belen** and scan the roadside beyond there. Back on the old main road to Madrid continue for a further 11 km, then turn east to Torrecillas de la Tiesa to reach more good habitat, especially via tracks leading south. The steppe around the sprawling town of Cáceres, west of Trujillo, is also well worth birding, especially the plain of the **Río Salor** to the southwest. To reach here turn southwest off the N630 (between Mérida and Cáceres) about 7 km south of Cáceres, on to a track, south of Valdesalor and just north of a bridge over the Río Salor, which leads to a railway line and the plain beyond (beware of dangerous old bridges and fast trains), or, alternatively, scan west from the railway station, accessible by road. At least 2,000 Little Bustards* were present on the plain in February 1995 and over 50 Great Bustards* have been seen west of the railway line at any one time.

Other areas worth scanning for bustards include the following: (i) alongside the N521 just east of Cáceres towards Sierra de Fuentes; (ii)

348

alongside the loop north of the N521 which rejoins this road further east towards Trujillo, via Santa Marta de Magastra; (iii) alongside the tracks linking the C520 and N630 north of the Embalse del Salor; and (iv) alongside the tracks linking the N630 and N523. Northwest of Cáceres towards the upper Río Tejo on the border with Portugal (p. 288) between 800 and 1,000 Great Bustards* are believed to be present, along with both sandgrouse, in the steppe grasslands between Membrío and **Brozas**. Spanish Sparrow has been recorded around the ruins about one km south of Brozas towards Herreruela. East of Brozas along the road to Garrovillas look out for the bustards from the high point about 500 m out of town, Black-shouldered Kite near the small lake after a few km and European Roller a few km before the turning on to the N630.

Accommodation: La Serena; Castuera del Buey—Hotel Los Naranjos. Trujillo and Cáceres—plenty to choose from.

The distinctive Black-shouldered Kite is one of the top birds in Extremadura

PARQUE NACIONAL DE MONFRAGUE

'Monfragway', as it is pronounced, is arguably the best place in Europe to see raptors, including Cinereous Vulture*, which is believed to be more common here than anywhere else on earth, and Spanish Eagle*. The park, which straddles a precipitous ridge running roughly west to east alongside the Río Tajo north of Trujillo, also supports Egyptian Vulture, Eurasian Griffon and all four other eagles which occur in Spain. It is possible to see the whole lot in a single day, if not a single hour, as well as Black Stork and White-rumped Swift, so any Spanish trip would be sadly incomplete without visiting this fantastic site.

The species listed below occur during the summer unless otherwise indicated.

Spanish Endemics
Spanish Eagle*.

Localised Specialities
Cinereous Vulture*, White-rumped Swift, Spanish Sparrow.

Other Localised Species

Great Spotted Cuckoo, Red-necked Nightjar, Azure-winged Magpie, Black Wheatear, Thekla Lark.

Others

Black and White Storks, Red and Black Kites, Egyptian Vulture, Eurasian Griffon, Short-toed, Golden, Bonelli's and Booted Eagles, Little Bustard*, Eurasian Thick-knee, Eurasian Eagle-Owl, Alpine and Pallid Swifts, European Bee-eater, European Roller, Red-billed Chough, Blue Rock-Thrush, Eurasian Crag-Martin, Red-rumped Swallow, Orphean, Sardinian and Subalpine Warblers, Rock Petronia, Rock Bunting.

(Other species recorded nearby include Black-shouldered Kite.)

The open cork-oak woods alongside the 50-km C524 road from Trujillo north to Monfrague support Great Spotted Cuckoo, European Roller, Azure-winged Magpie and Orphean Warbler, while on the approach to the park Cinereous Vultures* may be seen soaring overhead and there is a small colony of Spanish Sparrows in the valley (usually up from the road) signposted Arroyo de la Vid, north of Torrejon el Rubio. **Castillo de Monfrague** is the next place to head to, because this is one of the best places to watch raptors in Europe. Black Stork and Eurasian Griffon breed on the rocky pinnacle, known as Penafalcon, on the opposite side of the valley, and virtually anything else that soars may drift over. North of the turning to Castillo de Monfrague the C524 reaches the Río Tajo bridge (a good place to look for Alpine Swift and Rock Petronia) and then the park HQ at Villareal de San Carlos, where it is worth asking for the latest details on where it may be possible to see the nests of Cinereous Vulture*, Black-shouldered Kite and Spanish Eagle*. For example, in the late 1990s it was possible to see the nests of Cinereous Vulture* and Spanish Eagle* on the same wooded ridge viewable from the Mirador La Bascular. Otherwise head east from Villareal along the north side of the **Embalse de Torrejon** reservoir where Black Storks, Egyptian Vultures, Eurasian Griffons and Eurasian Eagle-Owls nest on

PARQUE NACIONAL DE MONFRAGUE

the rockfaces, and Cinereous Vultures* can be seen drifting over. This road descends into a valley towards La Bazagona where the cork-oak woods support Black-shouldered Kite and Azure-winged Magpie.

Spanish Eagles* (nesting on pylons) may also be seen along the road west from Torrejon el Rubio to Cáceres, especially by the village of **Monroy**, about 25 km west of Torrejon. Where this road crosses Río Almonte, west of Monroy, look out for Spanish Sparrow.

Accommodation: Pension Monfrague, Paseo Pizarro 25, 10694 Torrejon el Rubio, Cáceres, Spain (tel: 927 455026). Campsite—just north of the Parque Nacional near Estacion de Palazuelo (Red-necked Nightjar).

The huge Cinereous Vulture is one of the many raptors which can be seen with some ease at Monfrague*

CENTRAL SPAIN

Between Trujillo and Madrid in central Spain the roads off the N501 surrounding **Navalcan** and Rositarío pass through cork-oak woods which support Black-shouldered Kite, Spanish Eagle* and Azure-winged Magpie. The rugged, snow-capped **Sierra de Gredos**, which rises to 2592 m (8504 ft) at Pico de Almanzor, north of Navalcan, supports extensive pine forest and alpine-like pastures where Cinereous Vulture* and Spanish Eagle* occur in important numbers, along with Eurasian Griffon, Booted Eagle, Great Spotted Cuckoo, Red-necked Nightjar, Rufous-tailed and Blue Rock-Thrushes, the largest population of Bluethroats ('White-spotted' *cyanecula*) in Spain (in broome thickets on otherwise open slopes), Black Wheatear, Orphean and Spectacled Warblers, Alpine Accentor, Citril Finch and Rock Bunting, as well as Spanish ibex. Bird alongside the minor roads leading out of Arenas de San Pedro, especially those to the north and west, but take care off the beaten track because it is forbidden to carry binoculars, telescopes and long camera lenses in certain key wilderness areas of these mountains. The small town of Navarredonda de Gredos or Candeleda would make good bases for birding these mountains.

At least 20 pairs of Spanish Eagle* are thought to survive in the **Sierra de Guadarrama**, the mountain range northwest of Madrid which rises to 2469 m (8100 ft) at Penalara near Segovia. This range also supports a few pairs of Black Stork, Cinereous Vulture*, Rufous-tailed Rock-Thrush and Citril Finch (around the ski-lift at Puerto de los Cotos, northwest of Segovia via the N607, Jardines and the C604).

South of Madrid in the La Mancha region, about 25 km northeast of Ciudad Real, lies the **Las Tablas de Daimiel**, a national park which was established to protect seasonally flooded marshes which support huge numbers of ducks, especially Red-crested Pochard, as well as Common Crane (winter), Collared Pratincole, Whiskered and Gull-billed Terns, Moustached Warbler and Spanish Sparrow (which roost in the reedbeds). The huge cereal fields surrounding the park support Little* and Great* Bustards, and Pin-tailed Sandgrouse. Turn west off the Sevilla–Madrid road at Manzanares (if arriving from the south) or Puerto-Lapiche (if arriving from the north) to Daimiel, from where the park, with visitor centre, nature trails and hides, is signposted to the northwest. There is accommodation in Daimiel. To the northeast of here via Alcazar, White-headed Duck* occurs on the **Laguna de Pedro Munoz**, near Mota del Cuervo on the N301 southeast of Madrid.

NORTHERN SPAIN

Southwest of Santander on Spain's northwest coast, accessible via vehicular ferries from England which cross the Bay of Biscay (p. 69), the deep forested gorges and jagged limestone peaks, which rise to 2648 m (8688 ft) at Torre de Cerrado, in the often wet and misty **Picos de Europa**, support Eurasian Griffon, Black Woodpecker, Red-billed and Yellow-billed Choughs, Wallcreeper (between Fuente Dé (reached by cable-car from nearby Espinama) and Refugio de Aliva), Chiffchaff ('Iberian' *brehmii*), Bonelli's Warbler ('Western' *bonelli*), White-winged Snowfinch (between Fuente Dé and Refugio de Aliva) and Alpine Accentor. The areas around Las Arenas and Canales, in the north, and Espinama and Potes, in the south, are, arguably, the best.

The largest population of Dupont's Larks in Europe (2,000-3,000 pairs) inhabits the barren limestone lands between Madrid and Zaragoza, and the area around **Baraona**, north of Medinaceli which is situated on the N11, is one of the best places to look for this elusive species.

ZARAGOZA AREA

The dry steppe near the sprawling city of Zaragoza in northeast Spain supports several hundred pairs of Dupont's Lark and other steppe specialists such as both sandgrouse, and the largest natural lake in Spain, Laguna de Gallocanta, attracts one of the largest autumn and early winter concentrations of Common Cranes in Europe (up to 28,000), as well as internationally important numbers of wintering waterfowl, including 75% of the Western Palearctic population of Red-crested Pochards (over 8,000).

The birds listed below occur during the summer unless otherwise indicated.

Localised Specialities
Dupont's Lark.

Other Localised Species

Pin-tailed and Black-bellied Sandgrouse, Great Spotted Cuckoo, Spotless Starling, Black Wheatear, Lesser Short-toed and Thekla Larks.

Others

Red-crested Pochard, White Stork, Egyptian Vulture, Eurasian Griffon, Short-toed Eagle, Lesser Kestrel*, Red-legged Partridge, Common Crane (most in autumn and early winter), Little Bustard*, Eurasian Thick-knee, European Bee-eater, Spectacled Warbler, Calandra and Greater Short-toed Larks, Rock Petronia.

The two main areas for Dupont's Lark are as follows: (i) the **Lomazas Steppe** reserve which lies to the east of the C222 Mediana–Belchite road, southeast of Zaragoza. No vehicles are allowed on this fragile reserve so it is necessary to look for the larks on foot. They have been seen within 200 m of the car park but they are likely to prove much more elusive than that, for this is one of the hardest birds to see on earth. They favour the flat tops of low hillocks (*lomazas*) near outcrops of white chalky rocks and are most likely to be located (but not necessarily seen) at the crack of dawn when they are singing. Vocal territorial activity peaks in late March and early April, but they can still be heard up to at least early June, and by watching them return to the ground after their songflights, the best area to search can be pinpointed. Look out for the birds feeding, or more likely, sprinting, between scattered clumps of low vegetation; and (ii) at **Los Monegros**, north of Osera. From Osera (look out for the White Stork's nest on the church spire) head north, fork left at the hut with red pipes sticking out of the ground, keep right at the farm and church, and, after passing under the electricity wires and a farm in a dip on the right, scour the area to the right. Head further north to look for isolated pools which have attracted up to 700 Pin-tailed and Black-bellied Sandgrouse.

ZARAGOZA, LERIDA and EBRO DELTA

During the spring and autumn most of the Common Cranes which breed in northeastern Europe and northwestern Russia stop to rest and feed at the **Laguna de Gallocanta** reserve, about 70 km southwest of Belchite and about 30 km northwest of Monreal del Campo. During the late autumn the majority of cranes usually move on (to Extremadura or North Africa) for the winter, but in some years many overwinter here. To visit the reserve it is necessary to obtain a permit (from the address given below), but the lake where the cranes roost can be viewed from near the village of Gallocanta. The scrubby hills and neglected fields to the southeast of the lake support Little Bustard* and Pin-tailed Sandgrouse (which visit the lake at dusk to bathe and drink).

For more information on Lomazas Steppe and Laguna de Gallocanta reserves contact Servicio Provincial de Agricultura, Ganaderia y Montes, Seccion de Conservacion del Medio Natural, C/. Vasques de Mella, No. 10, 50009 Zaragoza, Spain.

Accommodation: Daroca—hotel (basic) and hostel (basic). Osera.

The plains and rocky outcrops around **Lérida** (Lleida), about half way between Zaragoza and Barcelona, support Black-shouldered Kite (two pairs in 1998) and Dupont's Lark, as well as Egyptian Vulture, Lesser Kestrel*, Little Bustard* (around Aspa), Pin-tailed and Black-bellied Sandgrouse, Great Spotted Cuckoo, Red-necked Nightjar, Alpine and Pallid Swifts, Lesser Grey Shrike (around Aspa), Black Wheatear, Spectacled Warbler, and Lesser Short-toed and Thekla Larks. The whole area is worth birding but if time is short try along the rough track which leads southeast off the Candasnos–Alcolea de Cinca road, a few km south of Ontinena (this area is sometimes referred to as **Aragones Monegros**).

SPANISH PYRENÉES

The Pyrenées extend for about 400 km from the Atlantic in the west to the Mediterranean in the east and rise to 3404 m (11,168 ft) at Pic de Aneto in Spain. This is splendid birding country, with clearwater streams and rivers running down from jagged snow-capped peaks through scree, boulder fields and montane meadows to silver fir and Scots pine forests, deciduous woods, rather arid scrubby hillsides (compared to the lusher French foothills, p. 188) and olive groves, all completed by such brilliant birds as Lammergeier, Wallcreeper and White-winged Snowfinch.

The species listed below occur during the summer unless otherwise indicated.

Localised Specialities
Lammergeier.

Other Localised Species
Black Wheatear, Wallcreeper, White-winged Snowfinch, Citril Finch.

Others
Egyptian Vulture, Eurasian Griffon, Short-toed, Golden, Bonelli's and Booted Eagles, Red-legged Partridge, Eurasian Eagle-Owl, Alpine Swift,

European Bee-eater, Black Woodpecker, Red-billed and Yellow-billed Choughs, Rufous-tailed and Blue Rock-Thrushes, Eurasian Crag-Martin, Orphean, Sardinian and Subalpine Warblers, Rock Petronia, Alpine Accentor, Rock Bunting.

Other Wildlife

Chamois, Alpine marmot, beech and pine martens, Eurasian otter. Late June and early July is the best time for plants and butterflies, when it is possible to see many of the 50 or so endemic plants and 70–80 species of butterfly (out of 100 or so).

(Other species recorded here include Rock Ptarmigan, Eurasian Capercaillie (both most likely in the national park at Aigues-Tortes, accessible from Espot, southeast of Viella), Tengmalm's Owl (most likely in Cadi-Moixeroi Natural Park, west of Ripoli) and White-backed Woodpecker (probably fewer than 100 pairs in the whole Pyrenées), as well as brown bear, Pyrenean desman, small-spotted genet and Spanish ibex.)

Most birders approach the best area of the Spanish Pyrenées, around Jaca, from Zaragoza to the south, in which case the first place to stop at is near **Huesca**, because there is a chance of Wallcreeper. Head east from Huesca on the N240 for 7 km to the Castillo de Montearagon (Black Wheatear), then take the minor road to Sasa del Abadiado and continue for 9 km to the end of the road, where Wallcreeper occurs. Back at Huesca head northwest on the N240 to the turning northeast to Riglos. This small village is situated at the base of the towering red crags known as **Los Mallos de Riglos**, a good place, especially when the

SPANISH PYRENÉES

SAN JUAN DE LA PEÑA

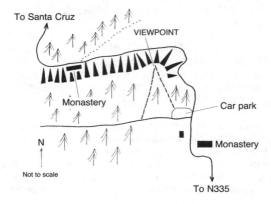

rock climbers are absent, to look for Lammergeier, Alpine Swift, Blue Rock-Thrush, Black Wheatear, wintering Wallcreeper (also at Castillo de Loarre, northeast of Ayerbe), Orphean and Sardinian Warblers, Rock Petronia (in the church tower) and wintering Alpine Accentor. Walk up from the car park at the foot of the crags to look for these birds. Back at the turning to Riglos continue north on the N240 then turn northeast towards Jaca. Along here turn west on to the HU230 to reach **San Juan de la Peña** where Black Woodpecker occurs in the woods and raptors such as Lammergeier and Bonelli's Eagle may be seen soaring over.

There are a number of sites worth visiting west of Jaca (where European Scops-Owl is usually fairly easy to locate in the town parks and botanical gardens). Turn south off the C134 about 19 km west of Jaca (1 km east of Camping Los Pirineos) on to a minor road towards **Alastuey** which traverses a good valley for raptors, and the rocky and scrubby slopes between the two river bridges in the valley, support Eurasian Eagle-Owl (look east from the second bridge), Orphean Warbler, Rock Petronia and Rock Bunting. This is also an excellent place for butterflies. West of the turning to Alastuey turn north off the C134 on to the HU210 which traverses the **Valle de Hecho**, another excellent place to look for raptors, including Lammergeier (which roosts here), and one of the better areas for Wallcreeper, which occurs on the rock walls of

Look out for the brilliant white bib of the White-throated Dipper along the stony streams and rivers of the Pyrenées

356

Boca del Infierno, around the tunnel entrance north of Hecho and above the Selva de Oza campsite west of Hecho. To the west of the turning to the Valle del Hecho, along the C134, European Scops-Owl can be seen in the hilltop town of **Berdun** where the streetlights attract moths such as giant peacock. For close-up views of Eurasian Griffon head for the gorge known as **Fos de Binies**, north of Berdun. White-backed and Black Woodpeckers, and Citril Finch occur alongside the road through the **Valle del Roncal** which leads to France, north of the Berdun–Lumbier road. Another good site for Lammergeier is **Fos de Arbayun**, west of the Embalse de Yesa (where there are also 150 pairs of Eurasian Griffon—one of Spain's largest colonies).

The **Col du Somport** area, on the border with France, about 25 km north of Jaca, is another good place to look for Wallcreeper (check the nearby quarry) and Citril Finch, as well as White-winged Snowfinch and Alpine Accentor. Turn off the N330 just before the 1632-m (5354 ft)-high pass on to a minor road which leads to a ski-resort in the Valle de Astun, the best place to look for these birds.

East of Jaca head to Biescas and Torla to reach the superb **Parque Nacional de Ordesa** (look out for Lammergeier and Wallcreeper at the Río Ara bridge *en route*) which is situated on the opposite side of the Pyrenean crest to Gavarnie in France (p. 189) and supports Lammergeier, Rufous-tailed Rock-Thrush, Wallcreeper, White-winged Snowfinch, Alpine Accentor and Citril Finch. From the park visitor centre at Casa Berges walk east through the magnificent Valle de Ordesa, with walls nearly 1000 m (3281 ft) high, for about 10 km to reach the towering Circo de Soaso, complete with waterfall and Wallcreeper. The 'butterfly-bird' is most likely to be seen along the steep trail to the east (right) of the waterfall, along with snowfinches and accentors. This trail eventually reaches Refugio Delgado Ubada (another good place for Wallcreeper) and the top of Monte Perdido at 3355 m (11,007 ft), but reaching here, let alone the waterfall, and getting back to the visitor centre in a day will test even the fittest birders. It is possible, however, to reach Circo de Soaso and return to Casa Berges along the southern rim of the valley within about eight hours. Black Woodpecker, Wallcreeper and Citril Finch all occur along the southern rim, part of

PARQUE NACIONAL DE ORDESA

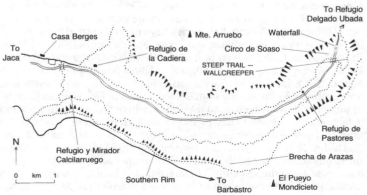

One of the many highlights of birding in the Pyrénées is the sight of a magnificent Lammergeier slowly drifting along the sheer rock walls of these mountains

which is also accessible by road. Otherwise spend the night at a refugio and take the time to absorb the mountain terrain and its avian delights. In the eastern Pyrenées the **Gorge de Montrebei** near Tremp is a good place to look for Wallcreeper, especially in winter.

The Pyrenean principality of **Andorra** (465 km^2), a major skiing area during the long winters, supports most of the mountain specialities, which are best looked for alongside: (i) the road over the Pas de la Casa and the 2409-m (7904 ft) Porto d'Envalira; (ii) the track north of Soldeu; (iii) the road from Andorra la Vella to Arinsal; and (iv) the road from Andorra la Vella to El Serrat and beyond.

Accommodation: Jaca—Hotel Ramiro and Camping Los Pirineos, 20 km west of Jaca on the C134, complete with cafe, shop, swimming pool, bar and Zitting Cisticola.

NORTHEAST COASTAL SPAIN

Some of Spain's best coastal marshes lie within **Aiguamolls de L'Emporda**, a natural park which is situated around the estuaries of Río Fluvia and Río Muga on the Costa Brava in the extreme northeastern corner of the country. Almost 300 species have been recorded here, including Greater Flamingo, almost the entire Spanish population of Great Bittern*, Little Crake (seven in mid-March 1998), an introduced population of Purple Swamphen (60 pairs), Marsh Sandpiper (five in late March 1998), Lesser Grey Shrike (six pairs in 1998), and Moustached and Orphean Warblers. The park lies to the east of Figueres, and can be approached from Ampurias to the south (where there is saltmarsh and a lagoon), and from Rosas to the north (where there is freshwater marsh). There is a visitor centre at El Cortalet, and several marked trails and hides. To the north, Black Wheatear and Thekla Lark occur at **Cabo de Creus** where, during the winter, Wallcreeper and Rock Bunting are also possible on the sea cliffs. To the south, the inland hills between La Escala and Estartit may support Marmora's Warbler (at the end of the 20th century no one was really sure whether this species was present on the Spanish mainland or not), and Cory's ('Scopoli's' *diomedea*) and Mediterranean Shearwaters have been recorded off Palamos. Almost the whole world population of 'Balearic' Shearwater (*mauretanicus*); between 8,000 and 11,000 birds, is believed to winter along the coasts of Catalonia and Valencia, and in January 1998 a total of 508 Mediterranean Shearwaters (505 'Balearic' *mauretanicus* and three 'Yelkouan' *yelkouan*) were seen off the **Llobregat Delta** just outside Barcelona. During the winter up to four Ferruginous Ducks* and 3,570 Mediterranean Gulls have been present in this delta, and during the summer up to 800 Audouin's Gulls* have been recorded.

EBRO DELTA

Despite the fact that over half of this 320-km^2 delta has been turned over to agriculture and just 12 km^2 actually lie within a reserve, it is still the second most important wetland in Iberia, after the Coto Doñana, and an excellent birding site. Over 300 species have been recorded in the marshes, paddies, salinas and scrubland, including huge breeding colonies of Audouin's* (11,600 pairs in 1997—the largest colony on earth) and Slender-billed (hundreds of pairs) Gulls.

The birds listed below occur during the summer unless otherwise indicated.

Localised Specialities
Purple Swamphen, Audouin's* and Slender-billed Gulls.

Other Localised Species
Greater Flamingo, Red-necked Nightjar, Spotless Starling, Lesser Short-toed Lark.

Others
Cory's ('Scopoli's' *diomedea*) and Mediterranean (mainly 'Balearic' *mauretanicus*) Shearwaters, Cattle Egret, Squacco Heron, Black-crowned Night-Heron, Little Bittern, Short-toed and Booted Eagles, Collared Pratincole, Snowy Plover, Whiskered and Gull-billed Terns, European Bee-eater, Zitting Cisticola, Moustached, Orphean and Sardinian Warblers.

(Other species recorded here include Marbled Teal*, Western Reef-Egret (a dark morph present from January 1995 to at least April 1997, and one white morph in April 1998), Great Egret (at least one pair bred in 1997, the first ever breeding record for Spain), Glossy Ibis (five pairs bred in 1998), Greater Spotted Eagle* (winter), Little Crake (three calling males were present in April 1996), Marsh and Broad-billed Sandpipers (both almost annual in autumn), Lesser Crested-Tern (one pair bred up to 1995, followed by a mixed pair in 1996 and three fledged juveniles in 1997) and Caspian Tern.)

The delta, which lies to the east of Tortosa on the Costa Dorada south of Barcelona, is accessible via several minor roads which lead east off the N340 between L'Ampolla, Amposta and San Carlos de la Rapita, and there is a visitor centre at Deltebre in the middle of the delta. In the

EBRO DELTA

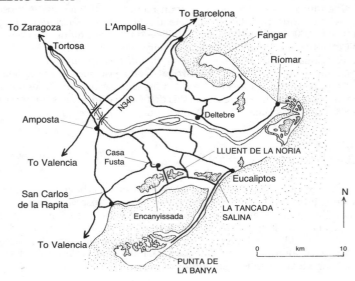

southern half which is, arguably, the best, despite the presence of many paddies, concentrate on the following areas: (i) **Lluent de la Noria**, the large reedbed near Casa Fusta, which supports a heronry and Moustached Warbler, with Orphean Warbler nearby; (ii) **La Tancada**, a large salina which is particularly good for shorebirds, gulls and terns (including Lesser Crested-); (iii) the saltings between there and the sea for Collared Pratincole and Lesser Short-toed Lark; and (iv) **Punta de la Banya**, at the end of the spit to the south, where the lagoons support Greater Flamingo, Audouin's* and Slender-billed Gulls (both of which may also be seen around San Carlos de la Rapita on the opposite side of the bay), and Gull-billed Tern. In the northern half of the delta Purple Swamphen occurs at the **Laguna de Canal Vell**.

Accommodation: San Carlos de la Rapita.

Up to four Lesser Crested-Terns were present in the ternery at Raco de l'olla, a 64-ha saltmarsh reserve in the natural park at **Albufera de Valencia** from 1994 to at least 1998 (one in 1999), breeding amongst themselves and, more often, with the Sandwich Terns also present. The **Cabo de la Nao**, between Valencia and Alicante, to the south, is a good place from which to seawatch, with possibilities including Audouin's Gull*.

ALICANTE

Few of the birds listed below actually occur in Alicante or the nearby resorts of the Costa Blanca such as Benidorm but birders in search of a budget birding break could do a lot worse than spend a while in this area, based at quieter resorts such as Santa Pola if preferred.

The species listed below occur during the summer unless otherwise indicated.

Localised Specialities
White-headed Duck*, Marbled Teal*, Audouin's Gull*, Dupont's Lark.

Other Localised Species
Greater Flamingo, Black-bellied Sandgrouse, Red-necked Nightjar, Spotless Starling, Black Wheatear, Lesser Short-toed and Thekla Larks.

Others
Cory's ('Scopoli's' *diomedea*) and Mediterranean (mostly 'Balearic' *mauretanicus*) Shearwaters, Squacco Heron, Black-crowned Night-Heron, Little Bittern, Glossy Ibis, Bonelli's Eagle, Lesser Kestrel*, Little Bustard*, Collared Pratincole, Whiskered Tern, Pallid Swift, European Bee-eater, Spectacled Warbler, Calandra Lark.

(Other species recorded here include Slender-billed Gull, Eurasian Eagle-Owl, Rufous-tailed Scrub-Robin and Orphean Warbler).

The **Salinas de Santa Pola**, together with their associated marshes and scrub, between the coastal N332 road to Santa Pola (Pallid Swift) and the major road to Elche, about 20 km south of Alicante, support Greater Flamingo, Squacco Heron, Audouin's Gull*, Whiskered Tern, Spotless Starling and Thekla Lark, while less regular visitors include Marbled Teal*, Glossy Ibis and Slender-billed Gull. The small island of **Tabarca**, 4 km offshore from Santa Pola and accessible on regular boat trips, is an excellent place to look for passage migrants such as warblers. Another excellent wetland site inland from Alicante near Elche is the natural park at **El Hondo**, the Spanish stronghold of Marbled Teal* (over 100 in September 1999) and a good site for White-headed Duck* (about 50 in September 1999). Greater Flamingo and Glossy Ibis also bred here for the first time in 1997. The plains accessible from **Alhama de Murcia**, southwest of Murcia, support Little Bustard*, Black-bellied Sandgrouse, Spectacled Warbler and Lesser Short-toed Lark. The plains around **Sierra Espuna**, also near Murcia, support Dupont's Lark.

Accommodation: Santa Pola—Hotel Polamar, Hotel Patilla.

ADDITIONAL INFORMATION

Addresses
Please send records of rarities to the Comite de Rarezas de la Sociedad Española de Ornitologia (SEO—Spanish Ornithological Society), Facultad de Biologia, Universidad Complutense, 28040 Madrid, Spain. The annual rarities report is published in *Ardeola*, in Spanish with an English summary, and can be obtained from SEO/BirdLife, Carretera de Humera, 63-1, 28224 Pozuelo, Madrid, Spain.

Books and papers
Where to watch birds in Spain. de Juana E (ed.), 1994. Lynx Edicions.
Where to watch birds in Spain and Portugal. Rose L, 1995. Hamlyn.
A Birdwatching Guide to the Costa Blanca (second edition). Palmer M,

1994. Arlequin Press.

A Birdwatching Guide to Southern Spain. Palmer M, 1997. Arlequin Press.

Where to watch birds in Southern Spain. Garcia E and Paterson A, 1994. Helm.

A Birdwatchers' Guide to Southern Spain and Gibraltar. Finlayson C, 1993. Prion.

Finding Birds in Southern Spain. Gosney D, 1993. Available from BirdGuides (address, p. 395).

Birds of the Strait of Gibraltar. Finlayson C, 1991. Poyser.

Las Aves de Doñana. Llandres C and Urdiales C, 1990. Lynx Edicions.

Portrait of a Wilderness. Mountfort G, 1955. This classic account of three ornithological expeditions to the Coto Doñana is out of print, but available in some second-hand bookshops and local libraries, and well worth reading.

A Birdwatching Guide to Extremadura. Muddeman J, 1999. Arlequin Press.

Artists for Nature in Extremadura. Hammond N (ed.), 1995. Wildlife Art Gallery.

Where to watch birds in North and East Spain. Rebane M, 1999. Helm.

A Birdwatching Guide to Eastern Spain. Palmer M, due 1999. Arlequin Press.

Finding Birds in Northern Spain. Gosney D, 1993. Available from BirdGuides (address, p. 395).

A Birdwatching Guide to the Pyrenées. Crozier J, 1998. Arlequin Press.

Andorra Birds. Crozier J *et al.* (eds.), 1995. ADN, Andorra.

Atlas de las Aves de España (1975–1995). SEO/BirdLife, 1997. Lynx Edicions.

Areas Importantes para las aves en Espana (Important Bird Areas in Spain). de Juana E (ed.), 1990. SEO.

Videos

Gosney in Spain. Gosney D. Available from BirdGuides (address, p. 395).

SVALBARD

This large, mountainous archipelago with stunning jagged peaks towering above the narrow coastal plain in the west, where most of the 3,000 people live, is situated 657 km north of mainland Norway, about half-way between there and the North Pole. Its deep, narrow fjords, rugged plateaux, glaciers and massive ice floes form a wild landscape, scarred in places by open-cast coal mines but still a wonderful place to see such delights as breeding Grey Phalarope, and Ivory and Sabine's Gulls. In addition, Svalbard also supports tens of thousands of Little Auks and up to a quarter of the world population of polar bears.

The best time for birds is in late June and early July and the species listed below occur during this period unless otherwise indicated. The best time for bears is August when the northern and eastern coasts they favour are most likely to be ice-free and therefore accessible by ship. From mid-April to late July the sun never sets and from mid-November to late January it never rises, hence this is the best time to see the Aurora Borealis (Northern Lights).

Localised Species
King Eider, Grey Phalarope, Ivory and Sabine's Gulls, Little Auk, Brünnich's Guillemot.

Others
Northern Fulmar (blue form), Pink-footed and Barnacle Geese, Long-tailed Duck, Rock Ptarmigan, Purple Sandpiper, Glaucous Gull, Arctic Tern, Long-tailed Skua, Black Guillemot, Atlantic Puffin, Red-throated Diver, Snow Bunting.

Other Wildlife
Polar bear, Arctic fox, narwhal, musk ox, reindeer, bearded, harp and ringed seals, walrus, beluga, bowhead, killer and minke whales.

(Other species recorded here include American Golden-Plover (a pair bred on Spitsbergen in 1997) and Ross's Gull.)

The best way to see the birds and mammals of Svalbard is to join one of the many cruises, especially those which attempt to circumnavigate the archipelago, since the likes of Ivory and Sabine's Gulls, and polar bear and walrus, are only likely to be seen along the northern and eastern coasts. Many cruises start in Tromso in north Norway, but it is possible to fly to Longyearbyen on the island of **Spitsbergen** and join the ships there. Most of the tour companies listed on p. 393 can provide details of cruises.

ADDITIONAL INFORMATION

Addresses

Please send records of rarities to the NSKF, Norsk Ornitologisk Forening, Seminarplassen 5, N-7054 Klaebu, Norway. The annual rarities report is published in *Var Fuglefauna*, in Norwegian with an English summary.

Books and papers

Svalbard: Portrait of an Arctic Summer. Fenton J and S, 1997.

The Ivory Gull is a bird of the Arctic pack-ice and its most accessible breeding colonies are on Svalbard

SWEDEN

INTRODUCTION

Summary

Most birders in search of the Scandinavian specialities combine Varanger in northern Norway with Finland rather than Sweden because such a trip is likely to include Red-flanked Bluetail and Yellow-breasted Bunting, two species which are very unlikely to be seen in this country. However, Sweden does support all the owls and many of the other forest specialities such as Siberian Jay which birders are after in Finland, and, as with that country, in order to see the majority of these birds it is necessary to make full use of local assistance on a trip which is likely to prove expansive and expensive.

Size

At 449,790 km², Sweden is 3.5 times larger than England and 60% the size of Texas.

Getting Around

Many visitors arrive by air, but Sweden is also accessible via vehicular ferries from England, Denmark and the Baltic states. Birders intending not to use the country's very efficient, fairly extensive, but expensive, public transport system, may want to take their own vehicle on these ferries because hire prices are very high in Sweden. The roads and many tracks are excellent, and there is little traffic away from the major centres, hence driving is a relatively pleasurable experience, although be sure to beware of elk and reindeer on the roads when driving in the north.

Many species are only likely to be seen with local assistance and even then it will probably be necessary to cover extensive areas on foot in order to see most specialities, particularly in the north.

Accommodation and Food

As in the rest of Scandinavia, accommodation, food and drink are expensive compared to the rest of Europe. However, camping, in campsites (many of which have chalets) or off-road, shopping in supermarkets and eating in fast-food joints, will enable birders prepared to 'rough it' to cut costs considerably. In most national parks, even those in the remotest areas, there are also refuge huts, linked by well-marked tracks and trails, which have been built specifically to provide cheap and comfortable overnight accommodation. Breakfast (*frukost*), normally included in the price of built accommodation, and the lunchtime *smorgasbord*, a mixture of cheese, eggs, fruit, herring, meat, potatoes and salad, which is normally put out by restaurants at lunchtime, are both substantial enough to last most birders for a day.

Health and Safety

Many birding sites, especially in the north, are cold, damp, remote and wild places, hence it is wise to bird such areas with a detailed map, a compass, plenty of food and drink, wellies, warm and waterproof clothing, and, if camping, the best gear available. During the summer it is also important to take plenty of insect repellent.

Climate and Timing

Sweden has short, warm summers and long, cold winters. The best time to look for owls, the other Scandinavian specialities and spring passage migrants is during late May and early June. In the north it is possible to bird for almost 24 hours a day from mid-May to late July, although the peak time to go birding is during the first few hours after midnight.

Habitats

The southern third of the country is relatively flat and low-lying, hence this is where most of the 9% of land used for agriculture is situated and where most of the small human population live. The country's numerous lakes account for another 10% of its area and they include the huge 5580-km^2 Lake Vanern which is also in the south, hence the remaining 80% of Sweden consists primarily of very sparsely populated mixed and boreal (*taiga*) forests (50%), and upland bogs and tundra (30%). With an average of just 19 people per km2, compared to 370 in England, northern Sweden has the largest expanses of wild country in Europe.

Conservation

The lowland beech forests of the southwest were cleared long ago to make way for agriculture and settlements. Contemporary conservation issues surround habitat loss and degradation, hunting and pollution, all of which need to be addressed in order to safeguard the future of the six threatened and near-threatened species as well as the relatively common and widespread birds which occur in Sweden. There are numerous 'protected' areas, including 20 National Parks, but lines on maps cannot stop international problems such as acid rain which has damaged about 20,000 of the 90,000 or so lakes and made about 4,000 of them so acidic that no fish are believed to survive in them. Fortunately some specific conservation projects have been successful. For example, the release of 2,759 captive-bred young Eurasian Eagle-Owls between 1969 and 1996 helped raise the total number of breeding pairs in the country to about 400 in 1996.

Bird Species

Notable species include Gyrfalcon, Great Snipe*, Broad-billed Sandpiper, Red-necked Phalarope, Caspian Tern, Long-tailed Skua, Eurasian Eagle-Owl, Ural and Great Grey Owls, Northern Hawk Owl, Eurasian Pygmy-Owl, Tengmalm's Owl, Siberian Jay, Eurasian Nutcracker, Bohemian Waxwing, Red-flanked Bluetail (a few pairs bred in 1996, an exceptionally good year), Siberian Tit, Pine Grosbeak (scarce in the north but occasionally moves south in large numbers, such as in winter 1998–1999 when about 1,000 were in the Stockholm area alone), Parrot Crossbill and Rustic Bunting.

FALSTERBO

During the autumn, raptors and passerines heading south for the winter cross the Baltic Sea between the southern tip of the Scandinavian peninsula, near Malmo in Sweden, and the east coast of Denmark about 20 km away. These birds concentrate at Falsterbo where over 14,000 raptors have been recorded in a single day and where seeing over 1,000 a day is not unusual during the peak period. High day counts include 1,864 European Honey-buzzards, 103 Red Kites and 611 Rough-legged Buzzards, and high autumn totals include 17,000 Eurasian Sparrow-hawks, 12,513 Common Buzzards, 7,000 European Honey-buzzards, 1,480 Rough-legged Buzzards, 295 Red Kites and 14 Lesser Spotted Eagles. Visible passerine migration is just as exciting during October when 100,000 birds have been recorded in a single day on several occasions, and on one very special day 1.2 million birds, mainly Chaffinches and Bramblings, were recorded passing over.

The best time to visit Falsterbo is from late August to October. Although unusual species such as Lesser Spotted Eagle are most likely to be seen at the end of August, the widest range of species occurs during the first half of September and peak numbers usually pass over in September and early October.

Regular Autumn Passage Migrants

Osprey, European Honey-buzzard, Red (most late Sep) and Black Kites, White-tailed Eagle* (scarce), Western Marsh-Harrier, Eurasian Sparrowhawk, Northern Goshawk, Common and Rough-legged Buzzards, Lesser Spotted Eagle (five in September 1998), Black Woodpecker, Eurasian Nutcracker, Red-throated Pipit (late Aug–late Sep), Chaffinch, Brambling (most late Sep–early Oct).

(Other species recorded here include Lesser White-fronted* and Red-breasted* Geese, King Eider, Pallid* and Montagu's Harriers, Greater Spotted*, Steppe and Imperial* Eagles, Gyrfalcon (Oct–Nov), Common Crane, Broad-billed Sandpiper, Red-necked Phalarope, Caspian Tern, Tengmalm's Owl and Bohemian Waxwing.)

FALSTERBO

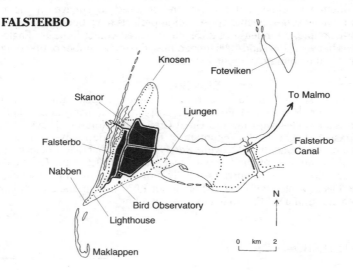

Falsterbo is about 25 km south of Malmo which is accessible by vehicular ferry from Copenhagen in Denmark. Bicycles can be hired in Skanor, the twin village just north of Falsterbo. In favourable conditions, usually fine days with light southwesterlies, large numbers of raptors rise above the heath at Ljungen on mid-morning thermals and they can be seen from the row of birches at the southwest end, near the campsite. During westerlies or northwesterlies birds tend to move along the coast, in which case the hill by the lighthouse car park or Nabben, further south, are the best viewpoints. Many birds often gather along the Falsterbo Canal further to the east and most birders concentrate their efforts here, along the road which runs by the canal, for if a rare raptor is located here it is then usually possible to follow it by car west to Ljungen and the lighthouse. In southerlies or easterlies the best place to be is in the Skanor harbour area. Passerine migration, which is usually best in southwesterlies, normally peaks between 0800 and 1000 hours and the best places to observe the mass overhead movement of birds are the lighthouse (where the garden, a good place for Black Woodpeckers and Eurasian Nutcrackers, can be checked at the same time) and Nabben (where seawatching is also possible). The inlet known as Foteviken, at the base of the peninsula between Holviksnas and Vellinge, is worth checking for passage shorebirds such as Broad-billed Sandpiper.

Accommodation: Falsterbo Fagelstation (Bird Observatory), Box 17, S-230 11 Falsterbo, Sweden, as well as two hotels, cottages and an official campsite, all three of which must be booked well in advance (if you intend to visit during the peak period) via the Malmo Tourist Information Office, Hamngatan 1, S-211 22 Malmo, Sweden.

The valley known as **Fyledalen**, just north of Ystad in eastern Skane, is an excellent place to look for raptors during the winter when up to 400 Red Kites occur, along with a few White-tailed* and Golden Eagles. During the autumn Lesser Spotted, Greater Spotted*, Steppe and Imperial* Eagles have all been recorded, and during the winter other possibilities include Smew, Eurasian Eagle-Owl, Eurasian Pygmy-Owl, Black Woodpecker, Eurasian Nutcracker and Bohemian Waxwing. Other wintering species in Skane include Horned Lark, Chaffinch (late January roosts have been estimated to contain as many as 2.5 million birds), Brambling, Twite and Snow Bunting, while outside possibilities include King and Steller's* Eiders, Gyrfalcon, Snowy Owl and Northern Hawk Owl.

To the north of Skane, the coast at **Aspet**, near Kristianstad, is a good place to look for wintering sea-ducks such as Long-tailed, and Eurasian Eagle-Owl is resident on the silos at **Ahus** harbour, nearby.

During the middle two weeks of April up to 5,000 Common Cranes gather to rest, feed and perform their courtship dances in the potato fields southwest of **Hornborgasjon**, a lake about 10 km southeast of Skara which is on the E3 about 125 km northeast of Göteborg in south-central Sweden. To reach here follow signposts for Falkoping (a good base) and scan the fields from the road southwest of Stora Bjurum church. At dusk and dawn the birds fly to and from their roost on the lake, and the trumpeting flocks can be seen passing over the road between Stora Bjurum church and Dagsnas. A few pairs remain to breed in the area, where there is a visitor centre and bird observation tower at Fageludden on the east shore, reached by turning west 1 km north of Brodedetorp church. **Store Mosse National Park**, about 50 km south of Jönköping, supports breeding Hazel Grouse, Jack Snipe, Wood Sandpiper, Eurasian Pygmy-Owl, Tengmalm's Owl, and Three-toed and Black Woodpeckers. Route 151 between Hillerstorp and Varnamo (on the E4) passes through this park where there are several car parks, marked trails and hides, as well as an observation tower overlooking Lake Kavsjon. All five European grebes, Common Crane and Black Tern breed on and around **Takern**, a 50-km² lake and popular resort about 70 km north of Jönköping east of Lake Vattern, but the area is better known as an important resting and refuelling station for Bean Geese. About 30,000 are usually present during the first half of October, although up to 47,000 have been recorded, along with occasional Lesser White-fronted Geese*. They roost on the lake and feed in the fields to the northeast, mainly around Hov. For more details on where to bird and where to stay contact Takerns Faltstation, Box 204, S-595 22 Mjolby, Sweden.

The large summer resort island of **Öland** in the Baltic Sea supports a fine range of breeding birds, including Corn Crake*, Little Gull, Black Tern, Black Woodpecker, Eurasian Nutcracker, Barred Warbler and occasional Caspian Terns and Collared Flycatchers, but it is more renowned amongst Swedish birders as the best place in the country to observe visible migration and to find regular rarities, most of which originate from the south and east, and have thus included the likes of Eleonora's Falcon, Cream-coloured Courser, Masked Shrike, Siberian and White's Thrushes, White-throated Robin, Siberian Accentor, and Rock and Cretzschmar's Buntings. Spring migration peaks between mid-April and early May, but the best time for spring rarities is during late May and early June, when the area around the Fagelstation (Bird Observatory) and lighthouse at Ottenby, at the southern tip of the island, is crowded with birders. Even more birders are usually present here during the autumn, especially in mid-October, when migrants such as Pallas's Warbler, Red-throated Pipit and Rustic Bunting are more or less regular visitors and other possibilities include Lesser White-front-ed* and Red-breasted* Geese, King and Steller's* Eiders, White-billed Diver and Tengmalm's Owl. A road bridge connects the island to the mainland at Kalmar, which is accessible by air, rail and road from Malmo or Stockholm. Most birders concentrate on the Ottenby area where news of unusual birds spreads fast, but it is also possible to find out 'what's about' in Stenasa Badet where there is a visitor centre (tel: 485 44148), with a cafe, bookshop and logbook, called *Stenhusa bod* and run by the Ornithological Society of Sweden (SOF). It is possible to stay at Ottenby Fagelstation, P1, 1500, S-380 65 Degerhaven, Sweden (tel: 485 61093), the youth hostel/campsite just to the north (tel: 485 62020) and in rooms at nearby Parboang (tel: 485 61011). For more details on accommodation and getting around contact the Ölands Turistforening (Tourist Information Office), PO Box 115, S-387 00 Borgholm, Sweden (tel: 485 89000).

The large summer resort island of **Gotland** in the Baltic Sea northeast of Öland, supports a strange mixture of breeding birds, including an isolated southern population of over 1,400 pairs of Barnacle Geese, Caspian Tern and a small population of Collared Flycatchers, here at the northern edge of this species' breeding range. During the winter flocks of Steller's Eiders* are regularly recorded around the coast. The island is accessible by air from Stockholm and via regular ferries from Nynashamn, Oskarshamn and Vastervik.

The extensive tract of coniferous forest in **Tyresta National Park**, on the southeast edge of Stockholm, supports Black Grouse, Eurasian Capercaillie, Hazel Grouse, Eurasian Pygmy-Owl, Tengmalm's Owl, Black Woodpecker and Parrot Crossbill, although seeing most of these birds will be very difficult without local assistance. Eurasian Eagle-Owl can be seen around the harbour at **Vasteras**, west of Stockholm, where one of these magnificent birds likes to perch, rather incongruously, on the cranes, especially number 21.

Eurasian River Warbler and Blyth's Reed-Warbler have been record-ed during the spring and early summer just north of **Sundsvall** on the west coast of the Gulf of Bothnia in central Sweden. North of Sundsvall turn off the E4 towards Alno, then follow the 'Alno K:A', 'Nacka 2' and '2 Eriksdal' signposts. After responding to the last signpost park 200 m further on and listen for the calm but brilliant mimicry of Blyth's Reed-Warbler, which usually sings at night (after 2230 hours). Head back to the '2 Eriksdal' junction and continue straight on to the next junction, then park and listen for the 'sewing machine song' of Eurasian River Warbler, which usually sings at dawn and dusk.

ANNSJON

The large shallow lake known as Annsjon, together with its surrounding marshes and forests, and the high Bunner Plateau to the south, near the border with Norway in west-central Sweden, support a fine range of forest and marsh birds, including Great Snipe*.

The species listed below occur during the summer unless otherwise indicated.

Localised Specialities
Great Snipe*, Northern Hawk Owl.

Other Localised Species
Rock Ptarmigan.

Others
Long-tailed Duck, Rough-legged Buzzard, Golden Eagle, Eurasian Capercaillie, Hazel Grouse, Temminck's Stint, Purple Sandpiper, Red-necked Phalarope, Eurasian Dotterel, Eurasian Pygmy-Owl, Tengmalm's Owl, Three-toed and Black Woodpeckers, Siberian Jay, Lapland and Snow Buntings.

Bird: (i) the extensive forests in the valley known as **Valadaten**, southeast of Annsjon via Underaker; (ii) **Storlien**, Sweden's best known Great Snipe* lekking area, which is situated to the west of Valadaten near the road to Trondheim in Norway and accessible from Storliens Hogfjallshotel. From there follow the blue-marked trail, turning west at Banggardsliften, to a hide overlooking the lekking area which is usually in use between 2300 and 0200 hours between late May and late June; (iii) the **Bunner Plateau**, which rises to 900 m (2953 ft) to the south of Annsjon; and (iv) around **Annsjon**.

Accommodation: Annsjon is a popular tourist area hence there is plenty to choose from, including campsites.

The **Holmoarna** archipelago in the northern Gulf of Bothnia is renowned for: (i) its impressive falls of passage migrants, which, during the spring, include regular Great Grey Owls and Yellow-breasted Buntings, and during the autumn, have included over 100 Rustic Buntings on single days; (ii) the large numbers of crossbills which often move through the islands at the end of July and have included over 100 'Two-barreds' in a day; (iii) often being the first place to record birds such as Northern Hawk Owl, Bohemian Waxwing, Arctic Redpoll and Pine Grosbeak when these species undergo periodic irruptions; (iv) lying alongside the flight path of migrating seabirds which regularly include King and Steller's* Eiders, Pomarine Skuas and White-billed Divers; and (v) hosting great European rarities such as Siberian and Black-throated Accentors. The peak time for seabird and landbird passage migrants is from mid-May to early June when breeding species such as Caspian Tern and Rustic Bunting are also present. The best island for passage migrants and rarities is **Stora Fjaderagg**, which is situated at the northeast end of the archipelago and is accessible from Umea on the mainland, which is connected by air to Stockholm, via a ferry during the summer and via ice-scooters during the winter, when the sea freezes over. It has a Fagelstation (Bird Observatory) and lighthouse. During the spring, especially late May to early June and autumn, many birders take day-trips from Umea to the island of **Holmon**, hire a bicycle in the village and pedal off in search of something special in the copses, fields and gardens which surround the village there. At this time of year Red-breasted Flycatchers and Greenish Warblers (*trochiloides*) often occur in good numbers, and other regular landbird passage migrants include Great Grey Owl, Eurasian River Warbler, Blyth's Reed-Warbler and Yellow-breasted Bunting. If there are few landbird passage migrants birders head for the Bergudden lighthouse and/or the harbour where large numbers of wildfowl, skuas and divers can often be seen passing by, especially during the last two weeks of May when over 4,000 Black-throated Divers have been seen in a single day. The rest of the island is largely covered with coniferous forests, in which few birds occur, but the forested island of **Angeson**, to the south of Holmon, supports breeding Tengmalm's Owl and Rustic Bunting. It is possible to stay at Stora Fjaderagg Fagelstation, Bjorn Olsen, Orrvagen 14, S-902 54 Umea, Sweden, and, on Holmon, in cottages or the campsite.

Between Lulea and Jokkmokk in northeast Sweden turn north off Route 97 at Padjerim, in response to the 'Letsi Kraftstation' signpost, to reach the **Serri** reserve, 18 km from the main road, where Siberian Jay, Bohemian Waxwing, Pine Grosbeak, Parrot Crossbill and Rustic Bunting occur along the 11-km-long Serri Loop Trail. Rustic Bunting also occurs in the damp spruce forest alongside the small lake which lies south of Route 97 about 2 km southeast of Vuollerim. Another excellent place to look for Arctic specialities in northern Sweden is **Muddus National Park** where over 100 species have been recorded, including Broad-billed Sandpiper, Northern Hawk Owl, Siberian Jay, Bohemian Waxwing, Siberian Tit, Pine Grosbeak, Parrot Crossbill and Rustic Bunting. The park is signposted from the Jokkmokk–Gallivare road. There are several walking trails with refuges for overnight stays but if only one day is available concentrate on the area between the waterfall and the two refuge huts to the north.

MUDDUS NATIONAL PARK

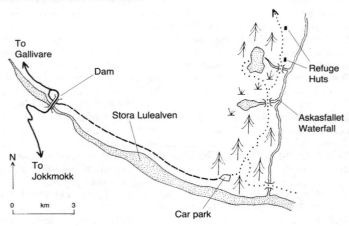

The largest wild area in Europe (over 5000 km²) lies within the three contiguous national parks of **Stora Sjofallet**, **Sarek and Padjelanta** in northwest Sweden, and it supports the likes of Lesser White-fronted Goose*, Gyrfalcon, and occasional Snowy Owls and Northern Hawk Owls. The area is situated about 120 km south of Narvik in Norway and is accessible from within Sweden from Vietas, which can be reached via a minor road off Route 88.

ABISKO NATIONAL PARK

This remote Arctic area which surrounds Lake Tornetrask near the border with Norway in extreme northwest Sweden supports plenty of high-Arctic breeding specialities, including Northern Hawk Owl, Arctic Warbler and Arctic Redpoll.

The species listed below occur during the summer unless otherwise indicated.

Localised Specialities
Northern Hawk Owl, Arctic Warbler, Arctic Redpoll.

Other Localised Species
Rock Ptarmigan.

Others
Greater Scaup, Long-tailed Duck, Velvet Scoter, Rough-legged Buzzard, Willow Ptarmigan, Temminck's Stint, Purple and Broad-billed Sandpipers, Red-necked Phalarope, Eurasian Dotterel, Arctic Tern, Red-throated and Black-throated Divers, Bluethroat ('Red-spotted' *svecica*), Brambling, Lapland and Snow Buntings.

Other Wildlife
Elk, reindeer.

(Other species recorded here include White-tailed* and Golden Eagles, Gyrfalcon, Long-tailed Skua and Pine Grosbeak.)

Abisko railway station, on the line between Kiruna in north Sweden and Narvik in Norway, is situated by the park visitor centre, which lies alongside Route 98 about 85 km northwest of Kiruna. There is a cable-car into the park from here and Linbana ski-lift also enables access to the high tops around the summit of Njulla. A good way to traverse the rest of the area is to buy an Abisko–Narvik return rail ticket and bird around the many small railway stations which are situated between these two main stops.

Accommodation: Abisko Turiststation, S-980 24 Abisko, Sweden, is a very expensive hotel which can be booked in advance via Svenska Turistforenin, Stureplan 2, Fack, S-108 80, Stockholm (tel: 8 227200). There are also some chalets, a youth hostel and a campsite here, as well as a fine network of refuge huts throughout the park (take sleeping bag, food and cooking utensils).

ADDITIONAL INFORMATION

Birdline
Information: 071 268300. Hotline: 020 768030.

Addresses
Please send records of rarities to the Swedish Rarities Committee, c/o Christian Cederroth, Segerstads fyr, S-38065 Degerhamn, Sweden. The annual rarities report is published in *Var Fagelvarld*, in Swedish with an English summary.

The Sveriges Ornitologiska Forening/Ornithological Society of Sweden (SOF), Box 14219, S-104 40 Stokholm, Sweden, publishes *Var Fagelvarld*.

Swedish Club 300, c/o Bjorn Christensson, Uttekilsvagen 22, S-124 30 Bandhagen, Sweden.

Books and papers
Finding Birds in Sweden. Gosney D, 1998. Available from BirdGuides (address, p. 395).

Birds at Falsterbo. Karlsson L (ed), 1994. *Anser* supplement No. 33.

SWITZERLAND

INTRODUCTION

Summary
Small, scenic Switzerland is one of the few countries in Europe where all of the best birds occur in compact areas and where the excellent integrated public transport system enables easy access to the high tops, which means it is possible to see such high-altitude specialities as Wallcreeper without hiring a vehicle. However, this is still an expensive country to visit and because some of the birds are very thin on the ground it may be necessary to cover large areas on foot.

Size
At 41,285 km^2, Switzerland is one third the size of England and over 6% the size of Texas.

Getting Around
Switzerland is one of the most expensive countries in Europe to travel around, even without hiring a vehicle. The integrated public transport system is renowned for its precision and together with bicycles which can be hired at all major railway stations, cable-cars, ski-lifts and the extensive trail network, it makes hiring a vehicle an unnecessary

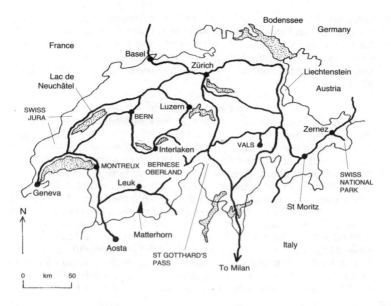

expense. Birders who prefer their own transport will have to pay to use the motorways (tickets are available at border crossings, petrol stations and tourist offices) and should drive carefully in the mountains where some stretches of road may terrify less confident drivers.

Accommodation and Food
Even campsites are expensive in Switzerland, although they are cheaper than hotels and 'Bed and Breakfast' places (*Zimmer frei*). Food and drink is also expensive when compared to the rest of Europe, although many products, including the excellent Swiss beer, are considerably cheaper in supermarkets.

Climate and Timing
Switzerland is a good place to visit at most times of the year, although the high tops, where the vast majority of the country's top birds occur during the summer, are usually only accessible between mid-May and October, when many parts of the country are actually wetter than during the winter. So, although it can be extremely cold during the winter, this is just as good a time to look for the high-altitude specialities, because they usually descend to lower altitudes and often occur near human habitation.

Habitats
The deep valleys and high mountains of the Alps extend across the southern half of land-locked Switzerland, rising to 4634 m (15,203 ft) at Monte Rosa on the border with Italy. For the most part, and especially in the Bernese Oberland, they fulfil many people's picture-postcard image of Swiss scenery, although most relatively flat areas are built-up or intensively farmed. The steeper slopes support diverse deciduous forest, montane beech and coniferous forest, alpine pastures, scree, snowfields and glaciers. North of the Alps lies the 40–50-km-wide forested

375

lakeland of the Mittelland Plateau, which encompasses about a third of the country, and extends from Lac Leman (Lake Geneva) in the southwest to Bodenssee (Lake Constance) in the northeast and on into Germany. In the northwest the predominantly limestone Jura Mountains run along the country's border with France, rising to 1679 m (5509 ft).

Conservation
Much of Switzerland's landscape may look beautiful, but beyond the dramatic veil lies a land ravaged by habitat loss and degradation. The Alpine tree-line was lowered centuries ago to increase the amount of grazing land, most of the original deciduous forest cover on the Mittelland Plateau has long been replaced with spruce plantations, about 30% of the remaining hedgerows were destroyed during the 1970s and 1980s, riverine forests have been felled, rivercourses altered, and since 1850 over 90% of the country's wetlands have been drained, mainly to make way for intensively managed farmland. The list goes on and, if it continues to be added to, there may not be much of a future for the three threatened species as well as the relatively common and widespread birds which occur in Switzerland, despite the presence of numerous 'protected' areas, including many reserves which are managed by Pro Natura—the Swiss League for the Protection of Nature (LSPN).

Bird Species
About 380 species have been recorded in Switzerland, of which about 200 have been known to breed. Notable species include Rock Partridge, Eurasian Nutcracker, Wallcreeper, White-winged Snowfinch, Alpine Accentor and Citril Finch.

Expectations
It is possible to see 100–130 species on a trip lasting one to two weeks during the spring and summer.

The wooded mountains of the **Swiss Jura**, which rise to 1679 m (5509 ft) alongside the border with France, support Hazel Grouse (most likely in the Col de Chasseral area, between St-Imier and La Neuveville at the north end of the Jura, and alongside the road through the Col du Mollendruz, which crosses the northern side of Mont Tendre, at the southern end of the Jura, northwest of Lausanne), Corn Crake*, Black Woodpecker, Eurasian Nutcracker, Wallcreeper (most likely at the cirque at Creux-du-Van and in nearby gorges along the River Areuse, in the middle of the Jura just south of Route 10 at Noiraigue, between Neuchâtel and Fleurier) and Citril Finch (most likely around Lac de Joux, which is situated at the south end of the Jura, south of Vallorbe, and along the track and trail to Col de Crozet, above Crozet, near Montoiseau, in the extreme south of the Jura).

Some of Switzerland's best wetlands are around **Lac de Neuchâtel** which supports large numbers of wintering waterfowl and attracts a wide range of passage migrants, especially during the spring when shorebirds such as Marsh Sandpiper and Temminck's Stint occur on an almost regular basis. Other species recorded here include Great and Cattle Egrets, Baillon's Crake, Red-necked Phalarope and Bluethroat ('White-spotted' *cyanecula*). The best marshes lie alongside the northeast shore, between the towns of Neuchâtel and Portalban, especially at the **Fanel** reserve which is accessible from the Gampelen–Cudrefin road. During the spring, passage shorebirds also occur on the old clay pits around **Chavornay** to the south of Lac de Neuchâtel. These can be reached by turning north off the Chavornay–Orbe road 2 km west of Chavornay. There is a visitor centre at the **Champ-Pittet Reserve**, at Cheseaux Noreaz, just east of Yverdon.

There are plenty of places worth birding near **Montreux** on the Lake Geneva shoreline. During the winter it is possible to see Wallcreeper on the old castle called **Chateau de Chillon**, just south of Montreux. The best birding area around Lake Geneva (Lac Leman) is between Villeneuve, just south of Montreux, and Bouveret, especially at **Les Grangettes** next to Villeneuve, where a Great Skua was present from November 1997 to at least May 1999 and passage migrants include Caspian Tern (seven in mid-April 1998). The foothills of the **Rochers de Naye** above Montreux support Tengmalm's Owl (near Sonchaux), Rufoustailed Rock-Thrush, Alpine Accentor and Citril Finch (all three along the Col de Jaman–Col de Bonaudon trail). The Col de Jaman and Sonchaux are accessible by road from Caux (where Wallcreeper occurs during the winter). Eurasian Pygmy-Owl has been recorded around **La Pierreuse**, southeast of Chateau-d'Oex, and accessible by minor road from L'Evitaz. The **Col de la Croix**, 15 km or so east of Aigle, is a well-known migrant hot-spot during the autumn when as many as 120 Citril Finches have been recorded on a single day during early October. For details about the ringing station which operates here contact Jacques Laesser, Progres IIla, 2300 LA Chaux-de-Fonds, Switzerland. In extreme southwest Switzerland the mountain pass on the border with France known as **Col de Bretolet** is reputed to be the best place in the Alps to witness the visible autumn migration of raptors, and one of the best for migrant Citril Finches during the autumn. To reach here head south from Montreux to Champery and continue for 6 km to the campsite at Barne (the only accommodation near the col). From here it is a 5-km walk up to the pass, via the track on the right-hand side of the creek above Barne. The area around the village of **Leuk**, just north of Route 9, supports all of the high-altitude specialities and one of the best places in Switzerland to look for Wallcreeper is from the old stone bridge over the Feschelbach Gorge about 3 km east of Leuk.

BERNESE OBERLAND

The extensive coniferous forest, juniper stands, alpine pastures, cliffs, snowfields and glaciers which adorn the beautiful mountains of central Switzerland, which rise to 3970 m (13,025 ft) at Eiger and 4195 m (13,763 ft) at Aletschhorn, support a typical Alpine avifauna.

The species listed below occur during the summer unless otherwise indicated. Some of the highest reaches may be inaccessible due to snow until mid-May and even June.

Localised Specialities
Rock Partridge.

Other Localised Species
Wallcreeper, White-winged Snowfinch, Citril Finch.

Others
Red Kite, Golden Eagle, Eurasian Pygmy-Owl, Alpine Swift, Black Woodpecker, Eurasian Nutcracker, Red-billed and Yellow-billed Choughs, Rufous-tailed Rock-Thrush, Eurasian Crag-Martin, Alpine Accentor.

Other Wildlife
Chamois, Alpine marmot and an exceptionally rich flora.

(Other species recorded here include Rock Ptarmigan and Three-toed Woodpecker.)

Interlaken is the main gateway to this huge area where most of the species listed above could be found almost anywhere in suitable habitat. However, some areas have proved to be better than others in the past and they are as follows. For Rock Partridge try: (i) the southern slopes of the mountains west of **Thun** and south of Gurnigel; and (ii) just below the hotel at the top of **Niesen**, accessible by rack-and-pinion railway from Spiez, as early in the morning as possible. For Eurasian Pygmy-Owl try the **Rotmos** reserve, reached by heading east out of Thun towards Luzern, then turning right to Eriz, continuing to the end of the road at Scheidzun and then driving on, to the reserve where the owl has been recorded a few hundred metres north of the reserve building. For Wallcreeper try: (i) **Pfinstegg**, accessible by cable-car from Grindelwald, where the cliff faces alongside the trail between the top station and Restaurant Stierbegg are worth a prolonged grilling; (ii) the **Lauterbrunnen** valley south of Interlaken, where Three-toed Woodpecker also occurs; (iii) above the ski-resort of **Wengen** which is connected to the Lauterbrunnen via various trails; (iv) the **Reichenbach Falls** near Meiringen, northeast of Interlaken beyond Brienz; (v) **Neiderhorn**; (vi) **Ifugen**, south of Lente; and (vii) during the winter, around the railway station at **Eigergletscher**, five minutes by train from Kleine Scheidegg, and about 25 minutes by train from Wengen. White-winged Snowfinch also occurs here, and, along with Citril Finch, around the summit of **Mannlichen**, accessible via the 6.2-km cable-car journey from Grindelwald Grund to the top station. From the summit it is possi-

Flocks of Yellow-billed Choughs riding the updraughts are a familiar sight in the high Alps

ble to return on foot to the base station via Kleine Scheidegg, Alpiglen and Brandegg.

Accommodation: plenty of campsites, including Gletscherdorf on the southeast side of Grindelwald.

Rock Partridge occurs above the old road at **St Gotthard's Pass**, above the 17-km tunnel (the longest road tunnel in the world) which links south-central Switzerland with Italy, along with White-winged Snowfinch and Alpine Accentor.

In southeast Switzerland the cliffs northeast of Route 6, southeast of the village of **Vals**, and a further km up the road near Balmentachli, are some of the best in the country for Wallcreeper, and the scree slopes above the tree-line on the south-facing slopes above Route 3 between **Maloya Pass and St Moritz**, further east, are some of the best in Switzerland for Rock Partridge.

Since 1914 the extensive forests and alpine grasslands on the mountains which rise above 3150 m (10,335 ft) in the 170-km² **Swiss National Park**, in extreme east Switzerland, have been left virtually untouched. There are no villages here and human interference is deliberately minimised, hence this is the site of a Lammergeier reintroduction programme and a good place to search for birds such as Eurasian Pygmy-Owl, Tengmalm's Owl and Wallcreeper, although none are easy to find. There is a visitor centre at **Zernez** and much of the park is accessible along marked trails from Route 28. The best place for Wallcreeper is at the bottom of Clemgia Gorge at the extreme northeast end of the park.

During the winter the **Swiss Bodenssee** (Lake Constance) in the northeast corner of the country on the borders with Austria (p. 59) and Germany (p. 201) supports Red-necked Grebe, Red-crested Pochard, Smew, and Red-throated and Black-throated Divers. The shore is accessible via several towns between Kreuzlingen and the Rhein Delta at the Bodenssee's southeast end. To the west of Bodenssee up to four Ferruginous Ducks* have been recorded on the River Rhein at **Stein-am-Rhein** during the winter.

ADDITIONAL INFORMATION

Birdline
Hotline (tel: 21 616 1222; updated daily in French and German).

Addresses
Please send records of rarities to the Schweizerische Avifaunistische Kommission, c/o Schweizerische Vogelwarte, 6204 Sempach, Switzerland. The annual rarities report is published in *Nos Oiseaux*, in French with an English summary, and in *Orn. Beobachter*, in German with an English summary.

Pro Natura—The Swiss League for the Protection of Nature (LSPN), Postfach, 4020 Basle, Switzerland (tel: 61 317 9191; fax: 61 317 9166).

Schweizer Vogelschutz—BirdLife Switzerland, Postfach, 8036 Zürich, Switzerland (tel: 1 463 7271; fax: 1 461 4778).

Ficedula, Societa pro avifauna della Svizzera Italiana, 6835 Morbio-Superíore, Switzerland (tel: 91 683 3379).

The quarterly journal, *Nos Oiseaux* (in French with English and German summaries), can be obtained via Administration de NOS OISEAUX, c/o Musee d'Histoire Naturelle de La Chaux-de-Fonds, Av. Leopold-Robert 63, 2300 La Chaux-de-Fonds, Switzerland (tel: 32 913 3976).

Books and papers

Where to watch birds in Switzerland. Sacchi M, Rüegg P and Laesser J, 1999. Helm.

UKRAINE

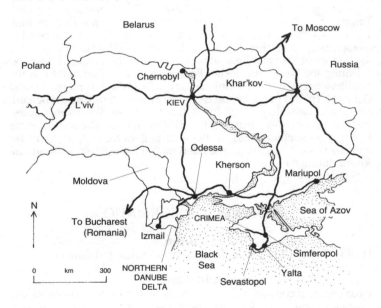

INTRODUCTION

If the tourist infrastructure is improved the Ukraine has the potential to become a popular birding destination in the 21st century, thanks primarily to the abundant birdlife of the wetlands and steppe along the north Black Sea coast, which includes several species at the northwestern edges of their ranges.

At 603,700 km^2 the Ukraine is 4.6 times larger than England and a little smaller than Texas. The major entry point by air is the capital Kiev, which is connected by air to Odessa on the Black Sea coast and Simferopol on the Crimean Peninsula, both of which are also accessible by ferry from the other countries bordering the Black Sea. The Ukraine can also be reached by road via Hungary, Poland, Romania and Slovakia, and vehicles can be hired in Kiev and on the Crimean Peninsula. The major problems for drivers are the erratic fuel supplies beyond the major cities, poor driving standards, Cyrillic roadsigns and frequent road blocks, at which it is sometimes necessary to barter over an often bogus fine before paying it and being allowed to continue. Although there is an extensive, cheap and fairly reliable bus, taxi and rail network, getting to the best birding sites will be very time consuming without a vehicle. A basic grasp of Russian will also make travelling around the Ukraine somewhat easier. The cheapest hotels tend to turn tourists away, in which case it will be necessary to stay in the expensive but basic larger hotels, hunt down the cheaper private flats and rooms which are also available, or use campsites, some of which also have chalets. Major foods include beetroot soup (*borshch*), casseroles and other meat dishes, dumplings, and, during the summer, fresh fruit and vegetables, which are all washed down with vodka, beer and wine. Immunisation against diphtheria is recommended. Thousands of square km around the nuclear power station at Chernobyl, north of Kiev near the border with Belarus, were contaminated by a leak of radioactive isotopes in April 1986, and this area should be avoided.

The best times to visit the Ukraine are during the summer when breeding species such as Demoiselle Crane are present, the spring, and, especially, the autumn, when masses of passage migrants pass through the country. The moderate continental climate includes warm summers and very cold winters.

Apart from the forested Carpathians, which rise to 2058 m (6752 ft) in the west, the mountains on the Crimean Peninsula (Krymski) in the south and the heavily industrialised cities in the Donetsk Basin and Dneiper Lowlands, the Ukraine is primarily a land of low-lying, very fertile, black earth steppe with extensive marshes. The country's southern boundary lies along the north Black Sea coast where there are a variety of important wetlands, ranging from part of the Danube Delta through shallow bays and saltmarshes to paddies and saline lakes. The two major problems facing the fifteen threatened and near-threatened species as well as the relatively common and widespread birds which occur in the Ukraine are habitat loss and degradation (large areas of the country have suffered serious environmental damage) and pollution (long stretches of some large rivers are heavily contaminated).

Over 400 species have been recorded in the Ukraine. Notable species include Pygmy Cormorant*, Great White and Dalmatian* Pelicans, Ruddy Shelduck, Black Stork (490–560 pairs in the mid-1990s), Cinereous Vulture*, Pallid Harrier*, Levant Sparrowhawk, Imperial Eagle* (50–75 pairs in the mid-1990s), Saker Falcon, Chukar, Little Crake, Common (490–560 pairs in the mid-1990s) and Demoiselle Cranes, Little* and Great* Bustards, Black-winged Pratincole*, Great Black-headed and Slender-billed Gulls, and Aquatic* and Paddyfield Warblers.

NORTHERN DANUBE DELTA

The Danube (Dunay) Delta is the largest and one of the most natural, richest and important wetlands in Europe. The vast majority of the delta is situated in Romania (p. 297) but parts of its northern edge extend into the extreme southwest corner of the Ukraine and here it is possible to see many of the birds associated with the whole delta, including Great White and Dalmatian* Pelicans, as well as Slender-billed Gull* and Paddyfield Warbler, both of which are rarely recorded within the Romanian sector.

The species listed below occur during the summer unless otherwise indicated.

Localised Specialities
Slender-billed Gull, Paddyfield Warbler.

Other Localised Species
Pygmy Cormorant*, Great White and Dalmatian* Pelicans.

Regular Passage Migrants
Black Stork, Marsh Sandpiper, Temminck's Stint, Broad-billed Sandpiper (most in Sep), Red-necked Phalarope (most in Sep), Caspian Tern, Collared Flycatcher (most in Sep).

Others
Ferruginous Duck*, Smew (winter), Squacco Heron, Glossy Ibis, White Stork, White-tailed Eagle*, Rough-legged Buzzard (winter), Red-footed Falcon, Little Crake, Collared Pratincole, Whiskered, White-winged and Gull-billed Terns, European Bee-eater, European Roller, White-backed (*lilfordi*), Syrian and Black Woodpeckers, Lesser Grey Shrike, Eurasian River, Moustached and Barred Warblers.

(Other species recorded here include Red-breasted Goose*, Ruddy Shelduck, Pallid Harrier*, Imperial Eagle*, Saker Falcon, Slender-billed Curlew*, Black-winged Pratincole* and Red-throated Pipit.)

The delta is three hours by road from Odessa and boats can be hired to explore the area. Slender-billed Gull* breeds in Tendra and Yagorlytski bays, which, together with their surrounding steppe, also attract passage migrants such as Black-winged Pratincole* and Caspian Tern, and rarities which have included Slender-billed Curlew*. The best place for Paddyfield Warbler is around Septima.

Accommodation: the two nearest towns are Bolgrad and Izmail.

Many of the species which occur in the Danube Delta area also occur on Tiligul Liman, a former rivermouth which has been flooded by the sea, about 35 km east of **Odessa**, as well as spring passage migrants such as Collared Flycatcher, Citrine Wagtail and Red-throated Pipit, while birds such as Pygmy Cormorant* and Little Crake can be seen at the Dnestr Delta to the southwest of Odessa.

The 111-km^2 arid steppe biosphere reserve known as **Askania-Nova**, together with its lakes and surrounding farmland, support steppe specialists such as Pallid Harrier*, Demoiselle Crane and Great Bustard*, as well as Ruddy Shelduck, Red-footed Falcon, Little Bustard* (winter), European Bee-eater, European Roller, Lesser Grey Shrike, and Pied and Isabelline Wheatears. The reserve is near Kherson, between Odessa and the Crimea. Nearby, over 280 species (over 150 of which have bred) have been recorded in the 719-km² **Black Sea Nature Reserve**, including Black-winged Pratincole* and Slender-billed Gull.

CRIMEA

The largest area of brackish and saltwater lagoons west of the Urals— known as the Syvash, together with the flat, low-lying farmland, steppe and isolated range of high rocky mountains on the 27,000-km² Crimean Peninsula combine to support a range of breeding, wintering and passage birds which matches anything Eastern Europe can muster and includes such cracking birds as Demoiselle Crane and Great Black-headed Gull, both of which are very rare northwest of here.

The species listed below occur during the summer unless otherwise indicated.

Localised Specialities
Ruddy Shelduck, Pallid Harrier*, Saker Falcon, Chukar, Demoiselle Crane, Great Bustard*, Black-winged Pratincole*, Great Black-headed and Slender-billed Gulls, Caspian Tern, Paddyfield Warbler.

Other Localised Species
Pygmy Cormorant*, Cinereous Vulture*, Imperial Eagle*, Semicollared Flycatcher, Pied and Isabelline Wheatears, Lesser Short-toed Lark.

Regular Passage Migrants
Lesser Spotted and Greater Spotted* Eagles, Terek and Broad-billed Sandpipers, Eurasian Dotterel.

Others
Ferruginous Duck*, Squacco Heron, Egyptian Vulture, Eurasian Griffon, Short-toed Eagle, Lesser Kestrel*, Red-footed Falcon, Little Bustard*, Collared Pratincole, Gull-billed Tern, Eurasian Eagle-Owl, Alpine Swift, European Bee-eater, European Roller, Lesser Grey Shrike, Rufous-tailed Rock-Thrush, Eurasian River, Moustached and Barred Warblers, Rock Bunting.
   (Other species recorded here include Steppe Eagle and Slender-billed Curlew* (including a flock of 48 in 1975).)

Yalta, a resort on the south coast of the peninsula 88 km south of Simferopol, which is accessible by air (one hour from Odessa) and rail (19 hours) from Kiev, is the best base for birding the **Ai-Petri Mountains** where Cinereous Vulture*, Imperial Eagle*, Saker Falcon (Karadag Reserve), Chukar (Angara Pass) and Semicollared Flycatcher (Crimean Reserve) occur, for there is an extensive trail system running through this range above the resort. Unfortunately, the other two top birding areas are at the north end of the peninsula, over 200 km away from Yalta. The shallow saltwater **Syvash Bay** (Syvash Zaliv) together with the marshes and steppe which surround it, at the northeast end, support breeding species such as Demoiselle Crane, Great Bustard* (most are usually present in the spring, on the island of Kuyuk-Tuk, but a few pairs breed), Black-winged Pratincole*, Great Black-headed and Slender-billed Gulls, Caspian Tern and Paddyfield Warbler, and during passage periods masses of grebes, waterfowl and shorebirds use this bay as a resting and refuelling site. Most of these birds also occur at the northwest end of the peninsula where the habitats are similar, and Paddyfield Warbler breeds around the fishponds and paddies by **Karkinitski Bay** (Karkinitski Zaliv). The Tarkhankut Peninsula is particularly good for Demoiselle Crane and passage raptors.

Accommodation: Yalta—numerous hotels and lots of touts offering private rooms in town, plus Polyana Skazok Campsite, with chalets, 3 km to the north.

Pallid Harrier* is one of several birds which are very difficult to see in Europe but relatively easy to catch up with in the Ukraine

The Ukrainian coast of the **Sea of Azov** (Azovskoye More) supports similar birds to the Crimea. The saline lake known as Molochny Liman has attracted passage migrants such as Red-breasted Goose* and Slender-billed Curlew*. Northeast of here, the bays and peninsulas, particularly Krivaya Kosa at the northeast end of the coast, are all worth grilling for species such as Black-winged Pratincole*, while the **Khomutovo Steppe**, 23 km inland, supports Demoiselle Crane.

Part of the Carpathian Range, known here as the **Karpatski**, is present in the far west of the Ukraine and these mountains, accessible from L'viv, support the same avifauna as those in the nearby countries of Poland, Slovakia and Romania, including Ural Owl and White-backed Woodpecker.

ADDITIONAL INFORMATION

Addresses

Please send records of rarities to the West Ukrainian Avifaunistic Commission, L'viv State University, Department of Zoology, Grushevsky str. 4, L'viv 290005, Ukraine.

YUGOSLAVIA

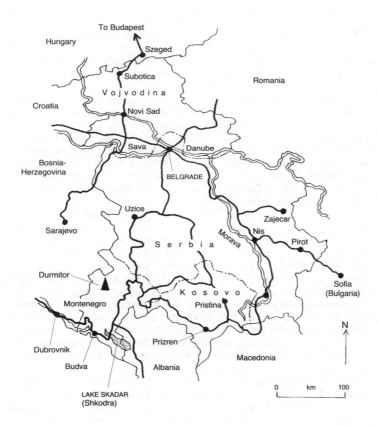

INTRODUCTION

Yugoslavia remained unsafe to visit at the end of the 20th century. The Montenegro region, adjacent to the Adriatic coast in the southwest, seemed set to rejoin the tourist circuit in the early 21st century but the Kosovo crisis which erupted in spring 1999 delayed that. This compact area was once a very popular birding destination because it offered some of the best birding in the Balkans for the price of a cheap package tour. There was a wide range of accommodation and vehicles could be hired in order to look for the likes of Lanner Falcon, Rock Partridge and Olive-tree Warbler.

At 102,170 km^2, Yugoslavia is 90% the size of England and 15% the size of Texas, and Montenegro is just 13,810 km^2. Immunisation against hepatitis, polio and typhoid is recommended. After the horrendous ethnic wars with Bosnia and Croatia in the early 1990s there were few clashes until 1998 when fighting again broke out, this time in the southern region of Kosovo, next to the border with Albania, and during early 1999 tens of thousands of Albanians were forced to flee Kosovo by Serb forces. Hence, it would be wise to contact the relevant foreign office for the latest information on travelling throughout Yugoslavia before considering a birding trip to this part of the world.

The best times to visit Yugoslavia are during the summer when breeding species such as Olive-tree Warbler are present, and during the spring and autumn when many passage migrants pass through the country, especially along the coast of Montenegro. The climate is continental, with hot summers and cold winters.

Yugoslavia is divided into four major regions: (i) Vojvodina, an area of intensively farmed lowland plains at the northern end of the country, crossed by numerous rivers, including the Danube (Dunav), Sava and Tisa. Some of Europe's finest riverine poplar and willow woods may survive here, as well as oak woods, unimproved flood-meadows, marshes, saline lakes, fishponds and steppe; (ii) Serbia, a mountainous area, split by the River Morava, in the middle of the country; (iii) Kosovo, a mountainous area at the south end of the country next to the borders with Albania and Macedonia; and (iv) Montenegro, another mountainous region at the southwest end of the country which borders the Adriatic between Bosnia, Croatia and Albania. Here there are olive groves and orchards amongst the mixed Mediterranean woods and important coastal wetlands, and forested mountains inland. Yugoslavia's natural evergreen oak woods were destroyed long ago, leaving maquis and garrigue on many lower mountain slopes. However, extensive areas, especially in the mountains, were relatively unspoilt up until the early 1990s when who knows what toll the terrible ethnic wars took on the region's habitats and the wildfe that inhabited them. Known contemporary problems facing the ten threatened and near-threatened species as well as the relatively common and widespread birds which occur in Yugoslavia include drainage, hunting, overgrazing and timber loss due to such activities as clearance for cultivation.

Notable species which may still be present in the north include Imperial Eagle*, Saker Falcon, Little and Baillon's Crakes, and Great Bustard*, while such species which are mainly restricted to the south and Montenegro in particular include Pygmy Cormorant*, Great White and Dalmatian* Pelicans, Levant Sparrowhawk, Lanner Falcon, Rock Partridge, Rufous-tailed Scrub-Robin, Rock Nuthatch, Wallcreeper, Olive-tree Warbler, Sombre Tit, and Cretzschmar's and Black-headed Buntings.

There used to be plenty of excellent birding sites in **Vojvodina**, north Yugoslavia, but whether any of those outlined below still support such a rich avifauna, let alone exist, remains to be seen. The wooded hills in **Fruska gora National Park**, along the River Danube near Novi Sad about 70 km northwest of Belgrade, may still support Saker Falcon, as well as Lesser Spotted and Imperial* Eagles. The once extensive marshes at the confluence of the Rivers Danube and Drava, just east of **Osijak** northwest of Fruska gora, may also still be worth visiting. The marshes and deciduous riverine forests on the floodplain along the east bank of the River Danube in northwest Yugoslavia in an area known as **Monostor** adjacent to Kopacki rit in Croatia (p. 145) may still support a fine range of waterbirds, including Little and Baillon's Crakes, as well as Saker Falcon and Collared Flycatcher. In extreme north Yugoslavia White-headed Duck* has been recorded during the autumn and winter on **Lake Palic**, and, during the summer, southeast of here, at **Lake Ludas**, which may also still support other breeding species such as Ferruginous Duck*, Squacco Heron and Moustached Warbler. The farmland, any remnant steppe, riverine woods and fishponds at **Jazovo-Mokrin**, also in extreme north Yugoslavia, may still support Red-footed Falcon and Great Bustard*, as well as Ferruginous Duck* and Squacco Heron. The best area used to be along the River Zlatica. Baillon's Crake has bred at **Soskopo**, a saline lake surrounded by farmland and remnant steppe, which also may still act as a resting and refuelling site for passage migrants such as Lesser Spotted and Imperial* Eagles, and Common Crane. This lake also used to attract rarities which have included Lesser White-fronted* and Red-breasted* Geese, Slender-billed Curlew* and Caspian Tern. Such species have also been recorded in the marshes alongside the **River Begej**, north of Belgrade, along with Greater Spotted Eagle*, Saker Falcon, and Little and Baillon's Crakes. The shallow lake known as Carska bara, as well as Ecka fishponds, Perleska bara and Tiganjica used to be the best areas. East of Belgrade one of the best birding sites used to be **Deliblatska pescara**, a special reserve set up to protect a tract of sand which was spreading north from the River Danube towards Vladimirovac and supported farmland, remnant steppe, woods and plantations which may still be inhabited by White-tailed*, Lesser Spotted and Imperial* Eagles, Saker Falcon and Corn Crake*. Near the border with Romania is **Donje podunavlje**, a flooded valley with poplar and willow woods, resulting from the construction of a hydroelectric power-station on the River Danube. Species which may still breed here include Pygmy Cormorant*, Ferruginous Duck*, Squacco Heron, Glossy Ibis and Corn Crake*. To the north, on the border with Romania, the farmland, remnant steppe and wooded hills at **Vrsacki breg** may still support Levant Sparrowhawk and White-backed Woodpecker.

Very little is known about the birdlife of the **Serbia** and **Kosovo** regions in southern Yugoslavia, although the mountains around **Zajecar** in the east, near the border with Bulgaria, may still support Ural Owl, as well as Lesser Spotted Eagle and Collared Flycatcher (the best areas used to be Beljanica Mountain, and the Klocanica, Resava and Zlot Gorges), and the **Sara Mountains** in the south may still support Rock Partridge, as well as brown bear and lynx (for more details see Macedonia, p. 251).

MONTENEGRO

The wetlands on the narrow Adriatic coastal plain and the forested limestone mountains, which rise abruptly inland to 2522 m (8274 ft) at Bobotov Kuk, of Montenegro in southwest Yugoslavia may still support one of the richest avifaunas in Europe.

The species listed below occur during the summer unless otherwise indicated.

Localised Specialities

Rock Partridge, Rufous-tailed Scrub-Robin, Olive-tree Warbler, Cretzschmar's Bunting.

Other Localised Species

Pygmy Cormorant*, Great White (winter) and Dalmatian* Pelicans, Levant Sparrowhawk, Lanner Falcon, Wallcreeper.

Others

Ferruginous Duck*, Squacco Heron, Glossy Ibis, Egyptian Vulture, Eurasian Griffon, White-tailed*, Short-toed and Booted Eagles, Lesser Kestrel*, Collared Pratincole, Whiskered Tern, Alpine and Pallid Swifts, European Bee-eater, European Roller, White-backed (*lilfordi*), Syrian and Black Woodpeckers, Yellow-billed Chough, Lesser Grey Shrike, Rufous-tailed and Blue Rock-Thrushes, Rock Nuthatch, Eurasian Crag-Martin, Moustached, Olivaceous, Orphean, Sardinian and Subalpine Warblers, Sombre Tit, Spanish Sparrow, Yellow Wagtail ('Black-headed' *feldegg*), Rock and Black-headed Buntings.

(Other species recorded here include Red-footed Falcon, Little Crake, and White-winged, Gull-billed and Caspian Terns.)

The package tour holiday resorts of Budva and Petrovac both used to make excellent base camps for birding Montenegro. The huge freshwater **Lake Skadar**, about 20 km inland from Petrovac, lies within Skadarsko Jezero National Park and extends eastwards into Albania where it is known as Lake Shkodra. The lake may still support the second most important population of Pygmy Cormorants* on the planet—up to 10,000 have been recorded during the autumn, a total exceeded only by the Danube Delta/Dobrudja area in Romania—as well as the only breeding colony of Dalmatian Pelicans* in Yugoslavia. Rock Partridge has been recorded in **Lovcen National Park**, reached by turning inland off the main coast road about 18 km west of Budva, and, further afield, below Bobotov Kuk in **Durmitor National Park**, about 85 km north of Titograd near Zabljak. Wallcreeper has been recorded around tunnels 9, 10 and 11 in **Moraca Gorge**, inland from Titograd.

REQUEST

This book is intended to be a first edition. If you would like to contribute to the second edition please send details of any changes, errors and sites you feel deserve inclusion, to:

Nigel Wheatley, c/o A & C Black (Publishers) Limited, 35 Bedford Row, London WC1R 4JH, UK.

It would be very helpful if information could be submitted in the following format:

1   A summary of the site's position (in relation to the nearest city, town or village), altitude, access arrangements, habitats, number of species recorded (if known), best birds, best times to visit, and its richness compared with other sites.
2   A species list, preferably using the taxonomic order and names in *Birds of the World: A Check List* (fifth edition), Clements J, due 2000.
3   Details of how to get to the site and where to look for the best birds once there, with information on trails etc.
4   A map complete with scale and compass point.
5   Any addresses to write to for permits etc.
6   Any details of accommodation.

Any information on where to look for the following species would also be very useful:

Europe
Black-shouldered Kite, Levant Sparrowhawk, Lesser Spotted and Greater Spotted* Eagles, Lanner Falcon, Gyrfalcon, Rock Partridge, Little and Baillon's Crakes, Red-knobbed Coot, Small Buttonquail (Andalusian Hemipode), Eurasian Eagle-Owl, Eurasian Pygmy-Owl, Tengmalm's Owl, Red-necked Nightjar, White-rumped Swift, Masked Shrike, Semicollared Flycatcher, Rufous-tailed Scrub-Robin (Rufous Bush Chat), Wallcreeper, Moustached, Olive-tree and Marmora's (in Spain) Warblers, Dupont's Lark, Citril Finch, and Parrot and Two-barred Crossbills.

Russia
Altai Falcon, Altai Snowcock, Daurian Partridge, Siberian Grouse*, Solitary and Swinhoe's Snipes, Black-winged Pratincole*, Sociable Lapwing*, Pallas's Sandgrouse, Blakiston's Fish-Owl*, Japanese Waxwing*, White-winged and Black Larks, and Asian Rosy-Finch.

Finally, I would be extremely grateful if you could also include a statement outlining your permission to use the information in the next edition, and, finally, your name and address, so that you can be acknowledged appropriately.

CALENDAR

The following is a brief summary of the best countries, islands and regions to visit according to the time of the year. This calendar is aimed to help those birders who have professions with set holidays to choose the best possible destinations.

Alternatively, if there are birders out there fortunate enough to have a year to go birding in Europe and Russia then following this schedule could produce the best birding and the most birds. If anyone tries this please let me know how they get on. Better still, if there is a willing sponsor out there, contact me immediately. Were such a dream to come true the following route may prove to be the most rewarding.

Start the year's epic journey in snowy Scotland where the endemic Scottish Crossbill* resides, as well as a good selection of wintering waterfowl. Then head south through eastern England and on to the Netherlands for more wintering waterbirds, which may include rarities such as Red-breasted Goose*. To ensure seeing this colourful goose travel to the Dobrudja in either southern Romania or northern Bulgaria where it winters in huge numbers. By mid-March it is time to head for the woods of central Europe where Hazel Grouse, owls and woodpeckers are setting up their breeding territories and relatively easy to track down while many of the trees are still leafless. Don't spend too long looking for these sparsely distributed birds though, for there will be another chance to catch up with them later in the spring, in Finland, towards the end of a wonderful journey from the Mediterranean to Varangerfjord in the Arctic, a trip first tried by Stan Bayliss Smith in the late 1960s and immortalised in the classic *Wild Wings to the Northlands*. He started in the Camargue but, better still, why not begin in the Coto Doñana, southern Spain, on 1 April. Once you have seen the Iberian specialities such as the endemic Spanish Eagle*, make sure of Audouin's Gull* at the Ebro Delta on the east coast of Spain before ascending the Pyrenées to look for the likes of Lammergeier, Wallcreeper and Citril Finch.

Bird the Camargue area in early May then return to the mountains, this time in the French Alps, to look for the tricky Rock Partridge, one of Europe's seven endemic species. From there continue east through the Swiss, Austrian and Bavarian Alps, where any missing high-altitude specialities can be looked for, then cross the Czech Republic, where Saker Falcon and Collared Flycatcher occur, to reach Poland by the end of May, the best time to see Great Snipe* and Aquatic Warbler*. Head north with the masses of migrant birds from there through the Baltic States of Lithuania, Latvia and Estonia, then catch a ferry to Finland. Work your way north through owl country, then spend a relaxing week in mid-June at Varangerfjord in north Norway, in the company of all the breeding shorebirds and other great birds such as Steller's Eider*, to complete what should be a memorable excursion across western Europe.

Unfortunately, mid-May to late June is also the best time to bird far east Russia, including Siberia, Kamchatka, the Amur-Ussuriland area and offshore islands such as Sakhalin, where it is possible to see over 300 species in three weeks, so you will either have to squeeze in a

Russian break at this time or concentrate on Europe one year and Russia the next.

The second half of June is a good time to look for the Caucasian specialities in Armenia and Georgia, by which time half of the year will be gone already. However, there is no time to relax and catch up with the notes yet, for early July is an excellent time to be on Corsica, where the endemic nuthatch and Marmora's Warbler can be seen along with a wealth of butterflies. From there fly north to the very different island of Iceland, the only place in Europe where Harlequin Duck and Barrow's Goldeneye occur. Early August is the only time available to look for the southeastern Europe specialities, including Spur-winged Plover and Rüppell's Warbler in Greece and Pied Wheatear in Bulgaria, and while ticking these off there may be time to catch your breath, update your notebook and take stock on a sunny beach before some serious sea-watching off southwest Ireland. To keep the blood circulating, and the adrenalin pumping, in between lengthy spells on the exposed headlands scour the coastal estuaries and lagoons for there is a strong possibility of spicing up your list with a few rare shorebirds at places such as Ballycotton and Tacumshin during the second half of August and the first half of September.

It would be nice to stay on the headlands of southwest Ireland throughout the autumn, in order to look for Nearctic passerines, but the only place to be during the second half of September is Fair Isle, where virtually anything can turn up, and the likes of Lanceolated and Pallas's Grasshopper Warblers, and Pechora Pipit, usually do. Come October, birders hoping to add American landbirds to their lists could stay on Fair Isle, although the records for the 1990s strongly suggest you will be better off in Iceland. However, birds, from the west *and* the east, can turn up almost anywhere in Britain and Ireland and the other countries bordering the North Sea and northwest France at this time of year, so it is a very difficult call to make as to which site is the best place to be. Shetland? Southwest Ireland? Cornwall? Isles of Scilly? Île d'Ouessant? Helgoland? Utsira? The choice is yours, although I would plump for a few, mostly relaxing, weeks mixing scarce migrants, great rarities and birding tales with old friends, on the Isles of Scilly.

In early November forget about rarities and head for the Hortobagy in Hungary to witness the spectacle of thousands of Common Cranes flying to their roosts, after which there will be plenty of time left to mop up any birds missed earlier in the year. Those who then may have a few days and enough energy to spare between Christmas and New Year may wish to end a memorable ramble through Europe with wintering white-winged gulls at Killybegs, northwest Ireland. The numbers of Glaucous and Iceland Gulls regularly reach double figures here and amongst them the diligent may find Kumlien's, Thayer's, American Herring and, maybe even Ivory.

JANUARY: Britain and Ireland, Bulgaria/Romania, Netherlands.
FEBRUARY: Britain and Ireland, Bulgaria/Romania, Netherlands.
MARCH: Britain and Ireland, Netherlands, Lithuania.
Late MARCH to early APRIL: Belgium, Czech Republic, Estonia, Portugal, Slovakia, southern Spain.
APRIL: Bulgaria, Crete, Denmark, Greece, Hungary, Portugal, Slovakia, Ukraine.

Mid-APRIL to early MAY: Balearic Islands, Hungary, Italy (Sicily), Russia (Volga Delta).

Early MAY: Southern France, Hungary.

MAY: Crete, Denmark, Estonia, Greece, Russia (Volga Delta), Ukraine.

Mid-MAY: Poland, Romania, the Russian far east.

Late MAY to early JUNE: Austria, Britain, Bulgaria, Finland & northern Norway (Varangerfjord), the Russian far east, southern and eastern Spain, Sweden, Switzerland.

JUNE: Armenia, Georgia, Greece, Italy, Latvia, Lithuania, Portugal, the Russian far east, Sardinia, Switzerland.

Early JULY: Armenia, Georgia, Corsica, Italy, Latvia, Lithuania.

Late JULY: Iceland, Latvia, Lithuania, Switzerland.

AUGUST: Southwest Britain and Ireland (seawatching).

Mid-AUGUST to early SEPTEMBER: Bay of Biscay, southern France (Camargue and Pyrenées), Greece, Hungary, Romania, Russia (Volga Delta), northern Spain (Pyrenées).

SEPTEMBER and OCTOBER: Britain and Ireland (Shetland, Fair Isle, southwest Ireland, Cornwall, Isles of Scilly), Bulgaria, Crete, France (Île d'Ouessant), Germany (Helgoland), Hungary, Norway (Utsira), Romania, Russia (Volga Delta), Sweden (Falsterbo), Ukraine.

NOVEMBER: France (northeast), Hungary.

DECEMBER: Britain and Ireland, Bulgaria/Romania, Netherlands.

USEFUL ADDRESSES

Clubs and Conservation Organisations

Association of European Rarities Committees, D'Haus vun der Natur, L-1899 Kockelscheuer, Luxembourg.

BirdLife International, Wellbrook Court, Girton Road, Cambridge, CB3 0NA, UK. Membership of this vitally important organisation costs from £25 per annum and members receive a quarterly magazine and an annual report.

VSO's WorldWise Tourism Campaign, 317 Putney Bridge Road, London, SW15 2PN, UK (tel: 0181 780 7233), aims to make sure local people benefit more from tourism and provides information on how travellers can play their part.

Trip Reports

Dutch Birding Travel Report Service (DBTRS), Postbus 737, NL-9700 AS Groningen, Netherlands (tel: 50 527 4993; fax: 50 527 2668; email: DBTRS@Natuurschool.com; website: www.Natuurschool.com/DBTRS). To obtain a copy of the catalogue which lists a very extensive selection of reports, covering most of the Europe and Russia region, send £3 or US$5.

Foreign Birdwatching Reports and Information Service (FBRIS), organised by Steve Whitehouse, 6 Skipton Crescent, Berkeley Pendesham, Worcester, WR4 0LG, UK (tel: 01905 454541). To obtain a copy of the catalogue, which includes over 450 trip reports and other privately published items, many of which deal with most of the birding sites in Europe and Russia in great detail, send £1.20 in the form of a cheque, postage stamps or postal order, or a US$5 bill.

Tour Companies

Animal Watch, Granville House, London Road, Sevenoaks, Kent, TN13 1DL, UK (tel: 01732 811838; fax: 01732 455441; email: mail@animalwatch.co.uk; website: www.animalwatch.co.uk).

Avian Adventures, 49 Sandy Road, Norton, Stourbridge, DY8 3AJ, UK (tel: 01384 372013; fax: 01384 441340; email: avian@argonet.co.uk).

Bird Holidays, 10 Ivegate, Yeadon, Leeds, LS19 7RE (tel/fax: 01133 910510).

Birding, Finches House, Hiham Green, Winchelsea, East Sussex, TN36 4HB, UK (tel: 01797 223223; fax: 01797 222911).

Birdquest, Two Jays, Kemple End, Birdy Brow, Stonyhurst, Lancashire, BB7 9QY, UK (tel: 01254 826317; fax: 01254 826780; email: birders@birdquest.co.uk).

Birdwatching Breaks, 26 School Lane, Herne, Herne Bay, Kent, CT6 7AL, UK (tel: 01227 740799; fax: 01227 363946; email: info@birdwatchingbreaks.com; website: www.birdwatching-breaks.com).

Branta, 7 Wingfield Street, London, SE15 4LN, UK (tel: 0171 635 5812; fax: 0171 277 7720; email: branta@netcomuk.co.uk).

Calandra Holidays, 6 Church Road, Hauxton, Cambridge, CB2 5HS, UK (tel: 01223 872107).

Field Guides Incorporated, 9433 Bee Cave Road, Building 1, Suite 150, Austin TX 78733, USA (freephone: (800) 728 4953; tel: (512) 263

7295; fax: (512) 263 0117; email: fgileader@aol.com; website: www. fieldguides.com).

Great Glen Wildlife, Sherren, Harray, Orkney, KW17 2JU, Scotland, UK (tel/fax: 01856 761604).

Greentours, Rock Cottage, High Street, Longnor, Buxton, Derbyshire, SK17 0PG, UK (tel/fax: 01298 83563; email: enquiries@greentours.co. uk; website: www.greentours.co.uk).

Ibis Excursions, Ganløseparken 46, Ganløse, DK-3660 Stenløse, Denmark (tel: 4819 5940; fax: 4819 5945; email: jeffprice@ibis-excursions.dk; website: www.ibis-excursions.dk).

Limosa Holidays, Suffield House, Northrepps, Norfolk, NR27 0LZ, UK (tel: 01263 578143; fax: 01263 579251; email: limosaholidays@ compuserve.com).

Naturetrek, Cheriton Mill, Cheriton, Alresford, Hampshire, SO24 0NG, UK (tel: 01962 733051; fax: 01962 736426; email: info@naturetrek.co. uk; website: www.naturetrek.co.uk).

Ocean Adventures, Two Jays, Kemple End, Birdy Brow, Stonyhurst, Lancashire, BB7 9QY, UK (tel: 01254 826116; fax: 01254 826780; email: expeditions@oceanadventures.co.uk).

Ornitholidays, 29 Straight Mile, Romsey, Hampshire, SO51 9BB, UK (tel: 01794 519445; fax: 01794 523544; email: ornitholidays@compuserve. com; website: www.ornitholidays.co.uk).

Speyside Wildlife, 9 Upper Mall, Grampian Road, Aviemore, Inverness-shire, PH22 1RH, Scotland, UK (tel/fax: 01479 812498; email: speyside_wildlife@msn.com).

Sunbird, PO Box 76, Sandy, Bedfordshire, SG19 1DF, UK (tel: 01767 682969; fax: 01767 692481; email: sunbird@sunbird.demon.co.uk; website: www.sunbird.demon.co.uk).

The Travelling Naturalist, PO Box 3141, Dorchester, DT1 2XD, UK (tel: 01305 267994; fax: 01305 265506; email: jamie@naturalist.co.uk; website: www.naturalist.co.uk).

Victor Emanuel Nature Tours, PO Box 33008, Austin, Texas 78764, USA (tel: 800 328 8368 or 512 328 5221; fax: 512 328 2919; email: VENTBIRD@aol.com; website: www.VENTBIRD.com).

Wildlife Worldwide, 170 Selsdon Road, South Croydon, Surrey, CR2 6PJ, UK (tel: 0208 667 9158; fax: 0208 667 1960; email: sales@wildlife-worldwide.com; website: www.wildlife-worldwide.com).

Wildwings, International House, Bank Road, Kingswood, Bristol, BS15 8LX, UK (tel: 0117 984 8040; brochureline: 0117 961 0874; fax: 0117 961 0200; email: Wildinfo@wildwings.co.uk; website: www.wildwings. co.uk). This is also a travel agency which specialises in arranging birding holidays.

Wings, 1643 North Alvernon Way, Suite 105, Tucson, AZ 85712-3350, USA (tel: 520 320 9868; fax: 520 320 9373; email: wings@rtd.com).

Zegrahm Expeditions, 1414 Dexter Avenue North, Suite 327, Seattle, WA 98109, USA (tel: 800 628 8747 or 206 285 4000; fax: 206 285 5037; email: zoe@zeco.com or zegrahm@accessone.com; website: www. zeco.com).

Booksellers

Natural History Book Service Limited (NHBS), 2–3 Wills Road, Totnes, Devon TQ9 5XN, UK (tel: 01803 865913; fax: 01803 865280; email: nhbs@nhbs.co.uk; website: www.nhbs.com

Subbuteo Natural History Books Limited, Pistyll Farm, Nercwys, Nr. Mold, Flintshire, CH7 4EW, UK (tel: 01352 756551; fax: 01352 756004; email: sales@subbooks.demon.co.uk; website: www.subbooks.demon. co.uk).

Centurion Books (mainly antiquarian and secondhand), 2 Roman Quay, High Street, Fordingbridge, Hampshire, SP6 1RL, UK (tel/fax: 01425 657988).

Maps

The Map Shop, 15 High Street, Upton upon Severn, Worcs., WR8 0HJ, UK (tel: 01684 593146; fax: 01684 594559; email: Themapshop@ btinternet.com; website: www.themapshop.co.uk).

Stanfords, 12–14 Long Acre, Covent Garden, London, WC2E 9LP, UK (shop tel: 0171 836 1915; shop/mail order fax: 0171 836 0189; mail order tel: 0171 836 1321).

Audio CDs and Cassettes, Books, CD-Roms, DVDs and Videos

BirdGuides Ltd, Jack House, Ewden, Sheffield, S36 4ZA, UK, England (freephone: 0800 919391; tel: 0114 283 1002; email: sales@birdguides. com; website: www.birdguides.com). BirdGuides' excellent range of exciting products include Dave Gosney's detailed birding guides to Bulgaria, Eastern Austria, Finland, Northern France, Southern France, Northern Greece, Hungary, Mallorca, Eastern Poland, Southern Portugal, Romania, Northern Spain, Southern Spain and Sweden.

WildSounds, Dept SP, Cross Street, Salthouse, Norfolk, NR25 7XH, UK (tel/fax: 01263 741100; email: sales@wildsounds.com; website: www. wildsounds.com).

RECOMMENDED BOOKS, VIDEOS, CASSETTES, CD-ROMS AND COMPUTER SOFTWARE

BOOKS

Regional Birding Guides
Where to watch birds in Eastern Europe. Gorman G, 1994. Hamlyn.
Where to watch birds in Scandinavia (including Denmark and Iceland). Aulen G, 1996. Mitchell Beazley.

Regional Field Guides
Birds of Europe with North Africa and the Middle East. Jonsson L, 1992. Helm.
Collins Bird Guide. Svensson L *et al.*, 1999. HarperCollins.
Collins Birdwatching: The Ultimate Guide to the Birds of Europe. Van den Berg A *et al.*, 1997. HarperCollins.
Collins Pocket Guide to the Birds of Britain and Europe with North Africa and the Middle East (fifth edition). Heinzel H, Fitter R and Parslow J, 1995. HarperCollins.
Field Guide to the Rare Birds of Britain and Europe. Alstrom P, Colston P and Lewington I, 1991. HarperCollins.
Hamlyn Guide to the Birds of Britain and Europe (second edition). Bruun B, Delin H and Svensson L, 1992. Hamlyn.
Identification Guide to European Non-Passerines. Baker K, 1993. BTO.
Identification Guide to European Passerines (fourth edition). Svensson L, 1992. Slate Creek Press, USA.
Photographic Guide to the Birds of Britain and Europe. Svensson L and Delin H, 1997. Hamlyn.
Photographic Handbook of the Rare Birds of Britain and Europe (second edition). Mitchell D and Young S, 1999. New Holland.
Pocket Guide to the Birds of Britain and North-West Europe. Kightley C *et al.*, 1998. Pica Press.
The Handbook of Bird Identification for Europe and the Western Palearctic (HBI). Beaman M, Madge S *et al.*, 1998. Helm.
The Macmillan Birder's Guide to European and Middle Eastern Birds. Christie D, Harris A and Shirihai H, 1996. Macmillan.
The Macmillan Field Guide to Bird Identification. Harris A, Tucker L and Vinicombe K, 1993. Macmillan.
A Field Guide to the Birds of North America (third edition). Scott S (ed.), 1999. National Geographic.
Wild Birds of Japan: a Photographic Guide. Kanouchi T *et al*, 1999. (Japanese text but English and scientific name photo captions.)

Handbooks and Reference Works
Birds of the Western Palearctic (BWP) Concise Edition (two volumes). Perrins C and Snow D (eds.), 1997. OUP.
Birds of the Western Palearctic (BWP): Handbook of the Birds of Europe, the Middle East and North Africa (Nine volumes). Cramp S (ed.),

1977–1994. OUP. Also available on CD-ROM (combined with the Concise Edition, 1998).

The EBCC Atlas of European Breeding Birds. Hagemeijer J and Blair M (eds.), 1997. Poyser.

Handbook of the Birds of the World. Volumes 1 to 5 and continuing to volume 12. del Hoyo *et al* (eds.), 1992 onwards. Lynx Edicions.

Bird Identification: A Reference Guide. Adolfsson K and Cherrug S, 1995. SkOF, Sweden.

The Birdwatcher's Year Book. Pemberton J (ed.), annual.

A Dictionary of Birds. Campbell B and Lack E (eds.), 1985. Poyser.

A Guide to the National Parks and other wild places of Britain and Europe. Gibbons B, 1994. New Holland.

Bird Families

Seabirds. Harrison P, 1985. Helm

Seabirds of the World: A Photographic Guide (second edition). Harrison P, 1996. Helm.

Photographic Handbook of the Seabirds of the World (revised edition). Enticott J and Tipling D, 1998. New Holland.

Cormorants, Darters and Pelicans of the World. Johnsgard P, 1993. Smithsonian Institute Press, USA.

Wildfowl: An Identification Guide to the Ducks, Geese and Swans of the World. Madge S and Burn H, 1988. Helm.

Photographic Handbook of the Wildfowl of the World. Ogilvie M and Young S, 1998. New Holland.

Herons and Egrets of the World: A Photographic Guide. Hancock J, 1999. Academic Press.

Storks, Ibises and Spoonbills of the World. Hancock J *et al*, 1992. Academic Press.

Birds of Prey in Britain and Europe. Burton P *et al*, due 2000. Helm.

Field Guide to the Raptors of the Western Palearctic. Clark W S and Schmitt N J, 1999. OUP.

Raptor In-hand Identification Guide. Clark W S and Yosef R, 1999. OUP.

The Raptors of Europe and The Middle East: A Handbook of Field Identification. Forsman D, 1998. Poyser.

Quails, Partridges and Francolins of the World. Johnsgard P, 1988. OUP.

Rails. Taylor B, 1998. Pica Press.

Bustards, Hemipodes and Sandgrouse: Birds of Dry Places. Johnsgard P, 1991. OUP.

Shorebirds: An Identification Guide to the Waders of the World. Hayman P, Marchant J and Prater T, 1986. Helm.

The Hamlyn Photographic Guide to the Waders of the World. Rosair D and Cottridge D, 1995. Hamlyn.

Gulls: A Guide to Identification (second edition). Grant P, 1986. Poyser.

Terns of Europe and North America. Olsen K M and Larsson H, 1995. Helm.

Terns and Skimmers. Wilds C and DiCostanzo J, due 2000. Pica Press.

Skuas and Jaegers: A Guide to the Skuas and Jaegers of the World. Olsen K M and Larsson H, 1997. Pica Press.

The Skuas. Furness R, 1988. Poyser.

The Auks. Gaston A J *et al.*, 1997. OUP.

Pigeons and Doves. Gibbs D *et al.*, due 2000. Pica Press.

Owls. Köning C and Becking J, due 1999. Pica Press (with accompanying CD).

Owls of Europe. Mikkola H, 1983. Poyser.

Nightjars. Cleere N and Nurney D, 1997. Pica Press (with accompanying CD).

Swifts (second edition). Chantler P and Driessens G, due 1999. Pica Press.

Kingfishers, Bee-eaters and Rollers. Fry C *et al*, 1992. Helm.

The Bee-eaters. Fry C, 1984. Poyser.

Woodpeckers (second edition). Winkler H *et al*, due 2001. Pica Press.

Crows and Jays. Madge S and Burn H, 1992. Helm.

Shrikes and Bush-Shrikes. Harris T and Franklin K, due 2000. Helm.

Shrikes. Lefranc N and Worfolk T, 1997. Pica Press.

Starlings and Mynas. Feare C and Craig A, 1998. Helm.

A Handbook to the Swallows and Martins of the World. Turner A and Rose C, 1989. Helm.

Warblers of Europe, Asia and North Africa: An Identification Guide. Baker K, 1997. Helm.

Tits, Nuthatches and Treecreepers: An Identification Guide. Harrap S and Quinn D, 1995. Helm.

New World Warblers. Curson J *et al.*, 1994. Helm.

Finches and Sparrows. Clement P *et al.*, 1993. Helm.

Buntings and Sparrows: A Guide to the Buntings and North American Sparrows. Olsson U *et al.*, 1995. Pica Press.

New World Blackbirds: The Icterids. Jaramillo A and Burke P, 1999. Helm.

Lists

The Birding World Complete List of the Birds of the Western Palearctic. Published by *Birding World* magazine, 1995.

British Birds List of Birds of the Western Palearctic. As published in the August 1997 issue of *British Birds* magazine.

Birdwatch Checklist of the Birds of the Western Palearctic. Solo Publishing, 1998.

Palearctic Birds: A Checklist of the Birds of Europe, North Africa and Asia North of the foothills of the Himalayas and the Yangtze River. Beaman M, 1994. Harrier.

Checklist of the Birds of Eurasia. King B, 1997.

Birds of the World: A Check List (fifth edition). Clements J, due 2000. Pica.

Birds of the World: A Check List—Supplement No. 1 and English Name Index. Clements J, 1992. Ibis.

Birds of the World: A Check List—1992–1997 Supplement. Clements J, 1997. Ibis.

A Complete Checklist of the Birds of the World (second edition). Howard R and Moore A, 1991. Academic Press.

Distribution and Taxonomy of the Birds of the World. Sibley C and Monroe B, 1991. Yale University Press.

A Supplement to the Distribution and Taxonomy of the Birds of the World. Sibley C and Monroe B, 1993. Yale University Press.

A World Checklist of Birds. Monroe B and Sibley C, 1993. Yale University Press.

European Bird Names in Fifteen Languages. Sandberg R, 1992. SkOF, Sweden.

World Bird Species Checklist (with alternative English and scientific names). Wells M G, 1998. WorldList.

General Reading

Great Auk Islands: A Field Biologist in the Arctic. Birkhead T, 1993. Poyser.
In Search of Arctic Birds. Vaughan R, 1991. Poyser.
Wild Wings to the Northlands. Bayliss Smith S, 1970. H F & G Witherby Ltd.

Conservation

Habitats for Birds in Europe: A Conservation Strategy for the Wider Environment. Tucker G and Evans M, 1997. BirdLife International.
Globally Threatened Birds in Europe: Action Plans. Heredia B, Rose L and Painter M (eds.), 1996. Council of Europe.
Birds in Europe: Their Conservation Status. Tucker G *et al.*, 1994. BirdLife International.
Important Bird Areas in Europe. Grimmett R and Jones T (compilers), 1989. BirdLife International.
Farming and Birds in Europe: The Common Agricultural Policy and its implications for Bird Conservation. Pain D and Pienkowski M (eds.), 1997. Academic Press.
Birds to Watch 2: The World List of Threatened Birds. Collar N *et al.*, 1994. BirdLife International.

Other Wildlife

Butterflies of Britain and Europe. Chinery M, 1999. HarperCollins.
Collins Field Guide to the Butterflies of Britain and Europe. Tolman T and Lewington R, 1997. HarperCollins.
Collins Wild Guide: Wild Animals of Britain and Europe. Burton J, 1998. HarperCollins.
Discover Whale and Dolphin Watching in Northern Europe. Hoyt E, 1995. WDCS.
Field Guide to Butterflies and Moths of Britain and Europe. Reicholf-Reihm H, 1991. Crowood Press.
Field Guide to the Mammals of Britain and Europe. MacDonald D, 1993. HarperCollins.
Collins Complete Mediterranean Wildlife. Sterry P, due 2000. Harper-Collins.
Mediterranean Wildlife: The Rough Guide. Raine P, 1990. Penguin.
The Atlas of European Mammals. Mitchell-Jones A *et al.*, 1999. Poyser.
Whales and Dolphins: The Ultimate Guide to Marine Mammals. Cawardine M *et al.*, 1998. HarperCollins.

Travel

Travel guides published by Lonely Planet, Rough Guides and Vacation Work (Travellers Survival Kits) cover most of the countries, islands and regions within Europe and Russia.

VIDEOS

A wide range of excellent videos are stocked by **BirdGuides** (see Useful Addresses, p. 395) and **Bird Images**, 28 Carousel Walk, Sherburn in Elmet, North Yorks, LS25 6LP, UK (credit card hotline: 01977 684666), including *The Birds of Britain and Europe* (a set of four videos), *The Raptors of Britain and Europe*, *Warblers of Britain and Europe* and *Eastern Rarities: Birds of Beidaihe*.

CD-ROMS

The CD-ROM Guide to all the Birds of Europe (Second Edition, 1997). Available from BirdGuides (address, p. 395).

The CD-ROM Guide to European Birds. Available from BirdGuides (address, p. 395).

Birds of Britain and Europe: The Ultimate Interactive Bird Guide (1997). Available from AA Multimedia, Broad Street, Bungay, Suffolk, NR35 1SP, UK.

BIRD SOUNDS

Bird Songs and Calls of Britain and Europe (4 CDs covering 396 species). Roche J-C.

COMPUTER SOFTWARE

A wide range of packages are available from **Wildlife Computing**, 6 Fiddlers Lane, East Bergholt, Colchester, CO7 6SJ, UK (tel: 01206 298345 or 0468 348867; fax: 01206 298030; email: sales@wildlife.co.uk; website: www.wildlife.co.uk).

BIRD NAMES WHICH DIFFER BETWEEN *CLEMENTS* AND VARIOUS OTHER BIRD BOOKS

Only those name differences which are not immediately obvious are given.

Name used by *Clements*	Name Used by other books	Latin name
Horned Grebe	Slavonian Grebe	*Podiceps auritus*
Black-necked Grebe	Eared Grebe	*Podiceps nigricollis*
Mottled Petrel	Peale's Petrel	*Pterodroma inexpectata*
Madeira Petrel	Zino's Petrel	*Pterodroma madeira*
Cape Verde Island Petrel	Fea's Petrel	*Pterodroma feae*
Streaked Shearwater	White-faced Shearwater	*Calonectris leucomelas*
Yelkouan Shearwater	Mediterranean Shearwater	*Puffinus yelkouan*
Band-rumped Storm-Petrel	Madeiran Storm-Petrel	*Oceanodroma castro*
Japanese Cormorant	Temminck's Cormorant	*Phalacrocorax capillatus*
Tundra Swan	Bewick's Swan	*Cygnus columbianus*
Brant	Brent Goose	*Branta bernicla*
Ferruginous Pochard	Ferruginous Duck	*Aythya nyroca*
Black Scoter	Common Scoter	*Melanitta nigra*
White-winged Scoter	Velvet Scoter	*Melanitta fusca*
Common Merganser	Goosander	*Mergus merganser*
Striated Heron	Green-backed Heron	*Butorides striatus*
Oriental Honey-buzzard	Crested Honey-buzzard	*Pernis ptilorhynchus*
Cinereous Vulture	Black Vulture	*Aegypius monachus*
Northern Harrier	Hen Harrier	*Circus cyaneus*
Japanese Sparrowhawk	Besra Sparrowhawk	*Accipiter gularis*
Rough-legged Hawk	Rough-legged Buzzard	*Buteo lagopus*
Willow Ptarmigan	Willow Grouse	*Lagopus lagopus*
Small Buttonquail	Andalusian Hemipode	*Turnix sylvatica*
Swinhoe's Rail	Yellow Rail	*Coturnicops noveboracensis*
Purple Swamphen	Purple Gallinule	*Porphyrio porphyrio*
Red-knobbed Coot	Crested Coot	*Fulica cristata*
Red-crowned Crane	Manchurian Crane	*Grus japonensis*
Latham's Snipe	Japanese Snipe	*Gallinago hardwickii*
Nordmann's Greenshank	Spotted Greenshank	*Tringa guttifer*
Red Phalarope	Grey Phalarope	*Phalaropus fulicaria*
Eurasian Thick-knee	Stone Curlew	*Burhinus oedicnemus*
Snowy Plover	Kentish Plover	*Charadrius alexandrinus*
Mongolian Plover	Lesser Sandplover	*Charadrius mongolus*
Mew Gull	Common Gull	*Larus canus*
Great Skua	Bonxie	*Catharacta skua*
Parasitic Jaeger	Arctic Skua	*Stercorarius parasiticus*
Dovekie	Little Auk	*Alle alle*
Common Murre	Common Guillemot	*Uria aalge*
Thick-billed Murre	Brünnich's Guillemot	*Uria lomvia*
Black Guillemot	Tystie	*Cepphus grylle*
Arctic Loon	Black-throated Diver	*Gavia arctica*

Common Loon	Great Northern Diver	*Gavia immer*
Yellow-billed Loon	White-billed Diver	*Gavia adamsii*
Oriental Turtle-Dove	Rufous Turtle-Dove	*Streptopelia orientalis*
Boreal Owl	Tengmalm's Owl	*Aegolius funereus*
Jungle Nightjar	Grey Nightjar	*Caprimulgus indicus*
Fork-tailed Swift	Pacific Swift	*Apus pacificus*
Crested Kingfisher	Greater Pied Kingfisher	*Megaceryle lugubris*
Grey-capped Woodpecker	Grey-headed Pygmy Woodpecker	*Dendrocopos canicapillus*
Grey-faced Woodpecker	Grey-headed Woodpecker	*Picus canus*
Yellow-billed Chough	Alpine Chough	*Pyrrhocorax graculus*
Rufous-tailed Shrike	Isabelline Shrike	*Lanius isabellinus*
Northern Shrike	Great Grey Shrike	*Lanius excubitor*
Scaly Thrush	White's Thrush	*Zoothera dauma*
Dark-throated Thrush	Black/Red-throated Thrush	*Turdus ruficollis*
Dark-sided Flycatcher	Siberian Flycatcher	*Muscicapa sibirica*
Red-throated Flycatcher	Red-breasted Flycatcher	*Ficedula parva*
Rufous-tailed Robin	Swinhoe's Robin	*Luscinia sibilans*
Thrush Nightingale	Sprosser	*Luscinia luscinia*
Orange-flanked Bush-Robin	Red-flanked Bluetail	*Tarsiger cyanurus*
Rufous-tailed Scrub-Robin	Rufous Bush Chat/Robin	*Cercotrichas galactotes*
Rufous-backed Redstart	Eversmann's Redstart	*Phoenicurus erythronota*
White-winged Redstart	Guldenstadt's Redstart	*Phoenicurus erythrogaster*
Zitting Cisticola	Fan-tailed Warbler	*Cisticola juncidis*
Asian Stubtail	Short-tailed Bush-Warbler	*Urosphena squameiceps*
Pallas' Warbler	Pallas's Grasshopper Warbler	*Locustella certhiola*
Pleske's Warbler	Styan's Grasshopper Warbler	*Locustella pleskei*
Sakhalin Warbler	Stepanyan's Grasshopper Warbler	*Locustella amnicola*
Lemon-rumped Warbler	Pallas's (Leaf-) Warbler	*Phylloscopus proregulus*
Inornate Warbler	Yellow-browed Warbler	*Phylloscopus inornatus*
Marsh Grassbird	Japanese Marsh Warbler	*Megalurus pryeri*
Bearded Reedling	Bearded Tit	*Panurus biarmicus*
Reed Parrotbill	Polivanov's Parrotbill	*Paradoxornis heudei*
Asian Short-toed Lark	Mongolian Short-toed Lark	*Calandrella cheleensis*
Horned Lark	Shore Lark	*Eremophila alpestris*
Rock Petronia	(Streaked) Rock Sparrow	*Petronia petronia*
Black-backed Wagtail	Kamchatka Wagtail	*Motacilla lugens*
Yellow-hooded Wagtail	Citrine Wagtail	*Motacilla citreola*
Spot-throated Accentor	Radde's Accentor	*Prunella ocularis*
Hoary Redpoll	Arctic Redpoll	*Carduelis hornemanni*
White-winged Crossbill	Two-barred Crossbill	*Loxia leucoptera*
Yellow-billed Grosbeak	Chinese Grosbeak	*Eophona migratoria*
Meadow Bunting	Long-tailed Bunting	*Emberiza cioides*
Ochre-rumped Bunting	Japanese Reed Bunting	*Emberiza yessoensis*
Chestnut-eared Bunting	Grey-headed Bunting	*Emberiza fucata*
Lapland Longspur	Lapland Bunting	*Calcarius lapponicus*

INDEX TO SITES

INDEX TO SPECIES

Index to Species